Wicked Enchantments

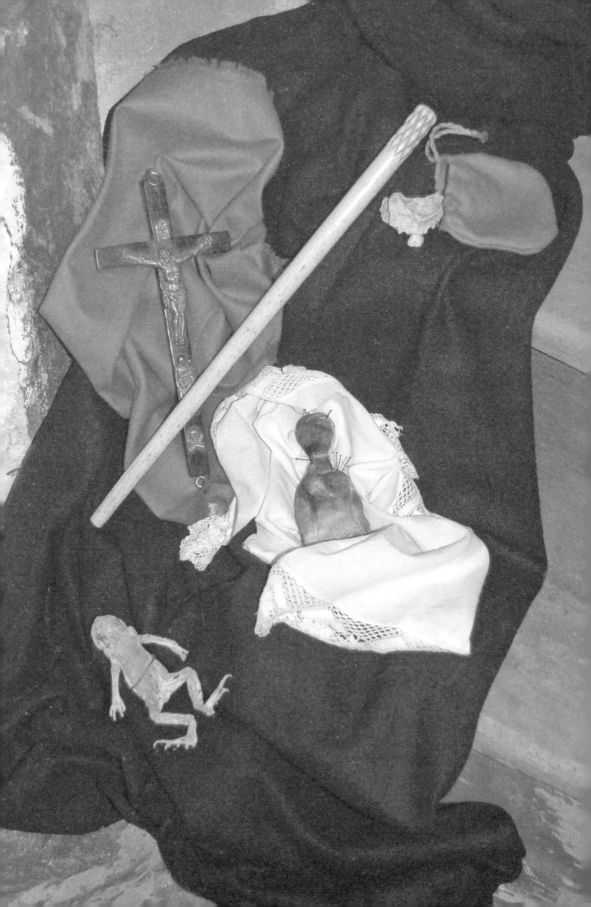

Wicked Enchantments

The Pendle Witches and their Magic

by Joyce Froome

It is necessary for men to know and understand the means whereby they work their mischief, the hidden mysteries of their devilish and wicked enchantments, charms and sorceries, the better to prevent and avoid the danger that may ensue.

The Wonderful Discovery of Witches in the County of Lancaster by Thomas Potts

IMPORTANT

You are strongly advised NOT to attempt any of the spells described in this book – particularly the one that involves removing a tooth from a live wolf.

Frontispiece Magical objects of the kind used by practitioners like the Pendle witches: a wand owned by the twentieth-century witch Alex Sanders; a crucifix from a collection of magical artefacts from the Netherlands; a skull fragment including a tooth (teeth and bone were used for healing and protection magic); a clay image made by the occultist Cecil Williamson, based on a description by the Pendle wise woman Elizabeth Sothernes; and a dried toad found hanging in the chimney of a house in Devon.
FROM THE MUSEUM OF WITCHCRAFT IN BOSCASTLE (IDENTITY NOS. MOW 977; 702; 497; 2007; 138).

Cover photographs see p.6 and p.295

Of related interest:
J. Lumby, *The Lancashire Witch Craze: Jennet Preston and the Lancashire Witches, 1612*;
Thomas Potts, *The Wonderfull Discoverie of Witches in the Countie of Lancaster*

Full up-to-date details and secure online ordering at
www.carnegiepublishing.com

Wicked enchantments

Copyright © Joyce Froome, 2010

First edition

Published by Palatine Books,
an imprint of Carnegie Publishing Ltd
Carnegie House,
Chatsworth Road,
Lancaster, LA1 4SL
www.carnegiepublishing.com

ISBN 978-1-874181-62-0

Typeset by Carnegie Book Production, Lancaster
Printed and bound in the UK by Short Run Press, Exeter

Contents

The main people connected with the 1612 Pendle witchcraft case

James Altham. Assize judge for the Northern Circuit.

James Anderton. Justice of the Peace who presided over formal examinations of prisoners in Lancaster Castle.

Nicholas Baldwyn. Magician living in the town of Colne near Pendle Forest (died in 1610).

Richard Baldwyn. Miller living at Weethead at the northern end of Pendle Forest. Employed Elizabeth Device to do casual work for him.

Nicholas Banester. Justice of the Peace living at Altham, south-west of Pendle Forest. Neighbour and colleague of Roger Nowell.

Edward Bromley. Assize judge for the Northern Circuit.

Christopher and **Jane Bulcock**. Farmers living at Mosse End in Pendle Forest. Probably employed the Device family to do casual work for them.

John Bulcock. Their son. Possibly friend of James and Alizon Device.

Henry Bulcock. Acquaintance of Alizon Device.

Thomas Covel. Jailer in charge of Lancaster prison.

Margaret Crooke. Daughter of Christopher Nutter and sister of John and Robert Nutter.

The Device family. Cunning folk living in Pendle Forest:-

Elizabeth Device, daughter of Elizabeth Sothernes, probably about forty years old in 1612.

John Device, Elizabeth's husband (died c. 1601).

Elizabeth's children:-

James, about nineteen.

Alizon, about seventeen (living at Malking Tower with her grandmother Elizabeth Sothernes).

Jennet, about nine.

William, probably about five; half-brother of James, Alizon and Jennet.

John Duckworth. Neighbour of the Towneleys, living at Lawnde in Pendle Forest. Employed James Device to do casual work (or perhaps perform magic) for him.

Alice Gray. Friend of the Sothernes/Device family, living in Colne. Possibly a wise woman.

Christopher and **Elizabeth Hargreives**. Clients of the Sothernes/Device family, living at Thurniholme, near Rough Lee, in Pendle Forest.

Henry Hargreives. Constable for the Pendle area, living in Goldshey Booth.

Jennet Hargreives. Client of the Sothernes/Device family, living in Barley in Pendle Forest.

Edmund Hartlay. Cunning man from south Lancashire, employed by Nicholas Starkie in 1595 to cure his sick children.

Katherine Hewit. Friend of the Sothernes/Device family, living in Colne. Possibly a wise woman.

Thomas Heyber. Justice of the Peace just over the border in Yorkshire. Father-in-law of Thomas Lister.

Christopher Howgate. Cunning man; son of Elizabeth Sothernes, and brother or half-brother of Elizabeth Device.

Elizabeth Howgate. Christopher's wife.

John Law. Peddler travelling the Pendle area.

Abraham Law. John Law's son. Cloth dyer living in Halifax.

Thomas Lister. Thomas Heyber's son-in-law. Neighbour of Jennet Preston.

Henry Mitton. Neighbour of Alice Nutter at Rough Lee.

Roger Nowell. Justice of the Peace for the Pendle area, living at Read, just off the south-western end of Pendle Forest. About sixty years old.

Alexander Nowell. Roger's son. Eighteen years old.

Alice Nutter. Member of a wealthy Pendle family living at Rough Lee. Client of the Sothernes/Device family.

Anthony Nutter. Client of the Sothernes/Device family, living in Goldshey Booth.

Anne Nutter, Anthony's daughter. Friend of Alizon Device.

Christopher Nutter. Landlord of the Redferne family, living at Greene Head in Pendle Forest.

John Nutter, Christopher's son.

Robert Nutter, Christopher's son.

John Nutter. Client of the Sothernes/Device family, living at Bulhole in Pendle Forest.

Thomas Potts. Court official at the Assizes. Author of the pamphlet about the case, *The Wonderful Discovery of Witches in the County of Lancaster*.

Jennet Preston. Friend of the Sothernes/Device family, living at Gisburne, just over the border in Yorkshire.

William Preston. Jennet's husband.

Anne Redferne. Wise woman living in Pendle Forest, daughter of Anne Whittle.

Thomas Redferne, Anne's husband.

Marie Redferne, Anne's daughter.

John Robinson. Acquaintance of the Sothernes/Device family, living in Barley.

James Robinson, his brother.

Elizabeth Sothernes. (also known as Elizabeth Demdike) Wise woman living at Malking Tower at the northern end of Pendle Forest. About eighty years old. Mother of Elizabeth Device and Christopher Howgate.

Nicholas Starkie. Roger Nowell's nephew, living at Huntroyde, just off the south-western end of Pendle Forest.

Anne Starkie. Nicholas's wife.

Anne (jr.) and **John Starkie**, their children.

Anne and **Henry Towneley**. Members of a wealthy Pendle family, living at Carre Hall in Pendle Forest. Employed the Device family to do casual work for them; perhaps also to perform magic.

Anne Whittle. (also known as Anne Chattox) Wise woman living in Pendle Forest, about eighty years old. Mother of Anne Redferne.

Preface

A few years ago it would have been impossible for me to write this book. The history of witchcraft is a subject full of horror, mystery and weirdness; but recently an increasing number of researchers have confronted its challenges, and I owe a great deal to their work, as well as to the encouragement, inspiration and support I have received from so many generous people.

It is important to be able to read our ancestors' own words if we are to have any hope of understanding a subject as complex and controversial as witchcraft. Fortunately a wide range of witchcraft case records, books of magic and accounts of folk magic are now accessible to modern readers, thanks to the efforts of editors, translators and publishers such as Richard Kieckhefer, Marion Gibson, Todd Gray, Hashem Atallah, Kessinger Publishing and Caduceus Books. Many important works can now be read online, for example on Joseph H. Peterson's remarkable *Esoteric Archives* website, and the Internet is also an invaluable way to track down books and articles. I hope the quotations I have included here will inspire readers to consult these often fascinating sources for themselves.

Two modern books have also had a crucial influence on me. Emma Wilby's *Cunning Folk and Familiar Spirits* demonstrated that it's possible to cut through the grim propaganda of witchcraft case records and uncover surprising glimpses of suspects' magical practices and beliefs. Jonathan Lumby's *The Lancashire Witch-Craze* revealed two enormously significant facts about the 1612 Pendle case – the campaign by Jennet Preston's family to clear her name, and the effect on Roger Nowell, the Justice of the Peace, of the earlier witchcraft case involving his close relatives the Starkies.

I would also never have written this book if I had not had access to the collection and library at the Museum of Witchcraft, and the help and support of my colleagues there – Graham King, Kerriann Godwin, Hannah Fox, Carole Talboys and Jack Evans. I should, however, perhaps make clear that the views I express are entirely my own. The museum exists simply to make magic-related objects available to the public, so that people can reach their own conclusions about them – not to promote any particular ideas, theories or beliefs.

Through the museum I have had many fascinating, thought-provoking and informative conversations, sometimes with anonymous visitors, and also with the many people who are regular supporters of the museum. Many are mentioned in the notes. In particular I would like to thank Steve Patterson, who made my scrying mirror; Martin Walker, who took part in the scrying experiment; Jason Semmens, who not only helped me with my work on *The Lenkiewicz Manuscript* but has also edited a wonderful collection of the writings of William Henry Paynter; and Liz Crow, who (among other things) reminded me of the importance of *The Egyptian Book of the Dead*.

I'm also extremely grateful to all the friends and acquaintances whose enthusiasm for this project has kept me inspired and motivated. And I owe a special mention to the people who actually read and advised me on the manuscript – my brother Peter, Christine Pritchard, Michael Howard, Helen Cornish, Lesley Heron, and Jenny and Chris Southern. The inspiration provided by my cats and Ben the (almost) black dog is harder to define but still invaluable.

Special thanks are also due to Vivienne Shanley and Tim, Mary, Tom and Kate Neale for their work on the illustrations, which extended to helping to research them and appearing in them. Recreating seventeenth century spellcraft led to some unexpected insights as well as helping me to define the central themes of the book. And I am also indebted to Nicky and Frank Grace for their hospitality and photographs on the field trip to Pendle, and to Rachel Turner for allowing us to explore the site of Malking Tower.

I would also like to mention the assistance I've received from libraries and record offices; and also Anna Goddard, Lucy Frontani and all the team at Carnegie Publishing, for having such a clear appreciation of what I was trying to achieve, and doing so much to help me achieve it.

But of course my greatest debt is to the cunning folk and magicians who are the subject of this book, and whose stories have left me with a profound respect for their resourcefulness, determination, humour and courage – and especially to Edmund Hartlay, whose fate illustrates so dramatically the complex, perilous status of cunning folk, and to James and Alizon Device.

CHAPTER ONE

Alizon the Witch

The evidence of John Law ... About the eighteenth of March last past, he being a peddler, went with his pack of wares at his back through Colne-field: where unluckily he met with Alizon Device ... who was very earnest with him for pins, but he would give her none: whereupon she seemed to be very angry; and when he was past her, he fell down lame in great extremity.

(*The Wonderful Discovery of Witches in the County of Lancaster* by Thomas Potts.[1])

'Unluckily he met with Alizon Device ...'. Eleven people died because John Law was at Colne-field that day. His argument with a teenage girl triggered one of the most dramatic and horrifying witchcraft cases in English history. The trials caused such controversy that a pamphlet, *The Wonderful Discovery of Witches in the County of Lancaster*, was written 'by commandment of his Majesty's Justices of Assize in the North Parts' to give the official version of what had happened.[2] It's a blatantly biased account; but in spite of all its distortions it still can't hide the fact that the defendants suffered an appalling miscarriage of justice.

At the heart of the case was the conflict between the local Justice of the Peace, Roger Nowell, and Alizon Device's family. *The Wonderful Discovery* includes the statements Roger Nowell took from them – from Alizon herself, her older brother James, her sister Jennet (about nine years old), her mother Elizabeth, and her grandmother Elizabeth Sothernes.[3] It's a disturbing record of a battle of wills fought out through a series of grim interrogations. Roger Nowell ruthlessly falsified evidence, but for a simple reason. He was convinced of his suspects' guilt.

Alizon and her family openly practised magic. Their lives and values were shaped by a complex magical culture – a strange fusion of Christian and pre-Christian elements. Magic gave them practical ways to deal with everyday problems – illness, bad luck and unhappiness in love. But it also had a profound effect on their spiritual beliefs. There was very little evidence that they had committed any of the crimes they were accused of, but their magic called on the help of supernatural forces that Roger Nowell sincerely believed were evil.

THE

WONDERFVLL

DISCOVERIE OF

WITCHES IN THE COVN-
TIE OF LAN-
CASTER.

With the Arraignement and Triall of
Nineteene notorious WITCHES, at the Assizes and
generall Gaole deliuerie, holden at the Castle of
LANCASTER, *vpon Munday, the se-
uenteenth of August last,*
1612.

Before Sir IAMES ALTHAM, and
Sir EDWARD BROMLEY, Knights; BARONS of his
Maiesties Court of EXCHEQVER: And Iustices
of Assize, Oyer *and* Terminor, *and generall*
Gaole deliuerie in the circuit of the
North Parts.

Together with the Arraignement and Triall of IENNET
PRESTON, *at the Assizes holden at the Castle of Yorke,
the seuen and twentieth day of Iulie last past,*
with her Execution for the murther
of Master LISTER
by Witchcraft.

Published and set forth by commandement of his Maiesties
Iustices of Assize in the North Parts.

By THOMAS POTTS *Esquier.*

LONDON,
Printed by *W. Stansby* for *Iohn Barnes,* dwelling neare
Holborne Conduit. 1613.

The case of the Pendle witches raises questions that are still important today. Questions about guilt and truth; about the relationship between the material world and the realm of the spirit; about good and evil; and about the nature of magic and the nature of power.

John Law, the peddler, encountered Alizon just outside the small town of Colne in Lancashire, on the edge of the spectacular moorland around Pendle Hill. Just 400 metres away was an inn, where no doubt he hoped to find some buyers for the goods in his pack. Mostly he sold small items such as ribbons and buttons. This was a rural community, and many people were paid not in cash but in farm produce. Money was scarce.

John travelled this route regularly, and for the local people he was also an important source of news and gossip. He may even have sold pamphlets and ballads about some of the more sensational recent news stories. The growth of printing and literacy meant that even in country districts people were well aware of current events and the latest controversies.[4]

The year was 1612, and one of the subjects most hotly discussed in early-seventeenth-century England was witchcraft. This was the mid-point of the English witch-trials period. It had begun fifty years before, and the last execution of an alleged witch would be in seventy years' time.[5] And on this particular March day it was especially topical. A local woman had just been tried for murdering a child by witchcraft (and found not guilty) at the Lent Assizes at York.[6] In fact, there was so much suspicion of witchcraft in the area that at the August Assizes at Lancaster there would be three unrelated witchcraft cases.

John probably felt uneasy as soon as he saw Alizon. He seems to have recognised her immediately,[7] and he would have known she was a 'wise woman' – someone who practised magic. Alizon would never have referred to herself as a witch. In the seventeenth century the word 'witch' had a very narrow meaning – someone who used magic to do harm. In fact many people regarded wise women and cunning men (as male practitioners were often called[8]) as their main defence *against* witches. Much of Alizon's magical power came from a healing charm that was handed down in the family from generation to generation, and which they claimed 'would cure one bewitched'.[9]

In fact one book written at the time accused wise women of stirring up the fear of witchcraft and encouraging the persecution of innocent people:

> He sent to the [wise] woman at R.H. and she said he was plagued by a witch, adding moreover, that there were three women witches in that town, and one man witch: willing him to look whom he most suspected: he suspected one old woman, and caused her to be carried before a Justice of the Peace … She was committed to the prison, and there she died before the Assizes.
>
> (*A Dialogue Concerning Witches and Witchcrafts* by George Gifford[10])

But wise women and cunning men could themselves be witches. When the cunning man John Walsh was arrested in 1566, his interrogators specifically asked 'whether they that do good to such as are bewitched, cannot also do hurt if they list [want to.]' He replied that 'he which hath the gift of healing, may do hurt if he list, but his gift of healing can never return again.'[11]

Also, of course, injuring someone physically was not the only way to harm them. It could be argued – and was – that all magic was essentially evil, even magic used for healing. It seduced both the practitioners themselves and their clients away from God, because it could only be performed with the help of the Devil and evil spirits:

> He [the Devil] worketh by his other sort of witches, whom the people call cunning men and wise women ... and by them teacheth many remedies, that so he may be sought unto and honoured as God.
>
> (*A Dialogue Concerning Witches and Witchcrafts*[12])

> By witches we understand not those only which kill and torment, but all diviners, charmers, jugglers, all wizards commonly called wise men and wise women ...; and in the same number we reckon all good witches, which do no hurt but good, which do not spoil and destroy, but save and deliver ... These are the right hand of the Devil, by which he taketh and destroyeth the souls of men.
>
> (*A Discourse of the Damned Art of Witchcraft*
> by William Perkins[13])

This was not a new idea. It had been the official view of the Church throughout the Middle Ages:

> Magic is ... a teacher of every kind of wickedness and evil-doing, [it] lies about the truth and in actual fact does harm to people's minds, it leads them astray from God's religion, persuades them to worship evil spirits, lets loose a degeneration of virtuous behaviour, and drives the minds of those who pursue it towards every type of crime and forbidden wickedness.
>
> (*Didascalion* by Hugh of St Victor[14])

Indeed, John Law, on his travels through Pendle, had heard many sinister rumours about Alizon and her family. There were stories that her grandmother's exceptional powers were the result of a visit from a spirit that had left her insane for weeks. It was said that Alizon's brother James – who was probably not yet twenty – had already murdered at least one person by witchcraft. And apparently Alizon herself, who was only about seventeen, had bewitched a child, although the child had recovered after a confrontation between Alizon and the father.[15]

But anyone in John's line of business must have been a tough character used to dealing with all kinds of strange people. Why didn't he just sell Alizon the pins and get rid of her?

Perhaps he didn't want to take off his pack at the roadside, when there was an inn so close. But he could easily have explained that politely, and got Alizon to go with him to the inn. Instead, things quickly became tense. According to John, Alizon became 'very earnest'. Alizon's own statement adds more details:

> This examinate [Alizon] demanded of the said peddler to buy some pins of him; but the said peddler sturdily answered this examinate that he would not loose his pack.[16]

'Sturdily' means more than just 'obstinately'. In the seventeenth century it meant 'harshly', or even 'violently'.[17] In Alizon's version, it seems clear that John didn't *want* to sell her the pins.[18]

Buying pins would have been quite an extravagance for a young girl like Alizon. It would have been unusual for her to be paid in cash, so she would have had very little actual money. Making pins by hand was labour intensive, so seventeenth-century pins were far from cheap. In fact it's likely that many country people normally used blackthorn points – pins made from the thorns of blackthorn trees. They were light, slender and sharp, and could be snapped off the tree for nothing.[19]

It's clear that Alizon was very determined to get hold of some metal pins, and John was equally determined that she shouldn't have them. It may seem strange that such a serious argument – which had such terrible consequences – should have started over something so trivial. But in fact pins were far less trivial then than they are now.

Today when we think of the tools of magic we think of wands, crystal balls and rings of power – glamorous and mysterious things. But in practice the object most often used for magic was the pin. It was used in spells for protection, for healing, for divination, to bring good luck, to curse, to reverse a curse, and for love magic. Its significance is recorded in a rhyme still often said today:

> See a pin and pick it up,
> All the day you'll have good luck.
> See a pin and let it lie,
> Sure to rue it by and by.[20]

It was love magic, of course, that was of particular interest to teenage girls:

The women have several magical secrets handed down to them by tradition … as, on St. Agnes' night, 21st day of January, take a row of pins, and pull out every one, one after another, saying a Pater Noster, or Our Father, sticking a pin in your sleeve, and you will dream of him, or her, you shall marry.

(*Miscellanies* by John Aubrey[21])

Another seventeenth-century spell was a little more complicated:

Yet I have another pretty way for a maid to know her sweetheart, which is as followeth. Take a summer apple, of the best fruit you can get, and take three of the best pins you can get, and stick them into the apple close to the head, and as you stick them in, take notice which of them is in the middle, and what name thou fancies best give that middle pin and put it into thy left-handed glove, and lay it under thy pillow on a Saturday at night but thou must be in bed before thou lays it under thy head, and when thou hast done, clasp thy hands together speaking these words:

> If thou be he that must have me
> To be thy wedded bride,

Researcher Kate recreates an early-twentieth-century love spell, using an onion to symbolise the young man's heart.

> Make no delay but come away
> This night to my bedside.[22]
>
> (*Mother Bunch's Closet Newly Broke Open* by T.R.)

A very similar version recorded in the early twentieth century used an onion instead of an apple, and is clearer about how the pins should be positioned. Nine pins were used, with eight forming a circle and the ninth 'given the name of the "true love"' and stuck in the centre. In this case, the spell had to be performed on St Thomas's Eve, and the saint was invoked in the charm:

> Good St. Thomas, do me right,
> Send me my true love this night,
> In his clothes and his array
> Which he weareth every day.
>
> (*Pins & Pincushions* by E.D. Longman and S. Loch[23])

As well as spells to summon a vision – or perhaps it would be truer to say the *spirit* – of her lover, a girl could also use magic to bring him to her in person:

If a lover did not visit his sweetheart as often as she wished, she roasted an onion stuck full of an ounce of pins. The pins must have never been through paper, and were supposed to prick his wandering heart and bring him to his lady's feet.

(Pins & Pincushions[24])

Again, this is a spell recorded in the early twentieth century, but it's based on the same principles as one recorded 500 years earlier, used by Matteuccia di Francesco, an Italian wise woman. A client wanted to regain the affection of her lover, who was ill-treating her. Matteuccia and her client worked a spell that involved melting a wax image over a heated tile, while the client recited a charm linking the image to her lover's heart and binding him to her will. Apparently the spell was a great success.[25] Wax images could be heart-shaped as well as in the shape of a human figure. One is mentioned in the seventeenth-century play *The Witch* by Thomas Middleton – 'Is the heart of wax stuck full of magic needles?'[26] In the play the image is used for a curse, but images were used just as often for love magic as for cursing. The methods were the same: it was the *intent* that was different.

In many ways, though, an apple or onion was a better representation of a lover's heart than a wax image. An apple would remind whoever worked the spell of the apple Eve gave Adam, which robbed them of their sexual innocence. An onion 'bleeds' when it's cut, and, as a root, contains the energy the plant needs to survive, just as the energy of the heart is essential to the survival of the human body.

So did John Law suspect that Alizon was about to use her evil powers to seduce some unfortunate young man? Or perhaps Alizon was not alone. She was, after all,

Pendle Hill from Pendle Forest.
COPYRIGHT NICKY AND FRANK GRACE

either leaving or heading into town. Perhaps she'd met up with a group of friends.[27] Perhaps John was confronted by a whole gang of teenage girls joking about the magical havoc they were about to wreak on Pendle's male population.

There was nothing noble or exalted about the aims of wise women and cunning men. They and their clients were very ordinary people. They wanted magic to get them out of difficulties, and bring them a little pleasure in life. And that was one of the things that made magic so abhorrent to the authorities – the God-fearing men of Church and State. What if it was true that a girl like Alizon could know a spell to turn a young man's heart? How could someone like her – an unruly, disrespectful, bad-tempered teenage girl – have some kind of strange power? Only if she was a tool of the Devil.

CHAPTER TWO

Love magic and pin magic

SEX AND MAGIC

Next, the master [i.e. the magician] drives the pins into the image, positioning one in the head, another in the right arm, the third in the left arm, the fourth where the heart is supposed to be, at that point saying, 'As this pin is driven into the heart of this image, so may love of N [the magician's name] be driven into the heart of N [the name of the desired woman], so that she cannot sleep, wake, rest, stay, go, until she burns with love for me'; the fifth [pin] in the navel, the sixth in the groin, the seventh in the right side, the eighth in the left side, the ninth in the anus … and says, 'I command, as follows, N [the woman's name], your head, your hair, your eyes, your ears …; I command, N, your kidneys, I command, N, your sides; I command, N, your anus; I command, N, your ribcage; I command, N, your womb …; I command, N, your whole self; I command, N, your whole essence; so that you cannot sleep nor settle nor rest nor have any skill at anything, until you have fulfilled my erotic purpose.'[1]

This remarkably intense and ruthless love spell is from a fifteenth-century book of magic named *The Munich Handbook* by its modern editor Richard Kieckhefer. It confirms just how important love magic was – to the educated magicians who wrote and read these books as well as to the wise women and cunning men who practised folk magic.[2] It's also clear that this spell was intended for the magician's own personal use – not to help a client.

The concept of the magician as sexual predator is an important element – with a rather off-key comic tone – in the pamphlet *News from Scotland*, published in London in 1591.[3] It's an account of the North Berwick witchcraft case, which began when the deputy bailiff of Trenent discovered that his servant Geillis Duncane was a wise woman.

This Geillis Duncane took in hand to help all such as were troubled or grieved with any kind of sickness or infirmity, and in short space did perform many matters most miraculous.

The deputy bailiff, suspecting 'it to be done by some extraordinary and unlawful means', had her tortured. She confessed to being a witch, and incriminated several other people, including a young schoolteacher, Dr John Fian.

John Fian, it seems, was already rumoured to be a magician, and *News from Scotland* recounts a bizarre story about him. Apparently he fell for the sister of one of his pupils, and decided to use a love spell on her. The spell required three of her pubic hairs, and he persuaded her brother to get them for him while she was asleep. However, the girl woke up, and complained to her mother, who got the story out of the boy, and then (being a witch herself) gave him three hairs from a cow to take to John Fian instead. John 'wrought his art upon them', with the result that the cow came 'leaping and dancing upon him' and followed him wherever he went 'to the admiration of all the townsmen'.[4]

In fact this is an updated version of a story from *The Golden Ass* by the Roman writer Lucius Apuleius.[5] It may have been added to *News from Scotland* by the pamphlet's author as a way of (literally) sexing it up; or it may have found its way into popular folklore and then attached itself to John Fian after he was suspected of being a magician.[6] However, the idea of a love spell that involved animal hairs was not completely ridiculous. The spell in *The Munich Handbook* involved various preparations, which included obtaining three hairs from the desired woman, and three from any red-coloured animal.

The fear of love magic was certainly very real, and was reflected in English law. The *Act Against Conjurations, Enchantments, and Witchcrafts* of 1563 made a year's imprisonment, with four six-hour sessions in the pillory, the punishment 'if any person or persons … shall use or practice any sorcery, enchantment, charm or witchcraft to the intent to provoke any person to unlawful love'. For a second offence, the punishment was life imprisonment. In 1604 the law was strengthened, making death by hanging the penalty for a second offence. In fact conditions in the prisons of the time were so appalling that even a year's imprisonment was often a death sentence.[7]

In another pamphlet, *Witches Apprehended*, it is a woman, Mary Sutton, who is portrayed as a sexual predator. Her technique is rather different, however. She puts a curse on someone and then tries to seduce him by offering to cure him:

> She drew nearer unto him, and sat by his bedside (yet all the while he had neither power to stir or speak) and told him if he would consent she should come to bed to him, he should be restored to his former health … He that before had neither power to move, or speak, had then presently by divine assistance free power and liberty to give repulse to her assault, and denial to her filthy and detested motion: and to upbraid her of her abominable life and behaviour, having before had three bastards and never married.[8]

Women accused of witchcraft often had a reputation for sexual misconduct. Ursley Kempe, the wise woman at the centre of the St Osyth case in Essex, had an illegitimate son;[9] and Alizon Device's mother Elizabeth supposedly put a curse on someone because he 'had chidden and becalled [her] for having a bastard child with one Seller'.[10]

In Thomas Middleton's play *The Witch*, Hecate (the witch of the title) cheerfully discusses taking on the form of a demon (an *incubus*) to seduce young men – blurring the distinction between human witches and evil spirits:

Hecate:	What young man can we wish to pleasure us
	But we enjoy him in an incubus?
	Thou know'st it Stadlin?
Stadlin:	Usually that's done.
Hecate:	Last night thou got'st the Mayor of Whelplie's son.
	I knew him by his black cloak lined with yellow;
	I think thou'st spoiled the youth; he's but seventeen;
	I'll have him the next mounting.[11]

Later, Hecate's son Firestone says, 'Mother, I pray you give me leave to ramble abroad tonight with the Nightmare, for I have a great mind to overlay a fat parson's daughter.'[12] This is a reference to the condition now known as sleep paralysis, which occurs when a person's body chemistry is disrupted during the transition from sleeping to waking. The person is temporarily paralysed and feels unable to breathe. This – in a way still not fully understood – triggers an altered state of consciousness. Sufferers experience panic and hallucinations – anything from a sensation that something is lying on top of them to a vivid and convincing vision of a hideous demon attacking them. Usually sufferers don't find anything sexual in this horrible experience, but to authors writing about witchcraft its potential for sexual overtones was obvious. It became one of the clichés of witchcraft that when a witch cursed someone she 'lay upon' them.[13] In his statement against Alizon Device, John Law's son Abraham claimed 'that he heard his said father further say, that the said Alizon Device did lie upon him'.[14]

METHODS OF LOVE MAGIC

Thomas Middleton's fictional witch Hecate is a comically sinister figure, but, even so, she has a steady stream of clients coming to her for help. One of them is a young man who wants a love spell, and he's not very impressed when Hecate tries to give him the brain of a black cat wrapped in a handkerchief.[15]

This is not just a grisly figment of Thomas Middleton's imagination. The use of bizarre animal ingredients was an important aspect of magic. It was based not on contempt for the lives of animals but – on the contrary – on a sense that the natural world was infused with hidden magical power.[16] Cat's brain was used for healing by a wise woman arrested in France in 1573.[17] It was included in a recipe for incense in Heinrich Cornelius Agrippa's influential *Three Books of Occult Philosophy*.[18] And its use in love magic was recorded by Reginald Scot, a Justice of the Peace who campaigned against the witch-hunts.

Reginald Scot's list of love magic ingredients also includes newts' and lizards' brains, hair from the tip of a wolf's tail, a wolf's penis, a bone from a frog, remora fish and swallow nestlings.[19] Most of them were probably used in love potions, which often consisted of a mixture of herbs and animal ingredients. *The Book of Secrets of Albertus Magnus* gives a typical recipe – periwinkle, houseleek and earthworms.[20] The Italian wise woman Matteuccia di Francesco made love potions out of eggs and herbs. She also instructed a woman whose husband was unfaithful to feed a baby swallow on sugar, then kill and burn it, and make the ashes into a potion by mixing them with wine and water she'd used to wash her feet.[21]

Unfortunately people were sometimes poisoned by love potions. In 1370 a French wise woman was executed after supplying a client with a potion that was intended to make his wife love him, but instead tragically killed her.[22] Even if the ingredients weren't dangerous in themselves, it must often have been difficult to keep them fresh until they could be put into the person's food without arousing suspicion.

Alternatively, the target could be tricked into wearing a magical object. The frog bone had to be made into a ring – presumably disguised by some more conventional form of decoration.[23] Or the object could be put in or under the person's bed. In 1394 an Italian woman was sentenced to be whipped and imprisoned for putting bread, charcoal, salt and a coin engraved with a cross in a man's bed to make him love her.[24]

An early twentieth-century spell sensibly used something less likely to be discovered – a willow catkin:

> Get some willow-knots [catkins], cut one of them, and put it into thy mouth, and say:
>
> > I eat thy luck
> > I drink thy luck
> > Give me that luck of thine
> > Then thou shalt be mine.
>
> Then if thou canst, hide the knot in the bed of the wished-for bride.
>
> (*The Book of Charms and Ceremonies* by 'Merlin'[25])

This demonstrates that the substances used in magic didn't necessarily have to be exotic. Salt is often mentioned. Another love spell recorded in the early twentieth century involved throwing salt on a fire and saying:

> > It is not the salt I wish to burn,
> > It is my lover's heart to turn;
> > That he may not rest nor happy be,
> > Until he comes and speaks to me.
>
> (*The Hand of Destiny* by C.J.S. Thompson[26])

A love charm consisting of a triangular box containing pubic hair, and incorporating the sacred name of God AGLA (MoW 748).

This had to be done on three consecutive Fridays – the day ruled by the planet Venus.

There were objects you could wear or carry to make you irresistibly attractive – henbane root, for example, or a purple geode.[27] *Liber de Angelis* (*The Book of Angels*) by Messayaac includes a ritual for persuading a spirit to give you one of these objects. It involved going to a crossroads or the site of a gallows and inscribing a circle on the ground using a cedar wand and a white-handled knife. The spirit – Zagam – was invoked by sacrificing three doves, and then tearing them apart and throwing the pieces into the air. The magician then appealed to the spirit for help:

> I request you, Zagam, and all your comrades, to bring me something that, if it is seen by any woman, will at once set her alight with the fire of love for me, and that has the power, in all things, to fulfil my purpose.

The next morning the magician would find the object lying where he had made the circle. Messayaac uses the word *figura* – a vague term meaning 'shape' or 'form' – which suggests that it could be some natural object that the magician would recognise by its significant shape – perhaps one of the doves' bones.[28]

Talismans – objects inscribed with pictures, words or symbols – were also important in love magic, and often used in a similar way to wax or clay images. *Picatrix*, a book of Arabic magic first used in Europe in the thirteenth century, gives instructions for a spell that involved engraving a picture of a woman on one piece of metal and a man on another. It was essential that this was done at exactly the right time astrologically, to draw on the magical influence of the correct planets and constellations. The two talismans were then placed together as if they were embracing, and buried beneath the main street of a town. 'And then men and women will like one another and have affectionate relationships' – an appealing picture of an entire town overwhelmed with romance.[29]

The Museum of Witchcraft has an early-twentieth-century love talisman that consists of a triangular box decorated with a heart pierced by an arrow (magical imagery still seen on Valentine's Day cards today), the initials J and F, Hebrew letters, and the letters AGLA. AGLA is one of the sacred names of God, almost certainly an acronym for 'Attah Gibbor Le'olam Adonai' – 'You are great forever, O Lord'.[30] The box contains pubic hair.[31]

Another spell in *The Munich Handbook* combined elements of talismanic and image magic with the use of animal bone. The name of the desired man or woman was written on the blade-bone of an ass, hare, goose or capon, together with the names of seven spirits. The bone was then placed on hot charcoal and the magician recited a long incantation. This involved invoking the seven spirits, compelling them to co-operate by using various sacred names of God, and then saying:

> Just as this blade-bone is heated and burns, so may you make this person N [name] burn and become hot with the fire of love for me, so that she (he) will never be able to rest until she (he) fulfils my purpose.[32]

Interestingly, in view of John Fian's supposed experience with the cow, this spell could also be used to tame animals.

INTENT

Using magic to make someone love you is obviously morally questionable, but anyone who's been in love will surely understand it. It's hard not to feel sympathy for the man who gave his wife a fatal potion because he wanted her to love him; or for Matteuccia di Francesco's client, mentioned in Chapter One, who was locked in an abusive relationship and desperately wanted her lover to treat her better.

But what are we to make of the kind of magician who would use the spell quoted at the beginning of this chapter? The violence of driving the pins into the image carries overtones of rape that simply cannot be ignored. This was exactly the kind of spell that gave magic a bad name and provided those who attacked magic with an easy target. But if we analyse it in full we can find some redeeming features – or at least intriguing ones.

The spell involved complicated preparations. The magician had to persuade a craftsman to make the pins specially at an astrologically favourable time. The wax for the image had to be ritually purified. The magician had to obtain three hairs from the woman and three from a red-coloured animal. He had to find two companions to assist him with the ritual itself – and who could be trusted not to betray him to the authorities. Interestingly (and rather touchingly) another book, *The Key of Solomon*, says that if the magician has no trustworthy human colleagues his dog can go with him instead.[33]

The magician and his assistants (or dog) then went to a place where there was a fruit-bearing tree (again at the astrologically correct time) and created a magical space for the magician to work in. This was done by clearing an area of bare ground, probably scattering a layer of ash or powdered clay, and then making a circle.[34] The instructions for this are quite specific: the magician had to invoke the help of three spirits – Belial, Astaroth and Paymon – by inscribing the circle on the ground with a white-handled knife and writing the names of the spirits around its edge.[35] Within the circle, the magician then shaped the image, softening the wax over hot charcoal.

And so, before the spell could even begin, the magician had to acquire magical tools, create a magical space, and gain the assistance of both human and supernatural allies. And no doubt these preparations were in part a test of his character and commitment – a way of weeding out the selfish bastards and the psychopathic stalkers. But they would also have had a significant effect on the spell's most important ingredient – the magician's mind. Before he could exert power over the woman, he had to draw on magical forces outside himself. As he stood in the circle holding the purified wax, he was no longer someone locked in the loneliness of hopeless desire – he was someone who now had a part of the Universe on his side.

Driving the pins into the image was just the beginning. Once that had been done the magician christened it, giving it the woman's name and immersing it in water three times. He then wrapped it in a clean cloth and laid it aside. Then he turned to face east and began his incantation, claiming power over each part of the woman's body in turn, and constantly repeating her name. He must, inevitably, have visualised her as he did so. He was using magic to fulfil his sexual desire, but he was also using his sexual desire to fuel his magic. As this section of the incantation ends, the wording is significant:

> I command, N, your whole self; I command, N, your whole essence; so that you cannot sleep nor settle nor rest nor have any skill at anything, until you have fulfilled my erotic purpose.

The magician does *not* say, 'until you have satisfied my lust' (*donec meam libidinem compleveris*), but 'until you have fulfilled my erotic purpose' (*donec meam libidinosam compleveris voluntatem*).

This concept of *voluntas* – purpose, intent or will – is central to magic, as in the notorious statement by Aleister Crowley:

Do what thou wilt shall be the whole of the law.[36]

Again, this demonstrates the crucial importance of the magician's mind. *Voluntas* represents an internal magical transformation. What began as ordinary sexual desire has become magical intent.

Magical intent was what made it possible to access the ultimate source of all magical power, invoked in the next stage of the incantation:

I command you ... by the true name Sabaoth [Lord of Hosts], by the true name Seraphin [an angel name associated with spiritual love], by the true name Emanuel [God With Us], by all the remains of the saints that lie in Rome, by the moon and the sun and the Lord who is greater still, and by the milk of the Virgin, by holy Mary, mother of our Lord Jesus Christ, by the holy eucharist, by the body and blood of Jesus Christ.[37]

Of course this spell is unashamedly sexual and disturbingly aggressive, but the magic itself pushes the magician *beyond* that and into contact with divine power. The word he uses repeatedly – *conjuro*, 'command' – means specifically 'command by invoking the sacred'.[38]

This is Christian magic, but obviously not conventional Christianity. Of course love magic pre-dates Christianity, and this is – to an extent – a pre-Christian spell that has been Christianised.[39] But it's also clear that the magic practised by magicians affected their Christianity – their view of the nature of divine power, and therefore of the nature of God.

But this was not simply blasphemy. Moral arrogance, perhaps – but the magician had to be sure that he had achieved some kind of inner justification. Because the divine power he invoked would judge him. As *The Sworn Book* by Honorius of Thebes says, 'Men have entitled this book ... the death of the soul, and that is true to them that work for an evil intent and purpose.'[40]

DREAMS AND DIVINATION

From the seventeenth to the twentieth century there are numerous records of spells that would enable a young woman to see her future husband in a dream. It's very tempting to think that these are love spells in disguise, that the aim was not just to see the future husband but to make it the right person – but without the spiritual and moral risks of obviously aggressive love magic, not to mention the risk of getting arrested. In their book *Pins and Pincushions*, published in 1911, E.D. Longman and S. Loch record a spell that seems deliberately vague about whether its aim is to foretell the future or gain power over the young man:

In some places they take the blade-bone of a rabbit, stick nine pins in it, and then put it under their pillows, and during the night they are sure to see the object of their affections.[41]

On the other hand, the spells recorded by the late-seventeenth-century writer John Aubrey are far more innocent-seeming, perhaps because love magic still carried the risk of the gallows at that point. One – which he calls charming the moon – involved standing astride a gate or stile on a new moon and saying:

> All hail to thee, moon, all hail to thee,
> I prithee good moon reveal to me
> This night who my husband (wife) must be.

Another involved knotting together a garter and a stocking with nine knots while reciting a charm, tying each knot at a pause in the charm:

> This knot I knit,
> To know the thing,
> I know not yet.
> That I may see,
> The man (woman) that shall my husband (wife) be,
> How he goes,
> And what he wears,
> And what he does,
> All days, and years.

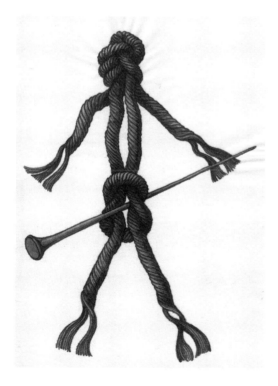

Love magic – an image made from knotted cord pierced with a pin. Picture in the Museum of Witchcraft's Richel Collection (MoW R/10/1293).

COPYRIGHT MUSEUM OF WITCHCRAFT,
PHOTOGRAPH GRAHAM KING

He also describes personally seeing a group of girls digging up plantains in the hope of finding a 'coal' that apparently formed beneath the root, which would be placed under the pillow like the rabbit bone.

Another of his examples was straightforward fortune telling. An egg-white was put in a glass and stood in the sun, and then examined for shapes that would indicate the future husband's profession – a process rather similar to reading tea leaves, which was, of course, a very popular form of divination in the nineteenth and twentieth centuries.[42]

Fortune telling was widely practised at Halloween, even in the seventeenth century. In 1641 a Scottish man was hauled up before his local presbytery for selling nuts for Halloween divination. In fact in the north of England Halloween used to be known as Nut-Crack Night.[43] The nuts were placed in a fire, and how they behaved was used to foretell the person's future health or fortunes in love. *The Folklore Calendar* by George Long, published in 1930, describes a typical method:

> The girls and boys, but especially the former, endeavour to discover the probable course of their love affairs by means of nuts. Two are placed side by side on the bars of the grate to represent a pair of lovers, or if a girl has two suitors she will name each nut after one of them, and place one in the middle to represent herself. If the nut cracks or jumps away the lover it represents will prove unfaithful, but if two blaze together they will be married.[44]

The Museum of Witchcraft has a humorous Halloween postcard from the early twentieth century depicting eight hazelnuts with little faces, smiling or frowning depending on whether the romantic prospects are good or bad.

This postcard has a companion by the same artist, Ellen Clapsaddle, which features cabbages instead of nuts. Exactly how cabbage divination would work was something of a puzzle, until a visitor to the museum revealed that she'd actually done it. On Halloween night she and a group of friends went out into a field of cabbages and each pulled one out by the root. The length of the root was supposed to indicate both the attractiveness of the future partner and the strength of the relationship. Remarkably, arcane folk magic practices like divination by cabbage are still happening out in the British countryside.[45]

Like Halloween, holy wells have also been associated with divination for centuries. In the early seventeenth century churchgoers on Palm Sunday would throw their palm crosses into Lady Nant's Well in Cornwall; if the cross sank, the person would die within the year.[46] A rather similar form of love divination was recorded in Wales in the nineteenth century: blackthorn points were thrown into the water at Ffynnon Saethon – if they floated the lover was faithful, if they sank he was unfaithful,[47] while if a pin thrown into St Helen's Well at Sefton in Lancashire landed on the bottom pointing towards the church, the person who threw it would be married within a year.[48] And if three pins were thrown into St Caradog's Well in Wales on Easter Monday, and the young woman then gazed into the water, she would see the face of her future husband.[49]

PINS FOR HEALING AND PROTECTION

Pins were also used for healing, and in particular for curing warts. A Welsh method – again recorded in the nineteenth century – involved pricking each wart with a pin, then rubbing it with sheep's wool found in the hedgerow. The pins were then bent and thrown into a holy well, and the wool hung in a hawthorn tree.[50] A simpler method, used by a wise woman, is described in *Pins and Pincushions*:

> It was also believed that pins would cure warts, and one way of doing this was to make the sign of the cross on each wart with a pin, and then throw it away. There is an old woman now living in Suffolk who cures warts in this way.

Pins and Pincushions also gives an attractive example of protection magic involving pins:

> Sailors, when starting on a voyage, are still often given, for luck, heart-shaped pincushions stuck full of bead-headed pins in fancy designs.

Sixteenth- and seventeenth-century pamphlets sometimes describe victims of witchcraft vomiting pins, and *Pins and Pincushions* suggests a convincing explanation:

> Sometimes … they were swallowed willingly, with the object of wounding the evil spirits of which the swallower believed himself to be possessed.[51]

Certainly pins were often used in counter-magic against curses. *The Evil Eye* by Frederick Thomas Elworthy includes a typical nineteenth-century example:

> Some of the old people declared it to have been a custom when a pig died from the 'overlooking' of a witch to have its heart stuck full of pins and white thorns, and to put it up the chimney, in the belief that as the heart dried and withered so would that of the malignant person who had 'ill wisht' the pig. As long as that lasted no witch could have power over the pigs belonging to that house.[52]

The Museum of Witchcraft has a dog's heart pierced with pins, which the museum's founder, Cecil Williamson, discovered outside his home shortly after moving to Cornwall in 1960 – probably counter-magic by someone who blamed him for the death of their dog.[53] Spells of this kind developed from the earlier practice of burning part of a bewitched animal. The pamphlet about the St Osyth witchcraft case includes a statement from a man who described cutting the ears off a pig and burning them to remove a curse.[54]

This type of counter-magic was based on the theory that by cursing someone a witch created a magical link between them – a link that could then be used in reverse to harm the witch. Around the beginning of the seventeenth century, cunning folk devised a method of exploiting that link using the curse-victim's urine rather than involving the removal of body parts – which was obviously preferable, especially if the victim was human.[55] This method was the witch bottle, described by Joseph Blagrave in his *Astrological Practice of Physick*, published in 1671:

> Another way is to stop the urine of the patient, close up in a bottle, and put into it three nails, pins or needles, with a little white salt, keeping the urine always warm: if you let it remain long in the bottle, it will endanger the witch's life, for I have found that they will be grievously tormented making their water with great difficulty, if any at all.[56]

An account in Joseph Glanvil's *Sadducismus Triumphatus* (1681) includes some interesting details. A rather mysterious 'old man' told the husband of a sick woman how to make the bottle. At first it was heated over a fire, but the cork blew out, so a second attempt was made, burying the bottle instead. This cured the woman, and killed the 'wizard' who had bewitched her. The use of the term 'wizard' indicates that the perpetrator was a cunning man, and he seems to have been paid to put a curse on the woman, rather than being a personal enemy. So this was evidently a battle between two cunning men.[57]

Witch bottles were intended to inflict an agonising death on the witch. It's clear that wise women and cunning men who set out to combat witchcraft could be just as ruthless as the authorities. But because a witch bottle could only work through the link created by the witch's curse, it could only harm someone who was guilty. If you were suspected of witchcraft by the authorities, however, being innocent wouldn't necessarily save you.

Modern forensic science has transformed crime detection. In the Early Modern period, getting a conviction for any crime, not just witchcraft, often depended on getting a suspect to confess. If the likely suspect protested their innocence, but the crime was so serious that releasing them seemed impossible, the authorities were faced with a problem. In many countries – including Scotland, but not England – the preferred method of resolving the dilemma was torturing the suspect.

After two sessions of torture, the pain and shock left the supposed magician John Fian unable to speak. When torture failed to produce instant co-operation, interrogators always tried to find reasons other than the shortcomings of their own methods. In witchcraft cases they had an obvious explanation – the suspect had used magic to resist the torture. According to *News from Scotland*,[58] John Fian's fellow-prisoners told his interrogators that his silence was the result of a charm he had in his mouth. It was found and removed, and John then confessed. The charm – we're told – consisted of two pins driven into his tongue.

CHAPTER THREE

The bewitching of John Law

After refusing to sell Alizon the pins, John Law strode past her – angry, but also unnerved by the strength of *her* fury. He walked on for some distance – according to Alizon about 40 rods (200 metres) – and then suddenly fell to the ground.[1]

Alizon was standing watching him – still seething after their quarrel – and saw him fall.[2] She started to go towards him, but he managed, with an effort,[3] to get to his feet and stagger to the nearby inn – another 200 metres. Alizon followed him, but she didn't catch up with him. She did, however, go into the inn briefly. At that point, in spite of her reputation for magical power, John didn't accuse her of doing anything to harm him, and no one made any attempt to question her or stop her leaving the inn again.

So far this seems like a simple and understandable accident. As John walked towards the town he was tense and angry, his mind still on Alizon on the road behind him. He was probably hurrying, wanting to get away from her as quickly as possible. He could easily have tripped. In those days roads were a mass of ruts and potholes. Celia Fiennes, who travelled widely at the end of the seventeenth century, gives a graphic account of nearly coming to grief on a Cornish road:

> My horse was quite down in one of these holes full of water but by the good hand of God's Providence which has always been with me ever a present help in time of need, for giving him a good strap he flounced up again, though he had gotten quite down his head and all, yet did retrieve his feet and got clear of the place with me on his back.[4]

There's nothing particularly strange about Alizon's behaviour either. She seems to have had a fierce temper, and to have given way to a fit of teenage rage when John embarrassed and disappointed her by refusing to sell her the pins. But when she saw him fall she went to help him: 'Before the peddler was gone forty rods further, he fell down lame: and this examinate [Alizon] then went after the said peddler.'

John's description of his collapse is highly emotive but remarkably vague. His statement says, 'He fell down lame in great extremity' – which could hardly be vaguer. In the seventeenth century 'lame' simply meant physically impaired in some way – anything from a twisted ankle to complete paralysis. 'In great extremity' sounds terrible, and does indeed mean in a desperate state – on the point of death, usually – but not only is that vague, it's also contradicted by the fact that he was able to get up again almost immediately, certainly before Alizon had time to reach him.[5]

His statement then describes him lying in the inn 'in great pain, not able to stir either hand or foot', which could easily have been the result of an injury – a back injury, for example – caused by his fall. He had been wearing a heavy pack, after all.

It's possible, though, that John fell because he'd had a stroke. If he already had high blood pressure and was predisposed to have a stroke, anything that caused his blood pressure to rise further – the stress of an argument, for instance – could have triggered one. But if he did have a stroke it couldn't have been a very serious one, if he was able to walk 200 metres unaided straight after it.[6]

Following John into the inn was in fact a serious mistake on Alizon's part. It seems to have made him even more uneasy about her. His statement mentions it and gives it a sinister quality: she 'stayed not long there, but looked on him and went away'. But we don't have Alizon's description of what happened. Her statement says, 'In a house [i.e. ale-house] about the distance aforesaid he was lying lame: and so this examinate went begging in Trawden Forest.' We can see from the way the account jumps abruptly from John lying lame to the apparently irrelevant fact of Alizon going begging that something has been cut here – her version of events.

This is because her statement was drawn up to be used as evidence *against* her, if she was sent to be tried for witchcraft. Anything that might suggest to a jury that she was innocent would *not* have been included.[7] Some parts of her statement contain vivid details that are surely close to her actual words – 'The said peddler sturdily answered this examinate that he would not loose his pack', for example. But in other places the wording is clearly *not* Alizon's. The account of John's fall uses the same phrase – 'fell down lame' – as John's statement. Obviously Alizon didn't use exactly the same phrase as John. What *did* she say? That she saw him trip, perhaps?

Since Alizon's account of what happened in the inn was cut from her statement, we can deduce that it must have been something that would have made a favourable impression on a jury. And in fact it's fairly obvious that she must have gone into the inn because she was concerned about John, and to offer to help him. John wasn't pleased to see her, but it was only after she'd made sure that he was being looked after that she decided there was no point in staying, 'and so [she] went begging in Trawden Forest'.

John was, however, in a very bad way – not only physically disabled, but mentally extremely distressed. He wasn't a young man; he had an adult son, Abraham, so he was probably at least fifty. His life as a peddler was tough and demanding. He needed to be perfectly healthy and fit. So as he lay tormented by pain, helpless and frustrated, he was also confronted by a terrible realisation – that he might never work again.

And it had happened in an instant. One minute he was fine – the next minute his life was in ruins. How could 'the good hand of God's Providence' (as Celia Fiennes put it) have struck him down so cruelly?

The answer seems to have dawned on him gradually. The disaster had befallen him immediately after he'd refused to sell a wise woman pins. It was the work not of God but the Devil. Alizon had bewitched him.

Even so, John did *not* send word to the local Constable, or to Roger Nowell, the local Justice of the Peace, accusing Alizon. He did, however, send for Abraham, his son. And eager though he would have been to see him, he must also have been anxious about his reaction. How would Abraham respond to the discovery that his father might be dependant on him, both financially and physically, for the rest of his life?

Abraham, who was a cloth dyer, lived in Halifax, about 25 kilometres from Colne, where John was now lying disabled. He made a statement against Alizon which is included in *The Wonderful Discovery*. It contains an obvious and rather stupid lie. It claims that John did in fact give Alizon the pins, but she bewitched him anyway. This can't be an honest mistake because it makes no sense. Why would Alizon put a curse on John if he'd given her the pins? It's clear that Abraham was trying to pretend that his father hadn't quarrelled with Alizon – that there was no reason for him to feel angry or agitated as he walked away from her. Is this because Abraham knew that the opposite was true – that his father had been very angry and agitated, and *that* could have been the reason why he collapsed, not witchcraft?

Abraham heard of John's plight three days after the quarrel. His statement says, 'He this examinate was sent for, by a letter that came from his father' – a letter either written by John, or perhaps more likely dictated by him.[8] But the statement then immediately contradicts itself by going on, 'That he should come to his father John Law, who then lay in Colne speechless, and had the left side lamed all save his eye'. Which was it? Was John well enough to write or dictate a letter himself, or did someone else send a message to Abraham saying that John was seriously ill?

Again, we have to remember that this was a formal statement drawn up to be read out in court. If Abraham's reference to a letter *from* his father had just been a slip of the tongue, the words 'by a letter that came from his father' would simply never have been included in the statement. Instead it looks as if what we have here are two statements pasted together – one where John was well enough to send a letter himself and one where he wasn't.

Could that have happened? Is it possible that a statement was drawn up after

Counter-magic against witch-craft – a dog's heart pierced with nine pins (MoW 518).

Abraham first told his story to Roger Nowell, the Justice of the Peace, but that once Roger Nowell had realised the full potential of Abraham's evidence he then encouraged him to make a second, improved statement, one that would make a better case against Alizon?

The claim that John 'lay in Colne speechless, and had the left side lamed' suggests that he'd suffered a stroke. And according to the statement, when Abraham reached Colne his father 'had something recovered his speech, and did complain that he was pricked with knives, elsons [awls] and sickles' – another classic stroke symptom. Perhaps John's fall had been caused by a slight stroke, which was then followed by a more severe stroke shortly afterwards. Or perhaps the stress of lying helpless and in pain had triggered a stroke – maybe days after the quarrel, giving him plenty of time to send a letter to Abraham before he was struck down.

However, John's own description of his condition doesn't really bear this out. Although his statement says he was 'in great pain, not able to stir', there's no mention that the pain was like being pricked or stabbed, or that he was more paralysed on the left side than the right. Most importantly, there's no reference to him ever having any difficulty speaking. And this isn't because he was too ill to make a clear statement. Most of his description of what happened is quite precise. He's only vague about his symptoms.

There's something else suspicious about Abraham's evidence too. He claims that John lost the power of speech and was paralysed on the *left* side. What he couldn't possibly have known, but we know now, is that in the vast majority of people the side of the brain that controls speech controls the *right* side of the body. As a result, people who have a stroke that affects their speech are normally paralysed on the *right* side, *not* the left. This is exactly the sort of mistake Abraham would have made if he was lying – if, say, he was describing a stroke victim he'd seen on some other occasion, and he'd forgotten which side they were paralysed on.[9]

Of course it's possible that John had suffered such a serious stroke that both sides of his brain were affected. There's another statement about John's condition, made about five months later.[10] It begins 'it was affirmed' without saying *who* affirmed it, but it was almost certainly Abraham – and if not him, someone acting on his and John's behalf. It gives a detailed description of some very serious symptoms:

> This John Law the peddler, before his unfortunate meeting with this witch, was a very able sufficient stout man of body, and a goodly man of stature. But by this devilish art of witchcraft his head is drawn awry, his eyes and face deformed. His speech not well to be understood; his thighs and legs stark lame: his arms lame especially the left side, his hands lame and turned out of their course, his body able to endure no travel [work]: and thus remaineth at this present time.

> This reads like an application for injury compensation – because that's exactly what it is. After hearing this statement, the Lancashire magistrates gave John a pension. Would Abraham have risked lying in those circumstances? That would depend – on whether he and John were really being compensated for John's disabilities, or paid to testify against Alizon.

In spite of the problems with John and Abraham's evidence, there's no reason to think that they cold-bloodedly made false accusations against Alizon. It's far more likely that they genuinely convinced themselves of her guilt. It must have been a

A witch bottle – protection against ill-wishing – found in the wall of a house in Plymouth. Its contents included pins, bird bones, human hair and a coral amulet in the shape of a hand. (MoW 14).

dreadful shock to Abraham to see his father in such a state – not only suffering physically, but also depressed, anxious and demoralised – when before he'd always been a tough and active person. Abraham needed to find an explanation that would make his father blameless, and also give him hope that things could still get back to normal.

What preyed on both their minds was the way John's suffering dragged on day after day with no relief. The evil that had struck him down still gripped him. As John's statement puts it, 'He was tormented both day and night with the said Alizon Device, and so continued lame.' Abraham's statement uses very similar words, describing him 'seeing his said father so tormented with the said Alizon'. Alizon was *still* bewitching John, and the only way to cure him was to stop her.

There was something else that would have confirmed their belief that John was Alizon's victim. About a year earlier there'd been a remarkably similar incident involving Alizon's brother James.[11] James had gone to Carre Hall, the home of a wealthy local family the Towneleys, probably because he regularly did casual farm work for them. But on this occasion Anne Towneley confronted him and accused him and his mother of stealing turfs. There was a rather one-sided quarrel – Anne became very angry, James tried to walk away, and Anne chased after him and hit him. A few days later Anne became ill, and about ten days after the quarrel she died – leaving her grief-stricken husband Henry convinced that James had killed her.

Carre Hall would have been on John Law's rounds, and John had probably met Anne many times. She may have been a valued customer. He would certainly have heard about her illness and death from other members of the household, and about Henry Towneley's terrible suspicions about James. At the time, John had probably been sceptical. There was no real evidence against James, certainly not enough to send him to Lancaster for trial, and James was not much older that Alizon; it would have been hard to believe that someone so young could be both powerful and vicious enough to kill someone by witchcraft.

Even so, there must have been something about James that had unnerved Henry Towneley, in the way that Alizon's fury had unnerved John Law. It's clear that James refused either to apologise to Anne or argue with her, and that infuriated her. Did it seem to Henry Towneley to be something more than just ordinary teenage sullenness – a sinister, covert malice?

Now, of course, John Law's views would have changed dramatically. As he lay wondering if he'd been bewitched by Alizon, he would also have wondered if Henry Towneley had been right about James. Henry's suspicions would have fed John's fears, and John's fears would have made Henry's suspicions more convincing. And another thought would no doubt have wormed its way into John's mind – perhaps he was going to die as Anne had died.

Alizon had to be stopped – but how? John and Abraham could have consulted a wise woman or cunning man, and fought magic with magic. But as we've seen, many people believed that all magic was evil, regardless of its purpose, and it's likely John and Abraham were among them.[12] Instead they considered the more dangerous route of reporting Alizon to Roger Nowell – dangerous because it would invite magical retaliation. It could make John's situation worse, not better.

Of course, if witches could kill anyone who accused or prosecuted them, it would never have been possible to put any witch on trial. But it was certainly believed to be a risk. As the Justice of the Peace Clement Sisley was about to write the warrant consigning Cecily Arnold to jail in 1574 he slipped and fell for no apparent reason, and dislocated his hip.[13] In the case of the Warboys witches, who were tried in 1593, a prison guard who chained the elderly Alice Samuel was struck down with fits and died a few days later. The jailer's son then became ill, and only recovered after Alice was taken to his bedside and he scratched her and drew blood – a common method of undoing a curse.[14] After Mary Sutton's unsuccessful attempt to seduce her curse-victim, described in Chapter Two, she was then accused of killing a child. The child's father attempted to 'swim' her; but 'all his men [were] presently stricken lame … Then taking courage, and desiring God to be his assistance, with a cudgel which he had in his hand, he beat her till she was scarce able to stir. At which his men presently recovered.'[15] And in France a guard leading a witch to the stake was struck down with leprosy after she blew in his face.[16]

However, incidents of this kind were surprisingly rare and the official view was that God would protect people who took action against witches.[17] In addition, although there were many ways witches could curse someone, it would obviously be harder for them to perform magic in prison, where they would be deprived of their magical tools and could be watched and guarded.[18]

It's likely that John and Abraham weighed up the possibility that Roger Nowell might be persuaded to arrest the whole family, not just Alizon. It must have occurred to them that if James had been prepared to curse Anne Towneley for accusing him and his mother of theft, he would think nothing of cursing *them* for accusing Alizon of witchcraft. But James could still be prosecuted for Anne Towneley's murder if he could be made to confess. And if James and Alizon were dangerous witches, they must have been taught their devilish arts by their mother and grandmother.

In England, unlike Scotland, the use of torture to extract confessions was technically illegal. But even so, it surely wouldn't be too difficult to force people like Alizon and James to co-operate. They might be witches, but, like most witches, they were 'of the meanest, and the basest sort both in birth and breeding'.[19] They would soon give way under pressure.

But the decision to go to Roger Nowell can't have been an easy one for John and Abraham to take. It was proof of their desperation. They would be caught up in a daunting process it would be hard to see through to the end. And they would have to be unflinching in their attitude to Alizon, because the aim would be to kill her.

CHAPTER FOUR

No man near them was free from danger

Roger Nowell was already investigating Alizon and her family. Along with other 'Justices of those parts' he was conducting an operation against witchcraft, bringing in members of the community for questioning about the 'proceedings and courses of life' of various 'suspected people'.[1]

Roger was a formidable figure: sixty years old, wealthy, respected and successful. He was a member of an important family of landed gentry, but three of his relatives had also been influential Protestant thinkers, including a Professor of Divinity at Cambridge University. In 1610 Roger had been Sheriff of Lancaster, which suggests that he was not only a very experienced Justice of the Peace but also an unsqueamish one, since one of the Sheriff's jobs was to supervise the executions after the Assizes.[2] He was astute, well read, and – no doubt – accustomed to winning arguments. He was also a family man, and one of his sons, Alexander, was similar in age to James and Alizon.[3]

The other Justices taking part in the operation were Nicholas Banester, the Justice for the area south of Pendle; Robert Houlden (Nicholas Banester's son-in-law); and Thomas Heyber, who lived just over the border in Yorkshire. Thomas Heyber, like Roger, was Protestant, while Nicholas Banester and Robert Houlden were Roman Catholics, but this doesn't seem to have prevented them from co-operating closely on this particular project.[4]

Another person who was almost certainly involved, although he wasn't actually a Justice of the Peace, was Nicholas Starkie, the son of Roger's half-brother. Roger and Nicholas lived only six kilometres apart, just off the south-western end of Pendle Forest – Nicholas at Huntroyde and Roger at Read.

Seventeen years earlier, Nicholas Starkie had sought help from a cunning man when his two children – John and Anne – had fallen ill. In a disastrous flirtation with magic, Nicholas assisted the cunning man in a ritual involving a circle. As a

GISBURNE
The home of witchcraft
suspect Jennet Preston

MARTON HALL
The home of
Justice of the Peace
Thomas Heyber

LANCASTER
YORK
AREA
OF MAP

MALKING TOWER
The home of
Alizon Device and
her grandmother
Elizabeth Sothernes

CLITHEROE

PENDLE HILL

NEWCHURCH

THE FOREST OF PENDLE

The road to Colne
where Alizon Device
quarrelled with John Law

COLNE

THE FOREST OF TRAWDEN

READ HALL
The home of Justice of the Peace
Roger Nowell

HUNTROYDE HALL
The home of Roger Nowell's
nephew Nicholas Starkie

CARRE HALL
Where James Device
quarrelled with
Anne Towneley

PADDIHAM
The home of witchcraft
suspect Margaret Pearson

ALTHAM
The home of
Justice of the Peace Nicholas Banester

BURNLEY

one mile
scale

N

V. S.

result, he became convinced that his family were being attacked by evil spirits, and eventually had to bring in two famous Puritan exorcists to end their ordeal. Both Nicholas and John were left with a deep-rooted hostility towards cunning folk.[5] In fact in 1634 John Starkie would supervise a second Pendle witch hunt.[6]

However, as John Law lay wondering whether to report Alizon, the Justices' campaign against witchcraft was not going well. Nicholas Banester had sent one suspect – Margaret Pearson – to Lancaster for trial twice, and both times she'd been acquitted.[7] Thomas Heyber's main target was a woman called Jennet Preston. He'd charged her with killing a child by witchcraft and sent her to be tried at

York, but his real reason for taking action against her was the fact that she was suspected of murdering his son-in-law's father. The York Assizes had just been held, and the jury had found Jennet not guilty.[8] Roger Nowell, of course, hadn't even been able to send James Device for trial.

The Wonderful Discovery tries very hard to convince us that the Justices' investigation was the result of a public outcry against witchcraft – 'the complaint of the King's subjects for the loss of their children, friends, goods and cattle'. It also portrays Alizon's family as a menace to everyone around them – 'Certain it is, no man near them was secure or free from danger'.[9] But in fact it gives us the names of just four people who gave evidence against the family. One of them was another suspected witch, Anne Whittle. When she was in prison in Lancaster Castle, and under a great deal of pressure, she made a statement against Alizon's grandmother.[10] The other three were John and Abraham Law and James's accuser Henry Towneley. The pamphlet tells us there were other witnesses, but gives us neither their names nor their statements. Significantly, it doesn't give us Henry Towneley's evidence either.

The Wonderful Discovery was commissioned by the trial judges, Sir Edward Bromley and Sir James Altham, and written by one of the court officials, Thomas Potts. He was given access to all the court documents, and also to statements taken by Roger Nowell that weren't actually used in court.[11] If a statement isn't included in the pamphlet, it's because Thomas Potts decided to leave it out.

The purpose of the pamphlet was to justify the killing of eleven people. Thomas Potts had to make the evidence against the executed prisoners look as convincing as possible, which meant missing out evidence that was obviously flimsy. And, of course, we know that the evidence that James killed Anne Towneley was unconvincing; if it hadn't been, James would have been sent for trial immediately after Anne's death.

However, even though James wasn't sent to the Assizes, he must have been arrested and questioned. The atmosphere would have been tense, perhaps even violent. At that point James was about eighteen years old, a 'labourer' (according to the trial records),[12] physically fit and tough, his social status low (officially at least), young enough to be unpredictable and old enough to be menacing. He was accused of killing a high-status woman in a particularly horrible manner. With no police force, just a single local Constable, it's likely that the victim's husband and his men assisted with the arrest. According to a legal handbook for Justices, 'When a felony is committed, every man may arrest suspicious persons that be of evil fame, etc. and if such person shall make resistance, the other may justify to beat him.'[13]

It seems inevitable that James would have been beaten up at some point. However, he kept his nerve and managed not to say anything that could incriminate him.

The Wonderful Discovery includes a description from James of his argument with Anne Towneley, and it's probably very similar to what he told Roger at that first interrogation:

> This examinate [James] went to the Carre Hall, and upon some speeches betwixt Mistress Towneley and this examinate; she charging this examinate and his mother to have stolen some turfs of hers, bade him pack [leave through] the doors: and withal as he went forth of the door, the said Mistress Towneley gave him a knock between the shoulders.[14]

This statement gives us some interesting clues about James's relationship with Anne. James was inside the Towneleys' house, and talking to Anne about some other matter when she made the accusation of theft. In spite of the difference in social status between them, it's clear they were on quite familiar terms. It is, of course, extremely unlikely that this argument – just before Anne's sudden illness and death – was a terrible one-off coincidence. It's far more probable that it was part of some ongoing tension between her and James.

Unfortunately the statement, as edited by Roger Nowell, doesn't tell us whether James and his mother *had* stolen the turfs. It's clear that Anne didn't summon James to accuse him of theft, but that the accusation grew out of some other discussion or dispute. James's explanation of how it arose has been cut, and the awkwardly unnatural phrase 'upon some speeches betwixt Mistress Towneley and this examinate' substituted. This is suspicious in itself, and James's behaviour suggests that he was disgusted by the accusation.

And it wasn't the theft that made Anne so angry, but James's reaction to the accusation. When she told him to leave and he turned to walk away, he did so in a manner that infuriated her so much that she hit him. It was his attitude that she objected to.

One of the surprising things about James's statement is that you wouldn't know from reading it that James was just a 'labourer' and Anne a woman of considerable importance. There's no sign that James regarded her as his social superior, and he obviously made no attempt to ingratiate himself with her.

At first sight it also seems strange that James described being hit by Anne. It seems a humiliating detail for him to mention – and it increased his motive for killing her. But James *wanted* to portray Anne as aggressive and unreasonable – to contrast her violence with his self-control.

This is very similar to Alizon's description of her confrontation with John Law – in particular the way she emphasised his aggressive rudeness when he 'sturdily' refused to remove his pack. And of course she then went on to make it clear that she went to help him when he fell, in spite of his unpleasantness towards her.

James and Alizon had a very definite image of themselves that they wanted to convey to Roger Nowell. They represented themselves as people who showed restraint in spite of provocation. It was Anne and John who were in the grip of uncontrollable anger.

Of course, Alizon wasn't being completely honest. John Law described her as 'very angry'. And his account of her standing looking at him in the alehouse gives her an air of menace that makes it clear he was genuinely afraid of her.

James, too, was more angry with Anne Towneley than he was prepared to admit – at least to Roger Nowell. He may have kept his self-control in Anne's presence, but he told his young sister Jennet about the incident, and betrayed his feelings to her. According to Jennet's own statement, she was at Carre Hall herself a week later, and 'saw the said Mistress Towneley in the kitchen there, nothing well: whereupon it came into [her] mind, that her said brother ... had brought the said Mistress Towneley into the state she then was in.'[15]

It's significant that Jennet was at Carre Hall, in the kitchen, *after* the quarrel between Anne and James. Since she was only about eight or nine, she was almost certainly with some other member of her family. This was most likely to have been her mother, who must have gone to Carre Hall fairly often, as she was included with James in the theft accusation. It seems obvious that the family worked for the Towneleys, and were still working for them even after the argument. In fact the most likely explanation for the theft accusation is that James and his mother took the turfs in payment for work they'd done. The glimpses of their characters that the pamphlet gives us suggest that they were quite capable of taking what they thought they were entitled to, without necessarily making sure they had permission. Perhaps the 'speeches' between James and Anne had consisted of James asking for some further payment, and Anne protesting that by taking the turfs he'd already gone too far.

In a rural community of this kind, people often did work on the basis of very informal agreements. Sometimes it seems it was closer to a vague system of people doing favours for each other. In particular, the more prosperous members of the community would help out the less well-off with gifts of produce, expecting them to do casual work in return. This relationship could often be soured by misunderstandings and disagreements.

It was a situation of this kind that led to the unfortunate pig getting his ears cut off in the counter-magic spell described in Chapter Two. Anne West had too many pigs and so offered one to her poorer neighbour Annis Herd. Annis hesitated, unsure if her landlord would agree, so Anne West sold the pig instead. Anne then asked Annis to spin some wool for her, but Annis refused, offended because she hadn't been given the pig. When one of the Wests' remaining pigs became ill, they suspected Annis of bewitching him. They considered burning him alive to save the rest of the animals from Annis's magic, but fortunately decided that was too drastic, so just cut off his ears and burned them.[16]

It's likely that the wealthy Towneleys had a similar rather uneasy relationship with the Devices. It's even possible that the work the Devices did for them was magical. That wouldn't rule out a disagreement about payment. Extraordinary as it may seem, people sometimes refused to pay cunning folk for magic they'd performed. The Essex wise woman Ursley Kempe was promised twelve pence by a client, Grace Thurlowe, if she cured her of a 'lameness in her bones.'

> For the space of five weeks after, she [Grace] was well and in good case as she was before. And then the said Ursley came unto the said Grace, and asked her the money she promised to her. Whereupon the said Grace made answer: that she was a poor and needy woman, and had no money: and then the said Ursley requested of her cheese for it: but she said she had none. And she the said Ursley, seeing nothing to be had of the said Grace, fell out with her, and said, that she would be even with her: and thereupon she was taken lame, and from that day to this day hath so continued.[17]

However, few cunning folk were full-time professionals. Most had a more conventional occupation and practised magic as a sideline.[18] So it's quite probable that James was indeed a 'labourer', doing casual work on the various farms in the neighbourhood. In fact that could have given him opportunities to build up a reputation as a cunning man – curing sick animals, and perhaps performing love magic for the other young men he worked with.

In fact, if James was a member of a gang of young farm workers, and if Anne Towneley was a tough employer who regularly gave them a hard time, James might have been under a certain amount of peer pressure to retaliate when she insulted him.

However, Anne Towneley had not been afraid of James and his magic. If she had, she would never have hit him. Even after she became ill, she didn't suspect him of bewitching her. She would certainly have mentioned it to her husband Henry, and it would have become part of his evidence – and Thomas Potts would definitely have included *that* in *The Wonderful Discovery*. But then Anne died, leaving Henry devastated and struggling to understand what had happened.

What if James had killed her? What if James was someone who could draw supernatural evil into the world and use it to commit murder? Then Anne's death was not some pointless cruelty of Providence, but part of a cosmic battle between the forces of good and evil. And destroying James would not only prevent him harming anyone else, it would strike a blow against the dark power that had made him its instrument. It would give Anne's death some kind of meaning.

This would have given Henry a compelling motive for accusing James. But the very fact that *The Wonderful Discovery* leaves out Henry's statement tells us something very important about him. He was not prepared to invent or exaggerate his evidence against James. All he had to offer Roger Nowell was the fact that Anne had become ill and died several days after the quarrel. It would have been easy for him to suggest that James had threatened Anne. He could have said that Anne told him that James 'lay upon' her. He could have convinced himself that some strange animal he'd seen was an evil spirit sent by James. Any of these things would have been regarded as powerful evidence in a witchcraft case.[19] But although Henry was convinced of James's guilt, and eager to testify against him,[20] he was only prepared to say what he was certain was the truth.

Alizon, too, had come under suspicion even before the incident with John Law. Just a few weeks after Anne Towneley's death she'd been accused of bewitching a child.[21] The child's father, Henry Bulcock, turned up at Malking Tower, where Alizon lived with her grandmother, and insisted that Alizon went with him to his home.

A sick child was even more likely than an adult to jump to the frightening and dramatic conclusion that their illness was caused by witchcraft. It's quite possible, too, that Henry Bulcock's child was a friend of Alizon's sister Jennet, and had been on the receiving end of one of Alizon's outbursts of anger. Henry may well have intended to get the child to scratch Alizon to undo the curse by drawing her blood.[22]

Carre Hall, the home of the Towneleys, photographed in 1954
FROM THE COLLECTION OF R. J. HAYHURST

Read Hall, Roger Nowell's home, early-nineteeth-century print
ENGRAVED BY N. G. PHILIPS

In a rural community like Pendle Forest word of the incident would quickly have spread, and Roger Nowell would have got to hear about it. Roger was conducting an operation against witchcraft and had just been frustrated in his attempts to build a case against James. *The Wonderful Discovery* tells us he was bringing people in for questioning. Henry Bulcock must have been one of those people, and Roger must have leant on him very hard to make a statement against Alizon.

However, there's no statement from Henry in the pamphlet, nor even a mention of one, and Alizon was never charged with the crime. We only know about the incident from one of James's statements. Alizon told him what had happened, and she may well have blamed him for it; his arrest for Anne's murder would have brought suspicion on the whole family.[23]

Henry Bulcock must have refused to make a statement. Of course he might have been more frightened of Alizon than of Roger Nowell – at least at first. But that would have changed as the balance shifted and Roger gradually got the upper hand over the family. Then, surely, Henry would have cooperated with Roger, if he'd been sure Alizon was guilty. Alizon must have tried to convince him of her innocence, and at least made him uncertain of her guilt.

Just as Henry Towneley had resisted the temptation to invent evidence against James, Henry Bulcock had let Alizon persuade him she might be innocent. Roger Nowell was thwarted once again. If everyone involved in the Pendle witch-hunt had behaved like Henry Bulcock and Henry Towneley, it would have ended very differently.

When the Essex wise woman Ursley Kempe was accused of witchcraft she insisted that 'though she could unwitch she could not witch.'[24] But when James and Alizon were accused, they took a different line. They represented themselves as people with the self-control to *choose* not to retaliate when provoked. It seems they may well have believed that they had the power to harm people by magic – but they chose not to use it.

Roger Nowell had no doubt about James's and Alizon's magical powers. But he saw them as people who had embraced evil magic, and been corrupted by it to the point when they would take malicious pleasure in doing harm for the most trivial of reasons.

And to kill or harm someone by witchcraft was a far worse crime than ordinary violence – particularly to a Justice of the Peace. When Roger investigated the rumours and accusations surrounding James and Alizon, he had to consider the threat they posed not just to individuals but to the peace and order of society – a society rooted in the Christian faith. The Essex Justice Brian Darcey campaigned to have the punishment for witchcraft changed from hanging to burning alive:

> The magistrates of foreign lands … kept a due analogy and proportion of punishment, burning them with fire, whom the common law of England (with more measure of mercy than is to be wished) strangleth with a rope. An ordinary felon, and a murderer, offending against the moral law of justice, is throttled: a sorcerer, a witch … defying the Lord God to his face; and trampling the precious blood of that immaculate lamb Jesus Christ most despitefully under feet is stifled: the one dieth on the gallows, and so doth the other: wherein doubtless there is a great inequality of justice.[25]

But in spite of widespread concern about witchcraft, no one believed it was *easy* to harm someone by magic. Witchcraft made beer spoil, or stopped cream turning into butter. It made a horse refuse to move, or a cow run wild. Sometimes, perhaps, it could make a person 'sore pained in his bones'.[26] But if someone was apparently maimed or killed by magic it was a rare and shocking event.

It's remarkable that anyone could have believed a young girl like Alizon was morally and magically capable of crippling John Law. It's evidence of her family's reputation for magical power, and her personal reputation for being a strong character with a fierce temper.[27] And when she and James were interrogated by Roger, their high opinion of themselves – dependant as it was on their belief in their magic – was to him evidence of their potential for evil. His certainty of their guilt was a distorted reflection of their self-belief.

And if the accusations against Alizon were remarkable, those against James were even more extraordinary. Eventually, Roger would claim that in the three years he'd been fully initiated into magic, James had killed four people – making him one of the most dangerous and powerful witches in European history.

CHAPTER FIVE

The tower and the charm

THE GREAT RESORT TO MALKING TOWER

The difficulty of proving James and Alizon guilty must have been very frustrating for Roger Nowell, particularly as *The Wonderful Discovery* tells us that he had another reason for taking action against the family. This was 'the great and universal resort to Malking Tower', the home of James and Alizon's grandmother, Elizabeth Sothernes.[1] This echoes a sentence in George Gifford's (fictional) *A Dialogue Concerning Witches and Witchcrafts*:

> There is also a [wise] woman at R.H. five and twenty miles hence, that hath a great name, and a great resort there is daily unto her.[2]

Evidently Elizabeth Sothernes also had a 'great name' as a wise woman. But to people like George Gifford, not only cunning folk but even their clients were guilty of witchcraft:

The wife of Samuell:
> There was one even now that said you are a witch.

The good wife R.:
> Was there one said I was a witch? You do but jest ...

The wife of Samuell:
> Did he not say she played the witch that heated the spit red hot, and thrust it into her cream, when the butter would not come? ...

The good wife R.:
> Is that witchcraft? ... Nay the good woman at R.H. taught it [to] my husband.[3]

Cunning folk lured their clients into performing magic. And as Roger Nowell knew, from his nephew's experiences, that magic was often a great deal more dangerous than just unwitching cream by plunging a hot spit into it.

Some people even campaigned for cunning folk to be executed for performing healing magic. One of them was William Perkins, a friend of another of Roger Nowell's relatives (the Cambridge professor).[4] In his book *A Discourse of the Damned Art of Witchcraft*, published in 1608, William Perkins wrote:

> As the killing witch must die by another law, though he were no witch; so the healing and harmless witch must die by this [biblical] law, though he kill not, only for covenant made with Satan.[5]

In theory, cunning folk could be hanged for 'feloniously entertaining evil spirits',[6] but in practice it was extremely difficult to get English juries to send people to the gallows unless they were accused of harming someone.[7]

HAST THOU KILLED GRIMALKIN!

According to *The Wonderful Discovery*, Alizon's grandmother 'dwelt in the Forest of Pendle, a waste place, fit for her profession'.[8] Pendle Forest curves round the eastern side of the moorland surrounding Pendle Hill. Even in the early seventeenth century it was certainly not a wasteland. It wasn't wooded – the name Forest came from its designation as a hunting ground under game conservation laws[9] – but, rather, was open countryside dotted with farms and smallholdings. It had two substantial houses – Carre Hall and Rough Lee – and a mill and a church.

It's unlikely that Thomas Potts, the author of the pamphlet, had ever been there. He came up from London for the trials,[10] and probably based his ideas about Pendle from what he'd heard about Pendle Hill itself. Clearly he didn't appreciate the wild beauty of moorland landscapes. The natural world untamed by man was, to him, both desolate and threatening. And the dark and dangerous energies that coursed through it were close kin to those of magic.

James and his mother Elizabeth lived at the smallholding that had belonged to Elizabeth's husband John Device, who had died eleven years earlier. One of the many ironies of this case is that, just as Roger Nowell had personal, family reasons for being a witch-hunter, so too did Alizon and James. As their father lay dying, he had insisted that he was bewitched – by Anne Whittle, another Pendle wise woman.[11]

The smallholding seems to have consisted of a cottage and outbuildings, and James may even have had his own room.[12] Alizon lived at Malking Tower, looking after her grandmother, who was about eighty years old and blind.[13] It's possible that Alizon was encouraged to move out of the Device smallholding to give James more space. He may have been starting to think about getting married and raising a family. Also it's clear that both he and Alizon were strong characters, and no doubt there were times when there was a degree of tension between them. Certainly, although he was quieter than Alizon, James could argue stubbornly when he had to. Alizon moving to Malking Tower may well have seemed like an excellent plan to everyone – except perhaps Alizon herself.

Malking Tower was at the northern end of Pendle Forest – the opposite end from Roger Nowell's home at Read – at the place now known as Malkin Tower Farm.[14] Malking Tower itself has disappeared, but that's hardly surprising. People quickly demolished empty buildings to re-use the stone and timber. Obviously it can't have been a huge tower like a medieval keep, or the mound or flattened area it was built on would still be visible. But it must have been a tower of some kind, as the name Malking Tower is used repeatedly in the pamphlet, not just in Thomas Potts's commentary but also in the statements taken by Roger Nowell.[15]

There are several possible meanings for the word Malking. Malkin was a woman's name – a familiar form of either Mary or Maud. It was sometimes used as a term for a poor or shabby woman. It was also used as a term for a cat, with 'grey malkin' – often spelled 'grimalkin' – used for an old cat.[16]

It was also a word associated with evil spirits, perhaps because the first part of the word, 'mal', can mean 'evil' – as in words like 'malice' or 'malevolent'. The Oxford English Dictionary mentions a thirteenth-century reference to a female spectre called Malekin. Malkin is the name of a cat spirit in Thomas Middleton's play *The Witch*,[17] and William Shakespeare used the name Grey-Malkin for a spirit in his play *Macbeth*.[18]

Malkin Tower Farm.

It's likely that both these authors were influenced by a book called *Beware the Cat* by William Baldwin, published in 1570. Essentially a comic novel in which a cat tells various amusing and unflattering stories about the humans around her, it also contains one distinctly dark and eerie episode – the death of Grimalkin. William Baldwin represents this as a true story from Ireland:

> There was a kern [soldier] of John Butler's ... who minding to make a prey in the night upon Cahir Mac Art, his master's enemy, got him with his boy (for so they call their horse-keepers be they never so old knaves) into his country, and in the night time entered into a town of two houses, and broke in and slew the people, and then took such cattle [livestock] as they found, which was a cow and a sheep ... But doubting [expecting] they should be pursued ... he got him into a church, thinking to lurk there till midnight ...
>
> He made his boy go gather sticks ... and made a fire in the church, and killed the sheep ... and roasted it. But when it was ready ... there came in a cat and set her by him and said ... 'Give me some meat.' He, amazed at this, gave her the quarter that was in his hand, which immediately she did eat up, and asked more till she had consumed all the sheep ... Wherefore they supposed it were the Devil, and therefore thinking it wisdom to please him, killed the cow ...
>
> Doubting lest, when she had eaten that, she would eat them too ... they got them out of the church and the kern took his horse and away he rode as fast as he could hie. When he was a mile or two from the church the moon began to shine, and his boy espied the cat upon his master's horse and told him. Whereupon the kern took his dart, and turning his face toward her, flung it and struck her through with it. But immediately there came to her such a sight of cats that, after a long fight with them, his boy was killed and eaten up, and he himself ... had much to do to escape.
>
> When he was come home ... he set him down by his wife and told her his adventure, which, when a kitling [kitten] which his wife kept, scarce half a year old, had heard, up she started and said, 'Hast thou killed Grimalkin!' And therewith she plunged in his face, and with her teeth took him by the throat, and ere that she could be plucked away, she had strangled him.[19]

The idea of Alizon and her grandmother living in a tower named after a demonic cat is extremely attractive, but unfortunately there's a problem. In *The Wonderful Discovery* the word is almost always spelled 'Malking', with a 'g'.[20] Possibly the name came from a story that one of Alizon's ancestors acquired the tower from a king, after working magic either for or against him. There were certainly many examples, both in legend and history, of wise women and witches becoming embroiled in politics.

Northern England no doubt had numerous local traditions about Morgan Le Fay, the sorceress lover of King Urien of North Rheged (Cumbria), for instance. The great medieval story *Sir Gawain and the Green Knight*, where the events are all part of one of Morgan's elaborate magical plots, was written somewhere around the Cheshire–Staffordshire–Derbyshire border.[21]

In the mid fifteenth century a London wise woman, Margery Jourdemayne, was a central figure in a sensational plot against King Henry VI.[22] Henry also suffered a series of defeats in the Hundred Years War because the French army was led by the young witch Joan of Arc – which inspired a vivid scene in William Shakespeare's *Henry VI Part 1*:

Alarum. Excursions. Enter Joan la Pucelle.

Joan:
The Regent conquers, and the Frenchmen fly.
Now help, ye charming spells and periapts,
And ye choice spirits that admonish me …
    Enter Fiends …
Now, ye familiar spirits that are culled
Out of the powerful regions under earth,
Help me this once, that France may get the field.
    They walk and speak not.
O, hold me not with silence overlong!
Where I was wont to feed you with my blood,
I'll lop a member [limb] off and give it you.[23]

Whatever the name's exact significance, it's clear that Alizon and her grandmother lived in a striking and distinctive building with a name full of connotations of magic and power. Malking Tower would have formed an eerie counterpoint to Roger Nowell's grand and civilised house at Read, at the other end of Pendle Forest.[24]

THAT FRIDAY SPELL

The tower suggests that Alizon's family may well have been practising as cunning folk for generations, and this is supported by the central element of their magic – their healing charm, which young Jennet told Roger Nowell 'would cure one bewitched'. It was included, in full, in the evidence used in court:

A CHARM

Upon Good Friday, I will fast while I may
Until I hear them knell
Our Lord's own bell,
Lord in his mess [feast][25]
With his twelve Apostles good,
What hath he in his hand
Ligh [blaze] in leath [healing][26] wand:
What hath he in his other hand?
Heaven's door key,
Open, open Heaven door keys,
Steck [fasten], steck hell door.
Let Crissom [new born] child
Go to it Mother mild,

What is yonder that casts a light so farrandly [splendidly],
Mine own dear Son that's nailed to the Tree,
He is nailed sore by the heart and hand,
And holy harne [brain] pan [i.e. skull],
Well is that man
That Friday spell can,
His child to learn [teach];
A cross of blue, and another of red,
As good Lord was to the Rood [cross].
Gabriel laid him down to sleep
Upon the ground of holy weep:
Good Lord came walking by,
Sleep'st thou, wak'st thou Gabriel,
No Lord I am sted [beset] with stick and stake,
That I can neither sleep nor wake:
Rise up Gabriel and go with me,
The stick nor the stake shall never deere [injure] thee.
Sweet Jesus our Lord, Amen.

James Device[27]

Usually these charms were handed down within families, something Jennet's charm refers to specifically:

Well is that man
That Friday spell can,
His child to learn.

Jennet told Roger that she and James had been taught the charm by their mother Elizabeth. In the record it's James's name that's written at the bottom of the charm, so it seems that after Jennet mentioned it to Roger, it was James who actually recited it to him. It's likely that they were being interrogated together at that point, with Jennet's presence being used to put pressure on James.

The eerie strangeness of the charm is partly due to the fact that it's a compilation of several shorter charms. It was quite common for cunning folk to use more than one charm – the Scottish wise woman Isobel Gowdie used seven[28] – but it was very unusual to combine them in this way. It's probable that someone in the family responded to the growing fear of witchcraft by deliberately creating a particularly powerful counter-magic charm. That person may well have been James's and Jennet's grandmother Elizabeth Sothernes. As she was about eighty in 1612, she would have been about thirty when the 1563 act against witchcraft was passed; Her career as a wise woman would have been taking off at exactly the same time that the English witch-hunts were. The use of the word 'stake' at the end of the charm is a specific reference to witchcraft – from the Anglo-Saxon words 'staca', meaning 'pin', and 'stacung', meaning the act of cursing someone by driving pins into an image.[29]

The origins of parts of this charm can be traced back several hundred years.

The lines

> Lord in his mess
> With his twelve Apostles good,
> What hath he in his hand
> Ligh in leath wand;

are closely related to – and almost certainly derived from – an important medieval fever charm:

> Archidecline [Lord of the Feast] sits on high and holds a virgin yard [wand] of hazel in his hand and says, also soth [truly] as the priest makes God's body in his hands and also soth as God blessed is mother Mary and also soth, I conjure thee, virgin yard of hazel, that thou close and be bote [remedy] of this evil fever to this man [name].[30]

Both English and Latin versions of this charm have survived in fifteenth-century manuscripts, but it's probably at least 200 years older than that.[31]

The phrase 'also soth as the priest makes God's body in his hands' is particularly significant, as it likens the process of summoning healing power into the wand to the transformation of the bread into the body of Christ by the priest performing the mass.

There is an account of the Derbyshire wise woman Elizabeth Wright using a wand and a charm to cure a bewitched cow:

> She came to the man's house, knelt down before the cow, crossed her with a stick in the forehead, and prayed to her God, since which time the cow continued well.[32]

We can reasonably picture James doing something similar – called from working in the fields by a farmer with a sick animal, and cutting a piece of hazel from the hedgerow. But as soon as he said the words

> What hath he in his hand
> Ligh in leath wand

he was no longer a labourer with a stick, but a member of a priesthood holding a wand blazing with spiritual power.

Even people like George Gifford had to acknowledge – and dismiss – this belief:

The wife of Samuell:
> Did he not say she played the witch that heated the spit red hot, and thrust it into her cream, when the butter would not come? …

The good wife R.:
> Is that witchcraft? … Nay the good woman at R.H. taught it my husband.

M.B.:
> Who do you think taught it [to] the cunning woman at R.H.

The good wife R.:

'She knelt down before the cow, crossed her with a stick in the forehead, and prayed to her God.' Cunning folk probably cut a fresh wand from the hedgerow each time they needed one.

AUTHOR COLLECTION

It is a gift which God hath given her, I think the holy spirit of God doth teach her.

M.B.:

You do not think then that the devil doth teach her?[33]

The description of Elizabeth Wright praying to '*her* God' is clearly intended to imply that her God was the Devil. Even in the nineteenth century the Shropshire wise women Betty Chidley and Priss Morris could cause consternation by apparently saying, '*My* God bless thee', instead of 'May God bless thee'.[34] But there was in fact an element of truth in the idea that the God of the cunning folk was *not* the same as the God of those who condemned them. William Perkins wrote:

This [witchcraft] and all other evils come to pass even by the will of God, who hath justly permitted the same ... to avenge himself upon man for his ingratitude, who having the truth revealed unto him will not believe or obey it.[35]

This remote and vengeful God was certainly very different from the Lord of the Feast who would lend his divine power for something as trivial as turning cream into butter.

PRAYER OR BLASPHEMY?

However, it would be a mistake to think that anyone expected cunning folk to be particularly saintly. One of the reasons they were popular was that they were ordinary people who *shared* the frustrations and problems of their clients. Often they were prickly and difficult – more like temperamental artists than priests. It's hard to excuse the behaviour of the Dartmouth cunning man Michael Trevysard, who refused to treat an injured child because he'd fallen out with the child's father:

> The said Trevysard then being in one Lovett's house at Hardness at cards at evening prayer time. On a sudden one came into the house and told him how the said Davye's child was scalded. Then Trevysard said that he could (if he would) help it in 24 hours, and being requested so to do by some there present, he answered he would never do the said George Davye good, nor any of his.[36]

With an attitude like that, it's not totally surprising that Michael found himself accused of witchcraft. The statement gives the impression of a disreputable, intemperate man, playing cards – and probably also gambling and drinking – when he should have been at church. The fact is, however, that as soon as the child was injured someone went rushing to him for help.

This kind of medical emergency was precisely when people most relied on cunning folk – making Michael's callousness all the more shocking. One particular charm for burns and scalds seems to have been so widespread it may well be the one Michael would have used if he'd been in a more compassionate frame of mind:

> There came three angels out of the east,
> The one brought fire, the other brought frost.
> Out fire; in frost.
> In the name of the Father, the Son and the Holy Ghost.[37]

The nature of the charms too was questionable. Jennet called her family's charm a 'prayer', Roger Nowell gave it the heading 'A Charm', and it refers to itself unashamedly as 'that Friday spell'.[38] The French witch-hunter Jean Bodin wrote, 'There is no blasphemy more evil than to call on God to make a spell';[39] while the Burgundian judge Henri Boguet objected to the ritual actions used along with the charms:

> I have seen another woman who cured several types of illnesses using prayers. But I observed that all these prayers were full of impieties and superstitions. For example,

for a horse stung [by flies], she said certain words in the form of prayers and drove a nail into the ground, which she did not pull out again. What power could the nail driven [into the ground] in that way have?[40]

The late-fifteenth-century witch-hunter's handbook *Malleus Maleficarum* (*The Hammer of the Witches*) distinguished between prayers and charms by arguing that a prayer only *requested* God's help. There must be no *expectation* that the prayer would have the desired effect.[41] But of course for cunning folk it was absolutely essential to be able to *expect* their charms to work. The confidence of their clients depended on it. Cunning folk had to believe that God made spiritual power available to them to draw on as they thought fit.[42]

But what kind of God would blithely make his power available to a cunning man like Michael Trevysard? The answer, of course, is the same kind of God who would make his power available to a magician performing the *Munich Handbook* love spell.

Certainly the Device charm has far more in common with the *Munich Handbook* spell than with a conventional prayer. They both invoke divine power, rather than appealing for divine help. And they employ techniques closer to art than religion to alter the practitioner's state of mind – and the client's, in the case of the charm.

The Device charm summons spiritual power by calling up in the imagination images of anguish and healing, authority and sacrifice. The use of rhyme gives the progression of ideas an air of inevitability, and the use of dialogue ratchets up the emotional intensity:

> What is yonder that casts a light so farrandly,
> Mine own dear Son that's nailed to the Tree.

Malleus Maleficarum was particularly scathing about this aspect of charms – the unorthodox conjunction of religion and art:

Some old women in their incantations use some such jingling doggerel as the following:

> Blessed Mary went a-walking
> Over Jordan river.
> Stephen met her, fell a-talking etc.

It was of course self-evident that 'the effect of them cannot be from God, who is not a witness to a lie.'[43]

When James recited the charm to Roger Nowell, he would have been well aware of all these objections to it. Even clients were sometimes offended when cunning folk used charms, as the Devices' rival, Anne Whittle, described:

She was sent for by the wife of John Moore, to help drink [i.e. beer or ale] that was forspoken or bewitched ... After which time this examinate [Anne] had used these prayers, and amended her drink, the said Moore's wife did chide this examinate, and was grieved at her.[44]

To James, the charm was evidence that he – like Roger – was fighting *against* witchcraft. But there was an element of defiance in his use of that defence. In his *Dialogue Concerning Witches and Witchcrafts*, George Gifford has his wise woman's client say, 'The good woman at R.H. ... doth more good in one year than all these scripture men will do so long as they live.'[45] Was James also – dangerously – implying criticism of Roger Nowell? When he recited the charm was he making the point that while people like Roger railed against magic and arrested suspects who might or might not be witches, it was cunning folk like James who actually helped the victims of witchcraft?

BEGGING IN TRAWDEN FOREST

However, alongside this evidence that Alizon and her family had a certain status in their community, there is also evidence that they were extremely poor. There are references in the statements to Alizon and her grandmother going begging, including, of course, Alizon's description of leaving John Law to go begging in Trawden Forest.

Being a wise woman or cunning man was certainly no way to get rich. Although wealthy people like Roger Nowell's nephew often consulted cunning folk, the majority of their clients were ordinary working people. You could save someone's life and just get a chicken in return – and if you thought that was a poor deal you were in the wrong profession.[46]

And for Alizon's family, John Device's early death – when James was about eight and Alizon about six – must have been a dreadful blow. In an age when childhood mortality was high, it's a tribute to Elizabeth Device's resourcefulness and determination that James and Alizon had survived to their late teens.

But in fact Alizon's reference to going begging in Trawden Forest may not be quite what it seems. Trawden Forest was a sparsely populated rural area, and Alizon's encounter with John Law happened in March, when supplies ran low in most farming communities.[47] Why would Alizon leave Colne, a busy town, and trek across several kilometres of countryside, to go begging in a place where people would have little spare to give her? If she was simply trying to scrounge money or food off strangers it makes no sense at all. She must have been going to someone she knew would definitely give her something.

There's evidence from the nineteenth century that cunning folk were often paid annual retainers by their clients, usually in the spring:

> While discussing the mysterious fraternity of wizards and witches with an old man well over eighty, he informed me that about forty-five years ago he attended the Assizes at Bodmin, and after the necessary business had been got through a dinner was held, at which all the chief of the county were assembled, including many prominent farmers. Just before the dinner was timed to commence a strange individual, dressed in a long white shirt, entered the room. He was at once hailed by the farmers present

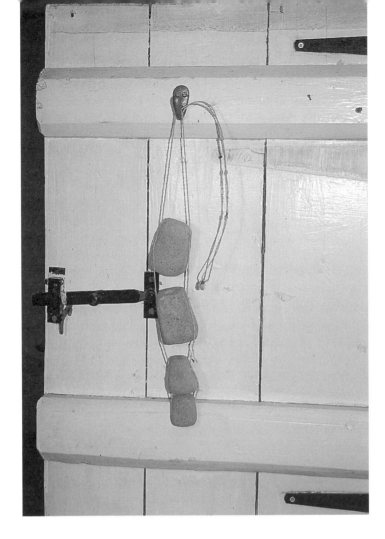

A farm protection charm made of clay. Cunning folk often demanded annual retainers in return for providing protection magic. (MoW 324).

as the 'Wizard of the West', and each in turn paid him a sum of money to keep 'witchcraft' off their farms during the ensuing twelve months.

(*Tales of Cornish Witches* by William Henry Paynter)[48]

In the mid twentieth century the occultist Cecil Williamson acquired a farm protection charm consisting of four clay wedge-shapes, and wrote:

The spell holds good for one year and one day, when, as is the case with your car licence, one is well advised to renew it – if trouble is to be avoided.[49]

By likening it to your annual car tax, Cecil Williamson was implying that the trouble could come from the wise woman or cunning man who issued it. Certainly one of the reasons that Roger Nowell's nephew Nicholas Starkie believed that evil spirits had been unleashed on his family was because the cunning man he'd employed had been dissatisfied with Nicholas's offer of a retainer of forty shillings a year.

Alizon's own father, John Device, paid the wise woman Anne Whittle a measure of meal every year, and went on paying her even after he'd married Alizon's mother Elizabeth – the daughter of an even more powerful wise woman. And when he did eventually stop paying, he soon became fatally ill, and was convinced Anne Whittle had bewitched him.

This wasn't simply protection *magic* – it was uncomfortably close to a gangster-style protection *racket*. If Alizon was collecting retainers for her grandmother, she might well have preferred Roger Nowell to think she was just going begging.[50]

CHAPTER SIX

The arts of the cunning folk

The status of cunning folk like Alizon and her family depended on two things – what they could achieve for their clients, and the techniques they used to achieve it. To understand how people viewed them we have to look at how their role reflected people's needs, and at the range and nature of the skills that made people believe in them.

WITCH-HUNTING

In the early fifteenth century, the Italian wise woman Matteuccia di Francesco offered her clients two main services – love magic and healing. And the majority of the illnesses she treated were regarded as natural, although some were attributed to evil spirits. The court record gives only two occasions when clients consulted her because they believed they were bewitched.[1] Two hundred years later, however, the fear of witchcraft had escalated so dramatically that Alizon Device's family had taken a fever charm and turned it into a charm against witchcraft.

By the early seventeenth century witch-hunting was an important part of the work of many cunning folk. An account of a typical consultation has survived from 1616. The father of a sick girl took a sample of her urine to a cunning man, who confirmed that she'd been bewitched. He then made the girl's father gaze into a mirror until he saw a vision of the witch's face – a form of divination known as scrying. The cunning man said that the girl had incurred the witch's anger by quarrelling with her over a hen, and gave instructions for the girl

> to make a cake with flour from the bakers, and to mix the same, instead of other liquor, with her own water [urine] and bake it on the hearth, whereof the one half was to be applied and laid to the region of the heart, the other half to the back directly opposite; and further, gave a box of ointment like treacle, which must be spread upon

that cake, and a powder to be cast upon the same, and certain words written in a paper, to be laid on … likewise.

(*A Treatise of Witchcraft* by Alexander Roberts[2])

Although helping to identify the witch would obviously impress the client, sometimes cunning folk refused to do so. One Lancashire wise woman was happy to treat a man who had been bewitched, but when she was asked to name the culprit she said 'she would not tell for a thousand pounds'.[3] And cunning folk certainly had nothing to gain if the client went to the authorities and had the suspect arrested. In their role as witch-hunters, cunning folk were usually *rivals* to the local Justices, not colleagues. Cunning folk wanted people to regard counter-magic as a *better* option than reporting suspects to the authorities.

In 1596 there was a revealing case in Derbyshire. Thomas Darling, a thirteen-year-old boy, started suffering from seizures. It was the local doctor who diagnosed witchcraft, although Thomas's family had assumed it was a 'natural disease'. Two family friends then consulted wise women:

There came one of them, having been of her own accord with Widow Worthington, the good witch of Hoppers, as they call her, and told them, 'she said that the boy was bewitched. Yet she could not help him, unless his mother or some of his nearest friends came to her.' The same answer was given by a witch around Coventry to another, looking for some help on the boy's behalf. But the mother of the child, detesting the Devil's help, thanked these two for their kindness towards her, but sharply reproved them for attempting a thing so unlawful.[4]

So instead of using counter-magic, the family went to the local Justice and reported the suspected witch – Alice Gooderidge, the daughter of the wise woman Elizabeth Wright. Alice died in prison.

It's also important to remember that although cunning folk fought witchcraft, they viewed it very differently from the authorities. Cunning folk, of course, didn't regard magic as essentially evil. To them, there was no cosmic conspiracy at work when someone put a curse on an enemy – just all-too-human feelings of anger, fear, bitterness and envy.

In fact cunning folk didn't always blame supernatural illnesses on witchcraft. Even George Gifford, in his *Dialogue*, has one of his characters say:

There was another of my neighbours had his wife much troubled, and he went to her [the wise woman at R.H.], and she told him his wife was haunted with a fairy.[5]

The Evil Eye was another source of illness and misfortune, similar to witchcraft; but unlike witchcraft it was not necessarily a deliberate act of malice. It could result unconsciously from any feelings of envy:

The believers in the gift assert that the evil eye may exist in man or woman, in friend or foe, and that it is prudent not to give causes for the feelings which give rise to it.

(Witchcraft and Second Sight in the Highlands and Islands of Scotland by John Gregorson Campbell[6])

In many Mediterranean countries you can still buy beautiful glass amulets resembling eyes, which counteract the Evil Eye by returning its stare. When my friend Kate visited Turkey, she brought me back (in her capacity as my research assistant) an eye amulet fridge magnet.

Magic to *prevent* harm – whether from the Evil Eye or witchcraft – was of course just as important as magic to undo harm already done. King James I, in his book *Demonology*, condemned wise women 'for healing of forspoken [bewitched] goods [livestock], for preserving them from evil eyes, by knitting rowan-trees [i.e. rowan wood], or sundriest kind of herbs, to the hair or tail of the goods.'[7] A traditional Scottish rhyme says:

> A rowan-tree and a red thread
> Gars [makes] all the witches dance to dead.[8]

The use of red thread to cure the Evil Eye is described in an early twentieth-century account:

A native of South Uist said that while different methods were employed to cure the Evil Eye, the most common, so far as she could judge, was the 'snaithnean' (thread) … The 'snaithnean' is simply a red woollen thread four or five inches long. The giver of it [i.e. the wise woman or cunning man] says some good words over it, hands it to the messenger with instructions to go straight home and tie the thread round the animal's tail till it recovers. In more important cases the professor may deem it advisable to fasten the string on himself.

(Evil Eye in the Western Highlands by R.C. MacLagan[9])

An English rhyme, recorded by the seventeenth-century writer John Aubrey, goes:

> Vervain and dill
> Hinders witches of their will.

Aubrey also wrote 'It is a thing very common to nail horse-shoes on the thresholds of doors: which is to hinder the power of witches that enter into the house.'[10]

Another popular amulet, again mentioned by John Aubrey, was a stone (usually a flint) with a natural hole in it. These were often hung in stables. 'It is to prevent the nightmare, viz. the hag [i.e. an evil spirit or a witch] from riding their horses.'[11] These stones – still known as hagstones – are used to this day as farm protection charms, often along with an old key, which combines the protective power of iron with the symbolism of 'Heaven's door key', referred to in the Device charm.[12]

Supernatural dangers were not the only threats magic was used against. The medieval book of magic *Picatrix* contains instructions for talismans against a whole range of distinctly unmagical problems, including mice, flies and mosquitoes.[13] In the late twentieth century a Cornish charmer (as they now prefer to be called) used a spoken charm to rid a house of an infestation of fleas.[14] A fifteenth-century charm offered protection against fire and thieves:

> In Bethlehem God was born. Between two beasts to rest he was laid. In that stead [place] was neither thief nor man but the Holy Trinity. That ilk self [same] God that there was born defend our bodies and our cattle from fire, from thieves and all other harms and evils, amen.[15]

This charm is also included in the *Lenkiewicz Manuscript*, an English book of magic from the late sixteenth or early seventeenth century;[16] but in that version the reference to fire is missed out, making it simply a charm against thieves. The fear of witches may have grown, but the fear of thieves certainly hadn't diminished.

In fact some of the methods for detecting witches were derived from thief-detection methods – the use of mirrors, for example:

> [The cunning man Miles Blomfield] brought with him a looking glass, (about 7 or 8 inches square), and did hang the said glass up over the bench in his said hall, upon a nail, and had the said examinate look in it, and said as far as he could guess, he should see the face of him that had [stolen] the said linen.[17]

Reginald Scot included several thief-detection spells in his book *The Discovery of Witchcraft*. One involved making a circle:

> Go to the seaside, and gather as many pebbles as you suspect persons in that matter; carry them home, and throw them into the fire, and bury them under the threshold, where the parties are likely to come over. There let them lie three days, and then before sun rising take them away. Then set a porringer [bowl] full of water in a circle, wherein must be made crosses every way, as many as can stand in it; upon the which must be written: Christ overcometh, Christ reigneth, Christ commandeth. The porringer also must be signed with a cross, and a form of conjuration must be pronounced. Then each stone must be thrown into the water, in the name of the suspected. And when you put in the stone of him that is guilty, the stone will make the water boil, as though glowing iron were put thereinto.[18]

Another particularly popular method was using a sieve and shears. The points of a pair of sheep-shearing shears were pushed into the rim of a large sieve, and the shears held up so the sieve was hanging from them. Two people – no doubt usually the practitioner and client – held the shears between them by pushing one finger up against the top. Reginald Scot writes, 'Ask [Saint] Peter and Paul whether A. B. or C. hath stolen the thing lost, and at the nomination of the guilty party,

Researchers Kate and her mother Mary demonstrate divination using a sieve and shears.
COPYRIGHT TIM AND MARY NEALE WWW.IDENNA.COM

the sieve will turn round.'[19] In fact the difficult thing is holding the sieve like this at all, as it will twist and fall at the slightest lapse of concentration. Again, this method was sometimes used to identify witches as well as thieves

Thief-detection could be a risky business, however. In 1663 a man accused of theft employed the cunning man Nicholas Battersby to clear his name by discovering the real culprits. After divining the thieves' identities, Nicholas went to the prison where his client was being held to demand his release, only to find himself put on trial for practising magic. Under English law the penalty for thief-detection was the same as for love magic – so Nicholas could have faced a year in prison and four six-hour sessions in the pillory. Fortunately, however, he was simply bound over to good behaviour and discharged.[21]

The people accused by the wise woman or cunning man could also react badly. When the Scottish wise woman Bessie Dunlop accused two brothers, Gabriel and Geordie Black, and their father John of theft, they seized her and took her to the Bishop of Glasgow. Bessie eventually confessed that she discovered thieves' identities by asking a spirit – Tom Reid, a local man who had been killed in battle and now lived in Elfland.[22]

There are similarities between Bessie's case and that of the Dorset cunning man John Walsh. Interrogated by a representative of the Bishop of Exeter, at first John claimed that he simply practised physic and surgery – i.e. herbal medicine and the treatment of minor injuries. However, it seems that someone reminded him that he'd had a 'book of circles' confiscated from him, and he then admitted making a circle to 'raise' a spirit 'of whom he would then ask for anything stolen, who did it, and where the thing stolen was left'. The account of the ritual is confused

– evidence of John's reluctance to talk about it and the stress he was under – but it involved candles of virgin (i.e. new) wax and the burning of frankincense and the herb St John's wort. The spirit apparently 'would sometime come unto him like a grey blackish culver [domestic pigeon], and sometimes like a brended [brown with stripes or spots] dog, and sometimes like a man in all proportions, saving that he had cloven feet'.[23]

HEALING

A more typical English case involving the Church occurred in Salisbury in 1614, when the wise woman Elizabeth Smith appeared before a church court accused of practising physic and surgery without a license, witchcraft, astrology, fortune telling 'and such like'.

> Concerning witchcraft she doth utterly deny the same to be true neither did she ever work by any familiar spirit, but she hath read in a book that there be ways to bring a familiar spirit into a vial or into a ring but she protesteth she never practised the same art neither will she, she being asked whether ever any hath resorted unto her for to request her to tell them of some things to come or to tell them of any thing that was or is lost she sayeth that she is altogether unacquainted of any such art. Being asked what skill she hath concerning calculation of nativities [i.e. drawing up horoscopes] she sayeth that she thinketh it is in God's hands only to know of any such matters or questions as are demanded of her; farther she sayeth she hath no skill in palmistry or fortune telling.

The reference to reading about familiar spirits shows that Elizabeth was literate – and, indeed, nearly a hundred years earlier, in 1526, the wise woman Margaret Williamson used books of love potions.[24] Strangely, though, it seems that Elizabeth wasn't questioned about her book, and the court was satisfied with her denials.

She did, however, admit

> that she doth sometimes give people some kind of purgation [cleansing] for agues [malaria] or fevers but for any great cure she meddleth not in any; and for her pains she receiveth not money unless any bring her some chickens or the like, she sayeth that her metson [medicine?] or purgation for the ague is pounding rue in a possett [a drink made with milk] and not otherwise with savory and bay salt [sea salt] laid onto their handwrists.[25]

She was given a formal warning not to practise physic and surgery, and discharged. She probably also had to pay court costs, which may well have been, to her, a considerable sum of money. However, it's clear that she was never in any danger of being imprisoned or executed.[26] This was just an example of the routine – and rather half-hearted – official harassment that English cunning folk learned to live with.

Elizabeth's treatment for the ague illustrates the way many cunning folk combined herbal medicines with magical remedies. Rue was recommended by the seventeenth-century herbalist Nicholas Culpeper as a treatment for the violent fits of shaking that are a symptom of malaria, and it's still used by medical herbalists today to relieve muscular spasms.[27] Putting salt and savory on the patients' wrists, however, seems clearly magical – at least to us. Elizabeth, though, may not have made the sharp distinction we make today.

In a rather similar case fifty years earlier, the Devon wise woman Margaret Lytlejohn attempted to cure a sick sow by getting the owner to tie herbs to the sow's head. The pig, however, was unco-operative, and the herbs 'would not abide upon the sow's head'. So instead Margaret 'did charm certain drink and did give unto the sow to drink'.[28]

This gives us a glimpse of the challenges cunning folk faced when they treated sick animals, and the importance of being able to improvise. The 'certain drink' may well have contained herbs, but it was something Margaret resorted to only after tying the herbs to the pig had proved unworkable. The charm spoken over the drink was also an important part of the cure. It was this part, in fact, that got Margaret into trouble with the Church – she was accused of 'incantation'.

It may be significant that Elizabeth Smith seems to have claimed at first that the rue was the only remedy she used – 'rue in a posset and *not otherwise*' – and probably only mentioned the salt and savory after further questioning. It may have been the use of salt that she was reluctant to admit to. Salt was used in love magic (as described in Chapter Two), and in types of healing that were far more obviously magical than Elizabeth's. The Burgundian judge Henri Boguet recorded an example he regarded as extremely suspect:

> She had herself shut up alone in a room with him [the child], after asking for a piece of flooring stone, a cake of salt and a blanket ... She heated the salt and the stone, then lifted the child out of the cradle and covered them both completely with the blanket ... It's likely that under the blanket this old woman used various words and rituals that she didn't want anyone to see.[29]

Another cure that involved a fusion of magic and herbalism was used by the Essex wise woman Ursley Kempe:

> About ten or eleven years past, she this examinate [Ursley] was troubled with a lameness in her bones and for ease thereof went to one Cocke's wife of Weley, now deceased, who told this examinate that she was bewitched, and at her entreaty taught her to unwitch herself. And bade her take hog's dung and chervil, and put them together and hold them in her left hand, and to take in the other hand a knife, and to prick the medicine three times, and then to cast the same into the fire, and to take the said knife and to make three pricks under a table, and to let the knife stick there: and after that to take three leaves of sage, and as much of herb John (St John's wort) and put them into ale: and drink it last at night and first in the morning, and that she taking the same had ease of her lameness.[30]

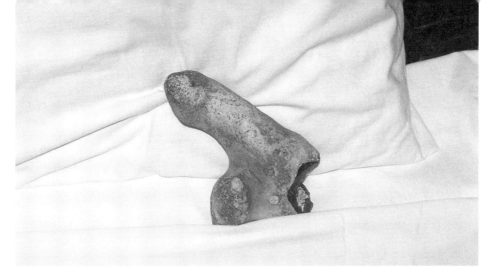

A phallic-shaped flint used as a fertility charm (MoW 1018).
COPYRIGHT MUSEUM OF WITCHCRAFT, PHOTOGRAPH AUTHOR

In this case the illness was attributed to witchcraft, but probably the remedy would have been the same if the disease had been regarded as natural – although pricking the table with the knife may have been intended to hurt the witch.

Throwing something into a fire was a common way to rid a patient of an illness. The Scottish cunning man Thomas Grieve used a particularly horrifying method – although the very fact that it was shocking no doubt increased its psychological impact on the client. In quite an elaborate ritual, a chicken was carried three times round a sick woman's house and then burned alive.[31]

Thomas also passed patients through a length of woollen cord made into a loop, and then burned the cord. Another Scottish cunning man, Andro Man, used the same method, but Andro also sometimes passed a cat through the loop after the patient, to transfer the illness to the cat.[32] An Anglo-Saxon spell for a woman whose children were stillborn or died in infancy also involved transferring the misfortune to someone else:

> The woman who cannot nourish her child, let her take herself a piece of her own child's grave, afterwards cover it in black wool and sell it to traders and then say, 'I sell it, you buy it, this black wool and seeds of this sorrow.'
>
> (*The Lacnunga Manuscript*[33])

The woman would probably have believed that if the trader was a man he wouldn't actually suffer any harm as a result – although he would surely have felt some consternation when he unfolded the wool and the graveyard dust fell out.

Matteuccia di Francesco was even more unscrupulous. To cure a paralysed patient she made a potion of thirty herbs and threw it into the street to transfer the paralysis to whoever next walked over it.[34] Similar spells were still in use in the twentieth century, when Cecil Williamson, researching folk magic in Cornwall, recorded the

A Get Lost Box. Pick it up at your peril! (MoW 68)

practice of leaving 'get lost boxes' in the road to transfer problems or illnesses to anyone foolish enough to pick them up. 'You find some strange things inside these boxes, from corns cut from toes to some unwanted husband's tobacco pouch.'[35]

The French witch-hunter Jean Bodin claimed that cunning folk never actually cured illnesses, but always transferred them to another person:

> If wizards cure a man who has been bewitched, they have to pass the spell on to someone else ... The Devil always wants to profit by the exchange, so that if the wizard removes the spell from a horse, he will pass it on to a horse who is worth more: and if he cures a woman, the illness will fall on a man.[36]

However, the Lancashire cunning man Henry Baggilie, with remarkable professional integrity, transferred the illnesses to himself. He told the Justices who interrogated him that he 'hath always been suddenly taken with sickness ... always in the same manner that the man or beasts that he blessed was troubled withal'.[37]

CHILDBIRTH AND FERTILITY

Wise women were frequently called upon to help women in labour. Bessie Dunlop's interrogators made a point of asking her 'if she could do any good to any women that were in travail [labour] of their child-bed'. She replied that the spirit Tom

Reid had given her 'a green silken lace, out of his own hand, and bade her attach it to their under-dress, and knit [it] about their left arm and without delay the sick woman would be deliver[ed]'. However, when Bessie looked for the lace to use it, it had vanished.[38]

Agnes Sampson, a wise woman caught up in the North Berwick witch-hunt along with her colleague Geillis Duncane, put 'moulds, or powder made of men's joints and members' from a churchyard under a pregnant client's bed, 'which moulds she conjured with her prayers, for staying and slaking of grinding the time of her birth'.[39]

The purple geode used in love magic was also 'profitable to women great with child', preventing miscarriage and reducing the dangers of labour.[40] As geodes are hollow stones containing crystals or other formations they were obvious symbols of female sexuality and fertility. The Museum of Witchcraft has a particularly fine example, used by Joan Long, 'a traveller working seasonally in the West Country', and which she called her 'fanny stone'. The Museum also has a large phallic-shaped flint which was placed under the pillows of couples who wanted to conceive a child, and was used until the 1920s.[41]

Of course there were also circumstances when women wanted to avoid becoming pregnant:

> A woman called Catarina from Città della Pieve approached her [Matteuccia], for a treatment to stop her becoming pregnant, as she was unmarried and sexually involved with a priest of the said town, and intended to spend time with him regularly and was afraid that if she had the misfortune to become pregnant, she would face public disgrace and her family would get to hear about it, Matteuccia told her to obtain a mule's hoof and burn it and reduce it to a powder, and drink the said powder with wine, saying these words as follows:

'The stone which is called *Aetites*... containeth always another stone in it.... This stone, hanged up in the left shoulder, getteth love between the husband and his wife. It is profitable to women great with child; it letteth [prevents] untimely birth.' (*The Book of Secrets of Albertus Magnus*) (MoW 275)

I take you in the name of sin and of the greater Devil so that I will never again be able to become pregnant.[42]

This was intended to transfer the mule's natural infertility to Catarina.

FORTUNE TELLING

As the accusations against Elizabeth Smith make clear, many cunning folk practised astrology or other even more suspect forms of fortune telling. The spirit Tom Reid sent Bessie Dunlop to warn a man that if his eldest daughter's marriage went ahead it would end in tragedy. The man heeded the warning and arranged for the fiancé to marry his other daughter instead.[43] When a client asked the Dartmouth cunning man Michael Trevysard whether her sick child would ever be able to run like other children, Michael terrified her by going into a trance-like state and saying 'No, it shall never run', 'repeating the same words, a dozen several times at the least, with great vehemence'.[44]

The blade-bone of a sheep was often used for divination. *The Munich Handbook* gives instructions for brushing the bone with olive oil to create a bright surface that was then used as a magic mirror.[45] In Scotland, however, cunning folk held the translucent bone up to the light and gazed through it like a crystal ball. If the prediction was bad, the situation wasn't hopeless – 'Then will they prescribe a preservative and prevention'.[46]

Another widespread divination method involved melting lead over a candle or fire, pouring it into water and studying the shapes it solidified into.[47] This still forms part of the New Year celebrations in many European countries, including Austria and Finland. In the run-up to the New Year, lead divination kits can be bought in every supermarket. In Austria, a shape resembling a pig is considered particularly favourable.[48]

During the witch-hunts it was sometimes used as a witch-detection method. The lead was supposed to take on a shape resembling the witch, and it could then be stabbed with a knife to reverse the bewitchment.[49]

Crystal balls have been used for centuries, but in the Middle Ages and early modern period they were much smaller than those used today. John Aubrey describes one in some detail. It was a sphere of clear reddish crystal, which he calls a beryl:

> This beryl is a perfect sphere, the diameter of it I guess to be something more than an inch: it is set in a ring, or circle of silver resembling the meridian of a globe: the stem of it is about ten inches high, all gilt. At the four quarters of it are the names of four angels, viz Uriel, Raphael, Michael, Gabriel. On the top is a cross patee [i.e. like a Maltese cross].

It was owned by a minister in Norfolk, who then gave it to his friend, a miller.

> Both did work great cures with it ... in the beryl they did see, either the recipe in

writing, or else the herb … Afterwards this beryl came into somebody's hand in London, who did tell strange things by it.

John Aubrey adds two other important details. Often the crystal's owner would persuade 'a little boy, or little maid … (for they say it must be a pure virgin) to look in the crystal'. Also:

There are certain formulas of prayer to be used, before they make the inspections, which they term a call.[50]

One of these 'calls' has survived in *The Lenkiewicz Manuscript*,[51] together with a talisman that had to be drawn out before the start of the ritual. The talisman consists of several sacred names of God, and the sigil, or seal, of the spirit who was being invoked – a group of symbols that the Italian magician Francesco Prelati aptly described as the magical equivalent of a heraldic emblem.[52]

The 'call' had to be read out either three or nine times, and is a long and repetitive invocation taking up a whole closely written page:

I conjure thee and charge thee and bind thee, that thou come and appear, in this stone of crystal, in a fair form and visible as one man seeth another, by all power and strength of all sprite, by the virgin Mary that bare our lord Jesus Christ, and by Michael Raphael and Gabriel … Also I conjure thee [Name] that thou come to this stone, by and by without any delay or tarrying, by all the host of Angels and Archangels and by all the holy company of good sprites; Also I bind thee thou sprite [Name], by the virtue of all herbs and stones and grass and spices and glasses, and by these holy names of God, Sother + Emanuell + Panton + Craton + Eleyson + Theamaton + agla + alpha + and omega + tetragramaton + Sabaoth + vermes + athanatos + Ely + Eloy + caramatos + Iesus + Also I conjure thee and bind thee thou, [Name], by all light and lights and stars and frost and cold, ice and snow … Also I bind thee thou sprite [Name], by these 3 words + tetragramaton + anatemate + anatematevethe + and by all that belongeth to these 3 words, Also I conjure charge adjure and bind thee, [Name], that thou come and appear in this stone of crystal and give me a true answer of all things that I shall ask thee of …

There is also a formula for dismissing the spirit at the end of the session:

Depart in peace from me ye sprite or spirit that have or hath appeared unto me, without any manner damage and hurt or disquiet unto me or any other creature. And be ye or you always ready and obedient unto me. And wheresoever I shall call you. In the name of the Father and of the Son and of the Holy Ghost Amen. And the peace of God be always between me and you Amen.

GOOD FORTUNE

Before the days of high street banks it was quite common for people to bury money and valuables to keep them safe. Stories of buried pirate treasure are just

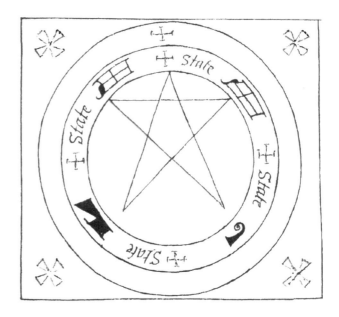

A talisman for treasure hunting, which was hung round the neck of a cockerel. The word '*State*' is a command in Latin: 'Stand!' From *The Lenkiewicz Manuscript.*

a particularly glamorous example of countless rumours of hidden wealth lying neglected in the ground. A letter among the papers of the nineteenth-century cunning man Cunning Murrell read:

> Mr Murls I have rote these few lines to ask you if you can tell us weather there is aney mony or Not hid in my fathers garden he is bin ded 4 years.[53]

Amateur archaeologists are still seduced by the prospect of discovering something lost by some unknown person centuries ago, even if it's only a belt-buckle or coin. Today we have metal detectors; in the seventeenth century they had … chickens:

> [To find] treasure of the earth: make this figure following with the blood of a black whelp [puppy] and hang it about a white cock's neck and go there as the [place] is suspected and cast your cock out of your hand and he shall go and stand right on it and crow, dig there and take it out of the ground … and your cock must have a cord or a line of seven yards long about his leg to have him again when you will.
>
> (*The Lenkiewicz Manuscript*[54])

There were also less ambitious types of magic that would simply guarantee you a good price for anything you sold. The Scottish wise woman Isobel Gowdie confessed:

> When my husband sold beef [cattle], I used to put a swallow's feather in the hide of the beast and [say]
>
> > [I] put out this beef in the Devil's name,
> > That mickle silver and good price come home![55]

She also confessed to calling the Devil 'our Lord' ('When we had ended eating, we looked steadfastly to the Devil, and vowing ourselves to him, we said to the Devil, "We thank thee our Lord for this!"'),[56] so it's quite likely that either she or her interrogators substituted the words 'the Devil' for 'our Lord' in the charms she quoted. This livestock-selling charm was probably originally, 'I put out this beef in our Lord's name.'

Isobel also had a charm to guarantee a good catch of fish, although again it's likely that it's become garbled as a result of pressure from her interrogators:

> The fishers are gone to the sea
> And they will bring home fish to me
> They will bring them home intill [in] the boat
> But they shall get of them but the smaller sort.[57]

Picatrix, too, includes 'a talisman to catch more fish'. It had to be made at the astrologically correct time, but the talisman itself was delightfully simple: 'make a picture of a fish'.[58]

British sailors travelling to Scandinavia found that the cunning folk there could sell them a fair wind:

Our own navigators, who trade in Finland, Denmark, Lapland, Ward-house, Norway, and other countries of that climate, and have obtained of the inhabitants thereof, a certain wind for twenty days together … and strings tied with three knots, so that if one were loosed, they should have a pleasant gale: if the second, a more vehement blast: if the third, such hideous and raging tempests that the mariners were not able once to look out.

(*A Treatise of Witchcraft* by Alexander Roberts[59])

And it seems that Isobel could do something similar:

When we raise the wind, we take a rag of cloth, and wets it in water; and we take a beetle [bat for cleaning clothes] and knock the rag on a stone, and we say thrice over,

> I knock this rag upon this stone,
> To raise the wind, in the Devil's name;
> It shall not lie until I please again![60]

These claims of being able to control the weather led inevitably to some cunning folk, such as Agnes Sampson, being accused of raising storms to sink ships.[61] Indeed, Michael Trevysard and his wife Alice could apparently sink ships even in fair weather. Their son Peter, however, used his power over boats simply for his own amusement and to impress his friends:

The examination of Christopher Honywell, aged 13 years or thereabouts …

This examinate sayeth that about Whitsuntide last, he was with Peter Trevysard, son of the said Michael Trevysard, at a place at Hardness where the fishermen use to hang their nets, where the said young Trevysard did put off his father's boat, saying 'go thy ways to new quay, and go in between the two lighters and I will meet thee there.' And further this examinate sayeth that he came with the young Trevysard to the new quay presently after and found the boat there between the two lighters, the said quay being distant near two flight shoots from the place where the boat was so thrust off as aforesaid and not right against the same place but on one side. The said two lighters also being so near together that there was but room enough for the boat to go in.[62]

As well as their anti-witchcraft charm, Alizon's family also used another, shorter, charm – 'Crucifixus hoc signum vitam eternam. Amen' ('The crucifix – this is proof of eternal life. Amen'). According to young Jennet,

> Her brother James Device ... hath confessed to her ... that he by this prayer hath gotten drink [i.e. beer or ale]: and that within an hour after the saying of the said prayer, drink had come into the house after a very strange manner.[63]

Roger Nowell's decision to include this in the evidence against James shows (apart from the bad effect the witch-hunts could have on a prosecutor's sense of humour) how important it was to him to represent magic as essentially blasphemous. He of course overlooked the fact that James was teaching his nine-year-old sister about magic, and so would naturally choose a less-than-serious example. In fact this gives us a poignant glimpse of their relaxed and affectionate relationship.

But James *was* making an important point – that magic was a way of dealing with everyday problems, as well as matters of life and death. A remarkable collection of mid-twentieth-century charms in the library of the Museum of Witchcraft also makes this clear:

> For all your needs any iota [least] thing you need in life do the Novena of the infant Jesus either nine complete hours during one day or nine days successively.[64]

Magic responded to the *needs* of the individual just as it worked through the individual's *intent*. It recognised the importance of small things in people's lives. It was there to help each individual achieve what mattered to *them*. If, after a hard day, James really needed a drink, magic would get it for him.

Magic declared and demonstrated the importance of the individual. And that did, arguably, make it blasphemous, at least to those who justified a rigid social order by claiming it reflected a divine order presided over by a God who demanded absolute self-denying obedience. People who practised magic, and were therefore so potentially useful to their communities, also potentially challenged some important social and religious assumptions. And, as we shall see in the next chapter, one of the crucial events that had led to the European witch-hunts had been an open act of rebellion against the authority of the Church, which had resulted in magic being condemned as the ultimate crime – high treason against God.[65]

CHAPTER SEVEN

Healers and heretics

THE ORIGINS OF THE WITCH-HUNTS

The European witch-hunts were fuelled by an image of magic that played on people's deepest fears. It portrayed magic as a link between the human world and the realms of supernatural evil. Not only did those who practised magic have access to the *power* to do terrible things, they were corrupted by magic until no crime was so horrible that it was beyond them. As the twelfth-century writer Hugh of St Victor wrote, 'Magic … drives the minds of those who pursue it towards every type of crime and forbidden wickedness.'[1]

This association of magic with evil spirits, and with cruelty, self-gratification and depravity, is still with us today. But it became part of the popular stereotype of magic only gradually, over a period of around 250 years between the early thirteenth century and the mid fifteenth. Four key events both illustrate this process and contributed to it – the creation of the greatest book of magic of the Middle Ages, the arrest of a French physician at the end of the fourteenth century, a persecution of wise women in Italy in the early fifteenth century, and one of France's most shocking criminal trials in 1440.

HONORIUS OF THEBES

In the twelfth century a revolution took place in European thought. For a number of reasons – including the Crusades – the works of Islamic thinkers flooded into the Christian world. Confronted by challenging new ideas on a whole range of subjects, such as mathematics, medicine and astronomy, Christian scholars responded with enthusiasm, developing their own new theories and experiments to test them. A typical example was Robert Grosseteste, the thirteenth-century Chancellor of Oxford University and Bishop of Lincoln, whose experiments on the nature of light led him to develop a version of the Big Bang theory 700 years before twentieth-century scientists, concluding that it was the propagation of light that created the dimensions of space.[2]

However, not all churchmen shared Robert's attitude. Many felt that the authority of the Church was threatened by uncontrolled speculation about the nature of the Universe. These concerns were one of the reasons why, in a series of moves between 1184 and 1233, three Popes created an organisation designed to take control of European thought and eliminate unacceptable ideas – the Inquisition.[3]

In the Middle Ages the distinctions we make today between art, science, philosophy and religion were blurred, and magic combined elements of all four. It shared with science the desire to understand the mysterious forces that governed the natural world and the human body and mind, and then to exploit that understanding to achieve practical results. Magic had thrived in the new intellectual climate – *Picatrix* was one of the Islamic books that arrived in Europe at this time – and now it was specifically targeted in the crackdown. At some point in the first half of the thirteenth century, the Pope declared all forms of magic punishable by death.[4]

However, many wealthy and influential people – including many churchmen – practised magic. One thirteenth-century thinker, Richard de Fourneville, owned thirty-six books of magic.[5] These people formed a loose-knit subversive community of magicians – and that, no doubt, was one reason the Church authorities were so concerned about them.

These magicians now had to decide how to respond to the Church's challenge. They considered and rejected using magic to overthrow the pope. A group of eighty-nine of them met to work out an alternative strategy.[6] Such a large meeting could hardly have been kept secret, so that was an act of defiance in itself. And the option they chose was a statement of the superiority of ideas over violence – they decided to write a book.

The man they selected to be the author was Honorius of Thebes – although this is almost certainly a pseudonym, to protect him and deny the Church authorities the propaganda coup that arresting the book's writer would have given them. But the book also had a co-author – a spirit, the Angel Hocroel, whose name probably means 'Wisdom of God'.[7]

It's now known as *The Sworn Book*, after the oath the magicians swore to protect it, which is its title in the British Library catalogue entry for one of the manuscripts.[8] However, the magicians called it both *The Sworn Book* and *The Sacred Book*:

> For in it is contained the 100 sacred names of God and therefore it is called sacred as you would say made of holy things, or else because by this book he [Honorius] came to the knowledge of sacred or holy things, or else because it was consecrated by angels, or else because the Angel Hocroel did declare and show unto him that it was consecrated of God.[9]

Honorius began *The Sworn Book* with an angry attack on the pope and cardinals. It was they, not magicians, who were acting 'through the instigation of the Devil'. It was they who were the servants of evil spirits intending to 'destroy all things profitable for mankind, and to corrupt all the whole world'. He then went on, 'Yet … we have gone about to set forth the principles of this art, and the cause of truth, and for that cause they had condemned this art and judged us to death.'[10]

Honorius was arguing that magic had been condemned by the Church precisely because it was a means to attain the truth. It offered spiritual insights and experiences far beyond anything the ceremonies of the Church could provide. And in fact the first section of *The Sworn Book* consists of instructions for a ritual to achieve a vision of God:

> O righteous God quicken me and visit me and my understanding clarify my soul and purge it … that like as thou didst show John and Paul the sight of thee when thou didst take them up into heaven even so Lord that I may while this my body liveth see and behold thy face.[11]

Honorius regarded magic as a mystical, visionary form of Christianity. It could have existed in partnership with conventional Christianity, but the pope's condemnation had made that impossible. Magic was now a counter-religion in opposition to the Church of Rome.

Honorius was well aware of magic's ancient origins. He refers to 'follow[ing] the steps and precepts of Solomon',[12] the biblical king who was renowned for his wisdom, had power over demons (according to the apocryphal *Testament of Solomon*[13]) and honoured pagan deities including Ashtaroth – the spirit invoked in the *Munich Handbook* love spell. Solomon was influenced by his foreign wives, one of them the daughter of the Pharaoh of Egypt, and Honorius's supposed place of origin, Thebes, may have been intended to link him with this source of Solomon's magic.[14] Honorius would also have been familiar with the account in the Gospel of St Matthew of the eastern magicians who visited the infant Jesus.[15] He would have read the bible in Latin, and the word used for these men, '*magi*' (a close equivalent of the original Greek word '*magoi*'), was used throughout the medieval and early modern periods as the Latin word for magicians.[16] It was only when the bible was translated into English that they were referred to as 'wise men'.[17] In Christian legend, these magicians were called Gaspar, Balthasar and Melchior, and their names came to be used as words of power in spells, an indication of how important this biblical vindication of their art was to Christians who practised magic.[18]

However, in spite of all this, and in spite of his enormous debt not only to Islamic learning but also to Jewish magical traditions,[19] Honorius emphasised that only Christians could perform truly effective magic. He also said that women should not be allowed copies of *The Sworn Book*.[20] Disappointingly, it seems that magic did not enable Honorius to transcend the prejudices of his time. However, at the root of this was Honorius's conviction that magicians were a Christian priesthood. Their Christianity uniquely empowered them because Christ's life (and sacrificial death) on Earth had created a unique link with divine power.

For all its mysticism, however, *The Sworn Book* was also a defence of the use of magic for a whole range of less exalted purposes, many of them familiar parts of the repertoire of cunning folk. Its rituals could be used 'to know all plants, herbs and beasts … and of their virtues', 'to heal all men of diseases', 'to have all treasures … hid in the ground', 'to bring again [what] a thief … hath stolen', and even 'to kill whom you will'.[21]

Crucially, though, all these things were obtained through invoking the help of spirits. This was done by making circles, burning incense, using incantations and drawing out an elaborate talisman called the Seal of God.[22] Through these rituals the magician drew on divine power to summon the appropriate spirits, and when they appeared he prevailed on them to do, or tell him, whatever he wanted. And although some of these spirits are referred to as 'angels', some are referred to simply as 'spirits', and others as 'demons'.[23]

If you hung a hagstone in a stable, tied herbs to a pig's head, or even stuck pins in an onion, you could argue that the magic worked because of some natural virtue in the objects you were using; but the magic of *The Sworn Book* depends entirely on the magician forming a relationship with supernatural beings, and as far back as the seventh century Church law had decreed that 'Christians must not abandon God's Church and go and summon angels'.[24] If summoning spirits was forbidden by the Church, then naturally, as far as the Church was concerned, any spirit that was prepared to be summoned was likely to be evil. Thus, if Honorius had set out to write a book that would convince the Church that magic was the worst kind of heresy, and all people who practised it were allied with the forces of evil, he could hardly have done a better job.

The Sworn Book was, indeed, condemned, vilified and labelled 'the death of the soul'.[25] Typically, later copies met this accusation head on:

> Men have entitled this book … the death of the soul, and that is true to them that work for an evil intent and purpose.[26]

This simply underlined the heretical assumption at the centre of the book – that individual intent was more important than obedience to authority. The magician must act according to his own conscience, stand by his decisions, and if necessary pay the price.

There's no doubt that Honorius was caught up in the intellectual self-confidence of what is now known as the Medieval Renaissance. To him there were no limits to what the human mind could achieve, and magic was a way 'to obtain all sciences'.[27] However, this sometimes unscrupulous individualism also seems to have been deeply rooted in magical culture itself, and perhaps even in the personalities of those who were drawn to practise magic. We see it in the *Munich Handbook* love spell. We see it in Nicholas Battersby recklessly demanding his client's release from prison; in James Device refusing to be deferential to Anne Towneley; in Michael Trevysard allowing his personal resentments to stop him treating an injured child.

The Sworn Book may have been a catastrophe for the relationship between magical

The Seal of God engraved on copper, used by the twentieth-century occultist Cecil Williamson, founder of the Museum of Witchcraft. Behind it is a seventeenth-century carving from a chest used to store magical artefacts by the collector Charles Wade. (MoW 2030 & 1009)

COPYRIGHT MUSEUM OF WITCHCRAFT, PHOTOGRAPH AUTHOR

practitioners and the religious authorities, but both its tone and content appealed to practitioners enormously. It remained Europe's most influential book of magic until it was gradually supplanted by Heinrich Cornelius Agrippa's *Three Books of Occult Philosophy* in the sixteenth century and *The Key of Solomon* in the seventeenth. Several good copies survive, one of which was owned by the Elizabethan magician John Dee and then by the playwright Ben Jonson; and it was translated into English in the sixteenth century.[28] Even very different books of magic such as Messayaac's *Liber de Angelis* and *The Lenkiewicz Manuscript* used words of power taken from its incantations.[29]

For Honorius, what lay at the heart of magic's individualism was the personal relationship between the magician and the spirits who worked with him – no doubt in his case, in particular, his relationship with his co-author, the Angel Hocroel. It would be easy for us to dismiss these claims of summoning spirits as wish-fulfilment fantasy, and the claim that *The Sworn Book* was written with the help of an angel as a cynical ploy to give it more authority. However, the magicians who attended the meeting believed that there was a good chance that some of them would be arrested, and admitting that they had dealings with spirits was the one thing most likely to guarantee a death sentence. Whatever these spirit encounters actually were, there can be no doubt that some of these magicians had experienced them. You don't risk your life for something you don't believe in.

No surviving records of arrests and executions can be linked with this meeting or the writing of *The Sworn Book*, but there is some evidence that Honorius himself may have been arrested. There are some important sections missing from the book – in particular, some crucial seals and a section on invoking spirits into objects (presumably things like mirrors and crystals).[30] It seems that *The Sworn Book* was never finished.

JEHAN DE BAR

In the early fourteenth century Pope John XXII launched another attack on magic, condemning practitioners for worshipping spirits and invoking their help using mirrors, images, rings and vials.[31] The magicians of the time were less restrained than Honorius and his colleagues. There were two plots to use magic to kill the pope, and at least one of the conspirators, Hugues Géraud (the Bishop of Cahors), was burned.[32]

Around the same time, there was an unusual case in London. A female magician, Juliana of Lambeth, was convicted of divination and image magic – probably love magic. Her punishment was to walk in a procession to St Paul's Cathedral holding a wax image and wearing her black philosopher's robe, and then stand on a platform in the cathedral while her books of magic were burned. To symbolise her repentance, and to indicate that she was lucky to get off so lightly, some of her hair was also burned.[33]

The Inquisition investigated a wide range of magical practices. An inquisitor's handbook written by Bernardo Gui in 1323/4 instructed investigators to question professional practitioners about thief-detection, fortune-telling, helping women become pregnant, improving married couples' relationships, finding hidden treasure and lost animals, and using healing charms. They should also be asked how many clients they had and what they were paid.[34]

However, healing magic was generally tolerated. John of Gaddesden, court physician to Edward II, cured the king's son of smallpox by wrapping him in a red cloth.[35] His influential book *Rosa Medicinae* (*The Rose of Medicine*) contained a number of magical remedies. One (for treating a haemorrhage) involved using the patient's blood to write the name of St Veronica on his or her forehead, and reciting a charm referring to the woman who was cured by touching Jesus's robe.[36] The eminent French surgeon Guy de Chauliac recommended a similar treatment for epilepsy – getting patients to write the names Gaspar, Balthasar and Melchior on parchment using their own blood. They also had to say conventional prayers – three Pater Nosters and three Ave Marias – daily for three months.[37]

At the end of the fourteenth century, however, something happened that changed everything. In 1398 the Department of Theology at the University of Paris produced a *Determinatio* listing forbidden magical beliefs and practices. The Paris *Determinatio* was so influential that nearly 200 years later the French witch-hunter Jean Bodin included it in full in the preface to his book *De la Démonomanie des Sorciers*. Through Jean Bodin's work it then went on to influence English Justices, including Roger Nowell.

The Paris *Determinatio* was itself strongly influenced by *The Sworn Book*. The first of its twenty-eight articles declared that the use of magic to obtain the help, friendship or familiarity (*familiaritas*, i.e. intimacy) of spirits was idolatry (which would make it forbidden by the first of the Ten Commandments). The final article condemned the belief that it was possible to use magic to obtain a vision of God. But the theologians were also familiar with other books of magic similar to *The Munich Handbook* and *The Lenkiewicz Manuscript*. Other articles condemned the use of images, mirrors and crystals. And one article, clearly aimed at cunning folk, condemned the use of counter-magic against witchcraft.

To publicise the *Determinatio* it was decided to make an example of someone, and the man selected was one of King Charles VI's court physicians, Jehan de Bar. Jehan owned several books of magic, and seems to have been arrested after making a circle in a wood in Brie. He was probably promised that he would be

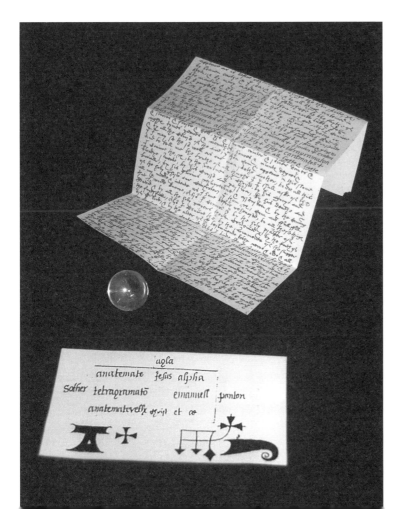

A modern crystal sphere of the size used by medieval and early modern scryers, with a talisman and 'call' for invoking a spirit copied from *The Lenkiewicz Manuscript*

71

treated leniently if he co-operated, and he made a detailed statement that was both a confession and a declaration of repentance. Parts of it reflect the *Determinatio* almost word for word, but since Jehan and the theologians had been studying the same kinds of books (although for very different reasons), it's probably still an accurate record of Jehan's magic.[38]

Jehan admitted practising 'invocations of devils' and wanting to have 'the familiarity and friendship of devils'. His books (which he had considered sacred but now accepted were 'wicked and execrable') contained 'errors against our faith, such as saying that some devils are good and benign'.

He performed rituals that involved wearing special robes, making circles, burning incense and using sacred names of God. He carried some of his own hair and nail clippings about with him in a small box to use as offerings to spirits. He believed his magic was empowered by performing it at the correct astrological times. He made an image to gain the favour of the Duke of Burgundy. He drew out talismans using animal blood and performed divination using a steel mirror. He gave clients horseshoe nails as amulets to protect their horses from going lame.[39] And he wrote out long invocations to spirits asking for the power to help the king, who was suffering from a mental illness.

Item five of his confession is remarkably similar to John Aubrey's description, 300 years later, of using a crystal ball. With a young boy looking into a 'stone of crystal', Jehan used an invocation to summon a spirit which he believed to be an angel, and which appeared to the boy in the shape of a bishop. Jehan's statement of repentance for this crime is both poignant and significant:

> I repent … and firmly believe that it was nothing but a delusion of the Devil and not in fact a good angel.

In spite of his cooperation, Jehan was sentenced to be burned. In most countries prisoners were strangled before burning, but the evidence from later witchcraft cases suggests that in France they were usually burned alive.[40] Since the authorities had taken action against Jehan to send an emphatic message to everyone who practised magic, it's likely they would have wanted his death to be as memorable and horrifying as possible. His books of magic were burned with him.

It's tempting to think that when Jehan admitted that his magic was 'a delusion of the Devil' he was just trying to save his life by saying what his interrogators wanted to hear. But it's possible that his repentance was genuine. Interrogators had an argument that it was hard for a helpless and desperate prisoner to answer – if your power was a gift from God and the spirits who helped you were angels, they would have protected you and kept you safe. The very fact that you were in this terrible situation was proof that the Devil had deceived you.

Jehan's capitulation shouldn't overshadow the courage he showed by continuing to practise magic even though he must have known that the University of Paris was preparing the *Determinatio*. His position at court, treating a sick king in the midst of all the intrigue that would have involved, was both high-profile and high-risk. He would have been well aware that the *Determinatio* could lead to serious trouble for him.

But it's also probable that he didn't realise that he was at risk of a cruel death. He'd used magic to try to help a king who was suffering from an intractable illness that more conventional treatments had failed to cure. It would have been hard for him to believe that anyone would regard that as a capital crime. He probably still couldn't believe it as they led him to the stake. He was a doctor. He'd never harmed anyone. Why would anyone want to kill him?

MATTEUCCIA DI FRANCESCO

Two years after Jehan's execution, the Black Death struck the Italian town of Siena. In the Hospital of Santa Maria della Scala a small group of people risked their own lives to do what they could for the dying. One of them was a twenty-year-old university-educated aristocrat called Bernardino. In spite of his wealth, Bernardino's life had already been difficult – his mother had died when he was three, his father when he was six, and the aunt who then cared for him when he was eleven. Bernardino survived the plague, but was then struck down by another serious illness.[41] Although he recovered, these experiences left him permanently traumatised:

> We have sweet things in this life, but mixed in with them is much bitterness. Look how many dangers there are in these delights, how many scandals! These are the stings of the world. And when you have meditated on them you will say: Oh treacherous world, I no longer believe in you! … Oh! believe you me, the world deceives you in every direction.[42]

Bernardino joined the Franciscan Order and became a travelling preacher, a life that often involved extreme hardship, and by 1417 he was beginning to become famous for his sermons. By the end of his life he was believed to be able to perform miracles, and within six years of his death the Church had declared him a saint.[43]

Bernardino's mission was to warn the ordinary people of Italy of the spiritual threats endangering them. His sermons were compelling dramatic performances, and at times he seems to have been like a particularly vicious kind of stand-up comedian, making his points by lurid exaggerations that were intended to provoke a combination of horror and laughter. In one of his many sermons against the Jewish community, he said:

> Beware of accepting cups or pots from the Jews, since I can't help believing that their women urinate into them in order to mock Christians.[44]

As he travelled Italy, Bernardino became increasingly concerned about the widespread use of magic:

There is neither town nor castle nor state that is not filled with seers, sorcerers, diviners and witches.[45]

The French theologians' campaign against magic was still concentrating on high-status physicians (the preacher Jean Gerson wrote an entire treatise criticising a doctor for using a talisman with a picture of a lion on it),[46] but Bernardino targeted the practitioners his audience of ordinary working people were most likely to encounter – wise women.

In Florence in 1425 he delivered a sermon that included a story he claimed was absolutely true. A young man lost a purse of money, and since his godmother was a wise woman he asked her to use her powers of divination to find it for him. Curious about her methods, he went back to her house that night.

> Lo and behold, in the first hours of sleep, this woman opens the door to her vegetable garden and comes out completely naked and her hair all undone, and she begins to do and say her various signs and conjurations, and to shriek out and call the Devil.

The Devil appeared and told the woman where her godson had dropped the purse, but insisted that instead of telling him the truth she should say that his wife was having an affair with a priest and had given him the money.[47]

Even if Bernardino didn't expect his audience to take this story completely seriously, its message was harsh. Wise women might appear to be practising simple forms of benign magic, but they were in fact summoning the Devil. And although they pretended to be helping their clients, their real purpose was to cause conflict and misery.

The tone of another sermon, preached in Siena in 1427, was deadly serious.

> Here is someone ... with parchment talismans, another with charms, another with sorceries, another with divinations. Some have visited the enchanter or diviner if they have been robbed of five cents. Do you know what you have done? You have caused men to renounce God, and you have caused the Devil to be adored ... Oh you who have used the charm of the three good brothers [a charm for wounds], what a great evil you do. Oh you who have used the charm for broken bones, to you ... I say, take heed! ... Know that she or he who claims to have the power to break a charm [i.e. curse] knows as well, be assured, how to work one. When such people say that they wish to cure anyone, do you know what you should do? There is nothing better to do than to cry, 'To the fire! To the fire! To the fire!'[48]

A year earlier, a similar sermon Bernardino preached in Rome prompted the citizens to denounce large numbers of cunning folk, both men and women. Alarmed, the head of the Franciscan monastery consulted the pope (Martin V), who agreed that only 'those who had done the worst' would be arrested. One of them, a woman called Finicella, 'confessed, without being put to torture, that she had killed thirty children by sucking their blood ... [and] that she had killed her own little son, and had made a powder out of him, which she gave people to eat in these practices of hers'. When she was asked which children she'd killed she gave the name of a child who had indeed died, which was considered proof of her guilt. Apparently another woman also confessed to similar crimes. Both were sentenced to be burned.[49]

Jehan de Bar's execution had been a major event, and now most of Rome turned out to watch the execution of the two wise women. Finicella was strangled before she was burned, but her colleague was burned alive. Perhaps she had retracted her confession, which would have been regarded not as evidence that she might be innocent but as proof that she was unrepentant.

Extraordinarily, to Bernardino the confessions of these two women were conclusive proof that all wise women fed on children's blood. In his Siena sermon a year later he called on his audience to accuse every 'worker of charms and spells' with the words, 'If it had happened that she killed one of your little children, what would you think about the matter then?'[50]

Bernardino also preached at the city of Todi.[51] There he not only made a great impression on the ordinary citizens, but also persuaded the city authorities to tighten their laws against magic – allowing suspects to be tortured and making the punishment for invoking spirits or using spells death by burning.[52]

Matteuccia di Francesco lived at Ripabianca, which was under the jurisdiction of Todi. She was arrested in March 1428.[53] It was not Bernardino, of course, who prosecuted her. He had preached his sermon and gone on his way. The man who took action against her was Lorenzo de Surdis, Captain and Justice of the Peace of the city of Todi.[54] The record that we have of the case is the statement of his judgment, and it consists of a detailed summary of Matteuccia's crimes together with the sentence passed on her.

Matteuccia was a successful professional with a large number of clients. Although Lorenzo de Surdis investigated only her activities of the previous two or three years, he recorded that she'd treated more than twenty people attacked by spirits[55] and – 'prompted by a spirit from hell and adding evil to evil' – 'numerous' people suffering from natural illnesses. She recited charms either over the patient or over a belt or cloak brought to her. Sometimes she threw salt into a fire or held a lighted candle and spat on to the ground, but sometimes she simply said the charm three times. It's likely that Matteuccia didn't fully appreciate that this was 'adding evil to evil', and recited her healing charms to Lorenzo to convince him she was *not* a witch, just as James and Jennet recited their charms to Roger Nowell two centuries later.

Matteuccia's love magic was mainly intended to improve relationships between husbands and wives:

> Adding evil to evil this Matteuccia evidently instructed countless numbers of women, who were beaten by their husbands, and who asked her for a remedy so that their husbands would love them and do their will, that they should take the herb called horsetail and pound it up and give it to their husbands in a drink or to eat, saying these words, as follows:

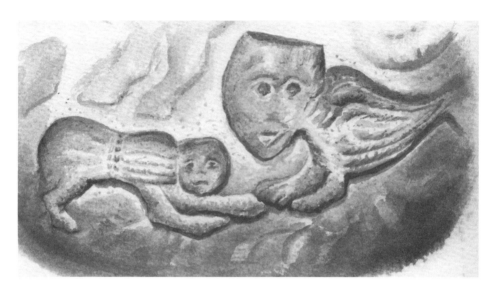

A carving of a witch – part-woman, part-owl – menacing a child; from the twelfth-century font in St Austell church in Cornwall.

> I give you this to drink in the name of phantom
> And of the invoked spirits
> And so that you can neither sleep nor rest
> Until you do what I wish to command you.

However, there are also some more detailed accounts of individual cases, which are probably taken from statements by people Lorenzo brought in for questioning, and who co-operated to avoid being prosecuted themselves. When a man was found drowned in the River Tiber, Matteuccia persuaded a local official to get her some flesh and fat from the corpse to make a healing oil.[56] She told a woman a spell to make her lover leave his wife. And when a young man came to her for help because the girl he was in love with was about to marry someone else, Matteuccia gave him instructions for a spell to make the bridegroom impotent, which could have resulted in the marriage being annulled.

But then the record claims that Matteuccia, like Finicella and her colleague in Rome, preyed on children by sucking their blood. Finicella could remember the name of only one of her thirty supposed victims,[57] but all of Matteuccia's five victims are identified by their parents' names and the places they lived. This strongly suggests that their parents – inspired by Bernardino's sermons and the burnings in Rome – accused her.

But there are also details that seem to have come from Matteuccia herself. To prey on the children she turned herself into a fly using an ointment made of bat's blood, vulture's fat and her victims' blood (it's not clear how she turned into a fly to attack her first victim).[58] She also used the ointment to travel (in the company of a demon in the shape of a goat) to meetings of witches and spirits held at a walnut tree and presided over by Lucifer. It was Lucifer who ordered Matteuccia and the other witches to carry out their attacks on children.

The belief that witches turned themselves into animals – usually owls or cats – and preyed on children dated back to Ancient Rome,[59] but by the Middle Ages it was widespread across Europe. A twelfth-century font in St Austell church in Cornwall is carved with a picture of two owls with women's faces menacing a child.[60] It provided an explanation for high rates of childhood illness and mortality, but there was confusion over whether these creatures were really women or evil spirits. Bernardino argued that the Devil attacked the children, but deluded the women into thinking they were responsible.[61] But there was still an ill-defined assumption that the women's involvement somehow gave the Devil his power to do harm.

Although Jehan de Bar was a royal physician and Matteuccia a small-town wise woman, they were prosecuted for essentially the same reasons. It's significant that Bernardino specifically condemned 'the charm of the three good brothers'. It was a charm used by educated physicians as well as cunning folk, and was included in a fifteenth-century version of John of Gaddesden's *Rosa Medicinae*. And, like the charm 'Archidecline sits on high', it was used to summon spiritual power into objects:

> Three good brothers went to the Mount of Olives to collect herbs and met our lord Jesus Christ who said to them 'Where are you going?' The three good brothers, replying, said, 'To the Mount of Olives to collect herbs to heal wounds.' And Jesus told them, 'I command you, three good brothers, to leave the herbs and take olive oil and black wool saying, 'I command you, wound, by the precious wound of Christ pierced by the soldier Longeus, which neither became septic, nor festered, nor bred maggots, nor caused severe pain, so you will not become septic, nor fester, nor breed maggots, nor cause pain, by the virtue of the oil and wool. In the name of the Father, the Son and the Holy Spirit'. Nor will you take payment, but do this in the name of the Father, the Son and the Holy Spirit.'[62]

To Bernardino that power came not from Jesus Christ but from the Devil. Using a charm was essentially the same as summoning an evil spirit – the same as Jehan summoning a spirit into a crystal, a spirit that was 'a delusion of the Devil'. And it was only one step further – albeit a terrible one – for Matteuccia, in some kind of delusional and ill-defined collusion with the Devil, to be responsible for the illness of five children.

Like Jehan, Matteuccia also confessed, apparently 'freely' – that is, without being tortured, although the knowledge that the city authorities had just given themselves the power to torture her must surely have influenced her. But it may not have been simply a matter of Matteuccia saying things she knew were untrue in order to avoid

pain. As with Jehan, it may be that Lorenzo used the threat of torture to increase Matteuccia's desperation, to make her wonder whether her magical power *was* in fact a delusion of the Devil. And if the Devil *had* tricked her into serving him, perhaps she was also somehow responsible for the children's illnesses.

Matteuccia had treated more than twenty people attacked by evil spirits, so she certainly believed that such attacks were possible. She may also have believed that people could make spirit journeys while they were asleep. One of the mid-twentieth-century charms in the Museum of Witchcraft's collection seems to refer to this idea:

> Protecting sprite who watches over me always ... during the night when my sprite finds itself in the unknown, take me to my loved ones.[63]

Lorenzo may well have been able to twist Matteuccia's own beliefs to convince her of her guilt.[64]

Although none of her supposed victims had died, Matteuccia was sentenced to be 'burned by fire until ... her soul is separated from her body'. We can only hope that, like Finicella, she was in fact strangled first.

The first letter of the manuscript recording her crimes is decorated with a small sketch of a woman's face. As the document's modern editor, Domenico Mammoli, suggests, this may be a portrait of Matteuccia. It is something of a caricature, but the way it depicts her, with a jutting determined jaw, a haughty nose, fierce dark eyes and loose, wild hair, gives the impression – perhaps in spite of the artist's intentions – of a formidable and dynamic woman.

CHAPTER EIGHT

The magician and the serial killer

The factors that had led to the killing of Jehan de Bar and Matteuccia di Francesco would develop into the European catastrophe that would engulf Alizon's family 200 years later. Before we return to the Pendle case in the next chapter, we can get an insight into how that happened from the fate of a magician born in Monte-Catini, north-west of Florence, who was a child when Matteuccia was killed.

Ten years after Matteuccia's death the persecution of wise women was spreading steadily northwards. Eustache Blanchet, a French priest who travelled regularly to Rome, noted with dismay that large numbers of women in Burgundy and Savoy were being hanged for having dealings with spirits.[1]

Eustache had reason to be uneasy. He had been commissioned by an aristocratic acquaintance to find and recruit a magician to join his household. He made discreet inquiries, and in Florence he was introduced to a young cleric called Francesco Prelati, a friend of Nicolas de Medici, a minor member of the powerful Medici family.[2]

Francesco, who was then about twenty-one, was a very charming young man and an entertaining conversationalist.[3] He had studied a wide range of arts and sciences, including poetry, alchemy, spirit-invocation and divination.[4] He also owned a book about alchemy and magic. Eustache was impressed, and persuaded Francesco to return with him to France.

Already there was dark talk about the rituals conducted by Eustache's aristocratic acquaintance. Apparently if you mentioned his castle at Machecoul, people in the surrounding area were likely to look at you in horror and mutter, 'They eat babies there.'[5] But Francesco – who had been about nine years old when Finicella sensationally confessed to her thirty child murders – would have been all too familiar with such allegations, and the way they were used to demonise magic. He couldn't know he was on his way to meet a man who in just eighteen months' time would be one of the most reviled criminals in French history – Gilles de Rais.

Gilles and Francesco met at one of Gilles's other castles, Tiffauges, in May 1439.[6] They liked each other immediately. Gilles regarded Francesco as 'exceptionally gifted', admired his learning and enjoyed his company.[7] Francesco, for his part, would show extraordinary loyalty to Gilles, and there was much about Gilles that Francesco might have found attractive. Thirty-five years old, he was a courageous soldier with formidable leadership qualities. He was generous, arrogant, impetuous and troubled. And he was certainly in need of Francesco's magical help.

For three generations France had been fighting the Hundred Years War, a territorial dispute between the kings of England and France, and the social and economic effects on both countries were disastrous. The war was fought not by national armies but by the private armies of the aristocracy, and in the lapses in the official fighting the aristocracy mimicked their kings and tried to seize each other's territory, using any excuse – a disputed marriage contract, a badly drafted will – and resorting to violence without hesitation. If a lord was to keep his lands he had to have a large retinue, and to keep his retinue loyal and his enemies daunted he had to have an impressively magnificent lifestyle.[8]

Gilles de Rais had inherited vast estates, but estates can drain money as easily as generate it. He had a natural taste for spectacle, and he was extravagantly lavish in his gifts to members of his household and his charity to his ordinary tenants.[9] For some time he'd been struggling to manage his finances. When he started to sell off some of his estates his brother and cousin took legal action against him and then tried to seize the lands by force. This aroused the unwelcome interest of Gilles's overlords, the Dukes of Brittany and Anjou, who tried to exploit the situation to get the lands for themselves.

By the time of Francesco's arrival at Tiffauges, Gilles had already lost another of his castles, Champtocé.[10] His brother had seized it, and although Gilles had negotiated its return he'd been forced to sell it to the Duke of Brittany. Gilles's brother had also briefly taken the castle at Machecoul.[11]

It was one of Gilles's brother's soldiers who started the rumour that Gilles was killing children. He claimed that the bones of two children had been found at Machecoul.[12] It's significant that the first stories claimed that Gilles and his confederates were eating babies. The persecutions that Eustache had witnessed further south had begun only months after Matteuccia's execution. They had already lasted for ten years, and around 200 people had been killed, many tortured to death. Like Matteuccia, they confessed to flying to meetings presided over by the Devil. And like Finicella they confessed to killing small children; but they also confessed to cooking and eating them.[13]

In 1438, at around the time the soldier started the rumour about Gilles, there was a particularly significant case at Tournon.[14] The suspect, Pierre Vallin, confessed to flying to meetings where children were eaten. But when he was forced to incriminate other people, his interrogators pressured him into naming wealthy men and aristocrats.[15] Although Bernardino of Siena attacked the cunning folk who worked for ordinary people, there was clearly still concern about upper-class magic.

While Pierre Vallin was being interrogated Francesco was still in Florence, but Gilles had already employed another magician, Jean de la Rivière. Jean had performed a ritual in a wood, and a spirit in the shape of a leopard had appeared. Jean interpreted this vision as ominous, and left Gilles's service abruptly – wisely, as it turned out.[16]

Even if Gilles had wanted to, it would have been impossible to keep his interest in magic secret. He was surrounded by a vast household,[17] and there was about as much privacy in a medieval castle as there is in a modern office building. Francesco's arrival no doubt triggered a renewed surge of gossip – and not just because he was a magician. Gilles had failed to produce a male heir – he had just one child, a daughter – and he was estranged from his wife.[18] He already had two attractive young male companions – Henriet Griart, a Parisian about twenty-five years old, who had joined Gilles's retinue about five years earlier, and Étienne Corrillaut, who was about twenty-one, and had become Gilles's page when he was ten.[19] If Gilles was not gay, he was certainly suspected of it. The homophobic nature of the accusations eventually made against him make that clear.

An early-twentieth-century talisman from the Netherlands; apparently copied from *The Secret Grimoire of King Hochmain* (MoW 673).

In fifteenth-century Europe homosexuality was a serious crime. In Florence, between 1432 and 1502 around 3000 people were convicted of 'sodomy' – a vague term used for all forms of sexual behaviour considered unnatural, but which was essentially homophobic. Bernardino witnessed – with great approval – a gay man being burned alive in Venice, and conducted a campaign against homosexuals that was just as virulent as his campaign against wise women. He also, like many of his contemporaries, assumed that all gay men were paedophiles.[20]

When Francesco became court magician, loyal friend and perhaps lover to Gilles de Rais he was certainly well aware of the risks. Eustache was getting jumpy, and they discussed not only the dangers of arrest but also the spiritual dangers of magic – in particular, whether magic ever involved getting power with the help of the Devil. Gilles was adamant that summoning the Devil was simply impossible, and Eustache joked that Francesco would summon the Devil just to get a jug of wine. (Later, when Henriet and Étienne mentioned this remark to their humourless interrogator, it was solemnly added to the evidence against Francesco.) Francesco insisted that the spirits he invoked were angels – 'begotten from material nobler than the Blessed Virgin Mary'.[21]

In fact Francesco began his association with Gilles in a particularly positive frame of mind, because he'd managed to acquire a second book – borrowed from a Breton physician – which contained a mixture of astrology, medicine and magic.

Using these books, Francesco and Gilles performed a ritual one evening in the lower hall at Tiffauges. With the help of Étienne, Henriet and Eustache, they drew out several circles on the floor with a sword, together with the seals of the spirits they were invoking. Étienne, Henriet and Eustache then left, and Francesco drew out a final seal using burning charcoal, which he sprinkled with an incense made of powdered magnetite, frankincense, myrrh and aloes. He and Gilles then read out incantations from one of the books.

Over the next few weeks Gilles and Francesco performed several similar rituals, and on one occasion Francesco and Étienne performed an outdoor ritual in a field, which apparently provoked a storm that left them soaked.[22]

Gilles also wrote out talismans and invocations using animal blood,[23] and he and Francesco planned some divination experiments using a crystal and a hoopoe. The bird's blood would probably have been used to write out the talisman incorporating the spirit's seal. But, luckily for the hoopoe, they had trouble obtaining a suitable crystal.[24]

In autumn 1439 Gilles went to Bourges on important business, and Francesco sent him a magical black powder which Gilles wore, enclosed in a silver vial, in a linen bag hung round his neck. The powder had been given to Francesco by a spirit called Barron.[25] Francesco may have performed a ritual similar to the one used to

Alchemical serpent, symbolising 'frozen mercury', a substance made by Francesco Prelati and Gilles de Rais. Picture in the Richel Collection (MoW R/7/1005).

obtain a love charm from the spirit Zagam.[26] Or Barron may have given Francesco instructions for making the powder – just as the owners of the crystal in John Aubrey's account were given instructions for making herbal remedies. Francesco and Gilles were conducting alchemical experiments, and they had apparently succeeded in making a substance called 'frozen mercury'.[27] This could well have been the powder Francesco sent to Gilles. It was believed to have protective, healing and transformative properties, and its formation was symbolised in books of alchemy by the highly charged image of a crucified serpent.[28]

Just before Christmas, Gilles moved his household to Machecoul. It seems that he was concerned that the Duke of Brittany, having gained possession of Champtocé, was now turning his attention to Gilles's other Breton castles, Machecoul and Saint-Étienne-de-Mermorte.[29] Things certainly seem to have been tense. Francesco, who had taken lodgings in the town, discovered his landlady in his room without permission, and was so angry and unnerved he nearly threw her down the stairs.[30]

Then Gilles received intelligence that Saint-Étienne-de-Mermorte was about to be attacked and decided to ambush the attackers, but as he was setting out he asked Francesco for advice. It seems that Francesco had some kind of natural magical ability that didn't require elaborate rituals, because he told Gilles, correctly, that the attack had been called off.[31]

However, sometime during the spring Saint-Étienne-de-Mermorte was seized by the Duke of Brittany's Treasurer, Geoffroy Le Ferron, who claimed Gilles had sold it to him. Geoffroy then left his brother Jean in command. On 15 May 1440 Jean went to the local church to hear mass, accompanied by representatives of the Duke, who had arrived with a restraining order to force Gilles's tenants to pay their rents and taxes to the Duke instead of Gilles.[32]

Gilles was lying in wait with sixty soldiers. He burst into the church and threatened to kill Jean. His words make it clear that he believed the castle and lands still belonged to him and were being held by violence: 'You have beaten my people and practised extortion from them!'[33]

Jean agreed to hand the castle back to Gilles, who imprisoned him and the Duke's representatives there as hostages.[34] But the whole situation may have been an elaborate trap. Jean Le Ferron was a member of the clergy. By taking him prisoner, Gilles had violated the authority of the Church.[35] It prompted the Bishop of Nantes (who also happened to be the Duke's Chancellor) to begin an investigation into the rumours that Gilles was killing children in Satanic magical rituals.[36]

At the same time the Duke of Brittany announced that he was fining Gilles 50,000 gold crowns. Gilles responded by transferring the hostages to Tiffauges, which was outside the Duke's jurisdiction. In July he arranged a meeting with the Duke, and again he asked Francesco for magical guidance. Francesco performed several rituals, and told Gilles that it would be safe to go ahead with the meeting.

Gilles did return from the meeting unscathed, but it had resolved nothing.

In August the Duke persuaded his brother, who was Constable of France, to capture Tiffauges and release the hostages, promising him one of Gilles's estates in return.

On 15 September the Duke's men arrived at Machecoul. Gilles surrendered without a fight. He probably thought that all the Duke wanted was the castle – that it was still just about land. Instead, he found himself under arrest for heresy, sodomy and murder. Francesco, Étienne, Henriet and Eustache were also arrested. Realising what they now faced, Henriet considered trying to snatch a knife from one of his guards to cut his own throat.[37]

The Bishop's initial inquiries were now followed up by the Duke's investigator, Jean de Touscheronde.[38] Many of the statements he took were hearsay – people simply saying they'd heard that children had disappeared. Even when he took statements from parents who claimed their own children were missing, they don't stand up to scrutiny. One set of statements is particularly poignant. A man testified that his son Olivier had been kidnapped while playing in the street outside his home. But Olivier's mother and grandmother told a very different story. According to them, they'd got separated from Olivier in the crowd while on a visit to Nantes. Olivier's father, desperate to find his son, told Jean de Touscheronde the story he thought was most likely to make him help him. Unfortunately, Jean de Touscheronde had no interest whatever in finding Olivier. All he wanted was to assemble statements that could send Gilles de Rais to the gallows or the stake.[39]

A talisman for purifying the fire used in magic, incorporating the sacred name of God AGLA, and invoking the help of Ophiel, a spirit associated with the planet Mercury. (MoW 814)

This was, of course, a country at war, with bands of soldiers regularly on the move. Many were undisciplined and dangerous. But they must also have seemed exciting and glamorous, particularly to older boys and teenagers. And in fact it was common practice for aristocrats to recruit boys from quite ordinary backgrounds and train them up to be soldiers or servants. Étienne Corrillaut had been such a boy himself – joining Gilles's household as a page at the age of ten, accompanying Gilles on his campaigns against the English, and leading a life of wealth and privilege, treated by Gilles more as a younger brother than a servant. Étienne seems to have been an approachable young man, and many of the boys in the areas round Gilles's various houses and castles sought him out to ask him to help them do as he had done – join Gilles's household or that of some other wealthy lord. And it seems that some of them may have run away from home after talking to him.[40]

It also seems that Étienne did recruit some of these boys to join Gilles's retinue. In one group of statements the witnesses claimed that they'd heard one of their neighbours complaining that her son was missing, and a local tailor testified that Étienne had visited his shop with the woman and the boy, and bought the boy a jacket. This suggests that Étienne ingratiated himself with the boy and his mother, took the boy away, and then the boy vanished. But in fact the dates are the wrong way round. Étienne, the boy and his mother visited the tailor *after* the date when, according to the witnesses, she'd said her son had disappeared. The obvious explanation is that the boy had joined Gilles's household and was perfectly all right; but that her neighbours misinterpreted some imperfectly remembered remarks – perhaps that she was concerned that she hadn't seen him lately – to mean that he was missing. Significantly, there's no statement from the woman herself.[41]

In fact in all these statements there is not one single shred of evidence that any of the children were dead, let alone that Gilles had killed them. But in spite of this, back in July the Bishop of Nantes had declared:

> We have become convinced that the nobleman, Milord Gilles de Rais … with certain accomplices, did cut the throats of, kill, and heinously massacre many young and innocent boys, that he did practise with the children unnatural lust and the vice of sodomy, often calls up or causes others to practise the dreadful invocation of demons, did sacrifice to and make pacts with the latter.[42]

It's strange that the Bishop apparently knew how the boys had been killed. No bodies had been found – in fact no trace of any bodies would ever be found, not so much as a bloodstain or a fragment of bone. Later, when they were tortured, Étienne and Henriet would confess that the boys' throats had been cut, but it's interesting that the Bishop knew what they were going to say two months before they were even arrested.

The evidence that Étienne and Henriet were tortured is fairly conclusive. As well as Henriet's desperate thoughts of suicide, out of the four statements taken from them, only one – a second statement by Étienne – says in the preamble that it was made 'without torture'.[43] This is a reliable indication that the other three were the result of torture. In addition, Perrine Martin, a woman who was arrested for allegedly procuring boys for Gilles, died during the trial.[44] And, of course, the victims of the witch-hunts further south were being tortured.

However, while Étienne and Henriet were held by the secular authorities, charged with murder, Francesco was held by the Church authorities, charged with the invocation of spirits. It's not clear whether Eustache was charged with any crime. He seems to have been released after making a statement playing down his relationship with Gilles and giving the impression that he disapproved of his magical activities.

There's no way of knowing whether Francesco was tortured, but his statement is very different from Étienne's and Henriet's, and very similar to statements made by later practitioners such as the cunning man John Walsh and Alizon and James Device. It shows signs of three different stages of interrogation. There's non-incriminating information that appears fluent and coherent, such as Francesco's description of meeting Eustache in Italy. Then there's information relating to magic that is incriminating but not fatally so, and which we know from other sources – such as books of magic – represents genuine magical practices; for example, Francesco's account of the circle ritual at Tiffauges. Finally, there are seriously incriminating accounts of devilish magical practices that we know fit the preconceptions of people hostile to magic. As the statement becomes more damaging it shows increasing signs of stress, such as confused details; and also increasing signs of editing, such as cuts, on the part of the interrogators.

Francesco was probably questioned by the Bishop of Nantes and the local Vice-Inquisitor.[45] The Bishop, of course, had already decided that Gilles and Francesco had practised 'the dreadful invocation of demons, [and] did sacrifice to and make pacts with the latter'.

Francesco confessed that the spirit Barron had appeared to him about ten or twelve times. Although *The Sworn Book* claimed that spirits would usually appear when summoned, other books of magic were more realistic, and gave instructions for rituals in which the *help* of spirits was invoked, but the spirits were not expected actually to put in an appearance. Indeed, in the ritual to obtain a love charm from Zagam the magician had to leave the site of the ritual and come back later to find the object, which Zagam would have left for him while he was gone.

But of course it would be difficult to make a pact with a spirit like Zagam who made a point of avoiding you. So it was important to make Francesco admit that he and Gilles had regular contact with Barron. However, Francesco seems to have tried to protect Gilles, insisting that Barron never appeared when Gilles took part in a ritual.

He did admit, however, that Gilles had prepared a written pact to be given to Barron. We know from Jehan de Bar's confession that magicians wrote out invocations asking spirits to give them magical powers, and perhaps it was only natural that opponents of magic would assume that these documents were contracts offering the spirits something in return. But Francesco emphasised that Gilles promised Barron anything he wanted *except* Gilles's life or soul. And he also said that, once again, Barron had failed to show up on that occasion, so the pact could not be given to him.

Eventually Francesco also said that he had seen the body of a baby at Tiffauges, but he insisted that the child hadn't been killed by Gilles, but by one of his companions who hadn't been arrested. Then, after further questioning, he added that Gilles had brought the baby's heart, hand, eyes and blood in a glass container to a ritual as an offering to Barron. But Barron, evidently unimpressed, had once again failed to appear, and the child's remains had been buried by the castle chapel.

This story could be a complete invention, but human remains were widely used in magic, particularly for healing. Matteuccia, as well as making a healing oil from the body retrieved from the Tiber, gave a client instructions to obtain a bone from a baby's grave to cure an illness caused by an evil spirit.[46] It's therefore not impossible that Gilles and Francesco dug up a child's remains for a ritual and then reburied them afterwards.[47]

It seems that these parts of Francesco's statement – very damaging both to himself and Gilles – were essentially distortions of what Francesco actually said. However, Francesco confirmed them in court – or more likely he didn't dispute them when his statement was read out.[48] It's clear that by then he was very frightened and demoralised, perhaps as a result of being tortured, but perhaps simply because he was facing death by burning. However, there were also things he steadfastly refused to say. He never said that Barron was an evil spirit or a delusion of the Devil, or that he or Gilles ever worshipped or obeyed the Devil or any spirit.

Meanwhile, however, Étienne and Henriet were confessing to very different crimes – horrible, impossible crimes – the sexual abuse and murder of dozens of boys.[49] Not only were Étienne and Henriet almost certainly tortured, they were also told that Gilles had betrayed them, making a deal to save his own life by incriminating them.[50] Their statements are almost identical, so they were probably interrogated together, and were desperate to save each other, as well as themselves. It's also possible that their interrogator – who we can reasonably assume was Jean de Touscheronde – played on their feelings of guilt about their sexuality.

Although today we find it easier to believe in paedophile serial killers than in shape-shifting witches, Étienne's and Henriet's confessions have no more right to our belief than Matteuccia's confession that she turned into a fly and sucked children's blood. What was happening to Gilles was essentially the same as what had happened to Matteuccia – she was blamed for children becoming ill, he was blamed for children going missing. Matteuccia was suspected because she practised magic, Gilles because he practised magic and was gay.

Étienne's and Henriet's statements are so horrifying it's hard to subject them to calm scrutiny, but if they are they immediately fall apart.[51] To believe them we have to accept that all these boys, many of them fifteen or sixteen, and two of them eighteen, allowed themselves to be abused and to have their throats cut or their heads hacked off without putting up any resistance whatsoever, and without even shouting for help, even though they were in castles full of people who could have saved them. We have to accept that although this resulted in an enormous amount of blood, every drop was cleaned not only from the walls, floor and furniture of the rooms where the murders took place, but also from the murderers' clothing, leaving not the slightest trace, and that the bodies were burned, in an indoor fireplace, quite literally to ashes, leaving not the smallest bone fragment. Étienne and Henriet described how the boys' clothing had to be cut up into small pieces to be burned, yet they said that the bodies were burned whole. And apparently all this happened while the rest of Gilles's household – probably at least a hundred people – went about their business all around without ever noticing anything suspicious.[52]

Étienne and Henriet confessed that far more children had been killed than the ones reported missing, but Jean de Touscheronde never asked about their identities so that he could contact their parents. Étienne and Henriet also confessed that one body, instead of being burned, was disposed of in a latrine. That body could have been retrieved, which would have been convincing proof of Gilles's guilt, and would also have enabled the parents to give their son a Christian burial. But there's no record of any attempt to recover it, either because none was made or because no body was found.

The statements have a sickening pornographic quality that originates not from Étienne and Henriet but from the nature of Jean de Touscheronde's questions. In one particularly appalling example, after Étienne and Henriet had described in graphic detail the horrifying methods used to kill the boys, Jean de Touscheronde demanded to know how many times Gilles achieved arousal with each victim.

It's hard not to conclude that Jean de Touscheronde knew perfectly well that none of these crimes had really taken place, and that he was deliberately constructing a ghastly but fictional moral fable, to illustrate the violent excesses homosexuality would lead to if it wasn't ruthlessly stamped out. It's also important to remember that he was an experienced interrogator working within a system where the use of torture was routine. During his career he would have tortured many people. These statements are not evidence of Gilles's guilt – they're evidence of the way torture warps the minds of those who use it.[53]

On 13 October 1440 Gilles de Rais appeared before an ecclesiastical court presided over by the Bishop of Nantes and the Vice-Inquisitor, and the Bill of Indictment against him was read.[54] After all the allegations had been listed, the final article announced:

> The said Gilles de Rais incurred the aforesaid authorities' sentence of excommunication and other punishments expected to be promulgated against like presumptuous people as are diviners, sorcerers, conjurors and summoners of evil spirits ... that, moreover ... he committed the crime of Divine high treason.[55]

At first Gilles was angry and defiant. He refused to accept the authority of either the Bishop or the Vice-Inquisitor, saying 'that he would much prefer to be hanged by a rope around his neck than respond to such ecclesiastics and judges'. He insisted 'that he was as good a Christian ... as they themselves ... and that he was shocked ... that they could accuse him of such abominable crimes'.[56]

On Thursday 20 October he was finally given access to the statements against him. He remained stubborn and uncooperative. The prosecutor asked for him to be tortured, and the judges agreed. The following day, Friday, they announced that

> even though they themselves had fixed and assigned Saturday to Gilles, the accused, to say or object, orally or in writing, anything he wanted against what had been produced in the case ... since it would not be illegal, however, they intended to proceed with the torture ...
>
> [Gilles] came and appeared personally before them in the said lower hall to submit to the said torture. And as the said Lord Bishop of Nantes and Vicar of the Inquisitor intended, in fact, to proceed with the application of the said torture ... the said Gilles begged them humbly to be willing to postpone the said application until the following day, which had been assigned [for his defence] as noted; saying that in the meantime he would deliberate somehow on the subject of the crimes and offences brought against him.[57]

The judges agreed to postpone the torture – but only until two o'clock that afternoon.

Gilles then asked to speak to the chief justice of Brittany (whose title was President of Brittany), who would be the judge at his later secular trial. At two o'clock, the time fixed for Gilles's torture, the President went up to the room where he was being held, with various other officials including Jean de Touscheronde, to question him.

Gilles made a brief confession that he had sexually abused and murdered children, and invoked and made sacrifices and promises to spirits. Although this confession was made at the time he was scheduled to be tortured, it was entered into the trial record as 'made voluntarily, freely, and under no constraint'.[58]

The President then asked Gilles 'who had persuaded him to the aforesaid crimes and taught him how to commit them ... surprised ... that the said accused would have accomplished the said crimes and offences of his own accord'. It's clear that the

President was trying to make Gilles confess to being part of a Satanic conspiracy obeying the orders of the Devil. 'Indignant at being solicited and interrogated in this manner', Gilles seems to have tried to impress on the President that he was falling victim to the growing paranoia about magic. 'Alas! My lord,' he protested, 'you torment yourself and me with you.'[59]

The President then ordered Francesco to be brought in, and he and Gilles were questioned about the spirits they invoked.[60] Apparently they admitted that the written pact with Barron had included a promise to obey the spirit's commands – although that's not what Francesco's statement had said. But again Francesco insisted that the pact had never been handed over to the spirit.

As Francesco was about to be taken back to his cell, Gilles said to him – using the Old French form of his name – 'Goodbye Francoys, my friend! We will never meet again in this world; I pray to God that he will give you fortitude and the faith in him that we will meet again in the true happiness of Paradise! Pray to God for me and I will pray for you.'[61]

Back in the courtroom, Gilles was taken through the various accusations against him and confessed to them all.[62] He was again questioned about why he had committed the crimes, and replied – with, I suspect, a certain amount of grim humour – that it was the result of his undisciplined upbringing and the unhealthy effects of too much mulled wine.

When Matteuccia confessed to sucking children's blood she said that she was acting on the Devil's orders. It seems extraordinary that Gilles was prepared to confess to being a paedophile serial killer and yet refused to make what seems the obvious excuse – that the Devil made him do it. But twelve years after Matteuccia's confession, Gilles and Francesco could see what she could not – that the persecutions flaring up across Italy and France were not some temporary paroxysm of brutality but just the beginning. They realised that they were caught up in the start of a Europe-wide witch-hunt, although they couldn't know that it would rage spasmodically for 250 years and kill tens of thousands of people.[63]

And they also realised that this witch-hunt depended on a crucial shift in people's perception of magic – away from the belief that magic was a power that could be used to help or harm according to the practitioner's own conscience, to the belief that magic was a power the Devil gave to those who served him.

Gilles knew from the persecutions further south that once his torture started it would continue until he either said what his interrogators wanted or died. And if he confessed to serving the Devil it could trigger a witch-hunt in Brittany. That's why, instead of confessing to the Bishop of Nantes and the Vice-Inquisitor, he confessed to Brittany's chief judge, who might be persuaded that a witch-hunt would be seriously misguided.

The ecclesiastical court found Gilles guilty of sodomy, 'perfidious apostasy' and 'the dreadful invocation of demons'.[64] Gilles, Étienne and Henriet were then tried for murder by the secular court. In spite of his earlier confession, Gilles again denied everything; and it seems that Henriet probably also tried to protest his innocence and had to be tortured again into a second confession. Étienne and Henriet were sentenced to be hanged and their bodies burned. The court spent some time debating whether Gilles should be hanged or burned alive, eventually deciding on hanging. Gilles then asked to be executed alongside Étienne and Henriet, so they would know it wasn't true that he'd betrayed them to save himself.[65]

Extraordinarily, Gilles – who had always had a taste for theatre and spectacle – managed to turn his execution into a religious pageant. Jean de Touscheronde wrote an account of it,[66] and seems to have been genuinely moved by the courage shown by all three prisoners. The vast crowd prayed for them, which surely indicates that there was still at least some doubt about their guilt. After the executions, Étienne's and Henriet's bodies were burned, but Gilles's body was symbolically scorched and then given a full Christian burial inside the Carmelite church of Nantes.

For Francesco, however, things were far from over.[67] Surprisingly, he was not sentenced to death. Apparently this was one case where the promises of mercy in return for co-operation were kept. It's also possible that Francesco's survival was a price Gilles demanded in return for his confession. Certainly Gilles's final words to Francesco – that they would not meet again this side of Paradise – show that he knew they would not be meeting at the execution site.

Francesco had probably been promised that he would be released – perhaps exiled back to Italy – but in fact he was sentenced to life imprisonment.[68] He wouldn't have survived long in prison, of course, but the Duke of Anjou engineered his release. It's likely that the Duke and his court took an interest in magic – Gilles had borrowed a book of magic from an Angevin knight, who was himself later imprisoned for heresy, probably for owning the book.[69]

However, Francesco was no longer just a charming enthusiast with a taste for the occult. The terrible experiences he'd been through had changed him. He had become tough and resolute. Instead of employing him as a court magician, the Duke made him Captain of La Roche-sur-Yon.[70]

This meant that Francesco had the power to arrest criminals in the territory under his jurisdiction. He discovered that Geoffroy Le Ferron – the Duke of Brittany's Treasurer, and the man whose seizure of Gilles's castle at Saint-Étienne-de-Mermorte had triggered the disaster that had engulfed them – was travelling through the area. In one of the most incongruous actions ever performed by a practitioner of magic, Francesco had him arrested.

In 1428 the Captain of Todi had arrested, tried and executed the wise woman Matteuccia di Francesco. Now, in an extraordinary mirror image of that case, Francesco Prelati, Captain of La Roche-sur-Yon, arrested someone for his part in persecuting the aristocratic magician Gilles de Rais.

But could a young Italian cleric invoke the power of the law to get justice against the Treasurer of the Duke of Brittany? Could someone who practised magic challenge the prejudices of those who believed it threatened their authority? Of course not. Geoffroy Le Ferron was released, and Francesco was hanged.

Francesco must always have known that would probably be the outcome. He was driven by fury and grief and survivor-guilt. Even though it was likely to cost him his life, he was determined to seize the chance to make one final protest of innocence – one final statement that people who practised magic were not servants of the powers of evil. And it is particularly remarkable that, after all he'd been through, he was prepared to face it all again – prison, torture, death – to make that statement to the world – to us.

CHAPTER NINE

Alizon denounces her father's murderer

As soon as he heard Abraham's accusation against Alizon, Roger Nowell summoned Pendle's law enforcement officer, the Constable, and gave him arrest warrants not only for Alizon but also for her brother James and her mother and grandmother.[1]

Arresting them would not have been an easy task. Although the elderly Elizabeth Sothernes was probably at Malking Tower, the others were people who spent most of their lives outdoors, and could be almost anywhere in Pendle Forest. And once they'd been located, there was always the risk that they might put up some kind of resistance, perhaps using magic.[2] Faced with these difficulties, the Constable, like an American sheriff, would have raised a posse of local people to help him.[3] And since the suspects, once they'd been arrested, would have to be stripped and searched for witch marks, he would also have had to recruit a group of respectable married women to search the female suspects.[4]

Abraham must have been both relieved and surprised to find everything happening so quickly. When he'd first arrived at Read he would have been a little unsure of the reception he would get. His father was a peddler – not part of Pendle's community, but one of the transients that Justices tended to regard as a potential nuisance. In fact peddlers were included in the list of rogues and vagabonds that Justices could have summarily whipped, along with other menaces to society, such as palm-readers and touring actors.[5]

However, to Roger Nowell, Abraham's arrival was a turning point, and a sign that God was on his side against the cunning folk – that, as *The Wonderful Discovery* puts it, 'God … had in his divine providence provided to cut them off, and root them out.'[6]

As the arrests were part of an official operation against witchcraft, no doubt they were made as public and humiliating as possible. A glimpse of what it must have been like is provided by a late-sixteenth-century woodcut which shows the witchcraft suspect Elizabeth Stile being taken to the Justice of the Peace by her accuser. She's dragged along by a rope tied round her chest, pulled by a man and a boy, and grabbing at the rope with her left hand as she struggles to keep up.[7]

However, Alizon and her family were in a significantly better position than Francesco had been. They were facing the possibility of being hanged, but not of being burned alive. They were very unlikely to be put on trial unless there was evidence that they had used magic to harm someone. If they *were* tried, their fate would be decided by a jury, which greatly increased their chances of being acquitted. And in England, torture was illegal, except in cases of high treason. This seems to have been a source of a certain amount of national pride:

> To use torment … or question by pain and torture in these common cases, with us is greatly abhorred, sith [since] we are found always to be such as despise death and yet abhor to be tormented, choosing rather frankly to open our minds than to yield our bodies unto such servile halings and tearings as are used in other countries. And this is one cause wherefore our condemned persons do go so cheerfully to their deaths, for our nation is free, stout, haughty, prodigal of life and blood … and therefore cannot in any wise digest to be used as villeins [serfs] and slaves, in suffering continually beating, servitude, and servile torments. No, our jailers are guilty of felony by an old law of the land if they torment any prisoner committed to their custody, for the revealing of his accomplices.
>
> (*The Description of England* by William Harrison[8])

But Francesco's statement was very similar to those of later English suspects, even though he could be tortured and they could not. Skilled interrogators could gradually put pressure on suspects, pushing them from talking freely about non-incriminating subjects to making potentially fatal confessions, whether or not torture was one of the methods available to them. Other techniques, such as psychological pressure and ill-treatment that stopped short of technical definitions of torture, but helped to confuse and intimidate prisoners, could be just as effective.

Even in England, although it was illegal to beat a prisoner to obtain information, subduing a prisoner was a different matter:

> If the party against whom any lawful warrant is granted, shall make resistance … the Officer may justify the beating and hurting of him.[9]

The search for witch marks – although it was primarily supposed to be a search for evidence – was also an effective way of reducing resistance to interrogation. Even in countries such as Scotland, where torture was legal, the search was often used in combination with it:

> They caused her [Agnes Sampson] to be conveyed away to prison, there to receive such torture as hath been lately provided for witches in that country: and forasmuch as by due examination of witchcraft and witches in Scotland, it hath lately been found

that the Devil doth generally mark them with a privy mark, by reason the witches have confessed themselves, that the Devil doth lick them with his tongue in some privy part of their body, before he doth receive them to be his servants, which mark commonly is given them under the hair in some part of their body, whereby it may not easily be found out or seen, although they be searched: and generally so long as the mark is not seen to those which search them, so long the parties that hath the mark will never confess anything. Therefore by special commandment [of King James] this Agnes Sampson had all her hair shaven off, in each part of her body, and her head thrawen [wrenched] with a rope according to the custom of that country, being a pain most grievous, which she continued almost an hour, during which time she would not confess anything until the Devil's mark was found upon her privities, then she immediately confessed whatever was demanded of her.

(*News from Scotland*)

In England prisoners weren't shaved, but it was still generally assumed that marks were likely to be found on a person's 'private place', making it a humiliating form of sexual assault which emphasised the prisoner's helplessness.[10]

In France and Scotland the marks were thought to be places where the Devil touched (or licked) witches when they pledged themselves to him.[11] In England they were places where witches fed their familiar spirits with their blood.[12] It doesn't seem to have worried the authorities that there were two different explanations for these marks – either way they were proof that a suspect was in contact with an evil spirit.

Although English searchers hoped to find something resembling a nipple, any unusual mark would do. This obviously made it a very convenient way to prove someone guilty. But there is some evidence that cunning folk themselves sometimes regarded a strange mark on their bodies as a badge of power. When a witch mark was found on the Scottish cunning man John Stewart, he claimed that his magical powers had been a gift from the King of the Fairies, and the mark was where the King had struck him with his wand.[13]

However, suspects were well aware that the discovery of a witch mark would be regarded as conclusive proof of their guilt. When Alice Gooderidge, the daughter of the Derbyshire wise woman Elizabeth Wright, realised she was about to be arrested, she cut a suspicious mark off her own body with a knife, leaving a bleeding hole 'of the bigness of two pence'.[14]

The searchers found a mark on Elizabeth Sothernes's left side. Her clothes were replaced in such a way that the mark could still be seen, and she was taken through to Roger Nowell, along with her daughter, Elizabeth Device.[15] Roger questioned them about the mark, and Elizabeth Device said that her mother had had it 'the space of forty years'.[16]

Roger hoped that the court would assume that Elizabeth was admitting that her mother had an incriminating mark. But Elizabeth Device was only in her early forties, so what in fact she was saying was that her mother had had the mark for

The blade bone of a sheep. Bones like these were used for scrying and love magic.

as long as she could remember – implying that it was a natural mark her mother had been born with.

Fourteen years earlier, Elizabeth Sothernes had received a visit from a spirit in the shape of a brown dog, and been left 'almost stark mad for the space of eight weeks'.[17] In a rural community like Pendle Forest you couldn't be mad for eight weeks without people talking. Elizabeth may even have encouraged the rumours. Some of her neighbours might have had doubts about the nature of the spirit, but everyone who believed in magic would have assumed that Elizabeth had emerged from the experience with enhanced powers.

Something similar happened to the Cornish wise woman Anne Jefferies. When she was nineteen years old she was accosted by 'six persons of small stature, all clothed in green, which she called fairies'. She was so frightened she collapsed in 'a kind of convulsive fit … and the long continuance of her distemper … almost perfectly moped her, so that she became even as a changeling'. However, as she started to recover she found that she'd been given healing powers, and 'people of all distempers, sicknesses, sores, and agues came not only so far off as the Land's End, but also from London, and were cured by her'. It might have been prudent to keep quiet about the source of her powers, but instead she seems to have told anyone who would listen, ending up in Bodmin jail as a result.[18]

No doubt Roger had found out about Elizabeth Sothernes's encounter with the spirit dog just as the Cornish Justices heard about Anne's encounters with the fairies. When he was shown the mark on Elizabeth's body, Roger probably asked her if that was where she fed the spirit. And her daughter protested, saying something like, 'She's had that mark for forty years, not fourteen!'

Divination by pouring molten lead into water – one of the methods used to identify witches (MoW 52).

It seems that Elizabeth Device quickly realised that Roger had distorted what she'd said, to make it incriminate, rather than clear, her mother. After that one brief statement she abruptly stopped cooperating, and from then on anything she said was dragged out of her only with the greatest difficulty.

✷ ✷ ✷

In fact Roger probably had no right to search Elizabeth Sothernes in the first place. The only person Abraham had accused was Alizon, and although Roger could reasonably interview other members of her family as potential witnesses, arresting them and searching them for witch marks was almost certainly exceeding his authority.

According to *The Country Justice* by Michael Dalton, published in 1618, the role of a Justice of the Peace was simple. A crime was committed, someone accused a suspect, the Justice took statements from the suspect, the accuser and any witnesses, and sent the suspect for trial.[19] In practice, however, many Justices took far greater responsibilities upon themselves. The Cornish Justice John Tregeagle sent Anne Jefferies for trial even though no one had accused her. On the other hand, the Devon Justice Sir Thomas Ridgwaye refused to take action against Michael and Alice Trevysard for more than two years, in spite of a number of accusations against them. And Elizabeth Stile's supposed victim wrote bitterly about the reluctance of the Mayor of Windsor and the local Justices to act on his complaints against her.[20]

When Roger and his colleagues embarked on their operation against witchcraft, they almost certainly based their campaign on the earlier one conducted by Brian Darcey in Essex in 1582,[21] and described in his influential pamphlet *A True and Just Record*. Brian Darcey gave one of his suspects, Elizabeth Bennet, a revealing account of how he saw his role:

> I calling her unto me, said, Elizabeth as thou wilt have favour confess the truth. For so it is, there is a man of great cunning and knowledge [the French witch-hunter Jean Bodin] come over lately unto our Queen's Majesty, which hath advertised her what a company and number of witches be within England: whereupon I and other of her Justices have received commission for the apprehending of as many as are within these limits, and they which do confess the truth of their doings, they shall have much favour: but the other they shall be burnt and hanged.[22]

In fact Queen Elizabeth did not respond to Jean Bodin's visit by changing the punishment for witchcraft from hanging to burning. Nor is there any evidence that she instructed Justices to eradicate witches. That was what Brian Darcey *hoped* would happen, *not* what had. However, the Queen had taken Jean Bodin's views seriously, in effect endorsing his newly published book *De la Démonomanie des Sorciers* (*On the Demon-mania of People who Practise Magic*), which Brian Darcey had studied enthusiastically. And this had sent a signal to Justices who wanted to take a proactive line against witchcraft and magic that they were free to do so.

By the time of the Pendle case, James I was on the throne – but he had actually written a book condemning magic, *Demonology*. Discussing whether magistrates who arrested witches were at risk from their magic, he wrote:

If … he according to the just law of God, and allowable law of all nations, will be diligent in examining and punishing them: God will not permit their master [the Devil] to trouble or hinder so good a work.[23]

The Wonderful Discovery specifically tells us that Roger brought in local people for questioning, to encourage them – perhaps even pressure them – into making accusations against the Pendle cunning folk:

The Justices of those parts … sent for some of the country [i.e. the community], and took great pains to enquire after their [the cunning folk's] proceedings, and courses of life.

It then adds:

In the end, Roger Nowell Esquire … a very religious honest gentleman, painful [conscientious] in the service of his country, whose fame for this great service to his country, shall live after him, took upon him to enter into the particular examination of these suspected persons.[24]

The discovery of the witch mark on Elizabeth Sothernes was very serious for the family. There was now – as far as Roger Nowell was concerned – strong evidence that three of them were guilty of witchcraft. But the family believed they had a powerful defence – they were not witches, but people who fought against witchcraft. To a certain extent, they and Roger were on the same side.

One way to prove you were a witch-hunter was to denounce a witch. And there was one person Alizon was more than willing to name – Anne Whittle, the wise woman her dying father had accused of killing him.

Alizon would have been well aware of the problems the Justices had experienced in their campaign so far – of the acquittals of Margaret Pearson and Jennet Preston. It would have seemed to her that she was in quite a good position to negotiate. She could offer Roger evidence against someone she was certain was genuinely guilty of witchcraft. And given the chance to save herself, and her brother and grandmother, by sending her father's murderer to the gallows, it would hardly have been a difficult decision.[25]

Alizon gave Roger a very incriminating account of her father's death:

Her father, called John Device, being afraid, that the said Anne [Whittle] should do him or his goods any hurt by witchcraft; did covenant with the said Anne, that if she would hurt neither of them, she should yearly have one aghen-dole [about 4 kilos][26] of meal [milled grain]; which meal was yearly paid, until the year which her father died in, which was about eleven years since: her father upon his then-death-bed, taking it that the said Anne Whittle … did bewitch him to death, because the said meal was not paid that year.[27]

Alizon then went on to accuse Anne of killing one of her friends:

> About two years agone, this examinate [Alizon] being in the house of Anthony Nutter
> … and being then in company with Anne Nutter, daughter of the said Anthony: the
> said Anne Whittle … came into the said Anthony Nutter's house, and seeing this
> examinate, and the said Anne Nutter laughing and saying, that they laughed at her
> … well said then (says Anne [Whittle]) I will be meet [even] with the one of you.
> And upon the next day after, she the said Anne Nutter fell sick, and within three
> weeks after died.

Finally, Alizon blamed Anne for the deaths of a man and a cow about six years
earlier, and gave Roger an account of the death of a child two years earlier that
included a description of Anne actually performing a curse:

> A child of the said John Moore, called John, fell sick, and languished about half a
> year, and then died: during which languishing, this examinate saw the said [Anne
> Whittle] sitting in her own garden, and a picture [image] of clay like unto a child
> in her apron; which this examinate espying, the said Anne … would have hid with
> her apron: and this examinate declaring the same to her mother, her mother thought
> that it was the picture of the said John Moore's child.[28]

There can be no doubt that Alizon believed that Anne Whittle used her magic to
harm people. She would never have lied about something as personal and traumatic
as her father's death, or the death of her friend Anne. She was only about six years
old when her father died, and would have had to do what she could to help care

for him, so his dying ravings about Anne Whittle must have made a horrifying impression on her.

However, her claim that she'd seen Anne holding an image of John Moore's young son seems suspicious. It's obviously extremely unlikely that Alizon just happened to be passing when Anne was unwisely performing a curse outside where anyone might see her. Did Alizon invent the encounter? In fact there's an even more likely explanation, indicated by the fact that Alizon asked her mother to help her interpret what she'd witnessed – an unnecessary detail she surely wouldn't have bothered to make up, as she'd already said the image was of a child. She was describing something she'd seen by divination.

As mentioned in Chapter Six, scrying with a mirror was often used to identify the witch when someone had apparently been cursed. It could be used to see what any kind of criminal or enemy was doing, and could apparently produce quite complex visions:

> Obtain a good plain looking glass, as large as you please, and have it framed on three sides only; upon the left side it should be left open. Such a glass must be held toward the direction where the enemy is existing and you will be able to discern all his markings, manoeuvrings, his doings and workings. Was effectually used during the Thirty Years' War.
>
> (*Egyptian Secrets*[29])

There's also another possibility. Just as dreams were an important form of love divination, they could also be used for thief-detection – and so no doubt for witch-detection as well:

> If [marigold] be gathered, the sun being in the sign Leo, in August, and be wrapped in the leaf of a laurel, or bay tree, and a wolf's tooth be added thereto … if any thing be stolen, if the bearer of the things before named lay them under his head in the night, he shall see the thief, and all his conditions.
>
> (*The Book of Secrets of Albertus Magnus*[30])

Alizon may have used a spell of that kind to induce a visionary dream. However, it seems likely that this experience happened not long after her friend Anne's death. It would have been natural enough for Alizon, grieving and angry, to dream about Anne Whittle just because of her suspicions about her. Today we would dismiss that as the suspicions *causing* the dream. But to Alizon it would have seemed that the dream was an *answer* to the questions in her mind. But, dream or vision, there was also an element of spirit-journey about it. Anne Whittle was aware of Alizon's presence, and tried to hide the clay image from her.

Alizon's grandmother included a similar account in a statement dated three days after Alizon's. She claimed to have seen Anne Whittle and her daughter Anne Redferne making clay images together. As Elizabeth passed them, the spirit who had appeared to her in the shape of a dog appeared again, this time in the shape of a black cat, 'and said, turn back again, and do as they do'.

> But this examinate denying to go back to help them to make the pictures [images] aforesaid; the said spirit seeming to be angry, therefore shove or pushed this examinate into the ditch, and so shed the milk which this examinate had in a can.[31]

This bizarre detail is very dream-like, but scrying could produce trance states similar to dreaming. An early-twentieth-century scryer had an experience just as dream-like and even more alarming than Elizabeth's, which began with him finding himself in a railway station:

> He entered the luggage-room, took his trunk and opened it. It contained a particularly horrible dead body, which leaped out of the portmanteau [trunk], and bitterly complained of being disturbed. It threw itself upon the sensitive, who immediately fled, pursued by the dead body … [the scryer] fell, and the dead body stopped and bent down to strike him. The visionary gave him a kick in the stomach, and stretched him at full length on the ground. The hallucination then ceased abruptly, and the sensitive found himself back in his room, in front of the crystal.
>
> (*Metapsychical Phenomena* by J. Maxwell.[32])

The spirit's presence in Elizabeth's account is a clear indication that this was an experience induced by magic, not a normal one. As the 'call' in *The Lenkiewicz Manuscript* demonstrates, in the early modern period scrying with a crystal involved summoning a spirit, and John Walsh and Bessie Dunlop called on the help of their familiar spirits when they discovered thieves' identities.

Elizabeth made her statement to back up Alizon's accusations against Anne Whittle. However, the actual dream or vision had occurred many years earlier, after Anne Whittle had been suspected of bewitching her landlord's son to stop him sexually harassing her daughter. The similarity between the two accounts is because Alizon was influenced by her grandmother's earlier experience, which is only to be expected – she was learning magic from her grandmother, using similar techniques and interpreting her experiences in the same way.

Alizon was certainly not a reluctant witness against Anne Whittle. She gave Roger five emphatic accusations with plenty of detail. She believed in and feared witchcraft, but she also saw herself as someone who could use magic to unmask witches and discover their activities. She denounced Anne because she believed that she'd killed her father, and to save herself and her family. But her statement also gives us an intriguing and slightly chilling glimpse of Alizon developing the skills to become a professional witch-hunter.

CHAPTER TEN

James Device betrays his sister

James, of course, had been through all this before, and talked his way out of it – or so he thought. He no doubt felt he'd handled himself rather well during his earlier interrogation. It must have been hard for a young man of around nineteen years old to keep his anger under control through the brutality and humiliation of arrest and the search for a witch mark. And it must have been particularly hard the second time, when he had to witness his sister, mother and grandmother enduring it all alongside him. But we know from the account of his argument with Anne Towneley that he was rather proud of his self-restraint.[1]

Now, as he waited his turn to be interrogated by Roger Nowell, he probably told himself that all he had to do was what he'd done before – keep his nerve and tell the truth. Perhaps he also told himself that he'd got Roger's measure now and didn't need to be afraid of him.[2]

Alizon may or may not have told James about her argument with John Law, but there's no reason to think that he knew why the family had been arrested.[3] He may well have assumed that *he* had come under some further suspicion. However, any relief he felt when he realised there was no new evidence against him would have quickly turned to dismay when Roger told him there had been accusations against Alizon. If Roger asked James about Alizon's confrontation with John Law, he got an unsatisfactory reply, because there's no record of it. But then Roger asked James about the incident when Henry Bulcock accused Alizon of bewitching his child, and James's statement in response is horrifying:

> About Saint Peter's Day last one Henry Bulcock came to the house of Elizabeth Sothernes ... grandmother to this examinate [James], and said, that the said Alizon Device had bewitched a child of his, and desired her, that she would go with him to his house: which accordingly she did: and thereupon she the said Alizon fell down on her knees, and asked the said Bulcock forgiveness; and confessed to him that she had bewitched the said child, as this examinate heard his said sister confess unto him this examinate.[4]

How could James have made such a damning statement against his own sister?

Even if they were going through a particularly rough patch in their relationship – not impossible if they were both teenagers – it was an incredibly stupid thing for James to do. Henry Towneley's accusation against James had helped to make Henry Bulcock and his child suspect Alizon. If Alizon was sent to be tried for witchcraft, James would find himself blamed for every mysterious illness and death in Pendle. His situation was already precarious. He couldn't afford to do anything that would add to the suspicions about him.

There are other problems with James's statement too. As discussed in Chapter Four, Henry Bulcock never testified against Alizon – which he surely would have done if she'd confessed to him. This was his child becoming ill, after all, not his ale being spoiled.

Then there are things that are odd about the wording of the statement. James doesn't say that Alizon confessed to him that she'd bewitched the child – he says that she confessed to him that she'd confessed to Henry. Yet surely as soon as Alizon mentioned that Henry had accused her, James would have asked her if she'd really done it – unless of course he was sure she hadn't.

Apparently Alizon described falling to her knees and begging Henry Bulcock to forgive her. But if she was on bad terms with James – such bad terms that he was willing to make a statement that could kill her – would she have described such a humiliating scene? Alizon begging in this way also seems out of character in view of what her other statements tell us about her. If Henry Bulcock had come at her brandishing a pin to scratch her she might have begged him not to do it; or she might have begged him not to report her to Roger; but confessing and begging forgiveness was almost *inviting* him to report her.

There are also things missing from the statement that should be there. There's no mention of Alizon offering to cure the child, or of Henry doing anything – such as getting the child to scratch her – to remove the curse. And yet if the only reason Henry had confronted her was to get her to confess so that he could report her, why *didn't* he report her? Also, there's no reason given for *why* Alizon bewitched the child – something Henry, James and Roger would all have wanted to know.

The first part of the statement has similarities to James's account of his quarrel with Anne Towneley. Henry Bulcock is portrayed as the aggressor – he's described not as a worried parent with a sick child but as an accuser invading Alizon's home – and Alizon is depicted as cooperative. But then both the tone and the style of the statement change, so that it no longer resembles James's other statement, but another account altogether:

> Leatherdall's wife being then in my house and … having her child there also … she this examinate burst out in tears and fell upon her knees and asked forgiveness of the said Leatherdall's wife … and confessed that she caused Newman's wife to send a spirit to plague the child.[5]

This is a description by the Essex Justice Brian Darcey of a confrontation he engineered between his suspect Ursley Kempe and a woman with a sick child. It was included in his pamphlet *A True and Just Record* – which Roger Nowell would certainly have studied when he and his colleagues began their investigation.

Roger had already twisted Elizabeth Device's statement about the mark on her mother's body. Now he was doing the same to James's statement about Alizon. The first part of the statement is genuinely something James said. But the second part is drawn from Brian Darcey's pamphlet.

In the case of Elizabeth Device's statement, her own words were cleverly made to seem incriminating by being taken out of context. But the second half of James's statement isn't even his own words. We can only speculate about what James really said, but probably he told Roger that Alizon had convinced Henry of her innocence.

Even in the 1970s some police officers were not above faking suspects' statements.[6] It would be naïve to think that someone trying to enforce the law with very few resources in the early seventeenth century would be more scrupulous. And it would be much easier for Roger to get away with it – for the simple reason that neither James nor Alizon would have a defence lawyer to check their statements, or any of the other evidence.

This may seem extraordinary – particularly to anyone familiar with William Shakespeare's play *The Merchant of Venice*, with its dramatic courtroom scene, where Portia, disguised as a lawyer, saves a defendant's life with a series of ingenious arguments. But Portia's client was the defendant in a *civil*, not a criminal case. He had rashly pledged a pound of his own flesh as security for a loan. If his life had been on the line because he was accused of a capital crime, Portia would never have been allowed anywhere near him.

By what now seems a cruel anomaly, defendants were allowed lawyers *unless* they were charged with felonies – crimes that carried sentences of imprisonment or death. The justification of this was the argument that no jury would convict someone of a felony unless the evidence was indisputable, making defence lawyers unnecessary. But the real reason was probably to spare lawyers the moral dilemmas involved in trying to save someone who might have committed a serious crime.[7]

There were also other aspects of the legal system that made it easy for Roger to fake evidence. As most suspects and witnesses were illiterate, statements were not written, or even read, by the people who made them. The Justice drew up the statement, and the Justice certified it as a true record of what the suspect or witness had said.[8]

When it came to the actual trials, the statement could be read out without the witness being present – and probably would be if the witness was another defendant.

If Roger decided to use James's statement against Alizon, James would not be in court to protest that the statement wasn't true, or to be challenged by Alizon.[9]

If defendants tried to dispute or retract any part of their statements during their own trials, the attitude of the judge would be crucial. A judge who was inclined to support the Justice could simply point out to the jury that it was the defendant's word against the Justice's, leaving them in no doubt which of the two they should believe.[10]

Roger Nowell was in the fortunate position of knowing that both of the judges on the Northern Circuit – Sir James Altham and Sir Edward Bromley – shared his views about witchcraft. It would in fact be Sir Edward Bromley who would try the Pendle suspects (the judges decided between them who would try which cases), and he had been appointed only two years earlier. His first year had conveniently happened to be the year Roger Nowell was Sheriff of Lancaster. It was the Sheriff's job to organise the Assizes – including the judges' accommodation and entertainment. One of the reasons Justices became Sheriffs was to ingratiate themselves with the judges, and we can be sure that Roger had been especially helpful to the inexperienced Sir Edward. It would also have given Roger the opportunity to sound him out on his views. In fact it's probably no coincidence that Roger and his colleagues began their operation against witchcraft at around the time Sir Edward was appointed.[11]

However, in spite of all this Roger Nowell spent a great deal of time and effort questioning his suspects closely, trying to manoeuvre them into genuine admissions. He was determined to make a moral point about magic, as well as remove the criminals from his community. It was important to him to make them acknowledge their guilt. Even when he changed James's statement it was only to make it describe what *should* have happened. Alizon *should* have confessed to Henry and begged his forgiveness.

The description of Alizon humble and on her knees bears a striking resemblance to a description of Gilles de Rais at his ecclesiastical trial:

> The aforesaid Gilles de Rais, the accused, falling to his knees and expressing contrition by great sighs, grievously and tearfully, begged humbly to be absolved in writing of the sentence of excommunication brought against him.[12]

In this not entirely convincing account the element of propaganda is painfully obvious. Gilles had expressed his defiance and contempt very eloquently. Once he'd been forced to back down it was essential to show him not just accepting the grim reality of the Church's power to kill him, but submitting to the Church's moral and spiritual authority.

Alizon was clearly not submissive by nature. She had unnerved a tough middle-aged peddler when she'd got into a disagreement with him. But she challenged authority in a far more serious way by practising magic in defiance of centuries of condemnation by both Church and State.

To Roger Nowell, Alizon on her knees begging forgiveness was a symbol of the restoration of the rightful order of things. It may not have really happened – yet. But it was something that ought to happen.

Changing James's statement was a means to an end – a step towards making Alizon and James admit their guilt. Roger had never believed James's protests of innocence, and he didn't believe him when he claimed Alizon was innocent. Now, however, Roger could go to Alizon and read her a statement in which James apparently betrayed her to save himself. That had worked well on Étienne Corrillaut and Henriet Griart. And it was recommended by Jean Bodin (who had studied the Gilles de Rais case) in his book *Démonomanie* – which Roger had probably read:[13]

And if he is determined to say nothing, he must be made to believe that his fellow prisoners have accused him, even if they have no intention of doing it: and then to take revenge on them he will perhaps retaliate.[14]

Even if Alizon didn't believe Roger, it would unnerve her and make her angry. A suspect's best hope was to say nothing, and so anything that provoked a suspect into speaking without thinking carefully first could be useful to the interrogator.

And James had, in fact, made a terrible mistake. Roger probably let him believe – or even told him – that Henry Bulcock had made a statement against Alizon. But of course that wasn't true. James's statement was the *only* evidence that Alizon had been accused of witchcraft by Henry. And even without Roger's embellishment it was very damaging to her. James, defending Alizon against a non-existent statement, had in fact given Roger valuable evidence against her.[15]

When James realised what had happened he must have been distraught. And it seems that Roger probably told him, because he then coerced James into making an even worse mistake.

Alizon's statement against Anne Whittle was extremely useful to Roger, but he had trouble getting other witnesses to back up her allegations.[16] So instead he concentrated on the incident mentioned by Elizabeth Sothernes – Anne Whittle's supposed murder by witchcraft of her landlord's son Robert Nutter.[17]

Robert Nutter had died eighteen years earlier, but the affair must have been a major scandal. Robert – himself a married man – had attempted to seduce a married woman, Anne Whittle's daughter Anne Redferne; and when she insisted on remaining faithful to her husband, he had threatened to have the whole family evicted.[18]

Not long afterwards, Robert had become ill, and claimed that Anne Whittle and Anne Redferne had bewitched him. But his father – no doubt thoroughly embarrassed and infuriated by Robert's behaviour – told him plainly that he was mistaken.[19] And even when Robert eventually died of his illness, it's clear that his father didn't blame Anne Whittle and her daughter, because the family was *not* evicted.[20]

Now, however, Roger Nowell took statements from Robert Nutter's brother and sister, and from a man who had worked for their grandfather. But all they were prepared to say was that Robert had believed that Anne Whittle and Anne Redferne had bewitched him, with Robert's sister adding that her father Christopher had also died shortly after Robert, and he too had claimed he was bewitched. But she was careful to point out that he hadn't named a culprit.[21]

However, Roger also had Elizabeth Sothernes's statement. Elizabeth's familiar spirit had helpfully identified the victims Anne Whittle and Anne Redferne were cursing:

> She [Elizabeth] asked whose pictures [images] they were? Whereunto the said spirit said; they are the pictures of Christopher Nutter, Robert Nutter; and Marie wife of the said Robert Nutter.[22]

It seems suspiciously convenient that the victims just happened to be the ones Roger was most interested in; particularly as Elizabeth had only started working with the spirit fourteen years earlier – four years *after* Robert's death. It's likely, therefore, that Elizabeth changed the victims' identities to give Roger the names he wanted to hear.[23] However, at least two members of the large Nutter family, John Nutter and Anthony Nutter (the father of Alizon's friend Anne), were Elizabeth's clients, so it's possible that one of them employed Elizabeth to discover whether Robert had been murdered, perhaps some years after Robert's death.[24]

Roger Nowell now had Anne Whittle and Anne Redferne arrested.[25] Confronted with the evidence against her, Anne Whittle made a desperate choice. To save her daughter, she confessed to bewitching Robert Nutter – but she insisted she'd acted alone, without Anne Redferne's help.[26]

This left Roger needing more evidence against Anne Redferne, and he persuaded James to give him a statement:[27]

> About two years ago, he this examinate saw three pictures of clay, of half a yard long, at the end of Redferne's house, which Redferne had one of the pictures in his hand, Marie his daughter had another in her hand, and the said Redferne's wife ... had another picture in her hand ... but whose pictures they were this examinate cannot tell. And at his returning back again, some ten rods off them there appeared unto him this examinate a thing like a hare, which spit fire at him.[28]

This statement is very similar indeed to parts of Elizabeth Sothernes's:

> This examinate [Elizabeth] went to the house of Thomas Redferne ... and there within three yards of the east end of the said house, she saw the said Anne Whittle ... and Anne Redferne ... the one on the one side of the ditch, and the other on the other: and two pictures of clay or marl lying by them: and the third picture the said Anne Whittle ... was making: and the said Anne Redferne her said daughter, wrought her [i.e. prepared] clay or marl to make the third picture withal ... Presently after that, the said spirit appeared to this examinate again in the shape of a hare, and so went with her about a quarter of a mile, but said nothing to this examinate, nor she to it.[29]

These similarities are far too great to be simply the result of James using the same magical techniques as his grandmother. In particular, the fact that the hare features in both accounts (although it's Elizabeth's familiar spirit in her account, and obviously the Redfernes' familiar spirit in James's) is damning evidence that James's statement is simply a version of his grandmother's, adapted to incriminate Anne Redferne and her husband and daughter.

Two things tell us this wasn't James's idea. Firstly, he would definitely have incriminated Anne Whittle, his father's murderer, regardless of how much other

evidence there was against her. Secondly, it's unlikely that James would have accused Anne Redferne's husband on his own initiative. Coming from a family of cunning folk himself, James would have known that magic was passed down from generation to generation through a combination of learned magical lore and *inherited* magical ability. Someone like Thomas Redferne (and James's father John Device), who just happened to have married a wise woman, would be unlikely to take such an active part in her magical practices.

It would have been easy for Roger to adapt Elizabeth's statement himself and simply attach James's name to it, but there were good reasons for him to coerce James into co-operating. Roger didn't intend to send Thomas and Marie Redferne for trial. Including them in the statement was just a way of putting pressure on Anne Redferne, in the hope that she would confess to save them just as her mother had confessed to save *her*.[30] And Roger didn't intend to send James for trial either unless he could get more evidence against him. Marie and Thomas would be certain to suspect James of incriminating them (even if Roger didn't tell them), and would probably confront him once he was released. If James convincingly denied any knowledge of the statement, it might unite the two families against Roger. It might even lose him the community's support.

What Roger wanted to achieve was the exact opposite. He wanted to increase the hostility between Pendle's two families of cunning folk and undermine the community's confidence in them. In fact he probably hoped that the Redfernes (as Jean Bodin had suggested) would retaliate with accusations against James.

Unfortunately there can be little doubt that in this statement James was knowingly giving false evidence against the Redfernes. But it's easy to see how Roger manipulated him into doing it. After tricking James into incriminating Alizon, he then gave him the chance to back up her accusations against Anne Whittle, just as his grandmother had done. Unlike Elizabeth Sothernes, who may have adapted her evidence to suit Roger, James was lying outright, but his horror at realising that he'd inadvertently endangered his sister had screwed up his judgment.

However, James wasn't simply Roger's desperate pawn. Like Alizon he believed in Anne Whittle's guilt, and he was probably willing to be convinced of Anne Redferne's. And like Alizon and his grandmother he was quite comfortable with the role of witch-hunter. It's significant that in James's statement the hare spits fire at him. This is further evidence that James was involved in drawing up the statement, because it not only suggests that the hare was an evil spirit but also that it felt the need to defend the Redfernes against him. It recognised him as someone magically powerful who was a threat to the Redfernes' malevolent magic.

James later made other statements where he freely admitted to bizarre paranormal experiences, and portrayed himself as someone with natural psychic abilities – and under psychic attack:

> ... this examinate heard a voice of a great number of children screiking and crying pitifully, about day-light gate [dusk] ... about ten rods distant of this examinate's said grandmother's house. And about five nights then next following, presently after daylight, within twenty rods of the said Elizabeth Sothernes's house, he heard a foul yelling like unto a great number of cats: but what they were, this examinate cannot tell. And he further sayeth, that about three nights after that, about midnight of the same, there came a thing, and lay upon him very heavily about an hour, and went then from him out of his chamber window, coloured black, and about the bigness of a hare or cat.[31]

Roger didn't quite know what to make of these statements, and they ended up in the bundle of unused evidence.[32]

In fact Roger did acknowledge the family's role as witch-hunters in one crucial respect. He must have known that Alizon's and Elizabeth's descriptions of Anne Whittle and Anne Redferne making images were magical evidence obtained by divination. And yet he was still prepared to use them – although of course he represented them to the court as ordinary eye-witness testimony.[33]

On the strength of James's statement Roger briefly arrested Marie Redferne, but not Thomas – an indication of how much more controversial it was to arrest a man for witchcraft than a woman.[34] But Anne Redferne steadfastly refused to confess. Remarkably, the Redfernes also resisted the temptation to make counter-accusations against James. But Anne Redferne was in a bizarre situation. She was suspected of witchcraft because she'd refused to be unfaithful to her husband. Robert Nutter had been so clearly in the wrong, and his accusation that she had bewitched him was so obviously tainted by malice and frustration, that it must have seemed extraordinary to Anne that Roger could even think of prosecuting her.[35]

In *The Wonderful Discovery* Thomas Potts says of James, 'He [was] but young, and in the beginning of his time.'[36] At this point in the Pendle witchcraft case James seems very young indeed. He had shown a complete disregard for the effects of his actions on Marie and Thomas Redferne, people he must have known were entirely innocent. And with a disastrous combination of naivety and over-confidence – following the lead of his younger and more impetuous sister – he had convinced himself that he could form some kind of alliance with Roger Nowell. Thinking that he'd retrieved the situation after his earlier mistake – that perhaps now Alizon would be all right after all – he was blind to the fact that he'd let Roger manipulate him into something that was both morally indefensible and a serious error of judgment. Because his willingness to give evidence against the Redfernes had started a new train of thought in Roger's mind – one that would lead to horrific consequences for many other people in Pendle as well as James himself.

However, there was also someone else who would have a profound effect on James's and Alizon's fate. He was a complex and ambiguous figure – protector, tempter, tormentor and redeemer. He had arrived on the southern edge of Pendle Forest, at Huntroyde, fifteen years earlier, summoned by a circle ritual – 'a thing like unto a Black Dog'.[37]

CHAPTER ELEVEN

A circle made at Huntroyde

When Roger Nowell manipulated Alizon and James so skilfully, he was no doubt helped by the fact that he had experience of handling teenagers from dealing with his own children. When he looked at James, did he see similarities between him and his own son, eighteen-year-old Alexander? Certainly James had something in common with Roger – the ruthless streak that allowed him to give false evidence against the Redfernes. But Roger probably saw far more similarities between James and someone else – another cunning man, Edmund Hartlay, the man who had been employed by Roger's nephew Nicholas Starkie. Roger had only met Edmund Hartlay three or four times, but the last two at least would have made a powerful impression on him.[1]

Roger believed that Edmund had nearly destroyed Nicholas's family, just as James had killed his employer Anne Towneley. The Towneleys, too, were related to Roger Nowell – although only distantly, and they were Roman Catholics, which might have lost them some of Roger's sympathy.[2] But still, the situation was basically the same – people of social standing and influence unwisely associating with a cunning man and being horrifically betrayed by him.

And there was a further connection. Although Edmund Hartlay was not from Pendle, he had performed magic at Huntroyde – on Elizabeth Sothernes's territory. That would have formed a magical link between them, and therefore between Edmund and Elizabeth's grandchildren. And, as we shall see, the circle Edmund made at Huntroyde did have a significant impact on the family's magic.

Nicholas Starkie was the son of Roger Nowell's much older half-brother, and so was in fact similar in age to Roger himself. In 1578 he married a wealthy heiress, Anne Parr, and went to live at her estate, Cleworth, which was near Leigh, to the west of Manchester.[3] But the early years of their marriage were devastated by

Huntroyde Hall, the home of Nicholas's father.

tragedy – their first four children died in infancy. It was an age of high childhood mortality rates, but that didn't make each individual death any less heartbreaking for the families concerned.

Anne Starkie became convinced that she had been cursed by her Roman Catholic relatives:

> Some of these, partly for religion, and partly because the land descended not to the heirs male, wished and vowed still to pray for the perishing of her issue [children] ... Some of Mistress Starkie's kindred, observing how one child after another pined away, moved with compassion told Mistress Starkie of the said unnatural vow. She hereupon conceived such a grief, that she made an estate of her land to her husband and his heirs, all issue failing herself.[4]

In other words, Anne made a will so that if she died childless all her lands would go to her husband and his family rather than her own blood relatives. A cynical person might suspect that while it was Anne's relatives who told her of the problem, it was one of Nicholas's relatives who suggested this solution.

However, it seemed to work. Nicholas and Anne had two more children, John and Anne junior, who thrived – until 1595, when Anne (then about nine years old) began suffering from seizures.

Seizures, although unusual, occur in about one in twenty-five children, and are rarely life-threatening. They're often related to a genetic predisposition to excess brain activity, and normally stop as the child gets older.[5] However, they *are* very alarming to witness. After the loss of their first four children, Nicholas and Anne were understandably terrified. And to make matters worse, John (who was then about ten) started having uncontrollable rages – no doubt the result of anxiety about his sister and jealousy at the attention she was getting.

Nicholas spent £200 – a huge amount in those days – on doctors' consultations, without success. He also spoke to a Roman Catholic priest, which shows that he was still worried about the curse. And then he heard about Edmund Hartlay.

Nicholas probably wasn't Edmund's first high-status client. It's likely that someone in Nicholas's circle recommended him. It seems that he lived some distance from the Starkies – when he visited them he had to stay at Cleworth. And Nicholas would have had plenty of choice if he wanted to consult a wise woman or cunning man. According to Reginald Scot there were sometimes seventeen or eighteen in a single parish – and since whole families practised that's not impossible.[6] There were probably more cunning folk than there were carpenters or blacksmiths. Edmund's reputation must have been particularly good.

However, from the start he seems to have been something of a disruptive influence on the Starkie family. He flirted with the servant girls and was demonstratively affectionate towards the children. But Anne's seizures were going to stop on their own, John's difficulties were purely emotional, and the real problem was their parents' anxiety. What the Starkies needed was someone confident and charismatic who could convince them that everything was going to be all right.

Using 'certain popish charms and herbs',[7] Edmund treated the children with remarkable success. For Anne's seizures, he may well have used a Latin charm vigorously condemned by both the Burgundian Roman Catholic witch-hunter Henri Boguet and the English Protestant sceptic Reginald Scot:

> Gaspar fert myrrham, thus Melchior, Balthasar aurum,
> Hoec tria qui secum portabit nomina regum,
> Solvitur a morbo Christi pietate caduco.[8]

> (Gaspar brought myrrh, Melchior frankincense, Balthasar gold, / Whoever carries the names of these three kings with them, / Will be freed from the falling sickness by the compassion of Christ.)

As the wording of the charm suggests, Edmund would probably have got Anne to write out the three names – though probably *not* with her own blood, the method recommended by Guy de Chauliac – and carry the paper with her.

His herbal remedy would almost certainly have included peony. *Egyptian Secrets* recommended 'water of peonies, mixed with the violet water … from thirty to forty drops every morning, before breakfast, and evening, before going to bed'.[9] And according to *The Book of Secrets of Albertus Magnus*,

> This herb [vervain] (as witches say) gathered, the sun being in the sign of the Ram, and put with grain or corn of peony of one year old, healeth them that be sick of the falling sickness.[10]

Anne and John were both cured, and remained healthy for almost eighteen months. Then Edmund announced that they no longer needed him, and he was going to stop visiting them. John immediately suffered some kind of haemorrhage – perhaps brought on by stress, although it's tempting to think it was the result of a self-inflicted injury.

Like burns and scalds, bleeding was the kind of medical emergency cunning folk often had to deal with – particularly in rural areas, where accidents with farm implements were commonplace. Again, the charm Edmund may have used has survived:

> Christ was born in Bethlehem, baptised in the fleam [river] Jordan. Also the fleam stood, also stand thy blood. N. [Name].[11]

Edmund stopped the bleeding, but it's clear that there was an even more fraught underlying problem – John had become dangerously emotionally dependent on him.

Nicholas offered Edmund a retainer of £2 a year to continue his association with the family. This was not exactly generous, considering that Nicholas had been prepared to pay £200 to conventional doctors. And Edmund was obviously aware that he needed to find some way of distancing himself from John, because he asked for a house to live in so that he wouldn't be staying at Cleworth Hall. Nicholas, however, thought that Edmund was trying to take advantage of him and refused. And Edmund was then rash enough to complain about Nicholas in the hearing of someone who reported back to him.

Edmund's irritation and frustration are understandable. He'd helped the Starkies enormously, but now Nicholas was making unreasonable demands and at the same time starting to resent his dependence on him. Nicholas had convinced himself that his family couldn't manage without Edmund, but he couldn't bring himself to fully trust him. The problem, of course, was Edmund's uncertain status. As someone who practised magic, he was essentially transgressive. And that, no doubt, was the main reason he was such an attractive figure to John. He had an aura of forbidden power about him that made his attention particularly gratifying, and which also appealed to the rebellious streak that was probably an important part of John's tantrums.

Edmund should have recognised the danger signs and extricated himself from the situation. But Nicholas seems to have been essentially a well-meaning person trying to do the best for his children, and he and Edmund had had a friendly relationship for eighteen months. And of course Edmund couldn't afford to alienate people as influential as the Starkies.

In November 1596 both children suffered relapses – although it's likely that Anne's problems were now in fact emotional, like her brother's. It seems obvious 400 years later that this was a result of the growing tension in the relationship between Edmund and the Starkies. But it clearly wasn't obvious at the time. Nicholas – once again growing increasingly desperate – decided to visit his father at Huntroyde, and took Edmund with him.

As Read was so close we can reasonable assume that Roger Nowell joined them at some point. No doubt they discussed not only John's and Anne's problems but also the curse put on Mistress Starkie by her relatives. Probably they sat up late into the night drinking and talking. Although Edmund was a confident and sociable man, he would have been aware that he was under scrutiny, and that Nicholas's father and uncle probably had reservations about him, even if they were not openly hostile.

When Edmund finally retired to his guest bedroom (or was he relegated to the servants' quarters?) he had a bad night. This was probably simply the result of a combination of tension and drinking too much, but he interpreted it as some kind of psychic attack. Although Nicholas must have mentioned the curse to him before, there's no evidence that up to this point Edmund had thought there was anything magical about the children's problems. Now, however, he decided that the herbs and charms he'd used so far were not enough, and he should try a different form of magic:

> The next day, being recovered, he went into a little wood, not far from the house, where he made a circle about a yard and a half wide, dividing it into four parts, making a cross at every division; and when he had finished his work, he came to Master Starkie, and desired him to go and tread out the circle, saying I may not tread it out myself.[12]
>
> This being also accomplished, he said, 'Well, now I shall trouble him that troubled me, and be even with him that sought my death.'[13]

John Walsh used a circle to summon a spirit, 'of whom he would then ask for any thing stolen, [and] who did it'.[14] *The Munich Handbook* includes a thief-detection ritual that involved a boy scrying in a circle after the magician had invoked the help of (literally) dozens of spirits.[15] Since methods for identifying witches were often derived from thief-detection methods, it seems likely that Edmund performed his circle ritual to identify, and retaliate against, a witch – the person he now believed had put a curse on the children and had also subjected him to a magical attack.

Getting the client to perform part of the spell or ritual was standard practice. However, making a circle implied the invocation of spirits. A circle was essentially a large talisman inscribed on the ground. It was a magical space – a point of contact between this world and the Otherworld – and also a spell in itself, which gave the practitioner power over spirits. Edmund must have known that it was

Researcher Kate (accompanied by Tom and 'a faithful and attached dog', as recommended by *The Key of Solomon*) recreates Edmund Hartlay's circle: 'He went into a little wood, not far from the house, where he made a circle about a yard and a half wide, dividing it into four parts, making a cross at every division.'

risky to involve Nicholas in a ritual of that kind. In spite of the tensions in their relationship, there must still have been some level of trust between them.

However, Nicholas does seem to have been slightly unnerved by the experience, and he later claimed that he lost confidence in Edmund after 'this wretched dealing of his'.[16] And he decided to consult another, very different type of magical practitioner – Dr John Dee, who Queen Elizabeth had consulted to determine the most astrologically favourable day for her coronation, and who was now Warden of Manchester College.[17]

Some years earlier John Dee had conducted a series of very successful magical experiments. Working with a gifted scryer called Edward Kelley, and using *The Sworn Book*, a crystal ball and a looted Aztec ritual mirror made of obsidian, he had made regular contact with a number of spirits. With their help he'd drawn up an improved version of Honorius's Seal of God.[18] It seems that Nicholas went to him for advice not only because he now believed his children were bewitched, but also because he was uneasy about Edmund's circle ritual.

John Dee wisely refused to get involved in attempting to cure the children. But he also summoned Edmund and, apparently, 'sharply reproved' him.[19] Undermining Edmund's relationship with his client in such dangerous times was indefensible. But just as cunning folk were trying to protect themselves by emphasising their role as witch-hunters, so highly educated magicians were trying to argue that they practised a rarefied magic quite different from the suspect kinds the authorities were rightly trying to suppress:

> Flee from earthly things, seek after heavenly things. Put no confidence in thine own wisdom; but look unto God in all things ...
>
> A magician therefore ought to be a man that is godly ... covetous of nothing but of wisdom about divine things ...
>
> We do detest all evil magicians, who make themselves associates with the devils with their unlawful superstitions ...
>
> Unprofitable and damnable magic ariseth from this; where we lose the fear of God out of our hearts ... there, even as the spider taketh the fly which falleth into his web, so Satan spreadeth abroad his nets, and taketh men with the snares of covetousness.
>
> (*Arbatel*[20])

Edmund was understandably offended. A month later he took the children to visit relatives in Manchester, and although they were also supposed to have a meeting with John Dee he refused them permission to go. The children went anyway – prompting Edmund to complain 'that it had been better for them not to have changed an old friend for a new', and to sulk on the journey home.[21] It's interesting, though, that Nicholas and Edmund were still on good enough terms for Nicholas to entrust his children to Edmund's care for the trip.

However, it seems that Edmund was instinctively right that the meeting with John Dee would be a mistake. It helped to encourage the children to believe they were under attack from evil spirits. As soon as they were back at Cleworth John collapsed, saying 'that Satan had broken his neck', and 'lying there pitifully tormented for the space of two hours'.[22] That night he had a spectacular tantrum, biting anyone who touched him and throwing his pillows into the bedroom fire.

There were also three other children in the Starkie household – Margaret and Elizabeth Hardman, aged fourteen and ten, and Elinor Holland, aged twelve, 'of whom Master Starkie had the education and tuition, with their portions committed unto him by their parents'.[23] No doubt it had seemed a good idea to have companions for Anne and John, but it meant that there were now five children aged between ten and fourteen in the house in an excitable state. Soon they were all behaving strangely, 'shrieking, barking and howling, in such a hideous noise as cannot be expressed'.[24]

It's also clear, however, that the adults around them were putting a sinister interpretation on their behaviour that it really didn't justify. For example, fourteen-year-old Margaret Hardman is described fantasising about dressing in the latest fashions, and chatting to an imaginary servant as she did so. It seems a little extreme to claim that this was proof she was demonically possessed by a 'spirit of pride'.[25]

Also staying at Cleworth, on a temporary social visit, was a 'poor kinswoman of Mistress Starkie's', Margaret Byrom, who was in her early thirties. It's very likely that she and Edmund had spent time together at Cleworth before. Now, in a catastrophic complication to an already fraught situation, she was discovered with Edmund in his bedroom in the middle of the night.

Margaret claimed that Edmund had suffered a night-time attack by evil spirits similar to the one he'd experienced at Huntroyde, and she'd gone into his room 'in a desire to comfort him'.[26] What they said the following day, however, suggests a less supernatural explanation:

> Hartlay said … I fear I have done her harm … Hartlay came to comfort her, for he pretended to bear a loving affection towards her: and it was thought he had kissed her … When he came to comfort Margaret, she could not abide his company. He demanded of her, why? She said for that she thought he had bewitched her. He asked the reason why she thought so? She answered, for thou art ever in mine eyes, absent and present.[27]

Margaret became increasingly unwell, with symptoms entirely consistent with stress, and which she may also have exaggerated as a form of self-defence. She was clearly in a state of emotional turmoil. In a way it was true when she said that Edmund had bewitched her. Like John, she was attracted to him because he defied the rules by practising magic. She and Edmund were both on the margins of the

Starkies' world of wealth and status, but Edmund had a transgressive power and freedom that Margaret must have envied and admired. But she was also horribly aware of what Edmund apparently refused to see – that this was going to end very badly for her, and even worse for him.

Eventually, after several days, Margaret seems to have had a sleep-paralysis-like incident – although normally they only last a few minutes, and this apparently lasted for 'a whole day and a night'. She was 'grievously molested and sorely frightened with a terrible vision. It appeared to her lying in bed, swelling and tumbling, like a foul black dwarf, with half a face, long shaggy hair, black broad hands and black cloven feet'.[28]

Margaret couldn't stand the atmosphere at Cleworth any longer, and went back to her home at Salford, where she lived with her mother. But Edmund went with her, quite openly – an act of madness that can only be explained by the fact that he was genuinely in love with her.

Edmund found somewhere in Salford to stay and spent every day with Margaret. Someone – perhaps Margaret's mother, or perhaps even Nicholas – alerted a local preacher. He went to the house and confronted the couple, demanding to know what Edmund was doing there. Edmund claimed he was using prayers to help Margaret. The preacher – no doubt rightly guessing that he meant charms – made a chilling response: 'Why man, you cannot pray.'

This was quite literally a deadly insult. It was believed that witches, as servants of the Devil, could not pray, and it was a standard test to ask a suspect to say the Lord's Prayer – which was exactly what the preacher now asked Edmund to do. 'And he began to fumble around it very ill-favouredly, and could not for his life say it to the end.'[29]

It's possible that Edmund was a Roman Catholic, so used to saying the prayer in Latin that, asked under stress to say it in English, his mind went blank. Or he may have been so choked up with fury and horror that it was more that he *would* not say it than that he *could* not. Whatever the reason, it was enough evidence for him to be arrested.

Margaret was now put under enormous pressure to make a statement against him. A day was fixed for him to be brought back to the house for her to confront him. For two nights Edmund appeared to Margaret in her dreams, urging her to tell the truth. Then, on the morning of the encounter,

> As she came to the fire, she saw a great black dog, with a monstrous tail, and a long chain, open mouth, coming apace towards her, and, running by her left side, cast her on her face hard by the fire.

The spirit then shape-shifted into a 'big black cat, staring fearfully at her', and then into a mouse 'that leapt upon her left knee'.[30]

When Edmund was brought in, Margaret collapsed and couldn't speak. But when he was taken out of sight behind the other people in the room – and just how many people had been brought in to pressure her into betraying him? – she made some unspecified accusations.

He was then taken to the Starkies' house. The children, faced with a man they had thought was their friend but had now been told had bewitched them, were understandably upset:

> They went at him all at once, attempting to strike him. It was much ado for two strong men to hold the least of them. And if they had not been forcibly restrained, the witch would have been in great danger, for they were as fierce and furious against him as if they would have torn him to pieces.[31]

However, a few days later, when the Justice of the Peace came to take statements from them, they all refused to testify against Edmund – although afterwards they made the excuse to the no doubt furious Nicholas that Edmund's witchcraft had prevented them from speaking.

Edmund was charged with bewitching John and Anne,[32] although not, apparently, with using love magic on Margaret, no doubt because of her reluctance to give evidence against him and to protect her reputation. The main witness – in fact probably the only witness – was Nicholas, and the trial quickly degenerated into a confrontation between the two men, each believing that the other had betrayed him.

However, Edmund was not facing a death sentence. John and Anne were still alive and, before the law was strengthened in 1604, non-fatal witchcraft carried the lesser penalty of a year's imprisonment and four sessions in the pillory. The chances of surviving a year in prison weren't good, and when he was helpless in the pillory there would be a real risk he would be seriously injured by the angry crowd. But on the other hand many of his clients probably believed that he was innocent, and they might be able to obtain a pardon for him.[33]

The court discussed this unsatisfactory situation, and apparently Nicholas 'called to mind the making of the circle',[34] and someone realised that according to the 1563 Act, 'if any person ... use, practise, or exercise, any invocations or conjurations of evil and wicked spirits ... every such offender ... shall suffer pains of death as a felon.'[35]

It's understandable that Nicholas hadn't mentioned the circle earlier – he would hardly have wanted to advertise his part in the ritual. But it seems strange that he should suddenly have realised its significance and decided to speak out. However, it's very likely that Roger Nowell was in court to give Nicholas his support, and it's also quite probable that Nicholas had told Roger about the circle. Was it in fact Roger who realised its legal significance, and prompted the reluctant Nicholas to speak?

This fresh accusation from Nicholas infuriated Edmund:

> Edmund stiffly denied it, and stood out against him. And he told him to his face
> that he should not hang him, let him do what he could. For the Devil had promised
> him that no halter would hang him.[36]

Edmund was arguing for his life, so it's hardly likely he would have admitted
being in league with the Devil. He may have been protesting that his powers were
God-given, and God had promised him that he wouldn't hang. Or he may have
been more defiant, and admitted having dealings with a spirit, but denied that the
spirit was evil. He may have had a similar experience to the Cornish wise woman
Anne Jefferies:

> The fairies appeared to her and told her that a Constable would come that day, with
> a warrant to carry her before a Justice of the Peace and she would be sent to jail. She
> asked them if she should hide herself. They answered, No, she should fear nothing,
> but go with the Constable.[37]

A new charge of spirit invocation was now added to the indictment, the jury
found Edmund guilty, and he was sentenced to death.

What happened at Edmund's execution would have profound consequences for the
Pendle cunning folk fifteen years later. Prisoners were executed one at a time, by
being pushed off a ladder leaning up against the gallows; and as they stood on the
ladder a Church minister asked them to confess and repent.[38] Officially, this was to
give them a final chance to save themselves from Hell, but of course a confession
would also conveniently justify their execution. Many witchcraft suspects obliged.
Joan Upney 'cried out saying: that she had grievously sinned, that the Devil had
deceived her, the Devil had deceived her'.[39]

Others, however, protested their innocence, and they were often put through the
test of being asked to say the Lord's Prayer. Agnes Samuel 'said the Lord's Prayer
until she came to say, 'But deliver us from evil,' the which by no means she could
pronounce'[40] – although the fact that she'd just watched her mother and father
being hanged may explain her loss of concentration. Mother Margaret of Windsor
proved herself a witch in an even more convincing fashion. She stopped partway
through the Lord's Prayer to put a curse on her accuser.[41]

There were also some prisoners who defiantly cut short the grim ritual – and
increased their chances of a quick death from a broken neck – by jumping from
the ladder instead of waiting to be pushed. However, that also increased the risk
of the rope breaking.[42] That, it seems, is what happened to Edmund – the rope
broke, and he fell to the ground still conscious.

He then had to wait, half-choked and in shock, while the executioner tied another
noose, before he was dragged up the ladder a second time, and asked, a second

time, to confess. The onlookers who had been in court remembered Edmund's claim that he'd been promised 'no halter would hang him'. The breaking of the rope now seemed horrible proof that the promise had been made by the Devil, and kept in this cruel twisted fashion. No doubt they used this to try to convince Edmund that the Devil had deceived him, and it seems they were successful:

> He penitently confessed that he had deserved that punishment and that all that Master Starkie had charged him with was true.[43]

Edmund's confession must have been profoundly important to Nicholas. It meant that he had saved his children, rather than murdered his friend. But it must also have had a considerable impact on Roger Nowell. It was horrifyingly dramatic confirmation that the centuries-old argument was true – whatever they might pretend, cunning folk were servants of the Devil.

> The day before Hartlay, his execution, was a sore day unto her [Margaret] ... After this time, she had more ease in the day ... but, in the night, she lay stiff and stark, quaking and trembling.[44]

Once Edmund had been arrested, Nicholas had an enormous emotional investment in believing him guilty, and so he naturally interpreted every symptom suffered by Margaret and the children as the work of witchcraft and evil spirits. And no doubt he unconsciously encouraged the children to produce the symptoms he expected.

With his confidence in counter-magic destroyed, Nicholas enlisted the help of two famous Puritan exorcists, John Darrell and George More.[45] They arrived a few days after Edmund's execution, and confirmed that Margaret and the children were actually possessed by evil spirits. One of the servants Edmund had flirted with, Jane Ashton, was talked into becoming his seventh 'victim', after being convinced that a throat infection she'd had a year earlier was the first sign of possession. And someone put forward the theory that Edmund had breathed devils into his victims by kissing them – a faint but still lurid echo of the charges of paedophilia against Gilles de Rais. After that,

> They had all and every one of them very strange visions and fearful apparitions, whereupon they would say, 'Look where Satan is. Look where Beelzebub is. Look where Lucifer is. Look where a great black dog is, with a firebrand in his mouth.'[46]

The exorcisms John Darrell and George More performed took two days and involved nearly fifty people gathering to pray at the Starkies' house. The spirits were successfully driven out, but although the victims were no longer actually possessed they continued to be haunted by disturbing visions. Edmund's ghost – or an evil spirit in his likeness – appeared repeatedly, telling them 'that they would never prosper'. And animal spirits also menaced them – a raven, an ape, a bear, 'divers whelps', and the black dog.

When John Darrell first arrived one of the children said to him, 'jocundly', 'They might hang Edmund, but they could not hang the Devil.' It's a chilling insight into the children's mental state by that point, that one of them could have seemed cheerful while saying something like that. However, it was certainly the truth. The Black Dog was far from dead.

Cleworth Hall, the home of Nicholas and Anne Starkie and their children.
ENGRAVED BY N. G. PHILIPS

CHAPTER TWELVE

I care not for thee, hang thyself

It was about a year after Edmund's execution that Elizabeth Sothernes had the defining experience of her magical career:

> Upon a Sabbath day in the morning, this examinate having a little child upon her knee, and she being in a slumber, the said spirit appeared unto her in the likeness of a brown dog, forcing himself to her knee, to get blood under her left arm: and she being without any apparel saving her smock, the said devil did get blood under her left arm. And this examinate awaking, said, Jesus save my child; but had no power, nor could not say, Jesus save her self, whereupon the brown dog vanished out of this examinate's sight: after which this examinate was almost stark mad for the space of eight weeks.[1]

The child may well have been Alizon, who would probably have been about two or three years old at the time; but Elizabeth also had a son, Christopher Howgate, and it may have been one of his children.

There's no doubt that there would have been a great deal of talk in Pendle about the Starkies' involvement with Edmund Hartlay. The fact that he had been sentenced to death for conjuring spirits at Huntroyde would have quickly become common knowledge throughout Lancashire, the gossip fuelled by the extraordinary circumstances of his execution. And if Nicholas had wanted to avoid scandal, he wouldn't have invited fifty people to the exorcism.

Elizabeth had probably got to hear about Edmund's visit to Huntroyde as soon as it happened, and she would have taken a keen interest in what he was doing there. Even if she didn't know about the circle until after his trial, she would easily have been able to find its traces in the wood. The plant enchanter's nightshade, which grows on disturbed ground in woodland, took its name from the fact that it grew where magicians and cunning folk made their circles.[2]

I can't imagine any wise woman being able to resist the temptation to visit the site of a circle that had cost a fellow-practitioner his life, and where he had summoned the spirits – in particular the Black Dog – who still haunted the Starkie family, punishing them for their involvement in his judicial murder.

Woodland at Huntroyde,
where Edmund Hartlay made
his circle.

COPYRIGHT NICKY AND
FRANK GRACE

It's unlikely that it was a coincidence that while all this was still fresh in Elizabeth's mind she herself had a spirit encounter with a brown dog, who went on to become her magical assistant.

Elizabeth says quite clearly that the vision occurred when she was 'in a slumber', and the dog vanished as she woke up. It was a particularly vivid dream, which managed to maintain its hold on her consciousness as she moved into a waking state. And it was no doubt a symptom, rather than a cause, of the illness that was about to strike her down and make her 'almost stark mad ... for eight weeks'.

However, the content of the dream was obviously influenced by the ideas about dog spirits already in her mind. And of course what mattered to Elizabeth was the interpretation she put on her experience. She certainly wouldn't have envied Edmund's trial and execution, but she might well have envied the notoriety he had acquired because of them. Edmund had summoned a black dog spirit and died a spectacular death as a result. Now Elizabeth encountered a brown dog spirit and went spectacularly mad for eight weeks. The parallels are almost certainly significant.

When Roger Nowell returned to Read after witnessing Edmund's execution he must have looked north towards Malking Tower with a mixture of anger and frustration. He must have wanted very badly to take action against the Pendle cunning folk, even at that point. And when the rumours about Elizabeth's spirit encounter began to reach him, it can't have been easy for him to restrain his fury. But there was nothing he could do.

Edmund's case illustrates perfectly just how complex the position of cunning folk was. They couldn't simply be dismissed as criminals; they helped desperate people in all sections of society, and their aura of forbidden power often added to their popularity. Bernardino of Siena's lurid stories of naked wise women summoning the Devil prompted many people to denounce them, but he also complained bitterly about the many people who rushed to their defence once they'd been arrested.[3] That was why Finicella's child murders became such an important weapon in his later attacks; no one could defend people who murdered children. And although Edmund had been sentenced to death for spirit invocation, the jury would never have convicted him if he hadn't also been accused of harming John and Anne Starkie. Thus as long as the Pendle cunning folk gave no one any cause to claim they were cursing people, there was nothing Roger Nowell could do about them.

There was, however, someone else who could have acted against them. The local Church of England minister could have reported them to the Bishop and had them tried by a Church court, as Elizabeth Smith was. They could have been forced to publicly renounce magic, or if they persisted in practising it they could have been excommunicated. But *The Wonderful Discovery* includes an account of James attending church and receiving the sacrament. It seems that his local minister was prepared to overlook his magical activities.

In fact many churchmen not only tolerated cunning folk but even practised magic themselves. John Walsh was given his 'book of circles' by a Roman Catholic priest,[4] and the crystal described by John Aubrey – together with its 'call' summoning a spirit – was used by a Church of England minister.

Eventually, however, fifteen years after Edmund's execution, and fourteen years after Elizabeth's encounter with the brown dog, Abraham Law, by 'divine providence' gave Roger Nowell the first real evidence against a member of Elizabeth's family. It's hardly surprising that Roger then exceeded his authority and had Elizabeth searched for the mark where she fed the brown dog with her blood. At some point Elizabeth gave Roger the account of her vision of the dog quoted at the start of this chapter. Once the witch mark had been discovered, she probably thought there was little point in refusing to tell him what she'd no doubt told all her clients. But even so, it's likely that she only admitted it *after* she believed that she'd secured her own safety by incriminating Anne Whittle and Anne Redferne. Accusing them had, after all, involved describing using divination with the help of the spirit.

Roger then questioned her about something that he'd probably heard about during his investigations – a quarrel between Elizabeth and Richard Baldwyn, the local miller.

> A little before Christmas last, this examinate's daughter having been to help Richard Baldwyn's folks at the mill: this examinate's daughter did bid her this examinate go to the said Baldwyn's house, and ask him something for her helping of his folks at the mill, (as aforesaid:) and in this examinate's going to the said Baldwyn's house, and

near to the said house, she met with the said Richard Baldwyn; which Baldwyn said to this examinate, and the said Alizon Device (who at that time led this examinate, [she] being blind) get out of my ground whores and witches, I will burn the one of you, and hang the other. To whom this examinate answered: I care not for thee, hang thyself: presently whereupon, at this examinate's going over the next hedge, the said spirit or devil called Tibb, appeared unto this examinate, and said, Revenge thee of him. To whom, this examinate said again to the said spirit. Revenge thee either of him, or his. And so the said spirit vanished out of her sight, and she never saw him since.

And further this examinate confesseth, and sayeth, that the speediest way to take a man's life away by witchcraft, is to make a picture [image] of clay, like unto the shape of the person whom they mean to kill, and dry it thoroughly: and when they would have them to be ill in any one place more than another: then take a thorn or pin, and prick it in that part of the picture you would so have to be ill: and when they would have any part of the body to consume away, then take that part of the picture and burn it. And when they would have the whole body to consume away, then take the remnant of the said picture, and burn it: and so thereupon by that means, the body shall die.[5]

This is a brilliant piece of editing by Roger Nowell. By putting Elizabeth's description of how to curse someone straight after the account of the quarrel, and using the word 'confesseth', he makes it look as if Elizabeth is confessing to using magic to harm or kill Richard Baldwyn or some member of his family. But of course the description of how a clay image was used was originally part of her evidence against Anne Whittle and Anne Redferne, explaining the clay images she claimed to have seen them making.

In her account of the argument with Richard all she admits to is having a protecting spirit who will avenge wrongs done to her. It's left to the spirit to decide what revenge is appropriate. There's nothing to suggest that Elizabeth intended the spirit to harm anyone. In fact there's nothing to suggest that Elizabeth believed anyone was accusing her of harming someone by witchcraft.

When Mary Sutton and her mother fell out with the miller Master Enger, they apparently made his horses break loose from the cart when he was sending a load of corn to market. That, not murder by witchcraft, was the stuff of everyday magical retaliation.[6]

And Richard Baldwyn was clearly in the wrong. Elizabeth Device had done work for him and now he was trying to get out of paying her. In fact millers were notorious for cheating people by not giving them all the flour they were entitled to when they milled their corn.[7] And it seems that Richard's wife wasn't very popular either. Anne Whittle confessed that her familiar spirit 'would have had [her] to have consented, that he might hurt the wife of Richard Baldwyn of Pendle; but this examinate would not then consent'.[8]

Roger also questioned Alizon about her grandmother's activities. He seems to have begun by asking her about a cow that had died – again, probably an incident uncovered by his investigations:

> One John Nutter of the Bulhole in Pendle aforesaid, had a cow which was sick, and requested this examinate's grandmother to amend the said cow; and her said grandmother said she would, and so her said grandmother about ten of the clock at night, desired this examinate to lead her forth; which this examinate did, [her grandmother] being then blind: and her grandmother did remain about half an hour forth: and this examinate's sister did fetch her in again; but what she did when she was so forth, this examinate cannot tell.[9]

Alizon was defending her grandmother, describing her performing healing magic to cure the cow. No doubt she knew perfectly well what Elizabeth had done, but was reluctant to tell Roger. Probably Elizabeth – too old to visit the cow in person – had recited the charm over a woollen thread, a piece of rowan wood or some herbs, which she would later have given to John Nutter to tie to the cow. However, the statement then adds:

> But the next morning this examinate heard that the said cow was dead, and this examinate verily thinketh, that her said grandmother did bewitch the said cow to death.[10]

As Edmund's case vividly demonstrated, if cunning folk treated people or animals who failed to recover they laid themselves open to being suspected of bewitching them. But, when it was an animal that was involved, admitting to a disastrous failure might have been even worse. Elizabeth might have preferred her clients to think that she was capable of witchcraft rather than that she was incompetent.

It's extremely unlikely that Alizon really said that she 'verily' thought that Elizabeth had killed the cow. In fact, since the cow had died during the night, Alizon may have been implying that there hadn't been time to deliver the charmed object, so the cow's death wasn't really a failure on her grandmother's part. However, she had told Roger that she didn't know what magic her grandmother had performed. Roger would have pushed her to admit that in that case she couldn't be sure that Elizabeth *hadn't* cursed the cow. And he would have seized on any hesitation or uncertainly Alizon showed and put his own interpretation on it. After all, Roger – influenced by Edmund's confession – would have assumed that all Elizabeth's promises to perform healing magic were just a way of deceiving her clients into trusting her.

But then Roger questioned Alizon about the confrontation with Richard Baldwyn, and Alizon's statement says:

> And further, this examinate sayeth, that Richard Baldwyn of Weethead within the Forest of Pendle, about two years ago, fell out with this examinate's grandmother, and so would not let her come upon his land: and about four or five days then next after, her said grandmother did request this examinate to lead her forth about ten of the clock in the night: which this examinate accordingly did, and she stayed forth then about an hour, and this examinate's sister fetched her in again. And this examinate heard the next morning, that a woman child of the said Richard Baldwyn's was fallen sick; and as this examinate then did hear, the said child did languish afterwards by the space of a year, or thereabouts, and died; and this examinate verily thinketh, that her said grandmother did bewitch the said child to death.
>
> And further, this examinate sayeth, that she heard her said grandmother say presently after her falling out with the said Baldwyn, she would pray for the said Baldwyn both still [soft] and loud: and this examinate heard her curse the said Baldwyn sundry times.[11]

However, the incriminating middle section – where Elizabeth apparently curses Richard Baldwyn's child – is simply the earlier section about the cow doctored to make it refer to the child. It even includes the same detail that it was Alizon's sister – Jennet – who brought Elizabeth back into the house. It's been inserted into the middle of what Alizon really said – that Elizabeth fell out with Richard and then cursed him in the sense that she told him to go hang himself, not in the sense that she bewitched him.[12]

What makes it quite clear that this is another example of Roger falsifying evidence is the fact that between the sections about the cow and the child there is a description of some milk mysteriously turning into butter:

> There was butter to the quantity of a quarter of a pound in the said milk, and the quantity of the said milk still remaining; and her grandmother had no butter in the house when this examinate went forth: during which time, this examinate's grandmother still lay in her bed.

This is not remotely incriminating. Roger put it in simply to separate the two other sections, so that when the statement was read out in court the similarities between them wouldn't be obvious to the jury.

CHAPTER THIRTEEN

What wouldst thou have me do unto yonder man

Satisfying though it must have been to trap Elizabeth Sothernes at last, she was not Roger Nowell's main target. When Roger's fellow Justice Thomas Heyber suddenly developed an interest in witchcraft, after his son-in-law's father was apparently bewitched, Roger joined him in his campaign not because of the diminishing threat posed by the ageing Elizabeth Sothernes, but because of the growing threat posed by her teenage grandchildren Alizon and James.

In his book *Discours des Sorciers* Henri Boguet discussed whether teenage suspects should be executed. Analysing the case of fourteen-year-old Christofle of Aranthon, who was sentenced to be banished after being forced to watch four of her fellow suspects burned alive, he concluded that she had been treated too leniently:

> Witches do not abandon the service of Satan whatever punishment one inflicts on them, except death ...
> I will always be of the opinion that, if there is the slightest doubt, one should put them to death ... [because] they never change their lives.[1]

This pessimistic view was shared by at least some English Justices. When, after more than two years of complaints, Sir Thomas Ridgwaye finally decided to take action against Michael and Alice Trevysard, he also decided to prosecute their son Peter. Since Peter had a thirteen-year-old friend he may well have been even younger than Alizon Device, and the eleven people who were falling over themselves to accuse his parents showed very little interest in accusing him. It took Sir Thomas considerable ingenuity to assemble the three statements necessary for a reasonable chance of convicting him.[2]

One was the story about the boat from Peter's friend Christopher – and since there was no law against using magic to move boats, it's likely that Christopher had no idea it could endanger Peter's life. Another was a fairly typical accusation that someone had fallen ill after refusing Peter a drink. The third, which claimed

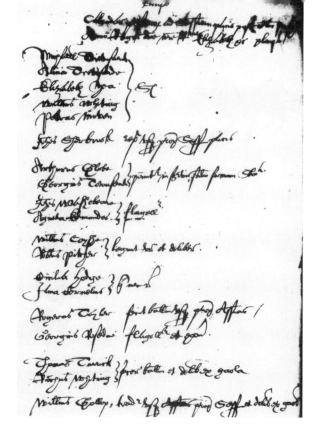

The Exeter Gaol Delivery Roll
recording the execution of
Michael and Alice Trevysard.
Their names are the first two
on the list.

that a woman had died after refusing to lend Peter a hatchet was prompted out of someone who was in the middle of giving a complex accusation against Michael. It's stuck into her statement in such a confusing and arbitrary way that the clerk put Michael's name in at one point by mistake.[3] It also relies on twisting Peter's polite offer, 'I will do thee a good turn, ere twelve months be at an end', into a sinister threat.

However, sometimes someone survived against the odds. The Gaol Delivery Roll that records the execution of his parents doesn't include Peter's name. It seems that he was never sent for trial. Perhaps the family realised the seriousness of the suspicions against them (maybe Christopher warned Peter), and his parents sent Peter to safety. If his expert knowledge of tides and currents is anything to go by he had the makings of a good seaman, so he may have joined the crew of a ship leaving Dartmouth. But whether he fled or not, at some point he managed to rebuild his life in Dartmouth – which must have taken considerable courage, since his parents had been executed for some of the most horrific crimes in the history of English witchcraft. Another record tells us that on 2 October 1615 Peter Trevysard married Joan Colman in St Clement's Church.[4]

Roger Nowell didn't intend to suffer the humiliation of having a suspect acquitted, as Thomas Heyber and Nicholas Banester had. He was determined to get a confession from Alizon.

As I've already mentioned, Alizon gave Roger an account of her quarrel with John Law that makes perfect sense:

> This examinate met with a peddler on the highway, called Colne-field, near unto Colne: and this examinate demanded of the said peddler to buy some pins of him; but the said peddler sturdily answered this examinate that he would not loose his pack; and so this examinate parting with him ... before the peddler was gone forty rods further, he fell down lame: and this examinate then went after the said peddler; and in a house about the distance aforesaid, he was lying lame: [missing section describing Alizon thinking there was no need for her to stay] and so this examinate went begging in Trawden Forest.[5]

However, this is not how her statement reads in *The Wonderful Discovery* – in the form it was drawn up to be used against her in court. In that version, between the words 'parting with him' and 'before the peddler was gone forty rods' there is a very damaging admission. The sentence reads perfectly well without this addition, and is almost certainly what Alizon originally said, but it does leave something unexplained – what Alizon was doing as John walked away from her. We can deduce that she was standing watching him, and we can reasonably assume that she was seething with fury. But Roger obviously pressed her to say explicitly what had happened. And eventually her statement read:

> ... and so this examinate parting with him: presently there appeared to this examinate the Black Dog, which appeared unto her as before: which Black Dog spoke unto this examinate in English, saying, What wouldst thou have me to do unto yonder man? to whom this examinate said, What canst thou do at him: and the dog answered again, I can lame him: whereupon this examinate answered, and said to the said Black Dog, Lame him: and before the peddler was gone forty rods further, he fell down lame ...

And Alizon also gave Roger a description of her first encounter with the dog (which is what is being referred to in the phrase 'appeared unto her as before'):

> About two years agone, her grandmother, called Elizabeth Sothernes ... did (sundry times in going or walking together, as they went begging) persuade and advise this examinate to let a devil or a familiar appear to her, and that she, this examinate would let him suck at some part of her; and she might have and do what she would. And so not long after these persuasions, this examinate being walking towards the Rough Lee, in a close of one John Robinson's, there appeared unto her a thing like unto a Black Dog: speaking unto her, this examinate, and desiring

COPYRIGHT PETER FROOME

her to give him her soul, and he would give her power to do anything she would: whereupon this examinate being therewithal enticed, and setting her down; the said Black Dog did with his mouth (as this examinate then thought) suck at her breast, a little below her paps [breasts], which place did remain blue half a year next after.[6]

Although this is a confession, this isn't the humble and repentant Alizon of the faked confession. Elizabeth Sothernes described the brown dog 'forcing himself to her knee, to get blood under her left arm', but Alizon is 'enticed' into a liaison with an obvious sexual element. Although the Black Dog asks for her soul, she does *not* say that she granted it to him. And instead of drinking her blood, he seems to take something less physical from her – some kind of spiritual essence.

When he appears after the argument with John Law, he behaves very much as if he was Alizon's boyfriend. Chivalrously outraged at John's treatment of her, he asks what she wants him to do about it. Alizon's response is slightly taunting – 'What canst thou do at him?' When he replies that he can lame him (not perhaps terribly impressive for a black hellhound) Alizon decides that's an appropriate retaliation and gives him permission.

This is an evocative account of a relationship where Alizon is very much in control. She enjoys the spirit's attentions and is not in the least afraid of him. It's very different from many of the other accounts of familiar spirits in witchcraft case records, where suspects portray their spirits as aggressive or even out of control.

Discussing interrogation techniques, Jean Bodin wrote:

> In order to draw out the truth from those who are accused or suspected, it is necessary for the [interrogating] judges to assume the appearance of feeling pity for them, and to say to them that it is not they, but the Devil who has forced and compelled them to make people die. And for that reason they are innocent.[7]

Brian Darcey seems to have used that technique on his suspect Elizabeth Bennet, getting her to describe a very hostile relationship with a spirit:

> She having a fire fork in her hand, and being a stirring of the fire in the oven, the spirit (called Suckin) came unto her and took this examinate by the hips, and said, seeing thou wilt not be ruled, thou shalt have a cause, and would have thrust this examinate into the burning oven, and so had (as this examinate sayeth) but for the foresaid fork, but this examinate striving and doing what she could to her uttermost, the said spirit burnt her arm.[8]

Elizabeth admitted that Suckin had killed one of her neighbours, but insisted it wasn't her fault:

> It told this examinate, it had plagued the said Byet's wife to the death. She this examinate saying it was done by the spirit, but not by the sending of this examinate. The said spirit saying, I know that Byet and his wife have wronged thee greatly, and done thee several hurts, and beaten thy swine, and thrust a pitchfork in one of them, the which the spirit said to have done, to win credit with this examinate.[9]

Alizon, however, makes it quite clear that it was she who made the decision that John Law should be lamed. But 'lame' was a very vague term, and we have to remember what Alizon actually saw. She saw John Law fall to the ground, but she then saw him get up again, and walk 200 metres to the alehouse. Just as there's no reason to think that Elizabeth Sothernes realised she was being accused of killing Richard Baldwyn's child, there's no reason to think that Alizon realised she was being accused of crippling John.

When Mary Sutton 'lamed' the men who were trying to 'swim' her they recovered completely in a few minutes. Alizon was confessing that the Black Dog had made John fall – that's all.

Even so, it seems very unwise of Alizon and her grandmother to have admitted to having familiar spirits. Elizabeth's formal statement is dated 2 April, and since the arrests were on 30 March it may have taken Roger four days of interrogation to get her to that point. But all Alizon's statements are dated 30 March, so it seems that Roger got everything he wanted out of her on the day of her arrest.[10]

However, prisoners are in fact most vulnerable to interrogation immediately after they've been arrested. Today this is known as 'the shock of capture', but sixteenth- and seventeenth-century interrogators were well aware of it, although they described it rather differently:

> It is always observed that when the witch is first apprehended at that point she feels that Satan has deserted her, and as if overwhelmed by fright she then voluntarily confesses what force and torture could not drag out of her.

> (*De la Démonomanie des Sorciers* by Jean Bodin[11])

Being arrested and charged with a serious crime was a terrifying experience in itself. Suspects suddenly found themselves in a situation where they had no control over what was happening to them. If Roger decided to prosecute them, Alizon and Elizabeth would be sent to Lancaster – more than a day's journey away – to spend four and a half months in terrible conditions in the prison there awaiting trial. They would have been desperate to avoid that, and would have seized on anything that gave them some hope of returning to their normal lives; while the search for witch marks would have impressed on them how completely they were in Roger's power.

Offering hope to a prisoner that everything could still be all right was another well-known technique:

> The said Brian Darcey then promising to the said Ursley, that if she would deal plainly and confess the truth, that she should have favour and so by giving her fair speeches she confessed as followeth ...

> (*A True and Just Record* by Brian Darcey[12])

And though these promises of 'favour' were often false, sometimes they *were* kept – particularly if, as well as confessing, the suspect gave evidence against someone else. Francesco Prelati's life was spared because his statement could be used against Gilles de Rais. When Matthew Hopkins began his notorious witch hunt in Essex, he had Rebecca West released after she made a statement incriminating her mother and four other women.[13] It's quite possible that it was common practice for Justices to make deals of that kind. We have no way of knowing how many accusations in witchcraft cases were made by people who were themselves suspects, giving evidence in return for the 'favour' of being released.

Justices of the Peace weren't supposed to hold prisoners in custody themselves, but to take a statement from them and then send them to the nearest jail immediately after their arrest.[14] In practice Justices often broke this rule, but it was something Roger could have used to put extra pressure on Alizon – telling her that if she was going to cooperate she had to do it at once, forcing her to make a quick decision before she had time to think it through.

Even so, Alizon didn't fall into the trap of confessing immediately. She cooperated, but only by incriminating Anne Whittle. But then, by giving Alizon the impression that she had done some kind of deal with him, Roger could have persuaded her that it was safe to talk about other things, and gradually drawn her on to more dangerous ground, such as Elizabeth's failed attempt to cure John Nutter's cow.

But with Alizon still failing to confess, Roger had to do something that would increase the 'shock of capture':

> A person's sense of identity depends upon a continuity in his surroundings, habits, appearance, actions, relations with others, etc. Detention permits the 'questioner' to cut through these links … Detention should be planned to enhance the subject's feelings of being cut off from anything known and reassuring.

This quotation, from the CIA's controversial *Human Resource Exploitation Training Manual – 1983*,[15] explains why James's statement incriminating Alizon was so important to Roger. It gave Roger a hold over James, but it was also a way to undermine Alizon's 'relations with others', to 'cut through [her] links' with her family.

It's not surprising that interrogators like Roger Nowell used techniques that are still recommended today. There's nothing new about wanting to get information from people reluctant to give it. Books and pamphlets by witch-hunters like Jean Bodin, Brian Darcey and Henri Boguet described techniques that had been proved to be effective over centuries of criminal proceedings. And no doubt Justices discussed their own personal experiences among themselves, particularly when they gathered at the Assizes.

Essentially, as the CIA manual explains, the aim of aggressive interrogation is to force the prisoner to regress into a state of child-like dependence on the interrogator. And central to that is the destruction of the prisoner's sense of identity.[16]

But to someone who believed in the existence of spirits, and who believed that it was possible for a person to have a protecting spirit who would defend and avenge them, describing their relationship with such a spirit could be a crucial way of asserting their identity.

Informed that her brother had betrayed her, Alizon responded with a challenging account of a relationship with a supernatural being who was a combination of guard-dog and lover. He was someone Roger could not trick or coerce into betraying her. Her relationship with him could not be undermined by her capture and detention.

Brian Darcey provoked another of his suspects, Ales Hunt, into admitting having familiar spirits by threatening to part her from them:

> The said Brian Darcey finding this examinate to be obstinate, and that she could be brought to confess nothing, said to this examinate, that he would sever and part her and her spirits asunder, nay sayeth she this examinate, that ye shall not, for I shall carry them with me.[17]

The sexual element in Alizon's relationship with the Black Dog may well have been deliberately intended to shock Roger. Sexual depravity had become a standard part of the accusations against witchcraft suspects, and Scottish and Continental suspects were often persuaded to confess to having sexual intercourse with the Devil. But the Scottish wise woman Isobel Gowdie used this accusation to humiliate her male interrogators:

> The youngest and lustiest women will have very great pleasure in their carnal copulation with him, yea much more than with their own husbands; and they will have an exceeding great desire of it with him … He is abler for us that way than any man can be.[18]

Like Alizon, Elizabeth Sothernes also had a hidden agenda when she described how she had responded to Richard Baldwyn's threats and insults by telling her familiar spirit to take revenge on him. She too was making it clear to Roger that she had the resources to resist his humiliating and aggressive interrogation.

And, like Alizon, she also at some point described her first meeting with the spirit.

> About twenty years past, as she was coming homeward from begging, there met her this examinate near unto a stone pit in Goldshey, in the said Forest of Pendle, a spirit or devil in the shape of a boy, the one half of his coat black, and the other brown, who bade this examinate stay, saying unto her, that if she would give him her soul, she should have anything that she would request. Whereupon this examinate demanded his name? and the spirit answered, his name was Tibb: and so this examinate in hope of such gain as was promised by the said devil or Tibb, was contented to give

her soul to the said spirit: and for the space of five or six years next after, the said spirit or devil appeared at sundry times unto her this examinate about day-light gate [dusk], always bidding her stay, and asking her this examinate what she would have or do? To whom this examinate replied, Nay nothing: for she this examinate said, she wanted nothing yet.[19]

Of course to an interrogator a confession like this was the proof he needed that the suspect was in league with an evil spirit. What's more, with the help of a spirit the suspect could commit any crime, however unlikely. Confessing to having a spirit was confessing to having a murder weapon.

But although admitting to a relationship with a spirit might imperil the prisoner's life, it was also an act of defiance that gave the prisoner a psychological advantage over the interrogator. Paradoxically, the prisoner was giving the interrogator what he wanted, and defying him.

However, when Alizon told Roger that her familiar spirit was 'a thing like unto a Black Dog', she was describing a creature with particularly diabolical and menacing associations, and of course with disturbing personal associations for Roger himself:

> Look where Satan is. Look where Beelzebub is. Look where Lucifer is. Look where a great black dog is, with a firebrand in his mouth.

Nicholas was now back living at Huntroyde. Was he still haunted by the Black Dog? Had the dog returned with him to the place where Edmund had originally summoned him?

Was Alizon deliberately trying to unnerve Roger by reminding him of Nicholas's terrible experiences? Perhaps, with typically teenage arrogance, thoughtlessness and casual spitefulness, she was indicating that she had a familiar spirit who could wreak the same havoc on Roger's family that Edmund's had wreaked on his nephew's. Was she even, perhaps, suggesting that her familiar spirit *was* Edmund's Black Dog, who had now transferred his allegiance to her?

Disused quarry near Newchurch – probably the 'stone pit in Goldshey' where Elizabeth Sothernes first met her familiar spirit Tibb.

CHAPTER FOURTEEN

Elves and angels

How much of what Alizon said about her familiar spirit was deliberate invention? When Elizabeth Bennet described her fraught relationship with Suckin, she had been told by Brian Darcey that she would have 'much favour' if she confessed, and probably also that she wouldn't be held responsible for what the spirit had done. That undoubtedly affected what she said. Alizon too was responding to the way she was being interrogated, using her description of the Black Dog to challenge and defy Roger Nowell.

However, she *did* believe in the existence of spirits. She believed that her grandmother had a shape-shifting spirit who sometimes took human form, and sometimes the form of a dog or cat. And she believed that she had inherited her grandmother's magical abilities. After her quarrel with John she had watched him walk away with vengeance in her heart. Under pressure from Roger, it wouldn't have been hard for her to believe that some kind of spirit had struck him down on her behalf.

JEAN BODIN RECORDS THE ACTIVITIES OF AN ANGEL

The idea that a person could have '*familiaritas*' with a spirit – a close association similar to the relationship with a family member – was specifically mentioned in the *Determinatio*, 200 years before Alizon told Roger about the Black Dog. Since the *Determinatio* was heavily influenced by *The Sworn Book*, the theologians were no doubt thinking of Honorius's relationship with Hocroel, the book's co-author.

Unfortunately *The Sworn Book* doesn't go into detail about how Honorius and Hocroel worked together. It simply tells us that Honorius wrote the book 'through the counsel of a certain angel whose name was Hocroel'.[1]

However, there is a surviving detailed account of the relationship between a human and an angel. Ironically, it's in *De la Démonomanie des Sorciers* by the dedicated opponent of magic Jean Bodin.[2]

He explains:

> I particularly wanted to make known what I was told by such a reputable person, to make people understand that having dealings with evil spirits should not be considered strange, if angels and good spirits can have such fellowship and affinity with men.

Of course Jean Bodin would have assumed that Hocroel was an evil spirit simply because Honorius was a magician; but as he tacitly admits, his account can at least give us some insights into the relationship magical practitioners had with spirits.

> This happened to him, as he said, after he had, for the whole of the previous year, prayed regularly to God with all his heart, morning and evening, that it would please him to send his good angel to guide him in everything he did ... Then he began, as he told me, to have dreams and visions full of guidance ... Then every morning, at three, or four o'clock, the spirit knocked on his door, and he got up, sometimes opening the door, and he couldn't see anyone ... And then the spirit made itself known when he was awake, knocking gently, the first day, when he was distinctly aware of several tapping sounds on a glass bottle, he was completely amazed ...
>
> From then on it was with him constantly, giving him a tangible sign, such as immediately touching him on the right ear if he was doing something wrong, and on the left ear if he was behaving well ... And sometimes when he began to praise God with some psalm, or to speak of his wonders, he felt himself seized by some kind of spiritual force, which gave him courage. And so that he could distinguish a dream that was the result of inspiration from other kinds of dreaming, which come when one is in a bad mood or troubled in spirit, he was woken by the spirit at two or three in the morning, and a little later he fell asleep: then he had the true dream about what he should do or believe, about doubts that he had, or about what was going to happen to him ...
>
> I asked him if he had ever seen the spirit in any kind of shape, he said to me that he had never seen anything while he was awake except a kind of light in the shape of a disc, intensely bright: but one day, his life in extreme danger, having prayed to God with all his heart that it would please him to preserve him, at daybreak, drifting between sleep and waking [*entre-sommeillant*] he said that he perceived, on the bed where he was lying, a young child dressed in a robe that changed in colour from white to purple, and with a face of supernatural beauty.

It's not surprising that after praying for a year for the help of an angel Jean Bodin's friend began to have dreams 'about what he should do or believe, about doubts that he had, or about what was going to happen to him'. Professor Deidre Barrett, of Harvard Medical School, has discovered that about half of us can train ourselves to have meaningful dreams – and these dreams can often provide us with solutions to problems that our brains have missed while we're awake. This is because the creative and intuitive parts of our brains are more active while we're dreaming. And although praying for a year, or putting marigold and a wolf's tooth wrapped in a bay leaf under your pillow, are no doubt effective ways of encouraging meaningful dreams, they're unnecessarily complicated. All you need to do is tell yourself that you want to dream about something just as you're drifting off to sleep.[3]

There's no doubt that dreams were regarded as a valid way for magical practitioners to make contact with spirits. According to the sixteenth-century book of magic *Arbatel*:

> Some do act with spirits openly, and face to face; which is given to few: others do work by dreams and other signs.[4]

When he gave instructions for summoning spirits, Honorius claimed that the magician would see them while he was awake, but it's clear that he also regarded dream experiences as just as real and meaningful. At a crucial point in the ritual to obtain a vision of God, the magician had to receive permission to proceed from an angel in a dream:

> Then in the night following shall be revealed unto you by an angel whether you shall obtain your petition or no.[5]

And in fact the vision of God itself was obtained in a dream. The ritual involved days of preparation, including fasting on bread and water, giving alms and reciting long prayers and pages of sacred names of God. The magician then had to 'make a couch of hay, and about it strew ashes that be clean sifted and in them write the hundred names of God ... Then let him sleep ...'.[6]

It's likely that these long and devout preparations – although not really necessary to induce a significant dream – helped to stimulate the magician's imagination, and to form ideas in his mind that would come together in the dream, and shape themselves into the vision he was so intent on experiencing.

It may be significant that Jean Bodin's friend had his dreams after waking in the early hours of the morning. This is a time when people suffering from stress often wake up (and it seems that Jean Bodin's friend had a rather stressful existence, with his life often in danger). But it's also a time when people wake up with their minds full of creative ideas. It's probable that this was the time when his mind was in a creative state most likely to produce vivid, coherent and meaningful dreams.

It seems that the angels who enabled Honorius and Jean Bodin's friend to experience their significant and even revelatory dreams were in fact not supernatural beings at all, but the creative and intuitive aspects of their own minds.

SPIRITS AND SCIENTISTS

A number of scientific discoveries have been the result of dreams. One with particularly magical elements was the discovery of the circular structure of the benzene molecule by Friedrich August Kekulé in 1865:

> I was sitting writing on my textbook, but the work did not progress; my thoughts were elsewhere. I turned my chair to the fire and dozed. Again the atoms were gambolling before my eyes ... long rows sometimes more closely fitted together all

twining and twisting in snake-like motion. But look! What was that? One of the snakes had seized hold of its own tail, and the form whirled mockingly before my eyes. As if by a flash of lightning I awoke.[7]

There are significant similarities to Elizabeth Sothernes's vision of the brown dog – she too was dozing in a chair, rather than asleep in bed, and then woke very suddenly, apparently as a result of what she'd seen in the dream. Both saw animals, and while Elizabeth's dog was probably inspired by stories of the Black Dog summoned by Edmund, Friedrich Kekulé's snake was almost certainly inspired by a symbol from alchemy – the Ouroboros serpent. This image – a snake devouring his own tail – occurs in many alchemical manuscripts, one of the earliest being an Egyptian manuscript of around the second century, *The Gold-Making of Cleopatra*, where the picture is accompanied by the words 'One is All'.[8]

Serpent imagery was extremely important in alchemy, and Friedrich Kekulé's dream also has similarities to one of Francesco Prelati's experiences which combined magic and alchemy, when his familiar spirit Barron showed him a vision of a winged serpent guarding a pile of gold.[9]

While Friedrich Kekulé's dream had some of the characteristics of a spirit encounter, another scientist, the astronomer George Ellery Hale, actually acquired a familiar spirit. George Hale, who was born in 1868, was the mastermind behind the 200-inch Hale Telescope at the Palomar Observatory in California.[10] Obsessive and driven, as well as extremely creative, George Hale suffered from severe nervous tension which led to headaches, stomach problems and insomnia.

One night, when he was sitting in his bedroom stressed out and unable to sleep (in fact in a mental state very similar to Jean Bodin's friend when he saw the vision of the child), he saw a small human figure – an elf. From then on, the elf not only appeared regularly, but also gave him advice. Although George Hale was understandably cautious about mentioning the elf to his colleagues, it seems probable that the spirit's advice contributed to his visionary achievement – the creation of the world's finest telescope.[11]

ANNE JEFFERIES AND THE FAIRIES

George Ellery Hale's experiences also resemble Anne Jefferies's fairy encounters. Her first vision was the result of a physical illness, but she continued to see them after she had recovered. By that time, however, she was under the stress of being accused of demonic magic:

> The great noise of the many cures Anne did, and also of her living without eating our victuals, she being fed, as she said, by these fairies, caused both the neighbouring magistrates and ministers to resort to my father's house, and talk with her ...
>
> The ministers endeavouring to persuade her they were evil spirits resorted to her, and that it was the delusions of the Devil. But how could that be when she did no hurt, but good to all who came to her for cure of their distempers? ... That night after the magistrates and ministers were gone, my father, with his family, sitting at a great fire in the hall, Anne being also present, she spoke to my father and said, 'Now they call!' meaning the fairies ... After she had been in [her] chamber some time, she came to us again with a Bible in her hand, and tells us that when she came to the fairies they said to her, 'What, hath there been some magistrates and ministers to you, and dissuaded you from coming any more to us, saying we are evil spirits, and that it is all delusions of the Devil? Pray desire of them to read in the 1st Epistle of St John, chapter 4, verse 1, 'Dearly beloved, believe not every spirit, but try the spirits whether they be of God.'[12]

Unfortunately one of the magistrates was the notoriously corrupt Justice of the Peace John Tregeagle. He had Anne arrested and imprisoned in Bodmin jail. She was tried at the Quarter Sessions, and the case was then passed on to the Assizes, where she faced the death penalty for entertaining evil spirits.[13] However, although she was questioned by the Assize judges, she was never actually tried. It's likely that the grand jury, who assessed the evidence before the trials, dismissed the case. But Anne must also have convinced the judges of her innocence, no doubt using the Biblical quotation so helpfully supplied by the literate and devoutly Christian fairies.

The account of Anne's case in unusual, because it was written by someone who was a personal friend of the suspected witch:

> It is the custom in our county of Cornwall for the most substantial people of each parish to take [as] apprentices the poor children, and to breed them up 'till they attain to twenty-one years of age, and for their services to give them meat, drink and clothes. This Anne Jefferies, being a poor man's child of the parish, by Providence fell into our family.

The writer, Moses Pitt, was a boy at the time the main events took place, and his account is so uncritically favourable to Anne it suggests that he had something of a crush on her. He describes her as 'a girl of a bold, daring spirit', and uncompromisingly labels John Tregeagle as her 'persecutor'. And even though he wrote his account fifty years later – by which time he was a publisher in London – it's clear that he never at any time had the slightest doubts about the reality of Anne's healing powers, or the fairies who had given them to her.

However, in spite of the fairies insisting that they were 'spirits ... of God', they were not quite as benign as that suggests. The first person Anne cured was Moses Pitt's mother, who had injured her leg in a fall – a fall it turned out the fairies had caused, after a minor quarrel between Anne and Mistress Pitt. Presumably that was something Anne did *not* mention to the Assize judges.

In an ironic final twist, John Tregeagle passed into Cornish folklore as a comic demon figure. According to the legend, after his death he was condemned to bail out Dozmary Pool on Bodmin Moor with a limpet shell.[14]

John Walsh also consulted fairies, as well as the spirit he raised with his circle ritual:

> He being demanded how he knoweth when any man is bewitched: he sayeth that he knew it partly by the fairies, and sayeth that there be 3 kinds of fairies, white, green and black. Which when he is disposed to use, he speaketh with them upon hills, where as there is great heaps of earth [i.e. burial mounds], as namely in Dorsetshire. And between the hours of 12 and one at noon, or at midnight he useth them. Whereof (he sayeth) the black fairies are the worst ...
>
> He being demanded whether that any of the three kinds of fairies when they did hurt, did it of their own malignity, or of the provocation of any wicked man? He answered that they do hurt of their own malignity.[15]

People had been acquiring magical powers from the fairies since long before the witch-hunts. In the thirteenth century, around the time Honorius and Hocroel were collaborating on *The Sworn Book*, the Scottish poet Thomas of Erceldoune was given the power of prophecy by the Queen of Elfland – as he was lying (perhaps 'in a slumber') on Huntlie bank under a hawthorn tree. The incident is described in the beautiful folksong *Thomas the Rhymer*:

> True Thomas lay on Huntlie bank,
> A ferlie [wonder] he spied with his eye,
> And there he saw a lady bright,
> Come riding down by the Eildon Tree ...
> 'Harp and carp, Thomas,' she said,
> 'Harp and carp along with me,
> And if ye dare to kiss my lips,
> Sure of your body I will be.'
> 'Betide me well, betide me woe,
> That weird [fate] shall never daunten me;'
> So he has kissed her rosy lips,
> All underneath the Eildon Tree ...

> She mounted on her milk-white steed,
> She's ta'en True Thomas up behind,
> And aye whene'er her bridle rung,
> The steed flew swifter than the wind …
> O they rode on, and farther on,
> And they waded through rivers above the knee,
> And they saw neither sun nor moon,
> But they heard the roaring of the sea.
> It was murk murk night, and there was no stern light,
> And they waded through red blood to the knee;
> For all the blood that's shed on earth
> Runs through the springs of that country.
> So they came to a garden green
> And she pulled an apple from a tree:
> 'Take this for thy wages, True Thomas,
> It will give the tongue that can never lie.'[16]

It's also important to remember that you don't necessarily have to see spirits to know that they're there. The fairies who gave Anne Jefferies healing powers are still helping people in Cornwall today, as this letter published in *Fortean Times* in March 2009 demonstrates:

... A few months ago, while I was putting out hay for my sheep, it [a medieval silver ring] slipped off my finger. It could have been anywhere, in deep straw, in a farm shed 40ft (12m) long and 35ft (11m) wide. My partner and I searched long and hard for it, but eventually we gave up. Just before Christmas, however, we went back to the job armed with a powerful metal detector ...

We went over the whole building, unearthing several rummy agricultural bits of metal buried deep in the earth floor – but the ring was not among them. Eventually I cried in desperation: 'Pixies, please help me!' Instantly – literally instantly – the headphones buzzed. The detector coil was right over a pile of hay-dust I'd scanned several times already. I scrabbled in the dust, and the ring fell out ...

Thank you pixies. How on earth do you do it?
Ali Barnes
Cornwall.[17]

SLEEP-RELATED HALLUCINATIONS

Many of these experiences happened when people were in the state described by Jean Bodin as 'entre-sommeillant' – when they were 'in a slumber' during the day; just before they woke up in the early hours of the morning, or just after they went back to sleep again; late at night when they were exhausted but unable to sleep, or at dawn when they were exhausted after a bad night; or when their sleep was disturbed by stress or illness.

The most likely explanation for Margaret Byrom's first encounter with the Black Dog, when he threw her down against the fire, is that she was in fact sitting by the fire, fell asleep and fell from her chair – not surprising considering that we know she'd been under extreme stress for the previous two nights.

Simon J. Sherwood, a modern researcher investigating Black Dog apparitions, had an experience similar to Margaret's:

> I had been in bed a couple of hours. I awoke to hear a patter of feet. I looked up thinking it was my dog, but to my terror I saw a massive black animal probably with horns but perhaps ears, galloping along the landing towards my bedroom. I tried to scream but I found it impossible. The creature's eyes were bright yellow and as big as saucers. The animal got to my bedroom door and then vanished as quick as it had appeared.[18]

This happened when he was four years old, and was in fact a hypnopompic hallucination – a hallucination that occurs as a person is waking up. In a survey published in the *British Journal of Psychiatry*, around one in eight people reported experiencing hypnopompic hallucinations, and over a third reported experiencing hallucinations as they were falling asleep (hypnagogic hallucinations). This type of hallucination includes seeing people or animals, or (more usually) coloured shapes; hearing sounds, or a sensation of being touched – the experiences described by Jean Bodin's friend. They're often experienced by people who are in a completely normal, healthy state, but insomnia and other sleep-related problems make it more likely.[19]

To Jean Bodin, his friend's experiences were enormously significant – they were proof not only of the existence of angels, but also of evil spirits. But the fact is that about half of us could train ourselves to have dreams similar to his, and more than a third of us have similar hypnagogic or hypnopompic hallucinations. There's nothing abnormal about such experiences. They don't require a brain that's different from other people's, or training in inducing altered states of consciousness.

However, Emma Wilby, in her groundbreaking book *Cunning Folk and Familiar Spirits*, draws attention to the similarities between the physical hardships – such as lack of sleep and lack of food – that were often facts of life in Early Modern Britain and the techniques deliberately used by shamans and mystics to induce visions.[20] We seriously underestimate our ancestors' resourcefulness if we imagine that they lived in squalor and misery,[21] but their lives could quickly be transformed from comfortable to desperate by misfortunes such as illness or crop failure.

Bessie Dunlop, for example, had her first encounter with Tom Reid when she was wide-awake, driving her livestock to pasture. But she was certainly not in a normal state, either mentally or physically. Her cattle and sheep were sick, her newborn baby was dying and her husband was seriously ill, and she herself hadn't fully recovered from giving birth.[22]

But, as Emma Wilby argues, how people responded to these visions was also crucial. Tom told Bessie that her husband would recover. Instead of dismissing the experience as a symptom of her abnormal mental state, Bessie believed him. Now convinced that her husband would live, she found the strength and determination to keep going. And with Tom as her mentor she went on to become a wise woman, helping other people as he had helped her.

People *valued* these experiences. They went over them in their minds, searching them for meaning. And once they'd had one, they often hoped to have more, and did everything they could to cultivate them. The tapping sounds and sensations of being touched that Jean Bodin's friend experienced began as hypnopompic hallucinations, but it seems that he then went on to experience them when he was fully awake – because he *wanted* to. He *encouraged* his brain to reproduce them. Praying to God to send him an angel told his brain to create one for him – and as well as leading to dreams 'full of guidance', it seems to have led eventually to dream-like and hallucinatory experiences when he was awake.

A SCRYING EXPERIMENT

[The cunning man Miles Blomfield] brought with him a looking glass, (about 7 or 8 inches square), and did hang the said glass up over the bench in his said hall, upon a nail, and had the said examinate look in it, and said as far as he could guess, he should see the face of him that had [stolen] the said linen.[23]

The scrying mirror made for me by Steve Patterson, inspired by medieval and early modern descriptions. The names of the four archangels are written round the steel scrying surface, and sacred names of God – AGLA, Eloy, Rex, Alpha et Omega, Sabaoth and Tetragrammaton – around the rim of the mirror. The wood is from a church.

AUTHOR COLLECTION

On some occasions, it wasn't the magically gifted cunning folk who saw visions, but their clients – ordinary people inspired simply by confidence in the practitioners they were consulting. If they could do it, it seemed worth experimenting to see if I could too. Usually it involved scrying with a mirror, so I asked Steve Patterson, an expert on traditional magical tools, to make me a steel mirror of the kind a magician, cunning man or wise woman might have used.

One of the Museum of Witchcraft's regular visitors, Martin, also agreed to experiment, using a fluorite sphere. After a couple of weeks' practice he was getting good results, seeing elvish-looking faces, and animals including a cat and a dog. He described it as similar to seeing shapes in clouds, although he never saw the same thing twice, even when he was gazing into exactly the same part of the sphere.

Meanwhile I was staring into my mirror, determined to see an animal spirit, without success – although one night, after looking into the mirror just before going to bed, I had a vivid dream about a black cat, which perhaps counted as a result of a kind.

Then one afternoon I decided that perhaps I should be more relaxed about it and let the mirror show me whatever it wanted. After a few moments I saw a dog's face. It appeared gradually, increasing in definition as I watched – vague and blurry at first, and then resolving itself into a recognisable image in a way that seemed familiar. Then I realised where I'd seen the effect before. In numerous films and television crime dramas, a police officer or member of the security services gazes at a CCTV or satellite picture on a computer screen and says, 'Can you enhance that for me?' The computer expert clicks the mouse a few times, and the grey blur on the screen crystallises into a scene containing a vital clue.

My brain had done the same as the computer. I wanted to see a dog's face, and so my brain had identified features in the mirror that could be constructed into a dog's face – small variations of light and shade that I probably wasn't even consciously aware of – and then enhanced them until the face appeared.

It's significant that the main use of mirrors was to identify thieves and witches. The human brain is particularly adapted to recognise faces, and so is also particularly inclined to seize on anything that resembles a face and turn it into one.[24]

Inside the dark cottage of a wise woman or cunning man, gazing into a mirror that didn't give the sharp reflections that modern mirrors do,[25] and perhaps with a candle or firelight creating a moving pattern of light and shadow, the client's brain built up a picture of the culprit's face. It was an optical illusion; but instead of being an accidental one it was one carefully, although unconsciously, constructed by the client's own brain.

In most cases the client probably saw the face of the person they already suspected; but sometimes the process may have worked like a problem-solving dream, bringing into play the creative and intuitive aspects of the client's mind to produce an unexpected result.

And if that could happen to a client, no doubt cunning folk themselves could develop it as a skill, practising until they could build up complex pictures.

SMOKE AND SHADOWS

This could also be a possible explanation for Honorius's claim that he could summon spirits in a visible form. His rituals involved using phenomenal quantities of incense.[26] In the early days of the Museum of Witchcraft, when it was run jointly by Cecil Williamson and Gerald Gardner, they burned a large quantity of incense during a ritual and Gerald Gardner fled in alarm after seeing the shape of a spirit forming within the incense smoke.[27]

William Bottrell, writing in the nineteenth century, recorded an account of a similar phenomenon:

Ef [if] any spells of witchcraft happen to strike, we must, after sunset, bring the ill-wished beast into a ploughed field, there bleed it on straw, and, as the blood and straw are burning together, the witch will either come bodily into the field or her apparition will appear in the smoke plain enow [enough] for us to know her.[28]

In fact when Daniel J. Driscoll produced the first printed edition of *The Sworn Book* in 1977, his translation of one of the Latin manuscripts included the lines:

Air is a corruptable, delicate, and fluid element which, if a suitable perfume be set to fire, is capable of receiving the qualities and forms of spirits who will then become visible for the magician to see.[29]

This is a rather free translation from John Dee's copy, which is in poor condition, but in struggling to decipher it Daniel Driscoll may have had a valuable insight into Honorius's magical experiences.

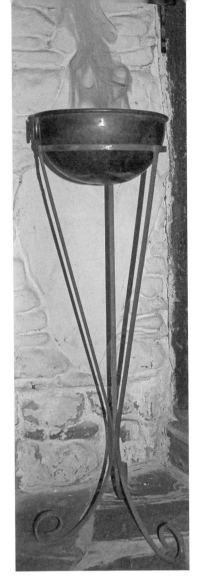

This incense burner is probably the one Gerald Gardner and Cecil Williamson were using when Gerald Gardner saw the shape of a spirit forming in the smoke (MoW 886).

This phenomenon could also explain other spirit encounters, such as glimpses of fairies in woodland, where light shining through moving leaves would create shifting patterns similar to those in incense smoke.

Elizabeth Sothernes's early encounters with Tibb always took place at dusk.[30] Although according to her statement she had a conversation with him on the first occasion and gave him her soul, apparently she then turned down his offers of help for the next six years. This seems very unlikely, since she was a professional wise woman. Even if she didn't personally need his help, she would have needed it for her clients. A far more likely explanation is that these encounters were no more than vague glimpses, leaving her unable to say definitely that Tibb had helped her on any particular occasion.

EDWARD KELLEY

However, there are some forms of scrying this theory can't explain. After John Dee acquired his Aztec obsidian mirror, many scryers began using dark mirrors, which have a completely featureless black surface. And there are also the complicated dream-like visions of the kind experienced by the unfortunate twentieth-century scryer who was chased by the corpse. It's possible, of course, that he had briefly dozed off. However, Theodore Besterman, in his book *Crystal Gazing* (published in 1924 but still the definitive book about scrying), cites the example of a scryer who was able to have complex visions while at the same time carrying on a lucid conversation with her clients.[31] It seems that some people may be able to induce experiences similar to meaningful dreams while they're awake, using gazing into the mirror or crystal as a way to achieve the right mental state.

One of the most talented of these scryers was Edward Kelley, who worked with

John Dee. The notes John Dee took during their scrying sessions have survived, and were published in 1659. Edward Kelley seems to have had a certain amount in common with Michael Trevysard, and to have been a cause of considerable anxiety to John Dee:

> E.K. had been ever since nine of the clock in the morning in a marvellous great disquietness of mind, fury, and rage, by reason his brother Thomas had brought him news that a commission was out to attach and apprehend him as a felon for coining of money ... and how Mr Husey had reported him to be a cosener [fraud], and had used very bitter and grievous reports of him now of late; and that his wife was at home with her mother at Chipping Norton.[32]

However, his visions (which, unusually, often featured female spirits) were frequently both beautiful and disturbing:

> E.K. said that Galvah her head is so bright fire, that it cannot be looked upon: the fore so sparkleth and glistreth as when an hot iron is smitten on an anvil, and especially at the pronouncing of every word. It is to be noted also that upon the pronouncing of some words, the beasts and also all creatures of the world every one showed themselves in their kind and form: but notably all serpents, dragons, toads and all ugly and hideous shapes of beasts; which all made most ugly countenances, in a manner assaulting E.K. but contrariwise coming to, and fawning upon Galvah.[33]

On other occasions, however, the spirits showed surprising flashes of humour:

> After a great silence and pause, appeared one ... like a woman having on a red kirtle and above that a white garment like an Irish mantle ... on her breast a precious stone of white colour, and on her back another precious stone; both which stones were set upon a cross, in the very centre of the cross.
>
> [John Dee said,] Your external apparel (you Daughter of Light) you perceive that we have somewhat noted: but by the power and mercy of the external Light, we trust and desire to understand somewhat of your internal virtue.
>
> She said, What do you think I am a jeweller's wife by my apparel?[34]

HALLUCINOGENIC DRUGS

There is also another way that incense could have been involved in the visions that Honorius and other practitioners saw. The ingredients of incense used in magic sometimes included powerful hallucinogens:

> Take black poppy seed, henbane, root of mandrake, the loadstone, and myrrh, and make them up with the brain of a cat or the blood of a bat.
>
> (*Three Books of Occult Philosophy* by Heinrich Cornelius Agrippa.[35])

If you inhaled large quantities of that it would certainly give you hallucinations – and probably make you extremely ill.[36]

In his book *Formicarius*, written in the 1430s, Johannes Nider described a wise woman using a hallucinogenic ointment to induce visions.[37] A number of recipes for these ointments were recorded, but usually in books hostile to magic, so they may not necessarily be accurate. One modern researcher, Karl Kiesewetter, died after trying one out.[38] Reginald Scot gives two: 'The fat of young children … eleoselinum [probably some plant related to hemlock], aconitum [wolf's bane], frondes populeus [poplar leaves], and soot;' and 'sium [water parsnip – perhaps in fact hemlock water dropwort[39]], acarum vulgare [sweet flag], pentaphyllon [cinquefoil], the blood of a flittermouse [bat], solanum somniferum [probably deadly nightshade], and oleum [olive oil].'[40]

People also sometimes took hallucinogens by accident. Ergot, a fungus that grows on rye, is the source of the modern drug LSD. It was used as a herbal medicine, but was also responsible for outbreaks of mass poisoning, though as rye wasn't widely grown in England that was more of a problem on the Continent.[41]

It's hard to be sure how important the use of hallucinogens was in Early Modern magic, but the hallucinogenic properties of a wide variety of plants were well known. The sixteenth-century Italian writer Giambattista della Porta suggested a rather unethical experiment:

> Take the roots of mandrake and but put them into new wine, boiling and bubbling up: cover it close; and let them infuse in a warm place for two months. When you would use it, give it to somebody to drink; and whosoever shall taste it after a deep sleep, will be distracted, and for a day shall rave: but after some sleep, will return to his senses again, without any harm: and it is very pleasant to behold. Pray make trial.[42]

Modern science is gradually revealing how complex the human brain is, and the important roles played by parts of it that are still essentially mysterious. Psychologist Ap Dijksterhuis of the University of Amsterdam has discovered that when people are faced with difficult decisions, they're much happier if they act on their instincts rather than considering the problem rationally. It seems that 'conscious' thought processes such as reason may play a far less significant part in our lives than we like to think; and it may really be 'subconscious' thought processes that motivate us and determine our sense of well-being (although terms like 'conscious' and 'subconscious' are themselves over-simplifications).[43]

Magical techniques such as scrying and inducing significant dreams helped people to utilise the 'subconscious' parts of their brains and come up with creative and intuitive solutions to problems. And they also gave people a supernatural justification for making a decision that might be hard to justify rationally. It's likely that one of the most important roles of magic was to give people permission, and confidence, to do what they wanted to do anyway.

However, as Emma Wilby points out, many spirit encounters didn't simply help people to solve their immediate problems, they completely transformed their lives. Bessie Dunlop, for instance, was on the point of physical and mental collapse when her encounter with Tom Reid gave her what she needed – both psychologically and practically – to survive. He enabled her to focus on the possibility that her husband might recover, and he then gave her a career as a wise woman. But he also made her realise that she wasn't someone insignificant, destined inevitably to be crushed by circumstances. Her fate mattered.

The spirit world accessed by magicians and cunning folk may perhaps have been an aspect of their own minds, but it was one they used to explore their relationships with others, with the natural world and with the forces that shaped and governed their existence.[44]

And the idea that the search for insight might take you into yourself would not necessarily have seemed strange to them. One of the spirits who appeared to Edward Kelley told him, 'The first plague that fell upon mankind was the want of science [i.e. knowledge] ... The want of science hindreth you from knowledge of yourself.'[45]

CHAPTER FIFTEEN

Black cats and black dogs

ANGELS OF THE EARTH

Apart from Hocroel, Honorius had dealings with three types of spirit – planetary spirits, spirits of the air and spirits of the earth. The planetary spirits had basically the same characteristics as the Roman gods who originally gave the planets their names, and were essentially updated versions of them:[1]

> Of the sprites that be under the planet Mars ... Their nature is to cause and stir up war murder destruction and mortality of people and all earthly things ...

> Of the sprites that be under planet of Venus ... Their nature is to provoke laughings enticements and desires to love women and to give flower, and fruits.[2]

Honorius's descriptions of the planetary spirits are evocative but lacking in detail:

> Their bodies are of a mean stature, dry and lean their colour is red like to burning coals burning red ...

> Their form or fashion is moveable clear like glass or the flame of white fire ...

> Their bodies are long and great, their countenance is whitish dim like crystal or like ice or a dark cloud ...[3]

The spirits of the air were linked with the planetary spirits, but some of them had animal characteristics. The spirits of the south – linked with Mars – had 'antlers in the manner of a stag, talons in the manner of griffins. They bellow like mad bulls.'[4]

Honorius's most vivid description, however, is of the 'angels of the earth', and if it's based on personal experience it certainly suggests he may have been high on henbane at the time:

Their bodies are as wide as they are tall, huge and terrifying, with ten toes on each foot, with talons in the manner of dragons, and their heads have five faces; one is of a toad, another of a lion, the third of a serpent, the fourth of a dead man lamenting and grieving, the fifth of a man beyond comprehension. They carry two tigers on their tail. They hold two dragons in their hands.[5]

But in spite of its hallucinatory quality, its combination of the grotesque and the awe-inspiring carries considerable poetic impact. And there is a haunting quality in the way it brings together images of the ugliness, violence and power of Nature with images of human death and transfiguration. As an expression of our anguished relationship with the natural world and our own mortality, it carries an uncomfortable core of truth within the bizarre nightmare.

In *Cunning Folk and Familiar Spirits*, Emma Wilby argues persuasively that British spirit encounters were a visionary tradition that had its origins in pre-Christian Shamanic practices. She points out that Siberian and Native American shamans place a high value on animal spirits, reflecting the respect they have for other species; and that our Early Modern ancestors had a far more interdependent relationship with animals and the natural world than we do today.[6]

And even today, cats and dogs – the shapes animal familiars took most often – bring the mysterious world of Nature into our homes in a particularly intimate way. It can still be an eerie experience to glance into a dark room and see the eyes of a cat as two bright discs in the blackness, or to be driving your car at night when someone comes towards you walking their dog, and the dog's eyes suddenly blaze as he turns his head towards you.

The final climax of the story of the death of Grimalkin, when the wife's pet kitten is suddenly transformed into a ferocious killer, capable of choking to death a tough and ruthless soldier, may be a slight exaggeration, but it reflects a sense that cats and dogs form a link between humankind and a natural world that is full of power and danger. And it may be significant that when Simon Sherwood had his hypnopompic hallucination of a Black Dog, when he was just four years old, he thought at first that the patter of feet was his own pet dog approaching. It seems possible that the demonic dog was the 'dark side' of his own dog.

GUARDIANS OF OUR FEARS

Animal spirits occur in British stories well before the witch-hunts. In *The Voyage of Mael Dúin*, written in Ireland in the eighth or ninth century, Mael Dúin and his companions are close to starvation on a sea voyage when they land on an island that appears to be deserted:

They came into the biggest house ... and there was no one there but a small cat which was in the middle, playing on four stone pillars. It was leaping from one pillar to the other ... They saw then three rows all round the wall of the house ... first there was a row of gold and silver brooches, with their pins in the wall; a second row of big collars of gold and silver, like the hoops of a barrel; and the third row of big swords with hilts of gold and silver … They saw then a broiled ox and a salt pig in the midst, and a big vessel of good intoxicating ale. 'Has this been left for us?' said Mael Dúin to the cat. It looked at them for an instant, and began to play again. Then Mael Dúin realized that it was for them that the meal which they saw had been left. They drank and dined and fell asleep … Then [they] considered leaving. One of Mael Dúin's three foster-brothers said, 'Shall I take one of these collars with me?' 'No,' said Mael Dúin, 'the house is not without a guard.' He took it with him all the same, as far as the middle of the courtyard. The cat came after him, and jumped through him like a fiery arrow, and burned him to ashes.[7]

In *The Dream of Rhonabwy*, a Welsh story written around the beginning of the thirteenth century, Owein, the son of the sorceress Morgan Le Fay, has a bodyguard of ravens who become involved in a skirmish with King Arthur's men:

Furiously and with exultation did they, with one sweep, descend upon the heads of the men … and they seized some by the heads and others by the eyes, and some by the ears, and others by the arms, and carried them up into the air; and in the air there was a mighty tumult with the flapping of the wings of the triumphant Ravens, and with their croaking; and there was another mighty tumult with the groaning of the men, that were being torn and wounded, and some of whom were slain.[8]

As well as the witch-owls depicted on St Austell font, a number of twelfth-century Cornish fonts feature carvings of cats. They too represent evil spirits – dangers that threaten children until they're protected by baptism. A remarkable picture in the Winchester Bible, dating from around the same time, illustrates a passage about idolatry with a scene showing the worship of a cat-headed deity. The figure is standing on an altar like a statue of a god, but is also reacting with dismay as two of its worshippers are beheaded. Meanwhile, in France, a greyhound who had saved a child from a snake was revered as Saint Guinefort, and sick children were taken to his grave, where their parents performed healing rituals with the help of a local wise woman.[9]

In the early fourteenth century Pope John XXII's condemnation of magic seems to have triggered one of Ireland's major witchcraft cases. The Bishop of Ossory conducted an Inquisition in his diocese and uncovered a group of witches, led by Alice Kyteler, who were apparently performing malevolent magic with the help of a spirit who sometimes took human form, sometimes the form of a cat and sometimes the form of a black dog.[10]

A hundred years later, during the persecutions witnessed by Eustache Blanchet, Jeannette Brunier confessed to having a familiar spirit called Brunet who took either human form or the form of a black cat, and Thomas Bèque admitted having a familiar called Mermet who appeared either as a man or a black dog.[11] And in England in 1450, during a rebellion against King Henry VI, the rebel leader Jack Cade 'reared up the Devil in semblance of a black dog'.[12]

Heinrich Cornelius Agrippa, the early-sixteenth-century author of the influential

Three Books of Occult Philosophy, wrote, 'Every man hath a threefold good demon, as a proper keeper, or preserver.'[13] According to Jean Bodin, Heinrich Agrippa's own demon took the shape of a black dog:

> All his life he was the greatest wizard of his time: and, unexpectedly, after his death … a black dog, which he called sir, was seen leaving his room, which went and threw itself into the Rhône, and was never seen again.[14]

A similar, but more grisly, story was attached to Newgate prison in London:

> In the reign of King Henry the Third there happened such a famine throughout England, but especially in London, that many starved from want of food, by which means the prisoners in Newgate eat up one another alive, but commonly those that came newly in, and such as could make small resistance. Amongst many others cast in this den of misery, there was a certain scholar, brought thither upon suspicion of conjuring, and that he by charms and devilish witchcrafts had done much hurt to the king's subjects; which scholar, maugre [in spite of] his Devil's Furies, sprites and goblins, was by the famished prisoners eaten up … This being done … the poor prisoners … supposed nightly to see the scholar, in the shape of a black dog, walking up and down the prison, ready with his ravening jaws to tear out their bowels.

The dog went on to haunt both the prison and its surroundings, 'gliding up and down the streets a little before the time of execution, and in the night while the sessions [trials] continued'.[15]

In 1577 a pamphlet by Abraham Fleming described the sensational events that had recently occurred during a thunderstorm at Bungay Parish Church in Suffolk:

> This black dog, or the Devil in such a likeness … running all along down the body of the church with great swiftness, and incredible haste, among the people … passed between two persons, as they were kneeling upon their knees, and occupied in prayer as it seemed, wrung the necks of them both at one instant clean backward.[16]

It's clear that by the start of the English witch-hunts there was already a well-established belief in animal spirits, and one of the earliest English cases featured Sathan, a spirit who initially took the shape of a 'white spotted cat'.[17]

Sathan belonged to Elizabeth Frauncis, and at first he resembles a sinister version of Puss in Boots (Charles Perrault wrote the most famous version of the fairy story in the late seventeenth century). According to Elizabeth, Sathan had to be kept in a basket and fed bread and milk, but he also asked her 'what she would have … in a strange hollow voice', and when she said sheep he 'forthwith brought sheep into her pasture'.

Sathan went on to kill Elizabeth's lover when he refused to marry her, and when she discovered she was pregnant by the dead man, 'he bade her take a certain herb and drink it which she did, and destroyed the child forthwith.' Elizabeth then married and had a baby daughter, but when the little girl was six months old she died, apparently because Elizabeth had asked Sathan to kill her.

Eventually Elizabeth gave Sathan to her sister Agnes Waterhouse.

A nineteenth-century Irish cunning man. Picture by E. Fitzpatrick, from *The Illustrated London News*, 31ˢᵗ December 1859 (MoW 462).

> Then when she had received him she [Agnes] (to try what he could do) willed him to kill a hog of her own which he did, and she gave him for his labour a chicken … and a drop of her blood … Another time being offended with one Father Kersye she took her cat Sathan in her lap and put him in the wood before her door, and willed him to kill three of this Father Kersye's hogs, which he did, and returning again told her so, and she rewarded him as before, with a chicken and a drop of her blood, which chicken he ate up clean … and she could find neither bones nor feathers.

Sathan performed more malevolent magic for Agnes, including killing her husband and another man. But apparently at some point Agnes turned Sathan into a toad:

> She kept the cat a great while in wool in a pot, and at length being moved by poverty to occupy [use] the wool, she prayed in the name of the Father, and of the Son, and of the Holy Ghost that it would turn into a toad, and forthwith it was turned into a toad, and so she kept it in the pot without wool.

Agnes's eighteen-year-old daughter Jone confessed,

> When her mother was gone to Breakstede, in her absence lacking bread, she went to a girl, a neighbour's child, and desired her to give her a piece of bread and cheese, which when she denied and gave her not … she going home did as she had seen her mother do, calling Sathan, which came to her (as she said) she thought out of her

mother's shoe from under the bed, in the likeness of a great dog, demanding what she would have, wherewithal she being afeared, said she would have him to make such a girl afeared naming this girl, then asked he her what she would give him, and she said a red cock, then said he no, but thou shalt give me thy body and soul, whereby she being sore feared and desirous to be rid of him, said she would.

Jone's victim, twelve-year-old Agnes Brown, testified in court that

She was churning of butter and there came to her a thing like a black dog with a face like an ape, a short tail a chain and a silver whistle (to her thinking) about his neck, and a pair of horns on his head, and brought in his mouth the key of the milkhouse door, and then my lord she said, I was afeared, for he skipped and leaped to and fro, and sat on the top of a nettle, and then I asked him what he would have, and he said he would have butter.

By the time he menaced Agnes Brown Sathan was obviously a spirit, but in his early days he may perhaps have been a mortal cat. There's evidence that people regarded even flesh-and-blood cats as magical animals. A picture of a nineteenth-century Irish cunning man, entitled *The Fairy Doctor*, depicts him with what are clearly the three essentials of his trade – herbs, a human skull and a mean-looking cat.[18]

There's also dramatic evidence of a belief that the spirits of dead cats could offer protection against a major threat to people's food supplies – rats and mice. Large numbers of naturally mummified dead cats have been found placed in the roof spaces of houses and outbuildings, sometimes carefully posed with dead rats. This practice continued until comparatively recently. In March 2009 the Museum of Witchcraft was given a pair of these cats, which were found in a house built in the late nineteenth century.[19]

Black Dogs also continued to haunt the British countryside well after the witch-hunts. In a Cornish story of uncertain date, the Black Dog, like the fairies in John Walsh's statement, is associated with an ancient burial mound:

On St Stephen's Down near Launceston, there was a large tumulus, or ancient burial mound, and there on Midsummer Eve the people lighted a great bonfire and indulged in wrestling and general merrymaking. Long years ago it is recorded they were so engaged when into their midst dashed a huge black dog, which so scared them that they all fled. Ever afterwards when wrestling matches were attempted there the contestants always came to serious hurt and the sport was abandoned. The idea of the miners and rustics was that the spirits of the giants buried in the tumulus resented sports at their burial place and had sent an evil spirit in the shape of a black dog to put a stop to the profanity or sacrilegious sport.

(*Cornish Ghosts and Other Strange Happenings in Cornwall* by William Henry Paynter.[20])

An encounter that took place in Norfolk around the 1930s sums up the ambivalence that seems to have characterised black dogs throughout their existence.

Mr E. Ramsey was cycling late at night when he was chased by a huge dog with eyes that 'shone like coals of fire':

> I heard him, coming up behind, his paws beating the grit road. 'My God, he's coming for me.' Instead, he passed me, so close I could smell his rankness … [He] suddenly stopped … in the middle of the road, facing me … I stopped, with my cycle between me and the hedge … Just then there was the roar of a vehicle … It came through with no lights, and was careering from side to side … The vehicle came so close that I fell into the hedge with my cycle on top of me … Picking myself up, thinking the hound had come to a bad end, I was amazed to see it still standing there … To my surprise he turned, and was gone. Neither left nor right, just vanished. They do say that anyone seeing him, is the sign of death, to one's self or next of kin. All I can say is, on that night he saved my life.[21]

SHAPE-SHIFTING

Every year, on May Day, an event takes place in Padstow in Cornwall that seems to support Emma Wilby's theory about the Shamanic origins of British magic. Accompanied by a band and a vast crowd playing and singing a folksong with a mesmeric drumbeat, a man dances wildly through the streets, wearing a fearsome masked costume that transforms him into a creature that is part-human, part-horse – the Padstow Oss. Periodically he sinks to the ground and 'dies', and is then brought back to life by a shout from the crowd that resembles a horse's neigh.

The event has similarities to descriptions of witches' Sabbats, but also to rituals performed by the Native American Hopi and Zuñi peoples, involving masks that embody the spirit of a deity.[22] The Padstow Oss ceremony could be viewed simply as a drama symbolising the renewal of life after the winter; but the Oss himself could also be viewed as a kind of familiar spirit, leading the people of Padstow in a magical ritual that will bring the town prosperity for the coming year.[23]

Richard Rudgley, in his book *The Encyclopaedia of Psychoactive Substances*, notes that aconite (wolf's bane), one of the plants used in hallucinogenic ointments, produces the sensation of having fur.[24] This too suggests a survival of ancient Shamanic rituals involving the practitioner's transformation into an animal – or perhaps into a being that was part-human, part-animal and part-spirit.

The confession of the Scottish wise woman, Isobel Gowdie, includes an eerie shape-shifting spell:

> I shall go intill [into] a hare,
> With sorrow, and sych [sigh] and mickle [much] care;
> And I shall go in the Devil's name,
> Aye [always] while I come home again!
>
> I shall go intill a cat,
> With sorrow, and sych, and a black shot [sudden pain]!

The Padstow Oss.

> And I shall go in the Devil's name,
> Aye while I come home again!
>
> I shall go intill a craw [crow],
> With sorrow, and sych, and a black thraw [convulsion]!
> And I shall go in the Devil's name,
> Aye while I come home again![25]

Continental witchcraft cases sometimes include accounts of witches turning themselves into wolves.[26] A pamphlet by George Bores, entitled *A True Discourse. Declaring the damnable life and death of one Stubbe Peeter, a most wicked sorcerer, who in the likeness of a wolf committed many murders*, was published in London in 1590. Although supposedly based on records of a German witchcraft case, it's obviously heavily fictionalised, and reads like an outline for a rather Gothic werewolf film:

> Stubbe Peeter ... surfeiting in the damnable desire of magic, necromancy and sorcery ... gave both soul and body to the Devil ... who ... gave unto him a girdle which, being put around him, he was straight transformed into the likeness of a greedy,

devouring wolf, strong and mighty, with eyes great and large, which in the night sparkled like unto brands of fire, a mouth great and wide, with most sharp and cruel teeth, a huge body and mighty paws ...

Often it came to pass that as he walked abroad in the fields, if he chanced to spy a company of maidens ... in his wolfish shape he would ... run among them, and ... who he had a mind unto, her he would pursue, whether she were before or behind, and take her from the rest, for such was his swiftness of foot while he continued a wolf that he would outrun the swiftest greyhound ...

Having a proper youth to his son ... in whom he took such joy that he did commonly call him his heart's ease, yet so far his delight in murder exceeded the joy he took in his son, that thirsting after his blood, on a time he enticed him into the fields, and ... in the shape and likeness of a wolf he ... there most cruelly slew him, which done, he presently ate the brains out of his head ...

Such is the compelling drama of the werewolf myth, even in this demonised and exaggerated form, that it seems plausible that it might have its origins in ancient rituals – rituals that sought to overcome the barriers of fear between human and predator, or to gain magical power by liberating aspects of the animal nature hidden within the human psyche.[27]

PAYMENTS AND PACTS

There are also stories of animals turning into humans. In one of Aesop's Fables, *Venus and the Cat*, a cat falls in love with a young man and persuades the goddess Venus to turn her into a woman. The couple marry, and all goes well until Venus mischievously releases a mouse in front of the ex-cat, with predictable results.[28] In the Scottish folksong *The Great Silkie of Sule Skerrie*, a young woman discovers to her dismay that the father of her child is in fact a seal – 'I am a man, upon the land, and I am a silkie in the sea.'[29]

According to a story recorded by William Bottrell, a family of Cornish cunning folk obtained their magical powers when one of them, Lutey, rescued a stranded mermaid. Since young seals are often washed ashore along the Cornish coast, it seems likely that in the original version of the story she was a shape-shifting seal woman rather than the half-woman half-fish of the mermaid stereotype.

She offered Lutey three wishes in return for rescuing her, and after careful thought he replied:

I only wish for the power to do good to my neighbours – first that I may be able to break the spells of witchcraft; secondly that I may have such power over familiar spirits as to compel them to inform me of all I desire to know for the benefit of others; thirdly, that these good gifts may continue in my family for ever.

However, as he carried her down to the sea she attempted to seduce him:

He felt so charmed with the mermaid's beauty and enchanted by the music of her voice that he was inclined to plunge with her into the waves ... Then, just in the nick of time, his dog, which had followed unnoticed, barked and howled so loud, that the charmed man looked round, and, when he saw the smoke curling up from his chimney, the cows in the fields, and everything looking so beautiful on the green land, the spell of the mermaid's song was broken.

When she then refused to let go of him he was forced to threaten her with his knife:

> The sight of the bright steel (which, they say, has power against enchantments and over evil beings), made the mermaid drop from his neck and into the sea. Still looking towards him, she swam away … 'Farewell my sweet, for nine long years, then I'll come for thee my love.' …
>
> Nine years after, to the day on which Lutey bore her to the waters, he and a comrade were out fishing one clear moonlight night; though the weather was calm and the water smooth as a glass, about midnight the sea suddenly arose around their boat, and in the foam of the curling waves they saw a mermaid approaching them … 'My hour is come,' said Lutey, the moment he saw her; and, rising like one distraught, he plunged into the sea, swam with the mermaid a little way, then they both sunk, and the sea became as smooth as ever.
>
> Lutey's body was never found, and, in spite of every precaution, once in nine years, some of his descendants find a grave in the sea.[30]

This appears to be derived from the idea of the pact with the Devil. Lutey's disappearance under the waves seems like a folklore version of the ending of Christopher Marlowe's play *Doctor Faustus*, when, after pledging his soul to the Devil in return for twenty-four years of magical power, Doctor Faustus is finally dragged down to Hell.

However, the opposite may in fact be true. The idea that obtaining magical power involved giving your soul to an evil spirit or the Devil – which was so central to the witch-hunts – may have been a crude over-simplification of older legends involving a human choosing to form a relationship with an Otherworld being. Another example, of course, is Thomas of Erceldoune's decision to go with the Queen of Elfland.[31] And this choice is in turn a symbol of whether humans should seek for experience, knowledge and power beyond the boundaries of the normal world – and whether the price is to lose your hold on life or gain a true understanding of it.

Both Thomas's and Lutey's stories have similarities to one that has elements that are probably not only pre-witch-hunt but pre-Christian – the story of Owein and the Lady of the Spring. Like Thomas and Lutey, Owein was a real person – King of North Rheged in the late sixth century. He was the son of King Urien and (depending on the legend) either the sorceress Morgan Le Fay or the Celtic goddess Modron. Although the Celts of Rheged were Christians, this suggests that they still worshipped a Celtic goddess alongside Jesus Christ. The earliest surviving version of Owein's story was written by the great French poet Chrétien de Troyes in the late twelfth century, but he drew heavily on earlier Celtic legends.[32]

At King Arthur's court, Owein hears stories of a magical spring:

The spring ... boils, though the water is colder than marble. It is shadowed by the fairest tree that ever Nature formed, for its foliage is evergreen, regardless of the winter's cold, and an iron basin is hanging there by a chain long enough to reach the spring. And beside the spring thou shalt find a massive stone ... whose nature I cannot explain, never having seen its like.[33]

Owein finds the spring, and uses the basin to pour water over the stone. At once a terrible storm lays waste to the surrounding countryside. A knight appears, and challenges Owein:

Their lances are splintered and ... the fragments are cast high in the air. Then each attacks the other with his sword, and in the strife they cut the straps of the shields away, and cut the shields all to bits ... At last my lord Owein crushed the helmet of the knight ... His head was split to the very brains, so that the meshes of his bright hauberk were stained with the brains and blood, all of which caused him such intense pain that his heart almost ceased to beat. He had good reason then to flee, for he felt that he had a mortal wound.[34]

Owein pursues the knight to a nearby town, and there a young girl gives him a magic ring that makes him invisible, and so saves him from being killed by the angry townspeople. Witnessing the dead knight's funeral procession, Owein falls in love with his widow – Laudine, the Lady of the Spring.

The young girl is Laudine's attendant, and she tells Laudine that she will find her another knight to defend the spring, and brings her Owein. Laudine easily guesses that Owein is in fact the man who killed her husband.

Then my lord Owein clasped his hands, and falling upon his knees, spoke like a lover with these words: 'I will not crave your pardon, lady, but rather thank you for any treatment you may inflict on me, knowing that no act of yours could ever be distasteful to me.' 'Is that so, sir? And what if I think to kill you now?' 'My lady, if it please you, you will never hear me speak otherwise ... I surrender myself altogether to you, whom I love more than I love myself, and for whom, if you will, I am equally ready to die or live.' 'And would you dare to undertake the defence of my spring for love of me?' 'Yes, my lady, against the world.' 'Then you may know that our peace is made.'[35]

Owein thus replaces the previous knight, who was married to Laudine for seven years.[36] 'So my lord Owein is master now, and the dead man is quite forgot.' Owein, like his predecessor, must now fight a series of duels at the spring, and while his challengers can admit defeat and appeal to him for mercy, Owein has no such choice – he must win or die. It is, of course, obvious that he can't go on winning forever; and it's equally obvious – though never explicitly stated – that Laudine is an immortal Otherworld being, and that her mortal husbands are destined to be killed and replaced every seven years.

However, unexpectedly Owein is offered a way out. King Arthur and his knights come looking for him, and Arthur asks him to return to his court. Laudine give Owein permission to go, but makes him promise to return in a year's time. But inevitably, once he's back in the normal world Owein forgets his promise.

In the story of Lutey and the Mermaid, Lutey's barking dog reminds him of the normal world and saves him from being carried off by the mermaid. In Owein's story the opposite happens. Laudine sends a messenger who accuses him of betraying her. And at once Owein realises that he's made a terrible mistake. Life at King Arthur's court suddenly seems empty and meaningless. 'He rises from his place among the knights, fearing he will lose his mind if he stays longer in their midst.' He goes mad, and lives in the forest like an animal. But then he saves a lion from a fire-breathing serpent, and with the lion's help he goes through a series of initiatory adventures that eventually lead him back to the spring and reconciliation with Laudine.[37]

Chrétien de Troyes went on to write one of the great Grail stories, *Perceval*. Unfortunately he died before completing it, but various later writers attempted 'continuations'. One of them, written by Gerbert de Montreuil, includes a scene that, again, has significant magical elements. Perceval, staying at an abbey in a forest, sees a wounded knight lying in a bed in the chapel. One of the monks tells him that the knight is King Mordrain, who was injured rescuing Joseph of Arimathea from imprisonment after Joseph brought the Grail to Britain. In gratitude, Joseph showed Mordrain the Grail, but Mordrain tried to gaze into it in the hope of seeing visions. An angel with a flaming sword drove him back, and a voice told him that in punishment his wounds would never heal, and he would be unable to die until saved by a knight free of sin. King Mordrain has been lying bleeding in the chapel for 300 years.[38]

Gerbert de Montreuil wrote this in around 1230 – about the time Honorius was writing *The Sworn Book*. *The Munich Handbook* includes a scrying ritual that involves gazing into a bowl,[39] and it seems likely that this account of King Mordrain gazing into the Grail is a reference to the way magicians like Honorius were trying to fuse magic and Christian mysticism. Gerbert appears to be condemning the attempt, but this may be too simple an interpretation, in view of Owein's acceptance of injury and death as a fair price for his relationship with Laudine. Maybe what King Mordrain glimpsed in the Grail before the angel drove him back was also worth the price.

It seems that, like the werewolf legend, the belief that magical practitioners gave their souls or their blood (or both) to spirits may be an echo of myths and rituals that wrestled with questions about our relationship with the forces that create and destroy us – and, in contrast to the witch-hunters' concept of the Satanic pact, found no easy answers.

In payment for his audacity, the Grail claimed King Mordrain's blood for 300 years, which makes the demands for blood by familiar spirits seem restrained. Of course, in the Middle Ages respectable physicians like John of Gaddesden and Guy de Chauliac advised patients to perform healing spells using their own blood. As a symbol of life, the blood represented their commitment to their own healing. It demonstrated commitment of a slightly different kind in a spell recorded in the early twentieth century:

> When you greatly wish to summon a person you must cut out a heart of red flannel, and thoroughly soak it with your blood. Stick a needle through it. At the stroke of midnight you must throw it into the fire saying:
>
> > 'It is not this heart I wish to burn
> > But the heart of [name] I wish to turn.
> > May he/she neither eat nor drink nor sleep
> > Until with me he/she come to speak.'[40]

Using blood in this way empowered the person working the spell. Rather than drawing power out of them, it enabled them to draw on their inner power to achieve magical results. Similarly, giving blood to a familiar wasn't a blood sacrifice to appease a threatening and demanding spirit. On the contrary, it gave the practitioner access to the spirit's powers. It established a relationship – a kinship – between human and spirit.[41]

This creation of a magical link between practitioner and familiar is evocatively described in Alizon's account of her first meeting with the Black Dog. In spite of his connection with Edmund's vengeful demon, and other threatening hellhounds such as the Black Dogs of Newgate and Bungay, he doesn't even break her skin as he draws out of her whatever mysterious essence it is that he takes. And he is then bound to help and defend her.

Whatever dark forces he represents, what he draws from Alizon gives *her* power over *him*. And whatever mysterious and awesome power he possesses as a spirit, within Alizon he finds a power that can merge with his own. He calls up from the innermost depths of her being a power that makes her his kin.

CHAPTER SIXTEEN

Lancaster Prison

Alizon's account of the Black Dog may well have been the final statement Roger Nowell took on 30 March. It would have been a successful, although unnerving, conclusion to what had been an extremely busy day. Roger had interviewed Abraham, organised the arrests, overseen the searches for witch marks, and then interrogated the four prisoners.[1] He'd kept the pressure on his suspects ruthlessly and skilfully. It must have taken formidable resolve and focus as well as unscrupulous ingenuity. At the end of the day he must have felt very satisfied with his progress – a witch mark found on Elizabeth Sothernes; damning evidence against Anne Whittle from Alizon; probably some statements from Elizabeth that could be used against her, Anne Whittle and Anne Redferne; a statement from Alizon that could be used against Elizabeth; and a statement from James that had helped Roger to provoke Alizon into a confession.

There was one important task, however, that it's unlikely Roger had time to do on that day – make the journey to Colne to interview the ailing John Law. That probably occurred on 31 March or 1 April, before the next round of major interrogations on 2 April.

In *The Wonderful Discovery* Thomas Potts represents John Law's evidence as testimony given in person in court. But Roger was legally obliged to take a written statement from John. And of course since John was apparently still suffering from the effects of Alizon's witchcraft he might be too ill to appear in court, or even dead – and then any written statement Roger had taken from him would be essential evidence.[2] Thomas Potts was a lazy thinker under a great deal of pressure to finish the pamphlet as quickly as possible, so he probably based the version he gives us of John's evidence on the written statement, adding a few extra details of what happened in the courtroom from his notes or recollections. Certainly his version must contain everything of importance that was in the original statement, or he would have given us that statement as well.

But two very important pieces of evidence are missing from John's statement that are included in Abraham's. Abraham claimed that his father was 'tormented' not only by Alizon but also by an 'old woman' – an obvious attempt to incriminate Elizabeth Sothernes. However, John's statement puts the blame solely on Alizon. And Abraham describes a crucial incident that John doesn't mention at all:

> This examinate [Abraham] made search after the said Alizon, and having found her, brought her to his said father yesterday being the nine and twentieth of this instant March: whose said father in the hearing of this examinate and divers others did charge the said Alizon to have bewitched him, which the said Alizon confessing did ask this examinate's said father forgiveness upon her knees for the same; whereupon this examinate's father accordingly did forgive her.[3]

It hardly seems likely that John would have forgotten to mention such a dramatic event that had happened only a couple of days earlier. Needless to say there are no statements from the 'divers others' who were apparently also present. And, suspiciously, once again Alizon is portrayed on her knees begging forgiveness – the humble Alizon of the faked section added to James's statement, not the coolly vengeful Alizon of her own statement.

After adding the section lifted from *A True and Just Record* to James's statement, Roger must then have persuaded Abraham to add a similar account to *his* statement. And we can tell that Abraham was fully aware of and involved in this falsification of evidence because of the little detail about his father forgiving Alizon – an attempt to show his father in as good a light as possible that echoes his earlier (also false) claim that his father gave Alizon the pins.

Of course Abraham had convinced himself that Alizon was guilty and that destroying her was the only way to save his father. Three days later James would betray the Redfernes far more cold-bloodedly.

However, John Law's statement also contains something missing from Abraham's. John had been unnerved when Alizon appeared in the alehouse – understandably, in view of how angry she had been just a few minutes earlier. But he now told Roger Nowell that he also saw the Black Dog there:

> As he lay there in great pain, not able to stir either hand or foot; he saw a great Black Dog stand by him, with very fearful fiery eyes, great teeth, and a terrible countenance, looking him in the face; whereat he was very sore afraid: and immediately after came in the said Alizon Device, who stayed not long there, but looked on him, and went away.[4]

Strangely, he failed to mention the dog to his son Abraham.[5]

It is, however, a very vivid and compelling description. And it fits in with the tone of the rest of John's statement, which gives the impression of a normally capable man suddenly left confused and frightened by a catastrophic misfortune. But he couldn't possibly have known when he first became ill that Alizon would confess that her familiar spirit took the form of a Black Dog.

John's claim to have seen the Black Dog just before Alizon came into the ale house is extremely unlikely to be true. It's possible that he invented the story as a

Cat spirits – they may look harmless but they want your soul. From the twelfth-century font in St Stephen-in-Brannel church in Cornwall.

VIVIENNE SHANLEY

result of prompting by Roger. But it's also possible that he really did have a dream or hallucination of the Black Dog at some point. Certainly the vividness of the description suggests it.

In fact if Abraham had gone back to his father on the night of 30 March and told him that Alizon had confessed to sending the Black Dog to attack him, that could well have caused John to have a dream about the dog that night. And when Roger interviewed him – probably the next day – John would of course have mentioned the dream to Roger. Either John or Roger could simply have changed what was actually a dream from the night before to a vision on the day of the argument.

Neither of them would have seen that as the kind of falsification of evidence that it looks to us now. Because if both of them were convinced that Alizon had a familiar spirit in the form of a Black Dog, then they would also have believed that a dream or hallucination of the dog was a genuine attack by the spirit.

Probably neither Alizon nor any of the other members of her family had any idea how the evidence was stacking up against her. On 2 April Elizabeth Sothernes was

A dead cat posed with a rat – protection magic against rats and mice (MoW 1494).

taken from Read to Fence, a village in Pendle Forest.[6] Anne Whittle and Anne Redferne were almost certainly already being held there. Elizabeth was questioned, no doubt in their presence, and probably simply confirmed a statement Roger had already drawn up after interrogating her on 30 March.[7] She incriminated Anne Whittle and Anne Redferne, still convinced that by doing so she would save both herself and Alizon. Then when Anne Whittle confessed but Anne Redferne did not, Roger went back to Read and persuaded James to incriminate the Redfernes – again, convincing him that it would save Alizon.

But then, probably on 3 April, Roger sent not only Anne Whittle and Anne Redferne, but also Alizon and Elizabeth, to Lancaster prison.

As both Anne Whittle and Elizabeth Sothernes were around eighty, no doubt they were transported in a cart, bound – or even chained – to prevent escape. The distance from Pendle Forest to Lancaster is about fifty kilometres, and it would have been a slow and miserable journey. It would probably have taken two days, with an overnight stop somewhere, but of course transporting prisoners to Lancaster was something Roger Nowell had organised many times before.[8] On this occasion, though, considering Alizon's hatred for Anne Whittle, and the role she and her grandmother had played in Anne Whittle's and Anne Redferne's arrest, the atmosphere between the prisoners must have been unusually tense.

However, their situation was not completely hopeless. How much they knew about the charges and evidence against them would have depended on how much Roger had decided to tell them. But they would have known that both Margaret Pearson and Jennet Preston had recently been charged with witchcraft and been cleared. And they would have known that only a very small proportion of suspects sent for trial for capital crimes were actually executed.

In fact on average out of every five people sent for trial for witchcraft only one was hanged.[9] However, although sometimes this was because judges or juries were sceptical about witchcraft, in most cases it was simply because of a lack of evidence. Many cases were not even tried, but dismissed by the grand jury that assessed the evidence before the trials. And there was nothing unusual about witchcraft in this respect. Justices were supposed to send anyone accused of a serious crime for trial, regardless of how little evidence there was against them. Their guilt was something a jury should decide, not the local Justice. Some Justices took this very seriously, and sent people for trial when they knew perfectly well they wouldn't be convicted. However, on other occasions the lack of evidence was simply laziness or incompetence on the part of the Justice. And, unluckily for the Pendle suspects, Roger Nowell was neither lazy nor incompetent.[10]

However, their trials at that stage may well have seemed a long way ahead. The Assizes were not until the middle of August, and what may have been chiefly occupying the prisoners' minds was how they were going to survive the four and a half months in Lancaster jail.

Early modern prisons were run as profit-making organisations. Anything the prisoners needed – even food – had to be paid for, and jailers charged far above normal prices. Prisoners even had to pay *not* to be chained.[11] The charming Robert Nutter, when he was hoping to get Anne Whittle and Anne Redferne sent to Lancaster jail for bewitching him, gloated over the fact that they would be so hungry they would be glad to eat the lice infesting the prison.[12]

An ex-convict who was held at Newgate, Luke Hutton, wrote a ballad exposing the conditions there, which he called *The Black Dog of Newgate*, using the legendary demonic dog as a symbol of the corruption and brutality of the prison system.[13] He describes how he was thrown into a completely dark cell, with his ankles fettered. After pleading with a guard he was allowed a candle, but it was almost immediately stolen by a rat.

The guard told him:

> Until thou pay a fine here must you bide,
> With all these bolts [fetters] that do aggrieve thy heart.
> No other place may here provided be,
> Till thou content the keeper [jailer] with a fee.

The jailer himself then appeared:

> 'If thou have any coin
> To pay for ease, I will a little wink,
> And bolts' releasement with discharge I'll join
> Of this close prison to some other ward,
> Paying thy fine, or else release is hard.'

> Like as the child doth kiss the rod for fear,
> Nor yet dare whimper though it have been beat,
> So with smooth looks this dog approach I near.
> Before the Devil a candle do I set,
> Treating him fair with fairest words maybe,
> Bidding him ask, he shall have gold of me.

> 'Why then,' quoth he, 'thy speeches please me well –
> Partners,' quoth he, 'strike off his irons all.'

However, Luke's money didn't last long, and once it had run out he was thrown back into a filthy underground cell, this time crammed with forty other sick and starving prisoners:

> Grief upon grief did still oppress my mind;
> Yet had I score compartners in my woe.
> No ease but anguish my distresses find.
> Here lies a man his last life's breath doth blow,
> And ere the sorry man be fully dead,
> The rats do prey upon his face and head.

Jailers were sometimes involved in drawing up the lists of defendants due to be tried, and missed off the names of their wealthier prisoners to keep them in jail paying their fees for longer. They also sometimes extorted money from prisoners by promising to rig the jury.[14] It's therefore not entirely surprising to discover that Thomas Covel, the jailer of Lancaster prison, became a very wealthy man.[15]

However, one of the worst threats facing prisoners was jail fever – typhus – and that didn't necessarily limit itself to them. At the Summer Assizes in Oxford in 1577 it spread from the jail into the courtroom and then into the town, killing the two judges, the sheriff, and nearly 400 other people.[16]

But there is also evidence of jailers and guards helping prisoners. John Fian escaped from prison after somehow obtaining a key – which strongly suggests he had the help of a guard.[17] And Henri Boguet complained that jailers obtained pain-killing drugs for torture victims.[18] Bribery no doubt often played a part, but jailers and guards must sometimes have developed a degree of camaraderie with their captives, and perhaps even moral scruples about the way they were treated.[19]

In addition, Justices of the Peace were obliged to raise money to provide food and clothing for prisoners – although the prisoners sometimes had to remind them of this duty;[20] and in 1613 the Constable of Padiham, near Pendle, was sent to Lancaster to take some clothes to a prisoner.[21]

And cunning folk were in a better position than many prisoners. They might not have much money, but they had skills they could trade. In fourteenth-century France the imprisoned wise woman Jeanne de Brigue was employed by her jailer to identify a thief.[22] And in Canterbury in 1570 the jailer actually allowed a wise woman out of the prison to make visits to clients in the town.[23]

As Alizon and her grandmother began their journey to Lancaster, her mother and James were released. If James had felt guilty about accidentally incriminating Alizon, he must have felt even worse when he realised that his false statement against the Redfernes hadn't saved her. And quite probably Roger Nowell made sure that Marie and Thomas Redferne, and the rest of the Pendle community, got the impression that James had betrayed not only the Redfernes but also his own sister to save himself.

However, there wouldn't have been much time for James to dwell on his mistakes. Although there's no information about it in the pamphlet, it's very likely that he, his mother and his uncle, Christopher Howgate, followed the prisoners to Lancaster. Alizon and her grandmother would have needed whatever money, food, bedding and clothing the family could scrape together. And it would be good for their guards to know that they had relatives still at liberty who would be taking an interest in the prisoners' fate.

Certainly the later statements Roger took from James show that James was very angry about Lancaster prison and very hostile towards the jailer, Thomas Covel. The most likely reason is that James had gone to Lancaster and seen the conditions his sister and grandmother were being held in. He must have been horribly aware of how vulnerable they were – Elizabeth elderly and blind, and Alizon an attractive young girl. As well as promising the guards any magical help they wanted if they treated their captives well, perhaps he also hinted at the magical retaliation they would face if they didn't.

CHAPTER SEVENTEEN

The great assembly of witches

GOOD FRIDAY

A week after the prisoners were sent to Lancaster it was Good Friday – a day that had particular significance in the family's magical tradition. Their charm contains repeated references to Good Friday and the Crucifixion:

> Upon Good Friday, I will fast while I may
> Until I hear them knell
> Our Lord's own bell ...
> What is yonder that casts a light so farrandly,
> Mine own dear son that's nailed to the tree,
> He is nailed sore by the heart and hand,
> And holy harne pan,
> Well is that man
> That Friday spell can
> His child to learn;
> A cross of blue, and another of red,
> As good Lord was to the Rood.

Some of the spells in *Egyptian Secrets* also show that Good Friday was associated with magic, and particularly protection magic:

Take elm wood on a Good Friday, cut the same while calling the holiest names [i.e. the Father, the Son and the Holy Spirit]. Cut chips of this wood from one to two inches in length. Cut upon them, in the three holiest names, three crosses. Wherever such a slip is placed, all sorcery will be banished ...

During Good Friday night between the hours of eleven and twelve, you must rub every animal, cattle or horse, etc., over the back, and stroke with your right hand in the three highest names, three times, and speak; This I do unto thee for boils and tumours, wild blood, griping pains and colic, and for all ailments and injuries, and for all bad people who will plague thee. Then you must cut a cross on the tail of the cattle, and also make a little incision on both points of the ears, thus nothing serious will happen during the entire year.[1]

On Good Friday 1612 there was some kind of gathering at Malking Tower. It was almost certainly an annual event. Roger Nowell and Thomas Potts would try to represent it as a 'great assembly of witches', like the Devil-worshipping Sabbats that were now a regular feature of Scottish and Continental witchcraft cases.[2] But an account by William Bottrell, who was familiar with similar festivities in nineteenth-century Cornwall, gives a more accurate picture:

> According to ancient usage, the folks from many parts of the west country make their annual pilgrimage to some white witch of repute, for the sake of having what they call 'their protection renewed'. The spring is always chosen for this object, because it is believed that when the sun is returning the Pellar [wise woman or cunning man] has more power to protect them from bad luck than at any other season ...
>
> There used to be rare fun among the folks in going to the conjuror in the spring, when they were sure to meet, at the wise man's abode, persons of all ages and conditions, many from a great distance. Then the inhabitants of the Scilly Isles came over in crowds for the purpose of consulting the white witches of Cornwall, and that they might obtain their protection, charms, spells, and counter-spells. Many of the captains of vessels, belonging to Hayle, St. Ives, and Swansea, often visited the Pellar before they undertook a voyage, so that, with seamen and tinners, there was sure to be great variety in the company.[3]

Of course on this particular occasion the fun must have been somewhat dampened by recent events.

THE DEATH OF A SHEEP

Questioned by Roger Nowell yet again after this gathering, James apparently told him that on the evening before Good Friday he 'stole a wether [male sheep] from John Robinson of Barley, and brought it to his grandmother's house ... and there killed it.'[4] A similar statement from Jennet, however, doesn't mention the sheep being stolen.[5] It may well have been John Robinson's annual payment to the family. After all, if Roger went to him and asked if he'd given the witches a sheep for their Devil-worshipping Sabbat, John Robinson was hardly likely to say yes. And if John denied giving James the sheep, Roger would assume James had stolen it.[6]

Jennet specifically mentioned that James killed the sheep in front of her – something that obviously made a great impression on her. The evening before Good Friday was of course the date of the Last Supper – also mentioned in the charm ('Lord in his mess / With his twelve Apostles good.') Jesus and the Apostles were commemorating the Passover, when the Israelites escaped from slavery in Egypt after Jehovah punished the Egyptians with the last of a series of plagues:

The blood of a sacrificed male sheep is used to protect a house from 'the destroyer', in a scene from Exodus prefiguring the death of Christ. Plaque from a medieval enamelled cross in the British Museum.

Then the Lord spake to Moses and to Aaron in the land of Egypt, saying ... let every man take unto him a lamb ... Your lamb shall be without blemish, a male of a year old ... And ye shall ... kill it at even.

After they shall take of the blood and strike it on the two posts, and on the upper doorpost of the houses where they shall eat it ...

For I will pass through the land of Egypt the same night, and will smite all the first born in the land of Egypt, both man and beast, and I will execute judgment upon all the gods of Egypt. I am the Lord.

And the blood shall be a token for you upon the houses where ye are; so when I see the blood, I will pass over you, and the plague shall not be upon you to destruction, when I smite the land of Egypt ...

Then Moses called all the Elders of Israel, and said unto them, choose out and take you for every of your households a lamb, and kill the Passover.

And take a bunch of hyssop, and dip it in the blood that is in the basin, and strike the lintel, and the door chekes [posts] with the blood that is in the basin, and let none of you go out at the door of his house, until the morning.

For the Lord will pass by to smite the Egyptians: and when he seeth the blood upon the lintel and on the two door chekes, the Lord will pass over the door, and will not suffer the destroyer to come into your houses to plague you.[7]

This was one of the Old Testament events that prefigured Jesus's crucifixion, and it was frequently portrayed in medieval art – for example on a beautiful twelfth-century enamelled cross now in the British Museum. In a stylised but vivid scene, the dying sheep slumps against the frame of a doorway, blood pouring from his throat, while a man stands calmly over him, using the blood to paint a cross above the door.[8]

This may well be the 'cross of red' referred to in the Device charm, and I think we can reasonably assume that James too, after ritually killing John Robinson's sheep, used the blood to paint the sign of the cross over the door of Malking Tower, as protection against 'the destroyer' for the following year.

Egyptian Secrets mentions using animal blood in this way to protect against witchcraft and evil spirits:

> The civet cat, also, abounds with sorceries; for the posts of a door being touched with her blood, the arts of jugglers [i.e. wizards] and sorcerers are so invalid, that evil spirits can by no means be called up.[9]

Animal blood was also used for writing out talismans – including the Seal of God, when it was used for summoning spirits rather than to obtain a vision of God:

> For it is made with the blood either of a mole or of a turtle dove or a lapwing [hoopoe in the Latin texts] or of bat or of them all and in virgin parchment of a calf or a foal or a hind calf. And so is the Seal of God perfect.[10]

Jehan de Bar also confessed:

> For my invocations I used blood from animals such as a hoopoe and a male goat and a pigeon, and with it I wrote letters and characters.[11]

William Bottrell describes the clients who attended annual gatherings being given written charms:

> [They] were furnished with a scrap of parchment, on which was written the ABRACADABRA, or the following charm:-
>
> SATOR, AREPO, TENET, OPERA, ROTAS.
>
> These charms were enclosed in a paper, curiously folded like a valentine, sealed and suspended from the neck of the ill-wished, spell-bound, or otherwise ailing person. The last charm is regarded as an instrument of great power, because the magical words read the same backwards as forwards.[12]

Both these charms were well known in the sixteenth and seventeenth centuries. *The Lenkiewicz Manuscript* explains that the word abracadabra was written out eleven times in a column, and then letters scraped out – one from the second line, two from the third, and so on – to symbolise the removal of the person's illness. 'Many hath healed diverse diseases this way, it wears by little and little away.'[13]

Even if James was illiterate – and we shouldn't necessarily assume that, just because the court record describes him as a 'labourer' – he would still have been quite capable of copying out simple written charms like these. And it's quite likely he used the sheep's blood to do it.[14]

Using animal blood didn't necessarily involve killing the animal. *The Key of Solomon* gives instructions for taking blood from a female bat without killing her, although the experience can't have left her feeling very well.[15] Heinrich Cornelius Agrippa wrote:

> We must know that there are some properties in things only whilst they live ... Hence is this general rule ...: That whatsoever things are taken out of animals, whether they be any member, the hair, nails, or such like, they must be taken from those animals whilst they be yet living; and, if it be possible, that so they may be alive afterwards.[16]

However, John Robinson's sheep was destined to be eaten as part of the Good Friday festivities. And he was also doomed because he was a symbol of Jesus's sacrificial death. Killing him was therefore a very significant act. It's interesting that the task was given to James rather than to his uncle (Elizabeth Sothernes's son) Christopher Howgate – in spite of James being so young, and in spite of the series of terrible mistakes he'd just made.

HUMAN TEETH

Written charms weren't the only things the cunning folk described by William Bottrell gave their clients:

> Some were provided with little bags of earth, teeth, or bones taken from a grave. These

precious relics were to be worn, suspended from the neck, for the cure or prevention of fits, and other mysterious complaints supposed to be brought on by witchcraft.[17]

Shortly after Good Friday the Constable, Henry Hargreives, went to Malking Tower to re-arrest James. While he was there he conducted a search – and found human teeth:

> And [James] further sayeth, that twelve years ago, the said Anne [Whittle] at a burial at the new church in Pendle, did take three scalps [skulls] of people which had been buried, and then cast out of a grave, as she the said [Anne Whittle] told this examinate; and took eight teeth out of the said scalps, whereof she kept four to herself, and gave the other four to the said [Elizabeth Sothernes], this examinate's grandmother: which four teeth now showed to this examinate, are the four teeth that the said [Anne Whittle] gave to his said grandmother, as aforesaid; which said teeth have ever since been kept, until now found by the said Henry Hargreives and this examinate, at the west end of this examinate's grandmother's house, and there buried in the earth.[18]

Confronted with this incriminating discovery, James once again lied, incriminating Anne Whittle. But at least this was an elegant and artistic lie. It also shows that James had quite a detailed knowledge of the laws against magic, because it was not illegal to be in possession of human remains; rather, it was illegal to dig them up.[19] In fact James, perhaps now regretting incriminating the Redfernes, didn't even claim Anne Whittle dug up the skulls. He claimed that she found them after they were accidentally exposed by a gravedigger.

No doubt it was really Elizabeth Sothernes who had dug up (or maybe found) the skulls, since there's no reason why Anne Whittle would have given something as valuable as human teeth to a rival – even though, if this was twelve years earlier, it would have been before their relationship was further soured by Anne's apparent murder of Elizabeth's son-in-law. It's also, of course, out of the question that Elizabeth would have kept four teeth for twelve years without using them. And

A fragment of a human skull including a tooth. 'These precious relics were to be worn, suspended from the neck, for the cure or prevention of fits, and other mysterious complaints supposed to be brought on by witchcraft.' (*Stories and Folk-Lore of West Cornwall*, by William Bottrell.) (MoW 497)

eight teeth would have been a very poor haul from three skulls, even if the bottom jaws were missing and the people had lost some teeth while they were alive.

Obviously the four teeth were all that were left from a far greater number that Elizabeth had been giving regularly to clients. But James made the idea that she herself had received them as an unwanted gift believable – by creatively claiming that there had only ever been eight teeth, and Anne Whittle had generously given Elizabeth half of them. And the lie worked, because Roger Nowell added this to the evidence against Anne, not Elizabeth.

A CLAY IMAGE

Unfortunately Henry Hargreives also found something else at Malking Tower:

> A picture [image] of clay [was] there likewise found by them, about half a yard over in the earth, where the said teeth lay, which said picture so found, was almost withered away.[20]

The two accounts make it sound as if James and Henry were conducting the search together, but what probably happened was that Henry noticed some disturbed ground and made James dig there. The teeth had no doubt been buried (perhaps in a box or wrapped in a cloth) so that they wouldn't be found if the building was searched, but could be retrieved later. And although it was unlucky that Henry found them, who knows what other magical objects James had buried there that Henry didn't find?

The supposed clay image, however, was 'almost withered away'. Henry Hargreives and Roger Nowell may have wanted to believe it was an image, but all Henry had actually found was a small lump of clay.

James, no doubt encouraged by Roger's acceptance of his explanation about the teeth, again blamed this 'picture' on Anne Whittle. He claimed it 'was the picture of Anne, Anthony Nutter's daughter' – Alizon's friend, who she believed Anne Whittle had cursed. James seems to have been saying that the image was at Malking Tower because his grandmother had found it in an attempt to unwitch Anne. According to John Walsh's examination:

> He being demanded whether that those which do heal men or women, being hurted by witches, can find out those images under ground, wherewith they were tormented? He affirmeth they can.[21]

However, there were also other magical uses for clay. There was a thief-detection method that involved writing the suspects' names on pieces of paper and rolling them up inside balls of clay, which were then dropped into water. The first clay ball to open up would be the one containing the culprit's name.[22]

The help of spirits was sometimes invoked by writing requests or drawing symbols on clay tiles. Honorius recommended this as a way of dealing with the fearsome 'angels of the earth':

But it is best to write the request on a new roofing tile with charcoal and put it in their circle, and thus you will not hear or see them.[23]

John Dee made his version of the Seal of God out of wax, and since clay was used as an alternative to wax for making images, it could well have been used for making talismans.

Protection charms involving substances enclosed in wax are also recommended by a rather unlikely source – the witch-hunters' manual *Malleus Maleficarum*:

> A second precaution is to be observed ... by the Judge and all his assessors ... they must always carry about them some salt consecrated on Palm Sunday and some blessed herbs. For these can be enclosed together in blessed wax and worn round the neck ... and that these have a wonderful protective virtue is known not only from the testimony of witches, but from the use and practice of the Church, which exorcises and blesses such objects for this very purpose.[24]

If cunning folk made amulets by enclosing magical substances in clay, it might cast some light on the otherwise enigmatic clay wedges in the Museum of Witchcraft described in Chapter Five.

JAMES THE MAGICIAN

One of the substances that had been widely used in protection magic for centuries was the Host – the bread transformed into the body of Christ during mass or communion.

> Equally insulting to God are such things as using the sacraments ... as instruments of sorcery – as may be seen in the example of a peasant keeping the body of Christ in his beehive.
>
> (*Anecdotes Historiques* by Etienne de Bourbon[25])

James told Roger that two years earlier his grandmother had sent him to church on the day before Good Friday to obtain the communion bread:

> He [James] sayeth that upon Sheare Thursday was two years [i.e. two years ago], his grandmother Elizabeth Sothernes ... did bid him this examinate go to the church to receive the communion (the next day after being Good Friday) and then not to eat the bread the minister gave him, but to bring it and deliver it to such a thing as should meet him in his way homewards: Notwithstanding her persuasions, this examinate did eat the bread: and so in his coming homeward some forty rods off the said church, there met him a thing in the shape of a hare, who spoke unto this examinate, and asked him whether he had brought the bread that his grandmother had bidden him, or no? whereupon this examinate answered, he had not: and thereupon the said thing threatened to pull this examinate in pieces, and so this examinate thereupon marked himself to God [crossed himself], and so the said thing vanished out of this examinate's sight.[26]

However, this account makes no sense. A spirit who would be frightened off by James crossing himself would certainly not want to be given the body of Christ. The contradiction may be because the description seems to have been inspired by two different sources. One is Henri Boguet's *Discours des Sorciers*:

> Within recent memory, Antide Colas ... confessed that the Devil had commanded her to bring him the Host when it was administered to her.[27]

The other is, once again, one of the confessions in Brian Darcey's *A True and Just Record*:

> The same evening she this examinate [Elizabeth Bennet] being set a milking of a red cow with a white face, sayeth that Suckin and Lierd [another spirit] came again unto her, and sayeth that Suckin appeared at that time in the likeness of a black dog, and Lierd in the likeness of a hare, the one being on the one side of her, and the other on the other side of her within less than two yards: and sayeth that the cow she was then a milking of, snorted and ran away ... and she praying to the Father, the Son, and the Holy Ghost, sayeth that they did depart, and that she saw them not a quarter of a year after.[28]

When James was arrested after Good Friday he was at first very reluctant to talk about what had happened at Malking Tower. *The Wonderful Discovery* tells us that Roger concentrated on interrogating James's young sister Jennet – 'By his great pains taken in the examination of Jennet Device, all their practices are now made known.'[29] It was at this point that Jennet, trying to explain the significance of Good Friday in her family's magic, told Roger about their charm, and that it was to 'cure one bewitched'.

It seems that Roger then confronted James with Jennet and her evidence. And in spite of his bad experiences only a couple of weeks earlier, which should have taught him the wisdom of saying nothing, James began to defend his family's magic stubbornly and defiantly – first by reciting the charm, and then by telling Roger about his grandmother asking him to obtain the Host. And no doubt he also told Roger that she intended to use it for protection and healing magic.

Of course James must have known that Roger would – at the very least – regard that as 'insulting to God'. But in fact it seems likely that a far worse thought entered Roger's head. He remembered Henri Boguet's account of the witch asked to obtain the Host by the Devil. And faced with two conflicting accounts, one by Henri Boguet, a senior French judge, and one by James Device, a young Pendle cunning man, he believed Henri Boguet's – which is perhaps not surprising.

In Roger's mind it would have seemed obvious that the Devil or an evil spirit had prompted Elizabeth to tell James to obtain the Host. And he would then have dismissed James's claims that the Host would have been used for benevolent magic as lies or delusion.

And so, once again, Roger added something to what James had said that would twist its meaning to fit Roger's interpretation of what the family's magic involved.

No doubt inspired by James's description of the hare spitting fire at him in his false statement against the Redfernes, and Alizon's description of her familiar spirit taking the form of a black dog, Roger remembered Elizabeth Bennet's account of being menaced by two spirits, and adapted it to create a new climax to James's account. While Elizabeth Bennet drove the hare and the dog away by praying to the Trinity, James supposedly drove the hare away by crossing himself.[30] Probably James had a habit of crossing himself in times of stress, and Roger had seen him do it. Perhaps he did it when he was brought in to be interrogated, and found his young sister Jennet already there.

However, it's significant that James told Roger that he did *not*, in fact, take the Host back to Malking Tower to his grandmother. He swallowed it. Once he'd made the decision to mention the Host, there was not much point in lying about whether he actually took it to Elizabeth or not, so that element of his account is likely to be true. And there were good magical reasons why he might have disobeyed his grandmother.

According to *The Sworn Book* it was necessary for a magician to receive the Host to prepare himself for performing magic:

> After mass he that shall work shall receive the sacrament saying the nineteenth and twentieth prayer, but let him take heed that he receive not the body of Christ for an evil purpose for that were death unto him.[31]

Good Friday was the day when their clients would expect the family's magic to be at its most powerful. To Elizabeth Sothernes that meant using the most magically powerful ingredients – human teeth, the Host – in the charms she gave to her clients. But to James it meant empowering himself by receiving the body of Christ. Influenced partly by natural teenage self-centredness, but also by the ideas of magicians like Honorius, James disagreed with his grandmother over what was the most important element of magic – the practitioner's tools, or the practitioner's own inner power.

NAMING A SPIRIT

As well as telling Roger about the charm, Jennet also apparently told him that the people who gathered at Malking Tower 'came to give a name to Alizon Device's spirit or familiar'. James's statement of about the same time puts it slightly differently, however – 'for the naming of the spirit which Alizon Device had'.[32] This phrase is ambiguous – 'naming' was occasionally used to mean 'invoking'.[33]

It looks as if James may have been rescued by his nine-year-old sister at this point. Had he been about to take his defiance too far and admit that there had been an attempt to invoke Alizon's familiar spirit? And had Jennet – perhaps remembering that Edmund had been executed for invoking spirits – interrupted, exploiting the fact that James had used the ambiguous word 'naming' to make Roger think that rather than invoking the spirit they had intended to give it a name?

It seems likely that James then remembered that the law had been changed, and it was now illegal even to 'entertain' a spirit, because he added, 'But [they] did not name him, because she [Alizon] was not there.'[34]

Humans did not, of course, give spirits names. The name of a spirit was a magically powerful thing in itself, something you could use to invoke the spirit's help. You learnt it from a book, or were told it by the spirit itself. However, invoking Alizon's familiar to ask him to protect her in Lancaster prison and get her justice at her trial was something her family and their clients would quite probably have done.

There was also magic specifically designed to help people in trouble with the law:

For releasing prisoners and the like, carve on a stone of crystallite the picture of a man sitting on a chair with a rooster on his head. His legs are those of an eagle, [and he has] a torch in his hand.

(Picatrix[35])

A particular Performance by which it is caused that a Person will always obtain Right before a Court of Justice

Take the herb called suntull (skunk cabbage) gathered during the month of August, while the sun stands in the sign of the lion, wrap a little thereof in a bay leaf, add a dandelion to it, carry this talisman on your person, and you will have the best of everybody, and receive the greatest advantage of it.

(Egyptian Secrets[36])

A porpoise, is a fish well enough known … If the tongue of it be taken … and if thou wilt bear it under thy arm hole [armpit], no man shall be able to have victory against thee; thou shalt have a gentle and pleasant judge.

(The Book of Secrets of Albertus Magnus[37])

James in particular would probably have been tempted to put a curse on Roger Nowell, but there were other, more pragmatic, alternatives:

```
2  9  4
7  5  3
6  1  8
```

The figure of Saturn … If you write it on a thin piece of lead, with Saturn in a favourable position and falling, and if you suffumigate it with a spider and carry it with you, you will fear neither the king nor anyone else who wishes to harm you, and you will get whatever you wish from them.

(Liber de Angelis by Messayaac[38])

This number square – the Square of Saturn – arranges the numbers 1 to 9 so that each row, column and diagonal adds up to the same number – 15. Saturn was the planet associated with obstacles and challenges, so this square could be used as a talisman by anyone facing some kind of unavoidable danger or difficulty. Messayaac also recommends it for childbirth, written on silk and tied to the woman's right thigh.

The instruction to 'suffumigate it with a spider' – that is, to burn a spider as a kind of incense to help to empower the talisman – probably refers not to a dead spider but to the external skeleton a spider sheds in order to grow.[39] The spider's successful emergence from this exoskeleton, involving an apparently re-created spider breaking free of its dead outer self, would be a particularly appropriate symbol.

CHAPTER EIGHTEEN

Charms and amulets

OPEN HEAVEN GATES

At night in the time of Popery when folks went to bed, they believed the repetition of this following prayer was effectual to preserve them from danger, and the house too.

> Who sains [protects with the sign of the cross] the house the night,
> They that sains it ilk a [every] night
> Saint Bryde and her brat [apron],
> Saint Colme and his hat,
> Saint Michael and his spear,
> Keep this house from the wear [were (danger)?].
> From running thief,
> And burning thief;
> And from an ill rea [ray?],
> That by the gate can gae [go],
> And from an ill wight [spirit],
> That by the gate can light [arrive].
> Nine reeds [roods, i.e. crosses] about the house;
> Keep it all the night,
> What is that what I see,
> So red so bright beyond the sea?
> 'Tis he was pierced through the hands
> Through the feet, through the throat,
> Through the tongue;
> Through the liver and the lung.
> Well is them that well may,
> Fast on Good Friday.
> (*Satan's Invisible World Discovered* by George Sinclair[1])

This charm, recorded in Scotland in the late seventeenth century, resembles parts of the Friday Spell (and they probably share a common source):

> Upon Good Friday, I will fast while I may
> Until I hear them knell
> Our Lord's own bell,
> Lord in his mess
> With his twelve Apostles good,
> What hath he in his hand
> Ligh in leath wand:
> What hath he in his other hand?
> Heaven's door key,
> Open, open Heaven door keys,
> Steck, steck hell door.
> Let Crissom child
> Go to it Mother mild,
> What is yonder that casts a light so farrandly,
> Mine own dear Son that's nailed to the Tree,
> He is nailed sore by the heart and hand,
> And holy harne pan,
> Well is that man
> That Friday spell can,
> His child to learn;
> A cross of blue, and another of red,
> As good Lord was to the Rood.
> Gabriel laid him down to sleep
> Upon the ground of holy weep:
> Good Lord came walking by,
> Sleep'st thou, wak'st thou Gabriel,
> No Lord I am sted with stick and stake,
> That I can neither sleep nor wake:
> Rise up Gabriel and go with me,
> The stick nor the stake shall never deere thee.
> Sweet Jesus our Lord, Amen.

Another charm incorporated into the Friday Spell was the White Pater Noster – which is invoked in a fourteenth-century house-protection charm in Geoffrey Chaucer's *The Canterbury Tales*:

> Therewith the night-spell said he anon-rights
> On four halves of the house about,
> And on the threshold of the door without:
> 'Jhesu Christ and Saint Benedight,
> Bless this house from every wicked wight,
> For night very, the White Pater Noster!
> Where wentest thou, Saint Peter's sister?'[2]

In his book *The Lancashire Witch-Craze*, Jonathan Lumby quotes an early-seventeenth-century version of the White Pater Noster itself:

> White Pater Noster, Saint Peter's brother,
> What hast in the one hand? White book leaves.
> What hast in the other hand? Heaven gate keys.
> Open heaven gates, and stek hell gates:
> And let every Crissom child creep to its own mother.
> White Pater Noster, Amen.

It was included in a book by a Lancashire minister John White, who condemned it as an example of 'the pitiful ignorance and confusion whereinto the Church of Rome plungeth her children'.[3] Perhaps fortunately for his peace of mind, his prejudice against Roman Catholicism blinded him to the fact that such charms were part of a heresy far older than the Church of Rome.

In *Demonology*, King James I wrote:

> But what I pray you shall be said to such as maintains this art [magic] to be lawful … [arguing] that Moses being brought up (as it is expressly said in the Scriptures) *in all the sciences of the Egyptians*; whereof no doubt, this was one of the principals … Affirming Moses to be taught *in all the sciences of the Egyptians*, should conclude that he was taught in magic, I see no necessity. For we must understand that the spirit of God there, speaking of sciences, understands them that are lawful: for except they be lawful, they are but *abusivè* called sciences, and are but ignorances indeed.[4]

This demonstrates how widely accepted it was that magic had its roots in Ancient Egypt. The White Pater Noster, with its line 'Open heaven gates, and stek [fasten] hell gates', promises access to heaven and avoidance of hell, which is also the aim of the charms in the Egyptian *Book of the Dead*.[5] And in fact the whole concept of the religious narrative charm can be traced back to *The Book of the Dead* – although no doubt it's even older than that.

The last section of the Friday Spell is a classic example of a charm where Jesus is described as performing an act of healing. Like the first part of the spell, it may originally have been a fever charm, as the phrase 'I can neither sleep nor wake' suggests.[6] But it also resembles a widespread charm for toothache:[7]

> As our Lord and Saviour Jesus Christ was walking in the garden of Gethsemane, He saw Peter weeping. He called unto him, and said, Peter, why weepest thou? Peter answered and said, Lord, I am grievously tormented with pain, the pain of my tooth. Our Lord answered and said, If thou wilt believe in Me, and My words abide with thee, thou shalt never feel any more pain in thy tooth. Peter said, Lord, I believe, help Thou my unbelief.[8]

There are charms in *The Book of the Dead* where the Egyptian god Ra is involved in healing the god Horus that are strikingly similar:

> It so happened that Ra said to Horus, 'Let me see your eye since this has happened

to it.' He looked at it and said: 'Look at that black stroke with your hand covering up the sound eye which is there.' Horus looked at that stroke and said: 'Behold, I am seeing it as altogether white.' And that is how the oryx came into being. And Ra said: 'Look again at yonder black pig.' And Horus looked at this black pig, and Horus cried out because of the condition of his injured eye, saying: 'Behold, my eye is like that first wound which Seth [Horus's wicked uncle] inflicted on my eye,' and Horus fainted before him. Then Ra said: 'Put him on his bed until he is well.'

I know the mystery of Nekhen; it is the hands of Horus of his mother's making which were thrown into the water when she said: 'You shall be the two severed portions of Horus after you have been found.' And Ra said, 'This son of Isis is injured by reason of what his own mother has done to him; let us fetch Sobk [the crocodile god] from the back of the waters, so that he may fish them out and that his mother Isis may cause them to grow again in their proper place.' And Sobk from the back of the waters said: 'I have fished and I have sought; they slipped from my hand on the bank of the waters, but in the end I fished them up with a fish-trap.'[9]

Of course some of the mythological aspects of these charms seem a little strange to modern readers; but the weirdest charm of all is not from Ancient Egypt but from Anglo-Saxon England:

In came a spider creature he had his mantle in his hand, said that you were his steed laid his thong on your neck, and they began to travel out of the land as soon as they came away from the land, then their limbs began to cool then in came [?]'s sister then she finished and swore oaths that this should never ail the sick nor whoever might understand this charm nor whoever might intone this charm. Amen, let it be.

(*The Lacnunga Manuscript*[10])

The concept that lay at the heart of Egyptian magic remained central even to the magic of the Pendle cunning folk. This was the belief that the spiritual power of the gods was continually active in the Universe – that a divine creative force permeated and connected everything. Through it the gods maintained the Universe's existence, and through it they gave the gifts of life, health and success to humankind.[11]

At the start of his *Three Books of Occult Philosophy*, Heinrich Cornelius Agrippa writes:

> The very original, and chief worker of all doth by angels, the heavens, stars, elements, animals, plants, metals, and stones convey from himself the virtues of his omnipotency upon us.[12]

Further on he adds, 'All virtues, therefore, are infused by God, through the Soul of the World' – later identifying the Soul of the World with the Holy Spirit.[13]

Magical techniques such as the use of narrative charms enabled humans to tap into this force, by reinforcing the link between the divine essence within humankind and the gods' divine natures. Sacred names fulfilled a similar purpose. They began as statements of a god's attributes:

> I know thee, and I know thy name ... 'Lady of victory, whose hand goeth after the Fiends, who burneth with flames of fire when she cometh forth, creator of the mysteries of the earth,' is thy name.
>
> (*The Book of the Dead*[14])

The fact that later magicians and cunning folk often didn't know the meanings of the names they used didn't deprive the words of their power to create a connection between the practitioner and the divine.

This use of narrative charms and sacred names is similar to the Buddhist practice of using visualisation to achieve identification with a deity. Visualising a deity who symbolises the enlightened state liberates the practitioner's own potential for enlightenment. This not only affects the person's long-term spiritual prospects, but also their more immediate health and well-being. Visualising the deity Tara, for example, and reciting her mantra 'Om Tare Tuttare Ture Soha', gives the power to overcome difficulties. Tare, Tuttare and Ture are sacred names meaning 'She who liberates', 'She who eliminates all fears' and 'She who grants all success'.[15] Similarly, a magical practitioner using a narrative charm was visualising a deity who symbolised divine healing power, which enabled the practitioner to access that power.

The similarity between the Devices' other charm – 'Crucifixus hoc signum vitam eternam. Amen' – and a Buddhist mantra is no coincidence. Short prayers were used to induce a meditative state in the Christian mystical tradition.[16] And the meaning of this charm – 'The crucifix – this is proof of eternal life' – demonstrates that the central principle of Christianity – the contact between the human and the divine in the person of Jesus Christ – harmonised perfectly with the central principle of magic, no matter what the religious establishment claimed.

THE SATOR SQUARE

Even the most widespread and pragmatic forms of magic were underpinned by an element of mysticism. Nothing illustrates this better than the charm mentioned by William Bottrell – SATOR AREPO TENET OPERA ROTAS. Usually written out as a square, and with similarities to the Square of Saturn, it had an impressive range of uses, as these examples from *Egyptian Secrets* demonstrate:

The Art of Extinguishing Fire without the aid of Water

Inscribe the following letters upon each side of a plate, and throw it into the fire, and forthwith the fire will be extinguished:

```
S  A  T  O  R
A  R  E  P  O
T  E  N  E  T
O  P  E  R  A
R  O  T  A  S
```

An Excellent way to Prove whether a Person is a Witch or not

First. Try to obtain St John's roots and one ounce of herb of the same plant called moto. Write the following letters upon a scrap of paper and put to the root and herbs:

```
S A T O R + Cross of Christ mildepos
A R E P O + Cross of Christ mesepos
T E N E T + Cross of Christ Habenepos
O P E R A
R O T A S
```

This must be sewed up in a piece of leather, and if you wish to see the witch, only carry the paper with you, but it must be taken in the hour when the first quarter of the moon occurs. You will then perceive that no witch can remain in the same room with you.

An Amulet for the Colic

```
S + a + t + o + r, A + r + e + p + o +
T + e + n + e + t, O + p + e + r + a +
R + o + t + a + s
```

When a Woman cannot Bear Easy

Inscribe upon a wooden plate the above amulet, then wash it off with wine, and give it to the woman to drink.[17]

As well as reading the same backwards and forwards and up and down, the Latin words also – rather surprisingly – form a sentence that makes sense. 'Sator' means 'the sower', and is one of the sacred names of the Roman god Jupiter, representing his aspect as a creator and fertility god[18] (the earliest surviving examples of the charm are from first-century Pompeii[19]). 'Arepo' cheats slightly, as it should have two 'r's, but in the days when every document had to be written out by hand such abbreviations were common. It means 'I crawl to' – in this case in the sense of humbly approaching the god. 'Tenet' means 'holds' or 'controls'. 'Opera' is 'achievements' or 'endeavours'. 'Rotas' means 'wheels', and refers either to the idea of the Wheel of Fortune or the cycle of life – or both, since they're closely connected. The charm can therefore be translated: 'The Creator, who I approach humbly, controls all my endeavours and all the changes of fortune that befall me.'

However, the charm also contains a hidden meaning. Not only is Rotas the word Sator written backwards, it also expresses the opposite concept. Sator represents the idea of a single, unifying force controlling the Universe; Rotas the idea of a Universe in a constant state of unpredictable change. Similarly, Arepo portrays the individual as insignificant and powerless in the face of the divine; but Opera reminds us that the divine is manifested through the actions and achievements of the individuals it has created.

Tenet forms a cross-shape at the centre of the charm. Long before the cross symbolised God's participation in human suffering it symbolised creation.[20] Here it also represents the tension between the opposites represented by the other four words, and indicates that it is that creative tension that is the key to the existence of the Universe.

THE PSYCHOLOGY OF MAGIC

The philosophical and religious ideas underlying magic were not a completely separate aspect, divorced from its practical applications. They were one of the reasons magic was effective – particularly in its most important application, healing.

In a book on medicine written around the beginning of the fourteenth century, the Italian physician Pietro d'Abano analysed the use of magic in medicine.[21] From his own experiences, Pietro was convinced that magic was an effective form of treatment, and he set out to develop a theory of how it might work. Surprisingly, rather than concluding that some kind of religious miracle or intervention by spirits was involved, he came up with an explanation that was purely psychological. He noticed a similarity between the effects of magic and another phenomenon that doctors had been observing for centuries – that patients experienced a better outcome if they had confidence in the doctor treating them.

However, Pietro d'Abano didn't simply conclude that claiming magical powers helped doctors to inspire confidence. Instead he argued that magic generated a different kind of confidence – it created a powerful concept of health in the patient's mind, and that concept then acted on the patient's body in a way similar to a physical medicine.

What Pietro was describing was what is now known as the placebo effect – when people who think they've been given a drug experience its beneficial effects (and even its unpleasant side-effects) when in fact they haven't been given it at all. In general, today, the placebo effect is dismissed merely as something that complicates drug trials. However, to some scientists it's important evidence that a person's mental state can have an effect on their body's biochemistry. According to Fabrizio Benedetti of the University of Turin, 'The relationship between expectation and therapeutic outcome is a wonderful model to understand mind-body interaction.'[22]

The placebo effect observed in modern drug trials depends on patients convincing themselves that something has happened when it hasn't – that they've taken a drug when they haven't. Magic, however, generated its placebo effect because of the philosophy behind it. The concept of health that it implanted in the mind of the patient was based on the belief that the forces that maintained the existence of the Universe also maintained human life and health. Behind everything that existed there was a creative power whose inherent tendency was to promote health and well-being. Magic was simply a way of restoring contact between the individual patient and that power – of enabling that power to fulfil its natural tendencies in that particular case.

However, although this philosophy can be expressed in intellectual terms, Pietro d'Abano placed particular emphasis on the role of the imagination in magic. In magic the appeal to the imagination is crucial, so that narrative charms, talismans, words of power and magic squares are far more important than any philosophical argument. This is probably because, as with spirit encounters, the power of the subconscious is involved. The knowledge that the Sator Square had a profound philosophical significance was essential to its hold on the imagination; but the wise woman or cunning man didn't have to explain its significance in detail.[23]

If implanting a concept of health in a person's mind can affect their biochemistry, alleviating symptoms and perhaps even curing some illnesses, then it's clear that implanting a concept of success could affect a person's mental attitude and enable them to handle difficult situations more effectively.

Professor Richard Wiseman, a psychologist at the University of Hertfordshire, has demonstrated that some people are 'luckier' than others – but the repeated success they enjoy in life is a result of their attitude, not of chance. One of the crucial factors he identifies is that 'lucky' people *expect* to be successful. His research also shows that good fortune often depends on getting other people to help you – and self-belief is obviously important if you're going to persuade someone that you deserve their help.[24]

Arguably the less control you have over your circumstances the more important your mental attitude becomes. Throughout history, soldiers have carried charms and amulets into battle. Reginald Scot's *The Discovery of Witchcraft* includes the popular Pope Leo's Amulet, supposedly given to the Pope by an angel, and used by the Emperor Charlemagne:

+ Jesus + Christus + Messias + Soter + Emmanuel + Sabbaoth + Adonai + Unigenitus + Majestas + Paracletus + Salvator noster + Agiros iskiros + Agios + Adanatos + Gasper + Melchior + & Balthasar + Matthaeus + Marcus + Lucas + Johannes[25]

The Museum of Witchcraft's collection of mid-twentieth-century charms includes one that was clearly originally a battlefield charm:

... Render their weapons to become as soft as the drops of blood shed by our saviour upon Mount Olives ... Jesus Christ ... leave me not that I may not die here.[26]

One of the most moving displays in the Museum is a collection of good- luck charms used by soldiers in the First World War. Many were made in the trenches by the soldiers themselves, using bullets, shell-cases or metal from munitions boxes. We should not dismiss these charms as something that gave soldiers a superstitious illusion of control. Instead we should see them as something that enabled them to focus on the possibility of survival, instead of being overwhelmed by the horror of their situation.[27]

Another type of good luck charm was manufactured in England for girlfriends and relatives to give to soldiers setting out for the Front. These were tiny figures – bizarre, and almost comical – of a cupid-like child, with hands raised in the thumbs-up gesture, and a wooden head to enable the soldier to 'touch wood' for luck.[28] The charm's role as a reminder of the family and friends the soldier hoped to return to was probably just as important as any belief that it would actually protect him. However, the explanatory card that was sold with the charm contained the poignant lines

> When Romans fought
> With sword and knife,
> The sign – thumbs up –
> Meant – spare his life.

CHAPTER NINETEEN

The magic of objects

CONNECTIONS

It's likely that the Device's short Latin charm 'Crucifixus hoc signum vitam eternam'
was repeated several times – at least three times and perhaps nine – and helped to
induce a meditative state in both the practitioner and client. However, it may also
have been used with an actual crucifix, as another account suggests:

> [The wise woman Mistress Pepper] call[ed] for a bottle of holy water, and took the
> same, and sprinkled it upon a red hot spot which was upon the back of his right
> hand; and did take a silver crucifix out of her breast, and laid it upon the said spot.
> And did then say that she knew by the said spot what his disease was, and did take
> the said crucifix and put it in his mouth.

> *(Depositions from the Castle at York*[1])

This was done either to send the crucifix's healing power into the patient, or to
transfer the illness to the crucifix.[2] Agnes Sampson used a healing charm that sent
the illness into the ground:

> All kinds of ills that ever may be,
> In Christ's name, I conjure ye;
> I conjure ye, both more and less,
> With all the virtues of the mass,
> And right so, by the nails so,
> That nailed Jesus, and no more;
> And right so, by the same blood,
> That reeked over the ruthful rood;
> Forth of the flesh and of the bone,
> And in the earth and in the stone.
> I conjure thee, in God's name.[3]

Another – probably earlier – version of the Archidecline fever charm created a different kind of connection between the illness and an object. Intended to cure a horse suffering from a sprain or strain, the wand or stick wasn't used to direct magical power; instead, a slit was made in the wood, and as the slit closed up the injury would heal:

> *Item for an horse that is wrench.* For to done [make] a yard [wand/stick] go together. 'Saint Architeclyn sat on his bench, in his left hand he held a yard of a briar and with his right hand he blessed the yard. And Father and Son and soothfast [true] Holy Ghost, help this horse that is wrench.' Pater Noster and Ave and say it till it go together.[4]

A nineteenth-century Lancashire cure for whooping cough involved a related type of symbolism. A live furry caterpillar – representing the unpleasant sensation of the cough – was put in a bag that was hung around the patient's neck. As the unfortunate caterpillar wasted away and died, so the illness would be cured.[5] Similarly, a charm bag in the Museum of Witchcraft, which was hung up in a house to bring good fortune, contained three bees symbolising prosperity.[6]

The range of creatures and objects that could be used for healing, protection and good luck was remarkable. Henri Boguet gives a list of items used as protection against witchcraft that includes date stones, alum, feathers and herbs such as St John's wort and rue.[7] The Lancashire minister John White, who objected so strongly to the White Pater Noster, also complained about people wearing the herb vervain as an amulet 'against blasts' (curses). He recorded the charm that was spoken when the herb was picked:

> Hallowed be thou, vervain,
> As thou growest on the ground.
> For in the Mount of Calvary,
> There thou wast first found.
> Thou healed'st our Saviour Jesus Christ,
> And staunched'st his bleeding wound;
> In the name of the Father, Son, and Holy Ghost,
> I take thee from the ground.[8]

The Book of Secrets of Albertus Magnus was an encyclopedia-like list of plants, minerals and animals that gave their magical properties as well as their medicinal uses:

> There be seven herbs that have great virtues ... The first is the herb of the planet Saturn, which is called *daffodillus*, daffodilly. The juice of it is good against the pain of the reins [kidneys], and legs; let them that suffer pain of the bladder, eat it, the root of it being a little boiled. And if men possessed with evil spirits, or mad men, bear it in a clean napkin, they be delivered from their disease. And it suffereth not a devil in the house ...[9]

> Take the stone which is called *adamas*, in English speech a diamond ... And if it be

bounden to the left side, it is good against enemies, madness, wild beasts, venomous beasts, and cruel men, and against chiding and brawling, and against venom, and invasion of fantasies ...

Take the stone which is called *corallus*, coral, and some be red and some white. And it hath been proved that it stemmeth anon blood, putteth away the foolishness of him that beareth it, and giveth wisdom ... And it is good against tempests, and perils of floods ...[10]

Upupa, the lapwing or black plover, is a bird sufficiently known ... And if the eyes of it be borne before a man's breast, all his enemies shall be pacified. And if thou shalt have the head of it in thy purse, thou canst not be deceived by any merchant.[11]

The Museum of Witchcraft has a house-protection amulet made from an oyster shell, painted with two heart shapes joined by an arrow and the sacred name AGLA. Although the symbolism resembles love magic, it is in fact a charm for protection against fire, from the Netherlands, dating from around the end of the nineteenth century.[12]

Picatrix contains numerous talismans that combine astrological and image magic with the use of magical stones:

A picture of a mouse between two cats is carved in the hour of Venus and, in its ascendant, is carved on a piece of coral. In this picture Venus functions to repel mice from the place of the coral ...

To repel snakes, carve the picture of a snake with this symbol [a crescent moon and a small circle] on its head on a stone of lapis azure or green *dahnaj* in its [the moon's] hour and ascendant.[13]

As literacy increased, charms that were originally spoken were also sometimes written down so that they could be carried as talismans. A Norfolk vicar, Robert Forbes, who died in 1709, wore a blue silk bag on a ribbon around his neck containing a paper on which was written, in code, another medieval fever charm:

When Christ saw the cross whereon he was to be crucified the Jews asked him art thou afraid or hast thou an ague Jesus said I am not afraid nor have not an ague whosoever wears these words shall never be troubled with an ague amen amen sweet Jesus.[14]

In George Gifford's fictional account of a wise woman consulted by a man whose wife was 'haunted with a fairy', the character Samuell says, 'I cannot tell what she bade him do, but the woman is merry at this hour. I have heard, I dare not say it is so, that she weareth about her Saint John's Gospel, or some part of it.'[15]

Reginald Scot describes a talisman that was used for childbirth and also offered protection against lightning, fire and drowning. It consisted of 'the Gospel of St John, written in fine paper' enclosed inside a small tablet made of wax, balsam (an aromatic resin) and holy water, with a picture of Christ's head on one side and 'a lamb carrying of a flag' (the Passover lamb symbolising Christ) on the other.[16]

A charm bag with the three
bees it contained. Bees were a
symbol of prosperity.
(MoW 262)

FOUND OBJECTS

Objects found by chance were believed to be particularly magical. Sea beans – large seeds carried across the Atlantic by the Gulf Stream – are occasionally washed up on Cornish and Scottish beaches, and were highly valued as amulets. A beautiful pearly grey bean was worn as a pendant by children to protect them from witchcraft and the Evil Eye, and the bean was believed to turn black if any evil threatened the child. Two other kinds – one looking remarkably like a kidney, and the other similar but smaller and with a cross-shaped indentation, were both known as 'Mary's kidneys' and used to ease childbirth.[17]

William Perkins, in his book *A Discourse of the Damned Art of Witchcraft*, mentions the belief that it was lucky to find a piece of iron:

> A man finds a piece of iron, he presently conceiveth a prediction of some good luck unto himself ... These and sundry other of the like sort, are merely superstitious. For the truth is, they have no virtue in themselves to foreshow any thing that is to come ... Therefore whatsoever divination is made by them, must needs be fetched from Satanical illusion.[18]

Significantly, William Perkins regarded this as a form of divination. He was apparently completely unaware of the fact that iron was regarded as a magical substance in itself, giving protection against witchcraft and evil spirits; and of the fact that finding a piece lying in your path would therefore indicate that the forces of the universe were actively well-disposed towards you.

What this demonstrates is that people who opposed magic were often surprisingly ignorant both about magical practices and about the philosophy behind them. This helps to explain how Roger Nowell could spend many hours interrogating James and Alizon Device and never even begin to understand them.

HEALING STONES

Other amulets were, specifically, gifts from the fairies:

> Sundry witnesses have gone to death with that confession, that they have been transported with the Fairy to such a hill, which opening, they went in, and there saw a fair Queen, who … gave them a stone that had sundry virtues, which at sundry times hath been produced in judgement.
>
> (*Demonology* by King James I[19])

When the Scottish cunning man John Brugh was arrested for witchcraft, part of the evidence against him was the fact that he used healing stones, which were put

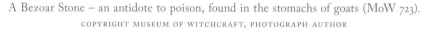

A Bezoar Stone – an antidote to poison, found in the stomachs of goats (MoW 723).

into water and the water then sprinkled over sick animals to cure them. However, when Sir James Lockart of Lee was examined by the Glasgow Synod because his family owned a healing stone, the Synod (possibly influenced by his social status) concluded that the use of the stone was acceptable because no spoken charm was involved.[20]

Often magical stones were believed to have come from, or been made by, animals:

> The country people retain a conceit that the snakes by their breathing about a hazel wand do make a stone ring of blue colour, in which there appeareth the yellow figure of a snake, and that beasts which are stung, being given to drink of the water wherein this stone hath been soaked, will therethrough recover.
>
> (*The Survey of Cornwall* by Richard Carew [21])

Carmarthenshire County Museum has a 'maen glain' (adderstone) which was found in the foundations of a house in 1836. It is a ring made of translucent greenish white glass with faint speckles.[22]

A nineteenth-century account of a Cornish adderstone, carried as protection against snakebites, describes it as a sphere of coralline limestone, resembling a ball of tangled snakes.[23] Another explanation for these stones was that they solidified from a foam spat out by hissing snakes when they fought during their courtship rituals.[24]

The Museum of Witchcraft has a fine example of a bezoar stone, a shiny brown stone-like object found in the stomach of a goat, which was believed to be an antidote to poison.[25] Another treatment for poison was the dragon stone:

> Take the stone which is called *Draconites*, from the dragon's head. And if the stone be drawn out from him alive, it is good against all poisons, and he that beareth it on his left arm, shall overcome all his enemies.
>
> (*The Book of Secrets of Albertus Magnus* [26])

However, the seventeenth-century writer Thomas Nicols sceptically suggested that the claim that the stone came from a dragon's head was just a fiction to increase the price. Also known as star stones, these objects were either small stones shaped like a five-pointed star or grey lumps of stone with a pattern of white stars – and were in fact fossils of the stems of a coral-like creature.[27] Since they date from the Jurassic period they may perhaps have been associated with dragons because they were found alongside dinosaur bones.[28]

MOLES, FROGS AND TOADS

Some animals were regarded as particularly magical, which of course was not necessarily good news for the animals involved. Jehan de Bar confessed that he believed that carrying the skin of a mole gave protection against being robbed.[29] The witchcraft suspect Cecily Arnold was 'searched by honest wives who between her kerchief and her hat found wrapped in a linen cloth swine's dung, the herb chervil, dill, red fennel and St John's wort, the right hand or forefoot of a mouldwarp [mole]'.[30] This may have been a protection charm she was using because she knew she was under suspicion, but more probably was a healing charm – the Museum of Witchcraft has a collection of moles' feet that were worn in bags as a cure for toothache or cramp.[31] And John Fian carried moles' feet in his purse, 'given to him by Satan, for this cause, that so long as he had them upon him, he should never want silver'.[32]

However, the animals that suffered the worst violence in the name of magic were frogs and toads. Toads exude a venom from their skins and, according to *News from Scotland*, Agnes Sampson confessed to collecting it:

> She took a black toad, and did hang the same up by the heels, three days, and collected and gathered the venom as it dropped and fell from it in an oyster shell.[33]

Supposedly she intended to use it to put a curse on King James. However, according to *Egyptian Secrets* it was used for healing, and its power depended (paradoxically) on the toad's 'natural aversion to man':

> That the toad may be prepared for a sympathetic remedy, disorders, such as the chills, epileptic fits, etc., and that our terror and natural hatred be more strongly imprinted in the toad, we must hang him in a chimney by the legs, and set under him a dish of yellow wax, to receive whatever may come down, or fall from his mouth; let him hang in this position, in our sight, for three or four days, at least till he is dead; not omitting to be present in sight of the animal, so that his terror and hatred for us may increase even to death.[34]

This cruelty may have increased the quantity of venom produced because of the stress caused to the toad.

The Museum of Witchcraft has a dried toad suspended from an elaborate metal holder, which was found in the chimney of a house in Devon.[35] Perhaps the venom was collected and the toad then left in the chimney as a house-protection amulet.

John Aubrey gives a remedy for oral thrush that is powerful evidence of the desperation caused by the disease:

> Take a living frog, and hold it in a cloth, that it does not go down into the child's mouth; and put the head into the child's mouth till it is dead; and then take another frog, and do the same.[36]

A cure for a cough recommended by Heinrich Cornelius Agrippa involved spitting into a frog's mouth.[37] Four hundred years later, in early-twentieth-century Cornwall, spitting into a frog's mouth was a cure for toothache.[38]

Several surviving magical rings are set with toadstones:[39]

Some say this stone is found in the head of an old toad; others say that the old toad must be laid upon a cloth that is red and it will belch it up … you may give a like credit to both these reports, for as little truth is to be found in them as may possibly be … It is reported of it that it is good against poison if it be worn so as it may touch the skin, and that if poison be present it will sweat, and that if any inflations procured by venomous creatures be touched with it, it will cure them.

(*Lapidary* by Thomas Nicols[40])

Similarly, the use of a ring set with the bone of a frog is described in detail in *The Lenkiewicz Manuscript*:

Take a frog … and put him into a pot, that is made full of holes and stop it fast and bury the pot in a cross highway in an ant hill … and let it be there nine days … and at the nine days' end go and take out the pot and thou shalt find two bones in it, take them and put them in a running water, and one of them will float against the stream … And make thee a ring and take thee of it that swum against the stream, and put it in the ring, and when you will have any woman and put it on her right hand.

And an account from the nineteenth century describes a young woman sticking pins in a live frog and shutting him in a box for a week – by which time he was dead – then keeping the remains until only a skeleton was left. Among the bones she found one shaped like a key, which she then contrived to fix to the coat of the young man she wanted to love her, saying:

> I do not want to hurt this frog
> But my true lover's heart to turn
> Wishing that he no rest may find
> Till he come to me and speak his mind.[41]

Around the same time, a number of cunning folk claimed that they had acquired their magical powers by obtaining a bone from a toad using the method described in *The Lenkiewicz Manuscript*.[42]

THE REMAINS OF THE DEAD

One of the changes to the law against witchcraft and magic introduced by King James was a clause regarding the use of human remains:

> If any person or persons ... take up any dead man, woman, or child, out of his, her, or their grave, or any other place where the dead body resteth, or the skin, bone, or any other part of any dead person, to be employed or used in any manner of witchcraft, sorcery, charm, or enchantment ... then every such offender or offenders, their aiders, abettors, and counsellors ... shall suffer pains of death as a felon or felons.[43]

James Device must have known the clause in some detail, since his claim that his grandmother received the human teeth as an unwanted gift cleared her of even being Anne Whittle's 'counsellor'. These two facts – the fact that King James felt it necessary to introduce the clause, and the fact that the young cunning man James Device knew the clause so intimately – are evidence of how important the magical use of human remains was.

The nineteenth-century illustration of the Irish cunning man mentioned in Chapter Fifteen, and the large number of skulls in the Museum of Witchcraft, suggest that in the nineteenth and early twentieth centuries having a human skull prominently on display was virtually essential for a wise woman or cunning man. The Museum also has some pieces of skull and a jaw fragment with a tooth attached, and the original caption by the Museum's founder, Cecil Williamson, defends their use robustly (if also a little picturesquely):

> ... A wooden bowl with human skull fragments used for grating as you do with a nutmeg so as to produce a sprinkling of skull powder, and a corpse candle set in a small bowl of grave dust with an unchurched dead man's tooth. Horrible – you say – fiddlesticks. The witch of gallows hill would soon demonstrate to you how you can from such things learn to acquire a moral strength – develop a state of fearlessness and thereby gain a great peace of mind. All of which can be won simply by accepting and learning to live with the living dead.[44]

According to Henri Boguet, writing 350 years earlier,

In order to cure the falling sickness, witches would have a man use the powder from the skull of a robber who had been hanged.[45]

Reginald Scot gives a similar epilepsy remedy: 'Drink in the night at a spring water out of a skull of one that hath been slain.'[46] In Dolgellau in Wales whooping cough and other illnesses were cured by drinking out of the skull of the Welsh hero Gruffydd ap Add ap Dafydd.[47] And a love spell by a wise woman in fifteenth-century Florence involved getting the man to drink a mixture of wine and water out of a skull.[48]

According to *Egyptian Secrets*, any small human bone inserted into a wound would stop it bleeding.[49] The Museum of Witchcraft has a collection of rings made from human bone, and although no record has survived of their precise use, they were probably worn as a cure for, or protection against, illness or witchcraft. In nineteenth-century Lancashire, rings made of metal from the hinges of coffins were worn to combat epilepsy, cramp and rheumatism.[50] The Museum of Witchcraft also has a remarkable stick or wand from a Dutch ritual magic collection, the upper part of which consists of a human hipbone, the ball joint of which is beautifully carved into the shape of a skull.[51]

The remains of someone who had died a premature death were believed to have particularly strong healing powers. In Paris in the early fifteenth century two midwives, Katherine and Perrette, were arrested and sentenced to the pillory after reluctantly obtaining the foetus from a miscarriage for a wealthy aristocrat suffering from leprosy.[52] Reginald Scot describes a common remedy for scrofula (an infection of the skin of the throat): 'Touch the place with the hand of one that died an untimely death.'[53] After hangings it was not unusual for people suffering from the disease to get the executioner's permission to use the dead criminal's hand as the body still hung on the gallows.[54]

Another (less accepted) use for the hand of a hanged criminal was the Hand of Glory, described in the eighteenth-century French book of magic *Secrets Merveilleux de la Magie Naturelle et Cabalistique du Petit Albert*.[55] The hand was cut off and mummified, and then used as a holder for a candle made with tallow from the corpse. 'The purpose of the Hand of Glory was to stupefy and immobilise anyone it was presented to.'[56] The same book also contains instructions for using a candle of human tallow, in a holder made from a forked branch of hazel, as a treasure-hunting device:

> If when the candle is lit in an underground place, it makes a great deal of noise, crackling and sparkling, it is a sign that there is treasure in that place; and the closer you approach the treasure the more the candle will crackle, and finally it will go out when you are very close; you must have other candles in lanterns so that you are not left without any light.

The eccentric collector Charles Wade, who turned his home Snowshill Manor in Gloucestershire into a private museum in the first half of the twentieth century, somehow acquired one of these candles, which is now in the Museum of Witchcraft.[57]

The gallows and the rope were also thought to absorb power from the prisoner's death. In the late fifteenth century a German wise woman made a potion by soaking pieces of wood from a gallows in beer – either for healing or love magic.[58] According to Heinrich Cornelius Agrippa, 'The halter wherewith a man was hanged hath certain wonderful properties.'[59] And a 'charm for the headache' given by Reginald Scot is, 'Tie a halter about your head, wherewith one has been hanged.'[60] A Devon doctor recording folk magic practices at the end of the nineteenth century wrote:

> Consumption can be cured by striking with a piece of hempen rope with which a man has been hanged, so that ropes used by suicides have a marketable value, and are sold in inch lengths.[61]

In William Shakespeare's play *Henry IV*, Falstaff compares his page to the human-shaped mandrake roots carried as good-luck charms – 'Thou whoreson mandrake, thou art fitter to be worn in my cap than to wait at my heels.'[62] According to John Gerard's *Herbal*,

> There hath been many ridiculous tales brought up of this plant ... That it is never or very seldom to be found growing naturally but under a gallows, where the matter that hath fallen from the dead body hath given it the shape of a man; and the matter of a woman, the substance of a female plant.[63]

'If when the candle is lit in an underground place, it makes a great deal of noise, crackling and sparkling, it is a sign that there is treasure in that place.' (*Secrets Merveilleux de la Magie Naturelle et Cabalistique du Petit Albert.*) This candle, supposedly made of human tallow, belonged to the collector Charles Wade. (MoW 346)

CHAPTER TWENTY

The magician of Colne

MAGICIANS AND CUNNING FOLK

The use of magical objects was so important, that James's decision not to take the Host back to his grandmother seems all the more remarkable. But although magical practitioners were working in an ancient tradition, based on certain essential core principles, it would be a mistake to think they were trapped in rigid formulas. In *Demonology*, King James I condemned both magicians and cunning folk for their 'restless minds' and 'curiosity'.[1] The evidence shows that many of them were creative, temperamental and individualistic people, quick to improvise and explore new ideas, and to exploit new sources of information and inspiration.

The Museum of Witchcraft's collection of mid-twentieth-century charms, used by expatriate St Lucian cunning folk in London, includes a beautiful charm for protection from thieves:

> Mary toiled and bore the child, three angels were her nurses. The first is named, Saint Michael, the other's name Saint Gabriel the third is called St Peter. Three thieves approach to steal the child of Mary; Mary spake, Saint Peter bind. Saint Peter said: I have bound it with iron fetters, with God's own hands that they must stand like a stick and look like a buck until they are able to count all the stars all the rain drops that fall into the ocean all grains of sand fro and to it they cannot do this they must stand like a stick must ever look like a buck till I may see them with my own eyes and with my tongue can bid them to arise and order them to go without ado thus I forbid the thieves my own my all and make the thief repent and fall. +.+.+ Give the thief three times strokes and bid him depart hence in the name of the Lord.[2]

However, although this is a classic religious narrative charm of the kind used by medieval and early modern cunning folk, it was in the repertoire of these twentieth-century London cunning folk not because they'd inherited it through some tenacious oral tradition, but because they'd taken it from the English translation of *Egyptian*

Secrets made by the influential occult publisher Lauron de Laurence in Chicago in 1914.[3]

Magic was a complex and varied art, as we can see from the differences between *The Sworn Book*, with its spirits and sacred names, and *Picatrix*, with its intricate talismans and their connections with astrology; from the way *Rosa Medicinae* included charms amongst its herbal remedies, and from the lists of the medicinal and magical properties of plants, stones and animals in *The Book of Secrets of Albertus Magnus*.

There were also different ways a person could acquire magical powers. You could be born into a family of cunning folk, like Alizon and James, and work your magic through a combination of natural ability and spells and charms handed down from generation to generation. You could be given magical power by a fairy or some other kind of spirit. You could learn specific spells and charms from a wise woman or cunning man. You could (although this seems to have been quite unusual) perform some kind of ritual, such as acquiring a toad bone. Some types of magic – in particular some love divination and counter-magic against witchcraft – seem simply to have been common knowledge. Or you could learn magic from books.

Of course there was no reason why an individual practitioner shouldn't use several different types of magic, or use different methods to acquire extra powers. John Dee may have 'sharply reproved' Edmund Hartlay for invoking spirits instead of sticking to charms, but techniques such as scrying and inducing dreams were common to both magicians and cunning folk, and often resulted in spirit encounters even if the spirits weren't specifically invoked. Honorius of Thebes might see a spirit of Mars called Samahel with a body 'red like to burning coals',[4] while Elizabeth Sothernes saw a black cat called Tibb, but the differences were superficial compared with what the experiences had in common. In the long and detailed account of the scrying experiments conducted by John Dee and Edward Kelley, one striking feature is the informal, often bantering, tone taken by the spirits – very similar to the exchanges between cunning folk and their familiars, such as Alizon's conversation with the Black Dog.

The love spell that involved throwing salt into a fire, described in Chapter Two, seems like straightforward folk magic, but had to be performed on a Friday, the day ruled by the planet Venus, linking it with the planetary spirits and astrologically significant times important in many books of magic. And a court magician like Jehan de Bar could use things like horseshoe nails and moles' skins as amulets just as cunning folk did.

One area where there was a complete overlap between the practices of magicians and cunning folk was image magic. Matteuccia di Francesco used an image to help a client gain power over her abusive partner; Jehan de Bar used an image to gain the favour of the Duke of Burgundy.

In a high-profile English case in the mid fifteenth century, the use of image magic led to a wise woman and two magicians finding themselves accused side by side of witchcraft.[5] In the summer of 1441 three clerics, Roger Bolingbroke, Thomas Southwell and John Home, were accused of plotting to use magic against the king, Henry VI. All three men were associated with Eleanor, Duchess of Gloucester, the wife of the king's uncle. Roger Bolingbroke was her personal clerk, John Home her chaplain and Thomas Southwell a local physician.

The previous October Roger and Thomas, using astrology, had predicted that the king would become seriously ill or die within two years. Roger was apparently an expert on divination, as he'd written a treatise on another kind – geomancy – for the Duchess.[6] It seems that Thomas also said a mass with incantations inserted into it to turn it into a magical ritual – a practice described in *The Sworn Book* and mentioned and condemned in the Paris *Determinatio*[7] – and it was claimed that this was intended to kill the king.

In July Roger was found guilty of practising magic by a Church court. His punishment was similar to Juliana of Lambeth's. He was made to sit on a platform at St Paul's Cross, on a painted chair he apparently used in his rituals, and with his magical tools, including wax images and images made of metal – presumably talismans like those described in *Picatrix* – on display around him. He made a public confession and statement of repentance that included admitting that magic was contrary to the Christian faith and involved having dealings with the Devil.

Unfortunately that wasn't the end of the matter. The case had complex political elements – like the case of Gilles de Rais, which had occurred only a few months earlier just across the Channel in Brittany. The Duchess, Eleanor, was arrested, and admitted that she had employed a wise woman, Margery Jourdemayne. When she was accused of using one of the images found in Roger's possession to try to kill the king, Eleanor insisted that it had in fact been intended to help her to conceive a child. Eleanor was a member of the minor aristocracy who had been an attendant of the Duke's first wife, and now she was also accused of employing Margery to help her bewitch the Duke into marrying her.

Thomas, Roger and Margery had all been using magic to help Eleanor (evidently an ambitious young woman) in her rather precarious position at court. She was almost certainly telling the truth (more or less) about the wax image, which may well have been made jointly by Roger and Margery to increase Eleanor's sexual hold over her husband. Since images were used to gain love and favour at least as often as they were used to put curses on people, there's no evidence that there was ever any real conspiracy against the king.

However, Margery Jourdemayne had been arrested for practising magic before. On that occasion, too, she had been imprisoned along with two clerics, raising the possibility that she may have been collaborating with magicians then as well. She had been released only after forswearing magic, as Roger had done. Now found guilty for a second time of heresy and witchcraft, she was burned alive – one of the few people burned for witchcraft in England.[8]

Thomas Southwell died in prison, but Roger Bolingbroke was put on trial again,

Moles' feet. The alleged magician John Fian was found to have moles' feet in his purse, 'given to him by Satan, for this cause, that so long as he had them upon him, he should never want silver'. (MoW 1038)

this time for treason, and hanged, drawn and quartered. Charges of treason against Eleanor were dropped, but she was found guilty of practising magic and sentenced to life imprisonment – although it took the comparatively comfortable form of a kind of house arrest. The other alleged conspirator, her chaplain John Home, was imprisoned but eventually pardoned.

The scandal destroyed the Duke of Gloucester's influence at court, which was probably one of the reasons behind the whole affair. However, as with the cases of Jehan de Bar and Gilles de Rais, it was also an opportunity for the authorities to make an example of some magical practitioners and send a warning to the aristocracy about their involvement with magic.

BOOKS OF MAGIC

Of course, if you wanted to perform a complex ritual involving elaborate seals and long invocations you had to work from a book. But, as literacy increased, more and more cunning folk were doing just that. By the early seventeenth century one in four people could read,[9] and cunning folk had more incentive to learn than most. Possession of a book of magic would not only enable them to increase the range of magical services they could offer, it was also an excellent way to impress their clients. It wasn't only the information inside a book of magic that was important; an aura of power surrounded the book itself. Gilles de Rais was rumoured to be writing out a book of magic using his victims' blood, 'and that, with this particular book, the said Gilles … would take all the fortresses he wanted; and that with this said book, thus written, nobody could harm him'.[10]

Owning a book of magic was an important factor in John Walsh's arrest. John had apparently not had much education – his interrogators tested his claim to be simply practising physic by asking him about the different 'humours' in plants (the prevailing medical theory of the time), 'whether he knew the natural operation of the herbs, as whether they were hot or cold and in what degree they were hot or cold, he answered he could not tell'. However, he had been in the service of a Roman Catholic priest, Sir Robert of Drayton, who had given him a 'book of circles'. John had used the book to summon his familiar spirit and, once the book had been confiscated by the local Constable, John could no longer invoke the spirit's help.[11]

Finding a successor to pass your book of magic on to was a heavy responsibility, and Robert must have had a good reason for choosing John. Perhaps John was from a family of cunning folk (although he said that he also learned his knowledge of herbs from Robert). Perhaps he had some natural magical ability – John Aubrey, in his account of the scrying crystal used by a Norfolk minister, wrote:

> To this minister, the spirits or angels would appear openly, and because the miller (who was his familiar friend) one day happened to see them, he gave him the aforesaid beryl and call.[12]

Or John might simply have been an enthusiastic pupil. It's also not stated just how literate John was, but he wouldn't have needed to read very well to use the pictures of circles in the book to remind him of what Robert had taught him.

Women, too, could acquire magical power in this way. Sixty years later, Anne Bodenham, who had been in the service (and perhaps the lover) of the magician Dr John Lambe, inherited his books of magic after he was beaten to death by a mob.[13]

The Wonderful Discovery contains an intriguing reference to a magical practitioner living in Colne, the town John Law was approaching when he met Alizon. Robert Nutter was clearly not the most popular person in Pendle, and even before his harassment of Anne Redferne some of his female relatives had asked Anne Whittle and two other wise women to use magic against him. However, Thomas Redferne persuaded Anne Whittle not to get involved.

> For which persuasion, the said Loomeshaw's wife [one of the other wise women], had liked to have killed the said Redferne, but that one Master Baldwyn (the late schoolmaster at Colne) did by his learning, stay the said Loomeshaw's wife, and therefore had a capon from Redferne.[14]

Nicholas Baldwyn, who had died in 1610,[15] seems to have been part cunning man and part magician – as many practitioners may have been. A magician like John Dee would probably not have been too pleased to be bracketed with a schoolteacher who protected people from curses and was given chickens in return, but Nicholas Baldwyn was certainly a magician in the sense that his magical powers were the result of his 'learning'.[16]

By the late sixteenth century there was a wide range of books Nicholas could have studied to acquire a knowledge of magic – particularly since, being a schoolteacher, he would have been able to read Latin. Not far away, in Manchester, John Dee had a copy of *The Sworn Book* – a book far too dangerous to be printed, but which was widely circulated in handwritten copies. Even if Nicholas couldn't afford to buy a copy, we know from the statements at Gilles de Rais's trial that magicians often borrowed books from each other. It's therefore possible that extracts, copied and recopied, gradually found their way from Manchester to Colne.

An English translation of *The Book of Secrets of Albertus Magnus* had been printed in 1550, and was so popular there were at least seven editions between 1550 and 1637.[17] Even more influential was Heinrich Cornelius Agrippa's *Three Books of Occult Philosophy* – a vast and complex study of every aspect of magic, from weasel's tails to sacred names, the Cabala to evil spirits, talismans to dreams. Taking a relentlessly philosophical tone, it condemned dealings with 'evil spirits' and 'wickednesses the foolish dotage of women is subject to fall into',[18] while recommending remedies such as 'a piece of a nail from a gibbet, wrapped up in wool, and hung about the neck' (for fevers).[19] Written in the early sixteenth century, it was controversial and attacked by writers such as Jean Bodin, but it was, nevertheless, printed, although an English translation wasn't published until 1651.[20]

In 1563, Johann Weyer, one of Heinrich Cornelius Agrippa's students, published a book entitled *Praestigiis Daemonum*, which included an appendix, *Pseudomonarchia Daemonum* (evidently an edition by Johann Weyer of an earlier work), consisting of a list of spirits, giving their names, appearance and attributes:[21]

> *Baell* … When he is conjured up, [he] appeareth with three heads; the first, like a toad; the second, like a man; the third, like a cat. He speaketh with a hoarse voice, he maketh a man go invisible …

> *Amon* … is a great and mighty marquis, and cometh abroad in the likeness of a wolf, having a serpent's tail, spitting out and breathing flames of fire; when he putteth on the shape of a man, he showeth out dog's teeth, and a great head like to a mighty raven; he is the strongest prince of all other, and understandeth of all things past and to come, he procureth favour, and reconcileth both friends and foes, and ruleth forty legions of devils …

> *Astaroth* is a great and strong duke, coming forth in the shape of a foul angel, sitting upon an infernal dragon, and carrying on his right hand a viper: he answereth truly to matters present, past, and to come, and also of all secrets. He talketh willingly of the creator of spirits, and of their fall, and how they sinned and fell: he sayeth he fell not of his own accord. He maketh a man wonderfully learned in the liberal sciences …[22]

Reginald Scot translated it into English and included it in his book *The Discovery of Witchcraft*, published in 1584. Campaigning against the witch-hunts on the grounds that all magic was ridiculous nonsense, Reginald Scot nevertheless put so many examples of spells, charms and rituals in his book it would have been a useful source for someone like Nicholas Baldwyn.

In the sixteenth century the first handwritten copies of *The Key of Solomon* began to appear. It gave detailed but concise instructions for every aspect of performing circle rituals, together with talismans for a wide range of magical purposes. Again too controversial to be printed, in spite of that it was very influential in the seventeenth and eighteenth centuries.[23] *Egyptian Secrets*, with its vast collection of herbal and magical remedies, and protection and counter-magic spells, was first printed in Germany in the early eighteenth century, but was no doubt compiled from earlier handwritten books of a kind that were probably common throughout Europe.[24]

The Lenkiewicz Manuscript is a remarkable surviving example of another type of book Nicholas Baldwyn may have owned. Rather than a copy of a well-known work of magic, it's a practitioner's personal compilation, where seals of spirits sit incongruously alongside a remedy for an embarrassing digestive problem that involves taking a mixture of saffron and turpentine. It contains a bit of everything – protection from enemies, divination, a love spell, a thief-detection method, a spirit invocation, a narrative charm. Compiled from many different sources over many years, it added up to a resource that guaranteed its owner would never be at a loss, whatever the situation and whoever needed help.

SCRYING ASSISTANTS

The call for invoking a spirit into a crystal in *The Lenkiewicz Manuscript* underlines the importance of this kind of divination. It's very likely that Nicholas Baldwyn's books also included instructions for scrying with the help of a spirit. If he couldn't get hold of a crystal, there were other things he could have used – a mirror, the blade bone of a sheep, a bowl, the blade of a sword or knife.[25] But there was one thing no magician could either buy or learn from books – a natural talent for scrying. John Dee's success in his experiments depended entirely on the help of Edward Kelley.

As John Aubrey's account mentions, it was thought that children were more likely to have this ability than adults. Jehan de Bar's scrying experiments involved a child gazing into the crystal. So too do several of the rituals described in *The Munich Handbook*.

As a schoolteacher, Nicholas of course had access to a considerable number of children he could have asked to help him. The twelfth-century writer John of Salisbury was tested for scrying ability as a boy by the priest who taught him Latin. The priest brushed one of John's fingernails with a magical oil and made

Researcher Tom (with his father Tim reading from a book of magic) demonstrates divination using a scrying mirror.

him gaze at it while he recited an invocation – not quite as bizarre as it sounds, since the size of the scrying surface isn't necessarily important.[26]

However, John – understandably – found the experience rather alarming. Since we know that Francesco Prelati and Gilles de Rais were considering scrying experiments, it's possible they too auditioned boys in this way – which could have fuelled the rumours that Gilles was kidnapping boys for Satanic rituals. By the late sixteenth century Nicholas Baldwyn would have been well aware of the risks of that kind of activity being misinterpreted.

But Nicholas had an alternative. About the time he was saving Thomas Redferne from being cursed by one of Anne Whittle's colleagues, Elizabeth Sothernes's daughter married John Device, one of Anne Whittle's clients. Not long afterwards, Elizabeth Device had two children – James and Alizon. From their statements against Anne Whittle, it seems very likely that Elizabeth Sothernes and Alizon were both gifted scryers, and James too may well have shared this family talent.

Nicholas Baldwyn would certainly have known of Elizabeth Sothernes, as well as having a connection with the Pendle cunning folk through his involvement with

Thomas Redferne. Although there's no direct evidence, it is in fact quite likely that James and Alizon scryed for Nicholas, first when they were children, but perhaps continuing the association until Nicholas's death in 1610. It would certainly have given Roger Nowell another reason to regard them as dangerous.

The Munich Handbook contains an invocation used when a child was scrying:

...Domine Ihesu Christe, fili dei vivi, qui ex voluntate Patris, cooperante Spiritu Sancto, per mortem tuam mundum vivificasti, illumina istius puer cor et mentem ... per hec sancta nomina tua: Jesus Nazarenus, Messyas, Sother, Emanuel, Fortis, Fons, Leo, Petra ...

Coniuro vos demones, per tres reges, Caspar, Balthasar, Melchior, et per tres pueros, Sydrac, Misac, Abdenago, ut omnes appareatis huic puero in hoc speculo vel ense, Abiniabyndo, Abyncola, Abracalos, Pyel, Thyel, Syel.[27]

(Lord Jesus Christ, son of the living God, who by the will of the Father, the co-operation of the Holy Spirit, by your death brought life to the world, grant illumi-nation to this boy, heart and mind ... by these your sacred names ... I command you demons, by the three kings, Caspar, Balthasar, Melchior, and by the three boys, Sydrac, Misac, Abdenago, that you all appear to this boy in this mirror or sword ...)

At the age of about ten years, no doubt James and Alizon would have found a ritual of that kind enormously impressive. It could well have inspired them to find out more about the contents of Nicholas's books. So when James told Roger that, in spite of his grandmother's request, he'd swallowed the communion bread – as *The Sworn Book* said a magician should, to prepare himself for performing magic – perhaps it was because he'd had access to the books of magic owned by Nicholas Baldwyn, the magician of Colne.

CHAPTER TWENTY-ONE

A witness unexpected

When Roger Nowell decided to hold Jennet for questioning he was, once again, basing his tactics on those used by Brian Darcey and described in *A True and Just Record*. Brian Darcey had used statements from four children (all against their own mothers) – Thomas Rabbet, about eight years old, Febey Hunt, also about eight, and Henry and John Selles, aged nine and six.[1]

Brian Darcey, in turn, was following Jean Bodin's recommendations in *De la Démonomanie des Sorciers*:

> And if it's not possible to get results by this method [promising suspects 'favour'], it's necessary to take the witches' young daughters into custody. Because it's generally found to be the case that they have been taught by their mothers and taken to assemblies: and at their tender age they are easy to persuade and reclaim with promises of immunity from prosecution, which their age and the fact that they were under the influence of their mothers ought to grant them. Then they name the people, the time and the place of the assemblies, and what happens there.[2]

The Burgundian judge Henri Boguet was also heavily influenced by Jean Bodin, and in his book *Discours des Sorciers* he describes in detail how he persuaded a twelve-year-old boy, Pierre Vuillermoz, to testify against his father. Guillaume Vuillermoz had been interrogated – perhaps tortured – for four months, but had refused to confess.

> Since this man was proving stubborn in his answers, it was decided to confront him with his son ... The son was asked if his father had taken him to the Sabbat, close to the village of Coirières: the son replied in the affirmative ... At that point the father became furious, began to shout, and flung out these words: 'Ah! my child, you have destroyed us both;' and then he beat his face against the ground, so violently that we thought he had killed himself ...
>
> A little later we asked the son, separately, to tell us if anyone had in any way made him say what he had testified in his father's presence. We remonstrated with him, even making sure that he understood that he risked being responsible for his father being

A Dragon Stone. These stones, containing fossils resembling pentacles, were thought to come from the heads of dragons. 'He that beareth it on his left arm, shall overcome all his enemies.' (*The Book of Secrets of Albertus Magnus*) (MoW 1944)

burned. In addition, he was threatened with being whipped. But he remained firm and definite without varying at any point. It was thought advantageous to confront him with his father again several days later ... The son added that when they went to the Sabbat, his father asked him to give himself to the Devil, but he would not do it.

It was very strange and also pitiable to be present at these confrontations, especially as the father was weak from prison, with his feet and hands in irons. He lamented, cried out, threw himself to the ground. I also remember that when he recovered himself, several times he said to his son, in an affectionate voice, that he could do whatever he wanted, but that he would always consider him his child. For all that, the son was not at all shaken and remained apparently indifferent, so much so that it seemed that Nature had provided him with weapons against herself, since his statements were likely to bring about, by a shameful death, the end of the man who had given him life. In fact I consider that there was in this a just and secret judgment of God, who would certainly not want a crime as detestable as witchcraft to remain hidden, without coming to light.[3]

This makes it look as if Pierre voluntarily gave evidence against his father, and that Henri Boguet and his fellow interrogators tried to dissuade him. However, several pages later, Henri Boguet reveals that fourteen-year-old Christofle of Aranthon

– herself under arrest – had confessed that she'd seen Pierre at a Sabbat.[4] Pierre had been arrested, charged with witchcraft, and imprisoned in the same jail as his father.

> The Aranthon girl admitted everything freely. But Pierre Vuillermoz lasted three days without it being possible to extract anything from him.[5]

In view of this, Pierre's unnatural indifference starts to look less like 'a just and secret judgment of God' and more like evidence that he was exhausted and traumatised. It also seems likely that his statement that his father had asked him to give himself to the Devil but he had refused began as a simple protest of innocence – that he had not and would never give himself to the Devil – which was then twisted to incriminate Guillaume.

Henri Boguet then gives another reason why Pierre was treated leniently – and the interrogators probably offered this to Pierre as a way out:

> Even though he had been to the Sabbat, that did not make him actually guilty, since he did not know where he was going at that point, and because he was taken there by his father, someone he did not dare to disobey.[6]

In spite of the confrontations with Pierre, Guillaume still refused to confess. And Pierre's evidence made no difference to his father's fate, because Guillaume died before he could be put on trial. As a result of his cooperation, Pierre was released without further punishment. So, arguably, Pierre had done the right thing – such were the terrible choices people faced when they were caught up in a witch-hunt.[7]

Bizarrely, when he writes about Pierre and Guillaume, Henri Boguet seems to have genuine sympathy for them, so that at times it's hard to remember that he was responsible for their plight. But of course as far as he was concerned he was witnessing a tragedy brought about by the Devil, who had deluded Guillaume into serving him.

Internal evidence in *The Wonderful Discovery* strongly suggests that Roger Nowell had studied Henri Boguet's book, as well as Jean Bodin's *De la Démonomanie des Sorciers* and Brian Darcey's *A True and Just Record*. It's therefore a little surprising to find Thomas Potts writing of Jennet, 'It pleased God to raise up a young maid … (a witness unexpected).'[8] Either Thomas Potts was extremely naïve or this was an unscrupulous piece of propaganda he knew perfectly well was untrue – and since he was a seventeenth-century lawyer, naivety seems unlikely.

In fact Thomas Potts admits that Roger had to take 'great pains' with Jennet to get what he wanted from her,[9] and we know that she began by emphasising her family's role as healers who cured the bewitched; and she may also have stopped James from admitting to invoking a spirit.

But Roger Nowell also had far more convincing evidence against Jennet's family than Henri Boguet had against Guillaume Vuillermoz. Henri Boguet had convinced himself that a sect of Devil-worshipping witches had managed to survive the persecutions in Burgundy witnessed by Eustache Blanchet – his book even includes quotations from a fifteenth-century account of the trials.[10] The Sabbats that Guillaume and Pierre were supposed to have attended almost certainly existed only in Henri Boguet's imagination, and Guillaume and Pierre were arrested only because other terrified and desperate suspects had incriminated them.

Jennet's family, however, *had* performed acts of magic at a gathering at Malking Tower; and, what's more, it was probably an annual event they made no attempt to keep secret. Jennet therefore had no reason whatsoever to feel guilty when she eventually admitted that it had taken place:

> Upon Good Friday last there was about twenty persons, whereof only two were men, to this examinate's remembrance, at her said grandmother's house, called Malking Tower aforesaid, about twelve of the clock: all which persons this examinate's said mother told her were witches, and that they came to give a name to Alizon Device's spirit or familiar, sister to this examinate, and now prisoner, in the Castle of Lancaster: and also this examinate sayeth, that the persons aforesaid had to their dinners, beef, bacon, and roasted mutton.[11]

It seems that as well as performing magic for their clients, the family also entertained them – although probably with food the clients themselves had provided.

Of course Jennet wouldn't have described her family and their clients as 'witches', but Roger was under no obligation to use her exact words.[12] The statement was his record of the examination he had conducted. It didn't even have to be written down until two days after the examination had taken place.[13] Roger Nowell, like George Gifford, believed that anyone involved in magic – even the clients of cunning folk – was a witch, and he wouldn't have hesitated to substitute the word 'witches' for whatever term Jennet really used.[14] And he was justified to a certain extent, since going ahead with the 'assembly', in spite of the arrests, was undoubtedly a show of strength and an act of defiance on the part of everyone involved.

Jennet claimed that she couldn't remember the names of most of the people there – unlikely, since many of them were friends or neighbours as well as clients – but she did identify six of them. Two of them were her uncle Christopher and aunt Elizabeth, who would obviously have been there and whose names she could hardly have pretended she'd forgotten. The others were Alice Nutter (another member of the important Nutter family), Jennet Hargreives, Christopher Hargreives and his wife Elizabeth.[15] Interestingly, these last three all have the same surname as the Constable, Henry Hargreives – and were never prosecuted.[16] It seems that the clients Jennet chose to name were the ones it would be most embarrassing for Roger Nowell to arrest.

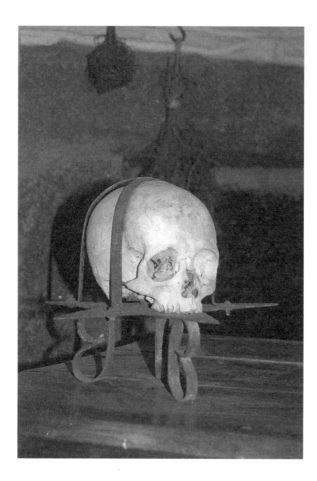

A skull on a stand incorporating a pentacle (MoW 198).

Thomas Potts doesn't tell us what happened to Jennet's aunt and uncle, and there are no statements from them in *The Wonderful Discovery*. Thomas Potts does say that some suspects who were released on bail fled before the Assizes, but it seems unthinkable that Roger would have bailed Elizabeth Sothernes's son.[17] The most likely explanation is that Christopher and Elizabeth Howgate fled before Roger could even arrest them – presumably taking any children they had with them. However, it's something they would have done only if they were certain their lives were in danger. It would have meant abandoning the rest of their family to their fate, leaving behind their smallholding and animals, and going on the run in a society where any travellers who couldn't explain where they were going and why could be summarily arrested and whipped as vagabonds.[18]

The gathering at Malking Tower had forced matters to a head. No doubt James and his mother and uncle hoped it would prove to Roger that they still had the support of a significant part of the community, and force him to back off. But instead it confirmed him in his determination to stamp out the practice of magic in Pendle once and for all. And Jennet's statement contains a probable clue to why he was willing to risk dividing the community. Although around twenty clients defiantly went to Malking Tower on Good Friday – a considerable number, under the circumstances – all but one of them were women. We know that John and Anthony Nutter were clients of the family, but it was their female relative Alice who went to Malking Tower, although she quite probably came away with charms for them as well.[19]

This would have helped Roger Nowell in his attempt to portray the gathering as a witches' Sabbat. In *Demonology*, King James wrote:

> What can be the cause that there are twenty women given to that craft [witchcraft], where there is one man? … The reason is easy, for as that sex is frailer than man is, so it is easier to be entrapped in these gross snares of the Devil.[20]

However, Roger didn't remove the Hargreiveses' names from Jennet's list, even though he didn't prosecute them, so it seems he didn't doctor her statement. The number of clients mentioned – twenty – may be Roger's substitution for some vaguer claim by Jennet, but it seems likely that Christopher Hargreives was indeed the only male client present.

The obvious conclusion is that the women of Pendle were more willing to defy Roger Nowell's authority than the men. The social system that gave Roger his power was based on the assumption that women were inferior to men, and excluded them from almost all positions of authority. But it was a simple fact that in the world of the cunning folk, men and women were equal. It's true that female magicians – like Juliana of Lambeth, with her books of magic and her philosopher's robe – were a rarity, but that was mainly because few women had the education necessary to study books that were generally in Latin. The magical power that cunning folk inherited from their parents, learned from other cunning folk, or were given by fairies or other spirits, was completely blind to gender. For every Michael Trevysard there was an Anne Jefferies; for every Edmund Hartlay there was an Elizabeth Sothernes.

So perhaps it's not surprising that when the magical power of the Pendle cunning folk was challenged by the secular power of Roger Nowell, it was the women of Pendle who sided with the cunning folk. But sadly it's also not surprising that the thought of alienating the women of Pendle didn't trouble Roger Nowell in the slightest.

Roger Nowell was, of course, not satisfied with Jennet's very limited list of names, and eventually Jennet and James both mentioned another person who had joined the gathering. According to James's statement, 'There was a woman dwelling in

Gisburne parish, who came into this examinate's said grandmother's house.' And Jennet later testified in court that 'there was a woman that came out of Craven that was amongst the witches at that feast.'[21]

This woman was Jennet Preston, from Gisburne in Craven, just over the border in Yorkshire – the woman Roger Nowell's colleague Thomas Heyber was determined to see executed, because he believed that she had killed his son-in-law's father.[22]

Jennet Preston had been tried at the Lent Assizes at York for killing a child by witchcraft, but the jury had found her not guilty.[23] The York Assizes were always held before the Lancaster Assizes, so the trial was probably around the middle of March, but *The Wonderful Discovery* tells us that Jennet was only released a few days before Good Friday.[24] There were various reasons why a person might not be released immediately. Even someone who had been acquitted had to pay various fees, in particular any money owed to the jailer.[25] And being acquitted by the jury didn't necessarily mean a person was regarded as innocent by the judge. Defendants were often only given a conditional discharge, and had to find people to stand surety for them before they could obtain their release.[26]

However, it seems a little suspicious that Jennet was released just before the Good Friday gathering. In fact it also seems suspicious that James and his mother Elizabeth were released by Roger Nowell. Technically, once Roger had decided not to send James and Elizabeth for trial along with the other prisoners, he was obliged to release them. But many Justices ignored such technicalities. Roger must have known about the Good Friday gathering, and he could easily have prevented it simply by keeping James and Elizabeth in custody for a few more days.

It's tempting to suspect that he released them because he wanted the Good Friday gathering to go ahead. And one reason he might have wanted it to go ahead was because he wanted Jennet Preston to be there. He saw a chance to oblige his colleague Thomas Heyber by providing him with some more evidence that Jennet Preston was a witch, confident in the knowledge that he could persuade James to incriminate Jennet just as he had incriminated the Redfernes.

In *The Lancashire Witch-Craze*, Jonathan Lumby draws attention to some very significant statements in *The Wonderful Discovery*, which reveal that Jennet Preston's family and friends believed that she was 'maliciously prosecuted', involving 'practice' – which Jonathan Lumby points out meant 'plot' or 'conspiracy' in the seventeenth century. *The Wonderful Discovery* adds that Jennet's family were spreading 'imputations and slander, laid upon the justice of the land to clear her'.[27]

Not only was Thomas Heyber the father-in-law of Jennet's main accuser, Thomas Lister, but (as Jonathan Lumby's research has revealed) her supposed victim, Thomas Lister's father, had actually collapsed and died during the wedding festivities when Thomas Lister married Thomas Heyber's daughter.[28] So there was not only a family connection between Thomas Heyber and the accuser; the Justice of the Peace had been present and caught up in the trauma surrounding the supposed victim's death. It's obvious that Thomas Heyber couldn't possibly have handled Jennet Preston's case with a proper degree of objectivity. But significantly, *The Wonderful Discovery* also tells us that Jennet's husband, William, turned up at the Lancaster trials of the Pendle suspects, where the prosecuting Justice was Roger Nowell, which makes it clear that William suspected Roger of also being part of the conspiracy.[29]

However, Roger's decision to send Alizon and her grandmother to Lancaster prison had clearly affected James's willingness to co-operate. All James would say was a vague admission that a woman from Gisburne had called at his grandmother's house. He avoided saying that she was present at the meal – clearly he wanted to give the impression that he hadn't actually seen her himself, and so didn't know who she was.

Although Jennet Device's testimony was given in court, she was obviously just repeating what she'd initially told Roger. The similarities between her evidence and James's again suggest that they were being interrogated together at that point. Jennet Device did let slip that Jennet Preston had joined the company for the meal, however – which obviously makes it particularly strange that she could remember that this woman came from Craven but had apparently forgotten that she'd just been tried for witchcraft.

James and Jennet were lying. They knew perfectly well who Jennet Preston was, but wouldn't admit it – partly to protect her, no doubt, but also to protect themselves. They knew that Roger was trying to make out that their Good Friday gathering was an assembly of witches, so naturally they were reluctant to admit that one of the guests had been arrested for witchcraft.

Of course in view of Roger's tendency to falsify evidence it's possible that Jennet Preston wasn't at the gathering at all. But if James's and his sister's statements were Roger's inventions, they would surely have given Jennet Preston's name. And Jonathan Lumby argues convincingly that the Devices might well have sent a message to Jennet Preston, asking her to come to Malking Tower to give them advice, since she'd just survived the ordeal of imprisonment and trial that now faced Alizon and her grandmother.[30] No doubt she was foolhardy to respond to their request, but the example of Francesco Prelati shows that people who survived accusations of witchcraft often responded with anger and defiance rather than being intimidated by their experiences.

So why did James and his sister even admit that a woman from Craven had been at Malking Tower? There's a possible clue in a statement by the Constable, Henry Hargreives:

> This examinate upon his oath sayeth, that Anne Whittle … confessed unto him, that she knoweth one Preston's wife near Gisburne, and that the said Preston's wife should have been at the said feast, upon the said Good Friday.[31]

This statement is dated 5 May, but the only time Henry and Anne were likely to have talked about Jennet Preston was when Anne was in custody around the 2 April. It's strange that this is a statement from Henry and not from Anne herself. Not only was she interrogated by Roger at Pendle, she was also interrogated by the jailer, Thomas Covel, at Lancaster prison.[32] Why did neither of them question her further about this important piece of information?

Could it be that this information wasn't from Anne Whittle at all, but from one of Henry's relatives? Did Roger Nowell and Thomas Heyber know that Jennet Preston was a friend or client of the Sothernes/Device family even before Good Friday, because Henry had told them? When Henry realised that his relatives had gone to Malking Tower on Good Friday, did he ask them if Jennet Preston had been there? Did he terrify them by telling them that Roger intended to charge everyone there with witchcraft? Did they give him other information too? Is that why he searched Malking Tower so thoroughly, and found the buried teeth and the lump of clay?

If Roger told James and Jennet Device that someone else who had been at Malking Tower had seen Jennet Preston there, that would explain their statements. And if young Jennet Device guessed that the informer was one of Henry's relatives, that would have given her another reason to name them.

Faced with James's insistence that he didn't know the name of the woman from Gisburne, Roger instructed Henry Hargreives to take James to see Jennet Preston, who was presumably back under arrest in Thomas Heyber's custody. According to the statement,

> Since the said meeting, as aforesaid, this examinate [James] hath been brought to the wife of one Preston in Gisburne parish aforesaid, by Henry Hargreives of Gold-shey to see whether she was the woman that came amongst the said witches, on the said last Good Friday ... and having had full view of her, he this examinate confesseth, that she was the self-same woman.[33]

It may seem strange that James, having lied about knowing Jennet Preston before, should admit to knowing her now. But there is an obvious explanation. Jennet Preston wouldn't have realised that James was pretending he didn't know her. When she was suddenly confronted with him, it wouldn't have occurred to her to disguise the fact that *she* knew *him*.

CHAPTER TWENTY-TWO

Therefore I have power of him

Young Jennet Device wasn't proving a very informative witness. But Roger Nowell wasn't holding her simply for what she could tell him; he was also holding her to put pressure on her mother and brother.

Guillaume Vuillermoz, after stubbornly defying his interrogators for four months, became distraught when his young son was arrested to be used as a witness against him. And there's another revealing account in the pamphlet *Witches Apprehended*, about the Mary Sutton case. Suspected by Master Enger of killing his seven-year-old son by witchcraft, Mary was beaten 'till she was scarce able to stir', bound and thrown into a millpond, stripped and searched for a witch mark, and then thrown into the millpond a second time.

> And then being taken up, she as boldly as if she had been innocent asked them if they could do any more to her … Master Enger told her it was bootless [useless] to stand obstinately upon denial … for her own son Henry had revealed all … when she heard that, her heart misgave her, she confessed all.[1]

Although unspoken, the threat is obvious: 'You killed my son, now I have yours, and unless you confess, something very bad is going to happen to him.'

Of course it's hard to believe that Master Enger, grief-stricken and violent though he was, would really have murdered Mary's son. It was also very unlikely that twelve-year-old Pierre Vuillermoz would be executed – although Christofle of Aranthon, only two years older, very nearly was. But Guillaume's anguished cry, 'Ah! my child, you have destroyed us both', makes it clear that he believed Pierre was in real danger. When it was your child, in those terrible circumstances, it must have been hard to assess the risk objectively.

What these two accounts show is that suspicions of witchcraft generated such an atmosphere of fear, anger and vengeance that any kind of cruelty and brutality seemed possible to those who found themselves defenceless suspects. And of course behind any threat to the child of a suspect lay the belief that the children of witches almost always went on to become witches themselves.

So how much danger was young Jennet really in? Pierre Vuillermoz convinced Henri Boguet that he was innocent by claiming that he didn't know his father was taking him to a Sabbat. But Jennet admitted that her mother had taught her the family's two charms; and not only had she been at the 'great assembly of witches' at Malking Tower, she actually defended the magic her family had practised there. Significantly, although Jennet is supposed to be a witness, not a suspect, Roger uses the phrase 'she confesseth' instead of just 'she sayeth' several times in her statements – betraying the fact that he regards her as a witch, just like her mother and her older brother and sister.[2]

Of course Roger could never have sent a nine-year-old girl to be tried at the Assizes. But in the early modern period it was quite common for adults in authority to use brutal physical punishments on children. When the schoolteacher John Fian fell in love with the sister of one of his pupils, he apparently persuaded the boy to help him with his love spell by promising 'to teach him without stripes' – in other words, without beating him.[3] Roger Nowell would not have needed a guilty verdict from a trial to have Jennet beaten.

Jennet also faced longer-term threats. If James and Elizabeth were sent to Lancaster, who would care for her while they were in prison awaiting trial? And if the worst happened, and all four older members of the family were executed, what would become of her then? Her aunt and uncle, Christopher and Elizabeth Howgate, had probably already fled.

What's more, Jennet wasn't the only child her mother and brother had to worry about. There was a young boy – William, half-brother to James, Alizon and Jennet. He's mentioned in later documents, but not in *The Wonderful Discovery*, so it seems that Roger Nowell didn't take any statements from him.[4] That suggests that he was significantly younger than Jennet – perhaps only about five.

Even if Jennet had relatives on her father's side they might be unwilling to care for William, who wasn't genetically related to John Device. In any case, it would be Roger Nowell's decision.[5] He might instead decide to hand Jennet and William over to another family, to be 'apprentices' like Anne Jefferies. But we can be certain that any family Roger would have chosen for them would not have been generous open-minded people like Moses Pitt and his parents.

Even in the most caring families children were at the mercy of disease and malnutrition. Few parents escaped the anguish of losing at least one child. It's likely that Elizabeth had painful memories of the death of a son or daughter – and James of the death of a younger brother or sister. And they would have been agonisingly aware of how Jennet's and William's chances of survival would plummet if they became little better than slaves in a household where the adults believed that Jennet at least had already been corrupted by the Devil.

When Henry Hargreives found the lump of clay at Malking Tower James had to make a difficult decision about how to handle the situation. Roger, of course, assumed that it was the remains of an image, and James had no hope of persuading him that he was wrong. After his success at blaming the teeth on Anne Whittle, blaming the image on her too must have seemed the obvious thing to do. And Roger did indeed use both accusations as evidence against her.

There may have been a germ of truth in James's story. Alizon had been present when Anne Whittle had apparently threatened Anne Nutter, and Anne Nutter's father, Anthony, was one of Elizabeth Sothernes's clients, so Elizabeth may well have performed some kind of counter-magic to try to save Anne Nutter from Anne Whittle's curse. However, the idea that Elizabeth had somehow located and retrieved the image Anne Whittle had used, and had then reburied it at Malking Tower, was not exactly convincing.

Also, Roger may well have expected to find an image at Malking Tower. Malking Tower was where Alizon lived, and Alizon had used magic to cripple John Law. Although it was the Black Dog who had lamed John immediately after the argument, John and Abraham believed that Alizon had then worked further magic to prevent John from recovering, and she might well have used an image to do it.

Roger's first thought, when Henry Hargreives told him about the lump of clay, must have been that it was an image used by Alizon against John Law. James must have been a very skilful liar if he had successfully distracted Roger from the idea, even temporarily. But it's also possible that Roger cynically decided to use James's statement against Anne even though he didn't believe it.

And because James had confirmed Roger's interpretation that the lump of clay was an image he was once again caught in a trap. If Roger now rejected James's claim that Anne Whittle had made it, and instead suggested that Alizon was responsible, James had only one way out. He would have to give Roger another perpetrator – one he would want to believe in even more than Alizon.

James's earlier attempts to protect Alizon had ended in disaster. Haunted by his past mistakes, but probably with no idea that she had confessed, he would have been desperate to believe that she could still be acquitted, and desperate to prevent anything else being added to the evidence against her.

And now he also had to try to protect Jennet and William. Roger's power over their fate was another bitter reminder of James's helplessness. And the more helpless James felt, the more inevitable it became that he would take the only opportunity left to him to influence what was going to happen, and to turn Roger's attention away from Alizon and Jennet, and *their* involvement in magic, and instead on to someone else – that he would confess to making the image himself, and using it to kill Anne Towneley.

Roger added James's confession to the end of the description of James refusing to give the Host to the hare spirit:

> In his coming homeward some forty rods off the said church, there met him a thing in the shape of a hare, who spoke unto this examinate, and asked him whether he had brought the bread that his grandmother had bidden him, or no? whereupon this examinate answered, he had not: and thereupon the said thing threatened to pull this examinate in pieces, and so this examinate thereupon marked himself to God, and so the said thing vanished out of this examinate's sight. And within some four days after that, there appeared in this examinate's sight, hard by the new church in Pendle, a thing like unto a brown dog, who asked this examinate to give him his soul, and he should be revenged of any whom he would: whereunto this examinate answered, that his soul was not his to give, but was his Saviour Jesus Christ's, but as much as was in him this examinate to give, he was contented he should have it.
>
> And within two or three days after, this examinate went to the Carre Hall, and upon some speeches betwixt Mistress Towneley and this examinate; she charging this

examinate and his said mother, to have stolen some turfs of hers, bade him pack the doors: and withal as he went forth of the door, the said Mistress Towneley gave him a knock between the shoulders: and about a day or two after that, there appeared unto this examinate in his way, a thing like unto a black dog, who put this examinate in mind of the said Mistress Towneley falling out with him this examinate; who bad this examinate make a picture of clay, like unto the said Mistress Towneley: and that this examinate with the help of his spirit (who then ever after bid this examinate to call it Dandy) would kill or destroy the said Mistress Towneley: and so the said dog vanished out of this examinate's sight. And the next morning after, this examinate took clay, and made a picture of the said Mistress Towneley, and dried it the same night by the fire: and within a day after, he, this examinate began to crumble the said picture, every day some, for the space of a week, and within two days after all was crumbled away; the said Mistress Towneley died.[6]

No doubt to Roger this made a logical narrative,[7] and again he was influenced by Elizabeth Bennet's confession in *A True and Just Record* (quoted in Chapters

A modern obsidian scrying mirror similar to the one used by John Dee and Edward Kelley. Behind it is a 17th century carving from a chest used to store magical artefacts by the collector Charles Wade. (MoW 1009).

COPYRIGHT MUSEUM OF WITCHCRAFT, PHOTOGRAPH AUTHOR

Thirteen and Seventeen).[8] Although the two accounts aren't exactly the same, Elizabeth's moves from the description of the two spirits – a hare and a black dog – menacing her to a description of them harming her enemies, just as the statement drawn up by Roger does. Significantly, one of the spirits, Suckin, reminds her of her grievances against the victims, and the Black Dog reminds James of his grievance against Anne Towneley.

The brown dog is of course Elizabeth Sothernes's familiar spirit. Both James and his mother eventually admitted seeing him on several occasions.[9] No doubt Roger asked James whether he had given the spirit his soul, since that had been a standard question since Francesco Prelati was interrogated in 1440. James's response, 'that his soul was not his to give, but was his Saviour Jesus Christ's,' was a theologically sound argument against the whole concept that it was possible to give your soul to the Devil. Another witchcraft suspect, Joan Prentice, put it in more detail – 'Her soul appertained only unto Jesus Christ, by whose precious blood shedding, it was bought and purchased.'[10] In fact it's surprising that Roger didn't cut it out of the statement, but he probably saw it as a way to confront and demolish James's claims to be a good Christian, since it would now be followed by James's confession of murder.

This statement is a complex mixture of elements from Roger and elements from James. James's ominous promise that instead of his soul he would give the spirit 'as much as was in him … to give' serves Roger's purpose of portraying James as someone allied with the forces of evil. But it also seems to reflect James's growing realisation that he faced paying a heavy price for his magic.

However, an important detail of the method used to kill Anne Towneley – *crumbling* the clay image – is clearly the result of Roger's input. It's not the method described by Elizabeth Sothernes in her evidence against Anne Whittle and Anne Redferne. She refers to drying the image and then pricking it with a pin or thorn, or burning parts of it.[11] Her description agrees with instructions in books of magic such as Messayaac's *Liber de Angelis*. If James had decided to curse Anne Towneley, that would have been the method he would have used. But no pins or thorns had been found with the lump of clay dug up at Malking Tower, and presumably it didn't have any scorch marks, so Roger altered the method to fit his piece of evidence. To him, there was probably little difference between piercing or burning an image and crumbling it. But magically, of course, there was a great difference. The use of fire and pins (and thorns were essentially a substitute for pins) were important aspects of magic, and occurred in many other spells, not only curses.

It is, of course, inconsistent that James makes his promise to the brown dog – his grandmother's familiar – but is then helped to kill Anne Towneley by 'a thing like unto a black dog' – a phrase used in Alizon's confession. It's possible that at this point Roger read Alizon's confession to James, and James tried to claim that the Black Dog was his familiar in another attempt to protect Alizon.

But there's also a statement from Jennet backing up James's confession:

She sayeth, that her brother James Device ... hath been a witch for the space of three years: about the beginning of which time, there appeared unto him, in this examinate's mother's house, a Black Dog, which her said brother called Dandy. And further, this examinate confesseth, and sayeth: that her said brother about a twelve month since, in the presence of this examinate, and in the house aforesaid, called for the said Dandy, who thereupon appeared; asking this examinate's brother what he would have him to do. This examinate's said brother then said, he would have him to help him to kill old Mistress Towncley of the Carre: whereunto the said Dandy answered, and said, that her said brother should have his best help for the doing of the same; and that her said brother, and the said Dandy, did both in this examinate's hearing, say, they would make away the said Mistress Towneley. And about a week after, this examinate coming to the Carre Hall, saw the said Mistress Towneley in the kitchen there, nothing well: whereupon it came into this examinate's mind, that her said brother, by the help of Dandy, had brought the said Mistress Towneley into the state she then was in.[12]

The last sentence, where Jennet describes seeing Anne Towneley looking ill and wondering if James was responsible, is very likely to be something Jennet really said, with the phrase 'by the help of Dandy' inserted by Roger. Anne's accusation of theft against not only James but also Jennet's mother had probably made Jennet very angry, and quite possibly she liked the idea that James had taken revenge on Anne. At least, she might have liked it when Anne was simply 'nothing well', rather than dead.

But there are also significant contradictions between Jennet's and James's statements, which would have worried Roger Nowell if the truth had been important to him. In Jennet's statement, the Black Dog is James's familiar spirit right from the start of his career as a 'witch' three years earlier, while in James's statement Dandy first appears after his quarrel with Anne. Even more importantly, Jennet doesn't mention the clay image.[13]

Jennet's statement is in fact closer to Alizon's confession, where Alizon and the Black Dog discuss harming John Law and then Alizon instructs the dog to do it.

This suggests a likely sequence of events for the creation of James's confession. Roger threatened to use the clay image as evidence against Alizon, so James confessed that he had used it to kill Anne Towneley. Roger then made James repeat his confession in front of Jennet, and James may even have told Jennet to cooperate and confirm his confession, to prevent Roger ill-treating her. Jennet admitted, truthfully, that it had crossed her mind that James might have put a curse on Anne. Roger then read Jennet Alizon's confession, and asked Jennet if James too had a familiar spirit – and Jennet found the idea that James had cursed Anne with the Black Dog's help both more interesting and more convincing than the idea that he'd used an image – partly, no doubt, because she hadn't seen him make one. Finally, Roger confronted James with Jennet's statement, and James agreed to his confession being modified to include the Black Dog, to protect Jennet.

Note, however, that this is one of the occasions when Roger uses the phrase 'she confesseth' in Jennet's statements – 'This examinate confesseth, and sayeth: that her said brother about a twelve month since, in the presence of this examinate, and in the house aforesaid, called for the said Dandy, who thereupon appeared.' By admitting that she was present when James summoned Dandy, Jennet was incriminating not only James but also herself. And perhaps like her sister Alizon she too betrayed the fact that she found the Black Dog a dangerously attractive figure.

Roger wasn't finished with James, however. Not content with getting him to confess to Anne Towneley's murder, he extracted a second confession from him:

> And he further sayeth, that in Lent last one John Duckworth of the Lawnde, promised this examinate an old shirt: and within a fortnight after, this examinate went to the said Duckworth's house, and demanded the said old shirt; but the said Duckworth denied him thereof. And going out of the said house, the said spirit Dandy appeared unto this examinate, and said, Thou didst touch the said Duckworth; whereunto this examinate answered, he did not touch him: yes (said the spirit again) thou didst touch him, and therefore I have power of him: whereupon this examinate joined with the said spirit, and then wished the said spirit to kill the said Duckworth: and within one week, then next after, Duckworth died.[14]

Yet again, this statement is not what it seems. Another earlier witchcraft suspect, Elizabeth Stile, had confessed 'that she herself did kill one Saddocke with a clap on the shoulder, for not keeping his promise for [to give her] an old cloak'.[15] Her case had been controversial, with two pamphlets written about it, and it was mentioned in Reginald Scot's *The Discovery of Witchcraft*.[16] Roger Nowell almost certainly knew about it. Did he suspect James of killing John Duckworth because during his investigations he'd heard that John had broken his promise to James, and it reminded him of the Elizabeth Stile case? Or was John Duckworth simply someone James had worked for who had died mysteriously, and did Roger invent the motive, drawing on Elizabeth's confession for inspiration? There is, of course, no testimony from any of John's family – or any mention of any.

Once we know that this statement too is probably corrupted by Roger Nowell's input, and we look more closely at it, we can see that in fact James was protesting his innocence. Only one lump of clay had been found, and James had explained it by confessing to killing Anne Towneley. So we see Dandy explaining to James that he was able to kill John Duckworth simply by touching him – as Elizabeth Stile had killed her victim. And no doubt this is because James initially denied killing John, protesting that there was no evidence of a second image. James even objects that he didn't so much as touch John – forcing Dandy to insist that he did. Dandy then becomes quite philosophical, explaining that James, by touching John, has given Dandy the power to harm him. It seems likely that the well-read Black

Dog not only knew of Elizabeth Stile's case but had also studied the analysis of the methods witches used to curse people in books like Henri Boguet's *Discours des Sorciers*.[17]

What we're seeing here is a statement that began as an argument between James and Roger – James objecting to being accused of two murders, when only one image had been found, and Roger arguing that James had killed John – with the help of the Black Dog – just by touching him.

Yet somehow that gets translated into an account of a spirit encounter. And that must have happened inside James's head, because Roger Nowell would never have put his own words into the mouth of an evil spirit. There's more evidence that at least some of this account is indeed James's own words in the phrase 'this examinate joined with the said spirit'. The use of the term 'joined with' to mean working with a spirit is very unusual – but it occurs in *The Sworn Book*.[18] This makes it far more likely to be used by someone who practised magic, like James, than by someone like Roger, whose ideas about magic were based on hostile stereotypes. Dandy's claim, 'Thou didst touch him, and therefore I have power of him', also sounds more like James trying to make sense of Roger's arguments than something it would have occurred to Roger to say.

Roger had managed to make Alizon think she might have a protecting spirit who had retaliated against John Law. Now James, too, was wrestling with the possibility that he had a protecting spirit who had killed John Duckworth. Obviously, though, James is not describing something that happened immediately after his visit to John. What he's describing is a spirit encounter that is a result of his interrogation by Roger – a dream or vision he experienced while he was Roger's prisoner.

James was under exactly the kind of extreme stress that was likely to trigger such an experience. And, of course, he was also someone who had probably trained himself to contact spirits – to encounter them in dreams and see them in mirrors. He was particularly likely to respond to psychological turmoil and disturbed sleep by having a dream or vision involving a spirit. And when he had that spirit encounter he would have regarded it as a valid magical experience. The Black Dog might not have existed for James before – but he existed for him now.

CHAPTER TWENTY-THREE

Curses

MAGICIANS, CUNNING FOLK AND CURSES

The procedure ... known as the Trojan Revenge

Take wax that is contaminated or deteriorated with age ... and make an image with it on the day and during the hour of Saturn ... saying as follows while wrenching and deforming the image: O spirits of Saturn, blazing and powerful, descend now from the exalted places! O spirits of grief, angry and restless, advance against this person [name]! ... The person's name should be written on the forehead, the name of the planet, which is Saturn, on the chest, and the seal of Saturn between the shoulders. Then it should be suffumigated with horses' hooves, old shoes, decomposed tin, human bones and hair. After that, wrap the image in a shroud, and it should be buried in some place that is horrible, foul and polluted ... If you want to harm a particular part of the body, tie cloth from the shroud around that part of the image and drive a pin through the spine ... And when you want to cure and restore the person to their original health, dig it up from the ground and unwrap it, and remove the pin, anoint the markings with oil and erase the writing, and also wash it in spring water.[1]

As this spell from Messayaac's *Liber de Angelis* indicates, magical practitioners did sometimes put curses on people – although probably not as often as those who thought they'd been cursed feared, or those who opposed magic would like us to believe.

In the early fourteenth century, when Pope John XXII embarked on a campaign against magic, the magician Hugues Géraud and his fellow conspirators attempted to kill him using wax images, baptised and wrapped in parchment inscribed with invocations. Three years later another group of magicians made a second attempt, this time using a silver image engraved with the names and seals of spirits. The ritual involved suffumigating the image with incense for nine nights, and then placing substances in a hole in the image's head and setting fire to them.[2]

In the nineteenth century, when attempting to harm someone by magic no longer carried the death penalty, it was not unusual for cunning folk to curse people quite openly. The Welsh cunning man Jac Ffynnon Elian took his name from his local holy well, Ffynnon Elian, which already had an established reputation as a cursing well. In 1831 he charged five shillings to put a curse on someone and nineteen shillings to remove it again; and although he didn't face the harsh penalties risked by his ancestors, he was in fact imprisoned twice.[3]

Putting a curse on someone generally involved Jac writing the target's name in a book, and inscribing his or her initials on a piece of slate, which he then put in the well.[4] He recited a curse, read passages from the bible and poured water from the well over his client's head. The client also had to drink some of the well water. If the target then wanted the curse removed, he or she had to walk round the well three times. Jac again read passages from the Bible, recited some kind of Latin invocation, and removed the slate from the well. The target took it home, ground it to powder, mixed it with salt and threw it on the fire. The target was also required to read parts of the Bible – from Job and the Psalms – and drink a bottle of the well water.

Near Padstow in Cornwall there is a bay named after a local wise woman, Mother Ivey – famous for a cruelly disproportionate but significantly political curse.

A knitted image used to curse a bullying ATS sergeant during the Second World War (MoW 231).

When a catch of pilchards failed to sell, the owner of the fishing boats spread the fish on one of his fields as fertiliser instead of giving them to local people as was the custom. Mother Ivey cursed the field, saying that if anyone ever disturbed the ground there, a member of their family would die. A number of tragedies followed, and even in 1997, when South West Water needed to lay a pipe across the field, the landowner wouldn't allow the work to go ahead until a local vicar had performed a service of blessing.[5]

In another – fortunately less extreme – Cornish case with political overtones, in the run-up to the 1906 General Election the wise woman Granny Boswell made a Tory campaigner's car break down.[6]

But there was a political dimension to many curses. Magic offered a way for people to hit back against those who abused their power. Anne Whittle's alleged killing of Robert Nutter is a classic example – a woman hitting back against a man, a tenant hitting back against a landlord. Magic was the only way she could defend her daughter against sexual harassment, perhaps rape, and her family from being thrown off their land and losing both their home and their livelihood.[7]

Of course pamphleteers tried to make out that curses were used to take revenge for the most trivial grievances – and extraordinarily Thomas Potts tries to do that even with Anne Whittle's curse. He quotes her statement in full, detailing Robert Nutter's appalling behaviour, and yet he then comments:

> I spare to trouble you with a multitude of examinations, or depositions of any other witnesses, by reason of this bloody fact, for the murder of Robert Nutter, upon so small an occasion, as to threaten to take away his own land from such as were not worthy to inhabit or dwell upon it, is now made by that which you have already heard, so apparent, as no indifferent man will question it, or rest unsatisfied.[8]

In attempting to demonise Anne Whittle, Thomas Potts betrays the ethical void at the heart of his propaganda.

In fact it was generally accepted that even a person without any special magical powers could put a curse on someone if the grievance was strong enough. A case from late-nineteenth-century Cornwall has some similarities to Anne Whittle's. A landowner claimed that a dog belonging to one of his tenants was chasing his sheep, and made it clear to the tenant that he must kill his dog or be evicted. The tenant took his dog to a nearby river and drowned him, but only after placing a savage curse on the landowner in front of a group of bargemen. Within days the landowner's cattle began to die, and in the end he was forced to approach his tenant and make him a gift of a piece of land in return for lifting the curse.[9]

In the Christian folksong *The Bitter Withy* (based loosely on the accounts of Jesus's childhood in some Apocryphal Gospels), the boy Jesus is described putting a curse on the willow tree after taking revenge – in a chilling but also eerily beautiful way – on some children who refuse to play with him:

So up Lincull and down Lincull
Our sweetest Saviour ran,
And there He met three rich young lords
Good morning! to you all.

Good morn! good morn! good morn! said they:
Good morning! then said He,
O which of you three rich young men
Will play at ball with me?

We are all lords' and ladies' sons,
Born in our bower and hall
And Thou art nothing but a poor maid's child,
Born in an ox's stall.

If you're all lords' and ladies' sons,
Born in your bower and hall,
I will make you believe in your latter end;
I'm an angel above you all.

So He made Him a bridge with the beams of the sun,
And o'er the water crossed He.
These rich young lords followed after Him,
And drowned they were all three.

Then up Lincull and down Lincull
These young lords' mothers ran,
Saying: Mary mild, fetch home your child,
For ours He has drowned all.

So Mary mild fetched home her child
And laid Him across her knee
With a handful of green withy twigs
She gave Him slashes three.

O withy! O withy ! O bitter withy
Thou hast caused Me to smart
And the withy shall be the very first tree
That shall perish at the heart![10]

Often the distinction between protection magic and cursing was blurred, as in this example from the Museum of Witchcraft's collection of mid-twentieth-century charms:

Oh great Saint Michael who was sent by the most high to harass Satan's pride which is the eternal enemy of humanity charge with your lance the enemy and watch with your self at my disposition I am daily attacked by the assignment [name] she is unchained against me for long and desires my downfall … by her perverseness and provocatious

An image with its tongue pierced with a needle – intended to stop the target spreading malicious gossip (MoW 223).

tongue and other wicked help she makes void all good that may be done for me ... O great St Michael protection of the children of God I pray thee ... take thy lance and go bravely forward to the home of [name] command her to leave me alone in peace command her to leave the home the community where she is if she still persist in staying strike with your lance and hurt her as you had hurt Satan make her disappear from my vicinity and chase all her friends who will be her allies.

Another of these charms is rather more brief and to the point:

In the name of God I do begin lame your hands and feet because you sin God grant that I may come out best or never I'll find peace nor rest.[11]

The Lenkiewicz Manuscript contains a spell that is both a curse and a thief-detection method:

For this experiment thou must take litharge of silver, that is to say, the purifying of silver, that goldsmiths make and bray [pound] him small, and form it upon a marble stone and distemper it with the white of an egg; and when it is tempered make an eye on the wall or in parchment and stick him on the wall then take a nail of latten [brass] of the weight of a penny and hammer of yew ... then say this charm; 'I conjure all the lookers on this eye, and all them that is in this thing be guilty of and is beholding of this eye, I conjure them by the virtue of the Father and of the Son and of the Holy Ghost, and by all the names of God, Alpha and Omega ... that all them that be guilty of such thing which is gone ... by the virtue of the holy names of our Lord Jesus Christ, beforesaid, that it never cease till his eye be out, or [he] give answer.'

Few curses were intended to kill. Most were reversible, allowing the perpetrator to decide when the target had suffered enough, or the target the opportunity to make amends for the wrong done to the perpetrator. One of the creepiest exhibits in the Museum of Witchcraft is an image of a face made of cloth, with buttons for eyes and a nylon stocking for hair, and with a needle driven into its felt tongue. But its main purpose was not to harm the target but to stop her spreading malicious gossip.[12]

Another cloth image in the museum, however, is deceptively beautiful. Made of pieces of fabric stolen from the target's clothing, it could be a child's cherished doll – if it wasn't for the small dagger driven viciously through its face.[13]

Two other examples provide eloquent evidence of the circumstances that prompted people to resort to this kind of magic. One is a photograph of a woman office worker with five pins stuck into it. Dating from the 1940s, it was hidden in the back of a filing cabinet in a local government building, and it's horribly evocative of the rivalries and tensions an office environment can generate. The other dates from the Second World War, and is a knitted doll hanging from a noose made from a bootlace, and represents a bullying sergeant in the ATS, the women's branch of the British army.[14]

THE PSYCHOLOGY OF CURSES

For someone seething with a sense of grievance, making an image or pronouncing a curse must have been a very satisfying act in itself – a way of liberating the perpetrator from the feeling of being a helpless victim, and a valuable antidote to frustration.

The effect on the target, however, obviously depended on the personality of the individual concerned. For many people, just knowing that someone hated you enough to curse you must have been very unnerving. And the awareness of that concentrated malice directed towards you, and perhaps of the existence of an image of you with pins in it, would be very likely to have an insidiously depressing or stress-inducing effect.

In the tough conditions of the early modern period, many people spent at least part of their lives suffering from exhaustion and malnutrition. Stress and depression would affect their appetites and digestions and disturb their sleep, making these problems worse. And increased physical weakness and mental tiredness would make accidents more likely.

But if healing magic could implant a concept of health in a person's mind, which then had a real physical effect on their body's biochemistry, could the opposite also be possible? Could there be some truth in the idea that those who could heal could also harm? Could a curse implant a concept of ill-health in someone's mind, and have a *damaging* effect on that person's biochemistry?

There is certainly now strong scientific evidence that psychological stress can suppress the immune system, making it easier for diseases to take hold. But research is also gradually revealing that many illnesses are caused not by outside threats overwhelming our defences, but by some of the chemicals produced by our immune systems turning against us, and poisoning us instead of defending us.

Cytokines are molecules that play a vital role in combating infections by enhancing the effectiveness of immune cells. However, if too many cytokines are produced, they can cause a range of unpleasant and even life-threatening illnesses, including inflammatory bowel disease, rheumatoid arthritis and septic shock. And psychological stress can affect the body's ability to regulate cytokine production.

It has also been discovered that a neurotransmitter that blocks cytokine production is released by the vagus nerve – the nerve that links the brain to the heart and other organs. Interestingly, people can be trained to slow their heart rate by controlling the activity of their vagus nerve. Theoretically, therefore, it's possible that people who believed they had been cursed could unconsciously reduce the activity of their vagus nerve, preventing it from blocking cytokine production, and so causing cytokine-related illnesses.[15]

It might seem that using curses went against the essential principle of magic – that the forces that maintain the existence of the Universe have a basic tendency to promote health and well being. But that was why the concept of revenge was so important in cursing. A curse would only work if the target had injured the perpetrator in some way. It was an instrument of natural justice, intended to restore the well being of the perpetrator as much as to harm the target.

However, there *was* a belief, particularly as the fear of witchcraft grew, that it was possible to lay curses that twisted this principle – curses that were disproportionate and *were* primarily motivated by malice. But when that happened, counter-magic could normally be used to reverse the curse and turn the magical force back on the perpetrator.

In fact, the belief in curses provided a very useful explanation for illness when cunning folk were performing healing magic. If the optimistic philosophy of magic was correct, and the forces of the Universe were essentially well-disposed towards humanity, why were illness and suffering so inescapable? Of course it was the very harshness of existence that made the optimism of magic so valuable. When often all that stood between people and death was their own determination to survive, pessimism was a luxury they couldn't afford. But illness had to be explained somehow, and the obvious explanation was that it involved some kind of conflict that disrupted the activity of divine power.

People were well aware that the body could be attacked by poisons and parasites, or that its own internal balance could be disturbed by things like the wrong diet. However, explaining an illness by claiming that it was an attack by an evil spirit, an easily offended fairy or witchcraft was in many ways more appealing. It made the patient's and practitioner's battle against the illness into a dramatic supernatural combat that captured the imagination, and gave recovery a spiritual as well as physical significance.

Anne Whittle's charm, which she described using to unwitch ale, but which was also probably used against all kinds of witchcraft, was brief but fiercely combative. It depicts the witch laying the curse with 'three biters' – 'the heart, ill eye, ill tongue' – and opposes these three instruments of evil power with the three persons of the Trinity:

> Three biters hast thou bitten,
> The heart, ill eye, ill tongue:
> Three [i.e. three times] bitter shall be thy boot [penance],
> Father, Son and Holy Ghost
> a [in] God's name
> Five Pater Nosters, Five Aves [Ave Marias],
> and a Creed,
> In worship of the five wounds
> of our Lord.[16]

But whether or not magic could really be used to harm someone, the fear of being cursed could have a very real effect on people's behaviour. In nineteenth-century Wales a cheating husband gave up his infidelities when he discovered that his wife had put an image of him in a cursing well.[17]

METHODS

Although an image stuck with pins was the usual way to curse someone (stereotypes aren't always inaccurate), there were a number of other methods. Isobel Gowdie's spoken charms included a curse:

> He is lying in his bed, – he is lying sick and sore;
> Let him lie intill [in] his bed two months and three days more![18]

Burying something under the threshold of the target's house was another popular method:

> A certain woman … approached Matteuccia saying that she had a sick daughter who couldn't be freed from her illness and that she believed her daughter had definitely been bewitched by a certain other woman whose husband her said daughter had slept with several times; and Matteuccia said to her that she should search in her daughter's house under the doorstep and there she would find spells and she should burn them. Then a few days later, the aforesaid woman came to Matteuccia with her daughter's lover and said that beneath the aforesaid doorstep they had found three black animals like mice wrapped up in linen and hemp yarn and burned them just as the aforesaid Matteuccia had said.[19]

Not long afterwards, in Lausanne, a magician called Staedlin confessed that he'd caused a woman to have a series of miscarriages by burying a snake under her doorstep. When the investigators tried to dig it up they found nothing, but they assumed the snake had disintegrated, and carefully removed all the earth, which apparently undid the curse.[20]

In a more reliable account from the nineteenth century, the Devon folklorist Sabine Baring-Gould wrote:

> I remember about thirty-five years ago a case brought before my father, as magistrate, of a man who had put nails, hair, and flesh, stuck with pins, by night under a neighbour's doorstep. He was observed doing this, and the person whose doorstep had been tampered with desired to have a summons taken out against the man who had tried thereby to bewitch him.[21]

Matteuccia was also approached by some people who believed that their nephew, who was mentally ill, had been bewitched, because they'd found a feather tied up in a piece of cloth in his pillow. During a seventeenth-century witchcraft trial in the Channel Islands, a witness claimed she'd found a similar curse:

> Susanne Le Tellier, widow of Pierre Rougier, deposed that … they also found forty-four witches' spells in her child's pillow, some of which were made like hedgehogs, others round like apples, and others again flat like the palm of the hand; and they were of hempen thread twisted with feathers.[22]

In the nineteenth century there was considerable excitement among folklorists when a length of string with feathers through it was found in the attic of a house in Wellington in Somerset. It's now in the Pitt Rivers Museum in Oxford, and there's a photograph of it on their website *England: the Other Within* (http://england.prm.ox.ac.uk). There was speculation that it might be a curse, but when Sabine Baring-Gould asked the Devon wise woman Marianne Voader about it she said it was probably a bird-scarer.[23]

Needless to say there was a method that involved cruelty to frogs. At a holy well in Anglesey a skewer was driven through a live frog, corks fixed to either end, and the frog left floating in the water. The target of the curse would suffer for as long as the frog survived.[24] Far more appealing is an exciting method from Devon that involved reciting the target's name while setting fire to a circle of gunpowder.[25]

IMPOTENCE

One of the problems particularly likely to be blamed on witchcraft was impotence. Around the time of the Pendle case a London magician, Dr Simon Forman, apparently used a wax image pierced with a thorn to prevent the Earl of Essex from consummating his marriage, so that his wife Frances could obtain an annulment and marry her lover, the Viscount Rochester.[26]

Two hundred years earlier, Matteuccia had helped a client in a similar situation – a young man desperate because the girl he was in love with was about to be forced to marry someone else:

Matteuccia ... said to the aforesaid young man that he should have a consecrated candle, burning, and hold it at a crossroads, and as the bride went to the wedding, he should extinguish the candle and bend it, saying the words written below and others even more wicked and devilish, as follows:

> As I bend this candle in my burning desire
> So may the bridegroom and the bride
> Never be able to join in the act of love.[27]

The most popular method for inducing impotence, however, was knot magic. In Thomas Middleton's play *The Witch* Hecate refers to tying knots in snakeskins for this purpose.[28] Jean Bodin learned a great deal about the subject from a rather surprising source:

> When I was in Poitiers at the Assizes as deputy royal prosecutor, in the year 1567, I was involved in the trials of some witches, and as I was describing what had happened at the trials to my hostess, who was a young lady with an impeccable reputation, she spoke like an expert in the science ... saying that there were more than fifty ways to tie the ligature ... The young lady also recited to us the different words that had to be used ... which were neither Greek, nor Hebrew, nor Latin ... I believe they had no relation to any other language either, and from what kind and colour of leather each type of ligature had to be made.[29]

It seems extraordinary that this young woman dared to reveal such a detailed knowledge of witchcraft to a man who was trying to have several people burned alive for practising it. No doubt it was a very pleasant dinner party, and the expensive wine removed some of her inhibitions. Jean Bodin was a highly respected thinker, and she probably found it gratifying to be able to hold his interest in this way. In some witch-hunts the fact that she was 'a young lady with an impeccable reputation' would not have protected her, but she'd judged her guest's character accurately. Jean Bodin seems to have been amused and impressed, and he mentally filed the information away to be used against others, not against her.

Knot magic could also be used to prevent a woman from giving birth, according to the folksong *Willie's Lady*. When his pregnant wife is bewitched by his mother, Willie (on the advice of a friendly fairy) makes a lifelike wax image of a baby to fool his mother into thinking the child has been born. In her surprise and annoyance, she reveals the way to undo her spells:

> Oh who has loosed the nine witch knots
> That was among that lady's locks?
> And who has ta'en out the combs of care
> That hangs among that lady's hair?
> And who's ta'en down the bush of woodbine
> That hung between her bower and mine?
> And who has killed the master kid
> That ran beneath that lady's bed?

> And who has loosed her left-foot shoe,
> And let that lady lighter be?[30]

However, knots were also often used in healing magic:

> A string with nine knots tied upon it, placed about the neck of a child, is reported
> to be an infallible remedy for the whooping-cough.
>
> (*Lancashire Folk-Lore* by John Harland and T.T. Wilkinson[31])

CURSING AND THE WITCH-HUNTS

In the sixteenth and seventeenth centuries, the authorities' relentless propaganda about the evils of magic increased the fear of curses to the point of paranoia, and accusations of cursing became central to the witch-hunts. However, in the vast majority of trial accounts there is no real evidence that the suspect had actually performed a curse. Usually it was only after a person had become ill or died that someone remembered a suspect making some kind of threatening remark. In fact, as we saw in the case of Peter Trevysard, sometimes a completely innocent remark – 'I will do thee a good turn, ere twelve months be at an end' – got twisted and interpreted as a threat.

Essentially, a curse was a way to explain and give meaning to an otherwise inexplicable and meaningless tragedy. And once the witch-hunts had got under way the majority of people accused weren't even cunning folk or magicians. If the power to curse was a gift from the Devil – one of his weapons in his battle for control of the Universe – then he could give it to anyone, not only people who had inherited a tradition of practising magic or spent long hours studying books.

However, cunning folk were still involved in many of the most influential cases. Jean Bodin was inspired to write *De la Démonomanie des Sorciers* by the case of the wise woman Jeanne Harvillier. When she was 'extremely young' – probably in her early teens – Jeanne was arrested and whipped, and her mother was burned alive. Even so, Jeanne began practising as a wise woman, moving frequently and changing her name to try to keep one step ahead of the authorities. She evaded capture for thirty years, marrying and having a daughter. Eventually she was approached by a girl who was being beaten by her father. Jeanne made a powder and scattered it on the ground where the man was expected to walk. But around the same time another man suddenly fell ill:

> [Jeanne] promised to cure him, and in fact she cared for the patient during his illness,
> and she confessed that … she had asked the Devil to cure the illness who had replied
> that it was impossible: and she then said to the Devil that he was always deceiving her
> and that he shouldn't come to see her any more … Two days later the man died.

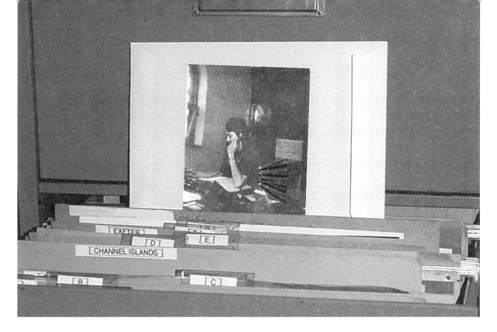

A photograph pierced with pins, found in a filing cabinet in an office in Cornwall in the 1940s (MoW 40).

At that point everyone, including Jeanne herself, seems to have become convinced that the curse had misfired and struck down the wrong person. Jeanne was arrested, and her daughter forced to flee.[32]

One of the most horrifying curses in any witchcraft trial record was apparently the work of Alice Trevysard:

The examination of Johan Baddaford …

This examinate sayeth that … she, with divers of her neighbours, coming from Townstall, from the house of Sir Thomas Ridgwaye, knight, where they had complained against the said Alice Trevysard, she, the said Alice, upon occasion of speech told this examinate saying 'thou or thine may be burned before long be'. From which time, being Monday till the Thursday following, this examinate made no fire at all in her house, but then beginning to make fire, laid some few coals in the chimney, her child setting upon the hearth, and this examinate, turning about to break some wood to put into the fire, heard the child suddenly cry out, and saw the band burning about the child's neck and looking into his neck found his flesh burned to the bone, the child having not fallen into the fire, but sitting on the hearth as before, and the fire not kindled at all, but the coals lying there, as she put them in. All which this examinate presently showed to divers of the chief of Dartmouth and sought the best remedy she could but found neither salve nor anything else that did any good but within three weeks after the child consumed and died.[33]

It's all too easy to see what must really have happened. Johan's statement admits that she was lighting the fire. Obviously a spark from the tinder set the child's neckband alight. But her horror and panic must have made it very difficult for Johan to remember the events clearly. It would have been one of those sudden shocking accidents that leave the person involved unable to think how it could possibly have happened. It would have been extremely difficult for Johan to accept that she was responsible – however innocently – for her child suffering such a terrible death. Then she remembered Alice's remark – which was no doubt in fact a response to Johan expressing the opinion that Alice and her family deserved to be burned as witches (just as Elizabeth Sothernes responded to Richard Baldwyn's accusations by telling him to go hang himself). And the only way Johan could live with the tragedy was to convince herself that it was the result of Alice's curse.

However, when there were stories of curses like that going around, it's hardly surprising that people were afraid of witchcraft.

THOU SHALT NOT SUFFER A WITCH TO LIVE

A key Biblical quotation used by William Perkins[34] and other writers in their condemnation of magic was Exodus 22:18, 'Thou shalt not suffer a witch to live.' Even in the sixteenth century there was some debate over whether this was an accurate translation of the original Hebrew. Reginald Scot wrote:

> Chasaph, being an Hebrew word, is Latinised *Veneficium*, and is in English, poisoning, or witchcraft; if you will so have it. The Hebrew sentence written in Exodus 22 is … in English, You shall not suffer any poisoners, or (as it is translated) witches to live … And because I will avoid prolixity and contention both at once, I will admit that *Veneficae* were such witches, as with their poisons did much hurt among the children of Israel; and I will not deny that there remain such until this day, bewitching men, and making them believe, that by virtue of words, and certain ceremonies, they bring to pass such mischiefs, and intoxications, as they indeed accomplish by poisons … Let us all abandon such witches and cozeners [frauds] … boasting they can do miracles, expound dreams, foretell things to come … Whatsoever they be that … take upon them to work such wonders, by soothsaying, sorcery, or witchcraft, are but liars, deceivers, and cozeners … Doth he not deceive himself and others, and therefore is worthily condemned for a witch? … So as, under this one sentence (Thou shalt not suffer a poisoner or a witch to live) is forbidden both murder and witchcraft; the murder consisting in poison; the witchcraft in cozenage or blasphemy.[35]

However, as this quotation itself illustrates, most people believed that witches should be severely punished – they just differed in their definition of a witch.

When cunning folk put pins and urine in a witch bottle they were quite happy to imagine the spell inflicting an agonising death on the witch – although of course that wasn't quite the same as prosecuting someone for witchcraft, watching the person being executed (perhaps burned alive), and then going on to prosecute someone else. Also, occasionally cunning folk would advise burning a sick animal alive, in the hope that would inflict suffering on the witch responsible for the illness; but as the case of the pig described in Chapter Four shows, most people who considered that option rejected it.[36]

But as far as cunning folk were concerned, using magic didn't make you a witch – in fact, even putting a curse on someone didn't necessarily make you a witch. Often what this amounted to in practice was the attitude that if someone put a curse on your client, *they* were an evil witch; but if your client asked *you* to put a curse on someone, you were an agent of natural justice.

However, as the case of Jac Ffynnon Elian demonstrates, sometimes the person who wanted someone cursed and the target of the curse could *both* be your clients – and cunning folk seem to have been able to take that in their stride. After all, they were dealing on a daily basis not with moral absolutes but with the messiness of real life. They did their best for each client who came to them, always working on the optimistic assumption that magic had a natural tendency to do good.

John Walsh, asked 'whether they that do good to such as are bewitched, cannot also do hurt', replied, 'He that doth hurt, can never heal again.'[37] If that was widely believed to be literally true, there wouldn't be so much evidence of magicians and cunning folk putting curses on people. However, it seems that Anne Whittle's reputation suffered once she was thought to have killed Robert Nutter, in spite of the provocation she'd suffered. One of her statements makes it clear that she was very upset after 'perceiving Anthony Nutter of Pendle to favour Elizabeth Sothernes'.[38] Quite possibly this was not because Anthony was grief-stricken by his relative's death, but because he'd lost confidence in Anne's ability to perform healing and protection magic.

The Sworn Book freely admitted that its rituals could be used 'for an evil intent and purpose' – but the magician would then risk 'the death of the soul'.[39] The crucial factor was the practitioner's state of mind – the practitioner's *intent* or *will*. Magic could be twisted away from its true, benevolent purpose if the practitioner's own will was twisted by malice.

Roger Nowell's unease at the prospect of Alizon and James practising magic in Pendle for the next fifty years was in fact justified. In that time, there can be no doubt that they would have been approached by clients wanting them to put curses on people. And at some point they would probably have obliged. But of course James and Alizon themselves also hated Anne Whittle for being a witch – perhaps not only because they believed that she'd killed their father, but also because, in order to kill him, she would have twisted the magic they regarded as sacred.

CHAPTER TWENTY-FOUR

Although she were their mother,
they did not spare to accuse her

Elizabeth Device … upon her examination, although Master Nowell was very circumspect, and exceeding careful in dealing with her, yet she would confess nothing, until it pleased God to raise up a young maid Jennet Device, her own daughter, about the age of nine years (a witness unexpected,) to discover all their practices, meetings, consultations, murders, charms and villainies …

   And then knowing, that both Jennet Device, her daughter, James Device, her son, and Alizon Device, with others, had accused her and laid open all things, in their examinations taken before Master Nowell, and although she were their own natural mother, yet they did not spare to accuse her of every particular fact, which in her time she had committed, to their knowledge; she made a very liberal and voluntary confession.[1]

The claim that Jennet was 'a witness unexpected' isn't the only inaccuracy in this passage by Thomas Potts – Alizon never said anything incriminating about her mother. But there *is* a fatally compromising statement from James:

About three years ago, this examinate being in his grandmother's house, with his said mother; there came a thing in shape of a brown dog, which his mother called Ball, who spake to this examinate's mother, in the sight and hearing of this examinate, and bade her make a picture of clay, like unto John Robinson, alias Swyer, and dry it hard and then crumble it by little and little; and as the said picture should crumble or mull [another word for crumble] away, so should the said John Robinson alias Swyer his body decay and wear away. And within two or three days after, the picture shall so all be wasted, and mulled away; so then the said John Robinson should die presently. Upon the agreement betwixt the said dog and this examinate's said mother, the said dog suddenly vanished out of this examinate's sight. And the next day, this examinate saw his said mother take clay at the west end of her said house, and make a picture of it after the said Robinson, and brought it into her house, and dried it some two days: and about two days after the drying thereof this examinate's said mother fell on crumbling the said picture of clay, every day some, for some three weeks together; and within two days after it was all crumbled or mulled away, the said John Robinson died.[2]

This is indeed similar to Elizabeth Device's own confession:

At the third time her spirit, the spirit Ball, appeared to her in the shape of a brown dog, at, or in her mother's house in Pendle Forest aforesaid: about four years ago the said spirit bid this examinate make a picture of clay after the said John Robinson, alias Swyer, which this examinate did make accordingly at the west end of her said mother's house, and dried the same picture away within a week or thereabouts, and about a week after the picture was crumbled or mulled away; the said Robinson died.

The reason wherefore she this examinate did so bewitch the said Robinson to death, was: for that the said Robinson had chidden and becalled this examinate, for having a bastard child with one Seller.[3]

The 'bastard child' may well have been young William Device.

This briefer statement by Elizabeth could certainly be a confirmation of James's, forced out of her once James had accused her, if it wasn't for a small but extremely significant contradiction between them.[4] In Elizabeth's statement, she mentions Malking Tower twice, on both occasions referring to it as her mother's house. In James's statement, Malking Tower is referred to as his grandmother's house the first time it's mentioned; but the *second* time, it's referred to as his *mother's* house. This isn't simply a slip of some clerk's pen. James's statement about the Good Friday gathering also starts by describing Malking Tower as his grandmother's house and then shifts to describing it as his mother's:

Upon Sheare Thursday last, in the evening, he this examinate stole a wether from John Robinson of Barley, and brought it to his grandmother's house … and there killed it: and that upon the day following, being Good Friday, about twelve of the clock in the day time there dined in this examinate's mother's house a number of persons, whereof three were men, with this examinate, and the rest women.[5]

And when James eventually gave a list of names of the people present, the statement reads:

The names of the said witches as were on Good Friday at this examinate's said grandmother's house, and now this examinate's own mother's, for so many of them as he did know, were these …[6]

What's more, Elizabeth Device then made a statement confirming James's list of names, and in that statement she too describes Malking Tower as her house:

The said Elizabeth Device being further examined, confesseth, that upon Good Friday last, there dined at this examinate's house, called Malking Tower, those which she hath said are witches, and doth verily think them to be witches: and their names are those whom James Device hath formerly spoken of to be there.[7]

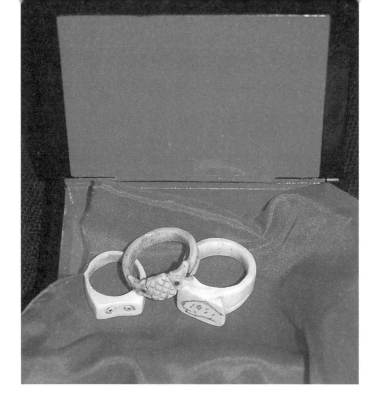

Rings made of human bone, probably worn to treat (or protect against) illness or witchcraft (MoW 496).

By Good Friday, of course, James's grandmother was in prison, but that was no reason for James to start referring to Malking Tower as his mother's house. He would have been hoping desperately that when the Assizes were held in August the cases against Alizon and his grandmother would be dismissed, or they would be acquitted, and by the end of August they would be back living at Malking Tower again.

Although James and his mother went ahead with the Good Friday gathering at Malking Tower, and entertained their clients there, it's very unlikely they would have gone to live there, moving out of the smallholding where Elizabeth had lived since she'd married John Device around twenty years earlier. The smallholding would have been an important part of their livelihood, with animals and crops providing them with essential food. There would have been work they needed to do there, particularly as it was April, an important time for planting vegetable crops. Admittedly it seems that James was arrested at Malking Tower, but all that shows is that he was spending part of his time there – not that Elizabeth Device had decided to live there.

Also, even if James and the rest of his family *had* decided to refer to Malking Tower as Elizabeth Device's house once Elizabeth Sothernes had been sent to prison – or if it was in fact Roger Nowell who decided to refer to it that way – then their statements made after Good Friday would *always* refer to Malking Tower as Elizabeth Device's house.[8]

But in fact something *did* happen *several weeks* after Good Friday that changed

Malking Tower from Elizabeth Sothernes's house to Elizabeth Device's. Elizabeth Sothernes died in Lancaster prison.

The statements from James and Elizabeth Device are dated 27 April. However, there is conclusive evidence in *The Wonderful Discovery* that Elizabeth Sothernes was still alive on 19 May.

Thomas Covel, the Lancaster jailer, had been interrogating Anne Whittle, and on 19 May Anne was examined by the Justice of the Peace James Anderton – a necessary formality because only a Justice of the Peace could take an official statement from her. Anne's statement incriminated Elizabeth Sothernes. It described how Elizabeth persuaded Anne to take up witchcraft and acquire a familiar spirit, and how as a result 'the Devil appeared unto her in the likeness of a man' at Malking Tower, along with Elizabeth Sothernes's familiar 'in the likeness of a spotted bitch', and provided them with a feast of 'flesh, butter, cheese, bread, and drink'.

> And she sayeth, that although they did eat, they were never the fuller, nor better for the same; and that at their said banquet, the said spirits gave them light to see what they did, although they neither had fire nor candlelight.[9]

This contradicts Anne's earlier statement to Roger Nowell, when she confessed to killing Robert Nutter, which said that the Devil appeared to her at her own house, and didn't mention Elizabeth Sothernes at all.[10]

Anne's Lancaster statement then went on to claim that she, Elizabeth and Loomeshaw's wife had bewitched Robert Nutter. Again, this contradicts Anne's statements to Roger. Then she had said there were two attempts to bewitch Robert Nutter, the first by the two Burnley wise women Loomeshaw's wife and Jane Boothman (after Thomas Redferne had persuaded Anne not to get involved); and the second by Anne herself entirely on her own.[11] Finally, Anne's Lancaster statement claimed that Elizabeth Sothernes 'had bewitched to death, Richard Ashton, son of Richard Ashton of Downeham Esquire'.

Roger Nowell must have decided that he needed more evidence against Elizabeth Sothernes and asked Thomas Covel to obtain this statement from Anne. It was added to the documents prepared for Elizabeth's trial – which were never used because she died before the Assizes. It's obvious that Anne would never have been formally examined by James Anderton, and the statement would never have been drawn up, if Elizabeth had already been dead at that point.

What all this strongly suggests, therefore, is that those parts of James's and his mother's statements that refer to Malking Tower as Elizabeth Device's house rather than Elizabeth Sothernes's were in fact made after 19 May, in spite of being included in the material dated 27 April. And this in turn, of course, provides us with information about the *order* of the statements.

✮ ✮ ✮

Both James's and his mother's statements begin by mentioning a spirit in the shape of a brown dog. Although this is supposed to be Elizabeth Device's familiar, it's almost certainly significant that there's no account of how Elizabeth acquired the spirit. Instead, her statement begins,

> The said Elizabeth Device, mother of the said James, being examined, confesseth and sayeth. That at the third time her spirit, the spirit Ball, appeared to her in the shape of a brown dog, at, or in her mother's house …

It's clear that Elizabeth Device also described two previous encounters with the brown dog, but Roger Nowell decided not to include those accounts in the evidence against her. The most likely explanation is that this was not her familiar at all, but her mother's familiar, who usually appeared as a brown dog.

James's statement, too, says that when he saw the brown dog with his mother it was in fact at his grandmother's house. And it's very likely that James, Alizon, their mother and grandmother would have performed rituals together at Malking Tower, when they invoked the help of Elizabeth Sothernes's familiar spirit.

Both these sections of James's and his mother's statements refer to Malking Tower as Elizabeth Sothernes's house, so no doubt they were made to Roger Nowell in April. The part of Elizabeth Device's statement where she describes making the image to kill John Robinson also refers to Malking Tower as 'her said mother's house', so that too no doubt dates from April. But when James's statement describes Elizabeth making the image, it reads, 'This examinate saw his said mother take clay at the west end of her said house' – which almost certainly means that it was made *after* Elizabeth's; in fact at least three weeks later, after 19 May.

So Elizabeth did *not* confess to killing John Robinson because James had already accused her of the crime. It seems that what really happened was that Elizabeth confessed to killing John Robinson in April to Roger Nowell, and then several weeks later, when James was in Lancaster prison, Thomas Covel extracted a statement from him confirming his mother's confession.

Why then did Elizabeth confess? Her statement describes her crumbling the image – the unusual method also described in James's statement confessing to the murder of Anne Towneley – the method almost certainly inspired by the fact that the supposed clay image found at Malking Tower was actually no more than a lump of clay. Elizabeth's reference to making the image at the west end of Malking Tower also links her image to the one found there, 'by the said Henry Hargreives and this examinate [James], at the west end of this examinate's grandmother's house'.[12]

There is, therefore, an obvious explanation for Elizabeth's confession. She too was confessing to making the image found at Malking Tower. She did indeed confess because of a statement made by James – but not a statement accusing her.

Researchers Tom and Mary suffumigate a Square of Saturn with the shed exoskeleton of a spider. The square was inscribed on a thin sheet of lead during the hour of Saturn on a Saturday evening while Mercury in Scorpio was sextile to Saturn in Virgo. The Square of Saturn was considered a powerful talisman for anyone facing difficulty or danger.

When Roger Nowell told her that James had confessed to making the image, she confessed that she had made it herself, in a desperate attempt to save James.

Of course, according to Roger Nowell's assumptions, Elizabeth must have been helped by an evil spirit. So it would hardly be surprising if he took some reference by Elizabeth to her *mother's* familiar and transformed it into a description of a spirit helping Elizabeth to commit her murder.

But what of Jennet's role in her mother's prosecution? There is certainly a damaging statement from her:

Jennet Device, daughter of Elizabeth Device, late wife of John Device, of the Forest of Pendle aforesaid widow, confesseth and sayeth, that her said mother is a witch, and this she knoweth to be true; for, that she hath seen her spirit sundry times come unto her said mother in her own house, called Malking Tower, in the likeness of a brown dog, which she called Ball; and at one time amongst others, the said Ball did ask this examinate's mother what she would have him to do: and this examinate's mother answered, that she would have the said Ball to help her to kill John Robinson of Barley, alias Swyer: by help of which said Ball, the said Swyer was killed by witchcraft accordingly; and that this examinate's mother had continued a witch for these three or four years last past. And further, this examinate confesseth, that about a year after, this examinate's mother called for the said Ball, who appeared as aforesaid, asking this examinate's mother what she would have done, who said, that she would have him to kill James Robinson, alias Swyer, of Barley aforesaid, brother to the said John: whereunto Ball answered, he would do it; and about three weeks after, the said James died.[13]

This bears a remarkable resemblance to Jennet's statement incriminating James for Anne Towneley's murder – except of course that it's missing the reference to Jennet seeing Anne in her kitchen looking 'nothing well', the detail that gives that part of Jennet's evidence the ring of truth.

Thomas Potts represents most of Jennet's evidence as testimony given in person in court, but some parts of it are given in the pamphlet as a written statement made on 27 April.[14] In reality, all – or almost all – of her evidence must have existed in written form. Roger was obliged to take written statements from all suspects and potential witnesses. With so many prosecutions failing for lack of evidence, a conscientious Justice like Roger, determined that his prosecutions would succeed, would know how important it was to get convincing evidence in the form of written statements. And we can see, from the many occasions in *The Wonderful Discovery* where Thomas Potts includes what he explicitly tells us are these written statements, that Roger went to a great deal of trouble to get them exactly how he wanted them.

Of course Roger knew there was a good chance that his suspects would deny everything when they appeared in court. But he took similar care with Abraham Law's statement. And Thomas Potts tells us that Abraham's written statement was read out in court, with Abraham then simply confirming it on oath.[15] The Assizes were run to a very tight schedule. Even when defendants' lives were at stake, each trial usually lasted less than half an hour.[16] Since there were no defence lawyers to dispute the evidence or cross-examine witnesses, reading out written statements was obviously the most efficient way to conduct a trial, as long as the statements had been prepared properly by the Justice.

In another of the trials, Thomas Potts implies that the evidence from Jennet, James and Elizabeth was all given in person in court, by saying the first statement was made 'against [the] prisoner at the bar, upon her arraignment and trial', and then punctuating the others with the phrase 'prisoner at the bar'. However, he then says, 'After these examinations were openly read ...'.[17]

There was no way someone like Roger Nowell would send a nine-year-old girl into a courtroom unless he could be sure he would be in control of what was going to happen. So we can reasonably assume that Jennet's written statements were read out, and she – like Abraham Law – simply answered yes when she was asked if they were correct.

However, she *did* answer yes – to statements she must have known could send her mother and brother to their deaths.

Jennet's statement incriminating her mother also refers to Malking Tower as Elizabeth Device's house, suggesting that it wasn't made until after 19 May, by which time James and Elizabeth had probably been in Lancaster prison for at least three weeks, leaving Jennet alone in Roger Nowell's hands.[18] It may also be significant that when Roger Nowell conducted his formal examination of Jennet, James and Elizabeth on 27 April, it was not at his own home at Read but 'at the house of James Wilsey of the Forest of Pendle'.[19] The obvious explanation is that the three prisoners were not all being held at Read – Roger had decided to separate them.

Perhaps James Wilsey and his family were the people Roger had selected to give Jennet and William a home, but in that case surely Jennet would have been taken back to Read for her examination. A more likely explanation is that once James and Elizabeth had confessed, Roger sent them to be held in custody at James Wilsey's house, and kept Jennet with him at Read to work on turning her against her family.

Jennet had been through a great deal. On 30 March her mother, grandmother, brother and sister had been arrested. At the beginning of April her sister and grandmother had been sent to Lancaster prison. And not long after Good Friday her mother and brother had been re-arrested, and Jennet herself taken into custody along with them.

Jennet's life was falling apart, and together with her fear for her family and herself she must also have felt anger at the older members of her family for letting it happen. In particular she must have asked herself why James and her mother had gone ahead with the Good Friday gathering, and why they hadn't escaped to safety as her uncle Christopher and his family had done.

And of course when James confessed to killing Anne Towneley that must have shaken Jennet, even if she believed that Anne's insulting behaviour deserved retaliation. Then Elizabeth confessed to killing John Robinson, and finally James admitted killing John Duckworth – although, interestingly, there's no statement from Jennet backing up *that* confession.

At first James and Jennet had both defended their magic equally vigorously, and it seems that James faltered before Jennet did. Stress, exhaustion, guilt and helplessness eroded his resolve, and he allowed Roger to convince him that he could have given the Black Dog the power to kill John Duckworth. The Black Dog who wormed his way into James's mind wasn't the seductive protector of Alizon's confession. He was born out of Roger Nowell's harsh accusations – that all James's magic was in fact the work of an evil spirit using James for its own ends. And Roger wouldn't have hesitated to tell Jennet that James had finally realised and accepted that terrible disillusioning 'truth'.

Behind everything Roger said to James and Jennet would have been his own sincere belief that the family were deluded by the Devil – that they were dangerous and wicked people who deserved the severest punishment, and yet at the same time ignorant and foolish people ensnared by a cunning and powerful supernatural adversary.

One of the most chilling passages in any book written during the witch-hunts is in Jean Bodin's *De la Démonomanie des Sorciers*:

> To tell the truth, whatever penalty one institutes against witches, such as to roast or burn them over a slow fire, that punishment is nowhere near as great as that which Satan makes them suffer in this world, not to mention the eternal punishments that are prepared for them, because the fire cannot last an hour or even half an hour before the witches are dead. But of all the sins that drag their own punishment in their wake, like avarice, envy, drunkenness, licentiousness, and others of a similar kind, there is none that punishes its servants more cruelly or protractedly than witchcraft, which brings retribution upon both the soul and the body.[20]

People like Jean Bodin were not deranged psychopaths. They were people who mistook their fear for a sense of justice, and their desire for order for a sense of what was right. They were brutalised by their own methods, but even so they could only nerve themselves to torture and kill by telling themselves that the enemy they were fighting was not the human being in front of them, but a faceless inhuman threat. By seeing the whole Universe as a battleground in a war between the forces of good and evil, and defining themselves and their colleagues as the forces of good, they could justify anything. It's ironic that such people could regard someone like Anne Jefferies as deluded by the Devil because she used magic to try to heal the sick, and yet not see that they were deluding themselves into a belief in the Devil that prevented them from recognising the horror of their actions.

Roger Nowell was a clever manipulator, and would have known very well how to cajole Jennet with promises and kindness as well as how to terrify her with threats – when to show sympathy, and when to show anger. He may have emphasised Jennet's responsibility to her younger brother William – perhaps threatened to separate them if Jennet couldn't prove that she was trustworthy. But Roger probably neither intended nor needed to make Jennet hate the rest of her family. What he had to do was make her believe what he had convinced himself was true – that her family's only hope was to acknowledge their crimes and renounce their association with the Devil. If Jennet's statements forced her mother and her older brother to confront their guilt, she might be helping to send them to the gallows, but she would also be saving them from eternal punishment in Hell.

CHAPTER TWENTY-FIVE

Such other witches as he knew to be dangerous

On 27 April Roger Nowell conducted his formal examination of Jennet, James and their mother Elizabeth. He was joined by his neighbour and fellow Justice of the Peace Nicholas Banester. It wasn't unusual for other officials to assist at examinations. William Sands, the Mayor of Lancaster, attended Anne Whittle's examination by James Anderton. Nicholas Banester would naturally have been interested in what was obviously an important case. But Roger may also have wanted Nicholas to be there because of the difficulties he was having with his suspects.

This examination was the climax of a series of interrogations that had not gone nearly as smoothly as the ones from 30 March to 2 April. We know that at first Elizabeth 'would confess nothing', that Roger had to take 'great pains' to get any information out of Jennet, and that James denied knowing Jennet Preston's identity and had to be taken to Gisburne for a confrontation with her.[1] It's also clear that when James gave Roger his hallucinatory description of killing John Duckworth with the Black Dog's help, he was in a very different state of mind from when he cleverly and unscrupulously blamed the human teeth at Malking Tower on Anne Whittle. And the change suggests that the two accounts were separated by several days of pressure.

Now Roger would confront his prisoners with what they had admitted. He'd probably already prepared draft versions of the statements that would be used at the trials, but he could quite legally edit them as much as his conscience allowed over the two days following the examination. The first time the suspects would know for certain what their statements contained would be when they heard them read out in court. And then it would be very difficult to challenge them – particularly if they were endorsed by Nicholas Banester as well as Roger himself.[2]

And what Roger had was James's confession to two murders, Jennet's evidence that James had killed Anne Towneley, and Elizabeth's confession to the murder of

John Robinson. He also had Jennet's and James's reluctant admission that Jennet Preston had been at Malking Tower on Good Friday, together with Jennet Device's list of six other people who had been there – her aunt and uncle, the three members of the Hargreives family, and Alice Nutter.

Young Jennet had been right to assume that Roger Nowell wouldn't arrest the Hargreiveses because of their connection with his Constable, Henry Hargreives. However, she'd miscalculated when she thought he wouldn't arrest Alice Nutter. According to local tradition, Roger had two other reasons for prosecuting Alice as well as her association with the Pendle cunning folk – he was involved in some kind of land dispute with her, and she was a Roman Catholic.[3]

However, Roger must have been very angry and frustrated that an important local family like the Nutters were so involved in magic. As well as the fact that Alice, John and Anthony were all clients of the Sothernes/Device family, there were the stories that some of Robert Nutter's female relatives had employed the two Burnley wise women to perform magic against him.[4] The temptation to make an example of Alice to shock the rest of her family out of their wickedness and folly – and to send a warning to other comparatively wealthy families in the area – must have been impossible to resist.

Apparently Elizabeth and James both made the same serious allegation against Alice. Elizabeth's statement reads:

> And further she sayeth, and confesseth, that she with the wife of Richard Nutter, and this examinate's said mother, joined altogether, and did bewitch the said Henry Mitton to death.[5]

However, the fact that the victim, Henry Mitton, is referred to as 'the *said* Henry Mitton' shows that he had already been mentioned. This statement of Elizabeth's is confirming some other earlier statement about the murder.

There's a statement from Jennet mentioning Henry:

> And this examinate also sayeth, that one other time she was present, when her said mother did call for the said Ball, who appeared in manner as aforesaid, and asked this examinate's mother what she would have him to do, whereunto this examinate's mother then said she would have him to kill one Mitton of the Rough Lee, whereupon the said Ball said, he would do it, and so vanished away, and about three weeks after, the said Mitton likewise died.[6]

But, according to this statement, Alice Nutter wasn't involved in the murder. Also, it's suspiciously similar to Jennet's account of her mother asking Ball to kill James Robinson – even down to the detail that Henry Mitton died about three weeks after the spirit's appearance.

The most revealing statement is James's. There are two versions of it, one drawn

Human-shaped mandrakes (thought to grow under a gallows) were carried as good luck charms. This mandrake was carved by the Dutch occultist Bob Richel (MoW 1393).

up for his mother's trial and one for Alice's, and they're not quite the same. The one used against Elizabeth reads:

The said James Device being examined, sayeth, that he heard his grandmother say, about a year ago, that his mother, called Elizabeth Device, and others, had killed one Henry Mitton of the Rough Lee aforesaid, by witchcraft. The reason wherefore he was so killed, was for that this examinate's said grandmother … had asked the said Mitton a penny; and he denying her thereof, thereupon she procured his death, as aforesaid.[7]

This statement indicates that Rough Lee has been mentioned before (Jennet mentioned it in her list of names as the place where Alice Nutter lived), but not Henry Mitton. Importantly, it contradicts itself. It begins by saying that Elizabeth Device, 'and others', killed Henry; but it then says that *Elizabeth Sothernes* 'procured his death' because he refused to give her a penny.

Significantly, there's no version of this statement included in the evidence Roger Nowell prepared to be used at *Elizabeth Sothernes's* trial – even though Roger *did* include far less incriminating evidence from James, such as an account of meeting the brown dog spirit near Malking Tower. The most plausible explanation is that this statement was made after Elizabeth Sothernes's death, when there was no point in preparing a version to be used against her.

This also suggests a likely explanation for the statement's contradictions. Thomas Covel, who interrogated James at Lancaster prison, was instructed by Roger Nowell to force James to incriminate his mother. Roger's investigations had turned up various suspicious deaths that could be blamed on Elizabeth Device, including Henry Mitton's. Confronted with the accusation that his mother had killed Henry,

PENDLE HILL

BARLEY

John and James Robinson

NEWCHURCH

Quarry where Elizabeth
Sothernes first met
the spirit Tibb

GOLDSHEY
BOOTH

MOSSE END

BULHOLE
John Nutter

Christopher, Jam
and John Bulcoc

Anthony and Anne
Nutter,

Henry Hargreives,
John Hargreives

FENCE

HIGHAM
Blaze Hargreives

V·S.

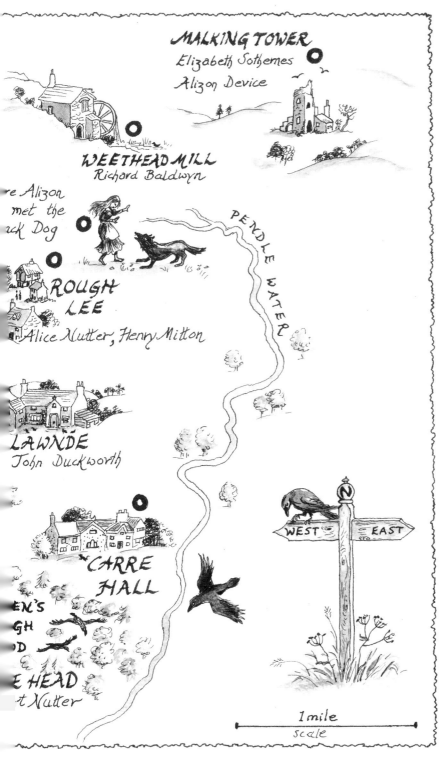

MALKING TOWER
Elizabeth Sothernes
Alizon Device

WEETHEAD MILL
Richard Baldwyn

re Alizon
met the
ck Dog

ROUGH LEE
Alice Nutter, Henry Mitton

LAWNDE
John Duckworth

CARRE HALL

EN'S
GH
D

E HEAD
t Nutter

PENDLE WATER

WEST   EAST

1 mile
scale

James – now increasingly confused as well as desperate – tried to blame the murder on his now dead grandmother, to protect his mother. Perhaps at that point he didn't know that Elizabeth had already confessed to killing John Robinson in an attempt to save *him*.

Probably it was only later that Roger Nowell decided that Henry Mitton's death could be used against Alice Nutter. Since Henry lived at Rough Lee, as Alice did, Roger would almost certainly have questioned Alice about Henry's death at some point. Alice no doubt defended Elizabeth, and ridiculed Roger's suggestion that Elizabeth had bewitched Henry. And when Jennet revealed that Alice had been at Malking Tower on Good Friday, Roger probably questioned Alice about *that*, and she defended Elizabeth on that occasion too.

If Alice refused to condemn Elizabeth, or to apologise for associating with her, it's not hard to imagine Roger developing a theory that it was Alice who had wanted Henry Mitton dead – that Alice had employed Elizabeth to curse him.

And so Roger doctored James's statement, extracted from him by Thomas Covel. Where it had originally read 'He heard his grandmother say, about a year ago, that she had killed one Henry Mitton', Roger changed it to read 'He heard his grandmother say, about a year ago, that his mother, called Elizabeth Device, and others, had killed one Henry Mitton.' And Roger then prepared another version of the statement, to be used against Alice, which began, 'He heard his grandmother say, about a year ago, that his mother, called Elizabeth Device, and his grandmother, and the wife of Richard Nutter of the Rough Lee aforesaid, had killed one Henry Mitton …'.[8] Finally, Roger either got Thomas Covel to force Elizabeth's statement out of her, or simply falsified it.

Thomas Potts admits that Alice Nutter was 'in the common opinion of the world, of good temper, free from envy or malice' – exactly the kind of person who would have tried to defend Elizabeth Device and her family, and gone on trying to defend them even when it put her own life at risk.[9]

Roger Nowell, of course, found Jennet's brief list of names unsatisfactory, and a statement from James contains a longer one:

> On Good Friday last, about twelve of the clock in the day time, there dined in this examinate's said mother's house, at Malking Tower, a number of persons, whereof three were men, with this examinate, and the rest women … The names of the said witches as were on Good Friday at this examinate's said grandmother's house, and now this examinate's own mother's, for so many of them as he did know, were these, *viz*. The wife of Hugh Hargreives of Barley; the wife of Christopher Bulcock of the Mosse End, and John her son; the mother of Myles Nutter [Alice]; Elizabeth, the wife of Christopher Hargreives, of Thurniholme; Christopher Howgate, and Elizabeth, his wife; Alice Gray of Colne, and one Mould-heeles's wife of the same: and this examinate, and his mother.[10]

Note how Christopher Hargreives is no longer included. He's been removed from the list so that John Bulcock can be added without contradicting the point Jennet had been so definite about – that only two men were present apart from James.

This indicates that Roger was hoping to have Jennet in court as a witness, but wasn't yet sure of her complete cooperation. He could now have James's list read out, saying that there were two men present including John Bulcock, then bring Jennet into the courtroom, and read out just the first part of her list, saying that two men were present. When Jennet confirmed that on oath, it would appear to corroborate James's statement naming John.[11]

Interestingly, when Roger prepared this cropped version of Jennet's list for John Bulcock's trial, he cut the word 'only' from the phrase 'only two were men'. This change was completely unnecessary, but it's an indication that Roger was aware of – and uneasy about – the fact that Jennet's list was clear evidence that John Bulcock was *not* at Malking Tower.

In fact there's also other evidence that Jane and John Bulcock weren't there, in a statement from Elizabeth Device:

> This examinate sayeth upon her oath, that she doth verily think, that the said Bulcock's wife doth know of some witches to be about Paddiham and Burnley.[12]

The use of the word 'witches' gives the impression – as it's intended to do – that Jane Bulcock made a habit of associating with people who performed curses. But when we remember that Roger Nowell regarded cunning folk (and indeed their clients) as witches, we can see that what Elizabeth probably really said was that Jane consulted cunning folk in Paddiham and Burnley – in other words, that Jane *wasn't* a client of the Sothernes/Device family. This was probably because Jane had lived at Paddiham or Burnley (which are both south of Pendle Forest) before she married Christopher Bulcock and moved to Pendle. We can therefore be reasonably certain that Jane and John Bulcock were *not* present at Malking Tower on Good Friday.

But it seems that Roger Nowell thought they *should* have been there, even if in fact they weren't. Mosse End, where Jane and John lived, was not far from Carre Hall, so it's very likely that the Devices did casual work for the Bulcocks, just as they had for the Towneleys before Anne Towneley's death.[13] Mosse End was also not far from the Lawnde, where James's other victim John Duckworth lived. That, again, raises the interesting possibility that Roger may have questioned the Bulcocks about the accusations against James, and the Bulcocks may have defended him. That would naturally have aroused Roger's suspicions, particularly after James confessed.

John Bulcock was probably a young, single man, since if he'd been married his wife would have been accused alongside him. Young men were also more likely to be accused of witchcraft than older men.[14] Perhaps he was similar in age to James and Alizon. Perhaps he was their friend.

Like Alice Nutter, Jane and John Bulcock weren't simply charged with attending the 'assembly of witches' at Malking Tower – they were charged with performing malevolent magic themselves. There's a statement from James incriminating them:

> And further he sayeth, that the said John Bulcock and Jane his said mother, did confess upon Good Friday last, at the said Malking Tower, in the hearing of this examinate, that they had bewitched, at the New-field Edge in Yorkshire, a woman called Jennet, wife of John Deyne, besides her reason; and the said woman's name so bewitched, he did not hear them speak of.[15]

Since the other evidence about Jane and John shows clear signs of distortions and tampering, the last part of this statement – 'the said woman's name so bewitched, he did not hear them speak of' – is particularly significant. How would James have known the name of the victim if Jane and John didn't mention it? And why would they give the name of the place where they bewitched their victim, and then not mention the *victim's* name? In fact it looks very much as if James was responding to a leading question – 'Did you hear Jane and John Bulcock talking about bewitching Jennet Deyne at the New-field Edge?' – and trying to *deny* it.

The other two people on James's list, Katherine Hewit (John Mould-heeles's wife) and Alice Gray, were also prosecuted for malevolent magic, and again the main evidence was a statement from James:

> The said witch, called Katherine Hewit … and one Alice Gray, did confess amongst the said witches at their meeting at Malking Tower aforesaid that they had killed Foulds's wife's child, called Anne Foulds, of Colne: and also sayeth, that they had then in hanck a child of Michael Hartley's of Colne.[16]

Jonathan Lumby points out in *The Lancashire Witch-Craze* that the term 'in hanck' is an ambiguous phrase meaning bound by magic. He suggests plausibly that Katherine Hewit and Alice Gray were wise women who attended the gathering at Malking Tower as colleagues of the Devices, and were discussing performing healing magic on the two children.[17] It may be that they'd come under suspicion of killing young Anne Foulds because their attempts to cure her had failed.

Even with the evidence helpfully provided by Roger Nowell that Jennet Preston had been at Malking Tower, Roger's colleague Thomas Heyber was struggling to build a case against her. The only real witnesses he had were his son-in-law Thomas Lister and a woman called Anne Robinson, who was probably one of Thomas Lister's servants.[18] As usual Thomas Potts claims that there were 'many other witnesses', but in a revealing little slip he says, 'Anne Robinson and others were *both* examined' (my italics).

However, their statements were certainly dramatic:

> In the end Anne Robinson and others were both examined, who upon their oaths declared against her, that Master Lister lying in great extremity, upon his death-bed, cried out unto them that stood about him; that Jennet Preston was in the house, look where she is, take hold of her: for God's sake shut the doors, and take her, she cannot escape away. Look about for her, and lay hold on her, for she is in the house: and so cried very often in his great pains, to them that came to visit him during his sickness.

Anne Robinson and Thomas Lister

> Being examined further, they both gave this in evidence against her, that when Master Lister lay upon his death-bed, he cried out in great extremity; Jennet Preston lies heavy upon me, Preston's wife lies heavy upon me; help me, help me: and so departed, crying out against her.
>
> These, with many other witnesses, were further examined, and deposed, that Jennet Preston, the prisoner at the bar, being brought to Master Lister after he was dead, and laid out to be wound up in his winding-sheet, the said Jennet Preston coming to touch the dead corpse, they bled fresh blood presently, in the presence of all that were there present.[19]

As Thomas Potts goes on to add, a dead body suddenly starting to bleed 'hath ever been held a great argument to induce a jury to hold him guilty that shall be accused of murder, and hath seldom, or never, failed in the trial'. In *Demonology*, King James wrote:

> In a secret murder, if the dead carcase be at any time thereafter handled by the murderer, it will gush out of blood.[20]

But, crucially, there was no evidence that Jennet Preston had ever threatened Master Lister, or shown any hostility towards any member of the Lister family. However, a statement from James solved that problem:

> There was a woman dwelling in Gisburne parish, who came into this examinate's said grandmother's house, who there came, and craved assistance of the rest of them that were then there, for the killing of Master [Thomas] Lister of Westby: because, as she then said, he had borne malice unto her, and had thought to have put her away at the last Assizes at York; but could not. And then this examinate heard the said woman say, that her power was not strong enough to do it herself, being now less than before-time it had been. And he also further sayeth, that the said Preston's wife had a spirit with her like unto a white foal, with a black spot in the forehead …
>
> And this examinate further sayeth, that all the said witches went out of the said house in their own shapes and likenesses, and they all, by that they were forth of the doors, were gotten on horseback like unto foals, some of one colour, some of another,

and Preston's wife was the last; and when she got on horseback, they all presently vanished out of this examinate's sight: and before their said parting away, they all appointed to meet at the said Preston's wife's house that day twelve-month; at which time the said Preston's wife promised to make them a great feast; and if they had occasion to meet in the meantime, then should warning be given that they all should meet upon Romles Moor. And this examinate further sayeth, that at the said feast at Malking Tower, this examinate heard them all give their consents to put the said Master Thomas Lister of Westby to death: and after Master Lister should be made away by witchcraft, then all the said witches gave their consents to join altogether to hanck Master Leonard Lister [Thomas's uncle], when he should come to dwell at the Sowgill, and so put him to death.[21]

Note the repetition, 'who came into this examinate's said grandmother's house, who there came, and craved assistance' – a briefly clumsy piece of editing, which marks the point where a later statement is pasted on to the end of James's original admission, when he said that he was vaguely aware that some woman from Gisburne had been at Malking Tower.

It's also significant that Jennet Preston's familiar spirit is described as 'like unto a white foal, with a black spot in the forehead'. A familiar spirit taking the form of a horse is quite unusual. But by now it probably won't surprise readers to discover that Ales Hunt, one of the suspects in Brian Darcey's *A True and Just Record*, 'had two spirits like colts, the one black, the other white'.[22]

Note too the attempts to make the gathering at Malking Tower out to be a Witches' Sabbat, like the meetings Matteuccia apparently flew to in the shape of a fly 200 years earlier. James is clearly pressured to admit that the guests shape-shifted, but insists that they all 'went out of the said house in their own shapes and likenesses'. The interrogator is forced to fall back on implying that they rode off on creatures that were not flesh and blood horses but spirits 'like unto foals', and that 'they all presently vanished out of this examinate's sight' in some vaguely supernatural way.

But by that point, was the interrogator Roger Nowell, or Thomas Covel, the Lancaster jailer? As I've already argued, the fact that James's list of names refers to Malking Tower as 'now this examinate's own mother's' strongly suggests that it was obtained from James after his grandmother's death, which can't have occurred before 19 May. In addition, *The Wonderful Discovery* specifically states that Thomas Covel interrogated James and forced him to name other suspects:

Master Covel, who hath the custody of the jail at Lancaster, having taken great pains with him [James] during the time of his imprisonment, to procure him to discover [reveal] his practices [plots], and such other witches as he knew to be dangerous.[23]

There is an undated statement from James made, like Anne Whittle's, before James Anderton at Lancaster. However, all this statement contains is a description of an encounter with the Black Dog. It doesn't contain any references to plots or other witches. The obvious explanation is that this important information, which

Thomas Covel took such 'great pains' to extract from James, was for some reason added to James's earlier statements – the ones dated 27 April.

All this points to the conclusion that James's list of names was part of the information obtained by Thomas Covel. And if this bare list – which simply says that Jane and John Bulcock, Katherine Hewit and Alice Gray were at Malking Tower on Good Friday – was the result of Thomas Covel's efforts, then the more incriminating evidence against them surely must be too.

It's extremely likely, therefore, that apart from James's admission that Jennet Preston was at Malking Tower, all his other evidence against her and these other four suspects, as well as all his evidence against his mother, was the result of the interrogations carried out at Lancaster prison. Roger Nowell may have given Thomas Covel instructions about the information he wanted from James, but it was Thomas Covel who forced James to give it. Roger may have convinced James that he'd been deluded by an evil spirit, but that was very different from making him admit that the clients who gathered at Malking Tower had gone there to gloat over cursing people.

It's perhaps surprising that Roger Nowell – who had taken such care with the statements he'd already drawn up himself – didn't go to Lancaster to assist in the interrogations. But if he had, there would surely be some Lancaster statements where his name appeared as one of the examining Justices. It seems that even when James was formally examined by James Anderton, Roger wasn't present.

Perhaps there were enough similarities between James and Roger's teenage son Alexander to make Roger decide that he didn't want to know what was going to happen to James at Lancaster prison. Perhaps as a Justice of the Peace, committed to upholding the law, he didn't want to know that Thomas Covel was going to break the law against torture.

CHAPTER TWENTY-SIX

The Devil's master

Now to proceed with felonies by statute …

Jailers (by duress and pain) enforcing their prisoner, to become an approver (that is an accuser of others as coadjutors with him in felony).

(*The Country Justice* by Michael Dalton[1])

The law against torture was clear and specific. However, *The Wonderful Discovery* tells us that Thomas Covel succeeded in making James 'an accuser of others'. If Roger Nowell had obtained all the information he wanted, there would have been no need for Thomas Covel to interrogate James. And Roger wouldn't have given up on questioning James himself, and sent him to Lancaster, if he hadn't been sure that Thomas Covel would succeed where he had failed.

When he was Sheriff, Roger would have co-operated closely with Thomas Covel to organise the Assizes, and no doubt they developed a good working relationship. But he could hardly expect the Lancaster jailer to share his outrage at the activities of a group of witches on the other side of the county.

However, it seems that when the Devices and their clients gathered at Malking Tower it wasn't only to practice magic. James, apparently, revealed another reason:

For the delivery of his said grandmother, this examinate's said sister Alizon; the said Anne [Whittle], and her daughter Redferne; killing the jailer at Lancaster; and before the next Assizes to blow up the castle there [the site of the prison], to the end the aforesaid persons might by that means make an escape and get away.[2]

And so – remarkably conveniently for Roger Nowell – Thomas Covel would be highly motivated when he interrogated James, because James had planned to blow Thomas Covel and his prison to pieces, and the people Thomas Covel would be forcing James to name were his fellow conspirators.

It would be tempting to dismiss this bomb plot as some fantasy of young Jennet's, if it wasn't for the fact that her statements make no mention of it. Elizabeth, too, insisted that she had no knowledge of the plan:

> But [she] denieth that any talk was amongst them the said witches, to her now remembrance, at the said meeting together, touching the killing of the jailer at Lancaster; blowing up of the castle, thereby to deliver ... her mother, Alizon Device her daughter, and other prisoners, committed to the said castle for witchcraft.[3]

If the phrase 'to her now remembrance' is an accurate record of Elizabeth's words, I imagine it was said with heavy irony.

So it seems that the idea of a bomb plot had its origins in something James said, and was probably a reflection of his anger at the conditions his sister and grandmother were being held in at Lancaster. As I've already suggested, it's likely he'd been to Lancaster and seen the prison for himself. But no doubt Jennet Preston also had horrific stories about what she'd experienced in the prison at York.

In fact it's quite possible that as well as performing magic to help the prisoners, the Devices and their clients discussed attempting to rescue them. Corruption and incompetence were so ingrained in the prison system that escapes were common.[4] One in particular is likely to have caught the imagination of the Pendle cunning folk – John Fian's escape, described in *News from Scotland*.

It's probably unlikely (though not impossible) that the Devices had actually read the pamphlet, but the main facts would have been common knowledge. Even by

A nineteenth-century French bowl depicting the Devil accompanied by a dog. Behind it is a Latin edition of Jean Bodin's *De la Démonomanie des Sorciers*. 'Des Sorciers' is translated '*Magorum*' – from the Greek word *magoi*, used in the Bible for the 'wise men' who visited the infant Jesus (MoW 1937 & 1447).

witchcraft standards, it had been a sensational case. The suspects – two of them, Geillis Duncane and Agnes Sampson, well-known wise women – had been charged with attempting to harm King James by wrecking his ship when he was on a visit to Denmark. The King had personally supervised the interrogations, and personally ordered the use of a level of torture unparalleled in British cases. He had also ordered a massive manhunt to recapture John Fian, the schoolteacher named as a magician by Geillis Duncane[5]

However, John Fian had escaped by the simple but effective method of getting hold of a key to his cell. Blowing up Lancaster prison and killing Thomas Covel would have been dangerous and unnecessary. Money spent on gunpowder would have been far better spent on bribes, as everyone at Malking Tower would have known.

Significantly, though, this was less than seven years after the notorious Gunpowder Plot of the 5th of November – an attempt by Roman Catholic extremists to blow up the Houses of Parliament with King James inside. The Malking Tower conspiracy seems like some kind of bizarre parody of the Gunpowder Plot. But perhaps that's because that's exactly what it was – someone's grim joke.[6]

It's certainly quite possible that some of the Device's clients were Roman Catholics who regretted the failure of the 5 November plot. Two members of the Nutter family had been hanged, drawn and quartered for being Roman Catholic priests – John Nutter at Tyburn in London in 1583, and his brother Robert at Lancaster in 1600, just twelve years earlier. This martyred Robert Nutter had been a close associate of one of the people supposedly involved in the Gunpowder Plot.[7]

However, this doesn't mean that James and his family were Roman Catholics. They would have known that the Protestant King James had killed the Scottish wise women Geillis Duncane and Agnes Sampson, but they would also have been well aware that the Roman Catholic church had a long history of killing cunning folk and magicians. Their branch of Christianity was the Christianity of Honorius of Thebes – who declared the pope in league with the evil spirits because he opposed magic. They used a Latin charm, perhaps in conjunction with a crucifix, and James crossed himself in times of stress – all things that would have made them look papist to Roger Nowell. But when Elizabeth Sothernes wanted James to obtain the Host for use in magic, she was quite happy to send him to a Church of England communion service.

It's clear that they believed that the bread turned into the body of Christ regardless of whether it was a Catholic priest or a Church of England minister who performed the ritual. But of course while Catholic and Protestant thinkers argued about whether what happened was transubstantiation, consubstantiation, or merely a symbolic gesture, to cunning folk it was an act of magic – just as their hazel stick turned into the 'ligh in leath wand' 'as the priest makes God's body in his hands'.

But the Devices had reason to be hostile towards King James himself, regardless of his religion. His book *Demonology* condemned all forms of magic, specifically mentioning the use of counter-magic against witchcraft:

> When such a cure is used, it may well serve for a short time, but at the last, it will doubtlessly tend to the utter perdition of the patient, both in body and soul.[8]

He then went even further:

> The consulters, trusters in, overseers, entertainers or stirrers up of these craft-folks, are equally guilty with themselves that are the practisers.[9]

But perhaps most importantly of all, in 1604 King James had revised the law against magic, and changed the penalty for harming someone by witchcraft from a year's imprisonment to death. It was only because of that change that Alizon was now at risk of dying on the gallows.

A stick or wand with a handle of human bone carved into the shape of a skull (MoW 1117).

It's therefore easy to believe that the conversation at Malking Tower on Good Friday might have turned to the Gunpowder Plot of 1605, and to revolutionary talk about how the prejudiced, sadistic dictator and his self-serving Parliament had deserved to be destroyed. Thomas Covel and his prison were part of the same vicious system, so it may well be that someone jokingly suggested that a similar explosion ought to be arranged for them.

And then at some point when James was being interrogated by Roger, something provoked him into mentioning it. James would almost certainly have complained to Roger about the conditions at Lancaster prison. Perhaps he wanted to shock Roger out of his patronising complacency – just as Alizon had done when she described her sexually charged relationship with the Black Dog.

But for Roger Nowell – and also for Thomas Potts, when he came to write his pamphlet – it presented an excellent opportunity to link the cunning folk and their clients with the Catholic traitors of 1605 – to underline the essentially treasonous nature of magic.[10] And then when James proved stubborn, it became a way for Roger Nowell to manipulate Thomas Covel into doing whatever was necessary to force James to cooperate.

Of course there was no real likelihood that anyone would hold Thomas Covel to account for his actions. And the law against torture wasn't the only law governing the treatment of prisoners. As *The Country Justice* explains,

> Though assaults and batteries be for the most part contrary to the peace of the realm, and the laws of the same, yet some are allowed to have a natural, and some a civil power (or authority) over others ...
>
> And therefore the parent (with moderation) may chastise his child ...
> So may the master his servant ...
> So may the jailer (or his servant by his commandment) his unruly prisoners.

It then gives an example:

> Note that the master may strike his servant with his hand, fist, small staff, or stick, for correction: and though he do draw blood thereby, yet it seemeth no breach of the peace.[11]

This aspect of the law was interpreted fairly freely by jailers. In the 1660s the 'small staff' used by the jailer at Leicester to beat prisoners was a quarterstaff – a two-metre pole with an iron tip. He also set his dog on them. His interpretation of 'unruly' was also remarkably inclusive – he beat Quaker prisoners for praying.[12]

However, the effectiveness of other, less violent, methods was also recognised. Jean Bodin suggested that

> Before the interrogation you should make a show of preparing a number of different instruments, and large quantities of rope, and guards to restrain them, and keep them for some time in that state of fear and helplessness.[13]

He added, 'The fear of torture is a form of torture'[14] – an observation echoed in the CIA's *Human Resource Exploitation Training Manual – 1983*:

> The threat of coercion usually weakens or destroys resistance more effectively than coercion itself. For example, the threat to inflict pain can trigger fears more damaging than the immediate sensation of pain.

Henri Boguet wrote:

> If the [examining] judge is unable to extract anything from the accused, he should have him locked in an extremely dark and cramped cell. Because it has been demonstrated that the stress of imprisonment usually forces witches to accept the need to confess, even if they're young people.[15]

This may well have been one of the methods he used so successfully on Pierre Vuillermoz. Lancaster prison certainly had solitary confinement cells of this kind – George Fox, the founder of the Quaker movement, was held in one in 1664.[16]

In addition, prisoners were routinely chained as a form of punishment and restraint. When Luke Hutton had the irons fitted to his ankles, he was warned by a sympathetic guard,

> To strive in fetters it will small avail:
> Seek first to ease thy legs, which will grow sore.

As well as their depressing psychological effect, the discomfort from the chains quickly became a constant background pain. Luke describes one desperate prisoner going down on his knees and begging the jailer to remove his shackles – getting the unsympathetic response,

> What now I know, if I had known before,
> Instead of these light chains thou shouldst have more.

Having experienced it for himself, Luke Hutton was in no doubt that the use of chains was a form of torture:

> Bolts, shackles, collars, and iron shears I spied,
> Thumb-stalls, waist-bands, torture's grief unfolding.[17]

Another well-known interrogation technique was the use of what are now known as 'stress positions' – where the prisoner is restrained or forced to stand or sit in an awkward position for long periods. John Gaule, campaigning against the witch hunt conducted by Matthew Hopkins and his colleagues in 1646, wrote:

> [The prisoner] is placed in the middle of a room upon a stool, or table, cross-legged, or in some other uneasy posture, which if she submit not, she is then bound with cords; there is she watched and kept without meat or sleep for the space of twenty-four hours.[18]

However, the use of stress positions had been routine in English jails for decades, as one prisoner described in 1596:

> Ten days I stood with both my hands stretched above my head against the wall in the standing stocks.[19]

According to the CIA Manual, this is one of the most effective interrogation methods:

The torture situation is an external conflict, a contest between the subject and his tormentor. The pain which is being inflicted upon him from outside himself may actually intensify his will to resist. On the other hand, pain which he feels he is inflicting upon himself is more likely to sap his resistance. For example, if he is required to maintain rigid positions such as standing at attention or sitting on a stool for long periods of time, the immediate source of pain is not the 'questioner' but the subject himself.

The surprising thing is not that Thomas Covel obtained the statements he required from James, but that the phrase 'having taken great pains with him during his imprisonment' suggests that it took him a great deal of time and effort.

✯ ✯ ✯

There are also statements from Elizabeth Device that were almost certainly obtained by Thomas Covel. She confirmed James's list of names and identified three other Good Friday guests – Anne Crouckshey of Marsden and 'two women of Burnley parish, whose names the wife of Richard Nutter doth know', although fortunately none of them were prosecuted. She also confessed 'in all things touching the christening [i.e. naming] of the spirit, and the killing of Master Lister, as the said James Device hath before confessed'.

> And she also sayeth, that at their meeting on Good Friday at Malking Tower aforesaid, the said Katherine Hewit, alias Mould-heeles, and Alice Gray, did confess, they had killed a child of Foulds of Colne, called Anne Foulds, and had gotten hold of another …
>
> And she further sayeth, that at the said meeting at Malking Tower, as aforesaid, Katherine Hewit and John Bulcock, with all the rest then there, gave their consents, with the said Preston's wife, for the killing of the said Master Lister.[20]

And she also confirmed Jennet's statement accusing her of killing John Robinson's brother:

> And this examinate further sayeth and confesseth, that she did bewitch the said James Robinson to death, as in the said Jennet Device her examination is confessed.[21]

The very brevity of these statements is chilling. It suggests a stubborn woman finally forced to confront her powerlessness – offered a last deceptive hope that she could still do something to protect her children, and clutching at it with a combination of disillusionment and desperation.

And there is evidence that Elizabeth, too, was tortured. After seeing her in the courtroom, Thomas Potts wrote:

> This odious witch was branded with a preposterous mark in nature, even from her birth, which was her left eye, standing lower than the other, the one looking down, the other looking up.[22]

Although he claimed this was a birth defect (and of course Roger Nowell would have been his only source of information about Elizabeth's early life), what Thomas Potts was actually describing – 'one [eye] looking down, the other looking up' – is a symptom of a serious eye injury: a fracture of the eye socket caused by a violent blow to the eye.

Surprisingly, the eyeball doesn't burst, but instead the force of the blow is transferred through the eyeball, and the eye socket splinters back into the head. As a result, the muscles that control the movement of the eye often become trapped in the broken bone. The impression that the damaged eye was set lower in Elizabeth's face than the other could have been caused by severe laceration of the lower eyelid. A blow from a fist isn't usually powerful enough to inflict such an injury – Elizabeth would have had to have been kicked in the face or hit with a staff or cudgel.[23]

Of course there's nothing that demonstrates conclusively that this was a torture injury inflicted by Thomas Covel. Elizabeth could have been hit during one of her arrests, or while she was in Roger Nowell's custody – or it could have been an accidental injury completely unconnected with the witchcraft case. But since what Thomas Potts describes is more likely to be the result of an injury than a birth defect, the fact that he's so insistent that it's a birth defect could be regarded as suspicious.

We also shouldn't underestimate the effect on James, Elizabeth and Alizon of Elizabeth Sothernes's death. Very probably she and Alizon were imprisoned in the same cell. There would have been no reason to separate them, and it would have been convenient for Thomas Covel to have Alizon looking after her grandmother. It would have been Alizon, therefore, who had to cope with her grandmother's increasing ill-health, and find ways to help her in spite of their desperate circumstances. However, it's clear that the statements from James and his mother were obtained only after Elizabeth Sothernes's death, which suggests it may have played a significant part in demoralising them.

But why was the evidence Thomas Covel extracted from James and Elizabeth at Lancaster presented in court as evidence obtained by Roger Nowell at Pendle? The clue is in something Thomas Potts tells us about Jane and John Bulcock:

> Among all the witches in this company, there is not a more fearful and devilish act committed, and voluntarily confessed by any of them, comparable to this [the bewitching of Jennet Deyne], under the degree of murder: which impudently now at the bar (having formerly confessed;) they forswear.[24]

In other words, at their trial Jane and John protested their innocence, in spite of having earlier confessed to bewitching Jennet Deyne. However, their confessions are not included in *The Wonderful Discovery*. If they'd confessed to Roger Nowell he would have turned those confessions into formal statements – in fact, as a Justice of the Peace he would have been obliged to do so. And then, of course, Thomas Potts would have included them in his pamphlet.

So Jane and John must have confessed to Thomas Covel – probably each confessing to try to save the other. Any information Thomas Covel obtained had to be confirmed in a formal examination conducted by a Justice of the Peace. And when Jane and John were brought before the Justice – probably James Anderton again – they must have retracted their confessions.

Elizabeth and James must have done the same. We know there was an official examination, conducted by James Anderton and with the Mayor of Lancaster also present, where a statement was taken from James Device describing an encounter with the Black Dog. That statement is included in *The Wonderful Discovery*. But James must have retracted everything else Thomas Covel had got from him.

All the evidence that Thomas Covel had so laboriously accumulated was now unusable. It would have been a serious humiliation for him. And he must have wondered how Roger Nowell would react to the news. And not just Roger – but also Thomas Heyber. Jennet Preston was due to be tried at York at the end of July – three weeks before the Lancaster trials. It had taken Thomas Covel a considerable time to piece together the necessary statements, and it's likely that Jennet's trial was getting close. James's statement was the only evidence that she was hostile towards the Lister family. It was essential for convicting her.

But Roger Nowell was a skilled manipulator. He knew how to manipulate the system just as he knew how to manipulate people. No doubt it seemed to him that it was just an irritating technicality that the statements drawn up by Thomas Covel had to be confirmed in the presence of a Justice of the Peace. There was a simple solution and Roger took it. He added the statements drawn up by Thomas Covel to the statements from the examinations he had conducted on 27 April.

Of course Roger's colleague Nicholas Banester had sat in on the 27 April examinations. Did he know that Roger was now using his name to legitimise these later Lancaster statements? It's unlikely he would have objected – particularly if Roger had involved him in the first place because James and Elizabeth were proving so uncooperative.

It must have taken considerable courage for James and Elizabeth to retract their statements. Thomas Covel would have emphatically discouraged any form of defiance by his prisoners. When Jane and John withdrew their confessions, no doubt they hoped that it would save their lives. James and Elizabeth, however, had already confessed to Roger, and during the long weeks in prison it must have been hard to hold on to any hope of survival.

It's possible that Jane and John persuaded James and Elizabeth to retract their statements. However, it's unlikely, because Roger would probably have waited until he had James's and Elizabeth's evidence before he arrested the other suspects. And James and Elizabeth were probably held separately from the other prisoners, at least while they were still being interrogated.[25]

However, there was, of course, one suspect who knew that James Device was under pressure to give evidence against her – Jennet Preston. She would have realised it when Henry Hargreives took James to identify her not long after Good Friday. And we know that her family fought hard to clear her. It's very likely that her husband William would have tried to find out more about James's testimony. Of course Thomas Covel wouldn't have allowed William to visit James in prison – if he'd known about it. But William might have been able to bribe one of the guards. Did William manage to see James, and plead with him not to give evidence against Jennet?

Certainly James didn't retract his evidence to save himself, because he didn't retract all of it. *The Wonderful Discovery* includes one final statement from him:

> The voluntary confession and declaration of James Device, prisoner in the castle at Lancaster.
>
> Before William Sands, Mayor of Lancaster, James Anderton, Esquire, one of his Majesty's Justices of Peace within the county of Lancaster: and Thomas Covel, gentleman, one of his Majesty's coroners in the same county. *Viz.*
>
> James Device, prisoner in the castle at Lancaster, sayeth; that his said spirit Dandy, being very earnest with him to give him his soul, he answered, he would give him that part thereof that was his own to give: and thereupon the said spirit said, he was above Christ Jesus, and therefore he must absolutely give him his soul: and that done, he would give him power to revenge himself against any whom he disliked.
>
> And he further sayeth, that the said spirit did appear unto him after sundry times, in the likeness of a dog, and at every time most earnestly persuaded him to give him his soul absolutely: who answered as before, that he would give him his own part and no further. And he sayeth, that at the last time that the said spirit was with him, which was the Tuesday next before his apprehension, when as he could not prevail with him to have his soul absolutely granted unto him, as aforesaid; the said spirit departed from him, then giving a most fearful cry and yell, and withal caused a great flash of fire to show about him: which said spirit did never after trouble this examinate.[26]

No doubt James repeated his assertion that 'his soul … was his saviour Jesus Christ's', since there's no other reason why Dandy would have insisted 'he was above Christ Jesus'. But at some point that was cut out, so that this unsatisfactory confession would at least be as incriminating to James as possible. To Thomas Covel and the other officials it was simply proof that James had dealings with the Devil, and James must have realised that would be their interpretation.

If the stress of being interrogated by Roger Nowell had triggered James's first dream or vision of the Black Dog, it would have been almost inevitable that what he went through at Lancaster would trigger others. But his relationship with the spirit had changed, and become more complicated. James now accepted that Dandy was not only an evil spirit but one so powerful he could claim to be above Christ – in fact, the Devil himself. And he also acknowledged that his lies and betrayals had given Dandy a claim to a part of his soul.

But in spite of that, at their final encounter James forced the Black Dog to retreat:

> The said spirit departed from him, then giving a most fearful cry and yell, and withal caused a great flash of fire to show about him.

'A flash of fire' was the term generally used in the seventeenth century to mean a flash of lightning. And the phrase 'withal caused' indicates that the 'him' was James. This was not the smoky fires of Hell swallowing up Dandy, it was a brilliant white light engulfing James.

In their earlier encounter, the Black Dog spoke with Roger Nowell's voice, and gained his power over James from Roger's accusations. But now James defeated the doubts those accusations had planted in his mind, as well as his own bitter sense of guilt and failure.

But the Black Dog was a complex figure. In this final encounter he took James out of the squalor and misery of Lancaster prison and across time and space, back to the countryside of Pendle and to freedom. And there, by challenging him, he gave him the chance to make one last *right* choice.

We can't know whether this vision of the Black Dog made James decide to retract his evidence against the other suspects, or whether his decision to retract triggered the vision, but it seems clear that they *are* linked. And so the last account we have from James is a description of a defining victory. He had access to a power imprisonment couldn't take from him.

> Everlasting God ... making both light and darkness ... Put forth thy hand and touch my mouth and make it like a sharp sword to declare and speak forth as well words as deeds ... to constrain and compel to come and to answer to stand and to go away such spirits unto me.
>
> (*The Sworn Book*[27])

The psychological importance of his vision to James himself is obvious. But it's less clear why he allowed it to become a statement that would be used against him at his trial. He could have retracted it along with his other evidence – but he did not.

In the late seventeenth century Moses Pitt asked his brother-in-law Humphrey Martyn to visit Anne Jefferies to get her version of her story. Humphrey Martyn wrote back:

> She replied that if she should discover it to you, that you would make either books or ballads of it; and she said that she would not have her name spread about the country in books or ballads, or such things, if she might have £500 for doing it.[28]

Any witchcraft case attracted a great deal of publicity, and James must have realised – from the number of people he'd been asked to incriminate – that he was caught up in a major case. He couldn't know that, thanks to Thomas Potts's pamphlet, every word of his official statements would be preserved, but he *did* know that there would be 'books or ballads' of some kind.

In 1900 Arthur Morrison wrote an article for *The Strand Magazine* about the famous nineteenth-century cunning man Cunning Murrell, and interviewed his son, Buck Murrell. At the end of their conversation, Buck Murrell said,

> You know now about my father, sir. Remember, sir, he were a good man – enemy to all witches, and the Devil's master. He never *put on* – he took off. Remember that, sir.[29]

James's final statement was not intended for William Sands and James Anderton. It was intended for the ordinary people of Lancashire, for the people who consulted cunning folk, the people who might one day consult Jennet and William. And perhaps it was also intended for Jennet and William themselves. James wanted them to know that he was not a servant of the Devil, or deluded by the Devil – he was the Devil's master.

CHAPTER TWENTY-SEVEN

The Trials

It's hard today to grasp the noise and chaos of a seventeenth-century trial. Even without a sensational witchcraft case, the Assizes were an important social and political event, attended by all the most influential people in the county. The courtroom was so packed with spectators it was sometimes hard for the judge to force his way through to the bench, and at a trial at East Grinstead the floor gave way under the weight. Security was limited to chaining any defendants regarded as dangerous – although that didn't stop them occasionally throwing things at the judge. There was no attempt to control the crowd, and it wasn't unknown for fights to break out, particularly during times of political tension.[1] One woman found guilty of witchcraft was afterwards asked why she didn't defend herself in court, and replied that 'when she was arraigned she would have answered for herself, but ... the throng [was] so great that she could not hear the evidence against her'.[2]

Doing his best to ignore the distractions, the judge conducted each trial with as much ruthless efficiency as possible. For him it was a gruelling process. His working day began at around seven in the morning and ended at around eleven at night. In those sixteen hours he might preside over fifty trials.[3] It must have been an enormous relief when he found himself working with a committed Justice of the Peace like Roger Nowell, who would take over much of the conduct of the trial, presenting statements and witnesses, and generally acting as prosecutor.[4] But the judge played a very active part in all trials, instructing the jury on how to interpret the evidence, and leaving them in no doubt about the verdict he expected. And juries could be fined or even imprisoned for a verdict that displeased the judge.[5]

It's therefore a credit to the jury at the York Lent Assizes in March that Jennet Preston had been acquitted. Thomas Potts explains that after murdering Thomas Lister's father, Jennet 'revenged herself upon his son, who in short time received great loss in his goods [livestock] and cattle by her means'.[6] He then adds:

> These things in time did beget suspicion, and at the Assizes and General Jail Delivery holden [held] at the Castle of York in Lent last past, before my Lord Bromley, she

was indicted and arraigned for the murder of a child of one Dodgsonne's, but by the favour and merciful consideration of the jury thereof acquitted.

Note how Thomas Potts unashamedly claims that Jennet wasn't acquitted because she was innocent, but because of the jury's misguided sympathy for her.

YORK SUMMER ASSIZES
Judge: Sir James Altham
27th July 1612
JENNET PRESTON[7]

Jennet Preston now found herself on trial for murder by witchcraft for a second time – this time finally charged with the murder of Thomas Lister's father. Thomas Lister and Anne Robinson were in court to confirm their evidence, but Elizabeth, James and Jennet were not;[8] their statements were read out in their absence. This meant, of course, that Jennet Preston was denied the chance to challenge these three vital witnesses in person – and that Elizabeth, James and Jennet were denied the chance to withdraw their evidence against her.

This is another indication that James and Elizabeth had in fact retracted their statements. They wouldn't appear in person as witnesses against any of their fellow suspects at the Lancaster trials either. There, too, their statements would be used but they would not appear in court except at their own trials. However, at Jennet Preston's trial Roger Nowell and Thomas Heyber may have argued that the distance from Lancaster to York made transporting James and Elizabeth to the York Assizes impractical.

But that argument couldn't have applied to Jennet Device. Thomas Lister and Anne Robinson lived only a few kilometres north of Pendle Forest.[9] If they could travel to York, Roger could have taken Jennet. So why *wasn't* Jennet Device in court to confirm her evidence against Jennet Preston? Was Roger afraid that she, too, would try to retract it?

Even if Roger was sure of young Jennet at this point, making her appear at the York Assizes carried obvious risks. It would expose her to the stress of appearing in court, and might unnerve her so much that she would become unreliable for the Lancaster Assizes, when her evidence would be even more important. In addition, if Jennet Preston was convicted and executed it would be hard to keep the news from Jennet Device. It would bring home to her the fact that her testimony had helped to cause someone's death, and that would be something Roger Nowell didn't want Jennet to have on her mind at the start of the Lancaster trials.

The Wonderful Discovery includes the judge's summing-up of the case against Jennet Preston:

> His Lordship commanded the jury to observe the particular circumstances; first, Master Lister in his great extremity, to complain he saw her, and requested them that were by him to lay hold of her.

After he cried out she lay heavy upon him, even at the time of his death. But the conclusion is of more consequence than all the rest, that Jennet Preston being brought to the dead corpse, they bled freshly, and after her deliverance in Lent, it is proved she rode upon a white foal, and was present in the great assembly at Malking Tower with the witches, to entreat and pray for aid of them, to kill Master Lister, now living, for that he had prosecuted against her.

And against these people you may not expect such direct evidence, since all their works are the works of darkness, no witnesses are present to accuse them, therefore I pray God direct your consciences.[10]

In spite of this, the jury deliberated 'for the most part of the day'[11] before finally delivering a verdict of guilty. At the end of the Assizes Jennet Preston was sentenced to death and hanged. She protested her innocence to the end.

Her family and friends, and in particular her husband William, reacted with horror and outrage. To counter their accusations of a conspiracy, Thomas Potts dashed off a pamphlet about the case. At that point he wasn't to know that he would soon be writing a much longer pamphlet that would include the Lancaster trials. He didn't know that William Preston would go to Lancaster to try to discredit James's evidence – to clear his wife's name, and also, no doubt, to try to save the other five people accused of being at the 'assembly of witches' and incriminated by James: Alice Nutter, Jane and John Bulcock, Alice Gray and Katherine Hewit.[12]

LANCASTER SUMMER ASSIZES
Judge: Sir Edward Bromley
18th(?) August 1612
MARGARET PEARSON[13]

Margaret Pearson had been tried twice before, once for murder by witchcraft and once for causing illness by witchcraft. Now she was charged with killing a horse. The Justice of the Peace who took action against her was Nicholas Banester.

It's not clear exactly when during the Assizes her case was heard. Thomas Potts puts it at the end of his account of the Pendle trials, but admits that this is simply because she wasn't facing a death sentence, but the lesser penalty of a year's imprisonment and four six-hour sessions in the pillory.

Just as Roger Nowell had provided evidence against Jennet Preston for Thomas Heyber, he also provided evidence against Margaret Pearson for Nicholas Banester – a statement from Anne Whittle. Thomas Potts implies that Anne's testimony was given in person in court, by beginning it, 'The examination and evidence of Anne Whittle ... Against Margaret Pearson, prisoner at the bar'. If Anne *did* appear in court in person, it suggests that Margaret's case was heard before Anne's trial, when Anne would still have had an incentive to present herself as cooperative. However, there are other occasions when Thomas Potts implies that evidence is given in person, only to reveal later that it was in fact a written statement read out, and very probably that's also the case with this evidence. In fact it's very likely that this statement was obtained by Thomas Covel at the same time he obtained Anne Whittle's statement against Elizabeth Sothernes, as the two are very similar:

> The wife of one Pearson of Paddiham, is a very evil woman, and confessed to this examinate, that she is a witch, and hath a spirit which came to her the first time in likeness of a man and cloven footed, and that she the said Pearson's wife hath done very much harm to one Dodgeson's goods, who came in at a loop-hole into the said Dodgeson's stable, and she and her spirit together did sit upon his horse or mare, until the said horse or mare died. And likewise, that she the said Pearson's wife did confess unto this examinate, that she bewitched unto death one Childer's wife, and her daughter.[14]

The other main evidence against Margaret was a statement taken by Nicholas Banester from one of her neighbours, Jennet Booth:

> This examinate was carding [wool] in the said Pearson's house, having a little child with her, and willed the said Margerie [either Margaret herself or a similarly named relative[15]] to give her a little milk, to make her said child a little meat, who fetched this examinate some, and put it in a pan; this examinate meaning to set it on the fire, found the said fire very ill, and taking up a stick that lay by her, and brake it in three or four pieces, and laid upon the coals to kindle the same, then set the pan and milk on the fire: and when the milk was boiled to this examinate's content, she took the pan wherein the milk was, off the said fire, and with all, under the bottom of the same, there came a toad, or a thing very like a toad, and to this examinate's thinking came out of the fire, together with the said pan, and under the bottom of the same, and that the said Margerie did carry the said toad out of the said house in a pair of tongs; but what she the said Margerie did therewith, this examinate knoweth not.[16]

Thomas Potts then says:

> After this were divers witnesses examined against her in open court, *viva voce* [in person], to prove the death of the mare, and divers other vile and odious practices by her committed.[17]

This suggests that Jennet Booth may *not* have been in court. And if we look closely at Thomas Potts's claim about the other witnesses, we can see that all he is able to say specifically is that someone made a statement saying that the horse was dead.

This tells us not only about the quality of the evidence presented against Margaret in court, but also about the way Thomas Potts then presents that evidence in *The Wonderful Discovery*. He includes the statements from Anne Whittle and Jennet Booth in full, clearly regarding them as conclusive proof of witchcraft. He then claims that there was other strong evidence given by witnesses anxious to accuse Margaret, but since he doesn't include it we can reasonably conclude that it was in fact far weaker than the statements he *does* include.[18] And this is supported by the one piece of definite information he does give us about this other evidence – that

A dead toad hanging from an elaborate holder. Found in the chimney of a house in Devon in the 1930s. (MoW 138)

it was 'to prove the death of the mare', not that Margaret Pearson was connected with the mare's death.

Of course, toads were animals associated with magic. In fact John Walsh described 'spirits in the likeness of toads' involved in cursing:

> As for the pictures of clay, their confection is after this manner. They use to take the earth of a new made grave, the rib bone of a man or woman burned to ashes ... and a black spider, with an inner pith of an elder, tempered all in water, in which water the said toad must first be washed ... Which toads being called the witches strike with two withy spars on both sides of the head, and sayeth to the spirit their Pater Noster backward ... And when he is stricken, they command the toad to hurt such a man or woman as he would have hurted. Whereto if he swell, he will go where he is appointed.[19]

Nevertheless, we can regard Jennet Booth's statement as a kind of benchmark.

If Thomas Potts doesn't include a statement, we can be sure it doesn't contain anything as damning as the unexpected appearance of a sinister toad.

Margaret Pearson was found guilty.[20]

18th August 1612
ANNE WHITTLE AND ANNE REDFERNE
Indicted with the death of Robert Nutter by witchcraft[21]

> This Anne Whittle ... was a very old withered spent and decrepit creature, her sight almost gone ... Her lips ever chattering and walking: but no man knew what.[22]

This vivid little caricature sketched out by Thomas Potts is a skilful journalistic touch, but it doesn't quite do Anne Whittle justice. She had survived the four and a half months in prison that had killed Elizabeth Sothernes. And she was not quite as 'spent' as Thomas Potts thought. He goes on:

> The example of this poor creature, would have moved pity, in respect of her great contrition and repentance, after she was committed to the castle at Lancaster, until the coming of his Majesty's Judges of Assize.[23]

But in spite of this apparent repentance, Anne Whittle pleaded not guilty. This ensured that she would be tried alongside her daughter Anne Redferne. As well as the evidence against Anne Redferne – Robert Nutter's accusations, relayed by his relatives and his grandfather's servant, James's statement incriminating the Redfernes and Elizabeth Sothernes's description of Anne Redferne and her mother making images – the jury would also hear the evidence against Anne Whittle. This of course included some damning testimony – such as James's claim that the image found at Malking Tower had been used by Anne Whittle to kill Anne Nutter, and Alizon's accusation that Anne Whittle had killed her father. But it also included Anne's own confession to Roger Nowell, insisting that she alone had killed Robert Nutter, and describing his sexual harassment of her daughter – which made it clear that his accusations against Anne Redferne were unreliable, tainted by his malice towards her.

And now, in the courtroom, Anne Whittle repeated her confession, and insisted once again that her daughter had not been involved in Robert Nutter's murder. And she did so coherently and convincingly, as Thomas Potts himself admits:

> Being oftentimes examined in open court, she was never found to vary, but always to agree in one, and the self same thing.[24]

From when she first confessed to Roger Nowell, everything Anne Whittle had done – her statements against Elizabeth Sothernes and Margaret Pearson, and all her admissions and expressions of repentance – had been intended to achieve a single aim: to make her appear a reliable and truthful witness, so that when she insisted that her daughter was innocent the jury would believe her.

But Anne would have to wait to discover whether she had succeeded. So many cases were tried at each Assizes, and it was so difficult to obtain enough jurors, that each jury heard several cases. This jury would hear two more, and then deliver their verdicts on all three cases after the third.[25]

ELIZABETH DEVICE
Indicted with the deaths of John Robinson,
James Robinson and Henry Mitton by witchcraft[26]

O barbarous and inhuman monster, beyond example; so far from sensible understanding of thy own misery, as to bring thy own natural children into mischief and bondage; and thyself to be a witness upon the gallows, to see thy own children, by thy devilish instructions hatched up in villainy and witchcraft, to suffer with thee, even in the beginning of their time, a shameful and untimely death.[27]

The tone of this passage, both gloating and accusing, is ugly but carefully calculated. Thomas Potts is using it to predispose his readers to take a certain view of Elizabeth's relationship with her children, to prepare us for his account of the most dramatic, but also one of the most controversial, moments in the trials – the confrontation between Elizabeth and her young daughter Jennet.

In fact it's impossible to imagine what Elizabeth was going through as she stood in the courtroom hearing her confessions read out, not only facing death herself, but knowing that her two older children would very likely hang alongside her, and her two younger children would be left to face a desperately uncertain future alone. When Roger Nowell led Jennet into court – something Elizabeth may not have expected, even though she probably knew he'd taken statements from her – it must have brought home to her, in a particularly brutal way, the full and terrible implications of her situation.

It's to her credit that she had the strength of character to react with anger. Thomas Potts describes her 'according to her accustomed manner, outrageously cursing'. Of course he wants us to think that her anger was directed entirely against Jennet – '[She] cried out against the child in such a fearful manner, as all the court did not a little wonder at her.'[28] But it's obvious that the main object of her fury would have been the man standing alongside Jennet, the man responsible for everything – Roger Nowell. And yet of course it's also possible that some of her anger did spill over on to Jennet – particularly if she realised, as she surely must have done, that if Jennet was being used as a witness against her, she would also be used as a witness against James.

In fact Elizabeth was perfectly entitled to object to the use of Jennet as a witness. Under normal circumstances, the evidence of young children was not allowed; and, in addition, the evidence of children of any age – even adults – could not be used against their parents. Continental lawyers like Jean Bodin and Henri Boguet argued that the normal rules should not apply to witchcraft, just as they did not apply to treason. In England, however, although Brian Darcey and other Justices had used child witnesses in earlier cases, the legality of using them had not been clearly established. We know this because, when Michael Dalton wrote *The Country Justice* in 1618, it was Sir Edward Bromley's decision to allow the use of Jennet Device that he gave as his legal precedent. This means that Elizabeth had every right to argue that the use of Jennet as a witness was illegal.[29]

However, the way Thomas Potts represents her protests is significant:

> No entreaty, promise of favour, or other respect, could put her to silence, thinking by this her outrageous cursing and threatening of the child, to enforce her to deny that which she had formerly confessed against her mother, before Master Nowell.[30]

It's hard to see what 'promise of favour' could honestly have been made to Elizabeth, since she was on trial for her life. More importantly, however, Thomas Potts betrays the fact that Jennet was simply being asked to confirm a statement 'formerly confessed against her mother, before Master Nowell', and that in practice it would have been extremely difficult for her to deny it. He also picks up Roger's use of the word 'confessed' to describe Jennet's evidence, to suggest, as Roger did, her guilt and involvement in her mother's magic.

But Jennet *did* hesitate:

> With weeping tears she cried out unto my Lord the judge, and told him, she was not able to speak in the presence of her mother.[31]

Again, Thomas Potts wants us to believe that this was because Elizabeth had terrified her, and to ignore the far more obvious explanation – that Jennet didn't want to testify against her mother. Edward Bromley, however, had Elizabeth dragged forcibly from the courtroom. By now there was such uproar that Jennet had to be made to stand on a table so that she could be seen and heard. But apparently she did confirm her statement.

Next, James's statements concerning the murders were read out. It seems that Elizabeth was then brought back into the courtroom, because Thomas Potts says:

> Being demanded by the court, what answer she could give to the particular points of the evidence against her, for the death of these several persons; impudently she denied them, crying out against her children, and the rest of the witnesses against her.[32]

But Elizabeth was also entitled to challenge James's evidence on the grounds that a son (of whatever age) couldn't be used as a witness against his mother. What's more, Elizabeth probably knew that James had never confirmed his evidence against her at a formal examination – and so it was illegal for that reason as well.

As for 'the rest of the witnesses against her', Thomas Potts doesn't even go so far as to say that anyone testified that Elizabeth's supposed victims were dead, so I think we're entitled to have serious doubts about whether these witnesses even existed.

But there's also something else that we should remember. William Preston was in court. Thomas Potts tells us specifically that he was present on the following day, 19 August,[33] and he must also have been in court on 18 August, as that was when Elizabeth and James were scheduled to be tried. He was there to discredit James's evidence, and when Elizabeth challenged James's statements against her, surely William would have begun his own angry protests. And it might well have been harder for Edward Bromley to have *him* extricated from the crowd and ejected. Thomas Potts tells us that it was not only Jennet Preston's family but also her friends who were determined to clear her name. William may well have been surrounded by a substantial group of supporters.[34]

Finally, abbreviated statements from James, Jennet and Elizabeth herself about the 'assembly of witches' at Malking Tower were read out. Thomas Potts implies that James and Jennet both gave this evidence in person, but from what he later says about James's trial James may not even have been in the courtroom at this point.[35] It also seems unlikely that Elizabeth would have been brought back into court while Jennet was still there, so Jennet's statement too was probably read out in her absence. And of course that's what would have happened if she had refused to give evidence earlier. Any risks involved in bringing her into court were worth the benefits. If she stopped cooperating at any point, she could simply be whisked away and her written statements used without her.

JAMES DEVICE

Indicted with the deaths of Anne Towneley
and John Duckworth by witchcraft[36]

So far the trials had not been an unqualified success for Roger Nowell. Anne Whittle had been unexpectedly convincing in her efforts to persuade the jury of her daughter's innocence. Elizabeth Device's denials and protests, and Jennet's obvious distress, must have made the jury uncomfortable, at the very least. And William Preston was probably heckling from the crowd. And now came the most crucial trial of all – the trial of James Device. If the other suspects incriminated by James were to be convicted, James had to be.

According to Thomas Potts:

> This wicked and miserable wretch, whether by practice, or means, to bring himself to some untimely death, and thereby to avoid his trial by his country, and just judgement of the law; or ashamed to be openly charged with so many devilish practices, and so much innocent blood as he had spilt; or by reason of his imprisonment so long time before his trial (which was with more favour, commiseration, and relief than he deserved) I know not: but being brought forth to the bar, to receive his trial before this worthy judge, and so honourable and worshipful an assembly of Justices for this service, was so insensible, weak, and unable in all things, as he could neither speak, hear, or stand, but was holden [held] up when he was brought to the place of his arraignment, to receive his trial.[37]

However, Thomas Potts later contradicts this claim that James could neither hear nor speak by saying that he denied some of the accusations against him – something Thomas Potts would hardly admit if it wasn't true. It seems that he couldn't stop himself revelling in and exaggerating James's suffering. But at the same time he seems to have recognised what William Preston must also have realised – that it was evidence that James had been illegally tortured.

Thomas Potts was obviously aware of the terrible conditions in the prison, but evidently he was also aware that they didn't provide an adequate explanation for James's condition. The claim that James was treated 'with more favour, commiseration, and relief than he deserved' is meaningless, since people like Thomas Potts

The Arraignement and Triall

THE ARRAIGNMENT
and *Triall of* I A M E S D E V I C E,
Sonne of ELIZABETH DEVICE, *of the Forreſt of Pendle, within the Countie of Lancaſter aforesaid, Laborer, for Witchcraft* ; *Vpon Tuesday the eighteenth of Auguſt, at the Assises and generall Gaole-Deliuerie holden at Lancaſter*

Before
Sir EDVVARD BROMLEY *Knight, one of his Maieſties Iuſtice of Assise at Lancaſter.*

James Deuice.

His wicked and miserable Wretch, whether by practise, or meanes, to bring himselfe to some vntimely death, and thereby to auoide his Tryall by his Countrey, and iuſt iudgement of the Law ; or ashamed to bee openly charged with so many deuillish practises, and so much innocent bloud as hee had spilt ; or by reason of his Imprisonment so long time before his Tryall (which was with more fauour, commiseration, and reliefe then hee deserued) I know not : But being brought forth to the and Roger Nowell believed that hanging James rather than burning him alive would be treating him with more favour than he deserved.

And so Thomas Potts suggests the unconvincing suicide attempt theory. Of course people did attempt suicide in prison – particularly people who were being tortured.[38] But in practice the only method available to most of them was to hang themselves. If James had attempted to hang himself with enough success to suffer permanent damage, his guards would have had to cut him down and revive him. Thomas Covel would have known about it and so would Thomas Potts – there would have been no doubt about it. Instead, Thomas Potts seems to be trying to imply that James somehow acquired poison – which is extremely unlikely, although it is perhaps very tenuous evidence that someone (maybe William Preston) did manage to visit him. Or perhaps we're meant to think that James attempted some kind of magical suicide.

Importantly, however, in witchcraft cases in particular, suicide or attempted suicide was regarded as evidence of guilt. Henri Boguet explains:

> We have encountered in the past witches who hanged themselves, which they probably did at the insistence of Satan; because, as he fears that witches condemned to death by the forces of justice may come to repent, he kills them, or else he urges them to put themselves to death, so that they will not be able to escape him.[39]

It's easy to see, therefore, why Thomas Potts might use the suggestion of attempted suicide to distract his readers from considering the possibility of torture.

Even if James wasn't literally too ill to speak, he was clearly too ill to defend himself effectively, and – conveniently – to protest effectively about the illegal use of the evidence obtained by Thomas Covel, or, for that matter, about how Thomas Covel had obtained it.

The trial began with Henry Towneley's testimony against James, and Thomas Potts makes a point of the fact that Henry Towneley 'attended to prosecute and give evidence against him', although he doesn't quote his statement.[40] Then James's confessions to the murders of Anne Towneley and John Duckworth were read. Then, once again, Jennet was brought into the courtroom, to confirm her statement about Anne Towneley's murder. This time, Thomas Potts tells us,

> Although she were very young, yet it was wonderful to the court, in so great a presence and audience, with what modesty, government, and understanding, she delivered this evidence against the prisoner at the bar, being her own natural brother.[41]

This account is so close to Henri Boguet's description of Pierre Vuillermoz, 'not at all shaken and … apparently indifferent', that it suggests that Jennet was in a similar emotionally damaged state.[42] Again it's impossible for us to imagine the pressure she was under: the culmination of weeks of stress and indoctrination, and added to all that the sudden shock of the crowds and noise of the courtroom, and the trauma of her confrontation with her mother.

But, according to Thomas Potts, James, unlike Elizabeth, made no attempt to dispute Jennet's evidence, 'which he himself could not deny, but there acknowledged in every particular to be just and true'.[43] This may simply be a distortion by Thomas Potts – twisting the fact that James was too ill to protest into an acknowledgement of guilt. But it's also possible that James realised that Jennet was traumatised, and could not bring himself to accuse her of lying.

But then, extraordinarily, in the middle of the trial, two new indictments were added to the charges against James – he was accused of the murders of two members of the Hargreives family, John Hargreives of Goldshey Booth and Blaze Hargreives of Higham. Two statements from Jennet were read, almost identical to her other statements accusing James and her mother except for the different names:

> Her brother James Device hath been a witch for the space of three years: about the beginning of which time, there appeared unto him, in this examinate's mother's house, a black dog, which her said brother called Dandy, which Dandy did ask her said brother what he would have him to do, whereunto he answered, he would have him to kill John Hargreives, of Goldshey Booth: whereunto Dandy answered that he would do it; since which time the said John is dead.

> And at another time this examinate confesseth and sayeth, that her said brother did call the said Dandy: who thereupon appeared in the said house, asking this examinate's brother what he would have him to do: whereupon this examinate's said brother said, he would have him to kill Blaze Hargreives of Higham: whereupon Dandy answered, he should have his best help, and so vanished away: and she sayeth, that since that time Hargreives is dead; but how long after, this examinate doth not now remember.[44]

At that point James *did* dispute Jennet's accusations. As Thomas Potts puts it, he 'slenderly [unconvincingly] denied them' – a grotesque comment, as it's hard to see how James could have produced a convincing defence against two charges of murder sprung on him completely without warning, even if he hadn't been seriously ill.

Thomas Potts adds:

> To this examination were divers witnesses examined in open court *viva voce*, concerning the death of the parties, in such manner and form, and at such time as the said Jennet Device in her evidence hath formerly declared to the court.[45]

So, like the witnesses who testified against Margaret Pearson about the death of the horse, these 'divers witnesses' were only testifying that John Hargreives and Blaze Hargreives were dead, and had died in an apparently unnatural way. And was one of these witnesses perhaps Henry Hargreives, the Constable, who was also from Goldshey Booth?[46]

It's clear from the phrase 'and at another time this examinate confesseth' that these statements from Jennet had been drawn up well in advance and probably over several days. So why wasn't James indicted with all four murders at the start of his trial? There seems to be only one possible explanation – that Roger Nowell (presumably with Edward Bromley's approval) wanted to be able to introduce these new charges into the trial at a point of his choosing – and the only likely reason

Researcher Mary recreates a spell worked by the Scottish wise woman Agnes Sampson, who used 'powder made of men's joints... conjured with her prayers' to ease the pain of childbirth.

he would want to do that would be to distract the jury from something else.

If James had been held in solitary confinement it might have been possible to prevent him from discovering that his Lancaster evidence – the evidence he had retracted – had in fact been used against Jennet Preston. But parts of that evidence would also be used against James himself. At some point during his trial James would realise what had happened, and start to protest. And by the beginning of James's trial Roger probably also knew that William Preston was in the courtroom.

We can't be sure what happened, but perhaps when James refused to deny young Jennet's first accusations, and seemed to be giving in, William Preston began to shout at him from the crowd. Hearing William Preston telling him that his evidence had helped to kill his wife would have had a considerable effect on James, ill though he was. Perhaps that was why Roger chose that moment to distract the jury with the two other murder charges.

The evidence about the Malking Tower meeting followed, and then James's description of his final encounter with the Black Dog. But it seems that the last evidence against James was Jennet's account of the family's two charms. James's trial ended with Jennet reciting – or, more probably, someone reading out on her behalf – the Friday Spell.

Anne Whittle – guilty
Anne Redferne – not guilty
Elizabeth Device – guilty of both murders
James Device – guilty of all four murders

Anne Redferne's acquittal was a serious blow for Roger Nowell. The following morning the Pendle trials were put aside and another witchcraft case was tried; it's tempting to suspect that Edward Bromley was giving Roger time to review his strategy. However, the disorganisation of the Assizes is probably just as likely an explanation. The Justice of the Peace in this other case was Nicholas Banester's son-in-law Robert Houlden. The chief witness and alleged victim was a fourteen-year-old girl, Grace Sowerbuts. The three defendants, Jennet Brierley, Ellen Brierley and Jane Southworth, were all acquitted.[48]

19th August 1612
ANNE REDFERNE
Indicted with the death of Christopher Nutter by witchcraft[49]

A major defeat was something Roger Nowell couldn't accept. Anne Redferne was now tried for a second time, charged with the murder of Robert Nutter's father Christopher.

Robert Nutter's sister, Margaret Crooke, had testified that her father had claimed that he was bewitched, but she had made a point of saying that he never named the person he suspected. However, Roger Nowell also had Elizabeth Sothernes's testimony, describing Anne Whittle and Anne Redferne making images, and saying that her spirit Tibb had told her they were images of Robert Nutter, Robert's wife Marie and his father Christopher. So there *was* evidence linking Anne Redferne to Christopher Nutter's death – a statement by a woman who had died before the trials, giving information that she had obtained from a spirit.

However, Roger also used the testimony from Margaret Crooke and her brother John Nutter, describing Robert Nutter's accusation that Anne Redferne had bewitched him. Importantly, though, he did *not* use Anne Whittle's written confession. Instead he had Anne Whittle brought into the courtroom, where she once again confessed – apparently to 'the making of the pictures of clay'[50] – and once again insisted that Anne Redferne was innocent.

Interestingly, Thomas Potts gives his own summing-up of the case *before* finally adding James's statement incriminating the Redfernes – which seems to suggest that this evidence from James was not used in this second trial.

Roger had originally taken James's statement as a way of putting pressure on Anne Redferne to confess, so she would have known about it before her first trial. It's very likely that she told the jury that James had lied in an attempt to save himself and his family from being prosecuted. It also seems to have been usual for prisoners waiting to be taken to the bar for their trials to be held together, perhaps at the back of the courtroom or in an anteroom.[51] So Anne might also have had a chance to confront James and demand that he admitted that his statement was false during his own trial. It is of course quite possible that James, even though he was so ill, had always intended to do that – just as he had withdrawn his evidence against the other suspects. The jury was the same for James's trial as for Anne's. That could be one of the reasons Anne had been acquitted.

But another, even more important, reason was no doubt the unreliability of Robert Nutter's accusations. Anne Whittle's confession had made it clear to the jury that Robert Nutter had hated Anne Redferne for rejecting him. But now Roger Nowell made sure that this information was not given to the new jury at this second trial. Anne Whittle's confession was not read out. The jury was given the testimony from Margaret Crooke and John Nutter that Robert Nutter had accused Anne Redferne. But they were not given the evidence of the malice he felt towards her.[52] And in the noise and confusion Anne Redferne may well not have realised that until she was already being dragged out of the courtroom at the end of her trial.

ALICE NUTTER
Indicted with the death of Henry Mitton by witchcraft[53]

There can be little doubt that Alice Nutter's trial was particularly controversial. We get an indication of that from the fact that Thomas Potts tries to imply, falsely, that James and Elizabeth gave their evidence in person, clumsily inserting the phrase 'prisoner at the bar, upon her arraignment and trial' into the middle of the preamble to Elizabeth's statement:

> The Examination of Elizabeth Device, mother of the said James Device.
>
> Against Alice Nutter, wife of Richard Nutter, prisoner at the bar, upon her arraignment and trial.
>
> Before Roger Nowell and Nicholas Bannester, Esquires, the day and year aforesaid.[54]

Three pages later he says clearly, 'After these examinations were openly read … '[55]

The only evidence against Alice was Elizabeth's statement about Henry Mitton's murder, James's statements about the murder and about the Malking Tower meeting, and evidence from Jennet that Alice had been at Malking Tower. The part of James's statement about the agreement to help Jennet Preston kill Thomas and Leonard Lister wasn't used against Alice, although the part about the bomb plot was. Thomas Potts makes no attempt to pretend that there were any other witnesses.

Jennet never accused Alice of murdering Henry Mitton. Her list of the six names of people present at Malking Tower, which included Alice's name, was read out.[56] But then

> his Lordship [Edward Bromley] being very suspicious of the accusation of this young wench Jennet Device, commanded one to take her away into the upper hall, intending in the mean time to make trial of her evidence, and the accusation especially against this woman, who is charged to have been at Malking Tower, at this great meeting. Master Covel was commanded to set all his prisoners by themselves, and betwixt every witch another prisoner, and some other strange women amongst them, so as no man could judge the one from the other ... then was the wench Jennet Device commanded to be brought into the court: and being set before my Lord, he took great pains to examine her of every particular point, what women were at Malking Tower upon Good Friday? How she knew them? What were the names of any of them? And how she knew them to be such as she named? In the end being examined by my Lord, whether she knew them that were there by their faces, if she saw them? she told my Lord she should: whereupon in the presence of this great audience, in open court, she went and took Alice Nutter, this prisoner, by the hand, and accused her to be one: and told her in what place she sat at the feast at Malking Tower, at the great assembly of the witches, and who sat next her: what conference they had, and all the rest of their proceedings at large, without any manner of contrariety.[57]

Of course, this proved very little. Jennet was simply being asked to pick out people she knew from strangers she didn't. And it's important to remember that she wasn't accusing any of these people of committing any crimes. All she was saying was that they had been at Malking Tower on Good Friday. Roger Nowell and Thomas Covel had drawn up statements from James and Elizabeth that represented the gathering as a meeting where witches plotted and boasted about killing people, but there are no statements from Jennet saying that. Thomas Potts, however, represents Jennet's identification of Alice as conclusive proof of guilt:

> This could be no forged or false accusation, but the very act of God to discover her.[58]

KATHERINE HEWIT AND ALICE GRAY
Indicted with the death of Anne Foulds by witchcraft[59]

The only evidence against Katherine Hewit and Alice Gray was, again, the Devices' testimony – mainly the statements from James and Elizabeth claiming that Katherine and Alice were at Malking Tower and talked about killing Anne Foulds. In their case, the references to the bomb plot were omitted. Jennet hadn't included their names in her list, but the first part of her statement was read out, saying that the guests at Malking Tower were 'witches' – Roger Nowell's choice of word, of course. And Jennet picked out Katherine Hewit in the absurd identity parade.

Anne Redferne – guilty
Alice Nutter – guilty
Katherine Hewit – guilty
Alice Gray – not guilty

It remains a mystery why Katherine Hewit was found guilty when Alice Gray was acquitted. Thomas Potts doesn't tell us that Alice Gray was picked out by Jennet in the identity parade – but he glosses over the fact that Alice Gray was tried at all, so reluctant is he to admit that she was found not guilty. It's possible that Jennet failed to pick her out – but could that really have made so much difference to the jury? Or did Alice somehow produce some evidence in her own defence? How could you prove you *hadn't* bewitched someone? Since Thomas Potts does his best to exclude anything that might cast doubt on the defendants' guilt from *The Wonderful Discovery*, we will never know.

JOHN BULCOCK AND JANE BULCOCK
Indicted that they had used witchcraft upon Jennet Deyne, so that she became mad[61]

The evidence against Jane and John Bulcock was even weaker. Elizabeth never confirmed James's statement claiming that they had talked about bewitching someone, and James's statement itself made it clear that he'd never heard them mention Jennet Deyne by name. However, the parts of James's statement referring to the bomb plot and the agreement to kill Thomas and Leonard Lister were both used against them.

Again the first part of Jennet's statement was read out, missing out (of course) the list of names that revealed that the only two men at Malking Tower had been her uncle and Christopher Hargreives.

> Then was the said Jennet Device commanded by his Lordship to find and point out the said John Bulcock and Jane Bulcock amongst all the rest: whereupon she went and took Jane Bulcock by the hand, accused her to be one, and told her in what place she sat at the feast at Malking Tower, at the great assembly of the witches; and who sat next her: and accused the said John Bulcock to turn the spit there; what conference they had, and all the rest of their proceedings at large, with any manner of contrariety.[62]

The reference to John Bulcock turning the spit seems like a convincing detail, but Jennet could easily have remembered it from some other social occasion. Jane and John insisted in court that they were not at Malking Tower on Good Friday, protesting their innocence in a 'very violent and outrageous manner'.[63] It might seem strange that they didn't produce witnesses to prove that they were somewhere else. But although it seems that they knew before their trial that they were suspected of bewitching Jennet Deyne, they almost certainly didn't know that the crucial evidence against them would be a claim that they'd talked about it at Malking Tower. Only when they stood in the courtroom would they have known, too late, that they needed to prove that they had *not* been at the 'great assembly'.

Thomas Potts then adds:

> She [Jennet] further told his Lordship, there was a woman came out of Craven to that great feast at Malking Tower, but she could not find her out amongst all those women.[64]

This, of course, was supposed to be Jennet Preston, and at that point William Preston stormed out of the courtroom. Thomas Potts writes that William 'cried out and went away, being fully satisfied that his wife had justice, and was worthy of death'.[65] We're expected to believe that a man who for months had stood by his wife in the face of all the accusations against her, had fought hard first to save her and then to clear her name, and had travelled to Lancaster to discredit James Device's detailed and damning statement against her, was suddenly convinced of her guilt just because Jennet Device suggested that she was at Malking Tower – something William almost certainly already knew.

ALIZON DEVICE

Indicted that she had used witchcraft upon John Law,
so that his body wasted and consumed[66]

Alizon was brought to the bar and the indictment read, but before she had a chance to plead guilty or not guilty, John Law, her accuser, was brought into the courtroom – not by Roger Nowell, but by another Justice of the Peace, Sir Thomas Gerrard, who would go on to arrange a generous pension for John after the trial.

It was of course illegal for a witness to be brought into court before the defendant had pleaded guilty or not guilty. And this wasn't a mere technicality. It was such an important point of law that a defendant could halt his or her trial by refusing to plead – and to prevent criminals using that as a way to escape justice, a person who persistently refused to plead could be executed.[67]

It's hard to understand how Thomas Gerrard could have made such an obvious mistake, and why Roger Nowell and Edward Bromley didn't prevent it. Evidently Thomas Gerrard was taking a particular interest in John Law, and wanted to orchestrate his arrival in court so that it achieved the greatest possible impact. It may also be significant that there was another witchcraft case still to be heard at the Lancaster Assizes, and Thomas Gerrard was the Justice involved in that case.[68] Edward Bromley dealt with the problem by simply ignoring it, and allowed Alizon's trial to proceed illegally without her pleading.

Thomas Potts gives an uncharacteristically vague description of John Law:

The poor peddler, by name John Law ... not well able to go or stand, being led thither by his poor son ... deformed by her witchcraft, and transformed beyond the course of nature.[69]

However, it's clear that John's arrival caused the stir Thomas Gerrard had intended, because evidently Edward Bromley couldn't hear what Alizon was saying, and she had to be brought forward from the bar closer to him.[70] Importantly this also means that most other people in the courtroom couldn't hear her – perhaps for most of her trial. Elsewhere in *The Wonderful Discovery* Thomas Potts may have been inhibited from lying too blatantly about what happened in court because of the large number of other people present (although his lie about William Preston was fairly blatant). But in this case it may well be that the spectators were unable to get a clear impression of what was happening.

What Thomas Potts *claims* happened is that 'there on her knees, she humbly asked forgiveness for her offence: and being required to make an open declaration or confession of her offence: she confessed as followeth ...'. He then gives the written statement drawn up by Roger Nowell on 30 March, claiming that Alizon 'declared [it] at the time of her arraignment and trial in open court', but then adding that it 'agreeth *verbatim* [word for word] with her own examination taken at Read ... the thirtieth day of March, before Master Nowell'.[71] This is of course a ridiculous assertion, because Alizon couldn't possibly have repeated exactly a statement drawn up four and a half months earlier by Roger Nowell – especially as Roger probably didn't tell her what it contained.

John Law then gave his evidence – or, more likely, his written statement was read out. And then John, 'in great passion', cried out to Alizon, 'This thou knowest to be too true' – loudly and clearly enough for all the court officials to hear him, in spite of the other noise.[72] Would he have accused her so emphatically if she'd just confessed and asked forgiveness?

Nevertheless, Thomas Potts goes on:

Thereupon she humbly acknowledged the same, and cried out to God to forgive her, and upon her knees with weeping tears humbly prayed him to forgive her that wicked offence; which he very freely and voluntarily did.

This humble weeping figure seems suspiciously familiar. It is of course the repentant Alizon of the false account of her confrontation with Henry Bulcock – and of Abraham Law's description of her confrontation with his father back in March, an event John Law himself strangely failed to remember, in spite of his perfect recall of other less significant details.

And in spite of the fact that Alizon was supposedly repeatedly incriminating herself, Roger Nowell now asked for Abraham Law's statement to be read out. Then the court heard the testimony (perhaps again from Abraham) listing John's disabilities.[73] And one of them at least – 'his speech not well to be understood'

– seems contradicted by Thomas Potts's description of John's clearly audible and articulate outburst a few minutes earlier.

But the trials of the Pendle witches ended with one final twist – and Alizon showed a keen awareness of the irony of it. Someone – probably Edward Bromley – asked Alizon if she could cure John. Alizon replied that she could not, but that if her grandmother had lived, 'she could and would have helped him'.

THE VERDICTS[74]

John Bulcock and Jane Bulcock – guilty

Although Alizon had been tried by a jury, and although the jury had continued to hear evidence from John and Abraham Law even after she had supposedly confessed in court, it seems that it was not the jury who decided her guilt. Edward Bromley declared her 'convicted upon her own confession'.[75]

of Witches at Lancaster.

The Verdict of Life and Death.

WHo vpon their Oathes found *Iohn Bulcock* and *Iane Bulcock* his mother not guiltie of the Felonie by Witch-craft, contained in the Indictment against them.

Alizon Deuice conuicted vpon her owne Confession.

Whereupon Master *Couel* was commaunded by the Court to take away the Prisoners conuicted, and to bring forth *Margaret Pearson*, and *Isabell Robey*, Prisoners in the Castle at Lancaster, to receiue their Triall.

Who were brought to their Arraignment and Trialls, as hereafter followeth, *viz.*

The Wonderful Discovery records the final verdicts in the Pendle case. The phrase 'not guiltie' is unfortunately a printer's error.

S 3   THE

CHAPTER TWENTY-EIGHT

Mocking Tower

THE WONDERFUL DISCOVERY

Thomas Potts's claim that William Preston was finally convinced of his wife's guilt no doubt reflects his hope that *The Wonderful Discovery* would convince its readers. Because it was now not only William Preston's voice that had to be drowned out by the official propaganda. There were four other angry and grieving families adding their protests to his – the Redfernes, the Nutters and the Bulcocks in Pendle, and Katherine Hewit's family in Colne. Apparently Alice Nutter's children were (in Thomas Potts's words) 'never able to move her to confess any particular offence'.[1] And the idea that she – like Jennet Preston – was the victim of a conspiracy involving Roger Nowell was mentioned in the mid nineteenth century as 'allegations which tradition has preserved'.[2]

Even by the end of the trials Edward Bromley was aware that the defendants' families would challenge the verdicts. As he passed the death sentence on the prisoners he said to them:

> You of all people have the least cause to complain, since in the trial of your lives there hath been great care and pains taken, and much time spent: and very few or none of you, but stand convicted upon your own voluntary confessions ... What persons of your nature and condition, ever were arraigned and tried with more solemnity, had more liberty given to plead or answer to every particular point of evidence against you? In conclusion, such hath been the general care of all, that had to deal with you, that you have neither cause to be offended in the proceedings of the Justices, that first took pains in these businesses, nor in the court that hath taken great care to give nothing in evidence against you, but matter of fact.[3]

Of course it was the awareness of the escalating controversy that led Edward Bromley to instruct Thomas Potts to write *The Wonderful Discovery*. No doubt someone would have written a pamphlet about such a major case, but Thomas

Potts was one of the officials at the trial. It was Thomas Potts, as he himself tells us, who handed Edward Bromley the list of prisoners to be sentenced. And Edward Bromley personally checked the text of *The Wonderful Discovery* before it was published.[4] And yet so confident were these people that they were right that, even as they were producing a work of unscrupulous propaganda, they had the arrogance to include details – such as the reference to Thomas Covel's interrogation of James – that give us revealing evidence of their malpractices.[5]

AFTERMATH

The community in Pendle Forest must have been torn apart. What did Henry Towneley make of it all – scrupulous Henry Towneley, who had gone to Lancaster eager 'to prosecute and give evidence against him [James] for the King's Majesty', and yet whose statement wasn't damning enough for Thomas Potts to publish? No doubt he'd felt a certain grim satisfaction when he saw James hang, but how did he react to the way James's evidence had been used to kill so many other people? Henry had been grief-stricken at the death of his wife – how did he now face his neighbour Christopher Bulcock, who had lost both his wife and his son?

Although Thomas Potts makes much of the fact that Henry Towneley appeared in court in person, he doesn't say the same of Margaret Crooke and John Nutter, Robert Nutter's sister and brother, whose evidence against Anne Redferne had been so ruthlessly manipulated. They too had been scrupulous in their testimony, simply reporting what their brother and father had said. It seems likely that they were reluctant witnesses, and may not have appeared in court at all. Perhaps they were left horrified by the outcome of the trials.

But there is also evidence that some people were convinced of the guilt of the accused. The following April Anne Redferne's sister, Besse Chattox, was in Lancaster prison, and the most probable explanation is that she too had been accused of witchcraft in the aftermath of her mother's and sister's convictions.[6]

And sadly it seems that Alice Gray didn't enjoy her escape from death for long: parish records suggest that she died in April 1613.[7]

Just as she'd been at the heart of the witchcraft case, young Jennet Device was no doubt at the heart of the controversy that followed. Whatever family had taken her in, Roger Nowell would have ensured that she was receiving religious instruction to keep her convinced of the evils of magic.[8] But at the same time William Preston, Christopher Bulcock, Alice Nutter's children and Katherine Hewit's family would all have been trying to persuade her to speak out against Roger Nowell.

It seems that one of Brian Darcey's child witnesses, Febey Hunt, later publicly denounced him.[9] However, Febey's mother Ales had been acquitted,[10] and obviously she would have encouraged Febey to help her clear her name. Jennet had no close relatives to support her if she decided to speak out. And she couldn't claim that she'd been coerced into inventing everything. There was no escaping the fact that her family had practised magic. After all, her testimony had included their two charms. Perhaps all she could do was concentrate on her own survival and the survival of her brother William. But Roger Nowell had deprived her of her grandmother, her mother, her older brother and her older sister, and no amount of propaganda could have closed the void that would have left in her life.

THE 1634 WITCH-HUNT

Roger Nowell died just over ten years later, in 1623. His eldest son (also called Roger) inherited his house at Read.[11] But in 1634, when Pendle once again became the location of a witchcraft case, it was not Roger Nowell's son who was the Justice of the Peace – it was John Starkie, the son of Roger's nephew Nicholas.

In February 1634, troubling rumours began to reach John Starkie and his colleague Richard Shuttleworth (Nicholas Banester's successor). A young boy called Edmund Robinson was saying that he'd witnessed a meeting of witches at an empty house called Hoarstones on the outskirts of Fence. The two Justices decided to bring Edmund in for questioning.[12] Edmund told them that on All Saints' Day he'd been picking wild plums at Wheatley Lane (between Carre Hall and Fence), when he'd encountered two greyhounds, one brown and one black. He tried to make them run at a hare, but they refused, so he beat them, and they turned into a boy he didn't recognise and one of his neighbours, Frances Dicconson. Frances then turned the boy into a horse, and carried Edmund with her on the horse's back to Hoarstones, where about sixty people had gathered, and were eating food produced by magic.[13]

> Seeing divers [some] of the said company going to a barn near adjoining, he followed after them, and there he saw six of them kneeling, and pulling all six of them six several ropes, which were fastened or tied to the top of the barn. Presently after which pulling, there came then in this informer's sight flesh smoking, butter in lumps, and milk as it were flying from the said ropes. All which fell into basins which were placed under the said ropes.[14]

Edmund was about ten or eleven years old – the same age John Starkie had been when he first met the cunning man Edmund Hartlay and formed the friendship with him that had sent Edmund to the gallows and left John believing himself possessed by evil spirits. Thanks to his own traumatic experiences John Starkie would easily have identified with young Edmund Robinson. Edmund's story of his neighbour unexpectedly revealing herself to be a witch, and carrying him off to this bizarre and sinister meeting, would have seemed like a slightly more outlandish version of John's own disastrous childhood encounter with magic.

But John's willingness to believe Edmund would have increased still further when Edmund gave the names of six people he'd recognised at the meeting. They were all already suspected of witchcraft, as Edmund himself explained, when he was questioned again five months later by a different Justice:

He framed those tales concerning the persons aforesaid, because he heard the neighbours repute them for witches. He heard Edmund Stevenson say that he was much troubled with the said Dicconson's wife in the time of his sickness, and that he suspected her, and he heard Robert Smith say that his wife, lying upon her death bed, accused Jennet Hargreives to be the cause of her death … and it was generally spoken that Beawse's wife, who went a-begging, was a witch, and he had heard Sharpee Smith say that the wife of John Loynd laid her hand upon a cow of his, after which she never rose.[15]

The other two reputed witches were Jennet and William Device. According to Edmund, 'he heard William Nutter's wife say that Jennet Device and William Device had bewitched her'. Edmund also told John Starkie that since the meeting he had seen Jennet with Frances Dicconson and John Loynd's wife (also called Jennet) 'several times in a croft or close adjoining to his father's house, which put him in great fear'.[16]

It's not surprising that Edmund was afraid of Jennet. Again, he admitted later:

He had heard the neighbours talk of a witch feast that was kept at Mocking Tower in Pendle Forest about twenty years since, to which feast divers witches came, and many were apprehended and executed at Lancaster.[17]

It's hard to believe he didn't know that Jennet Device had been at that earlier feast at 'Mocking Tower'. John Starkie would certainly have known it. And he would also have known that Jennet had confessed to being present when her brother James had summoned the Black Dog – perhaps the same Black Dog Edmund Hartlay had summoned with his circle ritual at Huntroyde, the Black Dog who had haunted John, his sister and the other members of the Starkie household Edmund Hartlay had bewitched.

But were Jennet and William now practising as cunning folk themselves? It would have been dangerous, but Jeanne Harvillier became a wise woman even though she was arrested and whipped when she was 'extremely young' – and probably forced to witness her mother burned alive. As Jennet and William grew older and struggled to live with the reality of their loss, they may have rebelled against Roger Nowell's indoctrination.

Were Frances Dicconson and Jennet Loynd suspected of witchcraft because they were not only Jennet Device's friends but also her clients? And could Edmund Robinson have misinterpreted the remark made by William Nutter's wife? After all, we know that several members of the Nutter family had been clients of Jennet's and William's grandmother, that Anne Nutter and Alizon had been friends, and that Alice Nutter had lost her life because she supported the Devices. Had Jennet and William *un*witched, not *be*witched William Nutter's wife? Or were they claiming annual payments in return for protection magic – that slightly suspect practice that carried the veiled threat that you might be bewitched if you didn't pay?

The Jennet Hargreives mentioned by Edmund Robinson wasn't the Jennet

Hargreives who had been at Malking Tower on Good Friday 1612 – but she *was* married to a close relative (perhaps the son) of Christopher and Elizabeth Hargreives, who had also been there.[18] Was she too one of Jennet's and William's clients?

Another suspect arrested by John Starkie and Richard Shuttleworth was a woman called Margaret Johnson – and it seems that she wasn't someone Edmund Robinson had named.[19] She confessed that she had a familiar spirit called Mamilion, who first appeared to her in the shape of a man dressed in black, and then as a white cat, a brown dog and a hare.[20] She also said 'that Good Friday is one constant day for a yearly general meeting of witches, and that on Good Friday last they had a meeting near Pendle Water-side'.[21] Waterside is on the west bank of the river Pendle Water near Fence, on the edge of Raven's Clough Wood.

In fact it might have been hard for Jennet and William *not* to become cunning folk. After the 1612 trials everyone would have known that Jennet had been taught the Friday Spell. People would have approached her, wanting her to practise magic for them. And it was a source of income she perhaps couldn't afford to turn down.

REPRIEVE

Under Richard Shuttleworth and John Starkie's questioning, Edmund added that at Hoarstones he'd seen Jennet Loynd and two of the other witches take three images pierced with thorns down from a beam in the barn. And eventually his statement ended with a long list of people he'd seen at the meeting – although the names vary in the different surviving copies.[22] At the Lent Assizes seventeen people were found guilty of witchcraft, but this time the judge reprieved all of them, although they remained in custody in Lancaster prison.[23]

In June the Bishop of Chester was instructed to investigate the case. By that time – after less than four months in prison – four of the defendants, including Jennet Loynd, were dead. The Bishop, however, doesn't seem to have thought that

Waterside. Margaret Johnson's evidence suggests that Jennet and William Device held a Good Friday gathering here in 1633.

COPYRIGHT NICKY AND FRANK GRACE

worth commenting on. What he did find significant, however, was the fact that just before the trials Edmund Robinson's father had approached John Dicconson, Frances's husband, and offered to get Edmund to withdraw his evidence against her in return for a payment of two pounds. That was a large amount of money in those days, but John would have paid, if Frances hadn't indignantly persuaded him not to. What's more, John had found a witness who had overheard the conversation.[24]

Frances Dicconson, Jennet Hargreives and Margaret Johnson, together with a fourth suspect, Marie Spencer,[25] were sent to London, and so too were Edmund Robinson and his father. While the four women were searched for witch marks by a panel of eight doctors and ten midwives,[26] Edmund's father was imprisoned, and Edmund questioned again.[27]

This time he admitted:

> He invented the said tale for that his mother … used him to fetch home her kine [cows], he was appointed one time to fetch home her kine but did not do it, but went to play with other children, and fearing his father or mother would beat him, he made this tale for an excuse.[28]

His father, desperately denying the Dicconsons' accusations of extortion, and with a member of the original trial jury now speaking out against him, insisted that 'Dicconson and his wife are neighbours … and there was never any cause of difference between them. Thinks them very honest harmless people.'[29]

The four suspects who'd been taken to London were returned to Lancaster to rejoin the others, and they were all probably given a conditional discharge at the Summer Assizes. However, that wouldn't mean they were immediately released. They still had fees to pay, and they would have had to 'enter recognisances with good sufficient sureties, to appear at the next Assizes at Lancaster, and in the meantime to be of good behaviour'[30] – in other words, they had to find people willing to pledge money to bail them out.

For Jennet and William that would have been particularly difficult, as John Starkie would have done everything possible to prevent them from being released. And they also faced another problem – the jailer at Lancaster was still Thomas Covel, and of course he remembered Jennet. He could hardly have forgotten her dramatic court appearances, and there's positive evidence that he remembered her. Jennet's surname is spelt Davies in Edmund Robinson's Lancashire statement, and Devys in the London documents, but in a list of prisoners drawn up by Thomas Covel it's spelt as it was twenty-four years earlier – Device.

This list dates from August 1636 – two years after Edmund Robinson's evidence had been discredited. Headed 'Witches remaining in his Majesty's Jail', it includes, as well as Jennet, Marie Spencer, Jennet Hargreives and Frances Dicconson – which is particularly surprising since from the start John Dicconson had clearly done everything he could to get her released. It also includes Alice Priestley, another of the suspects from Pendle. There are five other names, of people who seem not to have been accused by Edmund. Whether any of them were from Pendle or whether they were all people who had been reprieved or acquitted after other witchcraft trials it's not possible to say.[31]

What happened to the other Pendle suspects is also unknown. Some may have been released, but it's likely that at least some of them had died. One of the people missing from the list is William Device, and it's hard not to suspect that Thomas Covel had killed him, just as he had so nearly killed his brother twenty-four years earlier. However, given the social attitudes of the time, it would have been easier for a man to get someone to bail him than a woman. So perhaps it's not completely unreasonable to hope that William was free and working to secure his sister's release.

There is in fact some evidence that suggests indirectly that some of the Pendle suspects survived. The curate of Kildwick church in Craven, John Webster, spoke to Edmund Robinson in the run-up to the trials,[32] and also some years later when he was an adult. In 1677 John Webster published a book, *The Displaying of Supposed Witchcraft*, taking a similar sceptical line to Reginald Scot. The book describes his conversations with Edmund, and makes it clear that John Webster believed the suspects were innocent. However, it doesn't say what happened to them. If they had all died in prison, it would have caused such concern locally that John Webster would surely have mentioned it.[33]

One other record that may be relevant has survived. A leading Puritan, Henry Burton, was imprisoned at Lancaster in June 1637, and described indignantly how five witches were moved into a dark cell immediately under his. He seems to have thought it was done deliberately to annoy him, as they made a great deal of noise, and one of them had a small child with her. The reference to a child is intriguing, as Henry Burton also mentions that they'd been in prison for a long time, suggesting the child must have been born there. But unless some other documents come to light, we'll never know their identities or their ultimate fate.[34]

IF ENCHANTMENT OR DAEMON DISTURBS THIS PLACE

Over the next few decades the view held by people like Reginald Scot slowly but steadily prevailed. Magic was demoted from supernatural evil to fraud, and magicians and cunning folk from servants of the Devil to charlatans. The witch-hunts were deplored, but viewed as a grotesque superstition, which conveniently meant that the victims could be blamed along with their persecutors, since they could all be condemned as guilty of the same ignorance. The last person to be executed for witchcraft in England was Alice Molland, hanged at Exeter in 1685.[35] Two years later Isaac Newton published his law of universal gravitation.[36] The age of religion was over, and the age of science had begun.[37]

However, when he published his book *Optics* in 1704 Isaac Newton ended it with some philosophical speculations suggested by his research. One of them concerns the relationship between God and the Universe. Isaac Newton argues that while the sense impressions experienced by humans are only indirect images of the world around them, God 'in infinite space, as it were in his sensory, sees the things themselves intimately, and thoroughly perceives them, and comprehends them wholly by their immediate presence to himself'.[38] This concept of a pervasive divine power intimately involved with the Universe was the same ancient belief that was at the heart of magic.

In the early nineteenth century, as some men were demolishing a barn in West Bradford, just the other side of Pendle Hill from Malking Tower, a folded paper fell from one of the beams. It was a written protection charm, probably placed in the barn in the late eighteenth century. It was in code, but was deciphered by Richard Garnett of the British Museum in 1825.[39]

At the top of the charm is a magic number square, similar to the Square of Saturn, but with a six by six grid of numbers, with each column, row and diagonal adding up to one hundred and eleven – the Square of the Sun, which *Liber de Angelis* describes as 'the symbol of absolute power'.[40] Alongside the square is the seal of the Archangel Michael, whose help is invoked in many protection charms, but who also appears here in his role as a spirit associated with the sun. There are also three other seals of solar spirits. Below is an invocation, beginning with three lines of sacred names,[41] together with the Latin word 'fiat' ('so may it be') repeated three times; then (again in Latin) the words:

> As it is said in the seventeenth chapter of St Matthew at the twentieth verse by faith you may move mountains, so may it be in consequence of my faith, if there is, or shall be at any time, enchantment or daemon that frequents or disturbs this person, or this place, or this animal, I call on you, to depart without trouble, distress or disturbance of any kind, in the name of the Father, the Son and the Holy Spirit. Amen.[42]

The charm ends with the Lord's Prayer in Latin,[43] and the sacred names AGLA, On and Tetragrammaton are written on the outside of the folded paper. A similar charm, probably written by the same wise woman or cunning man, was also found at Foulridge, just north of Colne.[44]

Roger Nowell and John Starkie may have convinced themselves that they had won decisive victories in the battle against magic, but the existence of these charms makes a mockery of their efforts. In the eighteenth century there were still cunning folk around Pendle Hill – the spiritual, if not genetic, descendants of James, Alizon, Jennet and William. Magic had survived both demonisation and ridicule.

FEAR NOTHING

> Wise men and wise women ... all good witches, which do no hurt but good, which do not spoil and destroy, but save and deliver ... these are the right hand of the Devil, by which he taketh and destroyeth the souls of men.
>
> (*A Discourse of the Damned Art of Witchcraft* by William Perkins[45])

For the witch-hunters, magic was a source of constant gnawing fear, evidence of how easily people could be entrapped into damnation. Their fear of evil made them evil; their fear of Hell made them create their own small ugly hells – their places of torture and judicial murder.

But when Anne Jefferies was about to be arrested, and asked her familiar spirits, the fairies, if she should hide, they told her 'she should fear nothing'. Magicians and cunning folk offered their clients practical solutions to combat the things they feared – illness, misfortune, witchcraft or evil spirits. With the right magic – a spoken charm, a magic square, a hagstone or a human tooth – you need 'fear nothing'. And the very bizarreness of some of their methods is itself evidence of the ingenuity and resource-fulness (and sometimes even a certain dry humour) they brought to the task.

But the most bizarre aspect of magic – spirit encounters – remains as much of a challenge to us in our modern rationalist society as it was to the religious establishment in the seventeenth century. Spirit encounters were not the main purpose of magic, but they were an inescapable part of it – something that happened to many (perhaps most) people who practised magic, whether they tried to make it happen or not. They were life-changing experiences that motivated and inspired them; and they remind us that the spells intended to solve even the most ordinary problems gained their effectiveness from spiritual beliefs.

The spirits encountered by magicians and cunning folk were complex and ambiguous beings. They were the key to the hidden reality – the beauty, horror and strangeness of life that were masked by the routines of everyday normality. They were a personification of the central concept of magic – the existence of a divine creative force pervading and connecting everything. And they were a manifestation of the weirdly perceptive inner world of the subconscious and the imagination. For in the occult places of the human mind there were not only dark fears to be driven back, but also knowledge and power to be revealed by magic's 'great flash of fire'.

Researcher Vivienne puts a charm based on the ones found at Foulridge and West Bradford in the fireplace of her cottage.

Notes

For modern editions of sources quoted see Bibiography

Chapter One: Alizon the Witch

1 Thomas Potts, *The Wonderful Discovery of Witches in the County of Lancaster*, 'Published and set forth by commandment of his Majesty's Justices of Assize in the North Parts', 'Printed by W. Stansby for John Barnes, and are to be sold at his shop near Holborne Conduit', London, 1613, p. R4v. There was also a first edition published in November 1612 (see Marion Gibson's preface in her invaluable edition of witchcraft case pamphlets, *Early Modern Witches* (Routledge, Abingdon, 2000), p. 173ff.). There are a number of versions currently in print – see Bibliography. From now on this will be referred to in the notes as *WD*. Page numbers in seventeenth-century works are often a combination of letters and numbers, for example R4. Pages are also often only numbered on one side. By convention, the back of the page is designated by adding the letter v, for example R4v. When I quote any original source written in English, I have modernised the spelling and capitalisation, but left the grammar and punctuation unchanged. I have left place-names and proper names as spelt in the original.

2 *WD* title page. *WD* in fact covers four witchcraft cases – the trial of Jennet Preston at the York Assizes in July, and three cases tried at the Lancaster Assizes in August: the Pendle witches, the Salmesbury witches, and Isabel Robey. The Pendle case was the most complex – nine trials involving twelve people. It was also linked to the case of Jennet Preston, as part of the evidence against her was a crucial statement from James Device claiming she was involved with the Pendle witches.

3 I have opted to spell proper names as they are spelt in the original sources. Often names are spelt in a number of different ways; if one spelling seems generally preferred to the others I have used that one, otherwise I have used the spelling that appears easiest to read. For a number of reasons, I have opted to use first names when discussing people who feature prominently in the account. I sometimes use a combination of first name and surname, but to do that on a regular basis would quickly become tedious for the reader. It's obviously impossible to use surnames alone when so many of the people are related and have the same surname. In addition, today we generally refer to people by their first names, and although this would have seemed over-familiar in the seventeenth century, to do anything else would, in my opinion, distance these people from the modern reader – something I am anxious to avoid. In this (as in much else) I am following the example of Emma Wilby in her ground-breaking book *Cunning Folk and Familiar Spirits* (Sussex Academic Press, Brighton, 2005). Elizabeth Sothernes is also referred to as 'alias Demdike'. This was a legal formality – Justices of the Peace were obliged to note other names that suspects might be known by (Michael Dalton, *The Country Justice*, London, Printed for the Society of Stationers, 1618, p. 266). As today, these various names were usually the result of people marrying more than once, with women's maiden names also being given. Elizabeth is also referred to as 'old Demdike', a name Thomas Potts takes up with relish in his commentary (*WD* pp. Bv, F2v), no doubt

because of its ugly and vaguely insulting sound; but the epithet 'old' may have been purely descriptive – she certainly *was* elderly (around eighty (*WD* p. Bv)) – or even respectful. In Cornwall until very recently 'old' was used of someone particularly clever, regardless of their age (personal communication from Paul Tonkin).

4 See Joad Raymond, *Pamphlets and Pamphleteering in Early Modern Britain*, Cambridge University Press, Cambridge, 2006.

5 Agnes Waterhouse was executed in 1566, and Alice Molland in 1685. Incidentally, 18 March was technically still in 1611, as in early-seventeenth-century England the legal year began on 25 March.

6 Jennet Preston – more of her later. She lived at Gisburne, just over the border in Yorkshire. Although she wasn't released until early April, her trial was probably around the middle of March. The week Alizon and John Law had their confrontation was probably the last week the York Assizes could have been held. The Lent Assizes were generally held in March, and York always came before Lancaster. Also, Roger Nowell would almost certainly have gone to the Lancaster Assizes, and as he was at home for the week beginning 30 March, the Lancaster Assizes must have been held before then. *WD* p. Y.

7 He was a middle-aged man who'd no doubt travelled the same routes all his working life, and probably knew almost everyone in Pendle. There's no reference in his statement to making any inquiries about Alizon's identity.

8 The terms wise man and cunning woman were also used. The word witch was used for both men and women – although, of course, statistically women were far more likely to be accused of being witches.

9 *WD* p. Kv.

10 George Gifford, *A Dialogue Concerning Witches and Witchcrafts*, 'Printed by John Windet for Tobie Cooke and Mihil Hart, and are to be sold in Paul's Churchyard, at the Tiger's head', London, 1593, p. C. (George Gifford's surname is actually spelt Giffard on the title page of the pamphlet, but seems to have been usually spelt Gifford.) A discussion of witchcraft and magic by fictional characters. Gifford uses different characters to put forward a range of views and beliefs commonly held at the time, so that his protagonist can demolish them and demonstrate the evils of magic with a mixture of dubious logic and highly selective biblical quotations.

11 Anon, *The Examination of John Walsh*, 'Imprinted at London by John Awdely, dwelling in Little Britain Street without Aldersgate', 1566, p. A6v. In fact the pamphlet has 'he which hath but the gift of healing'; however, the word 'but' does not occur in the original record of the examination, Chanter MS 855B ff. 310–12, Devon Record Office.

12 George Gifford, *A Dialogue Concerning Witches and Witchcrafts*, p. A3.

13 William Perkins, *A Discourse of the Damned Art of Witchcraft*, Printed by Cantrell Legge, Printer to the University of Cambridge, 1618 (first published in 1608), Chapter 7, Section 4. Where sources have numbered chapters and/or sections, I give these instead of page numbers, since they are, in practice, more use to modern readers.

14 Hugh of St Victor, *Didascalion*, early twelfth century. Translated by P.G. Maxwell-Stuart in his fascinating anthology *The Occult in Mediaeval Europe* (Palgrave, Basingstoke, 2005), p. 71.

15 *WD* pp. B3, H3v, S2v, discussed in more detail later. The question of how old Alizon and James were is a tricky but important one. *WD* links them together and says of both of them that they were 'in the beginning of their time' (p. F2), suggesting that they were similar in age and both quite young. It then later says of James, 'He were but young, and in the beginning of his time' (p. I). In fact we don't even know for sure that James was older than Alizon, but he was charged with more serious crimes going back over a longer period, so it is a reasonable assumption. Rossell Hope Robbins, in *The Encyclopedia of Witchcraft and Demonology* (Spring

Books, Feltham, 1968 (first published 1959)), confidently asserts that Alizon was only eleven (p. 298), but that seems unlikely. Alizon is described in her indictment as a 'spinster', so she must at least have been *approaching* marriageable age. Life expectancy was of course lower in the early seventeenth century (although average life expectancy was slewed by high childhood mortality rates), which must have made a difference to people's perception of what would have been 'the beginning' of someone's life. Even 200 years later, in *Sense and Sensibility*, Jane Austen portrays Colonel Brandon (admittedly humorously) as 'an old bachelor' and of 'advanced years' at thirty-five. That makes it unlikely that you would be considered 'at the beginning of your time' at, say, twenty-five. On the other hand, Thomas Aikenhead, the Edinburgh University student sentenced to death for blasphemy in 1696, pleaded for mercy on the grounds of youth because he was only twenty when he committed the offence (see *A Complete Collection of State Trials*, compiled by T.B. Howell (T.C. Hansard, London, 1812) (aka *Cobbett's Complete Collection of State Trials*), vol. XIII, pp. 918–39, *Proceedings against Thomas Aikenhead*). As for internal evidence within *WD*, it's clear that Alizon was angry enough about the pins to frighten John Law – someone probably not easily scared – which suggests the kind of uncontrollable rage not unknown in teenagers. And it's clear that from very early in the case Roger Nowell based his strategy on the assumption that James would be vulnerable to interrogation. Taking these considerations into account, I would estimate a minimum age for Alizon of sixteen and a maximum for James of twenty-two, with their most likely ages being around seventeen and nineteen.

16   *WD* p. R3v.

17   *The Compact Edition of the Oxford English Dictionary*, Oxford University Press, 1971.

18   Later John's son Abraham made a statement claiming that Alizon didn't have the money to pay for the pins. But he wasn't there, and his statement is suspect for a number of reasons, which will be discussed in more detail later.

19   See E.D. Longman and S. Loch, *Pins and Pincushions*, Longmans, Green & Co., London, 1911, pp. 2, 20ff, 148, 153, 187, and Plate II Illustration 1. For the use of the term 'blackthorn point' see Francis Jones, *The Holy Wells of Wales*, University of Wales Press, Cardiff, 1954, p. 111.

20   There are, of course, several versions of this rhyme, including a more modern one that begins, 'See a *penny*, pick it up …' This is the version my mother taught me when I was a child. She told me that if I let the pin lie I would rue it because a witch would stick it in an image of me.

21   John Aubrey, *Miscellanies Upon the Following Subjects*, second edition, printed for A. Bettesworth, J. Battley, J. Pemberton and E. Curll, London, 1721, 'Magic'. First published in 1696.

22   T.R. Mother Bunch's Closet Newly Broke Open, printed by AM for P. Brooksby, London, 1685 (also quoted by C.J.S. Thompson, *The Hand of Destiny*, Rider & Co., London, 1932, p. 44.)

23   E.D. Longman and S. Loch, *Pins and Pincushions*, pp. 46–7.

24   E.D. Longman and S. Loch, *Pins and Pincushions*, pp. 40–41.

25   The original trial document, edited by Domenico Mammoli, and including an introduction and English translation, was published in Rome in 1972 as one of a series of papers about the history of Todi, *Res Tudertinae – 14*, entitled *The Record of the Trial and Condemnation of a Witch, Matteuccia di Francesco, at Todi, 20 March 1428*. Richard Kieckhefer discusses it in his book *Magic in the Middle Ages* (Cambridge University Press, Cambridge, 1990), citing Candida Peruzzi, 'Un processo di stregoneria a Todi nel 400', *Lares: Organo della Società di Etnografia Italiana-Roma*, 21 (1955), fasc. I–II, 1–17. He mentions this particular spell on p. 60.

26 Thomas Middleton, *The Witch*, Act 1, Scene 2, written around 1615 (see the Introduction by Elizabeth Schafer to the edition published by A. & C. Black, London, 1994).

27 It's only common sense that Alizon had a social life, and we shouldn't abandon common sense just because we're dealing with a witchcraft case. And as we shall see in Chapter Two, love divination was (and still is) often a social activity, and the line between love divination and more aggressive love magic was a thin one. It's also important to resist the propaganda in *WD* and other witchcraft accounts that portrays practitioners of magic as social outcasts. We know this wasn't true of Alizon because one of her statements describes her laughing and joking with a friend (*WD* p. E4v). The belief that Alizon had magical powers might have made some people avoid her, but it would have made other people cultivate her friendship. If there were other girls involved, that would explain why John doesn't mention his suspicions about the pins in his statement; but there are plenty of other reasons why that might not have been included: Roger Nowell might have told John that his son had said Alizon couldn't pay for the pins, and John might not have wanted to contradict him; John might have been reluctant to admit to knowing anything at all about magic; he might have thought Alizon wanted the pins to make a witch bottle – counter-magic to remove a curse, which would have put Alizon in too good a light to be mentioned; and even in the seventeenth century, pure speculation by a witness was generally not considered good evidence.

Chapter Two: Love magic and pin magic

1 *Codex Latinus Monacensis 849* in the Bavarian State Library, ff. 29v–31v. (Handwritten manuscripts do not in general have numbered pages, and so the pages are assigned sheet, or folio (f), numbers, with the front of the sheet being indicated by the letter r (*recto*), and the back by the letter v (*verso*).) Edited by Richard Kieckhefer and included in his book *Forbidden Rites: A Necromancer's Manual of the Fifteenth Century* (Sutton Publishing, Stroud, 1997), pp. 226–8, plus illustration on p. 359. He also includes a translation of parts of the spell and a scholarly analysis of it on pp. 86–9. His publication of this enormously important and fascinating manuscript is one of the most valuable contributions to the study of magic in the last fifty years. This is my translation from his edition of the Latin text. Notes on the translation: 'Drives' – *fingat*, obviously a mistake for *figit*, 'fixes', or in literary use 'drives in'. As these manuscripts were copied out by hand, mistakes are not unusual. 'Pins' – *acus*. This could mean either pins or needles, but it's actually quite difficult to drive a needle into wax (at least without using a thimble), so 'pins' is far more likely. 'Into the heart of N' – the Latin is in fact *in amorem*, but again this is obviously a mistake for *in cor*. 'Groin' – *femore*, literally 'thigh', but probably the upper inner thigh, i.e. groin, is meant – otherwise you'd need two pins, one for the left thigh and one for the right thigh. 'Command' – *conjuro*, see note 38.

2 For most of the Middle Ages and early modern period the people who used these books would have been men, because they were generally written in Latin and very few women would have received the kind of education necessary to read them. However, gradually more books of magic were translated or written in vernacular languages, and women's literacy increased, so that by the mid seventeenth century the painter David Teniers the Younger, in his picture *Witches Preparing for the Sabbat*, showed women working from books of magic.

3 *News from Scotland, Declaring the Damnable Life and Death of Doctor Fian, a Notable Sorcerer*, 'Published according to the Scottish copy. At London. Printed for William Wright.' 1591.

4 The town of Saltpans.

5 *The Golden Ass* was enormously popular throughout the Middle Ages and Early Modern period. It was translated into English by William Adlington in 1566. This particularly story (from the fourth chapter, *The Festival of Laughter*) was also quoted in *The Three Books of Occult Philosophy* by Henrich Cornelius Agrippa (see note 16), Book 1, Chapter 42.

6 It's not mentioned in the trial record, published in Robert Pitcairn, *Criminal Trials in Scotland 1488–1624*, Bannatyne Club, Edinburgh, 1833, first volume, second part, p. 209.

7 The various English laws against witchcraft are published in Rossell Hope Robbins, *The Encyclopedia of Witchcraft and Demonology*. The 1563 Act is on pp. 158–9, the 1604 Act on pp. 280–81. The pillory was a device on a platform in a public place, similar to the stocks, except that the prisoner was secured standing upright with his/her neck and (usually) wrists through holes in wooden boards. Standing in that position for six hours would have become extremely painful, and in addition the crowds that gathered often threw things at the prisoner – one alleged witch, sentenced to the pillory in Ireland in 1711, apparently had an eye knocked out (W.B. Yeats (ed.), *Fairy and Folk Tales of the Irish Peasantry*, Walter Scott, London, 1888, endnote). There is a vivid illustration from a sixteenth-century English chapbook on the Bridgeman Art Library website, www.bridgemanartondemand.com, and also one on p. 135 of Jonathan Lumby's book *The Lancashire Witch-Craze: Jennet Preston and the Lancashire Witches* (Carnegie, Preston, 1995).

8 *Witches Apprehended, Examined and Executed, for Notable Villainies by them Committed both by Land and Water*, 'Printed at London for Edward Marchant, and are to be sold at his shop over against the Cross in Pauls Churchyard, 1613', pp. B3v and B4.

9 Brian Darcey (W.W.) , *A True and Just Record of the Information, Examination and Confession of all the Witches, taken at St Oses in the County of Essex*, 'Imprinted in London at the three Cranes in the vinetree by Thomas Dawson 1582', p. 2A3v. (The title page gives the author as W.W., but this is if not, W.W. was little more than the editor of Brian Darcey's documents almost certainly a pseudonym for the Justice of the Peace Brian Darcey)

10 *WD* p. F4v.

11 Thomas Middleton, *The Witch*, Act 1, Scene 2. Strictly speaking an incubus was a male demon, and the female equivalent was known as a succubus.

12 Thomas Middleton, *The Witch*, Act 1, Scene 2.

13 See Owen Davies, 'The Nightmare Experience, Sleep Paralysis, and Witchcraft Accusations', *Folklore* 114 (no. 2, August 2003), pp. 181–203. Also personal communication from a sufferer of the severest form of the condition.

14 *WD* p. Sv.

15 Thomas Middleton, *The Witch*, Act 2, Scene 2.

16 See, for example, Heinrich Cornelius Agrippa, *The Three Books of Occult Philosophy*, one of the most influential works in magic. It was written in 1509–10, and became extremely popular even though it was then only available as handwritten copies. A revised edition was finally printed in 1533, and an edition in English was printed in 1651. It is still in print today, and can also be read on Joseph Peterson's website www.esotericarchives.com – which not only contains texts of numerous important occult works, but also includes succinct and authoritative introductions.

17 Jean Bodin, *De la Démonomanie des Sorciers*, Paris, 1580, Third Book, Chapter 2.

18 Heinrich Cornelius Agrippa, *The Three Books of Occult Philosophy* (see note 16), Book 1, Chapter 44.

19 Reginald Scot, *The Discovery of Witchcraft*, London, 1584, Book 6, Chapter 7. His opposition to the witch-hunts was based on the principle that most magic was nonsense, and although he argued that many people accused of witchcraft were innocent, he was extremely hostile to magical practitioners.

20 *The Book of Secrets of Albertus Magnus* was written anonymously, probably by one of Albertus Magnus's pupils, at around the end of the thirteenth century, with printed editions appearing from the late fifteenth century. The first English editions were printed in the mid sixteenth century. This love potion is from the section on periwinkle near the beginning of the First

Book, 'Of the Virtues of Certain Herbs'. The book is careful to say that its purpose is to make a husband and wife love each other.

21 Domenico Mammoli (ed.), *The Record of the Trial and Condemnation of a Witch* (*Res Tudertinae – 14*), Rome 1972. pp. 32, 34. Also discussed in Richard Kieckhefer, *European Witch Trials: Their Foundations in Popular and Learned Culture, 1300–1500*, Routledge & Kegan Paul, London, 1976, p. 58, and Richard Kieckhefer, *Magic in the Middle Ages*, pp. 59, 60; citing Candida Peruzzi, 'Un processo di stregoneria a Todi nel '400'', *Lares: Organo della Società di Etnografia Italiana-Roma*, 21 (1955), fasc. I–II, 1–17.

22 Richard Kieckhefer, *European Witch Trials*, p. 58, citing Augustin Chassaing (ed.), *Spicilegium brivatense: Recueil de documents historiques relatifs au Brivadois et à l'Auvergne*, Paris, 1886, pp. 438–46.

23 *The Lenkiewicz Manuscript*, a late-sixteenth- or early-seventeenth-century English book of magic owned by the Plymouth artist Robert Lenkiewicz who had a number of copies made so that the book's contents could be studied without damaging the original manuscript. Special thanks to Jason Semmens and Mark Davey for their invaluable help with my work on this document.

24 Richard Kieckhefer, *European Witch Trials*, p. 60, citing Gene A. Brucker, 'Sorcery in Early Renaissance Florence', *Studies in the Renaissance*, X (1963), pp. 7–24.

25 'Merlin', *The Book of Charms and Ceremonies*, W. Foulsham & Co., London, 1910, p. 15. For 'knot' meaning 'catkin', see *The Compact Edition of the Oxford English Dictionary*.

26 C.J.S. Thompson, *The Hand of Destiny*, p. 48.

27 *The Book of Secrets of Albertus Magnus*, First Book, 'Of the Virtues of Certain Herbs', and Second Book, 'Of the Virtues of Certain Stones' (the stone *Aetites*) (see note 20).

28 Messayaac, *Liber de Angelis, Annulis, Karecteribus & Ymaginibus Planetarum*, Cambridge University Library MS Dd.11.45, ff. 137v, 138r; the complete text, edited by Juris D. Lidaka, with a parallel translation, is published in *Conjuring Spirits: Texts and Traditions of Medieval Ritual Magic*, edited by Claire Fanger, Sutton Publishing, Stroud, 1998, pp. 45–75, together with an introduction on pp. 32–44. This manuscript, the only known surviving copy of Messayaac's book, dates from the fifteenth century, but as we know nothing about Messayaac (and indeed the name is probably a pseudonym) we can't be sure when the book was originally written. Although much shorter than *The Munich Handbook*, this is another wonderful and invaluable text. Juris Lidaka's translation is excellent, but I have opted to make my own, freer translation. Zaguam is given as one of the sacred names of God in the Latin versions of *The Sworn Book* (the English version has Zagnam) (see note 40).

29 Al-Majriti (attrib.), *Picatrix (Ghayat Al-Hakim – The Goal of the Wise)*. Translation by Hashem Atallah. Both the true author and date of this book are uncertain, but it is probably from the tenth or eleventh century. Numerous manuscripts – either in Arabic or Latin – survive, the earliest from the fourteenth or fifteenth century. There was, however, no English translation of this work – undoubtedly one of the most influential in the history of European magic – until Hashem Atallah made a modern translation from the Arabic, edited by William Kiesel and published by Ouroboros Press, Seattle, in 2002. This quotation is from p. 41.

30 See Joseph Peterson's note to his edition of Heinrich Cornelius Agrippa's *The Three Books of Occult Philosophy* (Book 3, Chapter 11), on his website www.esotericarchives.com.

31 Object identity number 748. The Museum of Witchcraft is in Boscastle, Cornwall. Its online database, which contains details of all the artefacts it houses, can be accessed from its website www.museumofwitchcraft.com. To find an object by its identity number, click on 'Advanced Search' and then use the dropdown menu and click on 'Museum Number' and enter the number in the box. See also Joyce Froome, 'The Symbolism of the Pierced Heart', *The Journal for the Academic Study of Magic*, Issue 2 (2004), pp. 287–99.

32 *The Munich Handbook*, ff. 32r–33r; in Richard Kieckhefer, *Forbidden Rites*, pp. 229–31, illustration on p. 360, analysis and translation on pp. 89–90. See note 1. Again this is my translation from the Latin.

33 *The Key of Solomon the King*, edited and translated by S. Liddell Macgregor Mathers, George Redway, London, 1889, Book II, Chapter III (p. 77). S. Lidell Macgregor Mathers compiled this edition from various eighteenth-century manuscripts. The dog isn't mentioned in all versions of *The Key of Solomon*, but does feature in an English version dated 1572 (again in the third chapter of the second book), *The Work of King Solomon the Wise, Called his Clavicle* (MS Sloane 3847 in the British Library), available on Joseph Peterson's Esoteric Archives CD which can be acquired from his website www.esotericarchives.com.

34 The use of clay or ash is described in *The Sworn Book* by Honorius of Thebes. See note 40.

35 The illustration in the manuscript suggests that the actual incantation was written round the edge of the circle, but, as Richard Kieckhefer points out, it's more likely that just the names were written, while the incantation was spoken. *The Sworn Book* describes writing the names of spirits round the edge of the circle. According to *The Book of the Sacred Magic of Abramelin the Mage*, by Abraham of Worms, Belial is one of the four Princes, and Astaroth and Paymon are two of the eight Sub-Princes. Ashtaroth was one of the pagan deities honoured by the Biblical King Solomon (1 Kings 11:5) (in the 1560 Geneva Bible; the name is spelt slightly differently – Ashtoreth – in the King James Version). Belial is mentioned as some kind of devil figure in 2 Corinthians 6:15.

36 Aleister Crowley (1875–1947) was undoubtedly one of the most influential figures in twentieth-century occultism. This quotation comes from *The Book of the Law (LiberAL vel Legis)* (Chapter One, No. 4), written in 1904, and first published in *The Equinox*, the journal of the O.T.O. (*Ordo Templi Orientis*), Vol. I, No. X (1913). According to Aleister Crowley *The Book of the Law* was in fact dictated to him by a spirit, Aiwaz. He was strongly influenced by the work of the Elizabethan magicians John Dee and Edward Kelley, who in turn worked from *The Sworn Book*, which was written by the thirteenth-century magician Honorius of Thebes with the assistance of the Angel Hocroel (see note 40). Aleister Crowley's analysis of the Gilles de Rais case, *The Forbidden Lecture* (Mandrake Press Ltd, Thame, Oxfordshire, 1990 (first published 1930)) should be read by anyone interested in witchcraft trials. As for the meaning and significance of the Latin word *voluntas*, it's worth remembering that 'the will of God' is 'voluntas Dei' in Latin (see, for example, Luke 22:42 in the Vulgate Bible: 'Pater si vis transfer calicem istum a me verumtamen non mea voluntas sed tua fiat.').

37 'True name' – the Latin is just *verum*, so either *nomen* ('name') or *deum* ('god') could be understood, but as one of the names, Seraphin, is strictly speaking an angel name, rather than a name of God (although it may refer to Jesus Christ), *nomen* seems to me more likely.

38 The primary meaning of both the Latin verb *conjurare* and the English *conjure* is to swear an oath with someone. From there comes the secondary meaning to bind someone to do something by making them swear an oath, and then to command or appeal to someone to do something by invoking something sacred – as we still do today when we say something like, 'For God's sake help me!' In magic, it generally meant to secure the assistance of spirits by using sacred names of God, such as AGLA, Sabaoth, Emanuel, Saday (Almighty), Adonay (Lord), Alpha et Omega (the first and last letters of the Greek alphabet, i.e. the Beginning and the End) and Tetragrammaton (literally 'word of four letters', referring to the Hebrew letters *yod heh vau heh*, the consonants of the name Jehovah). *The Sworn Book* by Honorius of Thebes (see note 40) contains pages of these names. The usual modern use of the word simply to mean to make something appear or happen by magic (or as if by magic) first occurs in the sixteenth century. See *The Compact Edition of the Oxford English Dictionary*.

39 See, for example, *The Leyden Papyrus*, which has been edited and translated by F.Ll. Griffith

and Herbert Thompson and published by Dover Publications, New York (a republication of an edition initially published in 1904). Although primarily drawing on the power of Ancient Egyptian deities, occasionally elements from the Judaeo-Christian tradition – such as the use of the sacred names Sabaoth and Adonay and references to the archangel Michael – creep in.

40 *The Sworn Book* by Honorius of Thebes (with the assistance of the Angel Hocroel) has been reliably dated to the first half of the thirteenth century by Robert Mathiesen in his article 'A Thirteenth-Century Ritual to Attain the Beatific Vision from *The Sworn Book* of Honorius of Thebes', in *Conjuring Spirits: Texts and Traditions of Medieval Ritual Magic*, edited by Claire Fanger. There are several known surviving manuscripts, all in the British Library; the only one in English (mainly) is Royal 17.A.XLII, which dates from the sixteenth century. This quotation is from f. 47r. of that manuscript. (In fact the Latin versions phrase this differently: 'Et hoc est verum male operantibus et propter effectum malum' – 'And that is true of those working evil and for evil outcomes'.) In 1977 Daniel J. Driscoll published a stunningly elegant version of *The Sworn Book*, a combination of Royal 17.A.XLII and his own translation of MS Sloane 313, a Latin manuscript from the late fourteenth or early fifteenth century at one point owned by the Elizabethan magician John Dee. A second edition was published in 1983 (both by Heptangle Books, Gillette, New Jersey). An edition of the Latin versions, *Liber Iuratus Honorii; A Critical Edition of the Latin Version of the Sworn Book of Honorius* by Gösta Hedegård (Almqvist & Wiksell International, Stockholm) was published in 2002. Robert Mathiesen quotes extensively both from Daniel Driscoll's edition and Royal 17.A.XLII in his article. Royal 17.A.XLII is now also available online, transcribed by Joseph H. Peterson on his excellent website www.esotericarchives.com – or, better still, support the website by buying the esoteric archives CD.

41 E.D. Longman and S. Loch, *Pins and Pincushions*, p. 44.

42 John Aubrey, *Miscellanies Upon the Following Subjects*, Section 13.

43 Ronald Hutton, *The Stations of the Sun*, Oxford University Press, Oxford, 1997, p. 380.

44 George Long, *The Folklore Calendar*, Philip Allan (no place of publication given) 1930.

45 Object identity numbers 1347 and 1339. See note 31.

46 Richard Carew, *The Survey of Cornwall*, 1602, Book 2, Pydar Hundred.

47 Francis Jones, *The Holy Wells of Wales*, p. 111, citing *Traethodydd* 1893 (quarterly journal), Denbigh-Holywell-Caernarvon, 1845–, p. 219–20.

48 E.D. Longman and S. Loch, *Pins and Pincushions*, p. 61.

49 Francis Jones, *The Holy Wells of Wales*, pp. 110, 111, citing J. Jones (Myrddin Fardd), *Llen Gwerin Sir Gaernarfon*, Caernarfon, 1908.

50 Francis Jones, *The Holy Wells of Wales*, p. 103, citing *Traethodydd* 1893 (quarterly journal), Denbigh-Holywell-Caernarvon, 1845–, p. 219–20. Special thanks to Judith Higginbottom for drawing this book to my attention.

51 E.D. Longman and S. Loch, *Pins and Pincushions*, pp. 30, 34–5, 184 and Plate XXXIX Illustration 2. They give examples of witchcraft victims vomiting pins from a case in Oxfordshire in 1606 and one in Renfrewshire in 1697. In 1702 Richard Hathaway was convicted of falsely accusing a woman of witchcraft after he was discovered to have faked vomiting pins.

52 Frederick Thomas Elworthy, *The Evil Eye*, John Murray, London, 1895, p. 53. There is an example of one of these hearts in Wells Museum.

53 Object identity number 518. See note 31.

54 Brian Darcey, *A True and Just Record*, p. Fv.

55 The term 'cunning folk', meaning wise women and cunning men, was used by George Gifford in his *Dialogue Concerning Witches and Witchcrafts*, and although it doesn't seem to

have been common in the Early Modern period, it has proved very popular with modern historians because of its convenience.

56 Joseph Blagrave, *Blagrave's Astrological Practice of Physick*, London, 'Printed for Obadiah Blagrave at the Bear and Star in St Paul's Church-Yard. 1689' (first published 1671).

57 Joseph Glanvil, *Sadducismus Triumphatus, or full and plain Evidence concerning Witches and Apparitions*, London, 1681. This account is one of the 'relations' (Relation Eight) appended to the end of the main text. It's clear from the account that neither the woman nor her husband had met the wizard who bewitched her. The term 'wizard' was often used for cunning men in church court trials (Owen Davies, *Cunning Folk: Popular Magic in English History*, Hambledon and London, London, 2003, pp. 14, 16). In later centuries, witch bottles seem to have been used as general protection magic. See Ralph Merrifield, *The Archaeology of Ritual and Magic*, Guild Publishing, London, 1987, pp. 163–75 for numerous examples and a discussion of the date of the incident included in Joseph Glanvil's book. Witch bottles were obviously a response to growing anxieties about witchcraft, making a late-sixteenth- or early-seventeenth-century date the most likely for their invention. See also Brian Hoggard's website www.apotropaios.co.uk.

58 Of course torture wasn't always used in Scotland, and when it was used it wasn't always used legally. Geillis Duncane's initial torture was technically illegal, and in the later stages of the North Berwick witchcraft case the situation was complicated by the fact that one of the suspects had confessed to using magic against the king. The question of interrogation methods is one we will (unfortunately) have to return to later. For other examples of the belief that people could use magic to resist torture see, for instance, Heinrich Kramer and Jacob Sprenger, *Malleus Maleficarum*, Cologne, 1486, Third Part; Henri Boguet, *Discours des Sorciers*, Jean Pillehotte, Lyon, 1610 (first edition 1602), *Instruction pour un Juge*, Article 22; and Reginald Scot, *The Discovery of Witchcraft*, Book 12, Chapter 17.

Chapter Three: The bewitching of John Law

1 John's encounter with Alizon and its aftermath are *WD* pp. R2v–S2. The author of *WD*, Thomas Potts, tries to give the impression that John's and Alizon's statements are records of what they said in court, but then admits that Alizon's was in fact a statement made to Roger Nowell in March, and the same is undoubtedly true of most of John's statement. This will be discussed further later.

2 This part of Alizon's evidence will be discussed in more detail later.

3 'By means' – see *The Compact Edition of the Oxford English Dictionary*.

4 Celia Fiennes's journals of her travels were first published as *Through England on a Side Saddle in the Time of William and Mary* in 1888, edited by Emily Griffiths; then as *The Journeys of Celia Fiennes*, edited by Christopher Morris (The Cresset Press, London, 1947). This quotation is from the section 'Through Devonshire to Land's End'. Celia Fiennes also describes a similar near-accident when her horse slipped on wet stones in Lancaster (in the section 'Lancashire and the Lake District'). Christopher Morris's introduction to his edition also has some interesting information about road conditions (pp. xxx–xxxii).

5 See *The Compact Edition of the Oxford English Dictionary*.

6 Kathleen M. Thies and John F. Travers, *Quick Look Nursing: Growth and Development Through the Lifespan*, Jones & Bartlett Publishers, 2006, p. 67; Tony Smith (ed.), *The British Medical Association Complete Family Health Encyclopedia*, Dorling Kindersley, London, 1990, p. 952ff. Also personal communication from Pam Steel, a physiotherapist with many years experience of treating stroke victims.

7 How statements were drawn up and trials conducted will be discussed in more detail later.

8 In view of the pain he was in. In addition, he may not have received much education, and may not have been literate.

9 Robert A. Wilson and Frank C. Keil (eds), *The MIT Encyclopedia of the Cognitive Sciences*, MIT Press, 2001, p. 369; Kathleen M. Thies and John F. Travers, *Quick Look Nursing: Growth and Development Through the Lifespan*, p. 67. Researchers estimate that over 95% of right-handed people and about 70% of left-handed people have language lateralised on the left side of the brain. Although a higher proportion of left-handed people have language lateralised on the right side of the brain, in general left-handedness indicates that the right side of their brains is dominant, not that the lateralisation of their brains is reversed.

10 Thomas Potts, the author of *WD*, saw John at this time and includes his own description in the pamphlet, but again it's extremely – and for Thomas Potts uncharacteristically – vague. It will be discussed later.

11 *WD* pp. H3, H3v, H4v. Incredible as it may seem, the evidence is contradictory over whether Anne Towneley had died one or two years earlier. This will be discussed later.

12 The name Abraham fell out of use during the Middle Ages, but was then revived by Protestants after the Reformation. Its use suggests that the Laws may well have been a strongly Protestant family. See E. G. Withycombe, *The Oxford Dictionary of English Christian Names*, Oxford University Press, Oxford, 1977. However, personal circumstances and experiences no doubt had even more effect on people's views about magic – James's accuser Henry Towneley was a Catholic (see Jonathan Lumby, *The Lancashire Witch-Craze* p. 143).

13 'A Memorial of Certain Most Notorious Witches' in *A World of Wonders*, by T.I., printed for William Barley, London, 1595, p. E3v; this account was discovered by Marion Gibson and included in her book *Early Modern Witches*.

14 Anon, *The Most Strange and Admirable Discovery of the Three Witches of Warboys*, 'Printed by the Widow Orwin, for Thomas Man, and John Winninton, and are to be sold in Pater Noster Row, at the sign of the Talbot', London, 1593.

15 Anon, *Witches Apprehended*, p. C2v. 'Swimming' was an ancient form of trial by ordeal, revived during the witch-hunts. The suspect was bound and thrown into a river or pool. If they floated it was considered proof of guilt. See Robert Bartlett, *Trial by Fire and Water: The Medieval Judicial Ordeal*, Oxford University Press, Oxford, 1986.

16 Henri Boguet, *Discours des Sorciers*, Chapter 37.

17 Henri Boguet, *Discours des Sorciers*, Chapter 37; King James I, *Demonology*, Edinburgh, printed by Robert Walde-grave, 1597, Second Book, Chapter 6.

18 Alexander Roberts describes a bewitched person recovering once the witch had been imprisoned in *A Treatise of Witchcraft*, printed by N.O. for Samuel Man, London, 1616.

19 *The Witches of Northamptonshire*, printed by Thomas Purfoot for Arthur Johnson, London, 1612, p. A3.

Chapter Four: No man near them was free from danger

1 *WD* p. B2.

2 However, the religious situation in many parts of England was complicated, and the half-brother of one of these fiercely Protestant Nowells had been one of the devoutly Roman Catholic Towneleys. Roger Nowell's background is detailed in Jonathan Lumby's *The Lancashire Witch-Craze*, pp. 115–18, which contains a great deal of fascinating research into the background of the Pendle witchcraft case. For the role of the Sheriff at executions see Susan Maria Ffarington (ed.), *The Farington Papers*, The Chetham Society, Manchester, 1856, p. 36ff. The Assizes were courts held once a year (in the Summer) in smaller counties, and twice a year (in Lent and in the Summer) in counties such as Yorkshire and Lancashire. They were presided over by Circuit judges from London, and tried serious crimes carrying

sentences of imprisonment or death (J.S. Cockburn, *A History of English Assizes 1558–1714*, Cambridge University Press, Cambridge, 1972).

3 Nicholas Assherton (edited by F.R. Raines), *The Journal of Nicholas Assheton*, The Chetham Society, Manchester, 1848, p. 62.

4 *WD* pp. T, L4v, Y2. Jonathan Lumby, *The Lancashire Witch-Craze*, pp. 130, 136–142.

5 John Darrell, *A True Narration of the Strange and Grievous Vexation by the Devil of Seven Persons in Lancashire*, London, 1600; George More, *A True Discourse Concerning the Certain Possession and Dispossession of Seven Persons in One Family in Lancashire*, London, 1600; Jonathan Lumby, *The Lancashire Witch-Craze*, pp. 119–28.

6 John Webster, *The Displaying of Supposed Witchcraft*, London, 1677, 'The Examination of Edmund Robinson', appended to the end of the book.

7 Or possibly the case had been dismissed for lack of evidence. Defendants were also often reprieved by judges, but this is unlikely in this case because both the Northern Circuit judges were believers in witchcraft. *WD* p. S4.

8 *WD* p. Y.

9 *WD* p. B2.

10 *WD* pp. B4, B4v.

11 These statements were nevertheless taken to the Assizes by Roger (*WD* p. B2), raising the possibility that Roger knew that a pamphlet was likely to be written about the trials, even before they were held.

12 *WD* p. Hv.

13 Michael Dalton, *The Country Justice*, 'Arrest, and Imprisonment', p. 295.

14 *WD* p. H3v. James's statement appears to say that this was two years earlier (p. H3), but his sister Jennet says it was one year earlier (p. H4v). However, James's statement (as will be discussed later) is clearly a paste job, while Jennet had almost certainly been coached by Roger Nowell, so Jennet's dating is more likely to be correct.

15 *WD* p. H4v.

16 Brian Darcey, *A True and Just Record*, pp. E8v–Fv.

17 Brian Darcey, *A True and Just Record*, p. 2A2v.

18 For example, in the case of Isabel Robey one of the accusers referred to a cunning man who was a glover (*WD* p. T3v); a cunning man who was a caulker is mentioned in Brian Darcey's *A True and Just Record* (p. C2), and the nineteenth-century Cornish cunning man James Thomas also worked as a miner (Jason Semmens, *The Witch of the West*, or *The Strange and Wonderful History of Thomasine Blight*, published by the author, Plymouth, 2004, p. 18).

19 For example, the appearance of a toad in Margaret Pearson's house was regarded as highly incriminating (*WD* p. T).

20 *WD* p. II2.

21 *WD* pp. C2, S2v.

22 Mary Sutton, as well as being swum, also had blood drawn (*Witches Apprehended*, p. C).

23 This statement of James's will be discussed in more detail later.

24 Brian Darcey, *A True and Just Record*, p. 2A2.

25 Brian Darcey, *A True and Just Record*, pp. A3v, A4. W.W., the initials that appear on the title page, are probably a pseudonym for Brian Darcey, and in any case the pamphlet consists almost entirely of statements taken by him, so that if W.W. is *not* Brian Darcey he should be considered more of an editor than the author; however, this section, at the start of the pamphlet, is one of the parts that may be by him. Even so, it is heavily influenced by Jean Bodin's ideas, as Brian Darcey's campaign against witchcraft was, so it is likely that it reflects Brian Darcey's thoughts on the matter (see Chapter Nine for more about Jean Bodin's influence on Brian Darcey's witch-hunt).

26 *WD* pp. Ev, E2; George Gifford, *A Dialogue Concerning Witches and Witchcrafts*, pp. M3, M3v; Gary St M. Nottingham, *Charms, Charming and the Charmed: Welsh Border Witchcraft*, Verdelet Press, Craven Arms, 2007, p. 23; Anon, *The Most Wonderful and True Story of a Certain Witch Named Alice Gooderige* printed for J.O., London, 1597, *WD* p. T3.

27 Ronald Hutton, summarising the latest research into the witch-hunts in a talk to the Friends of the Museum of Witchcraft on 6 December 2008, said that the people most likely to be accused of witchcraft were women prone to making verbal attacks on their neighbours.

Chapter Five: The tower and the charm

1 *WD* p. B2.

2 George Gifford, *A Dialogue Concerning Witches and Witchcrafts*, p. B.

3 George Gifford, *A Dialogue Concerning Witches and Witchcrafts*, pp. M3, M3v.

4 Jonathan Lumby, *The Lancashire Witch-Craze*, p. 118; see also pp. 110–14.

5 William Perkins, *A Discourse of the Damned Art of Witchcraft*, Chapter 7, Section 4.

6 'Certificate of the Committee for the county of Essex that the following offenders should be pardoned: … eight women for feloniously entertaining evil spirits.' Parliamentary Archives, HL/PO/JO/10/1/202, 5 Mar 1646–23 Mar 1646.

7 This was true not only for witchcraft cases. Juries regularly undervalued stolen goods to bring them below the value that would make the offender liable for the death sentence (J.S. Cockburn, *A History of English Assizes*, p. 128).

8 The actual word used is 'vaste' – in this case an archaic spelling of 'waste', not 'vast'.

9 Marion Gibson, *Early Modern Witches*, p. 182, note 7.

10 J.S. Cockburn, *A History of English Assizes*, pp. 70–85. *WD*, in the section on Jennet Preston's trial, contains the words 'these honorable and reverend judges, under whose government we live in these North parts' (p. Z3v), but it's very unlikely that a court official would have lived in northern England. The phrase was no doubt intended to give the impression that Thomas Potts was genuinely speaking for the people of Yorkshire and Lancashire, and that they supported the judges rather than Jennet Preston's family. Thomas Potts's position as a clerk involved in the trials is mentioned in *WD* p. A2v, and discussed in Marion Gibson, 'Thomas Potts's 'dusty memory'', Robert Poole (ed.), *The Lancashire Witches: Histories and Stories*, Manchester University Press, Manchester, 2002, pp. 42–57.

11 *WD* p. E4v. Anne Whittle was also known as Anne Chattox.

12 *WD* p. E4: A statement from Alizon reads, 'This examinate and her mother had their fire-house broken [into].' Malking Tower is referred to as Elizabeth Sothernes's house, so this must be a different house, and obviously it must be the house where Elizabeth Device had lived with her husband John Device, though as he isn't mentioned, the incident must have occurred after his death. The term 'fire-house' means 'dwelling house', and is used to distinguish a house from its outbuildings (*The Compact Edition of the Oxford English Dictionary*), which means that the Devices' house must have *had* outbuildings. On p. C2 a statement from James refers to '*his* chamber window', not '*the* chamber window'. (Alizon's account of the theft is part of her evidence against Anne Whittle; she claimed that she later saw one of Anne Whittle's daughters with one of the stolen items.)

13 *WD* contains several references to Alizon being at Malking Tower or being with her grandmother.

14 There is some debate about the location of Malking Tower, but one of Elizabeth Sothernes's statements describes her walking to the mill at Wheathead, with Alizon leading her (*WD* p. B3, with a reference to this being 'Weethead' on p. Cv). A possible site for the mill could be a field called the mill field just to the north-east of what is now Lower Wheathead at Admergill (see the article about Admergill on www.barrowford.org/page13.html). This would be a round trip of about three kilometres from Malkin Tower Farm – not an easy walk for

a blind eighty-year-old, but possible, particularly when the eighty-year-old was as tough and determined as Elizabeth Sothernes obviously was.

15 Sometimes Elizabeth Sothernes's home is referred to as the house *at* Malking Tower (e.g. *WD* p. G4), which could mean that Malking Tower was a place where Elizabeth had a house, but Jennet Device's statements refer to 'her said grandmother's house, called Malking Tower' (*WD* pp. G3v, I3v etc.).

16 E.G. Withycombe, *The Oxford Dictionary of English Christian Names*; *The Compact Edition of the Oxford English Dictionary*.

17 Thomas Middleton, *The Witch*, Act 3, Scene 3. Though Thomas Middleton could in fact have been influenced by the Pendle case, and named his spirit Malkin after Malking Tower.

18 *Macbeth*, Act 1, Scene 1; spelt Grimalkin in some editions. *Macbeth* was probably written in 1606.

19 William Baldwin, *Beware the Cat*, 1570. William A. Ringler prepared a modern text of this wonderful book from a transcript in the British Library of the lost first edition, which was published by Huntington Library, San Marino, California in 1988, and is the source of my text (pp. 12–14).

20 Obviously it's far more likely that an unusual word like Malking would lose the final g over time to turn it into a more familiar word, than that a familiar word would mistakenly get a 'g' added to the end.

21 J.R.R. Tolkien and E.V. Gordon, *Sir Gawain and the Green Knight*, Oxford University Press, Oxford, 1925; Simon Armitage, 'The Knight's Tale' in *The Guardian*, Saturday 16 December 2006.

22 Jessica Freeman, 'Sorcery at court and manor: Margery Jourdemayne, the witch of Eye next Westminster', *Journal of Medieval History* 30 (2004), pp. 343–57.

23 *The First Part of Henry VI*, Act 5, Scene 3 (probably first performed in 1592). Jean Bodin claimed that King Henry of Sweden used four sorceresses to help him in a war against the king of Denmark in the mid sixteenth century (*De la Démonomanie des Sorciers*, First Book, Chapter 5).

24 The folksong Alison Gross ('O Alison Gross, that lives in yon tower') may well refer to Alizon Device. Ballads were often written about witchcraft cases, and although the song wasn't collected until the late eighteenth century it incorporates elements from earlier songs. Today it's best known from the inimitable rendering by Steeleye Span, but there's also a version by the Scottish group Malinky, available on *Songs of Witchcraft and Magic* produced by the Museum of Witchcraft and WildGoose Records.

25 As in 'officer's mess' – literally, a group of people eating together at a feast (*The Compact Edition of the Oxford English Dictionary*).

26 *The Compact Edition of the Oxford English Dictionary*. OED gives 'lyghe' as a variant form of 'leye' – 'blaze' – and in view of the fact that much early-seventeenth-century spelling is phonetic, and this was taken down from someone reciting the charm, this is undoubtedly the meaning (there is no plausible alternative). *OED* has the meaning of 'leath' as 'rest', and cites a late-seventeenth-century dictionary giving the meaning as 'ease', 'rest' or 'ceasing', 'as no leath of pain'. In Scotland, healing cords were sometimes referred to as 'resting threads', particularly when they were used to cure fevers: 'A man in Yell, Shetland, had fever, and could not sleep. Barbara Stood in Delting gave him a resting thread which had to be wound about his head nine nights and then burned. This secured him rest.' (J.M. McPherson, *Primitive Beliefs in the North-East of Scotland*, Longmans, Green and Co., London, 1929, p. 249, citing John Graham Dalyell, *The Darker Superstitions of Scotland*, Edinburgh, 1835, pp. 118ff.).

27 *WD* pp. Kv, K2.

28 Robert Pitcairn, *Criminal Trials in Scotland*, third volume, pp. 602–16.

29 Stephen Pollington, *Leechcraft: Early English Charms, Plant Lore and Healing*, Anglo-Saxon Books, Hockwold-cum-Wilton, 2000, p. 56; John Richard Clark Hall and Herbert Dean Meritt, *A Concise Anglo-Saxon Dictionary*, University of Toronto Press, 1984.

30 British Library MS Sloane 962; published in Tony Hunt's fascinating collection of medieval charms and herbal remedies, *Popular Medicine in Thirteenth-Century England: Introduction and Texts* (D.S. Brewer, Cambridge, 1990), p. 93. There are in fact two versions of this charm. In one, the term 'archidecline' refers to the guest of honour at the marriage at Cana, not to Jesus, but in this version, the use of the phrase 'sits on high' and the reference to the transformation of the bread at mass clearly indicate that Jesus is meant. The other version will be discussed later.

31 According to Tony Hunt's assessment of the manuscript.

32 Anon, *The Most Wonderful and True Story of a Certain Witch Named Alice Gooderige*, London, 1597.

33 George Gifford, *A Dialogue Concerning Witches and Witchcrafts*, pp. M3, M3v. See also Emma Wilby, *Cunning Folk and Familiar Spirits*, pp. 216–17.

34 Gary Nottingham, *Charms, Charming and the Charmed*, p. 23, citing Georgina Jackson and Charlotte Burne, *Shropshire Folklore*, Trubner and Co., London, 1883.

35 William Perkins, *A Discourse of the Damned Art of Witchcraft*, Dedicatory Epistle.

36 The original manuscript statements are at Harvard University, but have been edited and published by Todd Gray under the title 'Witchcraft in the Diocese of Exeter: Dartmouth, 1601–1602' (the first of a series of articles publishing Devon witchcraft case records) in *Devon & Cornwall Notes & Queries*, Spring 1990, vol. 36, part 7, pp. 230–8. (Special thanks to Marion Gibson for alerting me to this source.) This is a statement by George Davye's wife Johan, and is intended to suggest that Michael in fact caused the child's accident by witchcraft. However, it's obvious that originally he was sent for in his capacity as a cunning man, because of his claim that he could cure the child. This can't mean that he can cure the child by lifting his own curse (although that could be what the statement is trying to imply), because he would hardly admit to the crime straightaway in front of a room full of people – and besides, that's clearly *not* what he actually says.

37 There are numerous versions of this charm; this version is from an entry in Samuel Pepys's diary (31 December 1664), quoted in Jonathan Roper, *English Verbal Charms*, Academia Scientiarum Fennica, Helsinki, 2005, p. 116. Some later versions say, 'One brought fire and two brought frost', since three angels are mentioned in the first line.

38 In the early modern period the term 'charm' was a synonym for 'incantation', and could be used for any form of magic involving spoken words.

39 Jean Bodin, *De la Démonomanie des Sorciers*, Third Book, Chapter 1 (my translation).

40 Henri Boguet, *Discours des Sorciers*, Chapter 35 (my translation).

41 Heinrich Kramer (aka Institoris) and Jacob Sprenger, *Malleus Maleficarum*, Part 2, Question 2, Chapter 6.

42 See Emma Wilby, *Cunning Folk and Familiar Spirits*, pp. 231–3.

43 Heinrich Kramer and Jacob Sprenger, trans. Montague Summers, *Malleus Maleficarum*, The Pushkin Press, London, 1948, Part 2, Question 2, Chapter 6, p. 181. I have opted for Montague Summers's translation because it captures the sneering tone frequently adopted by these writers.

44 *WD* p. E3. At the same time as Roger was questioning James, a Lancashire minister, John White, was complaining that such 'prayers' were an example of 'the pitiful ignorance and confusion wherein the Church of Rome plungeth her children' (Jonathan Lumby, *The Lancashire Witch-Craze*, p. 98). Of course Roman Catholic writers like Jean Bodin condemned the use of charms just as vigorously as Protestant writers.

45 'Scripture men' meaning men who used a detailed knowledge of the Bible to claim moral authority over everyone else. George Gifford, *A Dialogue Concerning Witches and Witchcrafts*, p. M3v.

46 *WD* p. D4.

47 The best source of information about daily life in a rural community in the early seventeenth century is the DVD set *Tales from the Green Valley*, produced and directed by Peter Sommer, and distributed by Acorn Video. Originally a BBC series, it follows five archaeologists and historians running a farm for a year as it would have been done in 1620. One of the historians involved, Stuart Peachey, has also written a book about the project, *The Building of the Green Valley: A Reconstruction of an Early Seventeenth Century Rural Landscape*, Heritage Marketing & Publications Ltd, Kings Lynn, 2006.

48 *Old Cornwall* 1, No. 9 (1929), republished in Jason Semmens (ed.), *The Cornish Witch-finder: William Henry Paynter and the Witchery, Ghosts, Charms and Folklore of Cornwall*, The Federation of Old Cornwall Societies, St Agnes, 2008, p. 79. Evidence from the nineteenth-century writer William Bottrell suggests this would have been the Lent Assizes held in March (*Stories and Folk-Lore of West Cornwall*, Penzance, 1880, p. 117).

49 Museum of Witchcraft id. no. 324 (see Chapter Two, note 31).

50 When I was discussing this with Jason Semmens, the author of *The Witch of the West: or, the Strange and Wonderful History of Thomasine Blight*, he remarked unprompted by me that Thomasine's husband James Thomas ran a 'protection racket'. See also John Swain, 'Witchcraft, economy and society in the forest of Pendle' in Robert Poole (ed.) *The Lancashire Witches*, pp. 73–87.

Chapter Six: The arts of the cunning folk

1 Domenico Mammoli (ed.), *The Record of the Trial and Condemnation of a Witch, Matteuccia di Francesco*.

2 Alexander Roberts, *A Treatise of Witchcraft*, p. H3.

3 Kirsteen Macpherson Bardell, 'Beyond Pendle: the 'lost' Lancashire witches' in Robert Poole (ed.) *The Lancashire Witches*, p. 110 (citing a Quarter Sessions record, Lancashire Record Office document ref. QSB 1/64/21).

4 Anon, *The Most Wonderful and True Story of a Certain Witch Named Alice Gooderige*. The Isobel Robey case also covered by *WD* includes an account of a cunning man apparently saying Isobel was 'no witch' (p. T4v), but as the rest of the statement is testimony that she *is* a witch this could be one of the pamphlet's several misprints.

5 George Gifford, *A Dialogue Concerning Witches and Witchcrafts*, p. Bv.

6 John Gregorson Campbell, *Witchcraft and Second Sight in the Highlands and Islands of Scotland*, James MacLehose & Sons, Glasgow, 1902, reprinted by E.P. Publishing Ltd., Wakefield, 1974, p. 59.

7 King James I, *Demononlogy*, First Book, Chapter 4. *Demonology* was first published in 1597, when James was still King James VI of Scotland.

8 John Gregorson Campbell, *Witchcraft and Second Sight in the Highlands and Islands of Scotland*, p. 11.

9 R.C. MacLagan, *Evil Eye in the Western Highlands*, David Nutt, London, 1902, p. 145.

10 John Aubrey, *Miscellanies Upon the Following Subjects*, 'Magic'.

11 John Aubrey, *Miscellanies Upon the Following Subjects*, 'Magic'.

12 Museum of Witchcraft object id. no. 487 (see Chapter Two, note 31).

13 Al-Majriti (attrib.), *Picatrix (Ghayat Al-Hakim – The Goal of the Wise)*.

14 Rose Mullins, *White Witches: A Study of Charmers*, PR Publishing, Launceston, p. 21.

15 British Library MS Sloane 962, included in Tony Hunt, *Popular Medicine in Thirteenth-Century England*.

16 See Chapter Two, note 23.

17 Chelmsford Quarter Sessions record, 1578, quoted in Alan Macfarlane, *Witchcraft in Tudor and Stuart England*, Waveland Press, Inc., London, 1991, p. 125.

18 Reginald Scot, *The Discovery of Witchcraft*, Book 12, Chapter 17.

19 Reginald Scot, *The Discovery of Witchcraft*, Book 12, Chapter 17.

20 Jean Bodin, *De la Démonomanie des Sorciers*, Fourth Book, Chapter 4.

21 Owen Davies, *Cunning Folk*, p. 10.

22 Robert Pitcairn, *Criminal Trials in Scotland*, first volume, second part, pp. 49–58. Bessie Dunlop's trial record is also published in full in the Preface of Emma Wilby, *Cunning Folk and Familiar Spirits*.

23 Anon, *The Examination of John Walsh*.

24 Owen Davies, *Cunning Folk*, p. 2.

25 Wiltshire and Swindon Archives, Document ref: D/1/39/2/7 fol. 90v. Thanks to Steven Hobbs of Wiltshire and Swindon Archives, Wiltshire and Swindon History Centre, for his help with the transcription, and for explaining the legal Latin.

26 For the procedures of church courts see Andrew Barrett and Christopher Harrison, *Crime and Punishment in England: A Sourcebook*, Routledge, Abingdon, 1999, pp. 75ff., and Owen Davies, *Cunning Folk*, p. 16.

27 Nicholas Culpeper, *Culpeper's English Physician and Complete Herbal*, London, c. 1794 (first published 1653); David Hoffmann, *The Herb User's Guide*, Thorsons Publishing Group, Wellingborough, 1987, pp. 45–6.

28 Published by Todd Gray and John Draisey in 'Witchcraft in the Diocese of Exeter: Part IV. Whimple (1565), Chawleigh (1571) & Morwenstow (1575)', *Devon & Cornwall Notes & Queries*, Autumn 1991, vol. 36, part 10, p. 367, from the manuscript Chanter 855b, f.28, Devon Record Office. This was a Church court hearing before the same Bishop of Exeter who sent his representative to interrogate John Walsh.

29 Henri Boguet, *Discours des Sorciers*, Chapter 35. It's possible that the term 'old woman' means 'wise woman', just as the term 'old man' seems to have indicated a cunning man in the account of the witch bottle in Joseph Glanvil's *Sadducismus Triumphatus* (see Chapter Two, note 57; also Chapter One, note 3).

30 Brian Darcey, *A True and Just Record*, pp. 2A7–2A7v.

31 Thomas Davidson, *Rowan Tree and Red Thread*, Robert Cunningham and Sons Ltd., London, 1949, p. 46.

32 Thomas Davidson, *Rowan Tree and Red Thread*, p. 47.

33 *The Lacnunga Manuscript*, remedy no. 170, edited and translated by Stephen Pollington in *Leechcraft*, p. 237.

34 Domenico Mammoli (ed.), *The Record of the Trial and Condemnation of a Witch, Matteuccia di Francesco*.

35 Museum of Witchcraft id. nos 68, 69, 70, 213 (see Chapter Two, note 31). A similar practice for getting rid of warts was recorded in 1931 by William Henry Paynter (edited by Jason Semmens *The Cornish Witch-finder: William Henry Paynter*, pp. 108–9).

36 Jean Bodin, *De la Démonomanie des Sorciers*, Third Book, Chapter 2, my translation. The French word 'sorciers' is usually translated 'witch', but I have here translated it as 'wizard'. In French there is no equivalent to the terms 'wise woman', 'cunning man' etc. When Jean Bodin's book was translated into Latin (the Frankfurt edition of 1603), the title was translated as *De Magorum Daemonomania – On the Demon-mania of Magicians*; so following the lead of that translator I have been flexible in my translation of 'sorciers', depending on the context.

37 A Quarter Sessions record of 1634, discovered by Jonathan Lumby and included in his book *The Lancashire Witch-Craze*, pp. 95–6. Quarter Sessions were courts presided over by county

Justices rather than Circuit judges, and with a jury. They usually tried less serious cases, and rarely – though occasionally – imposed the death penalty (J.S. Cockburn, *A History of English Assizes*, pp. 90ff.; Andrew Barrett and Christopher Harrison, *Crime and Punishment in England*, pp. 100–105, 116–20).

38 See note 22.

39 Robert Pitcairn, *Criminal Trials of Scotland*, first volume, second part, p. 237.

40 *The Book of Secrets of Albertus Magnus*, Second Book, 'Of the Virtues of Certain Stones' (the stone *Aetites*).

41 Museum of Witchcraft id. nos 275, 1018 (see Chapter Two, note 31).

42 Domenico Mammoli (ed.), *The Record of the Trial and Condemnation of a Witch, Matteuccia di Francesco*.

43 See note 22.

44 Todd Gray, 'Witchcraft in the Diocese of Exeter: Dartmouth, 1601–1602', pp. 230–8. The statement describes this incident in such a way that it could be interpreted as a casual encounter, but again from Michael's behaviour there's not much doubt this was a consultation. It's important to remember that people were often prosecuted for consulting cunning folk (Andrew Barrett and Christopher Harrison, *Crime and Punishment in England*, pp. 75ff.), so they would naturally gloss over the fact that they were clients (see also Chapter Five, note 36.)

45 Richard Kieckhefer, *Forbidden Rites*, p. 250.

46 Robert Kirk, *The Secret Commonwealth of Elves, Fauns and Fairies*, Helios Book Service Ltd, Toddington, 1964, p. 25 (written in 1691) (quoted in Emma Wilby, *Cunning Folk and Familiar Spirits*, p. 39). The marks on the bone could also be interpreted like reading tea leaves (sermon by Nicholas of Cusa, 1431, in P.G. Maxwell-Stuart, *The Occult in Mediaeval Europe*, p. 79).

47 Nicholas of Cusa listed a whole range of divination methods in a sermon in 1431, included in P.G. Maxwell-Stuart *The Occult in Mediaeval Europe*, p. 79.

48 Museum of Witchcraft id. nos 52, 1171, 1870 (see Chapter Two, note 31).

49 Henri Boguet, *Discours des Sorciers*, Chapter VI; probably drawing on Heinrich Kramer and Jacob Sprenger, *Malleus Maleficarum*, Part 2, Question 2.

50 John Aubrey, *Miscellanies Upon the Following Subjects*, 'Visions in a Beryl or Crystal'.

51 See Chapter Two, note 23. Special thanks to Jason Semmens for his help with transcribing this part of the manuscript.

52 During the trial of Gilles de Rais, a case that will be discussed later.

53 Arthur Morrison, 'A Wizard of Yesterday', originally published in the Strand Magazine in 1900, republished in Eric Maple and Arthur Morrison, *Marsh Wizards, Witches and Cunning Men of Essex*, Caduceus Books, Burbage, 2008, p. 33

54 See Chapter Two, note 23.

55 Robert Pitcairn, *Criminal Trials of Scotland*, third volume, p. 608.

56 Robert Pitcairn, *Criminal Trials of Scotland*, third volume, p. 612.

57 Robert Pitcairn, *Criminal Trials of Scotland*, third volume, p. 609.

58 Al-Majriti (attrib.), *Picatrix (Ghayat Al-Hakim – The Goal of the Wise)*, p. 41 in Hashem Atallah's translation (Ouroboros Press, Seattle, 2002).

59 Alexander Roberts, *A Treatise of Witchcraft*, p. D3.

60 Robert Pitcairn, *Criminal Trials of Scotland*, third volume, p. 607.

61 *News from Scotland*.

62 Todd Gray, 'Witchcraft in the Diocese of Exeter: Dartmouth, 1601–1602', pp. 230–8.

63 *WD* pp. K, Kv. In *WD* the word 'drink' generally means beer or ale (see pp. E2v, E3). Both were common drinks in the early seventeenth century. Home-brewed ale (which was low in alcohol and high in vitamins, and safer than the often contaminated water) was in fact

the main drink at that time, so running out of it would have been quite a serious matter. See *Tales from the Green Valley*, DVD set produced and directed by Peter Sommer.

64 Anon/unknown *Christian Charms/Prayers: Used by the Expatriate St Lucian Community in London 1960s+*, in the library of the Museum of Witchcraft, library id. no. 133.44 UNK 5076. Further details can be accessed on the museum's website www.museumofwitchcraft.com, by clicking on 'Library Collection'. Special thanks to Francilla Mangal Smart, who donated these documents.

65 For more information about the practices of cunning folk see Emma Wilby, *Cunning Folk and Familiar Spirits* (in particular, Chapter Two, 'Cunning Folk and Witches', pp. 26ff.) and Owen Davies, *Cunning Folk: Popular Magic in English History*.

Chapter Seven: Healers and heretics

1 Hugh of St Victor, (translated by P.G. Maxwell-Stuart) *Didascalion* in P.G. Maxwell-Stuart, *The Occult in Mediaeval Europe*, p. 71.

2 Charles Homer Haskins, *The Renaissance of the Twelfth Century*, Harvard University Press, Cambridge, Massachusetts, 1982 (first published 1927); A.C. Crombie, *Robert Grosseteste and the Origins of Experimental Science 1100–1700*, Oxford University Press, Oxford, 1971 (first published 1953), see p. 104 for his cosmological theories about light.

3 Rossell Hope Robbins, *The Encyclopedia of Witchcraft and Demonology*, pp. 266–7.

4 Honorius of Thebes and the Angel Hocroel, *The Sworn Book*. In this chapter I will be referring (unless otherwise stated) to the sixteenth-century English translation, British Library MS Royal 17.A.XLII (hereafter Royal in this chapter), transcribed by Joseph H. Peterson, and available on his website www.esotericarchives.com and on his Esoteric Archives CD available from the website. (The CD contains around a hundred works including many of the great books of magic of the Middle Ages and early modern period.) Although Gösta Hedegård, the editor of the Latin text (*Liber Iuratus Honorii*) has some reservations about parts of this translation, I feel it gives the reader a flavour of the impression *The Sworn Book* would have made on Early Modern practitioners. The book begins with an account of how it came to be written, and the reference to the Pope's condemnation of magic is Royal ff. 1r–2r. Harsh punishments for practising magic were not new, however. For example, a Church synod in Freising in 800 recommended that people practising magic such as divination should be imprisoned and tortured until they confessed and repented (Richard Kieckhefer, *Magic in the Middle Ages*, pp. 179–80).

5 His total library consisted of 260 books, suggesting he was very well-off indeed. Robert Mathiesen, 'A Thirteenth-Century Ritual to Attain the Beatific Vision', p. 144.

6 Royal has 811 (f. 2r), but the Latin versions have a more likely 89 (Gösta Hedegård (ed.), *Liber Iuratus Honorii*, p. 60).

7 Royal ff. 2r. The human author's pseudonym also refers to him as 'the son of Euclid', linking him symbolically to the great Greek mathematician whose works had been translated into Latin in the twelfth century. For the meaning of the name Hocroel, see Robert Mathiesen, 'A Thirteenth-Century Ritual to Attain the Beatific Vision', p. 160 note 25 (citing Gustav Davidson, *A Dictionary of Angels Including the Fallen Angels*).

8 For a summary of the various manuscripts and their dates see Joseph H. Peterson's introduction on his website www.esotericarchives.com.

9 Royal f. 2v.

10 Royal ff. 1v, 1r, 1v–2r.

11 Royal f. 39v.

12 Royal f. 6r.

13 Also available on Joseph H. Peterson's website www.esotericarchives.com.

14 1 Kings 11. Ashtaroth is the Goddess Astarte, and also one of the most important spirits in

magic. In the various different versions of the bible her name is spelled in several different ways. In 1 Kings 11 she is referred to as 'Astharthen deam' ('Astharthe the goddess') in the Latin Vulgate Bible used throughout the Middle Ages; 'Ashtaroth the god' in the Geneva Bible (1560); 'Ashtoreth the goddess' in the King James Version, and 'Astarthe the goddess' in the Douay-Rheims Bible (1609-10). In 2 Kings 23 she is referred to as 'Ashtharoth idolo' ('Ashtharoth the idol') in the Latin Vulgate; 'Ashtoreth the idol' in the Geneva Bible; 'Ashtoreth the abomination' in the King James Version, and 'Astaroth the idol' in the Douay-Rheims Bible.

15 Matthew 2.

16 When Jean Bodin's book *De la Demononmanie des Sorciers* was translated into Latin, in the Frankfurt edition of 1603, its title was *De Magorum Daemonomania*.

17 Interestingly, though, Honorius himself says that the word 'magic' means 'wise knowledge' (Royal f. 8v).

18 See for example the spell for epilepsy in Chapter Eleven.

19 Such as the Hebrew book of magic *The Sword of Moses*, also available on Joseph Peterson's website.

20 Royal ff. 7v–8r, 2v.

21 Royal ff. 4r–6r. Gösta Hedegård includes the section on killing people in his list of missing sections (*Liber Iuratus Honorii*, p. 28 note 114), but in my opinion it's covered in the section on Angels of Mars: 'Their nature is to cause and stir up war murder destruction and mortality of people' (Royal f. 67v.).

22 Royal ff. 8v–13r, 65v–80r. Royal stops before substantial sections on summoning spirits in the Latin versions. Gösta Hedegård's *Liber Iuratus Honorii* not only has the complete Latin text but a useful summary in the introduction (pp. 29–40).

23 Royal f. 2r refers to the magicians deciding not to use magic against the pope and cardinals because 'the wicked power of the sprites at our commandment would have destroyed them all.' The Latin text has 'hostilis demonum potencia' – 'the hostile power of the demons' (p. 60).

24 Dionysius Exiguus, *Canones*, 'Canons of the Council of Laodicea', edited and translated by P.G. Maxwell-Stuart in his book *The Occult in Mediaeval Europe*, p. 142. The wording of this condemnation clearly demonstrates that spiritual experiences that were not controlled by the Church were seen as a threat to its authority.

25 Richard Kieckhefer, *Magic in the Middle Ages*, pp. 155, 172–3.

26 Royal f. 47r.

27 Royal f. 4r.

28 See note 8.

29 The name of the spirit Zagam in *Liber de Angelis* seems to be derived from the sacred name Zaguam in *The Sworn Book*, and the 'call' in *The Lenkiewicz Manuscript* incorporates the sacred names Panten and Craton. *The Sworn Book* is also probably the origin of legends of a book written by the Devil, as in Roman Polanski's film *The Ninth Gate*.

30 The question of missing and misplaced sections is discussed by Gösta Hedegård in *Liber Iuratus Honorii*, pp. 27–8.

31 Rosell Hope Robbins, *The Encyclopedia of Witchcraft and Demonology*, pp. 287–8. Pope John also condemned image magic and using the Host for magic (which will be discussed later).

32 Richard Kieckhefer, *European Witch Trials*, pp. 109–10.

33 Valerie I.J. Flint, 'Magic in English Thirteenth-Century Miracle Collections', in Jan N. Bremmer and Jan R. Veenstra (eds), *The Metamorphosis of Magic from Late Antiquity to the Early Modern Period*, Peeters, Leuven, 2002, pp. 121–2 (citing Stubbs, *Chronicles*, Vol. 1, pp. 236, 275–6). The account isn't quite clear about whether it was actually her own robe she

wore, or whether she was made to wear one similar to the robes she was alleged to wear to perform her rituals. Special thanks to Tessel Bauduin for drawing my attention to this article.

34 P.G. Maxwell-Stuart, *The Occult in Mediaeval Europe*, pp. 87–9.

35 Tony Hunt, *Popular Medicine in Thirteenth-Century England*, pp. 26–7.

36 Tony Hunt, *Popular Medicine in Thirteenth-Century England*, p. 28. St Veronica was a woman who gave Jesus a cloth to wipe the sweat from his face when he was carrying his cross to the execution ground. The account of the woman cured by touching Jesus's robe (Luke 8:43–8) is interesting for Jesus's exclamation: 'Someone hath touched me: for I perceive that virtue is gone out of me' (*The Geneva Bible*).

37 Sachiko Kusukawa, 'Medicine in Western Europe in 1500', Peter Elmer (ed.), *The Healing Arts: Health, Disease and Society in Europe 1500–1800*, Manchester University Press / The Open University, Manchester, 2004, p. 19 (citing R. Porter, *The Greatest Benefit to Mankind*, Fontana, London, 1999, p. 118).

38 Jehan de Bar's confession is published in full (in French) in Jan R. Veenstra's book *Magic and Divination at the Courts of Burgundy and France*, Brill, Leiden, 1998, pp. 351–5, with a summary and analysis (especially of its links with the *Determinatio*) on pp. 343–350. For the circle in the wood, his books and general background, see pp. 68–9, 71. For the impact of his execution see p. 344. Translations are mine.

39 The text says 'a nail from a horseshoe given as a gift on a certain day of the year'. This could possibly mean that the nail should be given as an offering at a shrine; but I think it's more likely to mean given by the magician to his client as an amulet.

40 Jean Bodin, *De la Démonomanie des Sorciers*; Henri Boguet, *Discours des Sorciers*. Jeanne d'Arc (Joan of Arc), of course, was burned alive in 1431. She, like Jehan, was charged with having dealings with spirits that she believed to be an angel (St Michael) and St Catherine and St Margaret. The trial records can be read online at www.joanofarc.info.

41 Franco Mormando, *The Preacher's Demons: Bernardino of Siena and the Social Underworld of Early Renaissance Italy*, The University of Chicago Press, Chicago, 1999, pp. 29–30, 34.

42 Franco Mormando, *The Preacher's Demons*, p. 35. Franco Mormando's translation.

43 Franco Mormando, *The Preacher's Demons*, pp. 35–8.

44 Franco Mormando, *The Preacher's Demons*, p. 176. Franco Mormando's translation.

45 Franco Mormando, *The Preacher's Demons*, p. 52. Franco Mormando's translation.

46 Jan R. Veenstra, *Magic and Divination at the Courts of Burgundy and France*, p. 344 note 4.

47 Franco Mormando, *The Preacher's Demons*, p. 78. Franco Mormando's translation. A similar (but more humorous) story was told by the thirteenth-century French Dominican friar Etienne de Bourbon in his *Anecdotes Historiques*. P.G. Maxwell-Stuart includes it in his book *The Occult in Mediaeval Europe*, pp. 119–20.

48 Alan Charles Kors and Edward Peters, *Witchcraft in Europe, 400–1700: A Documentary History*, University of Pensylvania Press, Philadelphia, 2000 (2nd edition, revised by Edward Peters), p. 135. Translation by John Shinners. This text was first published in John Shinners's book *Medieval Popular Religion*, Broadview Press, Ontario, 1997.

49 Alan Charles Kors and Edward Peters, *Witchcraft in Europe*, pp. 135–6. Translations by John Shinners. For other accounts of the case, giving the woman's name as Finicella, see Franco Mormando, *The Preacher's Demons*, pp. 64–5. In his sermon Bernardino tries to imply that Finicella named more than one victim, but it's clear that in fact only one father confirmed that his child had died.

50 Alan Charles Kors and Edward Peters, *Witchcraft in Europe*, pp. 136–7. Translations by John Shinners. To their credit, the people of Siena were not convinced by Bernardino's argument that everyone who used healing charms must therefore be a vampire, and the accusations and arrests he hoped for did not occur (p. 133).

51 Todi is about halfway between Siena and Rome.

52 Franco Mormando, *The Preacher's Demons*, p. 73. It's likely that Bernardino preached at Todi twice – in 1426 when the laws were changed, and again in 1428, because there are references in the trial record of Matteuccia di Francesco to her performing magic in 1427 'before the visit of Brother Bernardino'.

53 Unless otherwise stated, all the information in this chapter about Matteuccia's case is taken from Domenico Mammoli's edition of the original trial document, *The Record of the Trial and Condemnation of a Witch, Matteuccia di Francesco, at Todi, 20 March 1428* (*Res Tudertinae – 14*, Rome, 1972). The translations are mine, from Domenico Mammoli's Latin text.

54 Literally, 'Preserver of the Peace'.

55 Probably possessed or perhaps just made ill by them – the Latin phrase is 'spiritatos ac fantasmata habentes' – literally, 'having spirits and phantoms'.

56 Domenico Mammoli discusses the identity of this man in his Introduction (p. 7), suggesting that some of Matteuccia's clients were influential people.

57 See note 49.

58 Matteuccia also apparently confessed that she 'struck' the children – a term still used in the South West of Britain to refer to someone being cursed.

59 P.G. Maxwell-Stuart, *Witchcraft: A History*, Tempus, Stroud, 2000, p. 26–7.

60 Intended to reassure parents that baptism would protect their children from such perils. The term 'owl-blasted' was still used in nineteenth-century Cornwall to mean 'cursed' (Jonathan Couch, *The History of Polperro*, Frank Graham, Newcastle-upon-Tyne, 1965 (first published 1871), p. 70).

61 Franco Mormando, *The Preacher's Demons*, p. 62. This is discussed by the Dominican friar Etienne de Bourbon in his *Anecdotes Historiques* (P.G. Maxwell-Stuart, *The Occult in Mediaeval Europe*, pp. 117–18), and it seems somewhat suspicious that a possible source for Bernardino's story about the wise woman asked to find the missing purse (see note 47) should also describe children being preyed on in this way. It seems that before Finicella was ever arrested Bernardino had read about the kind of crimes she confessed to.

62 Tony Hunt, *Popular Medicine in Thirteenth-Century England*, p. 29. British Library MS Add. 33996. My translation from Tony Hunt's Latin text. Once again, the word I have translated 'command' is '*conjuro*'.

63 Anon/unknown, *Christian Charms/Prayers: Used by the Expatriate St Lucian Community in London 1960s+*, in the library of the Museum of Witchcraft, library id. no. 133.44 UNK 5076. Further details can be accessed on the museum's website www.museumofwitchcraft.com, by clicking on 'Library Collection'.

64 For further discussion of the issues surrounding the origins of the witch-hunts and ideas about witchcraft and the Sabbat, see Norman Cohn, *Europe's Inner Demons: An Enquiry Inspired by the Great Witch-Hunt*, Book Club Associates/Chatto & Windus Ltd, London, 1975; Carlo Ginzburg, *Ecstasies: Deciphering the Witches' Sabbath* (trans. Raymond Rosenthal) Penguin, Harmondsworth, 1991; Éva Pócs, *Between the Living and the Dead* (trans. Szilvia Rédey and Michael Webb), Central European University Press, Budapest, 1997.

Chapter Eight: The magician and the serial killer

1 The trial records of this case, translated from Latin into French by Pierre Klossowski and then into English by Richard Robinson, and edited and annotated by Georges Bataille, have been published in Georges Bataille's book *The Trial of Gilles de Rais*, Amok Books, Los Angeles, 2004. Page references in the notes for this chapter will refer to this book. It also includes a substantial introductory section with some useful additional information and a helpful chronology, but this part was written in 1965 and so Georges Bataille's analysis of the case is fatally compromised by his complete lack of knowledge of fifteenth-century

magical practices and the other magic-related cases occurring in France at the same time.

Unless otherwise stated, the information in this chapter comes from Francesco Prelati's statement presented in court on 16 October 1440 (pp. 209–16). (In this edition of the text Francesco's name is given as François; this is a modernisation of the Old French form of the name, Francoys. Obviously Francesco was the name he was known by in Italy, but it does seem that Gilles called him Francoys, and that was the name he was generally known by while he was in France.)

The reference to the persecution of wise women is from Eustache Blanchet's statement presented in court on 17 October (pp. 216–23) p. 219. Eustache refers to these women as 'old women', which seems likely to be an alternative term for 'wise women', and not in fact anything to do with their age (see Chapter One, note 3; and the reference to a cunning man as an 'old man' in Joseph Glanvil's *Sadducismus Triumphatus*, mentioned in Chapter Two); the evidence from Hans Fründ's account of these persecutions (see note 13 below) suggests that the victims were not necessarily old.

2 Eustache's statement (Georges Bataille, *The Trial of Gilles de Rais*, p. 216).

3 Gilles de Rais questioned in court, 22 October (Georges Bataille, *The Trial of Gilles de Rais*, p. 200).

4 Specifically, 'geomancy', a term that was sometimes used for divination with a crystal, but more usually for a form of divination that involved making marks on the ground, sometimes throwing dice, and then interpreting the marks according to some kind of formula (Nicolas of Cusa, *Sermon*, in P.G. Maxwell-Stuart, *The Occult in Mediaeval Europe* (p. 79); Jean Bodin, *De la Démonomanie des Sorciers*, First Book, Chapter 6).

5 Statement from André Barbe, 28–30 September (Georges Bataille, *The Trial of Gilles de Rais*, p. 257). Translation by Pierre Klossowski and Richard Robinson. Machecoul is south-west of Nantes.

6 Eustache's statement (Georges Bataille, *The Trial of Gilles de Rais*, p. 217). Tiffauges is south-east of Nantes.

7 Gilles de Rais questioned in court, 22 October (Georges Bataille, *The Trial of Gilles de Rais*, p. 200). Translation by Pierre Klossowski and Richard Robinson.

8 For a succinct summary of the situation, see Margaret Wood, *The English Mediaeval House*, Ferndale Editions, London, 1981, p. 179.

9 Plays were a regular feature of the entertainments at his castles, and he founded a chapel of the Holy Innocents at Machecoul, complete with a college, and equipped it with ostentatiously rich crosses, candlesticks and vestments. Most of the singers, chaplains and other personnel travelled with him wherever he went. Georges Battaille's introduction, *The Trial of Gilles de Rais*, pp. 93–7. Statement of Jeanette Drouet, 28–30 September (p. 266).

10 Champtocé is east of Nantes, just west of Angers.

11 Georges Battaille's introduction, *The Trial of Gilles de Rais*, pp. 97, 99, 101, 103.

12 Statement of Étienne Corrillaut, presented in court on 17 October (Georges Bataille, *The Trial of Gilles de Rais*, p. 223); statement of Henriet Griart presented in court on 17 October (p. 233).

13 Of course once people were tortured into naming accomplices no doubt many people were incriminated who were not cunning folk; and although Eustache specifically mentioned women, many men were also arrested. Also some of the suspects were burned alive, although Eustache only mentions hangings. The persecutions were documented in a contemporary chronicle written by Hans Fründ, and extracts from his account can be read in the Wikipedia article *Valais witch trials* (http://en.wikipedia.org/wiki/Valais_witch_trials) (the full account was published in Joseph Hansen (ed.), *Quellen und Untersuchungen zur Geschichte des Hexenwahns und der Hexenverfolgung im Mittelalter*, Bonn, 1901, pp. 533–7). See also Robin

Briggs, "By the strength of fancie': witchcraft and the early modern imagination', *Folklore*, December 2004; Norman Cohn, *Europe's Inner Demons*, pp. 226–7.

14 On the River Rhône, in the Dauphiné region of south-eastern France, about halfway between Lyon and Avignon.

15 Norman Cohn, *Europe's Inner Demons*, p. 229 (citing Joseph Hansen (ed.), *Quellen*, pp. 459–66).

16 Eustache's statement (Georges Bataille, *The Trial of Gilles de Rais*, p. 221).

17 His travelling chapel alone consisted of about fifty people (see note 9).

18 George Bataille's introduction, *The Trial of Gilles de Rais*, pp. 80, 91.

19 Henriet's statement (Georges Bataille, *The Trial of Gilles de Rais*, p. 232), Étienne's statement (p. 223).

20 As a result of Bernardino's campaign many parts of Italy tightened their laws against homosexuality, making heavy fines the punishment for a first offence, and burning the punishment for a second. In Massa Marittima in Tuscany, any man over twenty-five who wasn't married could be prosecuted. The persecution wasn't limited to Italy. According to one of Bernardino's sermons, a mass persecution in Paris in the thirteenth century led to every known gay man in the city being burned alive – though he was no doubt exaggerating. Franco Mormando, *The Preacher's Demons*, pp. 115–16, 140, 152, 153, 158; and for a general discussion of attitudes to homosexuality and Bernardino's campaign, pp. 109–63.

21 Eustache's statement (Georges Bataille, *The Trial of Gilles de Rais*, pp. 219, 223); Étienne's statement (p. 230), Henriet's statement (p. 238). Translation by Pierre Klossowski and Richard Robinson.

22 Francesco's statement and Étienne's statement (Georges Bataille, *The Trial of Gilles de Rais*, p. 231).

23 Eustache's statement (Georges Bataille, *The Trial of Gilles de Rais*, p. 219). According to the statement Eustache assumed it was human blood; but from Jehan de Bar's confession we know that animal blood was used in magic, and of course Eustache was being pressured to back up the accusations that Gilles was killing children for ritual purposes.

24 The bird is simply described as 'crested', but Jehan de Bar used a hoopoe, so it's reasonable to assume that a hoopoe is meant here.

25 Francesco's statement, and Gilles questioned in court on 22 October (Georges Bataille, *The Trial of Gilles de Rais*, p. 199).

26 Some of Francesco's rituals apparently involved sacrificing birds, which was an important part of invoking Zagam's help. The powder may then have appeared as a result of the ritual.

27 Gilles questioned in court, 15 October (Georges Bataille, *The Trial of Gilles de Rais*, pp. 182–3).

28 Nicholas Flamel (attrib.) *Alchemical Hieroglyphics*, London, 1624. The origin of this image was the brazen serpent made by Moses to cure the Israelites bitten by poisonous snakes as a punishment for rebelliousness (Numbers 21). This was one of the Old Testament events believed to prefigure the crucifixion, and so was a frequent subject for medieval art. However, the similarity of the image to representations of the Serpent entwined around the Tree of Knowledge was not lost on alchemists and occultists.

The substance was made using a 'reflux apparatus' – a metal cylinder with a plate suspended inside. A mixture of metals and corrosive chemicals was heated inside the cylinder until it vaporised, and the substance then precipitated out on to the plate. According to the record, Barron gave Francesco the powder on a slate, which could mean that Francesco used a piece of slate, perhaps at Barron's suggestion, to make the plate inside the cylinder. (F. Sherwood Taylor, *The Alchemists: Founders of Modern Chemistry*, William Heinemann Ltd, London, 1951; special thanks to Jenny Southern for her insights into the workings of the reflux apparatus). Serpent imagery was extremely important in alchemy, and Francesco had another experience that combined magic and alchemy when Barron showed him a vision of a pile of gold guarded by a winged serpent.

29 Georges Bataille gives a valuable summary of the events of these final few weeks in his introduction, *The Trial of Gilles de Rais*, pp. 123–8. Saint-Étienne-de-Mermorte is south-east of Machecoul.

30 Statement by Perrine Rondeau, 28–30 September (Georges Bataille, *The Trial of Gilles de Rais*, p. 261). Francesco shared these lodgings with another Italian member of Gilles's household, the Marquis de Ceva. It's not clear why they weren't living in the castle, as Francesco was still spending most of his time there. Were they lovers? Was it so that they would have a refuge if the castle came under attack (as they were both Italians, perhaps Gilles hoped that they would not be pursued by the French authorities)? Or was the castle simply so crowded with soldiers there was no room for them to sleep there? After the incident with the landlady they moved out and rented a house in another part of town. The landlady, Perrine, later made a false statement against Francesco, claiming to have seen ashes and a bloodstained shirt removed from this other house after the arrests (p. 262). This can't be true, because if the Duke of Brittany's men had removed them, they would have been mentioned in the evidence; and if Gilles's men had removed them (unlikely since they weren't supposed to know anything about the alleged murders), they would certainly not have let Perrine see what they were doing. It's not impossible that Perrine had in fact been paid to spy on Francesco. A local man had certainly been paid to spy on the castle (statement by André Bréchet, 28–30 September, p. 262). Perrine also said that the Marquis de Ceva had provided Francesco with a page from a good family in Dieppe, and that after spending two weeks there the boy disappeared; however, Francesco told her that the boy had borrowed money from him and left (presumably to go back home) – a perfectly reasonable explanation.

31 The precise date of this event isn't clear.

32 Statement by Jean Rousseau, 19 October (Georges Bataille, *The Trial of Gilles de Rais*, pp. 241–2), 'Initial Complaints' in the record of the secular trial (pp. 250–51).

33 Statement by the Marquis de Ceva, 19 October (Georges Bataille, *The Trial of Gilles de Rais*, pp. 242–3). My translation, from the Old French given in a footnote.

34 At his secular trial Gilles was accused of having some of Jean's men beaten, but he angrily denied that he would ever ill-treat prisoners or tolerate them being ill-treated (Georges Bataille, *The Trial of Gilles de Rais*, p. 251).

35 Indictments at the ecclesiastical trial (Georges Bataille, *The Trial of Gilles de Rais*, p. 178).

36 Letter from the Bishop of Nantes, 29 July (Georges Bataille, *The Trial of Gilles de Rais*, p. 155).

37 Henriet's statement presented at his secular trial (Georges Bataille, *The Trial of Gilles de Rais*, p. 276).

38 Georges Bataille, *The Trial of Gilles de Rais*, pp. 253–74.

39 Statements of Jean Darel, Jeanne Darel and her mother Jeanne, 8 October (Georges Bataille, *The Trial of Gilles de Rais*, p. 272).

40 For example, Guillaume Rodigo testified that a boy called Bernard Le Camus, from Brest, who was staying with Guillaume to learn French, ran away after talking to Étienne. Although Bernard is referred to as a 'young boy' and a 'child', he was in fact fifteen (Georges Bataille, *The Trial of Gilles de Rais*, pp. 264–5).

41 Statements of Nicole Bonnereau, Philippe Ernaut, Jeanne Prieur, Raoulet de Launay, 2 October (Georges Bataille, *The Trial of Gilles de Rais*, p. 270). Étienne himself acquired a page, the ten-year-old son of Peronne Loessart, while he and Gilles were visiting La Roche-Bernard; Peronne testified that she hadn't seen the boy since (statement of 18 September, pp. 253–4). However, when Gilles had visited the area again Étienne wasn't with him,

and Gilles's men told Peronne that her son was with Étienne at Tiffauges or another of Gilles's estates, Pouzauges (south of Tiffauges). Another incident involved a thirteen- or fourteen-year-old boy who became page to one of Gilles's associates called Spadin. The boy disappeared while back visiting his family. Spadin was concerned about the boy and sent for his father to ask where he was. Inquiries were made and it was discovered that the boy had joined the household of a Scottish knight (statements of Jean and Nicole Hubert, 2 October (pp. 267–8), statement of Nicole Hubert, 8 October (pp. 272–3), statements of Jean Bureau and his wife, Jeanne Geoffroi and her daughter, and Guillaume Hemeri, 8 October (p. 273)). In another revealing account of a disappearance, a woman described how she had sent her two children aged ten and seven, alone (!), to Machecoul from her home near Port-Saint-Père, a round trip of thirty-five kilometres, to ask for charity at the castle. They failed to return (statement of Jeanette Drouet, 28–30 September (p. 266)). Gilles wasn't even at Machecoul at the time. He was at Tiffauges, entertaining the heir to the throne, the future King Louis XI – which you'd think was a fairly convincing alibi (Gilles questioned in court, 15 October (p. 183); George Bataille's introduction, p. 120).

42 Letter of the Bishop of Nantes, 29 July (Georges Bataille, *The Trial of Gilles de Rais*, p. 155), translation by Pierre Klossowski and Richard Robinson.

43 The statement taken from Étienne for his secular trial (Georges Bataille, *The Trial of Gilles de Rais*, p. 279). The main statements from Étienne and Henriet were presented in court on 17 October at Gilles's ecclesiastical trial (pp. 223–40). These statements from Francesco, Étienne and Henriet appear at first sight to be statements made verbally in the courtroom, but as they agree word for word with indictments read out on 13 October (pp. 168–80), it's clear that prepared statements were read out and Francesco, Étienne and Henriet simply confirmed them.

44 Statement of Jeannette Degrépie, 2 October (Georges Bataille, *The Trial of Gilles de Rais*, p. 266), prosecutor's statement in court, 15 October (pp. 183–4), Georges Bataille's footnote p. 184. In another important witchcraft trial in Arras twenty years later the interrogators used an effective combination of torture and false promises that the prisoners' lives would be spared if they confessed. One of the prisoners hanged himself. Extracts from the contemporary account of this case, by Jacques du Clercq, are included in P.G. Maxwell-Stuart, *The Occult in Mediaeval Europe*, pp. 122–9.

45 The Bishop of Nantes had personally questioned the local people who made statements about missing children, so it's likely he also personally questioned Francesco (letter of 29 July, Georges Bataille, *The Trial of Gilles de Rais*, p. 155).

46 A 'pagan bone' – that is a bone from someone who has not been baptised, which almost certainly means a child who died before being christened. It was probably not the fact that the child had not been baptised that gave the bone its power, but the fact that the child had died only shortly after being born, which would result in a life force still lingering around the remains (Domenico Mammoli, *The Record of the Trial and Condemnation of a Witch, Matteuccia di Francesco*).

47 This and other aspects of the case are discussed in E.M. Butler, *Ritual Magic*, Cambridge University Press, Cambridge, 1949 (mainly pp. 100–110).

48 See note 43.

49 See note 43.

50 Gilles speaking at his secular trial (Georges Bataille, *The Trial of Gilles de Rais*, p. 283).

51 Having already read Elizabeth Butler's astute analysis in her book *Ritual Magic* (see note 47), I approached the documents with considerable scepticism, otherwise reading them would have been near impossible.

52 As well as Étienne and Henriet, five other members of Gilles's household were listed in the indictments as alleged accomplices (Georges Bataille, *The Trial of Gilles de Rais*, p. 177).

53 For the connection between the use of torture and violent sexual perversion see Sam Vaknin, 'The Psychology of Torture', *Medical News Today*, 20 August 2005. The homophobia of the accusations is illustrated by the fact that although there are claims in Étienne's and Henriet's statements that Gilles occasionally abused and murdered girls, they emphasise that he was unable to rape them, and imply that this makes the crime even worse.

54 The record of the ecclesiastical court hearings is Georges Bataille, *The Trial of Gilles de Rais*, pp. 159–208.

55 Georges Bataille, *The Trial of Gilles de Rais*, p. 179. Translation by Pierre Klossowski and Richard Robinson.

56 Georges Bataille, *The Trial of Gilles de Rais*, pp. 166–7. Translation by Pierre Klossowski and Richard Robinson. At the next hearing, Gilles provocatively demanded the right to clear himself by trial by ordeal – a magical practice still used by some secular courts, but which the Church had outlawed in 1215 (see Robert Bartlett, *Trial by Fire and Water: The Medieval Judicial Ordeal*).

57 Georges Bataille, *The Trial of Gilles de Rais*, pp. 190–91. Translation by Pierre Klossowski and Richard Robinson.

58 Georges Bataille, *The Trial of Gilles de Rais*, p. 192. Translation by Pierre Klossowski and Richard Robinson.

59 Georges Bataille, *The Trial of Gilles de Rais*, p. 193. Translations by Pierre Klossowski and Richard Robinson.

60 By another of the officials, the Bishop of Saint-Brieuc.

61 Georges Bataille, *The Trial of Gilles de Rais*, p. 194. My translation, from the Old French given in a footnote.

62 There were, however, some discrepancies between what Gilles said and Étienne's and Henriet's statements. Most notably, Étienne's and Henriet's statements claimed that some of the boys had been suspended from hooks to terrorise them into silence. In his courtroom confession, Gilles said that these boys had been killed by being hanged from hooks – not the kind of mistake he would have made if the events had ever really taken place.

63 There has been a great deal of debate about the number of people killed during the European witch hunts, but with records so patchy, and many of those which do exist only just coming to light, an accurate figure is impossible. Current academic estimates put the figure at between 40,000 and 60,000 (Joanne Pearson, 'Wicca, Paganism and history: contemporary witchcraft and the Lancashire witches', Robert Poole (ed.), *The Lancashire Witches*, p. 192).

64 Georges Bataille, *The Trial of Gilles de Rais*, p. 208. Translation by Pierre Klossowski and Richard Robinson.

65 Étienne's and Henriet's statements – essentially abbreviated versions of their statements for the ecclesiastical trial, with a few additions – and their sentences are Georges Bataille, *The Trial of Gilles de Rais*, pp. 275–82. The fact that the preamble of Étienne's statement says that it was made without torture, and the preamble of Henriet's does not, strongly suggests that Henriet was tortured. Gilles's denials are p. 251 ('Initial Complaints'). The latter stages of the trial are an account by Jean de Touscheronde, pp. 282–4.

66 Georges Bataille, *The Trial of Gilles de Rais*, pp. 284–5.

67 This account is based on the information in Georges Bataille's introduction, *The Trial of Gilles de Rais*, p. 144 (citing Abbot A. Bourdeaut, *Chantocé, Gilles de Rays et les Ducs de Bretagne*, Rennes, 1924, pp. 128–30). Georges Bataille's interpretation of these events differs somewhat from mine; but owing to the lack of information about fifteenth-century magic at the time he was writing, he assumed Francesco was a fraud.

68 In a chilling passage, *Malleus Maleficarum* by Heinrich Kramer discusses the morality of making false promises to suspects that their lives would be spared, and suggests as one solution giving them the impression that they would be released but instead sentencing them

to life imprisonment on a diet of bread and water – which would, of course, result in them dying of scurvy within a few months (Third Part, Second Head, Question 14). Although *Malleus Maleficarum* was written about forty-five years after this case, it discussed methods of interrogation that were already well established.

69 Gilles de Rais questioned in court, 15 October (Georges Bataille, *The Trial of Gilles de Rais*, p. 182).

70 A town due south of Nantes.

Chapter Nine: Alizon denounces her father's murderer

1 Abraham's statement, Alizon's statement, James's first statement, and Elizabeth Device's first statement are all dated 30 March, and Elizabeth Sothernes's presence is mentioned in Elizabeth Device's statement (to be exact, her mark is described as being seen) (*WD* pp. S, R4, S2v, C2v). For arrest procedures see Michael Dalton, *The Country Justice*, 'Warrants' (pp. 287–93) and 'Arrest, and Imprisonment' (pp. 294–300).

2 As Mary Sutton did to resist the men attempting to swim her (Anon, *Witches Apprehended*).

3 Michael Dalton, *The Country Justice*, 'Posse Comitatus', pp. 301–3.

4 Brian Darcey, *A True and Just Record*, pp. C2v, C3.

5 William Harrison, *The Description of England*, 1587, Book 2, Chapter 10, and Michael Dalton, *The Country Justice*, 'Rogues and Vagabonds', pp. 96–7.

6 *WD* p. B2.

7 'Dragging a witch named Elizabeth Stile to the Justice of the Peace', 1579, The Bodleian Library, University of Oxford. This is used as the cover illustration of Marion Gibson's *Early Modern Witches*.

8 William Harrison, *The Description of England*, Book 2, Chapter 11.

9 Michael Dalton, *The Country Justice*, 'Arrest, and Imprisonment', p. 297.

10 Anon, *The Most Strange and Admirable Discovery of the Three Witches of Warboys*. I use the term 'witch mark' for convenience; in contemporary accounts they are usually just referred to as 'marks'. In France prisoners were shaved in the belief that they hid charms on their bodies that would help them to resist torture (as well as being searched for marks), and again the search helped to break their resistance. In some cases they may indeed have twisted charms into their hair, but no doubt more often it was the humiliation of the search that demoralised them (see, for example, Jean Bodin, *De la Démonomanie des Sorciers*, Fourth Book, Chapter 1, and Henri Boguet, *Discours des Sorciers*, Chapter 2).

11 See, for example, Jean Bodin, *De la Démonomanie des Sorciers*, Second Book, Chapter 4.

12 Or sometimes with a milk-like substance (Anon, *The Most Strange and Admirable Discovery of the Three Witches of Warboys*).

13 Described by John as a white rod (St John D. Seymour, *Irish Witchcraft and Demonology*, Portman Books, London, 1989 (first published 1913), p. 86).

14 Anon, *The Most Wonderful and True Story of a Certain Witch Named Alice Gooderige*.

15 How a search was conducted in England is described in Anon, *The Most Wonderful and True Story of a Certain Witch Named Alice Gooderige*.

16 *WD* p. C2v. The phrase 'the space of' emphasises the *length* of time.

17 *WD* p. B3.

18 Moses Pitt, letter to the Bishop of Gloucester, 1696.

19 Michael Dalton, *The Country Justice*, 'Examination of Felons, and Evidence against them', pp. 259, 260, 262.

20 Moses Pitt, letter to the Bishop of Gloucester; Todd Gray, 'Witchcraft in the Diocese of Exeter: Dartmouth, 1601–1602', Richard Galis, *A Brief Treatise Containing the Most Strange and Horrible Cruelty of Elizabeth Stile*, 1579.

21 In February and March, so this was 1581 by the old style legal calendar, with the new year beginning on 25 March.

22 Brian Darcey, *A True and Just Record*, pp. B6, B6v. Jean Bodin visited Queen Elizabeth as part of the entourage of the Duke of Anjou, one of the European nobles interested in marrying the Queen (Jonathan L. Pearl's Introduction to Jean Bodin, Randy A. Scott (trans.), *On the Demon-Mania of Witches*, CRRS Publications, Toronto, 2001, p. 10).

23 King James I, *Demonology*, Second Book, Chapter 6. At the time this was written, 1597, James was still only king of Scotland, so the magistrates he was referring to were Scottish ones, but English Justices would have interpreted this as referring equally to them, even though there were technical differences in their roles.

24 *WD* p. B2.

25 The fact that Roger had released James after Henry Towneley's earlier accusation would have helped to convince Alizon that she could persuade Roger of her innocence.

26 Edgar Peel and Pat Southern, *The Trials of the Lancashire Witches*, Hendon Publishing Co. Ltd, Nelson, 1985, p. 18.

27 Note that Alizon emphasises the 'protection racket' element of the agreement, claiming that her father believed right from the start that Anne would harm him if he didn't pay. Although John contracted with Anne not to harm him or his 'goods' – which meant livestock as well as other property – he didn't mention his family, so at that point he was not yet married to Elizabeth.

28 *WD* pp. E4–F.

29 Albertus Magnus (attrib.), (edited and translated by L.W. de Laurence) *Egyptian Secrets: White and Black Art for Man and Beast*, de Laurence, Scott & Co., Chicago, 1914, Volume I. First printed in Germany in the early eighteenth century, this book is very similar to medieval books combining charms and herbal remedies, although it's unlikely it was actually written by Albertus Magnus. The history of this book is discussed by Joseph H. Peterson on his website www.esotericarchives.com, and the text is available both on the website and on the Esoteric Archives CD, as well as in several printed versions.

30 *The Book of Secrets of Albertus Magnus*, First Book, 'Of the Virtues of Certain Herbs'.

31 *WD* pp. E–Ev.

32 J. Maxwell, *Metapsychical Phenomena*, London, 1905, pp. 195–6, quoted in Theodore Besterman, *Crystal-Gazing: A Study in the History, Distribution, Theory and Practice of Scrying*, William Rider & Son Ltd, London, 1924, p. 136.

Chapter Ten: James Device betrays his sister

1 Of course we only have James's version, but if Anne had given Henry a version that put James in a worse light, Roger Nowell and Thomas Potts would have made sure we had it.

2 Reading *The Wonderful Discovery*, it is easy to get the impression that the evidence it presents is a series of statements made freely and spontaneously by the people being questioned, and closely reflecting their own words. That, however, is misleading, and it is important to understand how this evidence was collected.

Alizon, for example, was questioned by Roger on 30 March, perhaps just once or more likely several times. Roger was a competent and conscientious Justice, so he probably took careful notes or had a clerk present to take notes for him. This was Alizon's 'examination of 30th March', and Roger was supposed to write it up within two days.

This is the type of record we have in Brian Darcey's *A True and Just Record*. But it is NOT what we have in *WD*. In *WD* we have the statements as they were drawn up by Roger to be read out in court. First of all, because the Assizes were run to a very tight schedule, statements had to be kept as brief as possible, so Roger would have cut his original records ruthlessly for this reason alone, quite apart from any desire to remove parts of what Alizon said that didn't suit his purposes. He then transformed the record of each examination into a series of statements to be read out at each trial. Thus, parts of Alizon's examination that might be used as evidence against her grandmother would be copied out and added to the pile of documents for her grandmother's trial; parts that could be used against Anne Whittle copied out and added to the documents for her trial, and so on.

At the end of this process, Roger had a series of piles of documents – one pile for each trial (there were nine trials eventually) – consisting of extracts from the records of the examinations. Some of these documents would be the same for more than one trial, if they were evidence against more than one suspect – and in *WD* some of the statements are repeated several times for this reason. Thomas Potts included the statements in the pamphlet exactly as they were prepared for use in court, except that he cut out some statements entirely, as discussed in Chapter Four.

Elizabeth Sothernes's statements are dated 2 April, not 30 March, but that doesn't mean she wasn't questioned on 30 March. In fact we know she *was*, because obviously she was present when her witch mark was shown to Roger and her daughter Elizabeth Device, and Elizabeth Device commented on it. She was questioned again on 2 April, probably as part of a staged confrontation with Anne Whittle and Anne Redferne, and this became the examination Roger used to draw up the trial statements, so no copies of any records of earlier interrogations have survived.

Because of this way that the statements are presented in *WD*, we have no way of knowing for certain the order the suspects were interrogated on any given day. Everything they said on a particular day would simply be recorded as part of their examination of that date, regardless of whether they were questioned once or several times. However, there is internal evidence within the statements themselves that can give us reliable clues, and it seems likely that both Alizon and Elizabeth Sothernes were interrogated several times. Certainly parts of Elizabeth's evidence were influenced by Alizon's, and parts of Alizon's influenced by James's.

Suspects were not supposed to be held in custody by either the Justice or the Constable. They were supposed to be questioned immediately they were arrested and then immediately sent to the nearest prison. In practice, however, that must often have been impossible, particularly if the prisoner was reluctant to respond to questioning and the nearest prison was many miles away. In *A True and Just Record*, Brian Darcey refers specifically to handing a prisoner over 'to the ward and keeping of the Constable' for the night (p. Bv), and many country areas must have had a local lock-up, or some outbuilding that doubled as one. Justices also sometimes simply ignored this rule – John Tregeagle imprisoned Anne Jefferies in his house for 'some time' (implying several days at least) (Moses Pitt, letter to the Bishop of Gloucester).

Alizon and Elizabeth Sothernes must have been held prisoner at Pendle between 30 March and 2 (or more likely 3) April, and it's likely that James and Elizabeth Device were too. Internal evidence within the statements also strongly suggests that Roger kept them separated from each other, at least during the time he was interrogating them on 30 March. Writers such as Jean Bodin and Henri Boguet show a keen awareness of the importance of sometimes keeping suspects separated and sometimes confronting them with each other.

See William Lambard, *Eirenarcha Or the Office of Justices of Peace*, London, 1581, First Book, Chapter 21; Michael Dalton, *The Country Justice*, 'Examination of Felons, and Evidence against them', pp. 259, 260; 'Arrest, and Imprisonment', p. 297; and for a general discussion of statements and judicial procedures see Marion Gibson, *Reading Witchcraft*, Routledge, London, 1999, pp. 50–72.

3 Abraham might have joined the posse, but Roger would probably have decided to keep the family in the dark at first about the evidence against them. (See the section 'Witnesses'

in Rossell Hope Robbins, *The Encyclopedia of Witchcraft and Demonology*, which shows how aware interrogators were of the issues involved in revealing the identity of accusers to suspects. On the other hand, Henri Boguet, in his *Discours des Sorciers*, recommended confronting suspects with fake witnesses who would pretend to have evidence against them ('Instruction pour un Juge', Article 12).)

4 *WD* p. S2v (dated 30 March) and p. C2 (dated 27 April).

5 Brian Darcey, *A True and Just Record*, p. 2A8v.

6 *The Real Life on Mars*, produced and directed by Steve Bradshaw and Simon Brown, broadcast on BBC4 on 11 August 2008.

7 J.S. Cockburn, *A History of English Assizes*, pp. 121–2. In Scotland defendants were allowed lawyers – see P.G. Maxwell-Stuart's detailed account of a Scottish witchcraft trial (of the wise woman Janet Cock) in *Witchcraft: A History*, pp. 98–108.

8 As the Justice had two days after conducting the examination to write it up, and the suspect was supposed to be sent to the nearest prison immediately after the examination, the final written version didn't have to be completed until after the prisoner had been sent away to jail. See note 2.

9 Michael Dalton, in *The Country Justice*, initially says that Justices must ensure that witnesses (including accusers) appear in person at trials; but when he then goes on to discuss whether witnesses should be examined by the Justice under oath, he makes it clear that sometimes in practice statements were used without the witness being present ('Examination of Felons, and Evidence against them', pp. 259, 264). *The Wonderful Discovery* itself makes it clear that this was the case. On p. Sv a witness's statement is read out in court, even though the witness is present, and on pp. Y3–Zv witness statements are read out in the witnesses' absence. On p. H4, Thomas Potts says that witnesses gave evidence in person 'notwithstanding' the fact that their written statements were available, implying that it was not strictly necessary.

10 Again, this was a problem suffered by defendants in the 1970s, when it was the defendant's word against a police officer's (*The Real Life on Mars*). Early Modern judges had far more freedom to influence the presentation of evidence than modern ones. A pamphlet published in 1702, *The Trial of Richard Hathaway for Endeavouring to Take Away the Life of Sarah Morduck for Being a Witch* (Isaac Cleave, London), is a rare example of an account of a trial that is an actual transcript of everything that was said. Even though in this case the defendant had a defence counsel, the judge's constant undermining of the defence's case meant the defendant stood little chance of being acquitted. See also J.S. Cockburn, *A History of English Assizes*, pp. 109, 117, 122.

11 J.S. Cockburn, *A History of English Assizes*, pp. 54–5, 65–9, 104–5, 286, 294–302. Jonathan Lumby, in *The Lancashire Witch-Craze*, draws attention to some important facts about Sir James Altham – his involvement in an Essex witchcraft case in 1607 and a heresy case in 1612 – and suggests reasonably that Sir Edward may have been influenced by Sir James's hardline views (pp. 61–5).

12 Court appearance, Saturday 15 October, 1440; Georges Bataille (ed.), Richard Robinson (trans.), Pierre Klossowski (trans.), *The Trial of Gilles de Rais*, p. 185.

13 It's clear from Brian Darcey's pamphlet *A True and Just Record* that Jean Bodin's visit to England sparked considerable interest in his book. Since *A True and Just Record* itself became something of a handbook for Justices involved in witchcraft cases, Brian Darcey's reference to Jean Bodin and the fact that he quoted from *Démonomanie* would in turn have added to the interest. And of course when Jean Bodin recommended interrogation techniques he was referring to practices that were already widely used and proven to be successful, so many Justices would already have been familiar with them.

14 Jean Bodin, *De la Démonomanie des Sorciers*, Fourth Book, Chapter 1.

15 This kind of second-hand evidence seems pretty feeble but was clearly acceptable. On p. Y4v

WD includes a statement in which a witness says someone else has told him that a suspect might have been going to do something.

16 Anne admitted some conflict with John Moore and Anthony Nutter, and confessed that she'd bewitched cows belonging to them; but did not confess to bewitching their children. There are no statements from them clarifying the situation. As usual, Thomas Potts claims there were numerous witnesses against Anne, but without telling us who they were. *WD* pp. E2v, E2.

17 Although Elizabeth's statement was dated 2 April, we know she was questioned about her witch mark on 30 March, and it's likely that she first described Anne Whittle and Anne Redferne making images shortly after Alizon's statement incriminating Anne Whittle, to back up Alizon's allegations. There is internal evidence in Alizon's and Elizabeth's statements (which will be discussed in Chapter Twelve) that demonstrates that other parts of Elizabeth's statement were made around the same time as Alizon was being questioned.

18 *WD* p. D3v.

19 *WD* p. O2.

20 Thomas Potts would definitely have told us if they had been; and they might well have been forced to become vagabonds and leave the area.

21 *WD* pp. O–O2, Ev–E2. The man who'd worked for Robert's grandfather also claimed that his ale had spoiled after Anne Whittle had drunk some when she was carding wool for him – but the fact that he was employing her to card wool strongly suggests that he didn't regard her as a murdering witch. Thomas Potts includes these statements in full, even though they are far from conclusively incriminating. This makes it clear that the numerous statements he tells us he hasn't bothered to include, if they existed at all, were even less convincing.

22 *WD* pp. E, Ev. It's likely that Roger Nowell questioned Robert's sister about her father's death because of this identification of one of the images as Christopher's. It's less likely that Elizabeth identified one of the images as Christopher because of Robert's sister's statement, because why then would she have mentioned Marie Nutter?

23 One might suspect that Elizabeth would most want to know whether her son-in-law John Device had been killed by Anne.

24 *WD* p. E3 (Anne Whittle is offended because Anthony Nutter 'favours' Elizabeth Sothernes), p. C. However, in the statement Elizabeth says that what she's describing occurred six months before Robert's death.

25 It's possible, of course, that Roger arrested Anne Whittle and Anne Redferne before he took the statements from Robert's relatives, but I think it's more likely he would have made sure he had the additional evidence against them before he arrested them.

26 *WD* pp. D3v, F Her insistence that Anne Redferne wasn't involved can be inferred from these accounts of what she said, and from the outcome of the trials, which will be discussed later.

27 This statement of James's appears in the pamphlet in a version dated 27 April. However, there is also a version of his statement about Alizon's confrontation with Henry Bulcock dated 27 April, as well as one dated 30 March. We know these are two different versions of the statement, not simply the result of Roger tagging it on to other statements, because Henry Bulcock's name is spelt differently. The second version of the statement about Alizon takes the form of an examination of James before Roger Nowell and his colleague Nicholas Banester. It seems that as the case progressed Roger decided it would be desirable to have his suspects' statements incriminating other people witnessed by a second Justice to give them extra credibility. So it was made to look as if James had incriminated Alizon a second time in front of Nicholas Banester as well as Roger. Of course it's out of the question that James would have repeated a statement that wasn't a true representation of what he'd said the first time. Roger simply added a version of the statement to the record of the later examination

without James knowing anything about it. There must also have been two versions of the statement incriminating Marie and Thomas Redferne – a 2 April version and a 27 April version – because *The Wonderful Discovery* states quite clearly that Marie was arrested on or shortly after 2 April (p. C2v). (The second version is however a slightly modified one: for example, it says that Anne Redferne is being held in Lancaster prison. James may have genuinely repeated this statement – or rather, confirmed it when it was read out to him. The 27 April statements will be discussed in more detail later.)

28 *WD* p. O2v.

29 *WD* pp. E–Ev.

30 It's also possible that Roger wanted to arrest both Marie and Thomas, even if only briefly. In *A True and Just Record* Brian Darcey described how he used the evidence of four children (the youngest aged six) against their parents. If Anne Redferne had any younger children, with both their parents and their elder sister under arrest there would be no one to prevent Roger interrogating them.

31 *WD* p. C2.

32 He seems to have considered using them as evidence against Elizabeth Sothernes.

33 It wasn't unheard of for evidence from cunning folk to be used to help incriminate witchcraft suspects. For example, several statements in Brian Darcey's *A True and Just Record* include references to cunning folk identifying the suspects as witches (e.g. p. 2A3), although we don't know whether they were actually used in court. In the trial of Isabel Robey in *WD* one of the statements mentions a witchcraft victim consulting a cunning man, who seems to have said Isabel was 'no witch', but because the rest of the statement is incriminating her, this may well be a misprint for 'a witch' (p. T4v).

34 *WD* p. C2v.

35 In fact this raises an interesting legal point that will be discussed later.

36 *WD* p. I.

37 *WD* p. R3v.

Chapter Eleven: A circle made at Huntroyde

1 The sources for this case are two pamphlets: George More, *A True Discourse Concerning the Certain Possession and Dispossession of Seven Persons in One Family in Lancashire*, and John Darrell, *A True Narration of the Strange and Grievous Vexation by the Devil of Seven Persons in Lancashire*. It is also analysed by Jonathan Lumby in *The Lancashire Witch-Craze*, pp. 119–28.

John Darrell and George More were Puritan exorcists, who responded to an appeal for help by Nicholas in March 1597. They based their belief in demonic possession on biblical descriptions of Jesus casting out demons (Matthew 12; Mark 9:25–6; Luke 8:26–39), but the Church of England was officially sceptical of possession and disapproved of both Puritans and exorcism. At the time they wrote their pamphlets, John Darrell and George More were in prison, convicted of 'counterfeiting' – conducting fake exorcisms of people only pretending to be possessed. Both men were desperate to get out of prison, with good reason – the terrible conditions would kill George More. Their pamphlets were intended to prove their innocence – and there's no doubt that Nicholas only called them in because he sincerely believed his family was under attack from evil spirits. There was no deliberate deception involved in Nicholas's or the exorcists' actions. However, the exorcists interpreted what Nicholas told them and what they witnessed happening in his home according to their preconceptions about possession. And no doubt when they wrote their pamphlets they unconsciously distorted the evidence to make their case. However, such an obvious bias is easy to allow for when analysing what they wrote. By the time they were called in, Edmund Hartlay's direct involvement with Nicholas's family was over, so the information in the pamphlets about Edmund and his magic is almost certainly based solely on what Nicholas told them. But Nicholas was trying to save his children, so we can be sure that what he told John Darrell and George More was the truth as he saw it. (For information about George More and John Darrell see Philip C. Almond, *Demonic Possession and Exorcism in Early Modern England*, Cambridge University Press, Cambridge, 2004, pp. 192–6, 240–43.)

2 Jonathan Lumby, *The Lancashire Witch-Craze*, pp. 118, 143–8.
3 Jonathan Lumby, *The Lancashire Witch-Craze*, pp. 119–121.
4 George More, *A True Discourse*.
5 Tony Smith (ed.), *The New Macmillan Guide to Family Health*, Macmillan Publishers Ltd/ Dorling Kindersley Ltd/Guild Publishing, London, 1987, pp. 690–91.
6 Reginald Scot, *The Discovery of Witchcraft*, Book 1, Chapter 2.
7 John Darrell, *A True Narration*.
8 Reginald Scot, *The Discovery of Witchcraft*, Book 12, Chapter 9. Henri Boguet's condemnation is in *Discours des Sorciers*, Chapter 35. To a Protestant like Reginald Scot this charm would be particularly suspect because it was in Latin, the language of Roman Catholic prayers.
9 Albertus Magnus (attrib.), L.W. de Laurence (trans.), *Egyptian Secrets*, Volume III.
10 *The Book of Secrets of Albertus Magnus*, First Book, 'Of the Virtues of Certain Herbs'.
11 British Library MS Sloane 962, in Tony Hunt, *Popular Medicine in Thirteenth-Century England*, p. 93. There are numerous variations of this charm, several given in Tony Hunt's book, and others in Jonathan Roper, *English Verbal Charms*.
12 John Darrell, *A True Narration*. 'Tread out' could either mean mark out the circle by walking round it or obliterate it by treading on the marks inscribed by Edmund. George More's account says the circle had 'many crosses and partitions'.
13 George More, *A True Discourse*.
14 Anon, *The Examination of John Walsh*, p. A5.
15 Bavarian State Library MS Clm 849, ff. 103r–105v, in Richard Kieckhefer, *Forbidden Rites*, pp. 339–42; 376. This circle was also divided into four parts.
16 John Darrell, *A True Narration*.
17 See Benjamin Woolley, *The Queen's Conjuror*, HarperCollins, London, 2001, p. 61. Nicholas also took a sample of John's urine to a physician in Manchester, who not surprisingly concluded that he wasn't suffering from any kind of physical illness.
18 John Dee, Meric Casaubon (ed.), *A True and Faithful Relation of What Passed for Many Years Between Dr John Dee and Some Spirits*, London, 1659. The crystal ball, obsidian mirror and a Seal of God inscribed in wax are all in the British Museum, and pictures of them are on the British Museum website, www.britishmuseum.org. The various versions of the Seal of God are discussed by Joseph Peterson on his website www.esotericarchives.com.
19 John Darrell, *A True Narration*. He and George More also claimed that John Dee advised Nicholas 'to crave the help and assistance of some godly preachers' (i.e. them).
20 Robert Turner (trans) *Arbatel of Magic, Or, The Spiritual Wisdom of the Ancients*, included in *Henry Cornelius Agrippa His Fourth Book of Occult Philosophy*, London, 1655, Aphorisms 4, 20, 26, 49. First published as *Arbatel de Magia Veterum* in Basel in 1575. *Arbatel* was another book of magic used by John Dee. See Joseph Peterson's introduction on his website www.esotericarchives.com. The website includes the original Latin text as well as Robert Turner's translation.
21 John Darrell, *A True Narration*.
22 George More, *A True Discourse*.
23 John Darrell, *A True Narration*.
24 George More, *A True Discourse*.
25 George More, *A True Discourse*. As with many of the possession incidents described in the pamphlets, the date this occurred is unclear.

26 George More, *A True Discourse*. This is the only point where there is a significant disagreement between the two pamphlets. According to John Darrell, *A True Narration*, Margaret was possessed after helping Edmund when he was attacked by evil spirits during the daytime, with several other people present. However, in view of subsequent events, George More's account seems the more likely. John Darrell would have had good reasons to modify his version – a desire to protect Margaret's reputation, and also an awareness that if Margaret and Edmund were sexually involved that offered an alternative explanation for her symptoms and seriously undermined his claim that she was possessed.

27 John Darrell, *A True Narration*.

28 George More, *A True Discourse*.

29 George More, *A True Discourse*. For another example of a suspected witch asked to say the Lord's Prayer, see Anon, *The Most Wonderful and True Story of a Certain Witch Named Alice Gooderige*.

30 John Darrell, *A True Narration*.

31 George More, *A True Discourse*.

32 It might seem to modern readers that there was a failure of logic in accusing Edmund of bewitching two children who were ill before he ever met them, but if witchcraft was a Satanic conspiracy, someone else could have bewitched the children initially, and the Devil then sent Edmund to finish the job.

33 For example, in 1602 Elizabeth Jackson was sentenced to a year's imprisonment for witchcraft, but soon pardoned (Merlin Coverley, *Occult London*, Pocket Essentials, Harpenden, 2008, p. 32–4, citing Michael MacDonald (ed.), *Witchcraft and Hysteria in Elizabethan London: Edward Jorden and the Mary Glover Case*, Routledge, London, 1991). Pardons were issued by the Court of Chancery or the Privy Council, and were the Early Modern equivalent of the modern Appeals system (J.S. Cockburn, *A History of English Assizes*, p. 130).

34 George More, *A True Discourse*. It could hardly have been correct procedure to discuss the sentence before the jury had delivered their verdict.

35 The full text of the 1563 *Act Against Conjurations, Enchantments, and Witchcrafts* is in Rossell Hope Robbins, *The Encyclopedia of Witchcraft and Demonology*, pp. 158–9.

36 George More, *A True Discourse*.

37 Moses Pitt, letter to the Bishop of Gloucester.

38 The gallows consisted of a long horizontal beam supported by posts at both ends. English illustrations of execution scenes generally depict the moment after the prisoner has been pushed, showing the executioner leaning across to check that the noose has pulled tight (see, for example, Jonathan Lumby, *The Lancashire Witch-Craze*, p. 150). One Continental illustration, however, shows the prisoner being dragged up the ladder by the executioner (Rossell Hope Robbins, *The Encyclopedia of Witchcraft and Demonology*, p. 179).

39 Anon, *The Apprehension and Confession of Three Notorious Witches*, 1589.

40 Anon, *The Most Strange and Admirable Discovery of the Three Witches of Warboys*.

41 Richard Galis, *A Brief Treatise Containing the Most Strange and Horrible Cruelty of Elizabeth Stile*.

42 Which happened to Robert Keyes, one of the Gunpowder Plot conspirators (see Antonia Fraser, *The Gunpowder Plot*, Weidenfeld and Nicolson, London, 1996).

43 George More, *A True Discourse*.

44 John Darrell, *A True Narration*.

45 Via John Dee, who gave Nicholas a letter of introduction to John Darrell, so it's regrettably clear that Edmund's execution did not affect John Dee's relationship with Nicholas.

46 George More, *A True Discourse*.

Chapter Twelve: I care not for thee, hang thyself

1 *WD* p. B3.

2 As I discovered after recreating Edmund's circle for the photograph for this book. The earliest surviving record of the name is in John Gerard's *Herbal*, published in 1597 (*The Compact Edition of the Oxford English Dictionary*); the plant's Latin name, *Circaea lutetiana*, which refers to the mythological sorceress Circe, was given to it by James I's court physician and botanist Matthias de L'Obel.

3 Alan Charles Kors and Edward Peters, *Witchcraft in Europe, 400–1700*, pp. 136–7.

4 Anon, *The Examination of John Walsh*.

5 *WD* pp. B3–3v. It's impossible to be sure exactly when Roger obtained this account from Elizabeth, since all her formal statements are the result of her examination on 2 April, and the order they appear in *WD* is not necessarily the order that Roger obtained the information. However, the tone of the references to Tibb strongly suggests that Elizabeth had already told Roger about the spirit in some detail by this point. It's interesting that Elizabeth apparently describes seeing the spirit in spite of the fact that she was blind – a vision that had nothing to do with ordinary sight, or evidence that either Elizabeth or Roger was exaggerating.

6 Anon, *Witches Apprehended*.

7 A dramatic medieval illustration of a woman setting fire to a mill after being cheated in this way is reproduced in Edward J. Kealey, *Harvesting the Air: Windmill Pioneers in Twelfth-Century England*, The Boydell Press, Woodbridge, 1987, pp. 204–5.

8 *WD* p. D3v.

9 *WD* p. C. Again, the order that Roger obtained these various accounts from Alizon has to be deduced from their content. The oddly precise reference to this event happening at ten o'clock and lasting for half an hour can't be what Alizon said, as it's very unlikely there would have been a clock at Malking Tower. It must be the result of Roger prompting Alizon. It does, however, suggest the possibility that the spell was linked to the moon in some way – perhaps Elizabeth began it at the rising of the moon.

10 *WD* pp. C–Cv.

11 *WD* p. Cv.

12 The reference to Elizabeth saying she would pray for him also probably has nothing to do with magic – she meant she would pray for him to see sense. Needless to say, there's no statement from Richard Baldwyn in *WD*.

Chapter Thirteen: What wouldst thou have me do unto yonder man?

1 Henri Boguet, *Discours des Sorciers*, Chapter 51. He did, however, say that they should be hanged rather than burned.

2 Todd Gray, 'Witchcraft in the Diocese of Exeter: Dartmouth, 1601–1602', pp. 230–8. Of course since the Trevysards lived in the busy port of Dartmouth eleven people were probably not a large proportion of their total acquaintances.

3 It's even possible that Sir Thomas substituted Peter's name for Michael's.

4 The execution record is in the Gaol Delivery Roll included in the Quarter Sessions Order Book for 1602 in Devon Record Office. The marriage record is one of the Bishop's Transcripts for St Clement's Church published on the Dartmouth History Research Group's website, www.dartmouth-history.org.uk.

5 *WD* pp. R3v–R4.

6 *WD* p. R3v.

7 Jean Bodin, *De la Démonomanie des Sorciers*, Fourth Book, Chapter 1.

8 Brian Darcey, *A True and Just Record*, p. B8.

9 Brian Darcey, *A True and Just Record*, p. C.

10 It's just possible that the arrests were on 29 March, but since the search for witch marks was on the 30th, that is the more likely date.

11 Jean Bodin, *De la Démonomanie des Sorciers*, Fourth Book, Chapter 1.

12 Brian Darcey, *A True and Just Record*, p. 2A7v.

13 Malcolm Gaskill, *Witchfinders: A Seventeenth-Century English Tragedy*, John Murray, London, 2005, pp. 57–60.

14 See Chapter Ten, note 2.

15 Section L. Obtained by the American press under the US Freedom of Information Act, and first published in the April 1997 issue of *Harper's Magazine*. This document can be read online on a number of websites. For example, there is a photocopy on the George Washington University website: www.gwu.edu/~nsarchiv/NSAEBB/NSAEBB27/02-01.htm.

16 See also Sam Vaknin, 'The Psychology of Torture'.

17 Brian Darcey, *A True and Just Record*, p. B5v.

18 Robert Pitcairn, *Criminal Trials of Scotland*, Third Volume, p. 611.

19 *WD* p. B2v–B3.

Chapter Fourteen: Elves and angels

1 British Library MS Royal 17.A.XLII, f. 2v. Transcribed by Joseph H. Peterson on his website www.esotericarchives.com and also available on his Esoteric Archives CD.

2 Jean Bodin, *De la Démonomanie des Sorciers*, First Book, Chapter 2. I have inserted paragraph breaks to make the account more readable. In his English translation *on the Demon-Mania of Witches* (Centre for Reformation and Renaissance Studies, Toronto, 2001, p. 59, note 78), Randy A. Scott suggests that this may be Jean Bodin's own experience, not that of a friend of his as he claims (citing P.L. Rose, *Jean Bodin and the Great God of Nature*, Droz, Geneva, 1980, p. 164).

3 *Horizon: Why Do We Dream*, Director/Producer Charles Colville, broadcast on BBC2 on 10 February 2009.

4 *Arbatel of Magic*, translation by Robert Turner (trans), Aphorism 38.

5 Royal f. 45r, transcribed by Joseph H. Peterson, www.esotericarchives.ues.com.

6 Royal ff. 61r, 64r transcribed by Joseph H. Peterson, www.esotericarchives.ues.com.

7 Translation by O.T. Benfey, *Journal of Chemical Education*, vol. 35. 1958, p. 21; quoted in Royston M. Roberts, *Serendipity: Accidental Discoveries in Science*, John Wiley & Sons, Inc., New York, 1989, p. 77 (special thanks to Jenny Southern for giving me this book).

8 F. Sherwood Taylor, *The Alchemists: Founders of Modern Chemistry*, pp. 52, 58.

9 Francesco Prelati's statement presented in court on 16 October 1440; in Georges Bataille, *The Trial of Gilles de Rais*, pp. 214–15.

10 It took fifteen years to build, and wasn't completed until more than ten years after George Hale's death.

11 Richard Preston, *First Light: The Search for the Edge of the Universe*, Scribners, London, 1991, pp. 36–51 (this account was pointed out to me many years ago by my father, a scientist whose curiosity extended to strange phenomena).

12 Moses Pitt, letter to the Bishop of Gloucester. This letter gives all the main details of Anne's case. A.K. Hamilton Jenkins also discovered some other sources referring to her, which he published in his book *Cornwall and Its People*, David & Charles, Newton Abbot, 1983, p. 277 (first published 1945). Anne couldn't read, but no doubt she had heard the biblical passage read.

13 The text of the 1604 *Act Against Conjuration, Witchcraft, and Dealing with Evil and Wicked Spirits* is published in full in Rossell Hope Robbins, *The Encyclopedia of Witchcraft and Demonology*, pp. 280–81.

14 See, for example, William Bottrell, *Traditions and Hearthside Stories of West Cornwall*, facsimile selection published by Llanerch Publishers, Felinfach, 1989, 'Tregagle', pp. 131–3.

15 Anon, *The Examination of John Walsh*, pp. A5, A6v. Marion Gibson, in a footnote in her edition (*Early Modern Witches*, p. 29), suggests the 'great heaps of earth' must be burial mounds, in turn citing Barbara Rosen, *Witchcraft in England 1558–1610*, University of Massachusetts Press, Amherst, 1991, p. 68, note 8.

16 Francis James Child, *The English and Scottish Popular Ballads*, Boston, 1882–1898, No. 37C. A performance of this song by Ron Taylor and Jeff Gillett is included on the CD *Songs of Witchcraft and Magic* produced by the Museum of Witchcraft and WildGoose Records. The earliest account is a fourteenth-century poem entitled *Thomas of Erceldoune*. See J.A.H. Murray (ed.), *The Romance and Prophecies of Thomas of Erceldoune*, N. Trubner & Co., London, 1875.

17 *Fortean Times*, March 2009, FT246, 'It happened to me ...' p. 75.

18 Simon J. Sherwood, 'A Psychological Approach to Apparitions of Black Dogs' in Bob Trubshaw (ed.), *Explore Phantom Black Dogs*, Heart of Albion Press, Wymeswold, 2005, pp. 21–35.

19 Patient UK website *Hypnagogic Hallucinations*, , www. patient.co.uk, citing (for the survey) M.M. Ohayon, R.G. Priest, M. Caulet and C. Guilleminault (Centre de Recherche Philippe Pinel de Montréal, Québec, Canada), 'Hypnagogic and hypnopompic hallucinations: pathological phenomena?', *British Journal of Psychiatry*, Oct. 1996, 169(4), pp. 459–67. I myself experienced a hypnopompic hallucination when I was suffering from a bad cold that had stopped me sleeping properly for several nights. One night I finally dozed off only to be woken in the early hours of the morning by a violent rainstorm. I heard someone call out outside my window, and then heard someone in the bedroom next to mine call out in reply, 'I'll just get my coat.' Then I heard the cupboard in the next-door room being opened. For a few moments I believed that the people were real, which I felt was strange but not exactly frightening, but within a few seconds I realised it was a hallucination. If I had been a seventeenth-century person, however, I might well have assumed I had heard spirits of some kind.

20 Emma Wilby, *Cunning Folk and Familiar Spirits*, pp. 59–76, 244–52.

21 *Tales from the Green Valley*, DVD set produced and directed by Peter Sommer. This re-creation of rural life in the early seventeenth century by a group of historians and archaeologists gives an accurate picture of the hard work and ingenuity involved, but also shows that our ancestors had developed a sustainable lifestyle that delivered a reasonable standard of living for most people most of the time.

22 Emma Wilby, *Cunning Folk and Familiar Spirits*, Preface and pp. 66–70.

23 Chelmsford Quarter Sessions record, 1578, quoted in Alan Macfarlane, *Witchcraft in Tudor and Stuart England*, p. 125.

24 See, for example, Elizabeth Svoboda, 'Faces, Faces Everywhere', *New York Times*, 13 February 2007, which can be read on the New York Times website, www.nytimes.com.

25 Most early modern mirrors were made of polished steel, even though they were often referred to as 'looking glasses'.

26 Gösta Hedegård, *Liber Iuratus Honorii*, Introduction, pp. 36–40.

27 Gerald Gardner was an extremely influential figure in the development of modern Wicca and the modern pagan witchcraft movement in general. They may have been using the incense burner still in the museum, object id. no. 886 (see Chapter Two, note 31).

28 William Bottrell, *Stories and Folk-Lore of West Cornwall*, p. 120 ('Annual Visit of the West-Country Folks to the Pellar').

29 Daniel J. Driscoll (ed. and trans.), *The Sworn Book of Honourius the Magician*, Heptangle Books, Gillette, New Jersey, 1977, p. 97.

30 *WD* pp. B2v–B3.

31 Theodore Besterman, *Crystal-Gazing*, Chapter IX, 'The Mechanism of Scrying'; and see also Chapter VIII, 'The Procedure of Scrying and the Genesis of Visions'. See also Emma Wilby's section 'Trance-Inducing Techniques' in *Cunning Folk and Familiar Spirits*, pp. 177–184.

32 John Dee, Meric Casaubon (ed.), *A True and Faithful Relation of What Passed for Many Years Between Dr John Dee and Some Spirits*, 'Wednesday [15 June] a Meridie circa 2d 1583'.

33 John Dee, Meric Casaubon (ed.), *A True and Faithful Relation of What Passed for Many Years Between Dr John Dee and Some Spirits*, 'Tuesday Junii 18 An.1583. ante meridiem circa 9'.

34 John Dee, Meric Casaubon (ed.), *A True and Faithful Relation of What Passed for Many Years Between Dr John Dee and Some Spirits*, 'Wednesday [15 June] a Meridie circa 2d 1583'.

35 Heinrich Cornelius Agrippa, *The Three Books of Occult Philosophy*, translated by J.F., Book One, Chapter 44; hallucinogenic incenses are also mentioned in Chapter 43. (Incidentally, Heinrich Cornelius Agrippa's name was often anglicised as Henry Cornelius Agrippa, including in this translation.)

36 For the effects of a wide variety of plants used in magic see Richard Rudgley's fascinating book *The Encyclopaedia of Psychoactive Substances*, Abacus, London, 1999.

37 Rossell Hope Robbins, *The Encyclopedia of Witchcraft and Demonology*, pp. 355, 364; Richard Rudgley, *The Encyclopaedia of Psychoactive Substances*, p. 267. Johannes Nider's account is, however, third-hand.

38 Rossell Hope Robbins, *The Encyclopedia of Witchcraft and Demonology*, pp. 364–7; Richard Rudgley, *The Encyclopaedia of Psychoactive Substances*, pp. 262–70.

39 Rossell Hope Robbins, *The Encyclopedia of Witchcraft and Demonology*, p. 366.

40 Reginald Scot, *The Discovery of Witchcraft*, Book 10, Chapter 8.

41 Emma Wilby, *Cunning Folk and Familiar Spirits*, p. 249; Richard Rudgley, *The Encyclopaedia of Psychoactive Substances*, pp. 95–8. Psilocybe mushrooms may also have been eaten – they produce a sensation of physical warmth and euphoria that would have been very welcome after a hard day working outside in the cold and wet; but they're only hallucinogenic in very large quantities (Richard Rudgley, *The Encyclopaedia of Psychoactive Substances*, pp. 206–10).

42 John Baptista Porta, *Natural Magic*, Book 8, Chapter 2; anonymous English translation printed in London in 1658 (seventeenth-century translators had a habit of anglicising authors' names).

43 Kate Douglas, 'The other you', *New Scientist*, 1 December 2007, Vol. 196, No. 2632, pp. 42–6 (the cover headline is 'The smart, strange world of the subconscious').

44 For an intriguing account of Slavic cunning folk and their relationship with spirits see Andrija Filipovic and Anne Morris, 'Milking the Moon: Cunning-Folk in Southern Slavic Folklore', *The Cauldron*, May 2007, no. 124, pp. 29–34. Also special thanks to folk myth researcher James Downs for his thought-provoking correspondence.

45 John Dee, Meric Casaubon (ed.), *A True and Faithful Relation of What Passed for Many Years Between Dr John Dee and Some Spirits*, 'Wednesday [15 June] a Meridie circa 2d 1583'.

Chapter Fifteen: Black cats and black dogs
1 In his *Three Books of Occult Philosophy*, Heinrich Cornelius Agrippa argued that the pagan gods were simply aspects of the Christian God (Book 3, Chapter 10).

2 British Library MS Royal 17.A.XLII, ff. 67r–67v; 68r. Transcribed by Joseph H. Peterson on his website www.esotericarchives.com and also available on his Esoteric Archives CD.

3 Royal ff. 67v, 68v, 69r.

4 My translation from the Latin text in Gösta Hedegård, *Liber Iuratus Honorii*, p. 127. This section is not in the Royal manuscript.

5 My translation from the Latin text in Gösta Hedegård, *Liber Iuratus Honorii*, p. 143. This section is not in the Royal manuscript.

6 Emma Wilby, *Cunning Folk and Familiar Spirits*, pp. 129, 225–31, 254–7.

7 Translation by Kenneth Hurlstone Jackson, in his book *A Celtic Miscellany*, Penguin, Harmondsworth, 1986, p. 154.

8 Translation by Charlotte E. Guest in *The Mabinogion*, Longman, Brown, Green and Longmans, London, 1849.

9 Stephen de Bourbon (d. 1262) wrote an account of the cult in his *De Supersticione*, which can be read on the Internet Medieval Sourcebook website (editor Paul Halsall), www.fordham. edu/halsall/source/guinefort.html. The illustration in the Winchester Bible accompanies an account in the apocryphal Old Testament Book of Macabees of an attempt by King Antiochus to force the Israelites to worship idols. See Claire Donovan, *The Winchester Bible*, The British Library/Winchester Cathedral, London/Winchester, 1993, pp. 58–9. The deity bears a remarkable resemblance to the Egyptian cat goddess Bast. There may also be a connection between Bast and the cats depicted on Cornish fonts. Cornwall had been trading with the countries around the Mediterranean for centuries, and Cornish tin was one of the ingredients of Ancient Egyptian bronze; and Bast was the Egyptian goddess of childbirth.

10 St John D. Seymour, *Irish Witchcraft and Demonology*, pp. 25–53. This was a complicated case with political issues and conflict between Alice and other members of her family also playing a part.

11 Norman Cohn, *Europe's Inner Demons*, p. 227.

12 Chris Huet, *The Dark Companion: The Origin of 'Black Dog' as a Description for Depression*, on the Black Dog Institute website, www.blackdoginstitute.org.au/docs/Huet.pdf, citing C. Lindahl, J. McNamara, J. Lindrow (eds), *Medieval Folklore: An Encyclopedia of Myths, Legends, Tales, Beliefs and Customs*, ABC-Clio, Santa Barbara, 2000, Vol. 1, p. 233.

13 Heinrich Cornelius Agrippa, *The Three Books of Occult Philosophy*, translated by J.F., Book Three, Chapter 27. 'Threefold' because three different aspects of the spirit oversee three different aspects of the person's life.

14 Heinrich Cornelius Agrippa, *The Three Books of Occult Philosophy*, First Book, Chapter 3.

15 Note to the 1638 edition of Luke Hutton's pamphlet *The Discovery of a London Monster* (originally written c. 1596 under the title *The Black Dog of Newgate*). Republished in A.V. Judges (ed.), *The Elizabethan Underworld*, Routledge & Kegan Paul Ltd., London, 1965, p. 507. King Henry III ruled from 1216 to 1272. Phantom Black Dog researcher Alby Stone suggests that the Black Dog of Newgate, with his association with executions, may be linked to canine psychopomps – mythological beings who accompany the spirits of the dead to the Otherworld – such as the Egyptian jackal god Anubis ('Infernal Watchdogs, Soul Hunters and Corpse Eaters', Bob Trubshaw (ed.), *Explore Phantom Black Dogs*, pp. 36–56). Anubis was often depicted as black – the colour that symbolised life and renewal to the Egyptians, because it was associated with the black silt deposited by the Nile floods.

16 *A Strange and Terrible Wonder Wrought Here Very Late in the Parish Church of Bongay*.

17 Anon, *The Examination and Confession of Certain Witches at Chensforde in the County of Essex*, printed by William Powell for William Pickering, London, 1566. Elizabeth Frauncis is also one of the subjects of the pamphlet *A Detection of Damnable Drifts*, London, 1579, which describes her as Agnes Waterhouse's sister.

18 The picture is by E. Fitzpatrick, and appeared in the *Illustrated London News* on 31 December 1859. Museum of Witchcraft object id. no. 462 (see Chapter Two, note 31).

19 Object id. no. 2010. The museum also has two others – nos 1196 and 1494 (see Chapter Two, note 31). See also Brian Hoggard's folkmagic website www.apotropaios.co.uk.

20 Written in 1949, but first published in William Henry Paynter (edited by Jason Semmens), *The Cornish Witch-finder: William Henry Paynter and the Witchery, Ghosts, Charms and Folklore of Cornwall*, p. 162.

21 Quoted by Jennifer Westwood in 'Friend or Foe? Norfolk Traditions of Shuck', in Bob Trubshaw (ed.), *Explore Phantom Black Dogs*, pp. 57–8. Originally published in Christopher Reeve, *A Straunge and Terrible Wunder: The Story of the Black Dog of Bungay*, Morrow and Co., 1988, pp. 67–8.

22 There are some evocative descriptions of these rituals in Tony Hillerman's novel *Dance Hall of the Dead* (published in Britain in the collection *The Leaphorn Mysteries*, Penguin, London, 1994).

23 Since 1919 there have in fact been two Osses. Another important figure in the ceremony is the Teazer, who dances in front of the Oss. See Donald R. Rawe, *Padstow's Obby Oss and May Day Festivities*, Lodenek Press, Wadebridge, 1999; Violet Alford, *The Hobby Horse and Other Animal Masks*, The Merlin Press Ltd, London, 1978. The name may be linked to the verb 'oss' which means to wish good luck (*The Compact Edition of the Oxford English Dictionary*).

24 Richard Rudgley, *The Encyclopaedia of Psychoactive Substances*, p. 1.

25 Robert Pitcairn, *Criminal Trials of Scotland*, third volume, pp. 607–8.

26 For example, Henri Boguet, *Discours des Sorciers*, Chapters 24 and 46. He specifically says witches use ointments to change into wolves. According to Richard Rudgley in *The Encyclopaedia of Psychoactive Substances* (pp. 32–6), deadly nightshade (belladonna) – another ingredient of hallucinogenic ointments – can provoke a state of frenzy, which again suggests that these ointments could have been used to take on characteristics associated with wolves. Perhaps the association of wolf's bane (aconite) with wolves came originally from the fact that it was used to *turn into* them rather than to poison them.

27 Special thanks to folk myth researcher James Downs for his thought-provoking ideas on vampires, werewolves and other related subjects.

28 Aesop was a Greek writer (620–560 BCE); the first printed English edition of his Fables was published by William Caxton in 1484.

29 Francis James Child, *The English and Scottish Popular Ballads*, No. 113.

30 William Bottrell, *Traditions and Hearthside Stories of West Cornwall*, First Series, published by the author, Penzance, 1870, 'The Old Wandering Droll-Teller of the Lizard, and his Story of the Mermaid and the Man of Cury', pp. 61–7. Special thanks to Cassandra Latham for drawing my attention to this story.

31 See Emma Wilby, *Cunning Folk and Familiar Spirits*, pp. 100–105.

32 The famous Welsh poet Taliesin was bard to both Urien and Owein, and his poems have been edited, giving the original Celtic with English translations, and with an excellent introduction, by Meirion Pennar (*Taliesin Poems*, Llanerch Publishers, Felinfach, 1988). There is also a version of Owein's story in *The Mabinogion*, and the relationship between this version and Chrétien's is discussed by Jeffrey Gantz in the introduction to his translation of *The Mabinogion* (Penguin, Harmondsworth, 1976). For general information about Owein see the CeltNet website www.celtnet.org.uk.

33 Translation by W.W. Comfort, 'Yvain', in Chrétien de Troyes, *Arthurian Romances*, J.M. Dent & Sons Ltd, London, 1976 (first published 1914), p. 185. Yvain is the medieval French form of Owein's name. I have used the spelling given in the Celtic poems in Meirion Pennar's *Taliesin Poems*.

34 Chrétien de Troyes, *Arthurian Romances*, p. 191. Translation by W.W. Comfort.

35 Chrétien de Troyes, *Arthurian Romances*, p. 206. Translation by W.W. Comfort'

36 Seven is a magical number, representing the sun, moon and the five planets known before the invention of the telescope. It may also be a combination of the number three representing time – past, present and future – and the number four representing space – the four directions north, south, east and west (or in front, behind, right and left). The number of years Lutey had before his death, nine, is three times three. Three is a magical number in itself, perhaps

representing time, but also associated with the numerous trinities of gods in mythology. Three times three is therefore especially magical.

37 Chretien de Troyes, Arthurian Romances, p.208 and p.216, translation by W.W. Comfort. There is a fascinating Jungian analysis of this story by Heinrich Zimmer in his book *The King and the Corpse: Tales of the Soul's Conquest of Evil*, Princeton University Press/Bollingen Foundation, Princeton/Washington, 1973 (first published 1948). See also Paul Broadhurst, *The Green Man and the Dragon*, Mythos, Launceston, 2006, in particular the section 'The Sacrifice of the Green King', pp. 70–74. The various myths about kings who had to fight to retain their kingship were first studied in detail by James G. Frazer in his monumental work *The Golden Bough*. (1st edition Macmillan London, 1890, with a more accessible abridged edition published in 1922)

38 Chrétien de Troyes and Gerbert de Montreuil, (translated by Nigel Bryant), *Perceval*, D.S. Brewer, Cambridge, 1982, p. 257. This story seems to be connected with the *Corpus Christi Carol* and the folksong *The Bells of Paradise* (aka *Down in Yon Forest*). There is a suitably eerie version of the *Corpus Christi Carol* by Jeff Buckley on his CD *Grace* (Columbia); and there is a version of *The Bells of Paradise* by Alva on the CD *Songs of Witchcraft and Magic* (Museum of Witchcraft / WildGoose Records).

39 Bavarian State Library MS Clm 849 ff. 49r-v, in Richard Kieckhefer, *Forbidden Rites*, pp. 252–3.

40 This spell was collected by the folklorist and witchcraft researcher Margaret Murray, and published in Caroline Oates and Juliette Wood, *A Coven of Scholars: Margaret Murray and her Working Methods*, FLS Books, London, 1998, p. 57.

41 Emma Wilby discusses the giving of blood to familiars in *Cunning Folk and Familiar Spirits*, pp. 107–11; 143–5, 240.

Chapter Sixteen: Lancaster Prison

1 Abraham might have gone to Roger on 29 March, and it's possible that the family was also arrested then. The 29th was a Sunday, and on the one hand Abraham might have been nervous of interrupting Roger's day of rest, and on the other hand he might have felt that Sunday was an appropriate day to take action against witchcraft. However, we know that the search for witch marks happened on the 30th, and that makes the 30th the most likely day for the arrests at least.

2 Another reason Justices were obliged to take written statements was to combat witness intimidation. See Michael Dalton, *The Country Justice*, p. 264, 'Examination of Felons, and Evidence against them'; J.S. Cockburn, *A History of English Assizes*, p. 127.

3 *WD* p. Sv. This fixes the 29th as the earliest the family could have been arrested, since even if this evidence is untrue Abraham would hardly have given a date after Alizon had already been arrested.

4 *WD* p. R4v.

5 A number of things rule out the possibility that this was a flesh-and-blood dog belonging to Alizon: Abraham doesn't mention him, John doesn't say that he saw him when he was arguing with Alizon over the pins, and the dog appears before Alizon enters the ale-house, not with her. It's just possible that John was interviewed by Roger on the 29th, and this story about the Black Dog led Roger to prompt Alizon to include the dog in her confession; but in that case Abraham would surely have mentioned the dog in his 30 March statement.

6 *WD* p. F4. According to local tradition, to the house now known as Ashlar House (Jason Karl, *The Secret World of Witchcraft*, New Holland Publishers, London, 2008, p. 21).

7 It's possible that Alizon was also there; but it's likely that Roger was keeping Alizon separate from the rest of her family so that they wouldn't realise she'd confessed.

8 Prisoners who could afford it were supposed to pay for being transported to jail, and their

goods could be confiscated if they refused; if the prisoner couldn't afford to pay, the Justice raised the money from the local community by a special tax (Michael Dalton, *The Country Justice*, p. 79). The accounts of the landowning Shuttleworth family show that three months later they paid three shillings and tenpence towards the cost of transporting Margaret Pearson to Lancaster prison, so presumably the local landowners also paid for the transport of the Pendle suspects (Edgar Peel and Pat Southern, *The Trials of the Lancashire Witches*, pp. 141–2).

9 C. L'Estrange Ewen, *Witch Hunting and Witch Trials*, Kegan Paul, Trench, Trubner & Co. Ltd, London, 1929, pp. 31, 98ff.

10 Michael Dalton, *The Country Justice*, pp. 260, 262, 'Examination of Felons, and Evidence against them'; J.S. Cockburn, *A History of English Assizes*, pp. 102–4, 126–33. For crimes as a whole, on average only one in ten of those indicted for capital crimes were executed, but the majority of those who escaped were thieves saved by juries who undervalued the goods they had stolen to below the amount that would result in the death penalty.

11 Letter from John Wortham to the Justice of Assize, York, August 1642; petitions from the prisoners in York Castle, 1654; petition from Oxford prisoners to the local Justices, 1687; all in Andrew Barrett and Christopher Harrison (ed.), *Crime and Punishment in England: A Sourcebook*, Routledge, Abingdon, 1999, pp. 131–3.

12 *WD* p. O2.

13 Written around 1596. Republished in A.V. Judges (ed.), *The Elizabethan Underworld*, pp. 265–91.

14 J.S. Cockburn, *A History of English Assizes*, pp. 107–8, 120; petition from the prisoners in York Castle, 1654, in Andrew Barrett and Christopher Harrison (ed.), *Crime and Punishment in England: A Sourcebook*, p. 132.

15 Edgar Peel and Pat Southern, *The Trials of the Lancashire Witches*, pp. 161–3.

16 J.S. Cockburn, *A History of English Assizes*, p. 53.

17 Anon, *News from Scotland*.

18 Henri Boguet, *Discours des Sorciers*, Chapter 43.

19 In fact some guards, such as the sympathetic guard who gave Luke Hutton a candle, were themselves prisoners.

20 Petition of Oxford prisoners, 1687, in Andrew Barrett and Christopher Harrison (ed.), *Crime and Punishment in England: A Sourcebook*, p. 133.

21 Edgar Peel and Pat Southern, *The Trials of the Lancashire Witches*, p. 142.

22 Jan R. Veenstra, *Magic and Divination at the Courts of Burgundy and France*, p. 81.

23 C. L'Estrange Ewen, *Witch Hunting and Witch Trials*, p. 69.

Chapter Seventeen: The great assembly of witches

1 Albertus Magnus (attrib.), L.W. de Laurence (trans.), *Egyptian Secrets*, Volume II.

2 *WD* p. Yv.

3 William Bottrell, *Stories and Folk-Lore of West Cornwall*, p. 117, 'Annual Visit of the West-Country Folks to the Pellar of Helston'.

4 *WD* p. I2v.

5 *WD* pp. I3v–I4.

6 Or John Robinson might have promised James the sheep and then refused to give it to him because Elizabeth and Alizon had been arrested, and James might have taken it anyway. It's also possible that after Jennet told Roger about the sheep, James lied to protect John.

7 Exodus 12, the Geneva Bible.

8 In fact a T-shaped tau cross. Ernst Kitzinger, *Early Medieval Art*, British Museum Publications Ltd, London, 1983, cover, plate 13 and pp. 126–7.

9 Albertus Magnus (attrib.), L.W. de Laurence (trans.), *Egyptian Secrets*, Volume III

(derived from a passage in Book 1 of Heinrich Cornelius Agrippa's *Three Books of Occult Philosophy*).

10 Transcription by Joseph H. Peterson of British Library MS Sloane 3853 – a mid sixteenth-century manuscript containing large portions of *The Sworn Book* – on his website www.esotericarchives.com and his Esoteric Archives CD. This description of the Seal of God is in Latin in MS Royal 17.A.XLII (f. 12r). The substitution of 'lapwing' for 'hoopoe' is presumably because hoopoes are extremely rare in Britain, and the lapwing, which is also a crested bird, was considered an acceptable alternative.

11 Jan R. Veenstra, *Magic and Divination at the Courts of Burgundy and France*, pp. 351–5 (my translation).

12 William Bottrell, *Stories and Folk-Lore of West Cornwall*, p. 118.

13 The abracadabra charm is also mentioned by Henri Boguet in *Discours des Sorciers*, Chapter 35. Parchment is a comparatively non-absorbent surface, and scraping letters off with a knife is not difficult. In later versions of the spell the letters were often simply missed out as the charm was written. The Sator Square will be discussed in more detail later.

14 It may be no coincidence that the most widely used sacred name of God – AGLA – was also the one easiest for an illiterate or semi-literate person to copy.

15 King Solomon (attrib), (edited and translated by S. Lidell MacGregor Mathers), *The Key of Solomon*, Book II, Chapter XVI.

16 Heinrich Cornelius Agrippa, *Three Books of Occult Philosophy*, Book 1, Chapter 21, translation by J.F. Since it would be very difficult to get enough blood from a small animal like a bat to write out a talisman, in practice magicians must often simply have added a few drops to more conventional ink.

17 William Bottrell, *Stories and Folk-Lore of West Cornwall*, p. 118.

18 *WD* p. E3v.

19 The text of the 1604 *Act Against Conjuration, Witchcraft, and Dealing with Evil and Wicked Spirits* is published in full in Rossell Hope Robbins, *The Encyclopedia of Witchcraft and Demonology*, pp. 280–1. This was one of the changes to the law made by King James. If the teeth were obtained 12 years earlier, that was before it was illegal, and the fact that James Device specifically mentions when the teeth were acquired is further evidence of his knowledge of the law.

20 *WD* p. E3v–E4.

21 Anon, *The Examination of John Walsh*, p. A8.

22 Emma Wilby, *Cunning Folk and Familiar Spirits*, p. 39.

23 My translation from the Latin text in Gösta Hedegård, *Liber Iuratus Honorii*, p. 143. This section is not in the Royal manuscript. For a love-magic spell involving drawing an image of the woman on a tile with a pin and then invoking various spirits, see Richard Kieckhefer, *Forbidden Rites*, pp. 80–81.

24 Heinrich Kramer and Jacob Sprenger, trans. Montague Summers, *Malleus Maleficarum*, Part 3, 2nd Head, Question 15.

25 Early thirteenth century. Translation by P.G. Maxwell-Stuart, in his collection *The Occult in Mediaeval Europe*, p. 75.

26 *WD* p. H3.

27 Henri Boguet, *Discours des Sorciers*, Chapter 60, translation by E. Allen Ashwin (*An Examen of Witches*, John Rodker, 1929; republished by Portrayer Publishers, Appleton, 2002, pp. 200–201). There were several editions of *Discours des Sorciers*, and this chapter is not included in my French edition.

28 Brian Darcey, *A True and Just Record*, pp. B8–B8v.

29 *WD* p. C3.

30 A suspiciously papist act in itself.

31 British Library MS Royal 17.A.XLII, f. 47r. Transcribed by Joseph H. Peterson on his website www.esotericarchives.com and also available on his Esoteric Archives CD.

32 *WD* pp. I3v, I2v.

33 The Oxford English Dictionary gives a sixteenth-century example: 'Thy holy name is invocate and named upon us.' (*The Compact Edition of the Oxford English Dictionary*).

34 The text of the 1604 *Act Against Conjuration, Witchcraft, and Dealing with Evil and Wicked Spirits* is published in full in Rossell Hope Robbins, *The Encyclopedia of Witchcraft and Demonology*, pp. 280–81.

35 Al-Majriti (attrib.), (translated by Hashem Atallah, edited by William Kiesel) *Picatrix*, p. 132.

36 Albertus Magnus (attrib.), (edited and translated by L.W. de Laurence), *Egyptian Secrets*, Volume I. This is an adaptation of a spell in *The Book of Secrets of Albertus Magnus* – the one involving marigold, a bay leaf and a wolf's tooth, which could be used for preventing people from speaking ill of you, as well as for inducing a thief-detecting dream.

37 *The Book of Secrets of Albertus Magnus*, Third Book, 'Of the Virtues of Certain Beasts'.

38 Messayaac, *Liber de Angelis*, edited and translated by Juris G. Lidaka in Claire Fanger (ed.), *Conjuring Spirits*, p. 65.

39 This occurred to me when we were working on the photograph re-creating this spell, and it became obvious that Tom would rebel if asked to burn a dead spider. I've never actually seen a spider emerging, but I have seen one sitting beside its shed exoskeleton shortly afterwards, with the slit in the exoskeleton clearly visible, so I'm sure our ancestors would have been familiar with the process.

Chapter Eighteen: Charms and amulets

1 Printed by John Reid, Edinburgh, 1685, Relation XXXV 'Anent some Prayers Charms and Avies used in the Highlands' (at the end of the book). Note the references to making the sign of the cross at various places around the house. This supports the idea that James made the sign of the cross with the sheep's blood over the door of Malking Tower. Graham King, Director of the Museum of Witchcraft, has suggested to me that the phrase 'a cross of blue' in the Friday Spell may originally have been 'a cross of blood'.

2 *The Miller's Tale*. There is some debate about the meaning of the phrase 'for night very', but I consider that the most likely meaning is simply 'for the whole night'.

3 Jonathan Lumby, *The Lancashire Witch-Craze*, p. 98.

4 King James I, *Demonology*, First Book, Chapter VII. The Biblical quotation is Acts 7:22. This is a wonderful example of false logic – the argument that magic must be lawful because the Bible says that Moses studied it is countered by the claim that the Bible can't say that Moses studied magic because magic is unlawful.

5 See the explanatory note to the night-spell by F.N. Robinson in his edition of *The Works of Geoffrey Chaucer*, Oxford University Press, London, 1966, p. 685. He argues that the White Pater Noster was personified as St Peter's brother or sister because it was believed to grant access to heaven.

6 However, the Angel Gabriel was particularly associated with a charm he was supposed to have given the biblical character Susanna, which cured a wide range of illnesses including worms, ulcers and tumours (Tony Hunt, *Popular Medicine in Thirteenth-Century England*, pp. 90–91).

7 As Jonathan Lumby points out (*The Lancashire Witch-Craze*, pp. 100–101), it was St Peter and the other disciples Jesus found sleeping in the Garden of Gethsemane.

8 *Devon & Cornwall Notes & Queries*, April 5, 1851, No. 75, pp. 258–9 ('Charms from Devonshire', contributed by H.G.T. of Launceston). For more information about this and other charms see

Jonathan Roper, *English Verbal Charms*, Tony Hunt, *Popular Medicine in Thirteenth-Century England*, and Graham King, *The British Book of Charms and Spells*.

9   Raymond O. Faulkner (trans.), *The Ancient Egyptian Book of the Dead*, Book Club Associates / British Museum Publications, London, 1985, pp. 108–9 (Spells 112 and 113).

10 Remedy no. 93, translation by Stephen Pollington, in his book *Leechcraft*, p. 221. Stephen Pollington surmises that this is probably either a fever charm or a charm against the Nightmare – sleep paralysis. There is a preamble in which it is described as being 'against a dwarf', and which includes instructions for writing the names of the legendary Seven Sleepers of Ephesus on seven holy wafers and hanging them around the patient's neck.

11 Werner Forman and Stephen Quirke, *Hieroglyphs and the Afterlife in Ancient Egypt*, Book Club Associates / Opus Publishing Limited, London, 1996, pp. 23–4. See also Ramses Seleem's introductory chapters to his two translations of *The Book of the Dead* – *The Illustrated Egyptian Book of the Dead*, Godsfield Press, London, 2001, and *The Egyptian Book of Life*, Watkins Publishing, London, 2004. Ronald Hutton also discussed this aspect, and the crucial role, of Egyptian magic in his lecture 'A General Framework for the History of European Magic' at the Conference *Magical Practice and Belief 1800 to the Present Day* at the University of Bristol's Department of Historical Studies on 25 April 2003 (for a summary of the conference see the August 2003 issue (no. 109) of *The Cauldron*).

12 Heinrich Cornelius Agrippa, *The Three Books of Occult Philosophy*, translated by J.F., Book One, Chapter 1. Heinrich Cornelius Agrippa develops this idea at some length in the early chapters of the *Three Books of Occult Philosophy*, citing numerous earlier authors, in particular Plato and the Neoplatonists.

13 Heinrich Cornelius Agrippa, *The Three Books of Occult Philosophy*, translated by J.F., Book One, Chapter 12, and Book Three, Chapter 8.

14 E.A. Wallis Budge (trans.) *The Chapters of Coming Forth by Day or the Theban Recension of the Book of the Dead*, Kegan Paul, Trench, Trübner & Co. Ltd, London, 1910 (2nd edition, 3 volumes), Volume III, Chapter CXLV. Heinrich Cornelius Agrippa discusses sacred names in his *Three Books of Occult Philosophy*, Book Three, Chapter 11.

15 Kathleen McDonald, *How to Meditate*, Wisdom Publications, London, 1984, pp. 110–13, 119–20 and 171–7. Tara gave this mantra to an Indian teacher to enable him to cure his translator, who had fallen ill. It once saved me when I was paralysed with vertigo on a scary path up a Cornish cliff. See also Lama Yeshe, *Introduction to Tantra*, Wisdom Publications, Boston, 1987. Visualisation is still very important in modern British magical practice – see, for example, Michael Howard, *Way of the Magus*, Capall Bann Publishing, Milverton, Somerset, 2001.

16 Daniel Goleman, *The Meditative Mind: The Varieties of Meditative Experience*, The Aquarian Press, Wellingborough, 1989, pp. 52–8. The charm's Latin construction is unusual. It would normally be 'hoc signum vitae eternae' – 'this is a sign *of* eternal life'. Using the accusative – 'vitam eternam' – instead of the genitive strengthens the meaning of 'signum' from 'sign' to 'proof' ('this is proof/proves eternal life to be'), and at the same time results in a more rhythmic sound when the charm is spoken aloud (*Cassell's Latin Dictionary*, Cassell and Company, Ltd, London, 1946).

17 Albertus Magnus (attrib.), (edited and translated by L.W. de Laurence), *Egyptian Secrets*; the first quotation is from Volume I, the other two from Volume II.

18 *Cassell's Latin Dictionary*.

19 Ralph Merrifield, *The Archaeology of Ritual and Magic*, Book Club Associates / B.T. Batsford Ltd, London, 1987, pp. 142–7.

20 See Ian McNeil Cooke, *Sun Disc to Crucifix – The Cross – A Short Illustrated History*, Men-an-Tol Studio, Penzance, 1999.

21 Matthew Klemm, *Incantations in the Medical Philosophy of Petrus de Abano*, published online

at www.aseweb.org/Papers/Klemm.htm, analysing Pietro d'Abano's *Conciliator*.

22 Michael Brooks, '13 things that don't make sense', *New Scientist*, 19 March 2005 (Vol. 185, No. 2491), pp. 30–31. Fabrizio Benedetti's experiments involved the ability of the placebo effect to control pain, so the belief widely held by witch-trial interrogators that prisoners could use magic to resist torture may have had some truth behind it. Reginald Scot gives several charms apparently used, including the biblical quotation, 'You shall not break a bone of him' (*The Discovery of Witchcraft*, Book 12, Chapter 18).

23 See also Patrick Harpur, *The Philosophers' Secret Fire: A History of the Imagination*, Ivan R. Dee, Chicago, 2003.

24 Richard Wiseman, *The Luck Factor*, Century, London, 2003. Although full of interesting research, this book is so relentlessly upbeat that I felt compelled to pencil in a quotation from the Chaos Magick group the Lincoln Order of Neuromancers (acronym LOON) – 'Getting it right = confidence = success. Bo-ring. Be wrong!' (Apikorsus, published online at www. philhine.org.uk)

25 Reginald Scot, *The Discovery of Witchcraft*, Book 12, Chapter 9. According to Reginald Scot this charm gave protection against a whole range of dangers, and was also used in childbirth. See also Rossell Hope Robbins, *The Encyclopedia of Witchcraft and Demonology*, p. 86, citing Thomas Ady, *A Candle in the Dark*, London, 1656.

26 *Christian Charms/Prayers: Used by the Expatriate St Lucian Community in London 1960s+*, library id. no. 133.44 UNK 5076.

27 Object id. nos 1507–12, 1516, 1523, 1532–6, 1562–5, 1568–70, 1572–82, 1590 (see Chapter Two, note 31). See also Vanessa Chambers, 'A Shell with my Name on it: The Reliance on the Supernatural During the First World War', *Journal for the Academic Study of Magic*, issue 2, 2004, pp. 79–102.

28 Object id. nos 1567 and 1738.

Chapter Nineteen: The magic of objects

1 *Depositions from the Castle at York*, James Raine (ed), p. 127; quoted in Owen Davies, *Cunning Folk*, p. 36.

2 In Switzerland today, illnesses are still sometimes cured by placing a piece of paper in the sick person's mouth, then putting the paper in a box and burning it (personal communication from visitors to the Museum of Witchcraft).

3 Robert Pitcairn, *Criminal Trials in Scotland*, first volume, second part, p. 237. I've put this charm into modern English; in the original it reads:

> All kindis of illis that ewir may be, In Crystis name, I coniure ye; / I coniure ye, baith mair and les, With all the vertewis of the mess, / And rycht sa, be the naillis sa, That naillit Jesus, and na ma; / And rycht sa, be the samin blude, That reikit owre the ruithfull rwid; / Furth of the flesch and of the bane, And in the eird and in the stane. / I coniure the, in Godis name.

4 British Library MS Sloane 962; in Tony Hunt, *Popular Medicine in Thirteenth-Century England*, p. 97. In this case Saint Architeclyn is probably not Jesus but the guest of honour at the marriage at Cana. The time taken for the slit to close would stop you putting your horse back to work too soon.

5 J. Harland and T.T. Wilkinson, *Lancashire Folk-Lore*, Frederick Warne & Co., London, 1867, p. 156. Special thanks to Graham King for drawing this book to my attention. This cure was also used in Cornwall (*Devon & Cornwall Notes & Queries*, Autumn 1969, W.P. Authers, 'Three Cornish Cures (Mullion District)'.

6 Object id. no. 262 (see Chapter Two, note 31).

7 Henri Boguet, *Discours des Sorciers*, Chapter 37.

8 *The Way to the True Church*, quoted in J. Harland and T.T. Wilkinson, *Lancashire Folk-Lore*,

p. 115. The reference to the herb healing Jesus's wounds suggests that this was originally a wound charm adapted for use against witchcraft. The term 'owl-blasted' was still used in nineteenth-century Cornwall to mean 'cursed' (Jonathan Couch, *The History of Polperro*, p. 70).

9   *The Book of Secrets of Albertus Magnus*, First Book, 'Of the Virtues of Certain Herbs'.

10 *The Book of Secrets of Albertus Magnus*, Second Book, 'Of the Virtues of Certain Stones'.

11 *The Book of Secrets of Albertus Magnus*, Third Book, 'Of the Virtues of Certain Beasts'.

12 Object id. no. 721. The oyster shell probably offered protection against fire because of its association with water, and heart symbolism is often associated with protection as well as love.

13 Al-Majriti (attrib.), (translated by Hashem Atallah, edited by William Kiesel), *Picatrix*, Ouroboros Press, pp. 131 and 136.

14 Owen Davies, 'Healing Charms in Use in England and Wales 1700–1950', *Folklore*, Vol. 107 (1996), pp. 19–32. Special thanks to Helen Cornish for drawing my attention to this article.

15 George Gifford, *A Dialogue Concerning Witches and Witchcrafts*, p. Bv.

16 Reginald Scot, *The Discovery of Witchcraft*, Book 12, Chapter 9.

17 Audrey Meaney, 'Drift Seeds and the Brísingamen', *Folklore*, vol. 94, no. 1 (1983), pp. 33–9 (citing, among others, Martin Martin, *Description of the Western Isles of Scotland* (London, 1703)). Museum of Witchcraft object id. nos 1800, 1945, 1946. For more information about sea beans see the DVD *The Wrecking Season*, written by Nick Darke, directed by Jane Darke, and produced by Boatshed Films.

18 William Perkins, *A Discourse of the Damned Art of Witchcraft*, Chapter 3, Section 2.

19 King James I, *Demonology*, Third Book, Chapter V.

20 David Hamilton, *The Healers: a history of medicine in Scotland*, Canongate, Edinburgh, 1981, pp. 83 and 88–9. Special thanks to James Downs for drawing my attention to these accounts.

21 Richard Carew, *The Survey of Cornwall* (1602) Book 1. Also quoted in Robert Hunt, *Popular Romances of the West of England*, John Camden Hotten, London, 1871, p. 419.

22 Item ref. 1975.2568. There is a picture of it at www.gtj.org.uk/en/item1/17703.

23 Robert Hunt, *Popular Romances of the West of England*, p. 418.

24 Marie Trevelyan, *Folk Lore and Folk Stories of Wales*, Eliot Stock, London, 1909; Michael G. Bassett, *'Formed Stones', Folklore and Fossils*, National Museum of Wales, Cardiff, 1982.

25 Object id. no. 723. Bezoar stones are described in Thomas Nicols, *Lapidary: or The History of Precious Stones*, Cambridge, 1652, Part III, 'Of Non-transparent and Common Stones', Chapter LII.

26 *The Book of Secrets of Albertus Magnus*, Second Book, 'Of the Virtues of Certain Stones'.

27 Object id. nos 1943, 1944. Thomas Nicols, *Lapidary*, Part II, 'Of Semi-transparent Gems', Chapter XXXV.

28 Chinese doctors used 'dragons' bones' which were in fact dinosaur fossils – see the Strange Science website, www.strangescience.net/stdino2.htm.

29 Jan R. Veenstra, *Magic and Divination at the Courts of Burgundy and France*, p. 355.

30 T.I. 'A Memorial of Certain Most Notorious Witches', p. E3v, in Marion Gibson, *Early Modern Witches*.

31 Object id. no. 1038. According to William Henry Paynter, writing in 1932, a Cornish cure for toothache involved applying mole's skin to the tooth, wearing a bag of moles' feet helped teething children, and carrying a mole's tooth cured gout (William Henry Paynter, edited by Jason Semmens), *The Cornish Witch-finder: William Henry Paynter and the Witchery, Ghosts, Charms and Folklore of Cornwall*, pp. 115–16).

32 Robert Pitcairn, *Criminal Trials in Scotland*, first volume, second part, p. 212.

33 *News from Scotland* actually calls her Agnes Tompson at this point, but seems to mean the same person as Agnes Sampson. Richard Rudgley discusses this venom at length in *The Encyclopaedia of Psychoactive Substances*, pp. 232–40.

34 Albertus Magnus (attrib.), (edited and translated by L.W. de Laurence), *Egyptian Secrets*, Volume III. Note however that the toad's suffering was recognised, and inflicted because it was considered magically necessary – there was no attempt to dismiss it by arguing that the toad was so inferior to humans he was incapable of real suffering.

35 Object id. no. 138.

36 John Aubrey, *Miscellanies*, 'Magic'.

37 Heinrich Cornelius Agrippa, *The Three Books of Occult Philosophy*, Book One, Chapter 51.

38 William Henry Paynter (edited by Jason Semmens), *The Cornish Witch-finder: William Henry Paynter and the Witchery, Ghosts, Charms and Folklore of Cornwall*, p. 116. William Paynter also recorded the use of a string used to hang up a toad as a cure for quinsy and wearing a toad's leg in a bag as a cure for epilepsy (p. 105).

39 The Victoria & Albert Museum has one on display in its jewellery gallery, and there are no fewer than ten in the British Museum, which can be viewed on its website www.british-museum.org. Richard Kieckhefer describes a fourteenth-century Italian example in his book *Magic in the Middle Ages* (pp. 102–3, with a photograph on p. 104).

40 Thomas Nicols, *Lapidary*, Part II, 'Of Semi-transparent Gems', Chapter XXXVI.

41 Sydney Oldall Addy, *Household Tales with Other Traditional Remains*, 1895, quoted in Jacqueline Simpson and Steve Roud, *A Dictionary of English Folklore*, Oxford University Press, Oxford, 2000, p. 218.

42 Andrew D. Chumbley, *The Leaper Between: An Historical Study of the Toad-bone Amulet*, published online on *The Cauldron* website, http://web.archive.org/web/2004l015023500/www.the-cauldron.fsnet.co.uk/toad.htm (citing L.R. Hubbard (ed.), *I Walked by Night: Being the Life and History of the King of the Norfolk Poachers*, Ivor Nicholson and Watson Ltd, London, 1935, pp. 13–14, *Eastern Counties Magazine*, 1901, and *Lincolnshire* magazine, 1936, no. 24).

43 *An Act Against Conjuration, Witchcraft, and Dealing with Evil and Wicked Spirits*, 1604; quoted in full in Rossell Hope Robbins, *The Encyclopedia of Witchcraft and Demonology*, pp. 280–1.

44 Object id. nos 198, 236, 288, 289, 292 (skulls), 237 (part of a skull), 1731 (skull fragments), 497 (skull fragment with tooth). The corpse candle (a candle used at a wake) was unfortunately lost in the 2004 flood. William Paynter recorded the practice of carrying a tooth from a skull as a cure for toothache in 1932 William Henry Paynter (edited by Jason Semmens), *The Cornish Witch-finder: William Henry Paynter and the Witchery, Ghosts, Charms and Folklore of Cornwall*, p. 115).

45 Henri Boget, *Discours des Sorciers*, Chapter 35. Translation by E. Allen Ashwin, *An Examen of Witches* (again, this section is not included in my French edition).

46 Reginald Scot, *The Discovery of Witchcraft*, Book 12, Chapter 14.

47 Francis Jones, *The Holy Wells of Wales*, p. 115, citing *Gwyneddon 3*, p. 235. A local parson mentioned the practice in the late sixteenth century.

48 Richard Kieckhefer, *European Witch Trials*, p. 58 (citing Gene A. Brucker, 'Sorcery in Early Renaissance Florence', *Studies in the Renaissance*, X (1963), pp. 7–24).

49 Albertus Magnus (attrib.), edited and tranlated by L.W. de Laurence, *Egyptian Secrets*, Volume II.

50 J. Harland and T.T. Wilkinson, *Lancashire Folk-Lore*, p. 75.

51 Object id. nos 496, 1117. The use of human bone may have been particularly common in Cornish magic because the practitioner didn't necessarily have to go digging for it. In the mid nineteenth century, shifting sands uncovered many of the medieval graves at St Piran's Oratory at Perran Sands. On 6 December 1861, the local newspaper, *The West Briton*, wrote, 'It has been a constant practice, since public curiosity, for persons to dig up bones of the

dead at this ancient cemetery & church, now obliterated by the encroaching sand. They would carry off 3 or 4 skulls, a dozen of teeth, then a thigh bone etc, day after day, year after year. It is well known some people have boasted of their success in this new kind of oryctology.' One of the most insightful accounts of the use of human bone in magic is Tanith Lee's novel *The Castle of Dark* (HarperCollins, London, 1984).

52 Thomas R. Forbes, *The Midwife and the Witch*, Yale University Press, New Haven, 1966, pp. 133–8 (citing the letter of pardon that enabled Perrette to continue practising, published in A. Delacoux, *Biographie des sages-femmes célèbres, anciennes, modernes et contemporaines*, Trinquart and Delacoux, Paris, 1834, pp. 130–37).

53 Reginald Scot, *The Discovery of Witchcraft*, Book 12, Chapter 14.

54 Peter Linebaugh, 'The Tyburn Riot Against the Surgeons', *Albion's Fatal Tree: Crime and Society in Eighteenth-Century England*, Penguin Books, Harmondsworth, 1977, pp. 109–11. This essay also demonstrates that the crowds who attended executions were very different from the stereotype of the blood-thirsty mob.

55 Published in Lyon in 1782. Available (in the original French) on Joseph H. Peterson's Esoteric Archives website and CD. A Hand of Glory features in the film *The Wicker Man*.

56 My translation.

57 Object id. no. 346. Candles of this kind may in fact have been made from 'grave wax', a waxy substance produced during decomposition, which apparently makes excellent candles (Stephanie Pain, 'The illuminating Irtyersenu', *New Scientist*, 20/27 December 2008 (vol. 200, no. 2687/2688) pp. 72–3).

58 Richard Kieckhefer, *European Witch Trials*, p. 64 (citing Dietrich Kohl and Gustav Rüthning (eds), *Oldenburgisches Urkundenbuch*, I (Oldenburg, 1914), pp. 216f.).

59 Heinrich Cornelius Agrippa, *The Three Books of Occult Philosophy*, translated by J.F., Book One, Chapter 16.

60 Reginald Scot, *The Discovery of Witchcraft*, Book 12, Chapter 14.

61 Dr R. Ackerley, 'Charms and Superstitions Encountered in a Country Practice', *Transactions of the Devonshire Association for the Advancement of Science, Literature and Art* (*Thirteenth Report of the Committee on Devonshire Folk-Lore, 1895*), Vol. 27, p. 70.

62 *The Second Part of Henry IV*, Act 1, Scene 2.

63 John Gerard, *The Herbal or General History of Plants*, London, 1636 (enlarged edition), Second Book, Chapter 51, 'Of Mandrake'. See also C.J.S. Thompson, *The Mystic Mandrake*, Rider & Co., 1934; Museum of Witchcraft object id. nos 297, 1393, 1911–21.

Chapter Twenty: The magician of Colne

1 King James I, *Demonology*, First Book, Chapters 3 and 4.

2 *Christian Charms/Prayers: Used by the Expatriate St Lucian Community in London 1960s+*, library id. no. 133.44 UNK 5076.

3 Albertus Magnus (attrib) (edited and translated by L.W. de Laurence), *Egyptian Secrets*. Vol. 1

4 British Library MS Royal 17.A.XLII, f.67v. Transcribed by Joseph H. Peterson on his website www.esotericarchives.com and also available on his Esoteric Archives CD.

5 This case is analysed in detail by Jessica Freeman in her article 'Sorcery at court and manor: Margery Jourdemayne, the witch of Eye next Westminster', pp. 343–57. It is also discussed in Richard Kieckhefer, *Forbidden Rites* pp. 176–7.

6 See Chapter Eight, note 4.

7 This is the origin of the idea of the Black Mass.

8 Burning was also the punishment for treason for women, but Jessica Freeman has discovered that Margery was not in fact tried for treason.

9 *Tales from the Green Valley*, DVD set produced and directed by Peter Sommer.

10 Translation by Pierre Klossowski and Richard Robinson, in Georges Bataille, *The Trial of Gilles de Rais*, p. 218 (statement of Eustache Blanchet).

11 *The Examination of John Walsh*, pp. A4v, A5v.

12 John Aubrey, *Miscellanies*, 'Visions in a Beryl or Crystal'.

13 Karin Amundsen, 'The Duke's Devil and Doctor Lambe's Darling: A Case Study of the Male Witch in Early Modern England', *Psi Sigma Historical Journal*, Volume 2, Winter 2004; available online on the website of the University of Nevada, Las Vegas, www.unlv.edu/student_orgs/psisigma/index.html.

14 *WD* pp. D3v–D4.

15 Marion Gibson, *Early Modern Witches*, p. 193, note 51 (citing Walter Bennett, *The Pendle Witches*).

16 John Fian was also a schoolteacher, of course; and as well as the sinister crime of carrying moles' feet in his purse he also seems to have predicted the deaths of two people (Robert Pitcairn, *Criminal Trials in Scotland*, first volume, second part, pp. 212–13). This suggests that he may have practised astrology, and upset some of his clients by making unfavourable predictions.

17 *The Book of Secrets of Albertus Magnus*, Introduction p. xii.

18 Heinrich Cornelius Agrippa, *The Three Books of Occult Philosophy*, translated by J.F., London, 1651, Book One, Chapter 39.

19 Heinrich Cornelius Agrippa, *The Three Books of Occult Philosophy*, translated by J.F., London, 1651, Book One, Chapter 51.

20 Joseph H. Peterson's introduction, on his website www.esotericarchives.com.

21 Joseph H. Peterson's introduction to *Pseudomonarchia Daemonum*, on his website www.esotericarchives.com. For more information about this and books of magic in general, see also Owen Davies, *Grimoires: A History of Magic Books*, Oxford University Press, Oxford, 2009

22 Translation by Reginald Scot, *The Discovery of Witchcraft*, Book 15, Chapter 2. There had been other lists of spirits before (there's one in *The Munich Handbook*), but this seems to have been an attempt to produce a particularly detailed and definitive one. It went on to form part of another influential book of magic, of uncertain date, *Lemegeton* aka *The Lesser Key of Solomon* (see Joseph H. Peterson's introduction). The sexist description of Astaroth as male is disappointing, particularly as John Milton, in the early scenes of *Paradise Lost*, shows that he was well aware of Astaroth's links with the goddess Astarte.

23 Joseph H. Peterson includes several versions of *The Key of Solomon* on his website www.esotericarchives.com and his CD, all with informative introductions.

24 Joseph H. Peterson's introduction, on his website www.esotericarchives.com.

25 The use of the blade of a sword for scrying is mentioned by Etienne de Bourbon in his *Anecdotes historiques*, published in P.G. Maxwell-Stuart, *The Occult in Medieval Europe*, p. 83.

26 Richard Kieckhefer, *Magic in the Middle Ages*, p. 151 (citing John of Salisbury's *Policratus*, in Joseph B. Pike (trans.), *Frivolities of Courtiers and Footprints of Philosophers*, Oxford University Press, London, 1938, ii.28, pp. 146–7). For the different sizes of objects used for scrying see Theodore Besterman, *Crystal-Gazing*, Chapters VIII and IX.

27 Bavarian State Library, MS Clm 849 f. 49v, transcribed by Richard Kieckhefer in *Forbidden Rites*, p. 253. Sydrac, Misac and Abdenago were Biblical characters saved by a miracle after being thrown into a furnace for refusing to worship pagan gods (Daniel 3).

Chapter Twenty-one: A witness unexpected

1 Brian Darcey, *A True and Just Record*, pp. 2A3v–2A4, 2A5v–2A6, D–Dv. Two boys, cousins, the eldest about ten or twelve years old, were also used as witnesses against their mothers

and grandmother (Joan Cunny) in another Essex case a few years later in 1589; the Assize judge made a point of commending them for giving evidence (*The Apprehension and Confession of Three Notorious Witches*).

2 Jean Bodin, *De la Démonomanie des Sorciers*, Fourth Book, Chapter 1.

3 Henri Boguet, *Discours des Sorciers*, Chapter 48.

4 This evidence may have been one of the reasons she was banished instead of being executed.

5 Henri Boguet, *Discours des Sorciers*, Chapter 51.

6 Henri Boguet, *Discours des Sorciers*, Chapter 51.

7 Evidence from Pierre was also used against another suspect, Rollande du Vernois, who was burned, but his testimony was not decisive in her case (Henri Boguet, *Discours des Sorciers*, Chapter 58).

8 *WD* p. F2v.

9 *WD* p. C3.

10 Henri Boguet, *Discours des Sorciers*, Preface. A history of witchcraft in a particular place seems often to have been a factor in the witch hunts. For example, England's first major witchcraft case – Agnes Waterhouse and Elizabeth Frauncis – took place in Essex; this was followed by Brian Darcey's Essex witch hunt, a number of other cases, and of course Matthew Hopkins's notorious campaign, which began in Manningtree in Essex.

11 *WD* p. G3v and p. I3v. This may seem inconsistent with the reference to fasting in the Friday Spell, but the family themselves may have fasted from the previous evening, when the sheep was killed; or even from midday the previous day.

12 Thomas Potts in general represents Jennet's evidence as being verbal testimony given in court, but a number of factors make it clear that in fact for most of the time she was simply confirming written statements that were read out – for instance, the fact that this statement is word for word the same in two different trials. This will be discussed in more detail later.

13 See Chapter Ten, note 2.

14 Reginald Scot also used the word 'witches' for cunning folk in *The Discovery of Witchcraft*, and in *Demonology* King James I wrote, 'What form of punishment think ye merits these magicians and witches? For I see that ye account them to be all alike guilty? ... They ought to be put to death according to the Law of God, the civil and imperial law, and municipal law of all Christian nations ... I see ye condemn them all that are of the counsel of such crafts ... No doubt, for as I said, speaking of *magie* [magic], the consulters, trusters in, over-seers, entertainers or stirrers up of these crafts-folks, are equally guilty with themselves that are the practisers' (Third Book, Chapter 6.)

15 *WD* pp. G3v–G4 and p. I4.

16 In fact Jennet gives Christopher Hargreives's name as 'Christopher Jackes of Thorny-holme', but this is clearly the same person as the 'Christopher Hargreives, of Thurniholme' mentioned in James's statement (*WD* p. G4), as Jonathan Lumby points out in *The Lancashire Witch-Craze* (p. 45). It's possible that the Hargreiveses fled to avoid standing trial, but there is evidence against that in the records of the 1634 witchcraft case (which will be discussed later).

17 *WD* p. R2. There's nothing in *WD* about them being sent to Lancaster prison, and their names aren't included in the list of defendants who were acquitted on p. X. In *The Country Justice*, Michael Dalton goes into considerable detail about bail ('Bailment and Mainprise', pp. 269–83). The conditions were strict, and the Justice had to take a statement from the suspect, which would surely have appeared in *WD* if Christopher and Elizabeth had been bailed but then fled.

18 William Harrison, *The Description of England*, Book 2, Chapter 10, and Michael Dalton, *The Country Justice*, 'Rogues and Vagabonds', pp. 96–7.

19 The death of John's cow wouldn't necessarily have made him lose faith in the family's powers – if Elizabeth Sothernes had indeed let him think she might have killed the cow deliberately, it might have made him even more likely to pay an annual retainer and stay on the right side of the family.

20 King James I, *Demonology*, Second Book, Chapter 5.

21 *WD* pp. Y3v–Y4, Z2v–Z3.

22 This aspect of the case is analysed in detail by Jonathan Lumby in *The Lancashire Witch-Craze*.

23 *WD* p. Y.

24 *WD* p. Y3. For the dates of the Assizes see J.S. Cockburn, *A History of English Assizes*, pp. 15–48.

25 C. L'Estrange Ewen, *Witch Hunting and Witch Trials*, p. 95.

26 *WD* p. X.

27 *WD* p. X4v. Jonathan Lumby, *The Lancashire Witch-Craze* pp. 5–6.

28 Jonathan Lumby, *The Lancashire Witch-Craze* pp. 70–77.

29 *WD* pp. Z2v–Z3. For William Preston's Christian name see Jonathan Lumby, *The Lancashire Witch-Craze*, p. 7.

30 Jonathan Lumby, *The Lancashire Witch-Craze*, pp. 19–20, 49–50, 60.

31 *WD* p. Y4v.

32 *WD* pp. B4–B4v.

33 *WD* p. Y4.

Chapter Twenty-two: Therefore I have power of him

1 Anon, *Witches Apprehended*, pp. C2v–C3v.

2 *WD* pp. K, I2, H4v, G, GV. Again, Thomas Potts represents these statements as verbal evidence given in court, but they are in fact written statements (as will be discussed in more detail later).

3 Anon, *News from Scotland*.

4 John Bruce (ed.), *Calendar of State Papers, Domestic Series, of the Reign of Charles I, 1634–1635*, Longman, Green, Longman, Roberts, and Green, London, 1864, p. 152 (16 July 1634, entry 97); see also Edgar Peel and Pat Southern, *The Trials of the Lancashire Witches*, p. 97. As William is simply referred to as Jennet's half-brother, it is of course just possible that he was the son of John Device by an earlier marriage, and so not mentioned in *WD* because he was much older and not genetically related to Elizabeth Device. Or, indeed, he could have been the much older son of Elizabeth by a previous relationship, but in that case he would probably have been at the Good Friday gathering. However, there is a reference in *WD* to Elizabeth 'having a bastard child with one Seller' (p. F4v), and the reference in the State Papers shows that William was closely associated with Jennet, so the interpretation that he was her half-brother by a relationship Elizabeth had after John Device's death is the one that best fits the evidence.

5 Pierre Vuillermoz was handed over to relatives, on condition they ensured he received religious instruction to prevent him from going astray in future; but they can't have been very close relatives, because his uncle and grandmother had also been arrested (his mother was presumably dead, or she would almost certainly have been arrested along with Guillaume).

6 *WD* pp. H3–H3v.

7 Although it did mean that in James's statement Anne Towneley died two years earlier, whereas in Jennet's (which is more likely to be accurate, as she was coached by Roger, and

this statement of James's is so obviously a paste job) Anne Towneley died only one year earlier.

8 Brian Darcey, *A True and Just Record*, pp. B8v–C.

9 As will be discussed later. A mention by James that he saw the brown dog coming from Malking Tower at dusk one evening is included in the same statement as his description of various other strange psychic experiences, discussed in Chapter Ten.

10 Anon, *The Apprehension and Confession of Three Notorious Witches*, p. Bv. Reginald Scot also gives this as an argument used to reason with a woman suffering from depression who had convinced herself she'd sold her soul (*The Discovery of Witchcraft*, Book 3, Chapter 10).

11 *WD* p. B3v.

12 *WD* p. H4v.

13 Note also the obvious additions by Roger emphasising the fact that Jennet was an eyewitness to these events – 'in the presence of this examinate' and 'in this examinate's hearing'.

14 *WD* pp. H3v–H4.

15 Anon, *A Rehearsal Both Strange and True, of Heinous and Horrible Acts Committed by Elizabeth Stile*, London, 1579, p. A7v.

16 Reginald Scot, *The Discovery of Witchcraft*, Book 3, Chapter 7. The other pamphlet was *A Brief Treatise* by Richard Galis.

17 Henri Boguet, *Discours des Sorciers*, Chapters 23–30.

18 Gösta Hedegård (ed.), *Liber Iuratus Honorii*, pp. 39, 140.

Chapter Twenty-three: Curses

1 Messayaac, *Liber de Angelis*, edited with a parallel translation by Juris G. Lidaka, in Claire Fanger (ed.), *Conjuring Spirits*, pp. 58–61; this is my rather freer translation from Juris G. Lidaka's Latin text. The word I have translated 'markings' is *vestigia* – 'markings' or 'traces' – so it could refer to the place where the image was buried. However, the context suggests it refers to the markings on the image.

2 Richard Kieckhefer, *European Witch Trials*, pp. 52–3, 164.

3 Francis Jones, *The Holy Wells of Wales*, pp. 119–22, citing a book by Jac Ffynnon Elian (also known as John Evans) himself: *Hanes Troion Rhyfedd cyssylltiol â Ffynnon Elian, ac offeiriad y Ffynnon*, ed. H. Humphreys, Caernafon (no date). The 1736 Act repealing the earlier laws against witchcraft did not make practising magic legal, it simply demoted it to fraud. The use of holy wells for putting curses on people had ancient origins – see Ralph Merrifield, *The Archaeology of Ritual and Magic*, pp. 138–42.

4 Sometimes the initials were written on parchment which was then wrapped in a piece of lead sheet.

5 Colin Gregory, 'SWW calls on vicar to lift field curse', *Western Morning News*, 31 March 1997. See also Howard Balmer, *Stone to Rock, River to Sea: The Old Stones, Barrows and Antiquities of the Padstow Area*, Howard Balmer, Padstow, 2004.

6 Kelvin I. Jones, *An Joan the Crone: The History and Craft of the Cornish Witch*, Oakmagic Publications, Penzance, 1999, pp. 41–2. The twentieth-century wise woman Mother Herne is still remembered with mixed feelings by the inhabitants of her Somerset village. According to one particularly dramatic story, when she discovered that a local landowner had caught a poacher, she warned him not to prosecute, telling him that if he did he would never walk again. The landowner ignored the threat, went ahead with the prosecution, and not long afterwards had a car accident that left him confined to a wheelchair for the rest of his life (Personal communication from a visitor to the Museum of Witchcraft).

7 It may not be coincidence that the other people suspected of trying to curse Robert Nutter were his *female* cousins.

8 *WD* pp. E2–E2v.

9 A.K. Hamilton Jenkins, *Cornwall and its People*, David & Charles, Newton Abbot, 1983, pp. 296–7 (originally published in the 1930s, and referring to this incident as having happened thirty or forty years earlier).

10 Cecil Sharp, *English Folk-Carols*, Novello & Co. Ltd, London, 1911. There are various performances of this song available on CD, including one by Peter Bellamy, and one by Tom Brown on the CD *Songs of Witchcraft and Magic* produced by the Museum of Witchcraft and WildGoose Records.

11 *Christian Charms/Prayers: Used by the Expatriate St Lucian Community in London 1960s+*, library id. no. 133.44 UNK 5076.

12 Museum of Witchcraft object id. no. 223. See Chapter Two, note 31.

13 Object id. no. 232.

14 Object id. nos 40 and 231.

15 Kevin Tracey, 'The monster within', *New Scientist*, 2 April 2005 (Vol. 186, No. 2493), pp. 38–41; Yong-Ku Kim and Michael Maes, 'The Role of the Cytokine Network in Psychological Stress', *Acta Neuropsychiatrica*, June 2003, Vol. 15, Issue 3, pp. 148–55; Gregory E. Miller, Sheldon Cohen and A. Kim Ritchey, 'Chronic Psychological Stress and the Regulation of Pro-Inflammatory Cytokines: A Glucocorticoid-Resistance Model', *Health Psychology*, 2002, Vol. 21, No. 6, pp. 531–41 (published online at www.apa.org/journals/releases/hea216531.pdf). Healing magic could have the opposite effect, increasing the activity of the vagus nerve, reducing cytokine production and relieving illnesses caused by cytokines.

16 *WD* pp. E2v–E3. The pentacle was often regarded as a symbol of the five wounds of Christ, for example in the poem *Sir Gawain and the Green Knight*. A similar charm was used by the Lancashire cunning man Henry Baggilie (Jonathan Lumby, *The Lancashire Witch-Craze*, p. 95).

17 Francis Jones, *The Holy Wells of Wales*, p. 123.

18 Robert Pitcairn, *Criminal Trials of Scotland*, Third Volume, p. 609.

19 Domenico Mammoli (ed.), *The Record of the Trial and Condemnation of a Witch, Matteuccia di Francesco*. This is my translation from Domenico Mammoli's Latin text.

20 Heinrich Kramer and Jacob Sprenger, *Malleus Maleficarum*, Part 2, Question I, Chapter VI. This account originated in Johannes Nider's *Formicarius*, written around 1435. See also Richard Kieckhefer, *European Witch Trials*, pp. 81–2, which includes an account of Staedlin performing a ritual similar to the one invoking Zagam in *Liber de Angelis*. Staedlin was caught up in the persecutions spreading north from Italy, but although many of the victims were not magical practitioners, it seems that Staedlin was.

21 Sabine Baring-Gould, *Transactions of the Devonshire Association for the Advancement of Science, Literature and Art* (*Thirteenth Report of the Committee on Devonshire Folk-Lore, 1895*), vol. 27, p. 63. Special thanks to Graham King for alerting me to this source.

22 John Linwood Pitts (ed. and trans.), *Witchcraft and Devil Lore in the Channel Islands: Transcripts from the Official Records of the Guernsey Royal Court*, Guille-Alles Library and Thomas M. Bichard, Guernsey, 1886.

23 Chris Wingfield, 'Witches' Ladder: the hidden history', *England: the Other Within: Analysing the English Collections at the Pitt Rivers Museum*, http://england.prm.ox.ac.uk/englishness-witchs-ladder.html. The witches' ladder is Pitt Rivers Museum number 1911.32.7.

24 Francis Jones, *The Holy Wells of Wales*, pp. 117–23. Nineteenth century.

25 Fabyan Amery, 'Folk-lore gleanings', *Transactions of the Devonshire Association for the Advancement of Science, Literature and Art* (*First Report of the Committee on Devonshire Folk-Lore, 1876*), Vol. 8, p. 53. Nineteenth century.

26 Beatrice White, *A Cast of Ravens*, John Murray, London, 1965, p. 33. As with the case of Eleanor, Duchess of Gloucester, in the reign of Henry VI, this attempt by a young woman

at Court to use magic to take control of her destiny ultimately ended badly; though not for Simon Forman, who died of natural causes before the scandal broke.

27 Domenico Mammoli (ed.), *The Record of the Trial and Condemnation of a Witch, Matteuccia di Francesco*. My translation from the Latin/Italian text edited by Domenico Mammoli.

28 Thomas Middleton, *The Witch*, Act 1, Scene 2. The play was partly inspired by the case of the Earl of Essex mentioned above.

29 Jean Bodin, *De la Démonomanie des Sorciers*, Second Book, Chapter 1.

30 Francis James Child, *The English and Scottish Popular Ballads*, No. 6. There is a performance of this song by Martin Carthy on the CD *Songs of Witchcraft and Magic*, produced by the Museum of Witchcraft and WildGoose Records. For the type of fairy involved, see Katherine Briggs, *An Encyclopedia of Fairies, Hobgoblins, Brownies, Bogies, and Other Supernatural Creatures*, Pantheon Books, 1977, p. 23.

31 J. Harland and T.T. Wilkinson, *Lancashire Folk-Lore*, p. 75.

32 Jean Bodin, *De la Démonomanie des Sorciers*, Preface, and Fourth Book, Chapter 1. To be precise, Jean Bodin's account says that Jeanne put a spell on 'celuy qui avoit battu sa fille' – which could possibly mean a man who had beaten Jeanne's daughter. However, Randy A. Scott, in his translation (*On the Demon-Mania of Witches*, CRRS Publications, Toronto, 2001), interprets this as meaning a man who had beaten his own daughter, and I agree with his interpretation – particularly in view of how often Matteuccia was approached by women whose husbands beat them. However, even if the other interpretation is correct, the fact that Jeanne was initially so confident that she could cure the man who fell ill makes it clear that she *was* a wise woman, not just a scapegoat picked on because she had a grudge against another neighbour.

33 Todd Gray, 'Witchcraft in the Diocese of Exeter: Dartmouth, 1601–1602', pp. 230–8.

34 At the very start of William Perkins, *A Discourse of the Damned Art of Witchcraft*, and also Chapter 7, Section 4.

35 Reginald Scot, *The Discovery of Witchcraft*, Book 6, Chapters 1–2. Reginald Scot also expresses a similar view about the other key biblical passage condemning certain magical practices, Deuteronomy 18:10–11. Although King James was extremely hostile to magic, the Authorised Version of the bible that he had produced is in fact no more anti-magic in its translations than the earlier Geneva Bible. Exodus 22:18 is exactly the same in both translations, and Deuteronomy 18:10–11 very similar – although it does have several differences that illustrate the difficulties of translating obscure terms in an ancient language.

36 This practice is also mentioned (for example) in George Gifford's *Dialogue Concerning Witches and Witchcrafts*, p. C3.

37 *The Examination of John Walsh*, p. A6v.

38 *WD* p. E3.

39 British Library MS Royal 17 A X LII, f. 47r. Transcribed by Joseph H Peterson, available on his website www.esotericarchives.com and his Esoteric Archive CD

Chapter Twenty-four: Although she were their mother, they did not spare to accuse her

1 *WD* pp. F2–F3.

2 *WD* pp. G2–G2v.

3 *WD* pp. F4–F4v. In view of the fact that Jennet's age is given in *WD* as about nine, and, according to Alizon, John Device had died about eleven years earlier, Jennet could also have been illegitimate. However *WD* never refers to Jennet as Elizabeth's 'base' daughter (the adjective used, for example, in Brian Darcey, *A True and Just Record* to describe Ursley Kempe's son Thomas (p. 2A3v)), and pamphlets usually liked to emphasise their subjects' sexual misdemeanours. It also stresses that James was Jennet's 'own natural brother' – not her half-brother (*WD* p. I). More likely, Jennet was nearly ten, and John Device had died

slightly less than eleven years earlier, and Elizabeth was pregnant with Jennet at the time of her husband's death.

4 As with James's confession and Jennet's confirming it, there are several contradictions in all. According to James's statement, John Robinson died three years earlier, after Elizabeth had spent three weeks slowly crumbling the image, with John dying two days after the image was finally crumbled away. In Elizabeth's statement, John Robinson died four years earlier, she only spent a week crumbling the image, but John died a week after she'd finished. These are the kind of details people might not remember very clearly if it was something trivial they were discussing, but since it's a murder, you might expect their memories of what had happened to be quite vivid.

5 *WD* p. I2v. Presumably the John Robinson of Barley whose sheep James killed the evening before Good Friday was a relative (perhaps the son) of the John Robinson of Barley James's mother was suspected of killing three or four years earlier. The situation is further complicated by the fact that one of Jennet's statements (p. G3v) says that the owner of the sheep was Christopher Swyer; another copy of her statement abbreviates this just to 'Robinson's' (p. I3v). Alternatively, the reference to John Robinson in James's statement might be a clerk's mistake for Christopher Robinson.

6 *WD* p. I3.

7 *WD* p. G3.

8 This would also be the case if the change was the result of final drafts of the statements being prepared by Roger after Elizabeth Sothernes's death. Curiously, the general impression given is that Malking Tower was owned by Elizabeth Sothernes, and bequeathed by her to her daughter. In the seventeenth century, however, it was very unusual for ordinary people to own property – most rented the homes they lived in. Of course in practice people often inherited the tenancy just as if their families actually owned the property. But if Malking Tower *was* rented, clearly the landlords were happy for Elizabeth Sothernes to live there in spite of her supposed reputation as a witch, and for Elizabeth Device to inherit the tenancy even after both she and her mother had been arrested.

9 The whole statement is *WD* pp. B4–B4v.

10 *WD* pp. D3–D3v.

11 *WD* pp. D3v–D4.

12 *WD* p. E3v.

13 *WD* pp. G–Gv.

14 *WD* p. Zv.

15 *WD* pp. S–Sv.

16 J.S. Cockburn, *A History of English Assizes*, p. 109; Marion Gibson, *Reading Witchcraft*, pp. 50–72.

17 *WD* pp. O4v–P2.

18 In this case, however, this isn't conclusive evidence, since this is part of Jennet's evidence that Thomas Potts was particularly keen to represent as evidence given by her verbally in court, so he may have edited it to enhance that impression.

19 *WD* p. F4 etc. It would seem that this is a different location again from the house at Fence where the 2 April examinations took place.

20 Jean Bodin, *Démonomanie des Sorciers*, Fourth Book, Chapter 1.

Chapter Twenty-five: Such other witches as he knew to be dangerous

1 *WD* pp. F2v, C3, Y4.

2 See Chapter Ten, notes 2 and 27.

3 Clifford H. Byrne, *Newchurch-in-Pendle. Folklore, Fact, Fancy, Legends, Traditions & Information*, Marsden Antiquarians, Nelson, 1982, p. 25. W. Harrison Ainsworth makes much

of the land dispute in his novel *The Lancashire Witches* (Routledge, London, 1884).

4 See Jonathan Lumby, *The Lancashire Witch-Craze*, pp. 181–2, for some interesting details about this. Jonathan Lumby also discusses the question of how wealthy Alice Nutter was on pp. 86–7.

5 *WD* p. F4v. See also p. O4v.

6 *WD* p. Gv.

7 *WD* p. G2.

8 *WD* p. O4.

9 *WD* p. O3v.

10 *WD* pp. G4–G4v; also (with minor differences) pp. I2v–I3. The inhabitants of this part of Lancashire certainly had some strange names, but the name Mould-heeles is the strangest. It was not the suspect's name, though, but the name of her husband John. It's possibly related to the woman's name Maud, rather than anything to do with fungus (see E.G. Withycombe, *The Oxford Dictionary of English Christian Names*). 'Hele' means a hidden or covered place; so the name may mean something like 'from Maud's Covert'.

11 *WD* pp. Q3v–Q4 and R.

12 *WD* p. Q4v.

13 Jonathan Lumby disputes the assumption that the Mosse End mentioned is the same as the Moss End in Pendle Forest today, on the grounds that a Christopher Bulcock is mentioned living further north-east, in Wheatley Booth, in a list of tenants dated 1608/9 (*The Lancashire Witch-Craze*, p. 180); but this could be a different Christopher Bulcock. In any case, that is still within about four kilometres of Carre Hall.

14 Karin Amundsen, 'The Duke's Devil and Doctor Lambe's Darling: A Case Study of the Male Witch in Early Modern England', *Psi Sigma Historical Journal*, Volume 2, Winter 2004; available online on the website of the University of Nevada, Las Vegas, www.unlv. edu/student_orgs/psisigma/index.html.

Roger Nowell never arrested Thomas Redferne, in spite of obtaining evidence against him from James.

15 *WD* p. Q4.

16 *WD* p. P4. The words 'and also sayeth' probably refer to James, not the two women themselves.

17 Jonathan Lumby, *The Lancashire Witch-Craze*, pp. 51–2.

18 Jonathan Lumby, *The Lancashire Witch-Craze*, p. 80. Jonathan Lumby's book gives a thorough analysis of Thomas Heyber's and Thomas Lister's actions against Jennet Preston.

19 *WD* pp. Y2v–Y3.

20 King James I, *Demonology*, Third Book, Chapter 6.

21 *WD* pp. Y3v–Y4v. The section I have omitted from the middle is James's description of being taken to Gisburne to identify Jennet. For information about Leonard Lister see Jonathan Lumby, *The Lancashire Witch-Craze*, p. 50–51.

22 A table at the end of the pamphlet. For a detailed analysis of the descriptions of familiar spirits in British witchcraft trial records, see Emma Wilby, *Cunning Folk and Familiar Spirits*.

23 *WD* p. I4v.

Chapter Twenty-six: The Devil's Master

1 Michael Dalton, *The Country Justice*, pp. 242 and 244.

2 *WD* p. I2v. This of course contradicts the other evidence saying that the 'witches' agreed to meet again in a year's time at Jennet Preston's house. An earlier part of this section of *WD* says that the meeting at Malking Tower was for three reasons (the other two being 'naming' Alizon's spirit and killing Thomas and Leonard Lister) 'as this examinate's said mother told

this examinate'; but this is clearly just a way to use the statement to incriminate Elizabeth as well as James.

3 *WD* pp. I4–I4v.

4 J.S. Cockburn, *A History of English Assizes*, pp. 107–8.

5 Robert Pitcairn, *Criminal Trials in Scotland*, First Volume, Second Part, pp. 211, 236; *News from Scotland*. Moses Pitt's letter to the Bishop of Gloucester about Anne Jefferies mentions the large number of ballad and pamphlets that were produced in the wake of any witchcraft case.

6 After all, Eustache Blanchet's joke about Francesco Prelati summoning the Devil in return for a jug of wine was taken completely seriously by the Vice Inquisitor and the Bishop of Nantes.

7 Jonathan Lumby, *The Lancashire Witch-Craze*, p. 104; Richard Wilson, 'The pilot's thumb: *Macbeth* and the Jesuits', in Robert Poole (ed.), *The Lancashire Witches: Histories and Stories*, pp. 139 and 134. These two executions of course took place during the reign of Elizabeth I.

8 King James I, *Demonology*, Second Book, Chapter 5. *Demonology* was written after the supposed magical plot against him, so no doubt that didn't improve his attitude to cunning folk.

9 King James I, *Demonology*, Third Book, Chapter 6.

10 See Stephen Pumfrey, 'Potts, plots and politics', in Robert Poole (ed.), *The Lancashire Witches: Histories and Stories*, pp. 22–41. Thomas Potts refers to the Gunpowder Plot on p. F3.

11 Michael Dalton, *The Country Justice*, pp. 149–50.

12 George Fox, edited by Rufus M. Jones, *George Fox: An Autobiography*, Friends United Press, Richmond, Indiana, 1976 (first published 1908), Chapter XV. The dog was a mastiff, a type specially bred (in those days) for fighting. However, he refused to attack Quaker prisoners. As dogs are very sensitive to body language he probably recognised that they weren't a threat.

13 Jean Bodin, *Démonomanie des Sorciers*, Fourth Book, Chapter 1.

14 Jean Bodin, *Démonomanie des Sorciers*, Fourth Book, Chapter 3.

15 Henri Boguet, *Discours des Sorciers*, Article 17.

16 George Fox, edited by Rufus M. Jones, *George Fox: An Autobiography*, Chapter XV. See also Jenny Paull, *Prisoners of Conscience and Prison Visitors: The Quakers of Lancaster Castle*, on the Lancaster Castle website, www.lancastercastle.com/html/people/tour.php?id=40.

17 Luke Hutton *The Black Dog of Newgate*.

18 *Selected Cases of Conscience Touching Witches and Witchcraft*, London, 1646; this extract is quoted in Rossell Hope Robbins, *The Encyclopedia of Witchcraft and Demonology*, p. 509.

19 Peter Linebaugh and Marcus Rediker, *The Many-Headed Hydra: The Hidden History of the Revolutionary Atlantic*, Verso, London, 2000, p. 50. The use of torture had complex effects on both the prisoner and the torturer; see Sam Vaknin, 'The Psychology of Torture'.

20 *WD* pp. G3, P4v–Q, Q4v.

21 *WD* p. F4v. Note once again how Jennet is referred to as having 'confessed'.

22 *WD* p. G.

23 Adam J. Cohen, *Facial Trauma, Orbital Floor Fractures (Blowout)*, published on the eMedicine website, www.emedicine.com/plastic/topic485.htm, Dec 18, 2006; James R. Gallagher and Peter Ramsay-Baggs, 'ABC of eyes: Injury to the eye. Orbital injuries should not be considered in isolation' (letter), *British Medical Journal*, 2004 (13 March), published online at www.bmj.com/cgi/content/full/328/7440/644-a.

24 *WD* p. Q3. I have moved the position of the first bracket – the original text has 'which impudently now (at the bar having formerly confessed;) they forswear', which seems clearly wrong.

25 Henri Boguet, in his *Discours des Sorciers* (Article 19), shows that interrogators were keenly aware of the effect on prisoners of being held either with or separately from their fellow suspects.

26 *WD* pp. I4v–K.

27 British Library MS Royal 17.A.XLII, ff. 33v and 34v. Transcribed by Joseph H. Peterson on his website www.esotericarchives.com and also available on his Esoteric Archives CD. I have modernised the spelling of the word 'sprytes' to 'spirits'. The manuscript also indicates that the names of the spirits should be inserted at that point in the invocation.

28 Moses Pitt, letter to the Bishop of Gloucester.

29 Arthur Morrison, 'A Wizard of Yesterday', republished in Eric Maple and Arthur Morrison, *Marsh Wizards, Witches and Cunning Men of Essex*, p. 35.

Chapter Twenty-seven: The Trials

1 J.S. Cockburn, *A History of English Assizes*, pp. 109–11; for the chaining of defendants, see Susan Maria Ffarington (ed.), *The Farington Papers*, Chetham Society, Manchester, 1856, pp. 44–5.

2 John Bruce (ed.), *Calendar of State Papers, Domestic Series, of the Reign of Charles I. 1634–1635*, Longman, Green, Longman, Roberts, and Green, London, 1864, p. 79 (June 15 1634, item no. 85). The woman was Marie Spencer – more of her later. For the difficulties defendants experienced, see also Emma Wilby, *Cunning Folk and Familiar Spirits*, pp. 203–4.

3 J.S. Cockburn, *A History of English Assizes*, pp. 109–11.

4 See, for example, *WD* pp. D3, H2 and S.

5 J.S. Cockburn, *A History of English Assizes*, pp. 94–6, 122–3; *The Trial of Richard Hathaway*, a transcript of an early 18th-century trial, also gives a good indication of the way the judge could influence jurors in a way that would be considered unethical today.

6 *WD* p. Y.

7 *WD* pp. X3–Z3v. At York James Altham tried the criminal cases and Edward Bromley tried the civil cases. At Lancaster they swapped, with Edward Bromley trying the criminal cases. Jonathan Lumby's book *The Lancashire Witch-Craze* gives a detailed analysis of all aspects of Jennet Preston's case, and includes the relevant section of *WD* as an appendix.

8 *WD* pp. Y2, Y3. Thomas Potts tells us that the Devices' written statements were 'sent to these Assizes from Master Nowell', which seems to suggest that Roger wasn't in court either. However, this may simply reflect the fact that Roger couldn't formally present this evidence in court himself, because he was a Justice of the Peace for Lancashire, not Yorkshire (Michael Dalton, *The Country Justice*, p. 264). It seems hard to believe that Roger wouldn't have been present to give Thomas Heyber his support. Henry Hargreives's statement about Anne Whittle saying that Jennet Preston 'should have been at the said feast' at Malking Tower was also read out (p. Y4v).

9 Westby is about 8½ kilometres north of Newchurch as the crow flies.

10 *WD* p. Z2. The reference to the fact that Thomas Lister 'had prosecuted against her' suggests that he was behind the earlier charge.

11 *WD* p. Z2. Thomas Potts uses very similar phrases for some of the Lancaster trials, so he is perhaps simply trying to emphasise the conscientiousness of everyone involved in the case; but I think we can still assume that the jury took some time to reach a decision.

12 *WD* pp. X4v and Z2v–Z3. Marion Gibson, in her footnotes to her edition of *The Wonderful Discovery* in her book *Early Modern Witches* (p. 256, note 211, and p. 257, note 213), suggests that the author of the section of the pamphlet relating to Jennet Preston may not be Thomas Potts. It seems clear that this part was originally intended to be a pamphlet in itself (with the reference to the Lancaster trials on pp. Z2v–Z3 added later); however, in my opinion the stylistic differences can be explained by Thomas Potts getting into his stride as he wrote.

The author of the Jennet Preston section also refers to 'these honourable and reverend judges, under whose government we live in these north parts', implying that he lives in the northern counties, but in fact all the officials at the Assizes lived in London, so this must be just a propagandist device to give the impression that he's speaking for the local inhabitants.

13 *WD* pp. S3v–Tv.

14 *WD* p. S4v.

15 The statement begins with the words, 'The Friday next after, the said Pearson's wife, was committed to the jail at Lancaster,' which seems to mean that Jennet Booth was at the house after Margaret Pearson had been arrested, in which case the Margerie referred to can't be her. However, these words could perhaps have been transposed from the end of the statement, so that Jennet was saying that shortly after she'd been at Margaret's house Margaret was arrested. The fact that Margerie is referred to as 'the *said* Margerie' certainly suggests that Margaret is meant.

16 *WD* p. T.

17 *WD* pp. T–Tv.

18 Remembering that Nicholas Banester would have had to have taken written statements from all these people before the trial, and Thomas Potts would have had access to these written statements as well as his own recollections of what had happened in court.

19 *The Examination of John Walsh*, pp. A7–A8.

20 *WD* pp. V–Vv.

21 *WD* pp. Dv–Fv; the fact that Anne Redferne was charged jointly with her mother is revealed by Thomas Potts at N3v–N4.

22 *WD* p. D2.

23 *WD* p. Dv.

24 *WD* pp. F and D2.

25 In fact the two or three cases heard by each jury in these trials are rather less than normal (see J.S. Cockburn, *A History of English Assizes*, pp. 117–18); it's possible each jury also heard other cases not involving witchcraft that Thomas Potts doesn't mention. Of course this practice meant that if the cases were related the jury would inevitably be influenced by the evidence from all the cases they heard.

26 *WD* pp. F2–H.

27 *WD* p. F2.

28 *WD* p. F4v.

29 Jean Bodin, *Démonomanie des Sorciers*, Fourth Book, Chapter 2; Henri Boguet, *Discours des Sorciers*, Articles 53 and 56; Michael Dalton, *The Country Justice*, p. 261 ('Examination of Felons, and Evidence against them').

30 *WD* p. G.

31 *WD* pp. F4v–G.

32 *WD* p. G2v.

33 *WD* pp. Z2v–Z3.

34 *WD* p. X4v. In the 17th century the word 'friends' could mean relatives, but Thomas Potts uses the phrase 'friends and kinsfolks', and certainly gives the impression that there were a significant number of them.

35 At the end of Elizabeth's trial Thomas Potts says, 'She being taken away, the next in order was her son James Device' (p. H). His description of James then strongly implies that his first appearance in court was after his mother's trial. Even if James was physically in the courtroom, what Thomas Potts says about him makes it clear he didn't give his evidence in person. Interestingly, Michael Dalton also says in *The Country Justice* that James's evidence against Elizabeth was all in the form of written statements (p. 261).

36 *WD* pp. Hv–K2v.

37 *WD* pp. Hv–H2.

38 The Scottish cunning man John Stewart hanged himself (St John D. Seymour, *Irish Witchcraft and Demonology*, p. 87), and the German witchcraft suspect Rebecca Lemp wrote a letter to her husband pleading with him to obtain poison for her (Rossell Hope Robbins, *The Encyclopedia of Witchcraft and Demonology*, p. 304).

39 *Discours des Sorciers*, Chapter 45. The claim that the Devil sometimes killed prisoners himself was of course a useful explanation for prisoners dying as a result of ill-treatment.

40 *WD* p. H2. We can be quite sure here that Thomas Potts had access to a written statement from Henry Towneley – Roger Nowell would definitely have taken one, and Thomas Potts had access to all the statements taken by Roger, including the ones drawn up for Elizabeth Sothernes's trial, which were never used. So even if Henry gave his evidence in person and his statement wasn't read out, and Thomas Potts couldn't remember what Henry said in court, he could have consulted Henry's written statement to remind him, if he'd wanted to include his evidence in the pamphlet.

41 *WD* p. I. Thomas Potts says on p. H2 that Roger Nowell brought written statements into court to be used as evidence against James; but then on p. H4 he says, 'My lord Bromley commanded, for their better satisfaction, that the witnesses present in court against any of the prisoners, should be examined openly, *viva voce*, that the prisoner might both hear and answer to every particular point of their evidence; notwithstanding any of their examinations taken before any of his Majesty's Justices of Peace.' He then goes on to give what is clearly a written statement by Jennet, although he puts at the beginning, 'Being examined in open court, she sayeth ...' (p. H4v). Also, of course, we know that (in spite of this 'command' by Edward Bromley) Abraham Law's statement was read out. In fact what this seems to mean is that *if* witnesses (and this clearly did not include fellow prisoners) were present in court they were asked to confirm their statements on oath, and were perhaps asked to clarify certain points by the judge. Note that the statement that the defendants 'might both hear and answer to every particular point of their evidence' doesn't mean prisoners could actually question witnesses, but only try to explain or refute what witnesses had said.

42 Henri Boguet, *Discours des Sorciers*, Chapter 48.

43 *WD* p. I.

44 *WD* pp. Iv–I2.

45 *WD* p. I2.

46 *WD* p. Y4v.

47 *WD* pp. K2v and N3v–N4.

48 *WD* pp. K3–N3.

49 *WD* pp. N3v–O2v

50 *WD* p. O2.

51 George Fox, edited by Rufus M. Jones, *George Fox: An Autobiography*, Chapter XV.

52 According to Jean Bodin and Henri Boguet, the evidence of people who could be considered personal enemies of the accused was not admissible in Continental trials (Jean Bodin, *Démonomanie des Sorciers*, Fourth Book, Chapter 2; Henri Boguet, *Discours des Sorciers*, Article 55), although Henri Boguet argued that in witchcraft cases only mortal hatred should exclude a witness. Of course Margaret Crooke and John Nutter weren't Anne Redferne's enemies, but they *were* simply relating the accusations of someone who was. However, when Michael Dalton discusses the 'examination of felons, and the evidence against them' in *The Country Justice* (pp. 261–2), he only mentions evidence by known perjurers, and argues that a Justice should still take evidence from them, but make the objections to the witness clear to the judge, who should presumably then pass those objections on to the jury if he allowed the use of the witness. In English trials, therefore, the presumption seems to have been that unreliable witnesses could be used as long as the jury was aware of their unreliability.

53 *WD* pp. O3–P2v.

54 *WD* p. O4v

55 *WD* p. P2.

56 This included Christopher Hargreives's name instead of John Bulcock's, but that wouldn't matter because John Bulcock would be tried by a different jury.

57 *WD* p. P2.

58 *WD* p. P2v.

59 *WD* pp. P3–Qv.

60 *WD* p. Qv. Alice Gray's not guilty verdict is not mentioned, but she's included in a list of people who were acquitted on p. X. This list includes four other names – Elizabeth Astley, John Ramsden, Isabel Sidegraves and Lawrence Hay – who may also have been suspects in the Pendle case who were acquitted; but Thomas Potts gives no information about them. He does, however, include the name Grace Hay in a list of people who were at Malking Tower on p. Rv (the other names in this list are all people mentioned in the statements). Confusingly, he includes this list of acquitted suspects – including Alice Gray – in his list of the witches in Robert Houlden's case on p. C4, although this could be a printer's error.

61 *WD* pp. Q2–R.

62 *WD* p. R. This suggests that the identity parade was repeated at each trial; and it's certainly likely that it was at this trial, as it involved a new jury.

63 *WD* p. Q3.

64 *WD* p. R.

65 *WD* p. Z3.

66 *WD* pp. R2v–S2v.

67 Andrea Mckenzie, "This Death Some Strong and Stout Hearted Man Doth Choose': The Practice of Peine Forte et Dure in Seventeenth- and Eighteenth-Century England', *Law and History Review*, vol. 23, issue 2; also published online by *The History Cooperative*, www.historycooperative.org/journals/lhr/23.2/mckenzie.html. This is a fascinating but at times harrowing article about people who refused to plead as an act of protest or defiance.

68 The case of Isabel Robey, *WD* pp. T2–V. Isabel was convicted and executed.

69 *WD* p. R3.

70 *WD* p. R3. Thomas Potts is quite clear that Alizon was already at the bar when John Law was brought in, although he then says that Edward Bromley 'commanded that she should be brought out from the prisoners near unto the court'. Presumably Jane and John Bulcock were still also at the bar, although elsewhere Thomas Potts says that Thomas Covel removed the prisoners at the end of each trial before bringing in the next defendant (e.g. pp. Fv and H). He does say, however, that Jane, John and Alizon were all brought into court together (p. Q2), so perhaps it depended on how long the trials were likely to last.

71 *WD* pp. R3–R4.

72 *WD* p. R4v.

73 Discussed in Chapter Three.

74 *WD* p. S3.

75 This seems to have been technically legal, assuming Alizon *had* confessed in court (Michael Dalton, *The Country Justice*, p. 268); but Anne Whittle's guilt had been determined by the jury even though she had confessed.

Chapter Twenty-eight: Mocking Tower

1 *WD* p. P2v.

2 By James Crossley in the introduction to his edition of *The Wonderful Discovery* (Chetham Society, Manchester, 1845) (which is also quoted in John Harland and T.T. Wilkinson, *Lancashire Folklore*, p. 193). James Crossley mentions the boundary dispute, but also says some

of Alice's 'nearest relatives' were involved. This seems to be contradicted by Thomas Potts's admission that Alice was universally liked, and may be the result of people interpreting his comment about her refusing to confess as meaning that her children tried to persuade her to (which was probably what he intended people to think); however, in close-knit communities family feuds can be as fierce as family loyalties, so there may be some truth in it.

3 *WD* pp. V3–V3v. Of course the fact that Alice Gray was acquitted shows that the jury recognised that James's and Elizabeth's evidence was unreliable. Yet Katherine Hewit, Jane and John Bulcock and Alice Nutter were all convicted on similar, equally suspect, evidence. Any objective judge would have decided that this was grounds for a reprieve, to allow the cases against them to be reassessed. Edward Bromley, however, did not grant any reprieves. (If the judge did not grant a reprieve when he sentenced the prisoners, they were executed the following day. This obviously meant that defendants and their families had very little time after they were found guilty to organise an effective challenge to the verdicts. This was so clearly unjust that it wasn't unknown for Sheriffs – who organised the executions – to reprieve prisoners themselves, although this was illegal and could result in the Sheriff receiving a heavy fine, as well as incurring the enmity of the judge he had overruled. (Susan Maria Ffarington (ed.), *The Farington Papers*, p. 43.))

4 *WD* pp. V2 and A2v–A3v.

5 No doubt Thomas Potts wanted to flatter Thomas Covel by giving him credit for an impressive achievement under difficult circumstances.

6 Edgar Peel and Pat Southern, *The Trials of the Lancashire Witches*, p. 142.

7 Edgar Peel and Pat Southern, *The Trials of the Lancashire Witches*, p. 146. Nicholas Banester died within a year of the trials; Thomas Lister died in 1619, aged 28. Edward Bromley tried another witchcraft case at Lancaster in 1614 – the defendant, Cicilia Dawson, was executed (Jonathan Lumby, *The Lancashire Witch-Craze*, pp. 135, 156, 65). Edward Bromley is also mentioned as one of the Assize judges in the witchcraft pamphlet *The Wonderful Discovery of the Witchcrafts of Margaret and Phillip Flower* (London, 1619). In 1615 Thomas Potts was made keeper of Skalme Park, which seems to have been a sign that he was in particular favour with King James (Stephen Pumfrey, 'Potts, plots and politics', in Robert Poole (ed.), *The Lancashire Witches*, p. 38). As regards the other suspects mentioned in this book, whose fates I have not yet recorded: Mary Sutton and her mother were both hanged (*Witches Apprehended*); so were Ursley Kempe and Elizabeth Bennet; Annis Herd was acquitted (Marion Gibson, *Early Modern Witches*, p. 88, note 41, p. 89, note 46, p. 118, note 147); Joan Prentice was executed (*The Apprehension and Confession of Three Notorious Witches*), and so were Elizabeth Stile (*A Rehearsal Both Strange and True*) and Cecily Arnold (*A Memorial of Certain Most Notorious Witches*); Jone Waterhouse was acquitted, but her mother Agnes was hanged (*The Examination and Confession of Certain Witches*), and Elizabeth Frauncis was executed after being accused of witchcraft again thirteen years later (*A Detection of Damnable Drifts*, London, 1579); there is no record of Isobel Gowdie's sentence, but as she confessed to murder by witchcraft she was almost certainly strangled and burned; Bessie Dunlop was strangled and burned (Emma Wilby, *Cunning Folk and Familiar Spirits*, Preface, p. xv); Jeanne Harvillier, like her mother, was burned alive (Jean Bodin, *Démonomanie des Sorciers*, Preface); John Fian was recaptured; he retracted his confession and maintained his innocence with remarkable courage and strength of will through even worse torture than he had suffered before; even so, he was strangled and burned (*News from Scotland*); Edward Kelley died in prison in Hnevin Castle in what is now the Czech Republic. Many records do not include information about a suspect's fate. The pamphlet *The Examination of John Walsh* seems to have been written because John's case could be used as anti-Catholic propaganda, since he had been given his book of magic by a Roman Catholic priest. It doesn't tell us what became of him, so we don't know whether his examination led to a Church court trial.

He had, however, been arrested, since the pamphlet tells us that he was being held in the Sheriff's Ward, a prison just across the river from the old city of Exeter (p. A4). John may have cooperated with the Bishop of Exeter's representative because he hoped that would lead to him being tried by a Church court rather than sent to the Assizes. If he *was* tried by a Church court he would probably have been released after publicly forswearing magic. If he was tried at the Assizes he would probably have been sentenced to a year's imprisonment and four sessions in the pillory for thief detection. He could theoretically have been executed for spirit invocation, but that is very unlikely, as he insisted he had never harmed anyone by magic, and his interrogators seem to have accepted that, suggesting that no one from his community had accused him. Luke Hutton was rearrested and hanged for robbery (A.V. Judges, *The Elizabethan Underworld*, pp. 506–7). It may be significant that he wrote in *The Black Dog of Newgate* 'I made choice of the Black Dog of Newgate to be a subject to write upon. Wherein I could not choose … but in that title shadow the knavery, villainy, robbery and cony-catching [confidence tricks involving false arrest] committed daily by divers [various people], who in the name of service and office, were as it were attendants at Newgate. … But … it is meddling with edge tools. As you comprehend them in the name of a dog, so if they be angry, they will bite, and play the Devil in their likeness.'

8   As Henri Boguet had with Pierre Vuillermoz (Henri Boguet, *Discours des Sorciers*, Chapter 51).

9   In another of his books about witchcraft, *A Brief Discourse Wherein is Declared the Subtle Practice of Devils by Witches and Sorcerers* (London, 1587, p. G4v), George Gifford mentions child witnesses revealing that they've been coerced, and he paraphrases Febey's statement referring to her mother feeding her familiars on milk (Brian Darcey, *A True and Just Record*, pp. 2A5v–2A6), although he doesn't mention Febey by name. (Robin Briggs quotes this passage by George Gifford in *Witches and Neighbours* (Fontana Press, London, 1997), p. 235, and points out that George Gifford lived close to where Brian Darcey's witch hunt took place.)

10 Marion Gibson, *Early Modern Witches*, p. 95, note 72. Since George Gifford refers to children, in the plural, it seems likely that Febey wasn't the only witness to speak out; of the other three children involved, Thomas Rabbet's mother Ursley Kempe was executed, and Henry and John Selles's parents died in prison, but Henry and John had an older brother who probably survived (Marion Gibson, *Early Modern Witches*, p. 88, note 41, p. 100, note 86).

11 Jonathan Lumby, *The Lancashire Witch-Craze*, p. 117. A search of the Access2Archives website reveals several documents referring to Roger Nowell junior.

12 Edmund's father insisted that he never accused any of the suspects, but was 'sent for by warrant to bring his son before Mr Shuttleworth and Mr Starkie' – John Bruce (ed.), *Calendar of State Papers, Domestic Series, of the Reign of Charles I. 1634–1635*, p. 144 (July 12, 1634, item 69). This document gives Edmund's place of residence as Newchurch. Edmund Robinson's official statement (which was taken at Paddiham) is included as a kind of appendix at the end of John Webster's book *The Displaying of Supposed Witchcraft* ('printed by J.M.', London, 1677); a slightly different version of Edmund's statement was included by James Crossley in his introduction to his edition of *The Wonderful Discovery*; and a version probably taken from James Crossley's was published in John Harland and T.T. Wilkinson, *Lancashire Folklore*, pp. 195–7. The spelling of the names varies considerably in the different documents. Where the names are clearly related to ones in *The Wonderful Discovery* I have used the spellings that occur there; otherwise I have used the spellings in the jail list in Susan Maria Ffarington, *The Farington Papers*, p. 27; otherwise the ones that seem easiest to read or make most sense. The original versions of Edmund's statement are dated 1633 because the legal year didn't begin until March. Hoarstones was empty because it had only just been built.

13 Edmund's statement suggests that as well as hearing stories about the earlier Pendle witchcraft case based on people's memories of what happened, he had also heard stories based on *The Wonderful Discovery*, because Thomas Potts's account of the case involving Robert Houlden includes evidence from fourteen-year-old Grace Sowerbuts that one of the suspects turned herself into a dog, and also a description of her being carried to a place where the three suspects offered her magical food (*WD* pp. L, L2v).

14 Edmund Robinson's statement published at the end of John Webster's *The Displaying of Supposed Witchcraft*.

15 John Bruce (ed.), *Calendar of State Papers*, p. 152 (July 16, 1634, item 97). John Bruce abbreviates the original documents, and in places slightly paraphrases what he does include. The examining Justice was George Long, one of the Justices of the Peace for Middlesex.

16 John Bruce (ed.), *Calendar of State Papers*, p. 152; Edmund's statement in John Webster, *The Displaying of Supposed Witchcraft*.

17 John Bruce (ed.), *Calendar of State Papers*, p. 152 (see note 15).

18 The Jennet Hargreives mentioned in 1612 was the wife of Hugh Hargreives; the Jennet Hargreives mentioned in 1634 was married to Henry Hargreives, according to the State Papers, but he's referred to as Henry Jackes in Edmund Robinson's statement; and Christopher Hargreives was also known as Christopher Jackes according to *The Wonderful Discovery*.

19 Her name isn't one of those included in the list at the end of Edmund's statement (see also note 23).

20 John Bruce (ed.), *Calendar of State Papers*, p. 78 (June 15, 1634, item 85). A statement taken by the Bishop of Chester on 13 June 1634.

21 This is in a manuscript of an earlier confession published in John Harland and T.T. Wilkinson, *Lancashire Folklore*, pp. 198–9, and which they say is from 'Dodworth's Collection of MSS, vol LXI, p. 47'. In his introduction to the Wonderful Discovery, James Crossley says that Margaret made this confesstion on 2 March 1634 before John Starkie and Richard Shuttleworth.

22 Edmund's statement at the end of John Webster's *The Displaying of Supposed Witchcraft*; John Harland and T.T. Wilkinson, *Lancashire Folklore*, pp. 195–7.

23 John Webster, *The Displaying of Supposed Witchcraft*, pp. 277–8. As well as Margaret Johnson, there were other suspects not named by Edmund – twenty-year-old Marie Spencer and her parents, from Burnley, were accused by a man called Nicholas Cunliffe (John Bruce (ed.), *Calendar of State Papers*, pp. 78–9).

24 John Bruce (ed.), *Calendar of State Papers*, pp. 77–9. Marie Spencer also told the Bishop than Nicholas Cunliffe had 'borne malice to her and her parents these five or six years'. Frances Dicconson also pointed out that Edmund Stevenson, who had made a statement against her, had just been accused of a felony himself (and it would be interesting to know if he was already suspected of the crime when he made the statement). The other three prisoners who had died were Marie Spencer's parents and a woman called Alice Higgin. Jennet Hargreives was seriously ill.

25 See notes 23 and 24.

26 John Bruce (ed.), *Calendar of State Papers*, pp. 129–30 (July 2, 1634, item 9). They found an extra nipple on Margaret Johnson, but noted that there was no issue of liquid from it.

27 John Bruce (ed.), *Calendar of State Papers*, p. 141 (July 10, 1634, item 57) and pp. 152–3.

28 John Bruce (ed.), *Calendar of State Papers*, p. 141 (see note 15).

29 John Bruce (ed.), *Calendar of State Papers*, pp. 144 and 152–3 (see note 15). It seems the juror had been contacted by John Dicconson.

30 *WD* p. X.

31 Susan Maria Ffarington, *The Farington Papers*, p. 27. The situation regarding names is confused by the fact that people often used more than one surname.

32 When he was being taken round the local villages by two men (one of them presumably his father) who claimed he could detect witches (John Webster, *The Displaying of Supposed Witchcraft*, pp. 277–8. Part of his account is also quoted in John Harland and T.T. Wilkinson, *Lancashire Folklore*, pp. 200–201). Kildwick church is not far from Jennet Preston's home, Gisburne.

33 John Webster, *The Displaying of Supposed Witchcraft*, pp. 277–8. See also Jonathan Lumby, *The Lancashire Witch-Craze*, pp. 152–61, for his account of John Webster and his book.

34 Alison Findlay, 'Sexual and spiritual politics in the events of 1633–4 and *The Late Lancashire Witches*', in Robert Poole (ed.), *The Lancashire Witches*, p. 162. Henry Burton had reason to be a little ill-tempered as he'd just had his ears cut off.

35 Alice Molland's execution is recorded in the Exeter Gaol Delivery Roll for March 1685 (dated 1684 at the time, as the legal year began on 25 March), quoted in C. L'Estrange Ewen, *Witchcraft and Demonialism*, Heath Grafton Limited, London, 1933, p. 444. The 1604 act was replaced in 1736 by an act condemning 'pretences to such arts or powers as are before mentioned, whereby ignorant persons are frequently deluded and defrauded', and making one year's imprisonment and four one-hour sessions in the pillory the punishment for anyone who should 'pretend to exercise or use any kind of witchcraft, sorcery, enchantment, or conjuration, or undertake to tell fortunes, or pretend, from his or her skill or knowledge in any occult or crafty science, to discover where or in what manner any goods or chattels, supposed to have been stolen or lost, may be found'. During the Civil War the radical group known as the Levellers made several attempts to get the legal system reformed, as well as calling for democracy and the abolition of the laws on heresy and blasphemy. The result was that the Levellers were ruthlessly suppressed. Two of their campaigning documents, the *Great Petition* of 11 September 1648 and *An Agreement of the Free People of England* of 1 May 1649, can be read online.

36 In his book *Philosophiae Naturalis Principia Mathematica*.

37 The last person to be executed in Britain for blasphemy was a scientist – the Edinburgh University medical student Thomas Aikenhead, who was hanged in 1697 for denying the existence of Hell, arguing that the bible was mythology, and suggesting that there might be a scientific explanation for Jesus's miracles. In a courageous pre-execution statement, he defended himself with the words, 'It is a principle innate and co-natural to every man to have an insatiable inclination to truth, and to seek for it as for hid treasure.' *A Complete Collection of State Trials*, compiled by T.B. Howell (T.C. Hansard, London, 1812) (aka *Cobbett's Complete Collection of State Trials*), vol. XIII, pp. 918–39, *Proceedings against Thomas Aikenhead*).

38 Isaac Newton, *Optics* (London, 1704), Query 28.

39 The complete decoded text of the charm is given by John Harland and T.T. Wilkinson in *Lancashire Folklore*, pp. 63–7; and there is a picture of the charm and an analysis of it by Ralph Merrifield in his book *The Archaeology of Ritual and Magic*, pp. 148–50. One of these charms is now at the Pendle Heritage Centre and the other in Clitheroe Museum.

40 Messayaac, *Liber de Angelis*, edited by Juris G. Lidaka, in Claire Fanger (ed.), *Conjuring Spirits*, pp. 67–8 (my translation).

41 Apanton, Hora, Camab, Naadgrass, Pynavet Ayias, Araptenas, Quo, Signasque, Payns, Sut Gosikl, Tetragrammaton, Inverma, Amo, Theos (abbreviated), Dominus, Deus, and Hora. Another name is missing where the paper has been damaged.

42 My translation.

43 With the word 'fiat' instead of Amen.

44 Ralph Merrifield, *The Archaeology of Ritual and Magic*, p. 150.

45 William Perkins, *A Discourse of the Damned Art of Witchcraft*, Chapter 7, Section 4.

Bibliography

PRIMARY SOURCES

In the main text and notes I have modernised title spellings, but here they are spelled as they were when originally published. Some modern editions keep the original spelling; others modernise it.

Abraham of Worms (translated by S.L. MacGregor Mathers), *The Book of the Sacred Magic of Abramelin the Mage*, The De Laurence Company Inc., Chicago, 1932. Modern editions include ones by Dover Publications, The Book Tree and Cosimo Classics. Also available on Joseph H. Peterson's website www.esotericarchives.com, and his Esoteric Archives CD. There's also a new translation by Steven Guth (edited by Georg Dehn) published by Ibis Press.

R. Ackerley, 'Charms and Superstitions Encountered in a Country Practice', *Transactions of the Devonshire Association for the Advancement of Science, Literature and Art* (*Thirteenth Report of the Committee on Devonshire Folk-Lore, 1895*), vol. 27.

Acts of Parliament. The 1563 and 1604 Acts are published in Rossell Hope Robbins, *The Encyclopedia of Witchcraft and Demonology*, Spring Books, Feltham, 1968; Barbara Rosen, *Witchcraft in England, 1558–1618*, University of Massachusetts Press, 1991; and C. L'Estrange Ewen, *Witchcraft and Demonianism*, Frederick Muller Ltd, London, 1933. The 1736 Act can be read on Owen Davies's website www.cunningfolk.com.

Sidney Oldall Addy, *Household Tales with Other Traditional Remains*, David Nutt, London, 1895. There are modern editions by Kessinger, HardPress and Cornell University Library.

Aesop, *Fables* (the first English translation was published by William Caxton in 1484). There are numerous modern editions, and it is also available online, for example on www.aesopfables.com.

Henrich Cornelius Agrippa, *Three Books of Occult Philosophy*, written 1509–1510. English translation by J.F. printed in 1651. This translation (with Agrippa's name given as Henry Cornelius Agrippa) is available on Joseph H. Peterson's website www.esotericarchives.com, and his Esoteric Archives CD. Modern editions of Book One (*Natural Magic*) include ones by Kessinger Publishing, BiblioLife and Cosimo. A new edition translated (with extensive notes) by Donald Tyson has recently been published by Llewellyn.

W. Harrison Ainsworth, *The Lancashire Witches*, Routledge, London, 1884. There are numerous modern editions of this novel.

Albertus Magnus (attrib.) (edited and translated by L.W. de Laurence), *Egyptian Secrets: White and Black Art for Man and Beast*, de Laurence, Scott & Co., Chicago, 1914. There are modern editions by Health Research and Kessinger Publishing. Also available on Joseph H. Peterson's website www.esotericarchives.com, and his Esoteric Archives CD.

Albertus Magnus (attrib.), *The Book of Secrets of Albertus Magnus*, late thirteenth century, with English translations printed from the mid-sixteenth century. There is a modern edition by Michael R. Best and Frank H. Brightman, published by Red Wheel/Weiser. A photographic copy of the 1604 London edition can be read online on the Farlang Gem and Diamond Foundation website, www.farlang.com.

Al-Majriti (attrib.) (translated by Hashem Atallah edited by William Kiesel), *Picatrix (Ghayat Al-Hakim – The Goal of the Wise)*, Ouroboros Press, Seattle, 2002.

Fabyan Amery, 'Folk-lore gleanings', *Transactions of the Devonshire Association for the Advancement of Science, Literature and Art (First Report of the Committee on Devonshire Folk-Lore, 1876)*, vol. 8, p. 53.

Anon, *The Apprehension and Confession of Three Notorious Witches*, 1589 (the record of the case of Joan Prentice and Joan Upney). There is a modern edition in Marion Gibson, *Early Modern Witches: Witchcraft Cases in Contemporary Writing*, Routledge, Abingdon, 2000.

Anon, *A Detection of Damnable Driftes*, London, 1579 (the record of the second case involving Elizabeth Frauncis). There is a modern edition in Marion Gibson, *Early Modern Witches: Witchcraft Cases in Contemporary Writing*, Routledge, Abingdon, 2000.

Anon, *The Examination and Confession of Certaine Wytches at Chensforde in the Countie of Essex*, printed by William Powell for William Pickering, London, 1566 (the record of the case of Elizabeth Frauncis, Agnes Waterhouse and Jone Waterhouse). There are modern editions in Marion Gibson, *Early Modern Witches* and Barbara Rosen, *Witchcraft in England, 1558–1618*, University of Massachusetts Press, 1991.

Anon, *The Examination of John Walsh*, printed by John Awdely, London, 1566. The original manuscript record of the examination is Chanter MS 855B ff. 310–12, in the Devon Record Office (a photocopy and transcript is available for study at the Museum of Witchcraft's research library). Modern editions of the pamphlet are included in Marion Gibson, *Early Modern Witches*; Barbara Rosen, *Witchcraft in England, 1558–1618*; and G.J. Davies, *Touchyng Witchcrafte and Sorcerye*, Dorset Record Society, 1985.

Anon, *The Lenkiewicz Manuscript*. A late sixteenth- or early seventeenth-century manuscript book of magic, which belonged to the Plymouth artist Robert Lenkiewicz. Robert Lenkiewicz had a number of facsimile copies made so that researchers could study the book without damaging the original manuscript. There is a copy available for study (together with a transcript) at the Museum of Witchcraft's research library.

Anon, *The Most Strange and Admirable Discovery of the Three Witches of Warboys*, Printed by the Widow Orwin, for Thomas Man, and John Winninton, London, 1593 (the record of the case of the Samuel Family). There are modern editions in Philip C. Almond, *Demonic Possession and Exorcism in Early Modern England: Contemporary Texts and Their Cultural Contexts*, Cambridge University Press, Cambridge, 2004 and (abbreviated) in Barbara Rosen, *Witchcraft in England, 1558–1618*.

Anon, *The Most Wonderful and True Story of a Certain Witch Named Alice Gooderige*, Printed for J.O., London, 1597. There is a modern edition in Philip C. Almond, *Demonic Possession and Exorcism in Early Modern England*.

Anon, *Newes from Scotland, Declaring the Damnable Life and Death of Doctor Fian, a Notable Sorcerer*, printed for William Wright, London, 1591. A modern edition is included in the edition of King James I's *Demonology* published by The Book Tree.

Anon, *A Rehearsal Both Straung and True, of Hainous and Horrible Actes Committed by Elizabeth Stile*, London, 1579. There is a modern edition in Marion Gibson, *Early Modern Witches*.

Anon, *The Tryal of Richard Hathaway for Endeavouring to Take Away the Life of Sarah Morduck for Being a Witch*, Isaac Cleave, London, 1702. This pamphlet is available for study in the Museum of Witchcraft's research library.

Anon, *The Witches of Northamptonshire*, printed by Thomas Purfoot for Arthur Johnson, London, 1612. There is a modern edition in Marion Gibson, *Early Modern Witches*.

Anon, *Witches Apprehended, Examined and Executed, for Notable Villainies by them Committed both by Land and Water*, printed for Edward Marchant, London, 1613 (the record of the case of

Mary Sutton). There is a modern edition in Marion Gibson, *Early Modern Witches*.

Anon/Unknown, *Christian Charms/Prayers, used by the expatriate St Lucian community in London 1960s+*, manuscripts in the library of the Museum of Witchcraft.

Lucius Apuleius, *The Golden Ass*; translated into English by William Adlington in 1566. There is a modern edition published by Murrays Book Sales.

Nicholas Assheton, (edited by F.R. Raines), *The Journal of Nicholas Assheton*, The Chetham Society, Manchester, 1848.

John Aubrey, *Miscellanies Upon the Following Subjects*, Second Edition, printed for A. Bettesworth, J. Battley, J. Pemberton and E. Curll, London, 1721 (first published in 1696). Modern editions include ones by The Echo Library, Kessinger, Centaur Press and BiblioLife. It can also be read online on the Project Gutenberg website, www.gutenberg.org.

W.P. Authers, 'Three Cornish Cures (Mullion District)', *Devon & Cornwall Notes & Queries*, Autumn 1969.

William Baldwin, *Beware the Cat*, 1570. William A. Ringler prepared a modern text of this book from a transcript in the British Library of the lost first edition, which was published by Huntington Library, San Marino, California in 1988.

Sabine Baring-Gould, *Transactions of the Devonshire Association for the Advancement of Science, Literature and Art* (*Thirteenth Report of the Committee on Devonshire Folk-Lore, 1895*), vol. 27, p. 63.

Andrew Barrett and Christopher Harrison (eds), *Crime and Punishment in England: A Sourcebook*, Routledge, Abingdon, 1999. Includes transcripts of Church court and Quarter Sessions trials, and accounts of prison conditions.

Georges Bataille (ed.), Pierre Klossowski (trans.) and Richard Robinson (trans.), *The Trial of Gilles de Rais*, Amok Books, Los Angeles, 2004. Georges Bataille's long introduction includes some important additional facts, but his analysis is fatally undermined by the fact that he was writing in the 1960s, when information about the other witchcraft cases that led up to Gilles's arrest was not available.

Bernardino of Siena's sermons, in Franco Mormando, *The Preacher's Demons: Bernardino of Siena and the Social Underworld of Early Renaissance Italy*, The University of Chicago Press, Chicago, 1999, and Alan Charles Kors and Edward Peters (ed.), *Witchcraft in Europe, 400–1700: A Documentary History*, University of Pensylvania Press, Philadelphia, 2000 (2nd edition, revised by Edward Peters), translation by John Shinners (this sermon also published in John Shinners, *Medieval Popular Religion*, Broadview Press, Ontario, 1997).

Theodore Besterman, *Crystal-Gazing: A Study in the History, Distribution, Theory and Practice of Scrying*, William Rider & Son Ltd, London, 1924. There are modern editions by Kessinger and University Books.

Bibles: Throughout the Middle Ages the version of the Bible generally used was the Latin Vulgate Bible. This can be read online at www.latinvulgate.com (which also includes the Douay-Rheims Bible (1609–10). The English translation mainly used in the early seventeenth century was the Geneva Bible (first published in 1560, available in a modern facsimile edition by Hendrickson Publishers, Inc.); it was only gradually replaced by the Authorised King James Version (first published in 1611).

Joseph Blagrave, *Blagrave's Astrological Practice of Physick*, Printed for Obadiah Blagrave, London, 1689 (first published 1671). There is a modern edition by Kessinger.

Jean Bodin, *De la Démonomanie des Sorciers*, Paris, 1580. The preface includes the Paris *Determinatio* of 1398. A facsimile edition was published by Georg Olms Verlag, Hildesheim, 1988. There is an English translation (abridged) by Randy A. Scott, with an introduction by Jonathan L. Pearl, *On the Demon-Mania of Witches*, published by The Centre for Reformation and Renaissance Studies, Toronto, 2001.

Henri Boguet, *Discours des Sorciers*, Jean Pillehotte, Lyon, 1610 (first edition 1602). There is a modern French edition, *Discours Execrable des Sorciers*, edited by Philippe Huvet with an introduction by Nicole Jacques-Chaquin, published by Le Sycomore, Paris, 1980. There is an English translation by E. Allen Ashwin, *An Examen of Witches*, John Rodker, 1929; republished by Portrayer Publishers, Appleton, 2002. There were several seventeenth century editions of *Discours des Sorciers*, so the chapter references I give for the quotations may differ by a chapter in E. Allen Ashwin's translation.

George Bores, *A True Discourse. Declaring the damnable life and death of one Stubbe Peeter, a most wicked sorcerer, who in the likenes of a woolfe, committed many murders*, London, 1590. This can be read online on a number of websites.

William Bottrell, *Stories and Folk-Lore of West Cornwall*, Third Series, published by the author, Penzance, 1880.

William Bottrell, *Traditions and Hearthside Stories of West Cornwall*, First Series, published by the author, Penzance, 1870. Modern editions of William Bottrell's books include ones by Llanerch Publishers, Kessinger and Cornell University Library.

John Bruce (ed.), *Calendar of State Papers, Domestic Series, of the Reign of Charles I. 1634–1635*, Longman, Green, Longman, Roberts, and Green, London, 1864 (records of the 1634 Pendle case, on pp. 77–9, 98, 129–30, 141, 144, 152–3).

E.A. Wallis Budge (trans.), *The Chapters of Coming Forth by Day or the Theban Recension of the Book of the Dead*, Kegan Paul, Trench, Trübner & Co. Ltd, London, 1910 (republished by Arkana in 1985).

John Gregorson Campbell, *Witchcraft and Second Sight in the Highlands and Islands of Scotland*, James MacLehose & Sons, Glasgow, 1902. There is a modern edition by E.P. Publishing Ltd.

Richard Carew, *The Survey of Cornwall*, 1602. There is a modern edition, edited by F.E. Halliday, published by Andrew Melrose Ltd, London, 1953.

Geoffrey Chaucer, *The Canterbury Tales*. Modern editions include F.N. Robinson (ed.), *The Works of Geoffrey Chaucer*, Oxford University Press, London, 1966.

Francis James Child, *The English and Scottish Popular Ballads*, Boston, 1882–1898. There are modern editions by Dover and BiblioLife. Also available online, for example on the Sacred Texts website, www.sacred-texts.com.

Chrétien de Troyes (translated by W.W. Comfort), *Arthurian Romances*, J.M. Dent & Sons Ltd, London, 1976 (first published 1914).

Chrétien de Troyes and Gerbert de Montreuil (translated by Nigel Bryant), *Perceval*, D.S. Brewer, Cambridge, 1982.

Jacques du Clercq, *Mémoires*, extracts translated by P.G. Maxwell-Stuart in his collection *The Occult in Mediaeval Europe*, Palgrave, Basingstoke, 2005. (The record of the Arras case.)

F.C. Conybeare (trans.), *The Testament of Solomon*, an apocryphal book of the Old Testament, first to third century, describing Solomon's power over demons. Available on Joseph H. Peterson's website www.esotericarchives.com, and his Esoteric Archives CD.

Jonathan Couch, *The History of Polperro*, Frank Graham, Newcastle-upon-Tyne, 1965 (first published 1871).

Aleister Crowley, (with the assistance of the spirit Aiwaz), *The Book of the Law (LiberAL vel Legis)*, *The Equinox*, (the journal of the O.T.O. (*Ordo Templi Orientis*)), Vol. I, No. X, (1913). There is a modern edition published by Red Wheel/Weiser.

Nicholas Culpeper, *Culpeper's English Physician and Complete Herbal*, London, c.1794 (first published 1653). There are numerous modern editions.

Michael Dalton, *The Countrey Justice*, printed for the Society of Stationers, London, 1618. A facsimile edition has been republished by The Lawbook Exchange, Ltd, Clark, New Jersey, 2003.

John Graham Dalyell, *The Darker Superstitions of Scotland*, Edinburgh, 1835.

Brian Darcey (W.W.), *A True and Just Recorde of the Information, Examination and Confession of all the Witches, taken at St Oses in the Countie of Essex*, Printed by Thomas Dawson, London, 1582 (W.W. is almost certainly a pseudonym for the Justice of the Peace Brian Darcey; if not, W.W. was little more than an editor for Brian Darcey's documents). (The record of the case of Ursley Kempe, Elizabeth Bennet, Ales Hunt, Cysley Selles and Annis Herd). There are several modern editions of this pamphlet: it is included in Marion Gibson, *Early Modern Witches* and Barbara Rosen, *Witchcraft in England, 1558–1618*; and there is a facsimile edition with an introduction by Anthony Harris published by Scholars' Facsimiles and Reprints.

John Darrell, *A True Narration of the Strange and Grievous Vexation by the Devil of Seven Persons in Lancashire*, 1600 (one of the records of the case of Edmund Hartlay). Republished in John Ashton, *The Devil in Britain and America*, Ward & Downey Ltd, London, 1896, with modern reprints by Kessinger Publishing and Newcastle Publishing Co.

John Dee (edited by Meric Casaubon), *A True and Faithful Relation of What Passed for Many Years Between Dr John Dee and Some Spirits*, London, 1659. There are modern editions by Askin Publishers and Kessinger Publishing.

Frederick Thomas Elworthy, *The Evil Eye*, John Murray, London, 1895. There are numerous modern editions.

Etienne de Bourbon, *Anecdotes Historiques*, extracts translated by P.G. Maxwell-Stuart in his collection *The Occult in Mediaeval Europe*.

Dionysius Exiguus, *Canones*, 'Canons of the Council of Laodicea', extracts translated by P.G. Maxwell-Stuart in his collection *The Occult in Mediaeval Europe*. Raymond O. Faulkner (trans.), *The Ancient Egyptian Book of the Dead*, Book Club Associates/British Museum Publications, London, 1985.

Susan Maria Ffarington (ed.), *The Farington Papers*, Chetham Society, Manchester, 1856 (includes a record of the 1634 Pendle case – Thomas Covel's list of imprisonned witches).

Celia Fiennes (edited by Christopher Morris), *The Journeys of Celia Fiennes*, The Cresset Press, London, 1947. (Originally published as *Through England on a Side Saddle in the Time of William and Mary*, edited by Emily Griffiths (1888).)

Nicholas Flamel (attrib.), *Alchemical Hieroglyphics*, London, 1624. A modern edition was published by Heptangle Books, New Jersey, in 1980.

Abraham Fleming, *A Strange and Terrible Wonder Wrought Here Very Late in the Parish Church of Bongay*, 1577. There is a modern edition published by Kessinger.

George Fox (edited by Rufus M. Jones), *George Fox: An Autobiography*, Friends United Press, Richmond, Indiana, 1976 (first published 1908). Available online on the Street Corner Society website, www.strecorsoc.org.

Hans Fründ's account of the Valais witch trials – extracts can be read in the Wikipedia article *Valais witch trials* (http://en.wikipedia.org/wiki/Valais_witch_trials)

Richard Galis, *A Brief Treatise Containing the Most Strange and Horrible Cruelty of Elizabeth Stile*, 1579. There is a modern edition in Marion Gibson, *Early Modern Witches*.

Jeffrey Gantz (trans.), *The Mabinogion*, Penguin, Harmondsworth, 1976.

Moses Gaster (trans.), *The Sword of Moses*, London, 1896. Available on Joseph Peterson's website www.esotericarchives.com, and his Esoteric Archives CD.

John Gaule, *Selected Cases of Conscience Touching Witches and Witchcraft*, London, 1646.

John Gerard, *The Herbal or General History of Plants*, London, 1636 (enlarged edition, first published 1597). There is a facsimile version of the 1633 edition published by Dover.

George Gifford, *A Dialogue Concerning Witches and Witchcraftes*, printed by John Windet for Tobie Cooke and Mihil Hart, London, 1593. A facsimile edition was published by The Shakespeare Association and Oxford University Press, London, 1931. There are also modern editions by Kessinger Publishing and Puckrel Publishing.

Joseph Glanvil, *Sadducismus Triumphatus, or Full and Plain Evidence Concerning Witches and Apparitions*, London, 1681.

Todd Gray (ed.), 'Witchcraft in the Diocese of Exeter: Dartmouth, 1601–1602', *Devon & Cornwall Notes & Queries*, Spring 1990, vol. 36, part 7, pp. 230–8. This is an edition of the statements against the Trevysard family. The record of the execution of Michael and Alice Trevysard is the Exeter Gaol Delivery Roll included in the Quarter Sessions Order Book for 1602 in Devon Record Office (ref. QS/1/2). Peter Trevysard's marriage record is one of the Bishop's Transcripts for St Clement's Church published on the Dartmouth History Research Group's website, www.dartmouth-history.org.uk.

Todd Gray and John Draisey (eds), 'Witchcraft in the Diocese of Exeter: Part IV. Whimple (1565), Chawleigh (1571) & Morwenstow (1575)', *Devon & Cornwall Notes & Queries*, Autumn 1991, vol. 36, part 10, p. 367 (the record of the case of Margaret Lytlejohn).

F.Ll. Griffith and Herbert Thompson (ed. and trans.), *The Leyden Papyrus: An Egyptian Magical Book*, Dover Publications, New York, 1974 (first published 1904).

Charlotte E. Guest (trans.), 'The Dream of Rhonabwy', in Charlotte E. Guest, *The Mabinogion*, Longman, Brown, Green and Longmans, London, 1849. Modern editions include ones by Dover, Llanerch and The Echo Library. Also available online on the Sacred Texts website, www.sacred-texts.com.

Bernardo Gui, *Practica inquisitionis heretice pravitatis*, extracts translated by P.G. Maxwell-Stuart in his collection *The Occult in Mediaeval Europe*.

H.G.T. of Launceston, 'Charms from Devonshire', in *Devon & Cornwall Notes & Queries*, 5 April 1851, No. 75.

John Harland and T.T. Wilkinson, *Lancashire Folk-Lore*, Frederick Warne & Co., London, 1867 (this includes the records of the Pendle 1634 case from James Crossley's introduction to *The Wonderful Discovery* (with modernised spelling, and with Margaret Johnson's confession slightly cut)). There is a modern edition by Kessinger. Also available online at www.archive.org/details/lancashirefolkloooharlrich).

William Harrison, *The Description of England*, 1587. There is a modern edition edited by Georges Edelen and published by The Folger Shakespeare Library and Dover Publications, Inc.

Honorius of Thebes and the Angel Hocroel, *The Sworn Book*, early thirteenth century. The first modern edition of this book was by Daniel J. Driscoll (as *The Sworn Book of Honourius the Magician*), published by Heptangle Books, Gillette, New Jersey, 1977 (a limited edition of 450; with a second edition in 1983). Daniel Driscoll used a surviving English translation (British Library MS Royal 17.A.XLII) and his own translation of British Library MS Sloane 313, a Latin manuscript owned by John Dee. He took some liberties with the text (although no more than his predecessor, the anonymous sixteenth-century translator), but produced a very elegant and (comparatively) accessible book. Unfortunately it's now rare and expensive. Royal 17.A.XLII has now been transcribed by Joseph H. Peterson, and can be read on his website www.esotericarchives.com and his Esoteric Archives CD. There is also a modern edition of the Latin text: Gösta Hedegård, *Liber Iuratus Honorii; A Critical Edition of the Latin Version of the Sworn Book of Honorius*, Almqvist & Wiksell International, Stockholm, 2002.

T.B. Howell (ed.), *A Complete Collection of State Trials (Cobbett's Complete Collection of State Trials)*, vol. XIII, T.C. Hansard, London, 1812.

Hugh of St Victor, *Didascalion*, extracts translated by P.G. Maxwell-Stuart in *The Occult in Mediaeval Europe*.

Robert Hunt, *Popular Romances of the West of England*, John Camden Hotten, London, 1871. There are modern editions by Llanerch Publishers and Forgotten Books.

Tony Hunt (ed.), British Library MS Sloane 962 and British Library MS Add. 33996 (fifteenth century charms); transcribed by Tony Hunt in his book *Popular Medicine in Thirteenth-Century England: Introduction and Texts*, D.S. Brewer, Cambridge, 1990.

Luke Hutton, *The Black Dog of Newgate*, c.1596 (republished as *The Discovery of a London Monster*, 1638). There is a modern edition in A.V. Judges (ed.), *The Elizabethan Underworld*, Routledge & Kegan Paul Ltd, London, 1965.

Kenneth Hurlstone Jackson (trans.), 'The Voyage of Mael Dúin', in Kenneth Hurlstone Jackson, *A Celtic Miscellany*, Penguin, Harmondsworth, 1986.

King James I, *Daemononlogie*, Printed by Robert Waldegrave, Edinburgh 1597. There are modern editions (using the spelling *Demonology*), by Filiquarian Publishing and The Book Tree (which also includes *News from Scotland*).

Francis Jones, *The Holy Wells of Wales*, University of Wales Press, Cardiff, 1954.

Friedrich August Kekulé's speech about his dream that led to the discovery of the structure of the benzene molecule, translated by O.T. Benfey (*Journal of Chemical Education*, vol. 35. 1958), quoted in Royston M. Roberts, *Serendipity: Accidental Discoveries in Science*, John Wiley & Sons, Inc., New York, 1989.

Richard Kieckhefer (ed.), *The Munich Handbook* (Codex Latinus Monacensis 849 in the Bavarian State Library), in his book *Forbidden Rites: A Necromancer's Manual of the Fifteenth Century*, Sutton Publishing, Stroud, 1997.

Robert Kirk, *The Secret Commonwealth of Elves, Fauns and Fairies*, written in 1691. There are numerous modern editions.

Heinrich Kramer and Jacob Sprenger, *Malleus Maleficarum*, Cologne, 1486. English translation by Montague Summers published by The Pushkin Press, London, 1948 (with modern editions by several publishers, and also available online on several websites). There is also a new translation by P.G. Maxwell-Stuart, Manchester University Press, Manchester, 2007.

William Lambard, *Eirenarcha Or the Office of Justices of Peace*, London, 1581. There is a modern facsimile edition published by Professional Books Limited, London, 1972.

George Long, *The Folklore Calendar*, Philip Allan, 1930 (no place of publication given). There are several modern editions.

E.D. Longman and S. Loch, *Pins and Pincushions*, Longmans, Green & Co., London, 1911.

R.C. MacLagan, *Evil Eye in the Western Highlands*, David Nutt, London, 1902. There are modern editions by Kessinger and BiblioLife.

J.M. McPherson, *Primitive Beliefs in the North-East of Scotland*, Longmans, Green and Co., London, 1929.

Domenico Mammoli (ed.), *The Record of the Trial and Condemnation of a Witch, Matteuccia di Francesco, at Todi, 20 March 1428*, Rome, 1972 (one of a series of papers about the history of Todi, *Res Tudertinae – 14*). The original Latin trial record, with an introduction and English translation.

Christopher Marlowe, *Doctor Faustus*.

J. Maxwell, *Metapsychical Phenomena*, London, 1905. There is a modern edition by Kessinger.

Merlin, *The Book of Charms and Ceremonies*, W. Foulsham & Co., London, 1910.

Messayaac, *Liber de Angelis, Annulis, Karecteribus & Ymaginibus Planetarum*, (Cambridge University Library MS Dd.11.45), edited by Juris D. Lidaka, with a parallel translation, in Claire Fanger (ed.), *Conjuring Spirits: Texts and Traditions of Medieval Ritual Magic*, Sutton Publishing, Stroud, 1998.

Thomas Middleton, *The Witch*, written around 1615. There is a modern edition with an introduction by Elizabeth Schafer published by A & C Black, London, 1994.

John Milton, *Paradise Lost*.

George More, *A True Discourse Concerning the Certain Possession and Dispossession of Seven Persons in One Family in Lancashire*, 1600 (one of the records of the case of Edmund Hartlay). There is a modern edition in Philip C. Almond, *Demonic Possession and Exorcism in Early Modern England: Contemporary Texts and Their Cultural Contexts*, Cambridge University Press, Cambridge, 2004.

Arthur Morrison, 'A Wizard of Yesterday', originally published in the Strand Magazine in 1900, republished in Eric Maple and Arthur Morrison, *Marsh Wizards, Witches and Cunning Men of Essex*, Caduceus Books, Burbage, 2008.

Isaac Newton, *Opticks*, London, 1704. There are modern editions by Dover, Prometheus Books and Cosimo Classics.

Nicholas of Cusa, Sermon, 1431, extracts translated by P.G. Maxwell-Stuart in his collection *The Occult in Mediaeval Europe*.

Thomas Nicols, *Lapidary: or The History of Pretious Stones*, printed by Thomas Buck, Printer to the University of Cambridge, 1652. Available online on the Farlang Gem and Diamond Foundation website, www.farlang.com.

William Henry Paynter (edited by Jason Semmens), *The Cornish Witch-finder: William Henry Paynter and the Witchery, Ghosts, Charms and Folklore of Cornwall*, The Federation of Old Cornwall Societies, St Agnes, 2008.

William Perkins, *A Discourse of the Damned Art of Witchcraft*, Printed by Cantrell Legge, Printer to the University of Cambridge, 1618 (first published in 1608).

Joseph H. Peterson (ed.), *Secrets Merveilleux de la Magie Naturelle et Cabalistique du Petit Albert*, Lyon, 1782. Available (in the original French) on Joseph H. Peterson's website www.esotericarchives.com and his Esoteric Archives CD.

Robert Pitcairn (ed.), *Criminal Trials in Scotland*, Bannatyne Club, Edinburgh, 1833 (records of the cases of John Fian, Agnes Sampson, Bessie Dunlop and Isobel Gowdie. Bessie Dunlop's trial record is also quoted in full in Emma Wilby, *Cunning Folk and Familiar Spirits*, Sussex Academic Press, Brighton, 2005.)

Moses Pitt, letter to the Bishop of Gloucester (the record of the case of Anne Jefferies). Published as *An Account of one Ann Jefferies*, Richard Cumberland, London, 1696. There are modern editions in Sabine Baring-Gould, *Cornish Characters and Strange Events*, Bodley Head, London, 1925, and Kelvin I. Jones, *Anne Jefferies and the Fairies*, Oakmagic Publications, Penzance, 1996.

John Linwood Pitts (ed. and trans.), *Witchcraft and Devil Lore in the Channel Islands: Transcripts from the Official Records of the Guernsey Royal Court*, Guille-Alles Library and Thomas M. Bichard, Guernsey, 1886. There are modern editions by BiblioLife, Hard Press and BookSurge Publishing. Also available online at http://infomotions.com/etexts/gutenberg/dirs/1/7/2/0/17203/17203.htm

Stephen Pollington (ed. and trans.), *The Lacnunga Manuscript*, in Stephen Pollington, *Leechcraft: Early English Charms, Plant Lore and Healing*, Anglo-Saxon Books, Hockwold-cum-Wilton, 2000.

Giambattista della Porta, *Natural Magic*; anonymous English translation (giving the author's name as John Baptista Porta) printed in London in 1658. There is a modern edition by Kessinger.

Thomas Potts, *The Wonderfull Discoverie of Witches in the Countie of Lancaster*, printed by W. Stansby for John Barnes, London, 1613 (2nd edition (with *errata*); the 1st edition was published in 1612). There are several modern editions of this book: a facsimile edition by Carnegie Publishing Ltd (*The Wonderfvll Discoverie of Witches in the Covntie of Lancaster*), Lancaster, 2007; an edition (with original page numbers) in Marion Gibson, *Early Modern Witches: Witchcraft Cases in Contemporary Writing*, and versions based on James Crossley's 1845 edition (published by the Chetham Society in Manchester) published by Dodo Press, Kessinger Publishing and BiblioLife. Substantial quotations can also be read on the website www.pendlewitches.co.uk. (James Crossley's introduction to his edition contains records of the 1634 Pendle case: a version of Edmund Robinson's Lancashire statement and Margaret Johnson's Lancashire confession.)

James Raine (ed.), *Depositions from the Castle at York*, Surtees Society, Durham, 1861.

Alexander Roberts, *A Treatise of Witchcraft*, printed bt N.O. for Samuel Man, London, 1616. Modern editions include ones by Hard Press, S.R. Publishers and BookSurge.

Reginald Scot, *The Discoverie of Witchcraft*, London, 1584. Modern editions include ones by Centaur Press, Dover Publications and E.P. Publishing.

Ramses Seleem (trans.), *The Book of the Dead – The Illustrated Egyptian Book of the Dead*, Godsfield Press, London, 2001.

Ramses Seleem (trans.), *The Egyptian Book of Life*, Watkins Publishing, London, 2004.

William Shakespeare, *Macbeth*.

William Shakespeare, *The First Part of Henry VI*.

William Shakespeare, *The Second Part of Henry IV*.

Cecil Sharp, *English Folk-Carols*, Novello & Co. Ltd, London, 1911.

George Sinclair, *Satan's Invisible World Discovered*, printed by John Reid, Edinburgh, 1685. There are modern editions by Kessinger and Scholars' Facsimiles and Reprints.

King Solomon (attrib.) (edited and translated by S. Liddell Macgregor Mathers), *The Key of Solomon the King*, George Redway, London, 1889. Modern editions include ones by Kessinger, Book Tree, Dover Publications and Red Wheel/Weiser. Also available on Joseph H. Peterson's website www.esotericarchives.com and his Esoteric Archives CD.

King Solomon (attrib.) (edited by Joseph H. Peterson), *Lemegeton Clavicula Salomonis: The Lesser Key of Solomon*, Red Wheel/Weiser, San Francisco, 2001.

King Solomon (attrib.) (edited by Joseph H. Peterson), *The Work of King Solomon the Wise, Called his Clavicle* (British Library MS Sloane 3847), 1572, transcribed by Joseph H. Peterson and available on his website www.esotericarchives.com and his Esoteric Archives CD.

Stephen de Bourbon, account of the cult of Saint Guinefort in *De Supersticione*, which can be read on the Internet Medieval Sourcebook website (editor Paul Halsall), www.fordham.edu/halsall/source/guinefort.html.

T.I., 'A Memorial of Certain Most Notorious Witches', in *A World of Wonders*, printed for William Barley, London, 1595 (the record of the case of Cecily Arnold). This account was discovered by Marion Gibson and included in her book *Early Modern Witches*.

T.R., *Mother Bunch's Closet Newly Broke Open*, printed by A.M. for P. Brooks, London, 1685. Republished in an edition by G.L. Gomme, The Villon Society, London, 1885 (part of the series *Chap-Books and Folk-Lore Tracts*). There is a modern edition published by BiblioLife. Also available online at www.archive.org/details/motherbunchsclosoovill.

Taliesin (edited and translated by Meirion Pennar), *Taliesin Poems*, Llanerch Publishers, Felinfach, 1988.

Thomas of Erceldoune (edited by J.A.H. Murray), *The Romance and Prophecies of Thomas of Erceldoune*, N. Trubner & Co., London, 1875.

J.R.R. Tolkien and E.V. Gordon (eds), *Sir Gawain and the Green Knight*, Oxford University Press, Oxford, 1925.

Marie Trevelyan, *Folk Lore and Folk Stories of Wales*, Eliot Stock, London, 1909. There is a modern edition by Kessinger.

Robert Turner (trans.), *Arbatel of Magic, Or, The Spiritual Wisdom of the Ancients*, included in Henrich Cornelius Agrippa (attrib.) (translated by Robert Turner), *Henry Cornelius Agrippa His Fourth Book of Occult Philosophy*, London, 1655. (*Arbatel* was first published as *Arbatel de Magia Veterum* in Basel in 1575.) A modern facsimile of the 1655 edition was published by Askin in 1978, with an edition just consisting of *Arbatel* published by Heptangle in 1979. Also available on Joseph H. Peterson's website www.esotericarchives.com and his Esoteric Archives CD. There's also a new translation by Joseph H. Peterson, published by Ibis Press.

Jan R. Veenstra (ed.), 'The Confession of Master Jehan de Bar', in Jan R. Veenstra, *Magic and Divination at the Courts of Burgundy and France*, Brill, Leiden, 1998.

John Webster, *The Displaying of Supposed Witchcraft*, printed by J.M., London, 1677. (Contains records of the 1634 Pendle case: Edmund Robinson's Lancashire statement and John Webster's own recollections of the case.) This book is available for study in the Museum of Witchcraft's research library.

Johann Weyer (ed.), *Pseudomonarchia Daemonum*, 1563 (an appendix to his book *Praestigiis Daemonum*). Translated into English by Reginald Scot and included in his book *The Discoverie of Witchcraft*.

Wiltshire and Swindon Archives, Document ref: D/1/39/2/7 fol. 90v (Record of the case of Elizabeth Smith). There is a photocopy and transcript of this document available for study at the Museum of Witchcraft's research library. Thanks to Steven Hobbs of Wiltshire and Swindon Archives, Wiltshire and Swindon History Centre, for his help with the transcription.

W.B. Yeats (ed.), *Fairy and Folk Tales of the Irish Peasantry*, Walter Scott, London, 1888. There are numerous modern editions.

MODERN WORKS

Violet Alford, *The Hobby Horse and Other Animal Masks*, The Merlin Press Ltd, London, 1978.

Philip C. Almond, *Demonic Possession and Exorcism in Early Modern England: Contemporary Texts and Their Cultural Contexts*, Cambridge University Press, Cambridge, 2004.

Karin Amundsen, 'The Duke's Devil and Doctor Lambe's Darling: A Case Study of the Male Witch in Early Modern England', *Psi Sigma Historical Journal*, Volume 2, Winter 2004; available online on the website of the University of Nevada, Las Vegas, www.unlv.edu/student_orgs/psisigma/index.html.

Simon Armitage, 'The Knight's Tale', *The Guardian*, Saturday 16 December 2006.

John Ashton, *The Devil in Britain and America*, Ward & Downey Ltd, London, 1896.

Howard Balmer, *Stone to Rock, River to Sea: The Old Stones, Barrows and Antiquities of the Padstow Area*, published by the author, Padstow, 2004.

Kirsteen Macpherson Bardell, 'Beyond Pendle: the 'lost' Lancashire witches', in Robert Poole (ed.), *The Lancashire Witches*, Manchester University Press, Manchester, 2002.

Andrew Barrett and Christopher Harrison (eds), *Crime and Punishment in England: A Sourcebook*, Routledge, Abingdon, 1999.

Robert Bartlett, *Trial by Fire and Water: The Medieval Judicial Ordeal*, Oxford University Press, Oxford, 1986.

Michael G. Bassett, *'Formed Stones', Folklore and Fossils*, National Museum of Wales, Cardiff, 1982.

Georges Bataille (ed.), Pierre Klossowski (trans.) and Richard Robinson (trans.), *The Trial of Gilles de Rais*, Amok Books, Los Angeles, 2004.

Steve Bradshaw and Simon Brown (producers and directors), *The Real Life on Mars*, broadcast on BBC4 on 11 August 2008.

Katherine Briggs, *An Encyclopedia of Fairies, Hobgoblins, Brownies, Bogies, and Other Supernatural Creatures*, Pantheon Books, 1977.

Robin Briggs, "By the strength of fancie': witchcraft and the early modern imagination', *Folklore*, December 2004.

Robin Briggs, *Witches and Neighbours*, Fontana Press, London, 1997.

British Museum website, www.britishmuseum.org.

Paul Broadhurst, *The Green Man and the Dragon*, Mythos, Launceston, 2006.

Michael Brooks, '13 things that don't make sense', *New Scientist*, 19 March 2005 (Vol. 185, No. 2491), pp. 30–7.

E.M. Butler, *Ritual Magic*, Cambridge University Press, Cambridge, 1949.

Clifford H. Byrne, *Newchurch-in-Pendle. Folklore, Fact, Fancy, Legends, Traditions & Information*, Marsden Antiquarians, Nelson, 1982.

Vanessa Chambers, 'A Shell with my Name on it: The Reliance on the Supernatural During the First World War', *Journal for the Academic Study of Magic*, Issue 2, 2004, pp. 79–102 (published by Mandrake of Oxford).

Andrew D. Chumbley, *The Leaper Between: An Historical Study of the Toad-bone Amulet*, published online on *The Cauldron* website, http://web.archive.org/web/2004101503500/www.the-cauldron.fsnet.co.uk/toad.htm

CIA, *Human Resource Exploitation Training Manual – 1983.* (Section L). Published online on a number of websites, for example the George Washington University website, www.gwu.edu/~nsarchiv/NSAEBB/NSAEBB27/02-01.htm.

J.S. Cockburn, *A History of English Assizes 1558 – 1714*, Cambridge University Press, Cambridge, 1972.

Adam J. Cohen, *Facial Trauma, Orbital Floor Fractures (Blowout)*, published on the eMedicine website, www.emedicine.com/plastic/topic485.htm, 18 Dec 2006.

Norman Cohn, *Europe's Inner Demons: An Enquiry Inspired by the Great Witch-Hunt*, Book Club Associates/Chatto & Windus Ltd, London, 1975.

Charles Colville (director/producer), *Horizon: Why Do We Dream?*, broadcast on BBC2 on 10 February 2009.

Ian McNeil Cooke, *Sun Disc to Crucifix – The Cross – A Short Illustrated History*, Men-an-Tol Studio, Penzance, 1999.

Merlin Coverley, *Occult London*, Pocket Essentials, Harpenden, 2008.

A.C. Crombie, *Robert Grosseteste and the Origins of Experimental Science 1100–1700*, Oxford University Press, Oxford, 1971 (first published 1953).

Aleister Crowley, *The Forbidden Lecture*, Mandrake Press Ltd, Thame, Oxfordshire, 1990 (first published 1930).

Thomas Davidson, *Rowan Tree and Red Thread*, Robert Cunningham and Sons Ltd, London, 1949.

Owen Davies, *Cunning Folk: Popular Magic in English History*, Hambledon and London, London, 2003.

Owen Davies, *Grimoires: A History of Magic Books*, Oxford University Press, Oxford, 2009.

Owen Davies, 'Healing Charms in Use in England and Wales 1700–1950', *Folklore*, Vol. 107 (1996), pp. 19–33.

Owen Davies, 'The Nightmare Experience, Sleep Paralysis, and Witchcraft Accusations', *Folklore* 114 (Number 2, August 2003), pp. 181–203.

Owen Davies and Lisa Tallis, *Cunning Folk: An Introductory Bibliography*, FLS Books, London, 2005.

Claire Donovan, *The Winchester Bible*, The British Library/Winchester Cathedral, London/ Winchester, 1993.

Kate Douglas, 'The other you', *New Scientist*, 1 December 2007, Vol. 196, No. 2632, pp. 42–6.

C. L'Estrange Ewen, *Witch Hunting and Witch Trials*, Kegan Paul, London, 1929.

C. L'Estrange Ewen., *Witchcraft and Demonianism*, Frederick Muller Ltd, London, 1933.

Claire Fanger (ed.), *Conjuring Spirits: Texts and Traditions of Medieval Ritual Magic*, Sutton Publishing, Stroud, 1998.

Andrija Filipovic and Anne Morris, 'Milking the Moon: Cunning-Folk in Southern Slavic Folklore', *The Cauldron*, May 2007, No. 124, pp. 29–34.

Alison Findlay, 'Sexual and spiritual politics in the events of 1633–4 and *The Late Lancashire*

Witches', in Robert Poole (ed.), *The Lancashire Witches: Histories and Stories*, Manchester University Press, Manchester, 2002.

Valerie I.J. Flint, 'Magic in English Thirteenth-Century Miracle Collections', in Jan N. Bremmer and Jan R. Veenstra (eds), *The Metamorphosis of Magic from Late Antiquity to the Early Modern Period*, Peeters, Leuven, 2002.

Thomas R. Forbes, *The Midwife and the Witch*, Yale University Press, New Haven, 1966.

Werner Forman and Stephen Quirke, *Hieroglyphs and the Afterlife in Ancient Egypt*, Book Club Associates/Opus Publishing Limited, London, 1996.

Fortean Times, March 2009, FT246 (letter from Ali Barnes, p. 75).

Antonia Fraser, *The Gunpowder Plot*, Weidenfeld and Nicolson, London, 1996.

J.G. Frazer, *The Golden Bough: A Study in Magic and Religion* (abridged edition), The Macmillan Press Ltd, London, 1976 (first published 1922).

Jessica Freeman, 'Sorcery at court and manor: Margery Jourdemayne, the witch of Eye next Westminster', *Journal of Medieval History* 30 (2004), pp. 343–57.

Joyce Froome, 'The Symbolism of the Pierced Heart', *The Journal for the Academic Study of Magic*, Issue 2 (2004), pp. 287–99 (published by Mandrake of Oxford).

James R. Gallagher and Peter Ramsay-Baggs, 'ABC of eyes: Injury to the eye. Orbital injuries should not be considered in isolation' (letter), *British Medical Journal*, 2004 (13 March), published online at www.bmj.com/cgi/content/full/328/7440/644-a.

Malcolm Gaskill, *Witchfinders: A Seventeenth Century English Tragedy*, John Murray, London, 2005.

Marion Gibson, *Early Modern Witches: Witchcraft Cases in Contemporary Writing*, Routledge, Abingdon, 2000.

Marion Gibson, *Reading Witchcraft*, Routledge, London, 1999

Marion Gibson, 'Thomas Potts's 'dusty memory'', in Robert Poole (ed.), *The Lancashire Witches: Histories and Stories*, Manchester University Press, Manchester, 2002.

Carlo Ginzburg, *Ecstasies: Deciphering the Witches' Sabbath*, Penguin, Harmondsworth, 1991.

Daniel Goleman, *The Meditative Mind: The Varieties of Meditative Experience*, The Aquarian Press, Wellingborough, 1989.

Colin Gregory, 'SWW calls on vicar to lift field curse', *Western Morning News*, 31 March 1997.

John Richard Clark Hall and Herbert Dean Meritt, *A Concise Anglo-Saxon Dictionary*, University of Toronto Press, 1984.

David Hamilton, *The Healers: a history of medicine in Scotland*, Canongate, Edinburgh, 1981.

Patrick Harpur, *The Philosophers' Secret Fire: A History of the Imagination*, Ivan R. Dee, Chicago, 2003.

Charles Homer Haskins, *The Renaissance of the Twelfth Century*, Harvard University Press, Cambridge, Massachusetts, 1982 (first published 1927).

Tony Hillerman, *Dance Hall of the Dead*, published in Britain in the collection *The Leaphorn Mysteries*, Penguin, London, 1994.

David Hoffmann, *The Herb User's Guide*, Thorsons Publishing Group, Wellingborough, 1987.

Brian Hoggard's website www.apotropaios.co.uk

Michael Howard, *Way of the Magus*, Capall Bann Publishing, Milverton, Somerset, 2001.

Chris Huet, *The Dark Companion: The Origin of 'Black Dog' as a Description for Depression*, on the Black Dog Institute website, www.blackdoginstitute.org.au/docs/Huet.pdf.

Tony Hunt, *Popular Medicine in Thirteenth-Century England: Introduction and Texts*, D.S. Brewer, Cambridge, 1990.

Ronald Hutton, *The Stations of the Sun*, Oxford University Press, Oxford, 1997.

A.K. Hamilton Jenkins, *Cornwall and Its People*, David & Charles, Newton Abbot, 1983.

Kelvin I. Jones, *An Joan the Crone: The History and Craft of the Cornish Witch*, Oakmagic Publications, Penzance, 1999.

Jason Karl, *The Secret World of Witchcraft*, New Holland Publishers, London, 2008.

Edward J. Kealey, *Harvesting the Air: Windmill Pioneers in Twelfth-Century England*, The Boydell Press, Woodbridge, 1987.

Richard Kieckhefer, *European Witch Trials: Their Foundations in Popular and Learned Culture, 1300–1500*, Routledge & Kegan Paul, London, 1976.

Richard Kieckhefer, *Forbidden Rites: A Necromancer's Manual of the Fifteenth Century*, Sutton Publishing, Stroud, 1997.

Richard Kieckhefer, *Magic in the Middle Ages*, Cambridge University Press, Cambridge, 1990.

Yong-Ku Kim and Michael Maes, 'The Role of the Cytokine Network in Psychological Stress', *Acta Neuropsychiatrica*, June 2003, Vol. 15, Issue 3, pp. 148–155.

Graham King, *The British Book of Charms and Spells* (work in progress).

Ernst Kitzinger, *Early Medieval Art*, British Museum Publications Ltd, London, 1983.

Matthew Klemm, *Incantations in the Medical Philosophy of Petrus de Abano*, published online at www.aseweb.org/Papers/Klemm.htm.

Alan Charles Kors and Edward Peters (ed.), *Witchcraft in Europe, 400–1700: A Documentary History*, University of Pensylvania Press, Philadelphia, 2000 (2nd edition, revised by Edward Peters).

Sachiko Kusukawa, 'Medicine in Western Europe in 1500', in Peter Elmer (ed.), *The Healing Arts: Health, Disease and Society in Europe 1500–1800*, Manchester University Press/The Open University, Manchester, 2004.

Benedek Láng, *Angels Around the Crystal: The Prayer Book of King Wladislas and the Treasure Hunts of Henry the Bohemian*, published online on www.staropolska.pl/sredniowiecze/opracowania/Lang.html

Tanith Lee, *The Castle of Dark*, HarperCollins, London, 1984.

Juris G. Lidaka, 'The Book of Angels, Rings, Characters and Images of the Planets', in Claire Fanger (ed.), *Conjuring Spirits: Texts and Traditions of Medieval Ritual Magic*, Sutton Publishing, Stroud, 1998.

The Lincoln Order of Neuromancers (LOON), *Apikorsus: An Essay on the Diverse Practices of Chaos Magick*, published online by the authors, 1986; available on Phil Hine's website, www.philhine.org.uk.

Peter Linebaugh, 'The Tyburn Riot Against the Surgeons', in Peter Linebaugh (*et al.*), *Albion's Fatal Tree: Crime and Society in Eighteenth-Century England*, Penguin Books, Harmondsworth, 1977.

Peter Linebaugh and Marcus Rediker, *The Many-Headed Hydra: The Hidden History of the Revolutionary Atlantic*, Verso, London, 2000.

Jonathan Lumby, *The Lancashire Witch-Craze: Jennet Preston and the Lancashire Witches*, Carnegie Publishing Ltd, Lancaster, 1999.

Kathleen McDonald, *How to Meditate*, Wisdom Publications, London, 1984.

Alan Macfarlane, *Witchcraft in Tudor and Stuart England*, Waveland Press, Inc., London, 1991.

Andrea Mckenzie, "This Death Some Strong and Stout Hearted Man Doth Choose': The Practice of Peine Forte et Dure in Seventeenth- and Eighteenth-Century England', *Law and History Review*, Vol. 23, Issue 2; also published online by *The History Cooperative*, www.historycooperative.org/journals/lhr/23.2/mckenzie.html

Robert Mathiesen, 'A Thirteenth-Century Ritual to Attain the Beatific Vision from The *Sworn Book* of Honorius of Thebes', in Claire Fanger (ed.), *Conjuring Spirits: Texts and Traditions of Medieval Ritual Magic*, Sutton Publishing, Stroud, 1998.

P.G. Maxwell-Stuart, *The Occult in Mediaeval Europe*, Palgrave, Basingstoke, 2005.

P.G. Maxwell-Stuart, *Satan's Conspiracy: Magic and Witchcraft in Seventeenth-Century Scotland*, Tuckwell Press, East Linton, 2001.

P.G. Maxwell-Stuart, *Witchcraft: A History*, Tempus, Stroud, 2000.

Audrey Meaney, 'Drift Seeds and the Brísingamen', *Folklore*, Vol. 94, No. 1 (1983), pp. 33–9.

Ralph Merrifield, *The Archaeology of Ritual and Magic*, Guild Publishing, London, 1987.

Gregory E. Miller, Sheldon Cohen and A. Kim Ritchey, 'Chronic Psychological Stress and the Regulation of Pro-Inflammatory Cytokines: A Glucocorticoid-Resistance Model', *Health Psychology*, 2002, Vol. 21, No. 6, pp. 531–41, published online at www.apa.org/journals/releases/hea216531.pdf.

Franco Mormando, *The Preacher's Demons: Bernardino of Siena and the Social Underworld of Early Renaissance Italy*, The University of Chicago Press, Chicago, 1999.

Rose Mullins, *White Witches: A Study of Charmers*, PR Publishing, Launceston.

Gary St M. Nottingham, *Charms, Charming and the Charmed: Welsh Border Witchcraft*, Verdelet Press, Craven Arms, 2007.

Caroline Oates and Juliette Wood, *A Coven of Scholars: Margaret Murray and her Working Methods*, FLS Books, London, 1998.

Oxford University Press, *The Compact Edition of the Oxford English Dictionary*, Oxford University Press, 1971.

Stephanie Pain, 'The illuminating Irtyersenu', *New Scientist*, 20/27 December 2008 (Vol. 200, No. 2687/2688), pp. 72–3.

Patient UK website, *Hypnagogic Hallucinations*, www.patient.co.uk

Jenny Paull, *Prisoners of Conscience and Prison Visitors: The Quakers of Lancaster Castle*, on the Lancaster Castle website, www.lancastercastle.com/html/people/tour.php?id=40.

Stuart Peachey, *The Building of the Green Valley: A Reconstruction of an Early Seventeenth-Century Rural Landscape*, Heritage Marketing & Publications Ltd, Kings Lynn, 2006.

Joanne Pearson, 'Wicca, Paganism and history: contemporary witchcraft and the Lancashire witches', in Robert Poole (ed.), *The Lancashire Witches: Histories and Stories*, Manchester University Press, Manchester, 2002.

Edgar Peel and Pat Southern, *The Trials of the Lancashire Witches*, Hendon Publishing Co. Ltd, Nelson, 1985.

Éva Pócs, *Between the Living and the Dead*, Central European University Press, Budapest, 1997.

Stephen Pollington, *Leechcraft: Early English Charms, Plant Lore and Healing*, Anglo-Saxon Books, Hockwold-cum-Wilton, 2000.

Robert Poole (ed.), *The Lancashire Witches: Histories and Stories*, Manchester University Press, Manchester, 2002.

Richard Preston, *First Light: The Search for the Edge of the Universe*, Scribners, London, 1991.

Stephen Pumfrey, 'Potts, plots and politics', in Robert Poole (ed.), *The Lancashire Witches: Histories and Stories*, Manchester University Press, Manchester, 2002.

Donald R. Rawe, *Padstow's Obby Oss and May Day Festivities*, Lodenek Press, Wadebridge, 1999.

Joad Raymond, *Pamphlets and Pamphleteering in Early Modern Britain*, Cambridge University Press, Cambridge, 2006.

Christopher Reeve, *A Straunge and Terrible Wunder: The Story of the Black Dog of Bungay*, Morrow and Co., 1988.

Rossell Hope Robbins, *The Encyclopedia of Witchcraft and Demonology*, Spring Books, Feltham, 1968.

Royston M. Roberts, *Serendipity: Accidental Discoveries in Science*, John Wiley & Sons, Inc., New York, 1989.

Jonathan Roper, *English Verbal Charms*, Academia Scientiarum Fennica, Helsinki, 2005.

Barbara Rosen, *Witchcraft in England, 1558–1618*, University of Massachusetts Press, 1991.

Richard Rudgley, *The Encyclopaedia of Psychoactive Substances*, Abacus, London, 1999.

Edmund H. Sedding, *Norman Architecture in Cornwall*, Ward & Co., London, 1909.

Ramses Seleem, *The Book of the Dead – The Illustrated Egyptian Book of the Dead*, Godsfield Press, London, 2001.

Ramses Seleem, *The Egyptian Book of Life*, Watkins Publishing, London, 2004.

Jason Semmens, *The Witch of the West: or, the Strange and Wonderful History of Thomasine Blight*, published by the author, Plymouth, 2004.

St John D. Seymour, *Irish Witchcraft and Demonology*, Portman Books, London, 1989 (first published 1913).

James Sharpe, *Instruments of Darkness: Witchcraft in England 1550–1750*, Penguin, London, 1996.

Simon J. Sherwood, 'A Psychological Approach to Apparitions of Black Dogs', in Bob Trubshaw (ed.), *Explore Phantom Black Dogs*, Heart of Albion Press, Wymeswold, 2005.

John Shinners, *Medieval Popular Religion*, Broadview Press, Ontario, 1997.

Jacqueline Simpson and Steve Roud, *A Dictionary of English Folklore*, Oxford University Press, Oxford, 2000.

Tony Smith (ed.), *The British Medical Association Complete Family Health Encyclopedia*, Dorling Kindersley, London, 1990.

Tony Smith (ed.), *The New Macmillan Guide to Family Health*, Macmillan Publishers Ltd/Dorling Kindersley Ltd/Guild Publishing, London, 1987.

Peter Sommer (producer and director), *Tales from the Green Valley* (DVD set), distributed by Acorn Video (made by Lion TV for BBC Wales).

Alby Stone, 'Infernal Watchdogs, Soul Hunters and Corpse Eaters', in Bob Trubshaw (ed.), *Explore Phantom Black Dogs*, Heart of Albion Press, Wymeswold, 2005.

Strange Science website, www.strangescience.net/stdino2.htm.

Elizabeth Svoboda, 'Faces, Faces Everywhere', *New York Times*, 13 February 2007, published online on www.nytimes.com.

John Swain, 'Witchcraft, economy and society in the forest of Pendle', in Robert Poole (ed.) *The Lancashire Witches: Histories and Stories*, Manchester University Press, Manchester, 2002.

F. Sherwood Taylor, *The Alchemists: Founders of Modern Chemistry*, William Heinemann Ltd, London, 1951.

Kathleen M. Thies and John F. Travers, *Quick Look Nursing: Growth and Development Through the Lifespan*, Jones & Bartlett Publishers, 2006.

C.J.S. Thompson, *The Hand of Destiny*, Rider & Co., London, 1932.

C.J.S. Thompson, *The Mystic Mandrake*, Rider & Co., London, 1934.

Kevin Tracey, 'The monster within', *New Scientist*, 2 April 2005 (Vol. 186, No. 2493) pp. 38–41.

Bob Trubshaw (ed.), *Explore Phantom Black Dogs*, Heart of Albion Press, Wymeswold, 2005.

Sam Vaknin, 'The Psychology of Torture', *Medical News Today*, 20 August 2005, also published in his book *Malignant Self Love*, Narcissus Publications, Czech Republic, 1999, and available online on www.samvak.tripod.com/torturepsychology.html.

Jan R. Veenstra, *Magic and Divination at the Courts of Burgundy and France*, Brill, Leiden, 1998.

Jennifer Westwood, 'Friend or Foe? Norfolk Traditions of Shuck', in Bob Trubshaw (ed.), *Explore Phantom Black Dogs*, Heart of Albion Press, Wymeswold, 2005.

Beatrice White, *A Cast of Ravens*, John Murray, London, 1965.

Emma Wilby, *Cunning Folk and Familiar Spirits*, Sussex Academic Press, Brighton, 2005.

Richard Wilson, 'The pilot's thumb: *Macbeth* and the Jesuits', in Robert Poole (ed.), *The Lancashire Witches: Histories and Stories*, Manchester University Press, Manchester, 2002.

Robert A. Wilson and Frank C. Keil (eds), *The MIT Encyclopedia of the Cognitive Sciences*, MIT Press, 2001.

Chris Wingfield, 'Witches' Ladder: the hidden history', in *England: the Other Within: Analysing the English Collections at the Pitt Rivers Museum*, published online at http://england.prm.ox.ac.uk/englishness-witchs-ladder.html.

Richard Wiseman, *The Luck Factor*, Century, London, 2003.

E.G. Withycombe, *The Oxford Dictionary of English Christian Names*, Oxford University Press, Oxford, 1977.

Margaret Wood, *The English Mediaeval House*, Ferndale Editions, London, 1981.

Benjamin Woolley, *The Queen's Conjuror*, HarperCollins, London, 2001.

Lama Yeshe, *Introduction to Tantra*, Wisdom Publications, Boston, 1987.

Heinrich Zimmer, *The King and the Corpse: Tales of the Soul's Conquest of Evil*, Princeton University Press/Bollingen Foundation, Princeton/Washington, 1973 (first published 1948).

Index